THE EARLY MIDDLE AGES

THE BIBLE AND WOMEN

An Encyclopaedia of Exegesis and Cultural History

Edited by Christiana de Groot, Irmtraud Fischer,
Mercedes Navarro Puerto, and Adriana Valerio

Volume 6.1: The Early Middle Ages

THE EARLY MIDDLE AGES

Edited by
Franca Ela Consolino and Judith Herrin

SBL PRESS

 PRESS

Atlanta

Copyright © 2020 by SBL Press

All rights reserved. No part of this work may be reproduced or transmitted in any form or by any means, electronic or mechanical, including photocopying and recording, or by means of any information storage or retrieval system, except as may be expressly permitted by the 1976 Copyright Act or in writing from the publisher. Requests for permission should be addressed in writing to the Rights and Permissions Office, SBL Press, 825 Houston Mill Road, Atlanta, GA 30329 USA.

Library of Congress Cataloging-in-Publication Data

Names: Consolino, Franca Ela, editor.
Title: The early Middle Ages / edited by Franca Ela Consolino and Judith Herrin.
Description: SBL Press, 2019. | Series: Bible and women ; Number 6.1 | Includes bibliographical references and index.
Identifiers: LCCN 2019014655 (print) | LCCN 2019017047 (ebook) | ISBN 9780884143819 (ebk.) | ISBN 9781589835757 (pbk. : alk. paper) | ISBN 9780884143802 (hbk. : alk. paper)
Subjects: Bible—Feminist criticism—Europe—History. | Women in Christianity—Europe—History. | Christian women—Religious life—History. | Church history—Middle Ages, 600–1500. | Bible and feminism—History.
Classification: LCC BS521.4 (ebook) | LCC BS521.4 .E275 2019 (print) | DDC 220.082/0902—dc23
LC record available at https://lccn.loc.gov/2019014655

Contents

Preface vii

Abbreviations ix

Introduction
    Franca Ela Consolino and Judith Herrin 1

"Woman's Head Is Man": Kyriarchy and the Rhetoric of Women's Subordination in Byzantine Literature
    Stavroula Constantinou 13

Women and the Bible in Byzantium
    Rosa Maria Parrinello 33

Kassia the Melodist (ca. 810–ca. 865) and Her Use of the Scriptures
    Anna M. Silvas 51

Byzantine Reception of Biblical Revelation on the Virgin Mary
    Mary B. Cunningham 71

The Virgin Mary and Ancient Jewish Literature
    Martha Himmelfarb 103

The Heavenly Guard of the Mother of God: Mary between the Angels in Early Byzantine Art
    Maria Lidova 121

Early Medieval Iconography of the Virgin Mary between East and West
    Giuseppa Z. Zanichelli 167

Women, Wine, and the Apostasy of the Wise: Sirach 19:2 in
   Medieval Latin Literature
   Giuseppe Cremascoli 205

The Women of the Old Testament in Early Medieval Poetry:
   Judith and the Others
   Francesco Stella 231

Women and the Bible in Latin Letter Collections of the Early
   Middle Ages (Sixth to Ninth Century)
   Christiane Veyrard-Cosme 259

Women Writers and Holy Writ in the Latin Early Middle Ages:
   The Bible in Dhuoda and Hrotsvit
   Franca Ela Consolino..277

The Reception of Biblical Texts and Their Normative Effect upon
   Marriage, Adultery, and Divorce from the Seventh to the
   Eleventh Century
   Ines Weber..321

Biblical Figures of Women in the Qur'an
   Ulrike Bechmann 345

Contributors..377
Primary Sources Index 381
Modern Authors Index...394

Preface

As we explain in the introduction, this series of twenty volumes devoted to the ways in which women have related to the Bible through the ages was set in motion many years ago by Adriana Valerio and Irmtraud Fischer, who had the ambitious vision of publishing an international edition in four languages. Kari Børresen played an important role both as a source of inspiration and as coeditor of volume 6.2, on women and the Bible in the Middle Ages (published in English in 2015), and volume 5.2, on ancient Christian authors (English edition in preparation). With her enthusiastic support we undertook to edit this volume on the early medieval period, which first appeared in its Italian edition in 2015. The German translation followed in 2019, and, finally, the English edition is now in print. A Spanish edition is also promised.

We wish most particularly to thank Irmtraud Fischer of the University of Graz, Austria, and Christiana de Groot of Calvin University, Grand Rapids, Michigan, USA, for their precise editorial work that ensured the appearance of these two editions. In addition, Sarah Bairstow provided careful translations of the Italian originals; Alyssa Gagnon assisted Professor de Groot in the preparation of the American edition with a grant from Gender Studies at Calvin University; and Nicole Tilford at the Society of Biblical Literature coped with numerous interruptions to the process of getting the book through the press. We are most grateful to them all.

Many of the authors submitted their chapters nearly ten years ago and would have liked to revise and update them, but this proved to be impossible. We therefore remind readers that most of the references date back to the early 2010s and regret that it was not possible to take account of more recent publications. It is important to emphasize how much we appreciate our contributors' forbearance during the many delays to this edition, and we wish it every success.

Franca Ela Consolino and Judith Herrin
April 2020

Abbreviations

AAAHP	*Acta ad archaeologiam et artium historiam pertinentia*
AAWG	Abhandlungen der Akademie der Wissenschaften in Göttingen, Philologisch-historische Klasse
Adv. Haer.	Irenaeus, *Adversus Haereses*
Alex.	Anna Komnene, *Alexiad*
Alleg.	Isidore of Seville, *Allegoriae quaedam Sacrae Scripturae*
AMBSR	Archaeological Monographs of the British School at Rome
Anal. hymn.	*Analecta hymnica medei aevi*. 55 vols. Leipzig: Reisland, 1886–1922.
ANF	Roberts, Alexander, and James Donaldson, eds. *The Ante-Nicene Fathers: Translations of the Writings of the Fathers Down to A.D. 325*. 10 vols. 1885–1887.
AntT	*Antiquité Tardive*
AOC	Archives de l'Orient Chrétien
Apoc. Paul	Apocalypse of Paul
Apocrypha	*Apocrypha: International Journal of Apocryphal Literature*
Append.	Hugh of Saint Victor, *Appendix ad opera dogmatic*
ArtBul	*Art Bulletin*
Arte praed.	Alanus de Insulis, *De arte praedicatoria*
Ascens. Dom.	Hrotsvit, *De ascensione Domini*
AScR	*Annali di Scienze Religiose*
b.	Babylonian Talmud
BAK	Beihefte zum Archiv für Kulturgeschichte
BAR	Biblical Archaeology Review
BARIS	Biblical Archaeology Review International Series
BCM	*Bulletin of the Cleveland Museum*
Bel. Cat.	Sallust, *Bellum Catilinae*
Ben.	Seneca, *De beneficiis*

Ber.	Berakhot
BISIME	*Bollettino dell'Istituto Storico Italiano per il Medio Evo*
BK	*Bibel und Kirche*
BN	*Biblische Notizen*
BolA	*Bollettino d'arte*
BSLT	Byzantine Saints' Lives in Translation
BW	Bible and Women
ByzSt	*Byzantine Studies*
ByzZ	*Byzantinische Zeitschrift*
CahA	*Cahiers Archéologiques*
Can. Wall.	*Canones Wallici*
Capit. episc.	*Capitula episcoporum*
Capit. Ital. episc.	*Capitula cum Italiae episcopis deliberate*
Capit. Olon.	*Capitulare Olonnense*
Capit. Silv.	*Capitula Silvanectensia*
Capit. Trev.	*Capitula Treverensia*
Cap. Jud.	*Capitula Iudiciorum*
CARB	*Corso di cultura sull'arte ravennate e bizantina*
Carm.	*Carmina*
Carn. Chr.	Tertullian, *De carne Christi*
Cath.	Prudentius, *Cathemerinon*
CCC	*Civiltà Classica e Cristiana*
CCCM	Corpus Christianorum: Continuatio Mediaevalis
CCSA	Corpus Christianorum: Series Apocryphorum
CCSL	Corpus Christianorum Series latina
CCT	Companions to the Christian Tradition
Cena Cypr.	Johannes Hymonides, *Cena Cypriani*
Cent.	Proba, *Centone*
CFHB	Corpus Fontium Historiae Byzantinae
CISAM	Centro italiano di studi sull'alto Medioevo
CM	*Classica et Mediaevalia*
Comm. in Eccl.	Rabanus Maurus, *Commentarius in Ecclesiasticum*
Comp. in Cant.	Alcuin, *Compendium in Cantica Canticorum*
Conc. For.	*Concilium Foroiuliense*
Conc. Meld.-Par.	*Concilium Meldense-Parisiense*
Conc. Par.	*Concilium Parisiense*
Conc. Rom.	*Concilium Romanum*
Conc. Suess.	*Concilium Suessionense*
Conc. Trib.	*Concilium Triburiense*

Conf. Ps.-Egb.	*Confessionale Pseudo-Egberti*
Cont. mundi	Innocent III, *De contemptu mundi*
Conv.	*Convivium*
Counc. Sav.	Council of Savonnières
CPG	Geerard, Maur
CRHCBM	Centre de Recherche d'Histoire et Civilisation de Byzance, Monographies
CSCO	Corpus scriptorum Christianorum Orientalium
CSEL	Corpus scriptorum ecclesiasticorum latinorum
CSHJ	Chicago Studies in the History of Judaism
CSMC	Cahiers de Saint-Michel de Cuxa
CSMC	*Cahiers de Saint-Michel de Cuxa*
CSS	Cistercian Studies Series
CWS	Classics of Western Spirituality
D.AR.FI.CLET	Dipartimento di Archeologia e Filologia Classica e loro Tradizioni
DCAE	*Deltion Christianikes Archaiologikes Etaireias*
Decr. lib.	Buchard of Worms, *Decretorum libri*
Decr. Verm.	*Decretum Vermeriense*
Deriv.	Osbern, *Derivationes*
Dial.	Justin, *Dialogus cum Tryphone*
Dip	*Diptycha*
DisAr	Diskurse der Arabistik
DMTS	Davis Medieval Texts and Studies
DOP	*Dumbarton Oaks Papers*
Dorm.	Andrew of Crete, *In dormitionem*
Dorm.	Germanus of Constantinople, *In dormitionem*
DOS	Dumbarton Oaks Studies
EAMA	La Collection des Etudes Augustiniennes, Série Moyen Âge et Temps Modernes
Ed. Roth.	*Edictus Rothari*
Elem. lit.	Papias, *Elementarium littera*
EME	*Early Medieval Europe*
ÉO	*Échos d'Orient*
Ep.	*Epistulae*
Ep. extra coll.	Ambrose, *Epistulae extra collectionem*
Ep. pontif.	Siricius, *Epistolae Romanorum pontificum*
ESMAR	Education and Society in the Middle Ages and Renaissance

Etym.	Isidore of Seville, *Etymologiae*
EUZ	Exegese in unserer Zeit
FIDEM	Fédération Internationale des Instituts d'Etudes Médiévales
FMSt	*Frühmittelalterliche Studien*
Fori Jud.	*Fori Judicum*
Form. extr.	*Formulae extravagantes*
Gen. Rab.	Genesis Rabbah
Git.	Gittin
GOTR	*Greek Orthodox Theological Review*
GRBS	*Greek, Roman and Byzantine Studies*
Greg	*Gregorianum*
Grim. leg.	*Grimvaldi leges*
Gub. Dei	Salvianus Massiliensis, *De gubernatione Dei*
GWR	Germanenrechte, Westgermanisches Recht
Hel.	Ambrose, *Helia et Jejunio*
Hist. arc.	Procopius, *Historia arcane*
Hist. eccl.	Nicephoros Kallistos Xanthopoulos, *Historia ecclesiastica*
Hom.	Basil of Caesarea, *Homiliae*
Hom. 2 in Dorm.	John of Damascus, *Homilia 2 in dormitione Mariae*
Hom. in Praes.	Germanus of Constantinople, *Homilia in praesentationem*
Hom. Matt.	John Chrysostom, *Homiliae in Matthaeum*
Hom. Ps.	John Chrysostom, *Homiliae in Psalmos*
Hor.	Gregory of Nazianzus
HTR	*Harvard Theological Review*
ICMR	*Islam and Christian-Muslim Relations*
Icon	*Iconographica*
IL	*Invigilata Lucernis*
Imag. Tetr.	Walafrid Strabo of Reichenau, *De imagine Tetrici*
In. Cant.	Bede, *In Cantica Canticorum*
Inst. coen.	John Cassian, *De institutis coenobiorum*
Inst. laic.	John of Orléans, *De institutione laicali*
IS	International Symposium
JAC	*Jahrbuch für Antike und Christentum*
JCH	*Journal of Cultural Heritage*
JCI	Judentum, Christentum und Islam
JECS	*Journal of Early Christian Studies*

JFSR	*Journal of Feminist Studies in Religion*
JML	*Journal of Medieval Latin*
JMNP	*Journal ministerstva narodnogo proscheshenia*
JÖB	*Jahrbuch der österreichischen Byzantinistik*
JRA	*Journal of Roman Archaeology*
JSJSup	Supplements to the Journal for the Study of Judaism
JSQ	*Jewish Studies Quarterly*
JTS	*Journal of Theological Studies*
JWAG	*Journal of the Walters Art Gallery*
KATE	Kommentar zum Alten Testament mit der Einheitsübersetzung
KEK	Kritisch-exegetischer Kommentar über das Neue Testament
Lam. Rab.	Lamentations Rabbah
Laud. cruc	Rabanus Maurus, *De laudibus crucis*
Laud. Dei	Dracontius of Carthage, *De laudibus Dei*
Laud. virg.	Aldhelm of Malmesbury, *De laude virginitatis*
Lect	*Lectio difficilior*
Lex Baiuv.	*Lex Baiuvariorum*
Lib. const.	*Liber constitutionum*
Lib. dec. cap.	Marbod of Rennes, *Liber decem capitulorum*
Lib. exhort.	*Liber exhortationis*
Lib. man.	Dhuoda, *Liber manualis*
Liut. Leg.	*Liutprandi Leges*
LXX	Septuagint
MAJ	*Melbourne Art Journal*
MDAI	*Mitteilungen des Deutschen Archäologischen Instituts*
MEFRA	*Mélanges de l'École française de Rome: Antiquité*
Metam.	Ovid, *Metamorphoses*
MF	Mittelalter-Forschungen
MGH	Monumenta Germaniae Historica
MJ	*Mittellateinisches Jahrbuch*
MilM	Millennio medieval
MM	Medieval Mediterranean
MNEA	*Mediterranean and Non-European Archaeology*
Mor. phil.	Hildebert of Lavardin, *Moralis philosophia*
Moral.	Gregory the Great, *Moralia*
MSB	Middeleeuwse studies en bronnen

MSKG	Millennium-Studien zur Kultur und Geschichte des ersten Jahrtausends n.Chr
MT	Masoretic Text
MW	*Muslim World*
Nat.	Andrew of Crete, *In nativitatem*
Nat.	Ephrem, *De nativitate*
Nat. grat.	Augustine, *De natura et gratia*
NEchtB	Die Neue Echter Bibel
NOB	Neue Orientalische Bibliothek
NRSV	New Revised Standard Version
OC	*Oriens Christianus*
Odes Sol.	Odes of Solomon
Off.	Cicero, *De officiis*
Or.	Theodore the Studite, *Orationes*
Ores. trag.	Dracontius of Carthage, *Orestis tragoedia*
OS	*Orientalia Sticcana*
P&P	*Past and Present*
Paen. Ambr.	Paenitentiale Ambrosianum
Paen. Cas.	Paenitentiale Casinense
Paen. Columb.	Columban, *Paenitentiale Columbani*
Paen. Finn.	Paenitentiale Finniani
Paen. Flor.	Paenitentiale Floriacense
Paen. Hub.	Paenitentiale Hubertense
Paen. Mart.	Paenitentiale Martenianum
Paen. Mers.	Paenitentiale Merseburgense
Paen. Oxon.	Paenitentiale Oxoniense
Paen. Par.	Paenitentiale Parisiense simplex
Paen. Ps.-Egb.	Paenitentiale Pseudo-Egberti
Paen. Ps.-Greg.	Paenitentiale Pseudo-Gregorii
Paen. Ps.-Rom.	Paenitentiale Pseudo-Romanum
Paen. Ps.-Theod.	Paenitentiale Pseudo-Theodori
Paen. Sang.	Paenitentiale Sangallense tripartitum
Paen. Sil.	Paenitentiale Silense
Paen. Vall.	Paenitentiale Vallicellanum
Paen. Vig.	Paenitentiale Vigilanum
ParOr	Parole de l'Orient
PG	Migne, Jacques-Paul, ed. Patrologia graeca. 161 vols. Paris, 1857–1886.
Phil	*Philologus*

PIAC	Pontificio Istituto di Archeologia Cristiana
PL	Migne, Jacques-Paul, ed. Patrologia Latina. 217 vols. Paris, 1844–1855.
Poen. lib.	Rabanus Maurus, *Poenitentium liber*
Praes.	Germanos of Constantinople, *In praesentationem*
Prot. Jas.	Protevangelium of James
PRSt	*Perspectives in Religious Studies*
Ps.-Matt.	Pseudo-Matthew
Psych.	Prudentius, *Psychomachia*
QFRM	Quellen und Forsschungen zum Recht im Mittelalter
QGM	Quellen zur Geistesgeschichte des Mittelalters
RAug	*Recherches Augustiniennes*
Reg.	Benedict, *Regula*
Reg.	Gregory VII, *Registrum*
Reg. brev.	Basil, *Regulae brevius tractatae*
Reg. can.	Chrodegang of Metz, *Regula canonicorum*
RevA	*Revue de l'art*
Rhet	*Rhetorica: A Journal of the History of Rhetoric*
RINASA	*Rivista dell'Istituto Nazionale di Archeologia e Storia dell'Arte*
RJK	*Römisches Jahrbuch für Kunstgeschichte*
Rom.	Dracontius of Carthage, *Romuleum*
RSR	*Recherches de science religieuse*
RSV	Revised Standard Version
RTAM	*Recerches de Théologie Ancienne et Médiévale*
San.	Sanhedrin
Sat.	Juvenal, *Saturae*
SBT	Studies in Biblical Theology
SBU	Studia Byzantina Upsaliensia
SC	Sources Chrétiennes
SCH	Studies in Church History
Scol.	Walter of Speyer, *Scolasticus*
Serm.	*Sermones*
Serm. cast.	*Sermo de castitate*
SH	Subsidia Hagiographica
Shab.	Shabbat
SHK	Schriften des Historischen Kollegs
SI	Scriptores Iberici
SISMEL	Societá internazzionale per lo Studio del Medioevo Latino

SL	Schriften zur Literaturwissenschaft
SLH	Scriptores Latini Hiberniae
SO	Symbolae Osloenses
Sobr.	Milo of Saint-Amand, *De sobrietate*
SOC	Studi sull'Oriente cristiano
SPBS	Society for the Promotion of Byzantine Studies
SPF	Studia Patristica Fennica
SSAM	Settimana di Studio sull'Alto Medioevo
StT	Studi e Testi, Biblioteca apostolica vaticana
SVTQ	St Vladimir's Theological Quarterly
SWR	Studies in Women and Religion
Syn. prim.	Synodus primus S. Patricii
Synthronon	Synthronon: Art et archéologie de la fin de l'Antiquité et du Moyen Âge
Tanh.	Tanhuma
TBN	Themes in Biblical Narrative
TFCI	Theologisches Forum Christentum-Islam
Theb.	Statius, *Thebaid*
Theol. Chr.	Abelard, *Theologia Christiana*
ThH	Théologie Historique
TM	Travaux et memoires
TQ	Theologische Quartalschrift
TS	Texts and Studies
TSAJ	Texte und Studien zum antiken Judentum
UB	Untersuchungen zu den Bussbüchern des 7, 8, und 9. Jahrhunderts
USQR	Union Seminary Quarterly Review
UTET	Unione tipografico-editrice torinese
VCSup	Supplements to Vigiliae Christianae
Virg.	Alcimus Avitus, *De virginitate*; Ephrem, *De virginitate*; Venantius Fortunatus, *De virginitate*
Vita Alc.	Vita Alcuini
Vita Mar. Jun.	Vita Mariae junioris
Vita Matr.	Vita Matronae
Vita Rad.	Baudonivia, *Vita Radegundis*
Vita sanct. abb.	Bede, *Vita sanctorum abbatum*
Vita Theod.	Gregory, *Vita Theodorae Thessalonicae*
Vita Thom.	Vita Thomaïs
W&I	Word and Image
WS	Wiener Studien

y.	Jerusalem Talmud
YSMT	York Studies in Medieval Theology
ZDP	*Zeitschrift für deutsche Philologie*
ZÖGDO	*Zeitschrift der österreichischen Gesellschaft für Denkmal und Ortsbildpelege*
ZRVI	*Zbornik Radova Vizantološkog Instituta*
ZSS	*Zeitschrift der Savigny-Stiftung für Rechtsgeschichte*

Introduction

Franca Ela Consolino and Judith Herrin

The early Middle Ages is a period of history often considered entirely Christian—meaning Roman Catholic—but, of course, other forms of Christianity as well as other faiths flourished between the fifth and eleventh centuries CE. Women who lived outside of the core of Western Europe, where the pope was the recognized head of Christendom as the successor to Peter, belonged to different churches, such as Greek Orthodox, Arian, Monophysite, Donatist, Nestorian, or to different religions, such as Judaism and Islam. Nonetheless, they were all influenced by the biblical texts that circulated widely and were known even to the illiterate and the uneducated. The Jewish tradition of the Old Testament had been accepted by the early Christians as the foundation for their revelation, documented in the New Testament, and both were known to the followers of Mohammad, whose teaching on submission to God (Islam) incorporated elements of both Judaic and Christian teachings.

In putting together this volume, it seemed appropriate to reflect these different realities, depicting as inclusively as possible the relationships that women from different geographical areas, classes, and levels of education had with the Bible. In some rarer and more fortunate cases, there was direct contact between individual women and the holy text—for instance, in the writings of nuns: Kassia in Byzantium, Hrotsvit in the West. More often, this contact was mediated by men, who drew on biblical models to inspire and guide women. For all of them, whether they could study the Bible on their own or knew it by hearing it read aloud or through commentary and stories regarding individual events or figures, the influence of the Judeo-Christian heritage was profound.

Although the entire Christian world was founded on the Holy Scripture as revealed truth, not all Christians related to the text in similar ways. In the Latin sphere, Jerome's direct encounter with the Hebrew text of the

Old Testament had brought about some discrepancies as compared to the Greek translation of the Septuagint, upon which the previously extant Latin versions had been modeled and which continued to circulate for some time while the Vulgate gradually became the key text for most readers. Similarly, establishing the canon of the Greek New Testament took many centuries—even the list of the books to include was not settled early on—and local martyrs with their cults and shrines, miracle stories, and hymns generated a remarkable variety of texts that directly or indirectly referred to the Bible.

The Bible did not always give clear or exhaustive answers to the questions raised by its readers. On the one hand, there were obscure passages that were difficult to interpret, and, on the other hand, there was the need to draw individual moral and behavioral lessons from the excerpts and episodes of Scripture; this was firstly the task of biblical exegesis, begun by Greek writers, but later practiced by Latin authors in an increasingly autonomous way. Less attention was given to certain questions—though they could have engaged even the less educated of the faithful—that remained unaddressed regarding the fate of figures on which the Bible gave little information, first among them the Virgin. In the East as in the West, this need found fulfillment in a series of apocryphal writings, composed with the precise intent—at times openly declared—of filling this gap. Coming from complementary but different spheres of research with distinct linguistic problems, we believed it best to compare and contrast such writings wherever possible.

While taking account of this group of texts, we see that various key elements dominated women's understanding of the Bible. Since late antiquity, two female figures had taken on critical importance: Eve, who was held responsible for the expulsion of the human race from paradise, and Mary, who redeemed it through her role in salvation. Within the Christian tradition, these polar opposites set up a general instruction: to avoid the sins of Eve and emulate the virtues of Mary. Sexual connotations reinforced the two models: since Eve was seduced by the serpent—that is, by the Devil—it was she who persuaded Adam to disobey God (hence the myriad warnings from the church fathers on the dangers of women) and who was further punished by subordination to man and the pain of repeated childbirths. By contrast, Mary had no knowledge of men and sexuality, having conceived through the Holy Spirit and given birth without pain.

Since no medieval women could ever fully realize the model of Mary—virgin and at the same time mother of God—they were all potentially condemned to that of Eve, and male authors constantly urged them to resist this essentially sinful image while aspiring to a higher, asexual existence akin to that of the angels. That many succeeded is clear from the numerous references to women embracing a celibate life as nuns and ascetics, who thus managed to throw off the inevitable comparison with Eve and draw nearer to the model represented by Mary. In encouraging devotion to her, the East and the West drew on different aspects of Marian worship, which, however, took on much greater importance in the Greek East during the early Middle Ages, as evidenced by the hymns to the Mother of God, which had no equivalent in the Latin West. Furthermore, a Life of Mary composed in Greek in the early Middle Ages and surviving only in a Georgian translation suggests that the Virgin served as a guide among the apostles, its feminist approach earning it much critical attention.

Educated women, who could select the biblical models most suitable to them (or to the men of the church, who sought to indicate them to women), could choose from a wide range of biblical figures for inspiration. On this matter, it is interesting to note that the figures used as models were not always the same. Thus in the East—where the presence and strength of the Marian model were more pervasive—biblical heroines such as Judith and Esther, for example, were much less often invoked than in the West; these models naturally had a tremendous appeal among medieval Jewish communities and even in some Muslim societies. For this reason, we felt that it was essential to include contributions from specialists in those fields, where biblical stories were well known and appreciated.

The theme of the relationship between women and the Bible can be articulated in various ways, as it can refer both to biblical precepts on women and for women; to biblical women as the subjects of action or objects of discussion, often as examples; and, lastly, to women who in their writings refer to the Bible as a moral authority and/or a narrative source that also includes the Apocrypha. In choosing the essays forming this volume, we have sought to represent each of these different ways, which intersect and overlap not infrequently.

Essays on the authoritative use of the Bible as a source of moral precepts have been contributed by Stavroula Constantinou for the Greek East and by Giuseppe Cremascoli for the Latin West. Cremascoli's essay gives a meaningful illustration of how the Bible has been used to warn against the risks of feminine appeal, addressing a readership primarily composed of religious figures, particularly monks. Starting with the Bible's indications regarding the risks—from which not even the wise are exempt—of straying from the straight and narrow path of faith, he notes how the greatest perils to which men's souls are exposed are wine and women; in particular, the nefarious influence that the latter exert are exemplified by the well-known vicissitudes of King Solomon. These oft-repeated thoughts form a constant element extending from late antiquity to the entire Middle Ages and beyond. It is a path of twists and turns, each of which accentuates or minimizes the negative role of women as an instrument of perdition, and in a way—as the scholar skillfully notes—it links the stability of the word and the biblical precept to a world of male unease held at bay but not entirely eradicated.

Constantinou, however, shows how in a heavily androcentric society (here the author speaks of kyriarchy), biblical precepts—of the apostle Paul in particular—on the submission of women were proposed, obviously by male authors, to a female public through exemplary stories; their female protagonists have introjected these precepts and adopted them as their own, abandoning the idea of a will independent of that of their husbands, who are often not their spiritual equals. These cases of harmonious couples are joined by others in which women protagonists, as an affirmation of their devotion, withstand without complaint (and at times provoke) the violence and mistreatment inflicted upon them by brutal husbands. The comparison with Procopius's commentary on the behavior of Belisarius and Justinian with their respective wives confirms the existence of socially shared parameters that base relations between the sexes on the total submission of women. When women apply the lessons of the Bible (and the men of the church who took on its interpretation) to themselves, at best they achieve the spiritual betterment of themselves and their husbands; at worst, they attain holiness through pious acts that will lead to the inevitable and expected cruelty of their spouse.

In addition to the two figures of Eve and Mary, set at opposite extremes by the earliest Christian interpreters of the Bible, Scripture offers a plentiful gallery of heroines on which to reflect and urge to reflect, and certainly one might suppose that their vicissitudes and problems could particularly engage a female public struggling with similar issues. Thus in societies to which the problem of fertility was of primary importance, all women who had trouble conceiving were likely attracted to stories of unexpected births, as in the case of Sarah, who succeeded in giving Abraham a son only in her old age, or Elizabeth, the aged mother of John the Baptist. Many empresses, queens, and women of the ruling elite shared the same problem of infertility with poor, ordinary women, and all of them are likely to have identified with the biblical protagonists of miraculous conceptions and prayed for a similar remedy to their barrenness. In the same way, a figure such as that of the repentant sinner (generally identified with Mary Magdalene) could have served as a warning not to lose the hope of divine mercy.

The written documentation available to us, however, did not always report this kind of reaction, and here the differences between East and West become apparent. For example, while Kassia succeeds in expressing the torment of the female sinner with extreme skill, the same cannot be said of the Latin writers, for whom the figure of Mary Magdalene did not receive special attention in the early Middle Ages, though it was established—quite firmly—shortly thereafter. Perhaps even more astonishingly, the Carolingian noblewoman Dhuoda, forcibly separated from her two sons (the eldest, William, sent to the court of Charles the Bald and the youngest taken from her for security reasons before he had even been baptized), did not seek identification with the Virgin, whom she never mentions, or the mother of Maccabees, but rather she likens herself to Job. Our book aims to reflect what emerges from the texts and grants the Virgin, who certainly dominates among the biblical heroines, much more room in the contributions regarding the Greek East, where her worship took on an all-encompassing dimension.

For the Latin West, Francesco Stella examines the success of certain female protagonists of the Old and New Testaments and illustrates their long duration in poetic texts ranging from late antiquity to beyond the early Middle Ages. The gallery of exemplary biblical women selected for readers' admiration—Judith and Esther chief among them—addresses a mixed readership; the texts urging consecrated chastity, however, address primarily and essentially women, who, though in different life conditions, are advised to imitate their virtues. Such an imitation could be achieved in various ways, given the adaptability of these figures, who can rise to models of behavior both sober and heroic (Judith in particular) but who when needed—as occurs with the empresses Judith and Ermengarde—may become the bearers of more concrete allusions to the political sphere and the management of power.

These women of the Bible, who find sufficient space and recognition in the Latin West, are all but eclipsed by the particular prominence of the Theotokos, the Virgin who generated God. Our volume acknowledges this reality, carefully analyzed by Mary B. Cunningham, who studies how the worship of the Virgin progressively established itself during the middle

Byzantine period (approximately the seventh to the twelfth century). Her worship became fully integrated in Byzantine society and was expressed among other things with the addition to the liturgical calendar of five feast days (Nativity of the Virgin, Presentation at the Temple, Conception, Annunciation, and Dormition) and other, minor commemorations, roughly between the sixth and the early eighth centuries. This study of liturgical sermons and hymns in honor of the Virgin is paired with a study of some lives of the Virgin Mary and shows how, despite differences of situation and literary genre, liturgical and hagiographical writings shared the tendency to portray Mary as a figure endowed with autonomous importance, thus granting her a role that takes its place beside that of Christ but that is not confined to it.

An indirect indication of the rising importance taken on by the Virgin in the East can also be found in ancient Hebrew literature. The essay by Martha Himmelfarb demonstrates this by examining three excerpts illustrating three different ways in which the ancient Jews reacted to the figure of the Virgin. The authors of such texts, produced in a period ranging approximately from the fourth to the sixth century and in environments under heavy Byzantine influence, appropriate certain aspects of her role, though perhaps to twist or turn them upside down. Not by chance, two of the heroines are mothers of the Messiah, and the other is the mother of seven children, her martyrdom portrayed in a key of redemption; the different fortunes of the three protagonists in the Middle Ages are also significant. The fate of Hephzibah is particularly revealing in this sense: the warrior-like, rather unfeminine mother of a Messiah lost her appeal as soon as the center of Jewish literature left the Byzantine Empire, thus eliminating the need to set her protective action against that which the Christians granted to the Virgin. By contrast, the mother of seven children, who had also appropriated a redeeming role that the Christians attributed to the Virgin, would maintain her validity as a model woman and mother throughout the Middle Ages, even beyond the Byzantine sphere.

The Old and New Testaments exercised a strong influence on Islam, the third great monotheist religion, which arose and established itself during the early Middle Ages. Therefore, an anthology on women and the Bible in the early Middle Ages would be gravely incomplete if it had not considered the biblical women present in the Qur'an; the work of Ulrike Bechmann fills this gap. In the Qur'an, which acknowledges not only the Bible but also the Bible and its reception, female figures of biblical origin appear relatively infrequently and their names are not given;

their importance is not linked to individual prerogatives or actions so much as—and this is a trait they share with the male protagonists—what they announce or signify in relation to the actions of God. The only one to be explicitly named is Maryam (Mary), who finds a place even in the mysticism and popular religion of Islam.

In addition to the written word, images had a highly important role, as they could teach the stories of the Bible (and the Apocrypha) and enable the establishment of devotional relationships not necessarily mediated by the voices of preachers or the reading of texts. The contribution of Giuseppa Z. Zanichelli on the depiction of the Virgin illustrates both what could be considered a common background in the East and West (the mosaics of Santa Maria Maggiore are particularly important in this regard) and the developments seen in each of the two areas, in a constant dialogue between these two different realities.

But the early Middle Ages were not only populated by many anonymous women who were more or less passive recipients of the Bible and its precepts, messages, and figures. This was also a period in which women wove an often profound dialogue with the word of the Bible and established a varyingly creative relationship with it. This more personal and direct involvement was expressed both in the exchange of letters—of which, moreover, only those of the primary intellectuals and spiritual leaders have been preserved—and in the Greek and Latin works written by women. Two essays are dedicated to the Bible in early medieval epistolography addressed to women: that of Rosa Maria Parrinello for the Greek East and that of Christiane Veyrard-Cosme for the Latin West; the essays dedicated to women authors are that of Anna M. Silvas on Kassia and that of Franca Ela Consolino on Dhuoda and Hrotsvit.

In volume 6.2 of the Bible and Women series on the twelfth to fifteenth century, Parrinello has already explored women's knowledge of the Bible at the end of medieval Byzantium; her contribution to this work has thus enabled us to establish a relationship of continuity with the later and certainly richer and more interesting developments, though—as is well illustrated in the introduction—it would be wrong to deny women's knowledge of the Bible in the period we cover here. Among those who had direct and in-depth knowledge of the Bible, the correspondents of Theodore the Studite—primarily but not exclusively nuns—stand out for their number and variety. Parrinello's research brings out both the different frequency of biblical citations (which at times are even absent) and their plurality of aim, whether consolation, catechesis, or spiritual direction. After all, the achievement of these various aims would have been impossible without the active cooperation of the women recipients, whom Theodore knows to be capable of recognizing the citations and putting them in context. In the dialogue that he thus comes to weave with his learned correspondents, Theodore makes of the Bible not only a shared reference but also an instrument that—combined with his rhetorical prowess—offers an answer to each of their needs for guidance and comfort.

For the Latin West, Veyrard-Cosme delves into letters addressed to women of high society who were capable of a direct and conscious approach to Scripture. Veyrard-Cosme investigates the ambiguities of these women's relationship with the Bible, seeking to determine how much these noblewomen were the subject and how much the object of the discussion of Scripture made with them by men of the church renowned for their learning, such as Alcuin of York, or for their position, like Pope Nicholas I (800–867). In the latter's correspondence with two Eastern empresses, whom he wished to take the side of the papacy, the pope turns to the Bible and its characters: male figures are used in the case of the empress Theodora (Moses, Aaron, Samuel, Zechariah, and even Jesus), while Esther is the model for the empress Eudoxia; in turn, Photius—the enemy of Nicholas—rises to the role of a new Eve. Within such a framework, the Bible is the point of comparison and behavioral parameters to which the two woman sovereigns are urged to conform.

An apparently more active role seems to have been played by some aristocratic nuns—chief among them Gisela, sister of Charlemagne and abbess of Chelles, and her niece Rotrude—in relation to Alcuin, whom they urged to reply to their exegetical questions. The reproposal of the relationship that had been established between Jerome and the pious women he wrote to thus legitimized a cultural exchange in which biblical doctrine and the curiosity of the women—though highly praised by their learned correspondent—become the backdrop for an exhibition that draws on Scripture to highlight the literary personality of the *magister* Alcuin.

Though the room given to female freedom and creativity with regard to Holy Writ cannot always be clearly defined, it becomes possible in the case of the three women who left testimony to it in their writings. The nun Kassia may have been one of the correspondents of Theodore the Studite, but her true importance lies in her poetic work, which offers a personal interpretation of scriptural themes, invoking them in her liturgical verses.

Through the analysis of certain hymns, Silvas shows how the close weave of biblical references offers space for re-evocation, commentary, and theological reflection, which are fully expressed in the liturgical form of the hymn. The author's sensitivity and her profound knowledge of Scripture find confirmation in the rest of her poetic work, which shows Kassia to be aware of the importance of women and their ability to take on a positive role, as long as it is allied with the truth.

A fellow nun, the Saxon Hrotsvit, a poet and author writing in Latin, was active a century after Kassia and lived in Ottonian Germany. The most interesting aspect of her personality is a strong self-awareness that in part translates into the deliberate choice to draw on apocryphal sources for those texts (a minority within her oeuvre) dealing with biblical themes. In justification, she states that one day such texts could be granted the authenticity that was then cast in doubt. In Hrotsvit we find no trace of male mediation (she addresses learned and male readers to ask forgiveness for her lack of skill, not to request doctrinal instruction), and her longest poem on an apocryphal subject is a biography of the Virgin that anticipates that attention to Mary that would be established a few years later with the arrival at court of the Byzantine Theophano.

But perhaps the most interesting case of all of an early medieval woman in direct contact with the Bible is a married laywoman, the duchess Dhuoda, who married into the high Carolingian aristocracy. About midway through the ninth century, after her fifteen-year-old son William was taken from her, Dhuoda decided to draft a manual that would guide him while he lived at the court of Charles the Bald, where his father had been forced to send him as a token of his loyalty. Dhuoda's case is made absolutely unique by both her condition as a married woman and by the use she makes of the Bible—as a layperson unmediated by men of the church—which sees the Bible as a book from which to draw maxims and examples that apply to the secular life of a young nobleman. In acting as a distance educator, this *mater dolorosa* turns to male biblical models, seeing her likeness in the role of the apostle Paul and expressing her affliction through the words of Job. The decision to discuss her and Hrotsvit together fulfills the dual purpose of bringing out both women's independence and the specificity of their respective positions.

Implicit in the stories of Kassia and Dhuoda, explicit in the letters of Nicholas I, the importance of the relationship between the Bible and political realities also emerges, though for a different purpose, in the essays by Maria Lidova and Ines Weber. Lidova's essay on the iconography of the

Virgin among the angels—widespread in the Byzantine East—shows how such an image, reclaiming contemporary symbolism of imperial power, suggests the queenly power granted to the Theotokos in the heavens and as a consequence reinforces her role as powerful intercessor to God on humanity's behalf. In other words, this is a case in which the perfect understanding of the message conveyed by the image is necessarily dependent on the perfect intelligibility of the system of symbols representing Byzantine power.

The study by Weber shows the profound influence that biblical precepts on marriage, adultery, and divorce exercised not only on the debate within the church but also on the laws governing such matters from the barbarian kingdoms on. The wealth of references reveal the breadth and extensiveness with which biblical precepts had informed the judicial world of the time. But the data gathered in this work also provide a legal background that, among other things, helps us understand a historical fact such as the well-known episode regarding the attempted divorce of Lothair II of Lotharingia (835–869) from his wife Teutberga, who had given him no heir, so as to marry his concubine Waldrada and legitimize the children she had borne him. The presence of extensive regulations before and after that infelicitous story (on which Hincmar of Reims had commented in his treatise *De divorcio Lotharii et Teulbergae*) provides the necessary framework for its context.

In investigating the series of references to women and their responses to the Bible's message, we found a very interesting contrast in the specific mechanisms with which the pervasive influence of Scripture was interpreted. One first, evident difference is both linguistic and geographic: examples such as those of Susannah or Judith receive attention almost exclusively in the West, and Esther, whom Nicholas I invoked as a powerful model for queens on the throne, is rarely cited in the Greek medieval texts; between the tenth and eleventh centuries, she also appeared in the coronation formula for the queens of Germany, while there is no parallel in the East, where the empresses were installed by virtue of being the emperor's wife. Theodore the Studite praises his correspondents in a way that differs greatly from that of his near contemporary Pope Nicholas I, but also from that of the monk Alcuin, who in addressing the nuns of the Carolingian elite reclaims for them and himself the role that had belonged to Jerome.

The comparison between Western Europe and Byzantium reveals, beyond their shared theological heritage, certain sensitive differences connected to the importance and cultural and liturgical centrality of the Theotokos, an importance that is also reflected by the Jewish reaction to the Christian interpretation of Scripture. Throughout the period, both verbal and visual images of women were adapted to particular functions and circumstances, with distinct developments in the Greek East and the Latin West, and yet another vision of the female biblical figures comes to us from the reinterpretation of the Bible—and its exegesis—proposed in the Qur'an.

A comparison with figurative arts also yields insights. For example, the depictions of episodes taken from the Apocrypha, especially as regards the life of the Virgin, corresponds to the attitude of Hrotsvit, who consciously chose apocryphal sources for her writings with biblical figures as protagonists. Hrotsvit, Kassia, and Dhuoda represent three different ways of dealing with the Bible and its characters, as a comparison between them reveals. And yet what they have in common appears even more important: a great determination, a direct way of coming into contact with Scripture not only to draw from it a moral lesson but also (one might say above all) to find therein a starting point and an inspiration for their own literary work.

Organizing such a great variety of aspects in a single book was no easy task, and we are grateful to Adriana Valerio, who entrusted its editing to us; to Irmtraud Fischer, who, along with Adriana, supported us in solving various practical problems; and to Kari Elisabeth Børresen, who was an invaluable resource during the initial phase of organization. Our dedication aims to pay a debt of gratitude that extends well beyond this particular occasion and regards her contribution as a scholar and her intellectual generosity.

Since the publication of the Italian edition of this volume we have learned with deep sorrow of Kari's death; she was our inspiring teacher and guide in exploring the relationship of early medieval women to the Bible. Our first encounters with this extremely energetic and commanding figure go back several decades. We both recall the insistent demands for our cooperation in her ambitious ventures; these arrived punctually in telephone calls made just after 8 am when Kari assumed we would be at work. From the 1970s onward, her determination to elucidate as fully as possible women's relationships with the Christian faith, from apostolic times through the late twentieth century, was irresistible. Her own scholarly work embodied this extremely broad interest—for example, in her studies of Christina of Sweden and her fierce and effective criticisms of patriarchy—and established a very high bench mark for everyone else. Thanks to her active engagement with the European Science Foundation, we both participated in a series of meetings held in exciting venues (Innsbruch, Göttingen, Strasbourg, Oslo, Rome), where a surprising range of scholars assembled to discuss particular aspects of female engagement with religion. Some of the debates in which we participated during those meetings have influenced our own work, and the present volume is most definitely a product of them; we could not have realized it without them. As the English edition of the volume goes to press, we add this warm appreciation of a leading feminist scholar, whose brilliant research, enthusiasm, and affection has influenced and inspired us so profoundly. We particularly thank Kari for opening up new viewpoints and perspectives that we had not yet considered, which was decisive in promoting a continuous exchange of views. This has enriched us immensely, has led to a shared approach, and, last but not least, has given us the rare pleasure of a scholarly collaboration resulting in a friendship.

In including certain aspects, any choice inevitably leaves others out or is forced to do so. Our volume is no exception to this rule, and we are well aware of it. We hope, however, that the variety of contributions and the differences in themes, environments, languages, and cultures have at least shown the world of the early Middle Ages to be richer and more problematic than one might imagine at first glance, pointing out further perspectives from which to observe the encounter and at times the clash between ideas and realities that influenced the development of later cultures.

With the publication of the English version of the book, we would like to express our gratitude to those who aided us in this undertaking in various ways. We wish, first, to thank the contributors for the texts they have given us and for the patience with which they have awaited their publication. Our special thanks also to the English editor Christiana de Groot and Nicole Tilford from SBL Press, who have given this volume so much care and attention.

"Woman's Head Is Man":
Kyriarchy and the Rhetoric of Women's Subordination in Byzantine Literature

Stavroula Constantinou

Throughout her pioneering work, Elisabeth Schüssler Fiorenza emphatically points out the great impact of biblical texts at various historical times on the ideology of gender and other constructs as well as the mentalities and values of Western societies.[1] Schüssler Fiorenza's insight finds its fullest application in the case of Byzantium, in that it was not just deeply Christian but also the theocratic empire par excellence. The Byzantine emperor was seen as the representative of God on earth. Just as God was the *kyrios* (κύριος, "lord," "master") ruling in heaven, the emperor was the *kyrios* ruling on earth and carrying out the divine commandments.[2] While the lord of the οἰκουμένη was the biblical God and while the emperor made in his image was the ruler of the Byzantine Empire, the *kyrios* of the οἶκος ("household")—around which Byzantine daily life was centered—was the *paterfamilias*, who was in turn the copy of the imperial master.[3] In other

---

1. See, for example, Elisabeth Schüssler Fiorenza, *But She Said: Feminist Practices of Biblical Interpretations* (Boston: Beacon, 1992), 47; Schüssler Fiorenza, *The Power of the Word: Scripture and the Rhetoric of Empire* (Minneapolis: Fortress, 2007).

2. For biblical influences on the Byzantine imperial and political ideologies, see Gilbert Dagron, *Emperor and Priest: The Imperial Office in Byzantium*, trans. Jean Birrell (Cambridge: Cambridge University Press, 2003). For the uses of the Bible in late eleventh- and twelfth-century Byzantium, see Margaret Mullett, "Food for the Spirit and a Light for the Road: Reading the Bible in the *Life of Cyril Phileotes* by Nicholas Kataskepenos," in *Literacy, Education, and Manuscript Transmission in Byzantium and Beyond*, ed. Judith Waring and Catherine Holmes (Leiden: Brill, 2002), 139–64.

3. On the Byzantine οἶκος, see Paul Magdalino, "The Byzantine Aristocratic Oikos," in *The Byzantine Aristocracy, IX to XIII Centuries*, ed. Michael Angold, BARIS 221 (Oxford: BAR, 1984), 92–111; as well as Leonora Neville, *Authority in Byzantine*

words, *kyriarchy*, "the social-political system of domination and subordination based on the power of the *kyrios*—the lord, slave master, pater familias and husband"—that Schüssler Fiorenza detects in the Bible and the societies influenced by it could also be used to describe the male-dominated structures of Byzantine society.[4]

The aim of the present chapter is to examine how Byzantine authors use biblical ideology and in particular the apostle Paul's famous notion that "woman's head is man" (1 Cor 11:3) in order to justify, reinforce, and sustain their society's kyriarchy, which was heavily based on gender inequalities.[5] Assisted by biblical texts, a number of Byzantine authors develop a powerful rhetoric enabling them to present women's position in a convincing and influential way. Their purpose is twofold: first, to encourage women to accept their submission to men as a divinely ordained destiny and in so doing to prevent them from undertaking any authoritative roles; second, to remind men of their responsibility to keep their women in their place. In order to achieve this double goal, they present as role models women who put the Pauline doctrine into practice by acknowledging their inferiority and by willingly accepting their lords' will

---

Provincial Society, 950–1100 (Cambridge: Cambridge University Press, 2004), 66–77. For the father's dominant role in Byzantine family, see Judith Herrin, "Toleration and Repression within the Byzantine Family: Gender Problems," in *Toleration and Repression in the Middle Ages: In Memory of Lenos Mavrommatis*, ed. Katerina Nikolaou, IS 10 (Athens: National Hellenic Research Foundation, 2002), 173–88.

4. Quote from Elisabeth Schüssler Fiorenza, "Yeast of Wisdom or Stone of Truth: Scripture as a Site of Struggle," in *Los caminos inexhauribles de la Palabra: Homenaje a Severino Croatto*, ed. Guillermo Hansen (Buenos Aires: Lumen, 2000), 70 n. 10. Instead of the narrow term *patriarchy*, which, as Schüssler Fiorenza has suggested, has a simple dualistic meaning—as it refers to the subordination of all women to all men without taking into account their racial, social, and other differences—I use here Schüssler Fiorenza's broader term *kyriarchy*, derived from the Greek word for lord (κύριος) and referring to various and reciprocally influential structures of domination and subordination manifested not only in sexism but also in other situations, such as racism, colonialism, and social position. See Schüssler Fiorenza, "To Follow the Vision: The Jesus Movement as *Basileia* Movement," in *Liberating Eschatology: Essays in Honor of Letty M. Russell*, ed. Margaret A. Farley and Serene Jones (Louisville: Westminster John Knox, 1999), 126.

5. Other social inequalities were created by factors such as age, health, sexuality, race, religion, and class. See, for example, Dion Smythe, ed., *Strangers to Themselves: The Byzantine Outsider; Papers from the Thirty-Second Spring Symposium of Byzantine Studies, University of Sussex, Brighton, March 1998*, SPBS 8 (Aldershot: Ashgate, 2000).

and domination, while they describe any women performing the opposite type of behavior as witches. They also harshly criticize any men who allow their women to transgress the limits that their gender imposes upon them, whereas they praise men whose wives are exemplary. The texts used for the purposes of this essay date from the sixth to the eleventh century, and they belong to various genres: hagiography (saint's life, beneficial tale), encomium (funeral oration), and history (emperor's life). By exposing the gender ethics of the examined texts, the following analysis aims to show how literary texts, in this case early and middle Byzantine literature, could function as a powerful tool that serves perfectly the kyriarchal structures and purposes of a given society.

In the *Life of Theodora of Thessaloniki*, a text written around 894 by a certain Gregory, a cleric in Thessaloniki, Greece, we read the following dialogue:

> She used reason to withstand her suffering, and became a support for her husband in his despondency, saying: "I have heard the Holy Writ explain that '*the head of the woman is the man*' [1 Cor 11:3] and that '*the members should have the same care for one another*' [1 Cor 12:25] and that '*the eye cannot say unto the hand, "I have no need of thee." Nay, much more, those members of the body which seem to be more feeble are necessary*' [1 Cor 12:21–22]. Therefore, since I, although feebler and lesser part, have the same care for you, I entreat you, my most respected head, do not be despondent at the loss we have now suffered of our children.... But give thanks to God Who granted <us these children>, and carry out this wish of mine. All men offer first fruits to God; let us also offer the first fruit of our children, the girl who is the sole child remaining to us...."
>
> Her good husband replied to her: "Wife, your wish is a good one, and your advice excellent. Come, let us quickly carry out your good plan. For one should not hesitate to carry out the best propositions." (*Vita Theod.* 8)[6]

This private conversation between the heroine Theodora and her unnamed husband is the only one that the couple is presented as having in the whole narrative. In other cases, it is the omniscient narrator's voice that presents the couple's thoughts, actions, and conjugal life. In this particular instance,

---

6. Translations from Alice-Mary Talbot, "Life of St. Theodora of Thessalonike," in *Holy Women of Byzantium: Ten Saints' Lives in English Translation*, ed. Alice-Mary Talbot, BSLT 1 (Washington, DC: Dumbarton Oaks, 1996), 169–70.

the hagiographer's decision to use the narrative technique of *showing*, in which the characters are presented talking together, is not innocent. As will be demonstrated, it is part of his didactic project that aims to influence his audience's views concerning female behavior: the *Life of Theodora*'s female listeners or readers are provided with the example of a woman whom they could emulate, and men are taught what kind of behavior they should expect from their wives.[7]

The way in which Theodora's words should be read and understood is determined by the narrator's comment that introduces the conversation. Just before giving the heroine's first words, the narrator eulogizes her for her sound judgment and wisdom, which are inextricably related to her virtue as an exemplary wife. Theodora's words that follow are intended to reinforce the earlier presentation of her as a perfect wife by illustrating her goodness in a more direct—and effectively more convincing—way. In addition, Theodora's direct speech is designed to provide a vivid display of the good wife's features—submission, obedience, pious initiatives, and conjugal support in misfortune—which in her case contribute to the acquisition of holiness.

Of course, all these purposes are achieved through the technique of showing, in which the heroine's words take the form of a highly stylized and powerful speech. Theodora starts her speech by employing citations from one of Paul's authoritative epistles, 1 Corinthians, in which the apostle describes the relationship between man and woman. In Paul's powerful rhetoric, effectively incorporated into Theodora's own discourse and further expounded, the relationship between man and woman is likened to that between the more and less important bodily parts (head to the rest of the body, or eye to hand).

It should be noted that the body metaphor employed by Paul is a complex one. As pointed out by Alcuin Blamires,

> To extract a hierarchized, gendered "head/body" metaphor from [Paul's epistles] is to do violence to a complex system of analogies within analogies. Christ, designated as head of the Church, is then imagined in a

---

7. In contrast to the large majority of saints, Theodora is not presented performing any extraordinary deeds. Her behavior and actions are rather closer to those of an ordinary woman than to those of a saint who is an extraordinary individual. This portrayal of Theodora reveals an attempt on the hagiographer's part to create a saint with whom contemporary women could identify.

spousal relation to the Church which is by extension "his body" and which he saves through self-sacrifice. Husbands are by analogy "heads" of their wives, and are urged to follow Christ's example in loving wives who are by extension "their own bodies" and "their own flesh." But husbands and wives are at the same time subsumed into "we" who are all "members" of Christ's/the Church's "body."[8]

Despite the metaphor's complexity, which seems to suggest a gender hierarchy and equality at the same time, church fathers and later Byzantine authors such as the ones discussed here use it to promote gender inequality rather than equality.[9] In Theodora's case, however, the notion of woman's inferiority coexists with a Christian wisdom incorporated by the heroine that her husband lacks. Even though Theodora declares her feminine frailty, she appears stronger and wiser than her husband before the tragedy of their family; she is the one who both manages through faith to eliminate their sorrow at the loss of their two younger children and who also has the God-pleasing idea to offer their oldest daughter to God. Nevertheless, Theodora's spiritual superiority does not provide her with autonomy; it is her husband as "her head" who decides and who puts into practice her suggestions, which he finds "excellent." Her husband is in turn described by the narrator as a "good" man for being aware of his wife's goodness and for seeing the righteousness of her judgment and advice.

It is remarkable that Theodora assumes a voice and takes the initiative to talk to her husband only when *he* needs her consolation and in order to influence him to make decisions according to God's will that would have an important effect on his spiritual improvement. In so doing, she puts into practice another Pauline injunction, "The woman was created for the good of the man" (1 Cor 11:9), which although not cited in the *Life of Theodora* is the subtext of Theodora's behavior and treatment of her husband: she is his servant and helpmate, caring for anything that suits his interests. Before undertaking the role of her husband's teacher in God-pleasing matters, however, Theodora, as already pointed out, does not fail to state her inferiority as a woman. It is this particular behavior that renders her wise and

---

8. Alcuin Blamires, "Paradox in the Medieval Gender Doctrine of Head and Body," in *Medieval Theology and the Natural Body*, ed. Peter Biller and A. J. Minnis, YSMT 1 (Woodbridge: York Medieval, 1997), 14.

9. For church fathers, see Elizabeth A. Clark, "Devil's Gateway and Bride of Christ: Women in the Early Christian World," in *Ascetic Piety and Women's Faith: Essays on Late Ancient Christianity*, SWR 20 (Lewiston, NY: Mellen, 1986), 23–60.

praiseworthy. By praising Theodora for her behavior in her role as a wife and by presenting this very behavior in a prominent way through the technique of showing, her hagiographer encourages the female members of his audience to identify with his heroine and to behave in a similar manner. If they follow her example, they will become perfect not only in men's eyes but also before God. In an analogous way, the married male members of the *Life of Theodora*'s audience are invited to follow the example of Theodora's "good" husband and to put into practice any pious advice or proposal of their wives.

It seems that the presentation of a woman, the saintly protagonist herself, as referring to Pauline passages on the relation between the two genders in order to show and justify woman's unfavorable position did not only serve the kyriarchal purposes of Gregory and those of his ninth- and tenth-century society. In fact, the citation of Paul's texts by female and not male characters becomes a common motif in hagiographical texts produced in different periods. Enjoying the highest popularity among the literary products circulating in Byzantium, hagiographical texts of various genres proved eminently suitable vehicles for promoting the hagiographers' and their society's kyriarchal ideologies. Thus hagiographical heroines who are cast in the wife's role are often depicted paraphrasing or quoting Paul in a way that resembles Theodora's reference to the apostle Paul. As in the case of Theodora's speech, their words are introduced with the narrator's praise. Like Theodora, these heroines appear to refer to Paul's gender notions when they find themselves in a difficult situation in which certain decisions and actions have to take place.

Another case in point found in a hagiographical genre other than the saint's life is the unnamed heroine of an edifying tale from the *Spiritual Meadow* (seventh century) of John Moschus (ca. 550–619). According to the tale, when an extremely beautiful woman visits her husband in prison, where he is kept for debt, she is seen by a rich and powerful man who asks her to go to bed with him and in return promises to give her the money she needs to secure her husband's release from prison. Then "she, who was very beautiful and very pure-minded, said to him: 'My lord, I have heard the Apostle say that a wife does not have authority over her own body: her husband has [1 Cor 7:4]. Let me go and ask my husband, sir, and I shall do what he commands.'"[10] "Sighing deeply and shedding tears," the hus-

---

10. Translation from John Wortley, *The Spiritual Meadow by John Moschus*, CSS 139 (Kalamazoo, MI: Cistercian, 1992), 162.

band rejects the offer.[11] Impressed by the couple's refusal of an offer that would end their misfortune, another prisoner, a robber and murderer who is soon to be executed, tells them where he has hidden the money he has stolen and asks them to take it. As soon as the prisoner is executed, the heroine asks her husband's permission to recover the money. She says to him: "Is it your wish, sir, that I go to the place revealed by the robber and see if he was telling the truth?"[12] Eventually she pays her husband's debts, and he comes out of prison (ch. 189).

This short story could be read as a literary treatise on ideal wifehood, since, as the following analysis will show, the female protagonist's exemplary character and behavior as a wife are the narrative's central themes and the kernels around which the plot unfolds. The unnamed heroine with whom every wife is invited to identify incorporates all the female characteristics praised by church fathers and later Byzantine authors who were influenced by Paul's teachings. Like Theodora, our heroine is moderate, pious, faithful, submissive, and aware of her inferior position. From the beginning to the end of the story, her only focus is on her husband, whose servant and helpmate she becomes. Caring only for her husband's welfare, she is prepared to do everything for him—even to sleep with a man she sees for the first time—if this will provide her with the means to satisfy his great desire for freedom. Her bodily beauty, which is emphasized by the narrator, is seen as a reflection of the beauty of her mind and character, which are the result of her qualities, listed above, that define her not as an independent individual but as a wife.

The heroine's discourse through which her wifely virtues are further illuminated does not have the stylized character of Theodora's words. This might be related to the fact that in contrast to Theodora's hagiographer, Moschus wants to provide his audiences with the portrayal of a wife who has no rhetorical abilities and who is unable to influence her husband's decisions through her speech. This might be the reason why his heroine speaks very little in comparison to Theodora. Despite her protagonist role, she speaks only twice (her words given above) in the whole narrative, and her speeches are reduced to a few short sentences. The anonymous heroine's words, however, serve the same purpose as those of Theodora: to

---

11. Wortley, *Spiritual Meadow*, 162.
12. Wortley, *Spiritual Meadow*, 163.

reveal a woman incorporating the ideals of a kyriarchal society who in so doing will influence the text's audiences.

The first time that the anonymous wife's voice is heard in the narrative is when she has to answer the powerful man's question about whether she would sleep with him if he discharged her husband's debt. In her reply, she first addresses the man with the formal "my lord," a phrase appropriate for a woman and an individual of a lower social class talking to a wealthy and powerful man. Such a form of address reveals, of course, another aspect of the kyriarchal ideology incorporated in the text: the distance that socially inferior people are expected to take from privileged men who are treated as masters. The heroine then goes on to give an answer to the powerful man's question by quoting the apostle Paul (1 Cor 7:4). Unlike Theodora and other hagiographical heroines, she does not refer to the head/body metaphor. Her whole behavior, however, shows that she is its very embodiment.

The second time that the heroine is presented talking is when she wants to find out whether the robber was telling the truth about his hidden money. Her speech this time is even shorter than the previous one. As in her brief conversation with the powerful man, she uses the formal "sir," with which she takes the distance expected in the author's society between a wife and husband. This time, however, she does not make any reference to a biblical authority, such as Paul. The words put in her mouth are again very carefully chosen and formulated by an author whose intention is to create the portrait of an obedient wife whose will is that of her husband. Instead of making a statement that would reveal a personal opinion, she addresses a question that her husband as her lord is invited to answer. She thus asks him if *he* wants her to go and "see if the robber was telling the truth." In fact, the question implies more than it says. The attentive reader realizes that the heroine means to ask if she could retrieve the robber's money in case it exists and if she could use it for her husband's liberation. The reason why she is not presented asking these questions is, I think, related to her construction as a wife without autonomous thought. The kind of question she is depicted asking shows a wife who behaves as if her head were her husband.

The narrative significance of the heroine's exemplary attributes and behavior lies in the fact that they determine the three heroes' own behaviors and actions through which the narrative progresses, reaches its peak, and comes to its natural end. In the first place, the heroine becomes her husband's companion in misfortune: she sees to it that she obtains the bread with which she feeds him, and her frequent visits and their shared meals in prison are meant to offer her husband all the emotional support he needs to continue his miserable life. Her presence in prison, associated with her exemplary behavior, not only consoles her husband, whose love for her increases, but it also attracts the attention of two other men—the powerful man and the prisoner—whose actions will eventually lead to the solution to the couple's problem and as a result the narrative will come to closure. The powerful man suggests a solution, and the narrative is set in motion. His *indecent* yet tempting proposal creates suspense through which the plot comes to a climax. The husband's rejection of the powerful man's proposal and his wife's goodness serve a twofold narrative function: they dissolve the feelings of suspense, and they activate the prisoner who becomes the couple's great helper by offering a solution acceptable to the husband. Through the prisoner's *decent* proposal the story ends.

As is obvious, the three men—husband, powerful man, and prisoner—are involved in a network of relations and actions established by the heroine. The powerful man makes an offer to the heroine, and she, as a submissive wife, lets her husband decide. His love for her as a result of her exemplary behavior prevents him from taking the only opportunity given to him to regain his freedom. His attitude is in accordance with the deutero-Pauline command according to which "husbands should love their wives as their own bodies" (Eph 5:28).[13] For this reason he is praised by the narrator, who calls him a "wise man." The prisoner, in turn, being edified by both of their reactions to the powerful man's offer, decides to help them without putting their integrity at risk. His offer, in contrast, takes the form of an act of penitence, which he gives in the hope of receiving God's forgiveness for his sins. By being an exemplary wife, the heroine becomes instrumental in improving both her husband's and the prisoner's situations. In the first place, the two heroes become better men. Despite his strong wish for freedom, the husband avoids sinning by preventing his wife from committing adultery on his behalf. The prisoner, on the other hand, is made to see his own sins and to repent. In the second place, the husband is released from prison through the prisoner's intervention, whereas the prisoner is released from his sins by performing a good deed motivated by the couple's righteousness.

---

13. In contrast to modern biblical scholars, Byzantine authors considered deutero-Pauline epistles as the apostle Paul's genuine writings.

The good wife's story proves uplifting for other men, too, who identify with the heroes. As Moschus informs us, he learned the story from a certain Eusebius, a priest living in the same city as the story's couple, who tells the tale to the men he comes across. Moschus, in turn, includes the story in his *Spiritual Meadow* for the benefit of both his friend Sophronius, to whom he dedicates his work, and his present and future audiences. In other words, this is a tale dominated by men's actions that is told by men and is originally addressed to men for their own edification.

As the preceding analysis has shown, the tale of the good wife could be described as the kyriarchal narrative par excellence. This is not just a story that originally circulated orally among men—in certain male monastic circles of the East—and that a man wrote down for another man in order to serve male spiritual needs; it is a tale dominated by kyriarchy. Kyriarchal ideologies permeate the story's entire architecture, since they may be detected in all levels: stylistic, thematic, structural, and narrative. In other words, the story introduces its audiences to a world in which only men decide and act. The sole female figure appearing in the narrative, who submits entirely to the kyriarchal ordering of female values, functions as a tool serving male intentions and interests.

"Women are good to think with," not only for hagiographers but also for authors writing in other literary forms, such as the encomium.[14] A case in point is Michael Psellos's (1017/18–1096) funeral oration for his mother Theodote, composed around 1054, in which the famous Byzantine author reveals more about himself than about the subject of his *logos*. As has been suggested by previous scholarship, in writing an encomium for his mother, Psellos aims at achieving a number of personal purposes. First, through his mother, Psellos wants to create an image of himself, to write his own autobiography.[15] Second, the encomium in question is a political document giving an answer to Emperor Constantine IX

---

14. The quote is a very famous aphorism of the French anthropologist Claude Lévi-Strauss (*Structural Anthropology*, trans. Claire Jacobson and Brooke Grundfest Schoepf [Harmondsworth: Peregrine, 1977], 61–62), which was also employed by Peter Brown to describe how men of late antiquity employed women to "verbalize their own nagging concern with the stance that the Church should take to the world" (*The Body and Society: Men, Women, and Sexual Renunciation in Early Christianity* [New York: Columbia University Press, 1988], 153).

15. Michael Angold, "The Autobiographical Impulse in Byzantium," *DOP* 52 (1998): 225–57.

Monomachos's attitude toward Psellos. Third, in praising his mother and presenting her as a saint, Psellos intends to exalt his own ascetic ideals. Fourth, through his mother, Psellos defends his own intellectual and philosophical motivations.[16] Finally, Theodote functions as a tool for Psellos's praise of rhetoric and his defense of rhetorical culture.[17] In his attempt, however, to present his work as an encomium devoted to his saintly mother, and thus to hide his real intentions and purposes, Psellos does not fail to discuss her way of life and to portray her as an exemplary individual in her various roles: as daughter, woman, wife, mother, and ascetic. When at some point Psellos describes Theodote's relation to her unnamed husband, he writes the following:

> To my father she was not only a helpmate and an aide, in accordance with divine degree, but also a prime agent and discoverer of the most noble things.... Since my father was such a man, on account of the equability of his soul everyone felt confident in approaching and speaking to him and not a single person feared to do so. Only my mother, on account of the sublimity of her virtue, did not associate and converse with him on an equal level, but as though she were inferior to him. It was only in this respect that she maintained an incongruity between them and did not speak to him in a manner according to his nature, since she did not seek to conform to his character, but rather to the ancient commandment.[18] (9a, 9d)

In contrast to the hagiographical texts examined so far, Psellos does not use the technique of showing in order to better illustrate his mother's behavior in her role as wife. The reason why he does not employ showing is probably related to the generic characteristics of the literary form he chose, to which this narrative technique does not belong. Another difference between Psellos and the other examined authors is that he does not quote Paul's words. His presentation of the wife Theodote, however, is permeated with Pauline gender doctrines, which are implied in the first and last sentences of the extract above. In spite of these differences, Psellos does not fail in the portrayal of his subject as an ideal wife whose exemplarity

---

16. Anthony Kaldellis, *Mothers and Sons, Fathers and Daughters: The Byzantine Family of Michael Psellos* (Notre Dame: University of Notre Dame Press, 2006), 29–50.

17. Jeffrey Walker, "These Things I Have Not Betrayed: Michael Psellos' Encomium of His Mother as a Defense of Rhetoric," *Rhet* 22 (2004): 49–101.

18. Translation from Kaldellis, *Mothers and Sons*, 67, 68.

lies in her endorsement of kyriarchal gender notions. Like the heroines previously discussed, Theodote is successfully depicted as a female role model for being aware of her inferiority in relation to her husband and for becoming his servant and helpmate. Since, as is the case with Gregory the hagiographer, Psellos's intention is to provide his mother with saintly attributes, he also adds to Theodote's wifely portrait her ability to act as a mediator of divine matters in her relationship with her husband.

Assisted by a biblically informed rhetoric and certain narrative techniques in their depictions of conjugal relationships, the authors examined so far kill two birds with one stone: they sustain and promote at the same time kyriarchal and religious values that might sometimes be antithetical. Laywomen, for instance, who are encouraged by hagiography to take religious initiatives, have to transgress the boundaries of the passive and submissive behavior assigned to them by their kyriarchal society. The authors in question manage to avoid giving antikyriarchal messages to their audiences by portraying harmonious marriages in which the heroines' involvement in religious matters is achieved through the consent of their husbands who share their religious interests. In fact, as has already been pointed out, the heroines are presented as having God-pleasing suggestions, which their equally pious husbands gladly put into practice. In this way, the heroines appear to the texts' audiences as religiously active without violating the head/body doctrine.

Of course, the texts that aim to strengthen both kyriarchal and Christian ideals among lay audiences are also addressed to women whose marital relationships are far from harmonious because their husbands are cruel, lead immoral lives, and do not share their religious aspirations. How, then, are these wives to be convinced to treat their husbands as their head, on the one hand, and at the same time adopt religious practices with which their husbands disagree, on the other? The answer to this question is given by a number of lay saints' lives (vitae) whose female protagonists achieve the crown of holiness both through acknowledging the authority of their brutal and impious husbands and by engaging in intense religious activities including charity, fasting, continuous prayer, and frequent visits to church, all of which meet the husbands' strong resistance—especially charity that affects the couples' economic situation.[19]

---

19. See Stavroula Constantinou, *Female Corporeal Performances: Reading the Body in Byzantine Passions and Lives of Holy Women*, SBU 9 (Uppsala: Acta Universitatis Upsaliensis, 2005), 162–92.

The hagiographers of holy wives resolve this contradiction—namely, to give the impression that their heroines do not deviate from the head/body doctrine while in fact they do so, since they do not follow their husbands' will but lead autonomous lives—by employing two methods. First, like the authors previously discussed, they present their heroines using a rhetoric influenced by that of Paul and his teachings. Mary the Younger, for instance, the protagonist of one of the vitae in question (an anonymous text written at some point in the eleventh century) says to her husband: "I know that I am not mistress of my body, but that you are my head, even if you do not think so" (Vita Mar. Jun. 7).[20] Second, our hagiographers depict their protagonists welcoming their husbands' violence, which in Schüssler Fiorenza's words "constitutes the heart of kyriarchal oppression."[21] Holy wives are humiliated and mercilessly beaten by their husbands, who cause their premature and sudden deaths. Thomaïs, for example, another holy wife whose anonymous life is dated to the mid-tenth century, finds her angry husband waiting for her when she returns home after performing her religious activities. He is described as a "violent tyrant with beetled brows, grimly regarding the blessed <Thomaïs>, and ... displaying a wild-looking glance and the coarse nature of his face" (Vita Thom. 15).[22] Without saying a word, he resorts to violence. His beatings cause such a great pain to the heroine that, as the hagiographer remarks, it cannot be "expressed in words" (Vita Thom. 9).[23]

The holy wives' bodily punishments are seen by both themselves and their husbands as natural and necessary. Since the wives disobey their husbands, they, as men whose authority has been questioned, have the absolute right and responsibility to punish them and, in so doing, to restore the order violated through their disobedience. For example, Thomaïs's hagiographer stresses how happily she receives her husband's unbearable and humiliating blows, which she both desires and enjoys: "She exulted and she rejoiced, '*My soul rejoicing shall exult in the Lord*, for He hath clothed me in the garment of salvation and the tunic of gladness'" (Vita Thom.

---

20. Translation from Angeliki Laiou, "Life of St. Mary the Younger," in Talbot, *Holy Women of Byzantium*, 263.
21. Elisabeth Schüssler Fiorenza, introduction to *Violence Against Women*, ed. Elisabeth Schüssler Fiorenza and Mary Shawn Copeland (London: SCM, 1994), x.
22. Translations from Paul Halsall, "Life of St. Thomaïs of Lesbos," in Talbot, *Holy Women of Byzantium*, 313.
23. Halsall, "Life of St. Thomaïs," 307.

7).²⁴ The more painful the husband's violence becomes, the more enjoyable it is. Thomaïs sees herself as a martyr who suffers at the hands of a tyrant for Christ's love. By behaving thus as true kyriarchs, the holy wives' husbands enable them to achieve holiness. It is through their husbands' violence, rather than through their own pious activities, that their sanctity is constructed.

Despite his kyriarchal teachings, Paul does not refer to husbands' use of violence against their wives. There are, however, other biblical texts such as 1 Peter that suggest that slaves and women should not resist their lords' or husbands' abusive and violent behavior. The violence addressed to them should be seen both as God's will and as the result of their own faults and inferior status. They are expected to suffer as followers of Christ. If they resist and do not forgive their lords, they cannot be Christ-like (1 Pet 2:18–24; 3). By echoing these ideas, the saints' lives of pious wives provide as role models for their female audiences women who welcome and stoically endure their husbands' or their lords' violence.

The Life of Mary the Younger in particular also appears to reflect the slave ideology of 1 Peter, as Mary's husband's treatment of the female servant who is close to her attests. Nikephoros—that is the name of Mary's husband—believes that his wife is having a sexual affair and threatens to kill her servant unless she reveals the name of Mary's assumed lover. The servant then reacts and is treated as follows:

> She said, "My lord, this day you hold in your hands my life and death, and I will suffer anything you wish. But I know nothing shabby about my mistress, nor have I heard such from others." He was filled with rage at this, and, having the slave stretched out on the ground, ordered her to be beaten mightily. Learning nothing more from her, even though she was whipped a good deal, he grudgingly allowed her to go free. (Vita Mar. Jun. 8)²⁵

Like Mary and the other violently treated holy wives, the servant is praised by the hagiographer for acknowledging her master's rights over her and for her bravery in the face of his inhuman violence. Following her mistress, and thus behaving in accordance with the exhortations of 1 Peter, the servant acquires the saintly attribute of endurance in suffering.

---

24. Halsall, "Life of St. Thomaïs," 307.
25. Laiou, "Life of St. Mary," 264.

All in all, the saints' lives of holy wives aim to teach laywomen married to impious and cruel husbands how to serve God without endangering their society's kyriarchal structures. These texts suggest that suffering in marriage is a natural and even necessary condition. Its endurance is a personal victory leading to spiritual growth. The wife who willingly undergoes violence at her husband's hands for Christ's sake achieves the greatest feminine virtue, which provides her with the crown of holiness. A wife such as Procopius's Theodora in the *Historia arcana*, on the other hand, who often becomes her husband's head, is an anti-woman that should be stigmatized and condemned.

"For Theodora was all too prone both to storm ... and to shew her teeth in anger" (Procopius, *Hist. arc.* 1.14).[26] In this short passage, which introduces Theodora into the narrative for the first time, the heroine is portrayed as a shrew-witch who easily loses her temper and "shows her teeth." As the narrative unfolds, the empress's representation as a witch is further developed and becomes more evident through the heroine's lurid premarital sexual life and her evil conduct. Theodora's portrayal as the witch-wife of Justinian, described in turn as the Antichrist, constitutes an inversion of that of the saintly woman who is the bride of Christ. Unlike the saintly woman, Theodora's goal is not to save but to destroy the world.

According to Procopius's *Historia arcana*, the strongest proof of Justinian's wickedness is his marriage with Theodora, a former prostitute of low origin possessing no virtue: "I need make mention of nothing else whatever in regard to the character of this man. For this marriage would be amply sufficient to shew full well all the maladies of his soul, since it serves as both an interpreter and a witness and recorder of his character" (*Hist. arc.* 10.3–4).[27] Procopius's literary treatment of Theodora is another instance in which a male author uses women to think with. In this case, however, the author employs an anti-woman because his main purpose is to attack Emperor Justinian for his character, failures, and bad judgments. Of course, through Theodora, Procopius also expresses his concern about conjugal relationships in which traditional hierarchy is inverted. Apart from being entertaining and highly sophisticated literature, the *Historia arcana* is a didactic work suggesting that husbands and wives ought to

---

26. Translation from H. B. Dewing, *Procopius, Anecdota, or Secret History*, LCL (London: Heinemann, 1935), 9–10.

27. Dewing, *Procopius*, 121.

perform their proper roles. Transgressive women are sources of disorder and agents of disaster, and as such they should not be tolerated.

The Pauline head/body metaphor describing Christ's relation to the church and man's relation to woman is also applied in monastic contexts where the abbot or the abbess is seen as the head of the monastic body: "The entire congregation of your sisterhood, together with your superior in Christ, resembles a complete body, composed and constituted of a head and different parts, which have different faculties and energies."[28] A number of monastic foundresses' and abbesses' vitae show that in the case of nunneries the head is often not the abbess but a male spiritual authority, such as a bishop, a patriarch, or an influential abbot. Female monastic foundation documents authored by women that claim woman's frailty and her incompetence in undertaking leadership roles confirm that the governance of a nunnery by a man is not a literary topos but a reality reflected in hagiographical literature.[29]

A hagiographical narrative that affords a very good illustration of the application of the gendered head/body metaphor in monastic contexts is the Life of Matrona, an anonymous text written around the middle of the sixth century. After spending her religious career as a pious wife suffering at her husband's hands for Christ's sake, as a cross-dressing monk in the monastery of the holy abbot Bassianos in Constantinople, as a nun in a convent in Emesa, Syria, and as an anchoress in various places, Matrona returns to Constantinople to satisfy her great desire to be close to her former abbot and spiritual father Bassianos. She eventually founds a nunnery in Constantinople after securing Bassianos's permission and assistance. Until his death, Bassianos acts as the heroine's spiritual father and as the head of her nunnery, which is constructed after the fashion of Bassianos's monastery.

---

28. Alice-Mary Talbot, trans., "Typikon of Theodora Synadene for the Convent of the Mother of God Bebaia Elpis," in *Byzantine Monastic Foundation Documents: A Complete Translation of the Surviving Founders' Typika and Testaments*, ed. John Thomas and Angela Constantinides Hero, DOS 35 (Washington, DC: Dumbarton Oaks, 2000), 1537.

29. Even though the female monastic foundation documents that have come down to us are mostly dated to the late Byzantine period, they seem to offer information about female monasticism that is also valid for previous periods. See Catia Galatariotou, "Byzantine Women's Monastic Communities: The Evidence of the Typika," *JÖB* 38 (1998): 290.

The narrator stresses repeatedly that Matrona always follows her spiritual father's will and that she "undertakes nothing without his consent" (Vita Matr. 36).[30] She is praised for becoming "an exact copy of her teacher" and "a flawless mirror of his way of life, having diligently preserved his legacy and passed it to those who came after her" (Vita Matr. 50).[31] Matrona goes so far as to adopt the girdles and the cloaks worn by Bassianos and his monks as monastic attire both for herself and for her nuns. In other words, Bassianos becomes the head of both Matrona and her nunnery, while the architecture of his monastery, his monastic attire and rules, and his way of life become the models by which Matrona's nunnery and the life within its walls are fashioned. Matrona's hagiographer suggests that her exemplarity as an abbess lies in the very fact that she has as her head such a holy man as Bassianos, who guides her in all her saintly deeds.

Earlier in the narrative and before starting her career as a monk in Bassianos's monastery, Matrona addresses a prayer to God, saying, "For without Thine inclination it is impossible for men to accomplish any good thing, and especially for women, who are easily disposed through weakness to evil's diversion" (Vita Matr. 5).[32] That these words are put into Matrona's mouth by the hagiographer is indicated by the comment that follows: "Such were probably the words with which the noble Matrona besought God" (Vita Matr. 5).[33] Obviously Matrona is another woman to be added to the list of Byzantine literature's heroines presented by the male narrators of their stories as adopting a kyriarchal rhetoric that aims to influence the audiences' gender perceptions. Matrona's words, I believe, offer the key to understanding her later behavior as an abbess. Seeing herself as a "weak" woman not being fit to act autonomously and to undertake such an authoritative role as that of the abbess, she surrenders the guidance of her monastic community to the hands of Bassianos. In so doing, Matrona behaves in accordance with biblical, patristic, Byzantine, and effectively kyriarchal gender dynamics, in which woman is by nature feeble, vulnerable, and unstable and consequently needs male control, protection, and guidance.

---

30. Translation from Jeffrey Featherstone and Cyril Mango, "Life of St. Matrona of Perge," in Talbot, *Holy Women of Byzantium*, 51.
31. Featherstone and Mango, "Life of St. Matrona," 63.
32. Featherstone and Mango, "Life of St. Matrona," 24.
33. Featherstone and Mango, "Life of St. Matrona," 24.

In one of her studies on Byzantine women, Alice-Mary Talbot concludes that

> the Byzantine attitude towards women was ambivalent. Under the influence of two stereotyped female images, the Virgin Mary, who miraculously combined virginity with motherhood, and Eve, the sexual temptress, they vacillated between revering women as mothers and criticizing them as weak and untrustworthy.[34]

As the preceding analysis has shown, however, the treatment of women in Byzantine literature is not *ambivalent*. The Theodora of the *Life of Theodora of Thessaloniki*, for instance, and the Theodora of *Historia arcana*, the ideal woman or saint, on the one hand, and the ideal anti-woman or witch, on the other, are two identities that—despite their obvious differences—represent consistently and unequivocally the same cultural practices, discourses, and ideologies. The two Theodoras who become their husbands' helpmates, either for good or for evil, are constructed to serve Byzantine kyriarchal ideologies in exactly the same ways. In the same way as the Virgin and Eve, these two figures are but two different sides of the same coin.

Bibliography

Angold, Michael. "The Autobiographical Impulse in Byzantium." *DOP* 52 (1998): 225–57.

Blamires, Alcuin. "Paradox in the Medieval Gender Doctrine of Head and Body." Pages 13–29 in *Medieval Theology and the Natural Body*. Edited by Peter Biller and A. J. Minnis. YSMT 1. Woodbridge: York Medieval, 1997.

Brown, Peter. *The Body and Society: Men, Women, and Sexual Renunciation in Early Christianity*. New York: Columbia University Press, 1988.

Clark, Elizabeth A. "Devil's Gateway and Bride of Christ: Women in the Early Christian World." Pages 23–60 in *Ascetic Piety and Women's Faith: Essays on Late Ancient Christianity*. SWR 20. Lewiston, NY: Mellen, 1986.

---

34. Alice-Mary Talbot, "Women," in *The Byzantines*, ed. Guglielmo Cavallo, trans. Thomas Dunlap, Teresa Lavender Fagan, and Charles Lambert (Chicago: University of Chicago Press, 1997), 143.

Constantinou, Stavroula. *Female Corporeal Performances: Reading the Body in Byzantine Passions and Lives of Holy Women*. SBU 9. Uppsala: Acta Universitatis Upsaliensis, 2005.

Dagron, Gilbert. *Emperor and Priest: The Imperial Office in Byzantium*. Translated by Jean Birrell. Cambridge: Cambridge University Press, 2003.

Dewing, H. B., ed. and trans. *Procopius, Anecdota, or Secret History*. LCL. London: Heinemann, 1935.

Featherstone, Jeffrey, and Cyril Mango. "Life of St. Matrona of Perge." Pages 13–64 in *Holy Women of Byzantium: Ten Saints' Lives in English Translation*. Edited by Alice-Mary Talbot. BSLT 1. Washington, DC: Dumbarton Oaks, 1996.

Galatariotou, Catia. "Byzantine Women's Monastic Communities: The Evidence of the Typika." *JÖB* 38 (1998): 263–90.

Halsall, Paul. "Life of St. Thomaïs of Lesbos." Pages 291–322 in *Holy Women of Byzantium: Ten Saints' Lives in English Translation*. Edited by Alice-Mary Talbot. BSLT 1. Washington, DC: Dumbarton Oaks, 1996.

Herrin, Judith. "Toleration and Repression within the Byzantine Family: Gender Problems." Pages 173–88 in *Toleration and Repression in the Middle Ages: In Memory of Lenos Mavrommatis*. Edited by Katerina Nikolaou. IS 10. Athens: National Hellenic Research Foundation, 2002.

Kaldellis, Anthony. *Mothers and Sons, Fathers and Daughters: The Byzantine Family of Michael Psellos*. Notre Dame: University of Notre Dame Press, 2006.

Laiou, Angeliki. "Life of St. Mary the Younger." Pages 239–89 in *Holy Women of Byzantium: Ten Saints' Lives in English Translation*. Edited by Alice-Mary Talbot. BSLT 1. Washington, DC: Dumbarton Oaks, 1996.

Lévi-Strauss, Claude. *Structural Anthropology*. Translated by Claire Jacobson and Brooke Grundfest Schoepf. Harmondsworth: Peregrine, 1977.

Magdalino, Paul. "The Byzantine Aristocratic *Oikos*." Pages 92–111 in *The Byzantine Aristocracy, IX to XIII Centuries*. Edited by Michael Angold. BARIS 221. Oxford: BAR, 1984.

Mullett, Margaret. "Food for the Spirit and a Light for the Road: Reading the Bible in the *Life of Cyril Phileotes* by Nicholas Kataskepenos." Pages 139–64 in *Literacy, Education, and Manuscript Transmission in Byzantium and Beyond*. Edited by Judith Waring and Catherine Holmes. Leiden: Brill, 2002.

Neville, Leonora. *Authority in Byzantine Provincial Society, 950–1100.* Cambridge: Cambridge University Press, 2004.

Schüssler Fiorenza, Elisabeth. *But She Said: Feminist Practices of Biblical Interpretations.* Boston: Beacon, 1992.

———. Introduction to *Violence against Women.* Edited by Elisabeth Schüssler Fiorenza and Mary Shawn Copeland. London: SCM, 1994.

———. *The Power of the Word: Scripture and the Rhetoric of Empire.* Minneapolis: Fortress, 2007.

———. "To Follow the Vision: The Jesus Movement as *Basileia* Movement." Pages 123–43 in *Liberating Eschatology: Essays in Honor of Letty M. Russell.* Edited by Margaret A. Farley and Serene Jones. Louisville: Westminster John Knox, 1999.

———. "Yeast of Wisdom or Stone of Truth: Scripture as a Site of Struggle." Pages 67–89 in *Los caminos inexhauribles de la Palabra: Homenaje a Severino Croatto.* Edited by Guillermo Hansen. Buenos Aires: Lumen, 2000.

Smythe, Dion, ed. *Strangers to Themselves: The Byzantine Outsider; Papers from the Thirty-Second Spring Symposium of Byzantine Studies, University of Sussex, Brighton, March 1998.* SPBS 8. Aldershot: Ashgate, 2000.

Talbot, Alice-Mary. "Life of St. Theodora of Thessalonike." Pages 159–237 in *Holy Women of Byzantium: Ten Saints' Lives in English Translation.* Edited by Alice-Mary Talbot. BSLT 1. Washington, DC: Dumbarton Oaks, 1996.

———, trans. "Typikon of Theodora Synadene for the Convent of the Mother of God Bebaia Elpis." Pages 1512–78 in *Byzantine Monastic Foundation Documents: A Complete Translation of the Surviving Founders' Typika and Testaments.* Edited by John Thomas and Angela Constantinides Hero. DOS 35. Washington, DC: Dumbarton Oaks, 2000.

———. "Women." Pages 117–43 in *The Byzantines.* Edited by Guglielmo Cavallo. Translated by Thomas Dunlap, Teresa Lavender Fagan, and Charles Lambert. Chicago: University of Chicago Press, 1997.

Walker, Jeffrey. "These Things I Have Not Betrayed: Michael Psellos' Encomium of His Mother as a Defense of Rhetoric." *Rhet* 22 (2004): 49–101.

Wortley, John. *The Spiritual Meadow by John Moschus.* CSS 139. Kalamazoo, MI: Cistercian, 1992.

Women and the Bible in Byzantium

Rosa Maria Parrinello

It is not a new idea that Byzantium was a world in which, for historical, social, and cultural reasons, women were excluded from both the world of passive culture, understood as learning, and active culture—that is, from literary production. As a result, some singular exceptions to this scene may seem a bit daunting, ranging from Kassia, a poet who lived in the mid-ninth century, to the famous historian Anna Komnene (1083–1153), who left us the most enjoyable work of all Byzantine literature, the *Alexiad*.[1] It is therefore a fact that even among the highest elite, educated women were a minority, although the situation improved in the last phase of the empire.[2] We can, however, say that in Byzantium, as will be apparent shortly, reading was not the only means that women had of knowing the Bible.

The texts that can be used to reconstruct the status of women include legal collections, which allow us to learn about the situation of women before the law; historical works regarding the empresses; biographies and hagiographies; and eulogies, which stand between hagiography and history.[3] For the period that interests us, we cannot add to these sources

---

I thank Professor Judith Herrin for valuable comments and bibliography.

1. For a series of broader general considerations, see the observations in my "Theodora Palaeologina and the Others: Women Scholars, Copists, and Exegetes in Byzantium," in *The High Middle Ages*, BW 6.2 (Atlanta: SBL Press, 2015).

2. Alice-Mary Talbot, "The Devotional Life of Laywomen," in *Byzantine Christianity*, vol. 3 of *A People's History of Christianity*, ed. Derek Kreuger (Minneapolis: Fortress, 2010), 201–40. See also Carolyn L. Connor, *Women of Byzantium* (New Haven: Yale University Press, 2004); Angeliki E. Laiou, "Women in the History of Byzantium," in *Byzantine Women and Their World*, ed. Ioli Kalavrezou (Cambridge: Harvard University Art Museums, 2003), 23–32.

3. See Joelle Beaucamp, *Le statut de la femme à Byzance (4ᵉ–7ᵉ siècle)*, 2 vols. (Paris: Boccard, 1992); Jean Grosdidier de Matons, "La femme dans l'Empire byz-

the rules governing female monasteries whose founder was a woman of the imperial family or aristocratic families, because these founding documents are later; the earliest dates to the tenth century.

There was in Byzantium a constant tension between the possible conditions of female life, ranging from the ideal of Christian ascetic virginity, feasible within the monastic life, to the promotion of marriage, which gave a legitimate outlet for sexual relations and the procreation of children. In marriage, the woman's primary role was to raise children, caring for them, teaching them the Psalms, and telling them Bible stories and the lives of saints. The ideal of feminine holiness was linked to the virginal condition or that of a widow: women still had to deny their femininity and become male (see, e.g., the Makrina of Gregory of Nyssa, a real γυνὴ ἀνδρεία).[4] If we examine the education of children, we note that for boys there were schools, but girls were educated at home by parents, guardians, or tutors from their sixth to seventh years because their education was destined to make them suitable wives and mothers; even young girls also learned to spin, weave, and embroider. The education given in monasteries was not that different. If girls were taught to read, the Psalter was intended to be their first reading. For a child in Byzantium, this education took place under the exclusive care of the mother in the *gynaeceum*, where children played games traditionally reserved for females and listened to fairy tales and edifying stories, mostly on religious subjects. In addition, the girl received a summary domestic education within the home, almost always directly from her mother.[5] Peter Hatlie adds that "Christian virtues of learning, discipline, nurturing, unwavering piety and indomitable spirit are among the characteristics epitomized by mothers."[6]

In addition to reading, girls learned to write, memorized various psalms by heart, and studied other books of the Septuagint. They also had access to the lives of the saints, and great care was given to learning the

---

antin," in *Histoire mondiale de la femme*, ed. Pierre Grimal, 4 vols. (Paris: Nouvelle Librairie de France, 1967), 3:12.

4. See Eva Nardi, *Né sole né luna: L'immagine femminile nella Bisanzio dei secoli XI e XII* (Firenze: Olschki, 2002), 199.

5. Judith Herrin, "Mothers and Daughters in the Medieval Greek World," in *Unrivalled Influence: Women and Empire in Byzantium* (Princeton: Princeton University Press, 2013), 80–114.

6. Peter Hatlie, "Images of Motherhood and Self in Byzantine Literature," *DOP* 63 (2009): 56.

liturgical chant.[7] Girls could be engaged at the age of seven or eight and, according to the old rule of Roman law in force in Byzantium, married at age twelve, although there are also examples of marriages at a very young age. The education that the child received up to the age of marriage (probably only three years at most) was happily defined by Elena Giannarelli as a "monastic pedagogy."[8] It was not meant to encourage genuine education or to provide a cultural foundation or critical spirit; rather, it was intended to provide the basic discipline for a life of devotion and prayer. Success involved a modest level of confessional literacy aimed at θαλάμευσις, or segregation in the θάλαμος ("inner chamber"), according to an already-established Roman and, above all, Greek practice.

Female domestic devotion thus provided the means for a spiritual reading, the veneration of icons, private prayer, and the performance of services in private chapels. The role of the mother figure was important, however, in the earliest education of children, boys and girls alike. We remember the beautiful example of Theodore the Studite's mother, Theoctiste, orphaned at an early age, who had been ἀγράμματος (illiterate), but once she came of age, through the love of God, as an autodidact, she learned to read and memorized the Psalter. She had not neglected the housework nor annoyed her husband, but before and after sleeping she studied intensively by candlelight (*Or.* 13.3 [PG 99:885B]). Further, we can cite the case of the great intellectual Michael Psellos (1018–1078), who in the *Epitaph* for his mother Theodote attributes to her the merit of understanding her son's great inclination to learn after having a vision of John Chrysostom and the Virgin, who invited her to make the child study![9]

The testimony of historian Anna Komnene, a Byzantine princess, is an exceptional case of female culture.[10] She recalls how her mother Eirene held a book in her hands during lunch and discussed the texts of the holy

---

7. Enrico Valdo Maltese, "Donne e letteratura a Bisanzio: Per una storia della cultura femminile," in *Dimensioni bizantine: Donne, angeli e demoni nel Medioevo Greco* (Torino: Paravia-Scriptorium, 1995), 114.

8. Elena Giannarelli, *La tipologia femminile nella biografia e nell'autobiografia del IV secolo* (Rome: Istituto storico italiano per il Medio Evo, 1980), 35, n. 21. Although Giannarelli refers to the education received by and given to Makrina, whose family situation is quite exceptional, in a period when consecrated virginity could also be lived in the home, according to Maltese ("Donne e letteratura a Bisanzio," 114–15), this is also valid for the following centuries.

9. Maltese, "Donne e letteratura a Bisanzio," 125–26.

10. See Parrinello, "Theodora Palaeologina and the Others."

fathers, specifically of Maximus the Confessor (Anna Komnene, *Alex.* 5.9.2-3). Maximus is certainly not an easy author to understand, being demanding and above all in his exegetical commentaries and even in non-exegetical works he makes continual reference to the Scriptures. We will return later to the significance of this choice.

Also from an earlier period, on the subject of reading and learning the Scriptures, we can quote a passage taken from the Life of Theophano (ch. 5), the future wife of Emperor Leo VI the Wise, who died in 895–896. At the age of six, Theophano began to be instructed by her father in the Holy Scriptures, and she learned quickly to memorize the Psalms, the hymns of vespers, and morning prayers. She spent her days reading and studying.

A significant aspect of matrilineal teaching involved devotion to icons (which could be venerated in the home as well as in the church), such as images of Christ holding the gospel or blessing (see the famous Sinai icon, probably dating to the sixth century, which shows Christ blessing with his right hand and holding the gospel in his left), of Peter holding the keys of paradise, and of the Virgin Mary with angels and saints.[11] The portrayal of the holy family was also important, and images were often closely related to the Bible. Many churches were decorated with images of miracles, such as the healing of the lame and the blind man, the resurrection of Lazarus, and the Samaritan woman at the well. Mothers could explain these images to their children and link them to the reading of the gospel during the liturgy. Thus we can talk about a sort of *Biblia pauperum*. Judith Herrin criticizes the tendency to think that the special veneration of icons by women derived from women being less rational than men and thus incapable of sophisticated theological understanding, showing that they were prey to their emotional natures and in need of a visual aid for their devotion, which explains their special bond with icons. In fact, as she has rightly objected, men were also quite close to icons, where the frontal image—as in the eyes and the face of Christ in the aforementioned Sinai icon—draws the attention of the spectators. She also emphasizes the personal relationship between the icons and the devotee as well as the immediacy of the message they carry. However, women had far fewer exchanges with the outside world than men, and

---

11. Judith Herrin, "The Icon Corner in Medieval Byzantium," in *Unrivalled Influence*, 281–301. This famous Sinai icon is the symbol of the monastery of Saint Catherine in Sinai; see the commentary in Herrin, "Women and the Faith in Icons in Early Christianity," in *Unrivalled Influence*, 57–59.

this enhanced their personal relationship with the icon in the domestic space. If the image is thus the bearer of a message, those who watch and pray at the same time welcome the message, and this contact intensifies in the space between them. This happens especially when the icon is at eye level and gives the illusion of an omniscient gaze that follows the devotee. When the figure appears to be directly addressing the viewer, its authority is greatly strengthened.[12] More specifically, the special bond between women and icons was born of and escalated into a situation of domestic imprisonment, limited access to the churches, and frustrated religious passion. In these conditions (and we must thank Herrin for highlighting this), icons had a special role in women's devotion because they offered a particular approach to religion, a special contact with the holy, enjoyed without any restrictions.

Although they were not part of the clergy, women were involved in private religious devotion: they transmitted their religion to their children, taught them the Psalms, and told them about saints' lives. This element of oral culture is important for women in all societies, and it is evident that in medieval Byzantium women had a real knowledge of Bible stories. In this sense, the hagiographies are precious sources. The Life of Athanasia of Aegina (the saint lived in the ninth century; the text is of the tenth) testifies that on Sundays and feast days she gathered the neighboring women and read them the Scriptures. Eirene of Chrysobalanton (tenth century) even preached to multitudes of women and girls.[13] There is no doubt that some, though few, women were educated and could read to others. We recall that in Byzantium, women copyists were exceptional and rare, as I have shown elsewhere.[14]

That is why, therefore, many women, excluded from participation in public life (although the empresses played a certain role in politics), became keen on the religious controversies of their time. The opposition movement to iconoclasm—that is, the struggle against images conducted by the Byzantine emperors from 726 to 843, with quite a few interruptions in phases during which the iconoclast party was victorious—often saw women as barricades fervently devoted to the icons. According to tradition, the first martyrs of iconoclasm were precisely the women who tried to prevent the soldiers from carrying out the order of Leo III to remove the

---

12. Herrin, "Women and the Faith in Icons," 57.
13. Nardi, *Né sole né luna*, 164.
14. See Parrinello, "Theodora Palaeologina and the Others."

icon of Christ from the Chalke gate of the palace of Constantinople. Later, two women, the basilissai (empresses) Eirene and Theodora, restored the official cult of icons in 787 and 843. In particular, Eirene, regent for her son Constantine VI after the death of her husband Leo IV (as well as one of the addressees of Theodore the Studite), convened the Second Council of Nicaea in 787 to rehabilitate the images, and Theodora, widow of Theophilus and regent for Michael III, put an end to the iconoclastic struggle.[15] Despite this close relationship that seems to be established between women and the Bible, the sources are not very generous in detailing the ways and practices of reading or their times and locations.

Religious faith and devotional practices played a significant role in the lives of Byzantine women, especially those of the middle and upper classes, whose religious life, as we have seen, was carried out within a limited scope (and often this life is also the only one about which we have historical information). Prayer, Bible study, and the veneration of icons in the home were able to offer spiritual comfort. Socially approved opportunities to get out of the house included participation in religious services (processions, Divine Liturgy), visits to sanctuaries, and charitable activities. Hagiographic sources, although they should be read with care, are precious primary witnesses to these occasions.

Why are the sources reticent to depict women reading and understanding the Bible? If we may identify a normative moment, it is represented by the Council in Trullo, convened by Emperor Justinian II in the same domed hall (*trullus*, hence the name of the council) where the Sixth Ecumenical Council (680–681) had met. This initial council did not issue canons; they were later issued by the Council of Trullo of 692. This is particularly important because canon 70, relying on Pauline magisterium, prevents women from talking during the Divine Liturgy.[16]

---

15. On these other figures of empresses and their ardent religious faith, see Judith Herrin, *Women in Purple: Rulers of Medieval Byzantium* (Princeton: Princeton University Press, 2001), and her articles in *Unrivalled Influence*: "Women and the Faith in Icons in Early Christianity," 38–79; "The Imperial Feminine in Byzantium," 161–93; "Political Power and Christian Faith in Byzantium: The Case of Irene (regent 780–790, emperor 797–802)," 194–207; "The Many Empresses at the Byzantine Court (and All Their Attendants)," 219–37; and "Theophano: Considerations on the Education of a Byzantine Princess," 238–60.

16. Judith Herrin, "Femina Byzantina: The Council in Trullo on Women," *DOP* 46 (1992): 97–105.

> Women shall not be allowed to speak during the holy mass, but in accordance with the words of Paul the Apostle: "They should be silent in the Churches: for they are not permitted to speak, but should be subordinate, as the law also says. If there is anything they desire to know, let them ask their husbands at home." (1 Cor 14:34–35)[17]

In general, the Council in Trullo was the culmination of a long process leading to the exclusion of women from active participation in the liturgy: the bishops of Trullo reduced women to silence, making them mere spectators and auditors of the liturgy.[18] This was not the only rule that affected women, however; canons 19 and 64 did as well. Canon 19 recommended that the Holy Scriptures be explained according to the established rules and the tradition of the fathers:[19]

> The superiors of the Churches must instruct all their clergy and their people in true piety every day, but especially on Sundays, choosing for them from divine Scripture the thoughts and judgments of truth and following unswervingly definitions already set forth and the tradition of the God-bearing Fathers [τοὺς ἤδη τεθέντας ὅρους ἢ τὴν ἐκ τῶν θεοφόρων πατέρων παράδοσιν]. If a scriptural passage should come up for discussion, they shall in no wise interpret it differently than the luminaries and Doctors of the Church [οἱ τῆς ἐκκλησίας φωστῆρες καὶ διδάσκαλοι] have set down in their writings. In this way shall they distinguish themselves, rather than by composing their own works, being at times incapable of this and thereby falling short of what is proper.[20]

In Byzantium, it was therefore forbidden to explain the Bible other than according to the established rules and the tradition of the fathers, without innovation.[21] To this we can add canon 64 in support:

> No layman is to hold a public lecture on dogma, nor to teach, thus arrogating to himself the office of teacher [ἀξίωμα διδασκαλικόν], but is to follow the order handed down by the Lord, and to lend an ear to those who have

---

17. Michael Featherstone and George Nedungatt, eds., *The Council in Trullo Revisited* (Rome: Pontificio Istituto Orientale: 1995), 152.
18. Herrin, "Femina Byzantina," 100.
19. Herrin, "Femina Byzantina," 94–96.
20. Featherstone and Nedungatt, *Council in Trullo Revisited*, 94–95.
21. Martin Jugie, "Exégèse médiévale," in *Dictionnaire de la Bible: Supplément* (Paris: Letouzey et Ané, 1945), 4:591.

received the grace of teaching [τὴν χάριν τοῦ διδασκαλικοῦ λόγου] and to be taught divine things by them.... If anyone is found undermining the present canon, he shall be excommunicated for forty days.[22]

In light of these canons, we understand why Eirene read Maximus the Confessor: he was one of those luminaries and doctors of the church, so she did not run the risk of breaking the canons.

Theodore the Studite (759–826) and Letters of Spiritual Direction to Women

Thus far we have learned that women were not permitted to speak during the liturgy, nor was it permissible for them to teach or interpret Scripture independently. What opportunities remained, then, if not passive reading?

I want to focus, albeit briefly, on women's spiritual direction in the letters of Theodore the Studite in order to see what role biblical quotations played.[23]

Theodore, the great reformer of moral laxity that was rampant among monks in his time, gave new rules for the monastery of Stoudios with his *Hypotyposis*. He was abbot of the monastery of John Prodromos Stoudios (which became known as the Stoudiou), which had been founded by a private benefactor, Stoudios, ὕπατος (consul) of the East in 454, in the district of Constantinople—precisely in the southwest corner of the old city in the region of Psamathia, near the Golden Gate. He promoted the activity of writing in his monastery. In fact, the Studite monastic confederation played an important role in the cultural and humanistic revival of the ninth century, since Stoudios may have been the driving force behind an

---

22. Featherstone and Nedungatt, *Council in Trullo Revisited*, 145–46.

23. See Julien Leroy, "La réforme studite," in *Il monachesimo orientale*, ed. Convegno di studi orientali (Rome: Pontificium Institutum Orientalium Studiorum, 1958); Leroy, "Le monachisme studite," in Théodore Studite, *Les grandes catecheses (Livre I), Epigrammes (I–XXIX)*, trans. Florence de Montleau (Bégrolles-en-Mauges: Abbaye de Bellefontaine, 2002), 39–116; Peter Hatlie, *The Monks and Monasteries of Constantinople, ca. 350–850* (Cambridge: Cambridge University Press, 2007); Rosa Maria Parrinello, *Il monachesimo bizantino* (Rome: Carocci, 2012), 49–69. Here I omit some epistles, like those to the hēgoumenissa Eirene, Maria the wife of Spatharios, and the nun Hypakoe, because there are no particular use of biblical quotations. Also in the letter to the virgin Tomaide, *On the Question of the Images*, there are no biblical quotations.

extraordinary phenomenon: μεταχαρακτηρισμός, the shift in script from uncial (upper case) to lower case (minuscule).

Theodore lived during a difficult period for monasticism, during iconoclasm (730-787/815-843). For his iconodule faith, he suffered excruciating torture, but he never ceased to exhort the monks, his spiritual children, to bear the new martyrdom in the same way as the glorious martyrs had during earlier persecutions against the Christians. After the end of the first phase of iconoclasm, there was an attempt inside the monasteries to return to the original cenobitism. Theodore the Studite in no way intended to eliminate the contemplative aspect, the *hesychia*, which he considered crucial for the ascetic experience, but he tried to eliminate the excesses that brought into question the coenobitic type of monastic experience.

In the first letter we examine (dated 797-799), for the mother Theoctiste, who was discovered to be seriously ill, Theodore quotes abundantly and especially from Paul (2 Tim 4:10; 2 Cor 5:8; Rom 11:33; 2 Cor 11:23ff.) but also from the Old Testament (Gen 25:8). The quotations function as a kind of consolatory letter and emphasize that she will walk along the road that leads to the Lord (Matt 7:14), dead but alive at the same time, fighting the good fight (2 Tim 4:7). (This is a reading that is heard in the Mass on the Sunday before Theophany.[24])

A letter written in 801 addressed to the basilissa Eirene, mother of Constantine VI, who was campaigning for a favorable policy toward the monks, gives thanks to her for having exempted the monks of Stoudios from some tax obligations. The letter opens with a quote from Jer 38:15 and is interwoven with quotations mostly from the Old Testament: the prophetic texts (Isa 58:6; Mal 17:4) and Genesis (33:11). (It is important to remember that the images used to undergird the ideology of Byzantine kingship come from the Old Testament, not the New Testament.[25]) After citing Matt 2:10 and quoting from Gregory of Nazianzus (*Hor.* 22.1 and 15.11), the letter closes with a kind of ring composition, again with a quote from Jeremiah (15:19).[26]

---

24. Georgios Fatouros, ed., *Theodori Studitae epistulae*, CFHB 31.1-2 (Berlin: de Gruyter, 1992), 21-23.

25. See Gilbert Dagron, *Emperor and Priest: The Imperial Office in Byzantium* (Cambridge: Cambridge University Press, 2003).

26. Fatouros, *Theodori Studitae epistulae*, 24-27.

Theodore also wrote a series of letters that could be called "on government," addressed to those who were in charge of female monasteries (the *hēgoumenissai*, ἡγουμένισσαι) or to all the nuns. In letter 59 to the *hēgoumenissa* of Gordina (between 821 and 826), he praises the fact that the nuns have withstood the iconoclastic persecution and urges them to persevere in purity of heart, in the way of virginity and orthodoxy. The *hēgoumenissa* is an example of orthopraxis, for the disciples must live with only one desire: for the law of the Lord. The farewell is given in the name of 2 Thess 3:18, a true doxology.[27] He wrote to the *hēgoumenissa* of Nicaea for the same reason (ca. 815–820). The letter is a series of quotations from the letters of Paul (Rom 8:35; 1 Cor 6:20; Phil 3:8; 2 Tim 2:5; Eph 4:1ff.; 1 Cor 9:27), plus a quote from Isaiah (8:18) and one from the Gospel of John (8:41).[28] Basically, the letters Theodore wrote to monastic communities are richer in biblical citations than those to individual women. For example, letter 65, sent to a monastic community of Prinkipos (in the years 821–826) and singing its praises, is a patchwork of quotations from Genesis (2:9, one of the readings for the Thursday of Lent), the Song of Songs (4:12, "garden enclosed, a fountain sealed"), the gospels (Luke 1:75, the visit of Mary to Elizabeth, a passage read during the service on November 25, and Matt 10:38, read on the Sunday of All Saints), Acts (15:30), and the Pauline letters (1 Cor 6:20; Rom 8:17; Phil 4:4, a reading for Palm Sunday, and 3:30). The quotations are intended to help to build the image of a holy body, a kind of garden of virginity and sanctity, in which Christ is in the midst as the tree of life.[29] I think that Theodore personalized the use of biblical quotations according to the addressee: if the addressee was the monastic community, which finds its cohesive identity through listening to the Holy Scriptures, the use of citations was intensified.

In about 818–819, Theodore wrote to a community of three hundred nuns that had endured imprisonment and beatings, that lacked their spiri-

---

27. Fatouros, *Theodori Studitae epistulae*, 170–71.

28. 1 Cor 6:20 was read on the so-called Sunday of the Prodigal Son. For this and other liturgical character notations, I am indebted to Stefano Rosso, *La celebrazione della storia della salvezza nel rito bizantino: Misteri sacramentali, feste e tempi liturgici* (Vatican City: Libreria Editrice Vaticana, 2010). Eph 4:1ff., the theme of which is to build the body of Christ in unity, in this case, monastic, was read on the eighth Sunday of Luke. See Rosso, *Celebrazione della storia della salvezza*, 610–11.

29. Fatouros, *Theodori Studitae epistulae*, 178–80. On the visit of Mary to Elizabeth, see the chapter by Mary B. Cunningham in this volume.

tual mother, and that had been separated from the monastery; three times he calls them blessed mothers, daughters of the heavenly Jerusalem. He quotes Mark 9:23 ("all things are possible to him who believes," a passage read during the fourth Sunday of Lent, in honor of John Klimakos, "The Ladder") and 1 Pet 1:8. Furthermore, he quotes the father perhaps most often mentioned in the monastic literature, in particular by the Studite, Basil of Caesarea (*Hom.* 19.6 [PG 31:20A]), who was at the base of the Studite monastic reform.[30] In the 818 letter of consolation to nuns Megalone and Mary for the death of the *hēgoumenos*, a man of God and dear friend of Theodore, he says that the abbot is not dead but now dwells where the true light shines and where the blessed rest. There are only two quotations from Paul's letters (1 Tim 3:15; Phil 2:15), concentrated at the point where the Studite stresses that the church rejoices for the pillars and the stars, of which the abbot is part, and who are a bulwark in the fight against heresy.[31]

Theodore also wrote consolatory letters to women living in the world, such as one to the wife of a military commander, Demoncharis, who had recently died (about 821–826). The woman loved her husband deeply, and Theodore knew that it was impossible to find the right words to alleviate her pain. He uses two quotations from Paul's letters (2 Cor 5:8 and 1 Thess 4:13ff.), from Genesis (3:19) and Job (1:21, "The Lord gave, and the Lord has taken away"), a passage read on Thursday of Holy and Great Easter Week, to convince the woman to resign herself in acceptance of the will of the Lord.[32] Furthermore, we have a letter to a woman who had lost her son; since she was a person of great culture, Theodore cites passages not only from Sirach (10:19), as well as the Psalms (102:15; 88:49; 49:14; 114:7; 117:6) and the Pauline letters (1 Thess 4:14; 1 Cor 15:52), but also the *Agamemnon* of Aeschylus (line 1343). In this case, the biblical and classical citations together help to create a letter that is a real consolation, written in a rhetorically elaborate way. In addition, he uses the quote from Job 1:21, as in the previous letter.[33]

One of the most full-bodied dossiers is that of nine letters written to the *hēgoumenissa* Euphrosyne in consolation for the death of her mother, Eirene. Eirene was the widow of a great imperial dignitary, an Armenian by birth. She became a nun along with her daughter Euphrosyne, who

---

30. Fatouros, *Theodori Studitae epistulae*, 559.
31. Fatouros, *Theodori Studitae epistulae*, 465–66.
32. Fatouros, *Theodori Studitae epistulae*, 643–44.
33. Fatouros, *Theodori Studitae epistulae*, 734–37.

became abbess after her mother. In the third letter of this series (about 823), Theodore urges the daughter to imitate maternal virtues. It is the richest letter of biblical quotations: he quotes Genesis (35:20 and 50:1) in reference to the figure of Rachel, Isaiah (8:18, a passage read on Monday of the second week of Lent), the Psalms (33:20), Deuteronomy (34:8), the Pauline letters (Phil 3:3; Eph 6:12, a passage of the tenth Sunday of Luke, and 2 Cor 11:2), and a passage from 1 Peter (5:4) in order to invite her to think of the other sisters of whom she is *hēgoumenissa*, following the example of her mother Eirene.[34] In the fourth letter (ca. 823–826), Theodore quotes the passage from Acts that in monastic ideology refers to the first coenobitic monastic community of Jerusalem, in which everyone had one heart and one soul (4:32). He cites the examples of Thecla, the first martyr, and of Febronia, and he urges Euphrosyne to be like other nuns: a bride of Christ, a coheir of Christ, and a light of the world.[35] The fifth letter (about 824) returns to the theme of the death of Euphrosyne's mother and cites Paul (1 Tim 6:12, a reading of the first of the Triodion; 2 Thess 1:7; Col 3:11, a passage read during the Sunday of the Holiest Forefathers of the Lord; 1 Thess 2:8), Matt 5:12, and again Acts 4:32. The *Catechetical Letter* (circa 824) is a kind of sermon on Lent; it is probably a text meant to be read for instruction or catechesis because here we have a rise in the style and tone and a more frequent inclusion of quotations, mostly from the Pauline letters (1 Cor 7:32; Phil 2:12; 4:7, a reading of the Feast of the Nativity of the Theotokos; 2 Cor 9:7, on the generosity of giving, a passage read on the fifth Sunday of Luke). To this he adds Matt 21:18, read on the Monday of Holy and Great Week, and again Acts 4:32, along with a quote from the liturgy of Chrysostom.[36]

To the patrician Eirene, who was married and then became a nun, he writes (perhaps around 818–820) to praise her for being a soldier of Christ. In fact, she gave up a comfortable life to enter the monastery. In addition to Luke 1:42ff., a passage read in the aforementioned feast of November 25, which celebrates the entry of Mary into the temple, Matt 5:12, and an oration of Gregory of Nazianzus (7.19), Theodore quotes John 14:23; he is therefore certain that the Father and the Son have taken up residence in her and asks for prayers for himself.[37]

---

34. Fatouros, *Theodori Studitae epistulae*, 666–67.
35. Fatouros, *Theodori Studitae epistulae*, 678–79.
36. Fatouros, *Theodori Studitae epistulae*, 705–10.
37. Fatouros, *Theodori Studitae epistulae*, 575–76.

To an anonymous recluse (815–818) who obviously must have sent a long letter, Theodore justifies himself for sending a short answer with a quote from Luke 6:30 ("Give to everyone who asks you"). He also quotes Acts 4:32 again and cites 2 Cor 12:20 and a passage in a letter of Basil (*Ep.* 262.2). He sums up the principles of the monastic life, reminding the nun to remain steadfast in her faith, especially in the tumultuous and difficult era of iconoclasm.[38]

In about 815–819, Theodore faced a difficult issue: the wife of a dignitary of the Byzantine court, a πρωτοσπαθάριος (originally a military position, which became an honorific title that allowed access to the Senate), wished to join a monastery and asked the Studite how she could get permission from her husband to do so. Theodore urged her to persuade her husband to embrace the monastic life with her, as a way of salvation, citing 1 Cor 7:16.[39] In addition to this, Theodore resorted to Ps 102:15 and to the citation of a Basilian Rule (*Reg. brev.* 8.1).

In several letters to the nun Maria (the first dated to 818, the second between 815 and 819), he writes that with her and all the other Christians he is part of μία ἐκκλησία κοινοβιακή (one cenobitic community) and defines Maria as no less noble than Febronia and Thecla, as a child of God and the bride of Christ. Alongside the Pauline citations (2 Cor 6:14, 1 Tim 6:12, a reading already found for the first Saturday of the Triodion; Phil 1:28; Rom 8:35; Gal 2:6), we also have a verse of a psalm (45:3) and a quote from the pagan epistolographer Aristaenetus (*Ep.* 1.13).[40]

Among the addressees of Theodore there is also Kassia, cited at the beginning of this essay.[41] Kassia was a beautiful girl, one of the candidates to become the wife of Theophilus. In 821, the dowager empress Euphrosyne decided it was time for her stepson Theophilus (829–842) to marry and proclaimed a beauty contest for the choice of the bride. Similar competitions were held frequently from the end of the eighth to the ninth century. Officials departed from the capital throughout the empire, provided with the so-called imperial meter, a table with the ideals of competing measures (height, breast, foot). Kassia was one of two girls (the other was the very Theodora who later ended iconoclasm) to parade in front of the emperor Theophilus, who, seeing that she was beautiful, said,

---

38. Fatouros, *Theodori Studitae epistulae*, 537–38.
39. Fatouros, *Theodori Studitae epistulae*, 549–51.
40. Fatouros, *Theodori Studitae epistulae*, 551–52.
41. See the chapter by Anna M. Silvas about Kassia in this volume.

"Woman was the source and cause of all human tribulations."[42] To this she promptly replied: "From a woman also derive the best things." This salacious response ruled her out of the contest and determined her subsequent choice of the monastery, a voluntary choice (we do not therefore think that it is the monkish hell of Arcangela Tarabotti). In fact, once deprived of the chance to become empress, she founded a monastery where she spent the rest of her life composing religious poems, epigrams (many of which are gnomic verses), and hymns.[43] Kassia was in close contact with Theodore, and we have some of his letters addressed to her. In later centuries, Stoudios played a central role in the new edition of liturgical books, including those of Kassia. She wrote not only spiritual poetry but also the music to accompany it, and thirty-three hymns can be safely ascribed to her.[44]

The first letter of the Studite to Kassia (from 816–818) contains no biblical quotations.[45] In the second (of the same period), there is a single quote each from the Psalms (132:1), John (1:29), and the Pauline letters (Phil 1:29). In the third (ca. 821–826) we find a greater selection of Old Testament (Num 23:3ff.; Ezek 7:3) and Pauline quotations (1 Thess 2:4; 2 Tim 2:15; Phil 3:8; 2 Tim 2:19), perhaps because the letter is longer and more articulate than the others. Theodore did not take particular care in the construction of the letters addressed to Kassia; she was, for the Studite, a nun like the others who turned to him, provided with the same love of Christ and the virginal life.

---

42. PG 109:685c; Enrico Valdo Maltese, "Donne a Bisanzio: misogamia culta e popolare tra l'XI e il XV secolo," in *Dimensioni bizantine*, 25.

43. See Hans-Georg Beck, *Kirche und Theologische Literaturim byzantinischen Reich* (Munich: Beck, 1959), 429, 461, 603, 604, 698, 797. He quotes Martha, the mother of Simeon Stylites the Younger, in the sixth century; Sergia, of the monastery of Holy Olympia in Constantinople, in the seventh century; Thecla, the author of a canon to the Theotokos, in the ninth century; Theodosia, in the ninth century; Theodora Palaiologina Raoulaina; and a Palaiologina author of canons in San Demetrius in the first half of the fourteenth century. On the other Byzantine hymnographers, see Eva Catafygiotu Topping, *Holy Mothers of Orthodoxy* (Minneapolis: Light and Life, 1987); Catafygiotu Topping, "Thekla the Nun: In Praise of Woman," *GOTR* 25 (1980): 353–70; Catafygiotu Topping, "Women Hymnographers in Byzantium," *Dip* 3 (1982–1983): 98–111.

44. In addition to the work of Anna M. Silvas in this volume, see Eva Catafygiotu Topping, "Kassiane the Nun and the Sinful Woman," *GOTR* 26 (1981): 201–9; Catafygiotu Topping, "The Psalmist, St Luke and Kassia the Nun," *ByzSt* 9 (1982): 199–210.

45. We have three letters of the Studite to Kassia: letters 217, 370, and 539 in the edition of Fatouros, *Theodori Studitae epistulae*, 339–40, 501–2, and 813–14, respectively.

A letter to Empress Theodosia, wife of Leo V, and her son Basil (ca. 821–824) dealing with the struggle against images deserves separate mention.[46] Against εἰκονομάχοι, Theodore reaffirms the legitimacy of the veneration of images of Christ and prays for the empress to defend the orthodox faith. He quotes the Pauline letters (1 Tim 2:5 and 6:12; Heb 11:38, a passage read on the Sunday of All Saints, and 12:4; 1 Cor 10:29) but also 2 Pet 1:5, Luke 6:44, Job 5:9, and Sir 4:5.

To conclude this first, brief exploration of the use of the Bible in the letters that Theodore wrote to women, I think we can conclude that the biblical quotes had different purposes in the writings of the Studite. They were certainly the spiritual food, the food for the journey, a means of consolation, and the framework of the epistles (but there are some that notably lack citations). At the same time, through Theodore's able pen, they were the instrument for the rhetorical construction of the letters. He addressed women who were in a position to retain the quotes (because they knew them), to contextualize them, and even to reuse them. He seemed to be aware that his letters could become an opportunity for catechesis; sometimes he wrote them with this purpose. He used the Old and New Testaments, especially the Psalms and the Pauline letters, although surely Paul was the most popular author. Some passages (e.g., Job 1:21) play special roles as citations for consolation letters, while others (e.g., John 14:23) connote female monastic communities as "the Father's house." The most cited passage is Acts 4:32, perhaps because the majority of letters were to nuns. In short, the Bible was, for the Studite, not only the great codex that he shared with them but also the main instrument—although, it does not seem excessive to say, secondary to the same letter—for the spiritual direction of women, not only nuns but also secular women, widows, women who had lost children, daughters who had lost mothers, and nuns as martyrs waiting for the consolation of the beloved spiritual father.

Bibliography

Beaucamp, Joelle. *Le statut de la femme à Byzance (4ᵉ–7ᵉ siècle)*. 2 vols. Paris: Boccard, 1992.

Beck, Hans-Georg. *Kirche und Theologische Literaturim byzantinischen Reich*. Munich: Beck, 1959.

---

46. Fatouros, *Theodori Studitae epistulae*, 811–12.

Catafygiotu Topping, Eva. *Holy Mothers of Orthodoxy*. Minneapolis: Light and Life, 1987.

———. "Kassiane the Nun and the Sinful Woman." *GOTR* 26 (1981): 201–9.

———. "The Psalmist, St Luke and Kassia the Nun." *ByzSt* 9 (1982): 199–210.

———. "Thekla the Nun: In Praise of Woman." *GOTR* 25 (1980): 353–70.

———. "Women Hymnographers in Byzantium." *Dip* 3 (1982–1983): 98–111.

Connor, Carolyn L. *Women of Byzantium*. New Haven: Yale University Press, 2004.

Dagron, Gilbert. *Emperor and Priest: The Imperial Office in Byzantium*. Cambridge University Press, 2003.

Fatouros, Georgios. *Theodori Studitae epistulae*. CFHB 31.1–2. Berlin: de Gruyter, 1992.

Featherstone, Michael, and George Nedungatt, eds. *The Council in Trullo Revisited*. Rome: Pontificio Istituto Orientale, 1995.

Giannarelli, Elena. *La tipologia femminile nella biografia e nell'autobiografia del IV secolo*. Rome: Istituto storico italiano per il Medio Evo, 1980.

Hatlie, Peter. "Images of Motherhood and Self in Byzantine Literature." *DOP* 63 (2009): 41–57.

———. *The Monks and Monasteries of Constantinople, ca. 350–850*. Cambridge: Cambridge University Press, 2007.

Herrin, Judith. "Femina Byzantina: The Council in Trullo on Women." *DOP* 46 (1992): 97–105.

———. "The Icon Corner in Medieval Byzantium." Pages 281–301 in *Unrivalled Influence: Women and Empire in Byzantium*. Princeton: Princeton University Press, 2013.

———. "The Imperial Feminine in Byzantium." Pages 161–93 in *Unrivalled Influence: Women and Empire in Byzantium*. Princeton: Princeton University Press, 2013.

———. "The Many Empresses at the Byzantine Court (and All Their Attendants)." Pages 219–37 in *Unrivalled Influence: Women and Empire in Byzantium*. Princeton: Princeton University Press, 2013.

———. "Mothers and Daughters in the Medieval Greek World." Pages 80–114 in *Unrivalled Influence: Women and Empire in Byzantium*. Princeton: Princeton University Press, 2013.

———. "Political Power and Christian Faith in Byzantium: The Case of Irene (Regent 780–90, Emperor 797–802)." Pages 194–207 in *Unri-*

valled Influence: Women and Empire in Byzantium. Princeton: Princeton University Press, 2013.

———. "Theophano: Considerations on the Education of a Byzantine Princess." Pages 238–60 in *Unrivalled Influence: Women and Empire in Byzantium*. Princeton: Princeton University Press, 2013.

———. "Women and the Faith in Icons in Early Christianity." Pages 38–79 in *Unrivalled Influence: Women and Empire in Byzantium*. Princeton: Princeton University Press, 2013.

———. *Women in Purple: Rulers of Medieval Byzantium*. Princeton: Princeton University Press, 2001.

Jugie, Martin. "Exégèse médiévale." Pages 591–608 in vol. 4 of *Dictionnaire de la Bible: Supplément*. Paris: Letouzey et Ané, 1945.

Laiou, Angeliki E. "Women in the History of Byzantium." Pages 23–32 in *Byzantine Women and Their World*. Edited by Ioli Kalavrezou. Cambridge: Harvard University Art Museums, 2003.

Leroy, Julien. "Le monachisme studite." Pages 39–116 in Théodore Studite, *Les grandes catecheses (Livre I), Epigrammes (I–XXIX)*. Translated by Florence de Montleau. Bégrolles-en-Mauges: Abbaye de Bellefontaine, 2002.

———. "La réforme studite." Pages 181–214 in *Il monachesimo orientale*. Edited by Convegno di studi orientali. Rome: Pontificium Institutum Orientalium Studiorum, 1958.

Maltese, Enrico Valdo. "Donne a Bisanzio: Misogamia culta e popolare tra l'XI e il XV secolo." Pages 25–48 in *Dimensioni bizantine: Donne, angeli e demoni nel Medioevo Greco*. Torino: Paravia-Scriptorium, 1995.

———. "Donne e letteratura a Bisanzio: Per una storia della cultura femminile." Pages 111–37 in *Dimensioni bizantine: Donne, angeli e demoni nel Medioevo Greco*. Torino: Paravia-Scriptorium, 1995.

Matons, Jean Grosdidier de. "La femme dans l'Empire byzantin." Page 11–43 in vol. 3 of *Histoire mondiale de la femme*. Edited by Pierre Grimal. Paris: Nouvelle Librairie de France, 1967.

Nardi, Eva. *Né sole né luna: L'immagine femminile nella Bisanzio dei secoli XI e XII*. Florence: Olschki, 2002.

Parrinello, Rosa Maria. *Il monachesimo bizantino*. Rome: Carocci, 2012.

———. "Theodora Palaeologina and the Others: Women Scholars, Copists, and Exegetes in Byzantium." Pages 181–201 in *The High Middle Ages*. BW 6.2. Atlanta: SBL Press, 2015.

Rosso, Stefano. *La celebrazione della storia della salvezza nel rito bizantino: Misteri sacramentali, feste e tempi liturgici.* Vatican City: Libreria Editrice Vaticana, 2010.

Talbot, Alice-Mary. "The Devotional Life of Laywomen." Page 201–40 in *Byzantine Christianity.* Vol. 3 of *A People's History of Christianity.* Edited by Derek Kreuger. Minneapolis: Fortress, 2010.

Kassia the Melodist (ca. 810–ca. 865) and Her Use of the Scriptures

Anna M. Silvas

1. The Historical Context

Kassia, Cassia, Kasia, Kassiane, Eikasia, or Ikasia, as her name is variously recorded or spelled, was a nun of ninth-century Byzantium. She is the outstanding female poet of the Greek Church. Of the four or five Greek-speaking women hymnographers positively identified, she is the only one known whose works gained admittance into the liturgical books.[1]

Kassia is the spelling of her name in two of Theodore the Studite's letters, and that will be our spelling here. She was born early in the ninth century to an aristocratic family of Constantinople. From the surname κανδιδατίσση, it is conjectured that her father held the high military post of *candidatus* at the imperial court.[2] Like other girls of a privileged circle, Kassia received a good education, achieving a high degree of literacy

---

1. On Theodosia, Thekla, Kassia, and Palaiologina, see Eva Catafygiotu Topping, "Women Hymnographers in Byzantium," *Dip* 3 (1982–1983): 98–111. On Phebronia, an early ninth-century nun and writer of poetry, grammar, and metrical works that have not survived, see also Peter Hatlie, *The Monks and Monasteries of Constantinople, ca. 350–850* (Cambridge: Cambridge University Press, 2007), 422–23.

2. The title κανδιδατίσση poses a problem, since it would normally mean *wife* of a *candidatus*. For the debates over this title and Kassia's life situation, see Ilse Rochow, *Studien zu der Person, den Werken und dem Nachleben der Dicterin Kassia* (Berlin: Akademie-Verlag, 1967), 24–25; George Fatouros, ed., *Theodori Studitae epistulae*, 2 vols. (Berlin: de Gruyter, 1992), 26; Judith Anne Bentzen, "A Study of the Liturgical and Secular Works of Blessed Kassia, Byzantine Nun and Poet" (MA thesis, University of New England, 1994), 14–15.

in the Greek language.³ She studied the Scriptures, the patristic classics (especially Gregory of Nazianzus), sacred music, poetry and meter, and possibly some Hellenic classics (e.g., Homer). The curriculum covered what we might call primary and early secondary studies, and it usually, but not always, stopped short of higher studies in rhetoric and philosophy. For women of Kassia's caliber in ninth-century Byzantium, there was a limited window of opportunity to develop their gifts; it soon closed, however, with the reassertion of traditional, misogynist sentiment from the tenth century onward. Though the iconodules triumphed—indeed, partly as a women's movement—it seems that the opportunity was not taken to remedy certain iconoclast dispositions.

We may assume (quite hypothetically) that Byzantine society of the eighth century, which was forced to struggle with the Arabs for its own survival, acquired a more patriarchal character than it had in the previous century. We may assume (even more hypothetically) that this patriarchal tendency incited women's resistance. If this is so, it would be another explanation for the active role of women in the anti-iconoclast movement. On the surface, iconoclasm was defeated in the mid-ninth century, and the veneration of icons was restored. Strangely enough, however, the principles of the iconoclasts proved more durable than their attitude toward holy images. If we assume that the victors of 843 CE inherited the iconoclasts' antifeminist position, the data collected above acquire a certain coherence: in the world of triumphant iconodules, women's role in cultural life was sharply curtailed (correspondence with women virtually ceased and women's poetry was supplanted), the traces of women's participation in the struggle against iconoclasm were obscured, and the celebration of saintly women who defended icon veneration was drastically curbed.⁴

---

3. The majority of Byzantine women were illiterate. But this was also true of men. On the education of girls in court circles, see Judith Herrin, "Theophano: Considerations on the Education of a Byzantine Princess," in *The Empress Theophano*, ed. Adelbert Davids (Cambridge: Cambridge University Press, 1995), 64–85, esp. 76–79. Herrin remarks on the quick pace of female education, which was expected to be accomplished by marriageable age (puberty): "It is important to remember that young girls were expected to learn fast. Princesses must have matured quickly, under pressure, for they were expected to cope with important affairs of state" (83). See also Ann Moffatt, "Schooling in the Iconoclast Centuries," in *Iconoclasm*, ed. Anthony Bryer and Judith Herrin (Birmingham: University of Birmingham, 1977), 85–92.

4. A. P. Kazhdan and A. M. Talbot discuss the changing role of women in "Women and Iconoclasm," *ByzZ* 84/85 (1991–1992): 401–4, esp. 404.

The great political, religious, and social context of Kassia's life was therefore the convulsion of Eastern Christendom by the iconoclastic controversy, which lasted from 729 to 843 CE. Iconoclasm was an attempt to stamp out the use of sacred icons in Christian worship, partly as a response to accusations of idolatry from Islam. Women—from all classes—and monks were the staunchest opponents of this misguided attempt to impose a pseudo-Christian archaism.[5] Kassia, who "belonged to the monachophile and Iconophile milieu, even though among her relatives there was at least one high-ranking Iconoclast," was active in this resistance even as a girl.[6] This experience formed her spirited character and her commitment to Christian piety and to a high conception of Christian womanhood. She was even something of a child confessor of the faith, being beaten for her aid to imprisoned monks and iconodule outlaws.[7]

Kassia sought the advice of the outstanding church father of the time, Theodore the Studite (759–826), the monastic reformer, champion of Christian marriage (against the imperial recourse to divorce and remarriage), and a great iconodule theologian.[8] In Theodore's three surviving letters to Kassia, he warmly commends her zeal for her orthodox faith and traditions, thanks her for aiding one of his imprisoned disciples, and at the same time praises the quality of her Greek style as outstanding for the times and remarkable in one so young.[9] They also reveal that the young Kassia had set her heart on the monastic life from an early age, and she

---

5. Cyril Mango concludes that the triumph of orthodoxy was due to an alliance of women and monks ("Historical Introduction," in *Iconoclasm*, ed. Anthony Bryer and Judith Herrin [Birmingham: University of Birmingham, 1977], 4), a point developed further by Judith Herrin in "Women and the Faith in Icons in Early Christianity," in *Unrivalled Influence: Women and Empire in Byzantium* (Princeton: Princeton University Press, 2013), 38–79.

6. A. P. Kazhdan with the collaboration of Lee F. Sherry and Christine Angelidi, *A History of Byzantine Literature, 650–850* (Athens: National Hellenic Research Foundation Institute for Byzantine Research, 1999), 316–17.

7. See Rochow, *Studien*, 20–26.

8. On the relationship between Theodore and Kassia, see Hatlie, *Monks and Monasteries of Constantinople*, 407–8, 424–25, 432.

9. The letters to Kassia may be found in Rochow, *Studien*, 20–22. They are discussed and translated into English at the end of my "Kassia the Nun, c.810–c.865: An Appreciation," in *Byzantine Women: Varieties of Experience, AD 800–1200*, ed. Lynda Garland (Aldershot: Ashgate, 2006), 32–37. Theodore asserts that in the struggle for Orthodoxy, men and women are equal (*Ep.* 142.19–21).

had sought Theodore's protection for this aim; he was somewhat ambiguous about endorsing this impulse, however, possibly out of respect for her family's say in the matter.

2. Two Kassias, One Identity

There is a famous legend, first attested by Symeon the chronicler in the tenth century, that Kassia appeared in a bride show arranged by the empress Euphrosyne for the crown prince Theophilos in the year 829. It is worth citing, since it shows a Kassia who uses a great theme of Scripture in favor of women:

> In the year of the world 6323, and of the divine Incarnation 823, the emperor of the Romans Theophilos, son of Michael the Stammerer, 12 years. His mother Euphrosyne, being resolved to give him a wife, assembled various maidens of peerless beauty, of whom there was a certain maiden, the fairest bloom among them, called Kassia, and another named Theodora.[10] Giving him a golden apple, Euphrosyne told him to give it to the one who pleased him the most. Astonished by Kassia's beauty, Emperor Theophilos said: "Ach, what deplorable things gushed forth through woman!" She answered, albeit with a certain modesty: "Yes, but also through woman the better things spring." Cut to the heart by this word, Theophilos passed her by and gave the golden apple to Theodora who came from Paphlagonia.[11]

---

10. The term ὡραιοτάτη possibly implies someone a little older than the others, nearer to the full bloom of young womanhood.

11. PG 109:685C: κόσμου ἔτος ϛτκγ΄, τῆς θείας σαρκώσεως ἔτος ωκγ΄, Ῥωμαίων βασιλεὺς Θεόφιλος ὁ υἱὸς τοῦ Μιχαὴλ Τραυλοῦ Εἰκονομάχος, ἔτη ιβ΄. τῆς δὲ μητρὸς αὐτοῦ Εὐφροσύνης βουληθείσης δοῦναι αὐτῷ γυναῖκα, ἄγει κόρας διαφόρους ἀσυγκρίτους τῷ κάλλει, μεθ᾽ ὧν μία τις ἐξ αὐτῶν κόρη ὡραιοτάτη ὑπῆρχεν Εἰκασία λεγομένη καὶ ἑτέρα Θεοδώρα ὀνομαζομένη. τούτῳ δοῦσα ἡ μήτηρ χρυσοῦν μῆλον εἶπεν δοῦναι τῇ ἀρεσάσῃ αὐτῷ. ὁ δὲ βασιλεὺς Θεόφιλος τῷ κάλλει τῆς Εἰκασίας ἐκπλαγεὶς ἔφη, ὡς ἄρα διὰ γυναικὸς ἐρρύη τὰ φαῦλα. ἡ δὲ μετ᾽ αἰδοῦς πως ἀντέφησεν· ἀλλὰ καὶ διὰ γυναικὸς πηγάζει τὰ κρείττονα. ὁ δὲ τῷ λόγῳ τὴν καρδίαν πληγεὶς ταύτην μὲν εἴασεν, Θεοδώρᾳ δὲ τὸ μῆλον ἀπέδωκεν, οὔσῃ ἐκ Παφλαγονίας. The legend was repeated many times with slight variations. Rochow discusses the versions of Leon Grammatikos, Theodosius Melitenos, Georgios Monachos, Zonaras, Glykas, and Ephrem (*Studien*, 5–19). They are all recorded and translated in Kurt Sherry, *Kassia the Nun in Context* (Piscataway, NJ: Gorgias, 2013), 120–32.

Is this the same Kassia whom we know from the letters of Theodore and from her own literary monuments? Among more recent scholars, Judith Anne Bentzen discounts its historical character, yet she says that this legend "proves how well remembered she was and how important to the Byzantines, that she should be included in the literature."[12] The *Prosopography of the Byzantine Empire* includes two entries, "Kassia I" and "Kassia II," concluding the latter entry by saying: "Possibly identical with Kassia I."[13] Marc Lauxterman highlights the difficulties of assuming that there were *two* Kassias: "Kassia is a very unusual name, and it requires much imagination to assume that there were two girls called Kassia, both with a literary talent, and both desiring to become a nun, living in exactly the same period." To this we might add: both living in the city (presumably) and both from aristocratic families.[14] All these factors in common are surely too much to ascribe to coincidence. Hence we infer that we are dealing with one and the same Kassia.

Still, determining the identity of these two Kassias requires some chronological negotiations, namely, the dating of the bride show, the dating of Theodore's letters, and the estimation of Kassia's age. In an earlier survey, my solution was to agree with Karl Krumbacher and Hans-Georg Beck in placing her birth circa 810 and to accept that Theodore's letters were written in the 820s when Kassia was in her postpuberty early teens.[15] In accounting for her comparatively "elderly" status as a nine-

---

12. Bentzen, "Study of the Liturgical," 7.

13. Dion Smythe and J. R. Martindale, *Prosopography of the Byzantine Empire I (641–867)* (Farnham: Ashgate, 2001), 762–63.

14. Marc Lauxtermann, "Three Biographical Notes," *ByzZ* 91 (1998): 391–405, esp. 392. Lauxtermann argues that Kassia did not intervene on what he takes to be her uncle's deathbed because she had softened in her stance as an iconophile and that her presence at the bride show was a later invention of her nuns, who, he supposes, wrote a *vita* to rehabilitate their mother's reputation with iconodules. This supposititious *vita* did not survive but was pillaged for this incident by the chroniclers. The theory is largely an edifice of conjecture.

15. Silvas, "Kassia the Nun," 17, 33; see Karl Krumbacher, "Kasia," in *Sitzungsberichte der Bayerischen Akademie der Wissenshaften: Philosophisch-philologische und historische Klasse* (Munich: Verlag der Kaiserlichen Bayerischen Akademie, 1897), 3.7:305–70, esp. 315; Hans-Georg Beck, *Kirche und theologische Literatur im byzantinische Reich* (Munich: Beck, 1959), 519; see also Kazhdan, *History of Byzantine Literature*, 316; Diane Touliatos, "'Kassia' (c. 810–c. 843–67)," in *Women Composers: Music through the Ages*, ed. Martha Furman Schleifer and Sylvia Glickman (New York: Hall, 1996), 1:1–24. In Theodore's second letter, he addresses her as a κόρη ἀρτιφυεῖ

teen- or twenty-year-old in the bride show of 829–830 (in itself a sign that she had already been reserving herself from marriage), I bracket Bentzen's assertion that any girl in a bride show could not have been older than fourteen years.[16]

The character of the Kassia of the bride show resonates entirely with the character of the later woman poet. Here is a young woman inclined to candor and prompt with wit, who did not consider accepting an insult on account of her sex an option—yet not from any stance of arrogance, still less of misandry, but as a Christian perfectly well aware of the age-old Eve/Mary typology of the church fathers.[17] Persuasive of the identity of the two is the quiet but firm defense of woman and the unservile attitude toward lofty rank. This reminder to Theophilos of Mary as the antitype of Eve reappears in Kassia's troparia to Barbara and Christina and, indeed, throughout her religious writing. Moreover, as Lauxtermann points out, the Kassia who replies here with a dodecasyllabic verse would be entirely in

---

("a maiden lately sprung"), which is surely to be understood as "lately emerged into maidenhood," that is, early to mid-teens, not infancy.

16. The 830 dating was established by Warren T. Treadgold in "The Problem of the Marriage of the Emperor Theophilos," *GRBS* 16 (1975): 325–41. For Bentzen's assertion, see Bentzen, "Study of the Liturgical," 20; in evidence, he apparently cites (on p. 42) Angeliki E. Laiou, "The Role of Women in Byzantine Society," *JÖB* 31 (1981): 236. In Roman law, seven years was the minimum age for betrothal, and the twelfth year was the minimum age for the marriage of girls. Since, according to Gregory of Nyssa's *Life of Macrina*, she was promised for betrothal in her twelfth year and yet had to wait for some years, it is clear that Christians in that area and time preferred their girls to be a little more mature for marriage. In the *Great Asketikon* (Longer Rule 15), Basil affirms that profession of virginity should be deferred until the age considered suitable for marriage. In canonical letter 199, he nominates sixteen or seventeen as the earliest age suitable for the profession of virginity or marriage. Confirming evidence is the case of Theodoret of Cyrrhus's mother, who was finally cured of infertility at age thirty, after thirteen years of marriage. Thus in late antiquity, at least, Christian girls tended to marry in the age bracket of fifteen to eighteen rather than twelve to fifteen.

17. The Eve/Mary theme was drawn from the Adam/Christ typology of Rom 5:14 and 1 Cor 15:22–45. It can be traced back almost to subapostolic times and is found across all the ancient Christian traditions. See Justin, *Dial.* 100 (PG 6:709–12); Irenaeus, *Adv. haer.* 3.22.4 (SC 211:438–45); 5.19.1 (SC 153:248–51); Ephrem, *Nat.*; John Chrysostom, *Hom. Ps.* 44.7 (PG 5:93); John of Damascus, *Hom. 2 in Dorm* 3 (SC 80:130–35); Hesychius, *Sermo 5 in Deiparam* (PG 93:1464); Tertullian, *Carn. Chr.* 17 (SC 2:904); Jerome, *Ep.* 22.21 (PL 22:408); Augustine, *Serm.* 51.2–3 (PL 38:335); 232.2 (PL 38:1108).

keeping with the Kassia who was a writer of epigrams and maxims.[18] There is a play on words between Theophilos's verb ἐρρύη and Kassia's πηγάζει. Kassia switches to the present tense, indicating that Mary's role reversal of Eve is an ongoing source of "the better things" for human beings, hinting that this salutary role of woman, exemplified supremely in the Theotokos, might be instantiated in any woman given to holiness.[19]

According to the chroniclers, after the final collapse of iconoclasm in 843 (after the death of Theophilos), Kassia founded a monastery of nuns. Symeon says it was in disappointment at missing out on becoming empress.[20] This is a romantic spin that can be thoroughly discounted. No, Christ the bridegroom was not Kassia's peeved second choice. As a youthful aspirant to monastic life of spirited character, her presentation as a candidate in the imperial bride show looks at best like a family ploy. She was under constraint. Her failure cannot have been but, for her personally, a win. It reminds one strongly of Polonius's speech in Shakespeare's *Hamlet*: "To thine own self be true, and it must follow as the night the day, thou canst not then be false to any man" (Act 1, Scene 3). Kassia was given an unexpected opportunity to express something of her true mind to Theophilos. She seized the moment, which had the happy consequence of saving them both from an ill-sorted future together.

The fact that Kassia had the resources to found a monastery some twelve or thirteen years later suggests that her parents had by that time

---

18. Lauxterman, "Three Biographical Notes," 367.

19. Or, for that matter, men, who are given to holiness. In Kassia's maxims on the monastic life, Mary is the archetype of every perfect Christian: "'A monk is an abode of God, a royal throne, a palace of the Holy Trinity.' "Her allegorical description of the monastic state borrows the familiar liturgical titles of the Theotokos. In other words, Kassia asserts that the true monastic ... is a *theotokos* in that he or she brings forth God in his or her own soul" (Sherry, *Kassia the Nun*, 40).

20. According to Symeon the Chronicler (PG 109:685), ἡ μὲν Εἰκασία τῆς βασιλείας ἀποτυχοῦσα μονὴν κατεσχεύασεν. See Hatlie, *Monks and Monasteries of Constantinople*, 327–30, 347–52, on the expansion of monastic foundations that preceded the Triumph of Orthodoxy in 843; and Rosemary Morris, *Monks and Laymen in Byzantium, 843–1118* (Cambridge: Cambridge University Press, 1995). According to Peter Charanis, after the end of iconoclasm, there was a "rash of new monasteries" ("The Monk as an Element of Society," *DOP* 25 [1971]: 68). Many foundations previously committed to iconoclasm, such as the Chora monastery, reverted to the control of iconophile monks.

passed away.[21] Her monastery was in the west of the city near the men's monastery of Stoudios, which tended to confirm and extend her youthful association with Theodore.[22] As the nuns' ἡγουμένη, she followed in the tradition of her spiritual fathers, Basil the Great and Theodore, being entirely committed to cenobitism (the practice of ordered life in community) as an imperative of the Christian life. As can be seen from her intense aphorisms on the monastic vocation, she expected of herself and her nuns considerably more than the genteel, minimally ascetic life of aristocratic women in retirement observable in the later Byzantine period.[23]

In her monastic community, immersed at last in a lifestyle of liturgy, work, and continuous scriptural meditation, Kassia flourished as an exceptionally skilled and prolific writer of sacred chants and melodies and also of nonliturgical verse. Manuscripts from the eleventh to the sixteenth century ascribe to her some forty-nine hymns, of which twenty-three are included in the liturgical books and some 261 nonliturgical verses in the form of either epigrams or aphorisms called gnomic verse.[24] Her literary skill is revealed by comparing her work with that of contemporary hymnographers. While their style tends to be conventional, prolix, and mannered, Kassia's tends to originality, a simpler vocabulary, and a subtler, more concise use of words.

It was the proximity and the link between Kassia and the monastery of Stoudios that facilitated her literary survival. The Studite monks played a pivotal role in the revision and updating of the Constantinopolitan liturgical books in the ninth to the twelfth century. They gave their female colleague and friend a unique memorial, not by writing her *vita* but by incorporating a selection of her hymns into the liturgical books, which

---

21. She may have been an only child, since there is never a mention of siblings.

22. On the location, see Antonia Tripolitis, *Kassia: The Legend, the Woman, and Her Work* (New York: Garland, 1992), 15; Bentzen, "Study of the Liturgical," 8.

23. See the study of Kassia's "philosophy of monasticism" in Sherry, *Kassia the Nun*, 63–91, 111–17. Compare also her sticheron for the nativity of John the Forerunner, the exemplar of all monks (Tripolitis, *Kassia*, 50–51), studied by Kosta Simić, "Kassia's Hymnography in the Light of Patristic Sources and Earlier Hymnographical Works," *ZRVI* 48 (2011): 28–30.

24. The liturgical books are listed and discussed by Rochow in *Studien*, 32–46. The corpus of Kassia's noncanonical hymns was amplified by the discoveries in two manuscripts on Mt. Athos. See Sophronius Eustratiades, "Κασιανὴ ἡ Μελωδός" [Kassia the Melodist], Ἐκκλησιαστικὸς Φάρος 31 (1932): 92–112. For an edition of Kassia's canonical and noncanonical works in Greek and English translation, see Tripolitis, *Kassia*. The nonliturgical verses were given their first edition by Krumbacher, "Kasia," 336.

they were in an unequalled position to endorse and disseminate. All the same, we would have been grateful for the survival of a decent *vita*.

3. Kassia and the Patristic Approach to the Scriptures

It perhaps needs to be pointed out that many of the unconscious assumptions that surround the term *Bible* in the West, particularly from the time of the Protestant Reformation in the sixteenth century and from the rise of scientific biblical studies in the nineteenth century, were unknown in the religious culture to which Kassia was heir. The very term Bible was unheard of, being the result of medieval Latin commentators who recycled the Greek neuter plural βίβλια ("books") as a Latin feminine singular *biblia* ("the book"/"the Bible"). Of course, in the earlier era, there was no plethora of printed "Bibles" on tap. The acquisition of the word in those days required time-consuming manual labor and the toil of the mind, at some cost. Even when the written text was acquired, this was largely done in the context of a highly oral, communal, and ecclesial culture.

The patristic hermeneutic of Scripture was based on listening to the sacred words in what one might call a range of *keys*. In ascending order, they are (1) the literal (the immediate narrative context), (2) the moral (the lesson for conduct that might be derived from this text), (3) the typological (how this text fits into salvation history), and (4) the anagogical (how this word leads upward to ultimate spiritual realities). The most prayerful approach to Scripture aspired to this last outcome: the kindling of the spiritual senses by the Holy Spirit. Patriarch Bartholomew I captures something of this tradition of the spiritual senses thus:

> We seek to draw on a rich Patristic teaching, dating to the early third century and expounding a doctrine of the five spiritual senses. For listening to God's word, beholding God's Word, and touching God's Word are all spiritual ways of perceiving the unique divine mystery. Based on Proverbs 2.5 about *the divine faculty of perception* [αἴσθησις], Origen of Alexandria exclaims: "The sense unfolds as sight for contemplation of immaterial forms, hearing for discernment of voices, taste for savoring the living bread, smell for sweet spiritual fragrance, and touch for handling the Word of God, which is *grasped by every faculty of the soul*."[25]

---

25. Patriarch Bartholomew I of Constantinople, address to the Synod of Bishops on the Word of God, Sistine Chapel, October 18, 2008. *L'Osservatore Romano*, weekly edition in English, October 22, 2008.

The spiritual senses are variously described as the "five senses of the soul," as "divine," or as the "inner faculties," and even as "faculties of the heart" or "mind." This doctrine inspired the theology of the Cappadocians (especially Basil the Great and Gregory of Nyssa) as much as it did the theology of the desert fathers (especially Evagrius of Pontus and Macarius the Great).[26]

This sapiential, aspirational approach to the Scriptures had as its nurturing matrix the life of the church and above all participation in its liturgy. To make use of a classic term from western monasticism, the liturgy is, in a very real sense, the church's corporate *lectio divina*, her contemplative and doxological reading of the saving words and acts of God. Kassia's engagement with Scripture operates entirely in this ancient ecclesial modality. In the liturgy, all the narratives, prophecies, symbols, commandments, parallels, and antitheses of Scripture are sung—and they are *theologized* in the singing, especially in the splendid and imaginative hymns that increasingly found entry into the Constantinopolitan tradition in those centuries, not least through influences from the Syriac-speaking church. As in the liturgy, so in personal prayer, the pondering of Scripture was ordered for the awakening of spiritual interiority and sublimely for the assimilation of Christian believers' bodies, souls, and spirits to the Logos, the Word behind the words, the Godman Jesus Christ.

Kassia's version of Scripture was the canonical version of the Greek-speaking church (i.e., the original Greek New Testament, in its Byzantine recension), and for the Old Testament, the Greek canonical version was the Septuagint. Since she was never called upon to preach publicly, we do not have the extensive commentaries on Scripture in the form of recorded homilies that have come down to us from the fathers. Instead, she fills her verses and poetry with her interpretations of scriptural themes, particularly as they are called forth by the liturgy.[27]

---

26. Patriarch Bartholomew I of Constantinople, address to the Synod of Bishops on the Word of God, p. 5.

27. According to Kurt Sherry, Kassia deserves to be recognized as a church mother: "I contend that Kassia's works should be placed in the same category as those of the Church Fathers who were her contemporaries: John of Damascus, Photius the Great, and Theodore the Studite, her own spiritual father.... Kassia's written legacy of hymnography and its theological content place her, as a Church Mother, on par with those counted as Fathers" (*Kassia the Nun*, 7–12, quote at 11–12).

4. Kassias as Interpreter of Scripture in Liturgical Verse

An excellent introduction to Kassia's hermeutic of Scripture may be found in her hymn for the Forefeast of the Theophany at Vespers.[28] It is in the form of a dramatic dialogue that patterns itself over three stichera. Kosta Simić elucidates Kassia's manner:

> Here, the poetess elaborates upon the dialogue between Christ and John the Forerunner, as it is described in the Gospel of Matthew (Matt 3:13–15), simultaneously dramatizing and theologically amplifying it. Christ's words are preceded by an introduction spoken by the narrator, i.e., Kassia, who introduces the person of Christ in the drama. Christ asks John to baptize Him in the waters of the Jordan, where He wants to regenerate human nature that is "enslaved by the serpent's cunning" (lines 9–10).[29]

This entering into the gospel event with imagination, and elucidating its inner meaning in the disposition of theological wonder, is very much the manner of Byzantine liturgical dramatization. Kassia brings her hymn to a crescendo in the third sticheron, in which she, the theologian who sings, articulates the awe of John's response to Christ's request for baptism at his hands:

> "O my Maker, how shall I who am *grass*, (Ps 89:5, 102:15)
> lay hands upon you who are *fire*? (Heb 12:29 et al.)
> How shall the streams of the *river* receive you,
> who are a great *sea* (Sir. 24:31) of *divinity* (Col 2:9) and the inexhaustible *fountain of life*? (Ps 35:9)
> How shall I baptize you who, having no defilement remove the filth of men? (Ezek 22:15 et al.)
> For which, for our sake, you were born of the Pure One," said he who was born of the Barren One:
> "*It is I who have need of baptism from you!*" (Matt 3:14)
> Glory to you O Lord![30]

The ear familiar with the accents of Scripture will sense immediately the many scriptural allusions along which Kassia threads this sticheron,

---

28. See text in Tripolitis, *Kassia*, 30–33.
29. Simić, "Kassia's Hymnography," 16–18.
30. Translated from the Greek in Tripolitis, *Kassia*, 32.

entirely in the manner of patristic liturgical and theological discourse. There is, however, something more to understand. Simić explains how the whole hymn might work *musically* in its liturgical enactment. Indeed, this complex interweaving, this symphony of the musical, the liturgical, the emotional, is theologically attentive; the doxological and ecclesial/communitarian applies to all of Kassia's treatment of Scripture:

> The dramatic effect would have been greatly augmented, particularly in the second and third *stichera*, by the antiphonal performance of these poetic works by two choirs. The alternating chant would bring the choirs into a dialogue; they would assume the voices of the protagonists, with one choir performing the role of Jesus, voiced in the second *sticheron*, and the other performing the role of John from the third *sticheron*. The faithful assembled in the church, who were not part of the alternating choirs, would also participate in the dramatization of the Gospel narrative through the repetition ... of the final words of each *sticheron*: Κύριε, δόξα σοι.[31]

Kassia composed many troparia in which martyrs, holy women, and the Cappadocian fathers predominate among her themes. For major liturgical festivals, she composed one canonical and eight noncanonical troparia for the Nativity of the Savior, three for the eve of Theophany or Epiphany, three noncanonical troparia for the Feast of the Meeting or Presentation of the Lord in the Temple, one for the Feast of Annunciation and one for the Feast of the Dormition of the Theotokos, two for the first Sunday of Lent (Sunday of the Publican and the Pharisee), one for Friday of the first Week of Lent, and one for Wednesday of Holy Week. One of her canons was for the Easter vigil and another, a long one, for the dead.[32]

All the hymns that Kassia composed are strongly theological and liturgical in sensibility, economic yet sensitive in rhetorical expression. Several themes recur: her favorite invocation of Christ as savior (σῶτερ), the saving of souls, the importance of tears, and the supplication of divine mercy. She was greatly inspired by the image of the myrrh-bearing women

---

31. Simić, "Kassia's Hymnography," 16–18.

32. The canonical troparion for the nativity of the Savior, *When Augustus Was Monarch upon the Earth*, is considered to be her finest after the one on the sinful woman. For the text, see Tripolitis, *Kassia*, 18–19. See also the study of this troparion by Simić, "Kassia's Hymnography," 8–12. On the toparia for the Feast of the Meeting or Presentation of the Lord in the Temple, see Tripolitis, *Kassia*, 38–41.

on the morning of the resurrection of Christ and their role as the first heralds of that culminating event. Not surprising in an iconodule and disciple of Theodore, Kassia is particularly attentive to the humility and abasement of Christ's incarnation and the condescension and compassion that prompted it. She returns constantly to the term "kenosis" (κένωσις; see Phil 2:7)—"self-emptying" or "abasement"—usually with a qualification highlighting the paradoxes (e.g., Christ's *divine kenosis*). She also uses the closely related term συγκατάβασις ("descent" or "condescension") in describing the divine self-abasement of the incarnation. Similarly, in her hymns on the nativity discovered by Sophronius Eustratiades, she is arrested by the *poverty* of the newly born Savior, pondering the Scripture: "*For your sakes he became poor, so that by his poverty you might become rich*" (2 Cor 8:9).[33] Simić notes how often Kassia uses the language of "seeing" God the Word "in the *flesh*," by way of stressing the reality of Christ's humanity as a remedy of the mistaken ideas of the iconoclasts.[34]

It is remarkable that a canon composed by Kassia found its way, in part and disguised, into the very heart of the most sacred of all Christian festivals: the Paschal Vigil. For a time, it was considered unseemly that it be attributed to a woman, and her authorship was obfuscated and diluted. Understandably, it is considered among the finest of her longer works.[35] It begins by remembering the singing of Miriam and the women after the deliverance at the Red Sea. It was not unfitting, then, that its first composer was a woman and its first singers the choir of her nuns:

> But let us like the maidens, Sing now to the Lord,
> for he has been wonderfully glorified!

Included here in full is Kassia's troparion to Barbara, one of the popular women saints of the Christian East. Its theology of woman echoes the riposte given to Emperor Theophilos in the bride show and recurs in the troparia to Christina. Kassia portrays Barbara as sharing in Mary's role reversal of Eve. In Kassia's mind, this is the potential role of every woman in the age-old contest between the mercy that saves and the malice that destroys:

> The malign Enemy,
> who once gained the Fore-mother as an instrument for sin,

---

33. See Eustratiades, "Κασιανὴ," 102–5.
34. Simić, "Kassia's Hymnography," 20, 25.
35. See Eustratiades, "Κασιανὴ," 97–100.

has been put to shame, worsted by a woman,
for He who was incarnate of a Virgin, the Word of the Father,
simple and immutable, as only He knows,
has undone the curse of Eve and Adam.
Now Christ has worthily crowned Barbara the Martyr,
and extends to the world through her atonement and great mercy.[36]

Kassia uses Scripture typologically to illumine Scripture. In the fourth ode of her *Tetraodion for Holy Saturday*, she applies the expectation of a coming fearful theophany in Hab 3:1–19 to its realization in the incarnation and the passion of Christ, weaving in an allusive use of Hab 3:14:

Habbakuk, foreseeing
your divine self-emptying [κένωσις] cries out *in ecstasy*:
"You have *broken through* the power *of the mighty*, O Good One,
preaching to those in Hades
as the Almighty."

In her three stichera on the meeting or presentation of Christ in the temple (Luke 2:22–38), she applies the vivid image of the burning coal born by a seraph in Isa 6:6–7 to the Christ child born in Mary's arms as in a "pair of tongs."[37] Mary hands him over to Simeon the Elder as the coal that is not consumed with fire.

Kassia's most famous work is her troparion for Orthros on Wednesday of Holy Week, Κύριε, ἡ ἐν πολλαῖς ἁμαρτίαις, which enters into the experience of the sinful woman of Luke 7:36–50 as she approaches Christ, combined with some elements from the anointing at Bethany in John 12:1–8. This troparion is included in many anthologies of Greek and religious poetry.[38] As with her other hymns, Kassia also set this one to music, so that she is properly called μελῳδός.

O Lord, she who had fallen
into many sins,
discerning your divinity,
takes up the rank of a myrrh-bearer,
and mourning, brings you myrrh, before your burial.

---

36. Translated from the Greek text in Tripolitis, *Kassia*, 12.
37. See the text and translation in Tripolitis, *Kassia*, 38–41.
38. E.g., C. A. Trypanis, *The Penguin Book of Greek Verse* (Harmondsworth: Penguin, 1971).

Alas for me! she says,
for the night smothers me—a goading of passion
murky and moonless, a craving for sin!
Receive the fountains of my tears, You who disperse from clouds
the waters of the sea.
Stoop down to me,
to the groaning of my heart,
You who bowed down the heavens
in your ineffable self-emptying [κένωσις]!
I shall fervently kiss your undefiled feet,
and then I shall wipe them with the hairs of my head,
at whose sound in Paradise,
breaking upon her ears in the cool of the evening,
Eve hid in fear.
O who can fully trace out the multitude of my sins
and the depths of your mercies, O Savior of souls, my Savior?
Turn not aside from me your handmaid, O bearer of great mercy unmeasured![39]

In this hymn Kassia recapitulates the entire Lenten experience of μετάνοια ("repentance") as the church pauses on the brink of entering into Christ's passion. Kassia uses a language of psalm-like emotional immediacy with a stripped-down economy of words to portray the woman's unequal struggle with the habit of sin that has enslaved her, the point of crisis at which she has arrived, her resolve to approach Christ, and her appeal to him. This sinful, suppliant woman assumes the cry of a whole needy world, which cannot save itself, to its savior.

Unlike her male colleagues, Kassia does not bluntly name the woman she portrays as a ἁμαρτωλός ("sinner") or a πόρνη ("harlot"). Nevertheless, she wonderfully expresses her moral desperation. Paradoxically, it is this fallen woman who perceives that the one in their midst is God—not Simon and the Pharisees, who doubted he could even be a prophet. By her coming to anoint the Savior, Kassia assigns the woman a place with the holy myrrh-bearing women who were the first to herald the resurrection.

The poem then becomes a dramatic monologue in the person of the woman herself: "In the words of the sinful woman Kassia unfolds the *pathos* of a troubled and contrite soul searching for salvation," drawing the hearer to participate in her exodus from the "moonless night" of sensual

---

39. Translated from the Greek text in Tripolitis, *Kassia*, 76–79.

captivity to the "fathomless abyss" of the Lord's mercies.[40] Such a journey of repentance is possible, for through the ineffable kenosis of his incarnation, God has stooped down to become present and compassionate, approachable and touchable in Jesus. Eve, in her sin, had once run *from* him, but this woman dares the very opposite: in her very captivity to sin, she runs *to* him, staking everything on his goodness and condescension, supposing not that his purity could be contaminated by her impurity but that it should be its remedy instead.

Kassia's masterpiece is an exquisite hymn to the humility and compassion of Christ the Savior of souls. The author of this sacred poetry cannot but have understood from the inside what a deeply penitent spirit before God was. We may be sure that as a poet, so also as a spiritual mother, Kassia was concerned to foster such dispositions in others. It is shallow to suggest that Kassia herself had to experience the actual sins of the woman portrayed to express these sentiments. Like any mature Christian who has gone any distance in a serious life in Christ, she has been made to measure her own spiritual indigence. She knows what utter dependence on the saving mercy of God is about.

5. Kassia's Use of Scripture in Nonliturgical Verse

We turn briefly to Kassia's use of Scripture in her nonliturgical verse. On the topic of woman, Kassia revisits some of the Old Testament wisdom sayings and epigrams of Palladas in the *Greek Anthology*. On feminine beauty, she seems ambivalent—it is either an unwelcome distraction or at best an ancillary help. Then she makes a startling utterance. Kassia lights on a text in 1 Esdras, which in every way confirms her experience of feminine solidarity in the crisis of the church and accords with her Eve/Mary typology. She adapts the text to give her strongest affirmation of the strength of women—when they are in alliance with truth: "Esdras is witness that the race of women together with truth prevails over all."[41] The text comes from the book known in the Greek Septuagint as 1 Esdras and in the Latin Vulgate as 3 Esdras, which is not to be confused with the book Ezra of the

---

40. Catafygiotu Topping, "Psalmist, St Luke and Kassia the Nun," 206.

41. φῦλον γυναικῶν ὑπερισχύει πάντων·ντωὶ μάρτυς Ἐσδρας μετὰ τῆς ἀληθείας. Bentzen misses the full scriptural context ("Study of the Liturgical," 148) and so translates it in a secular feminist key: "The race of women dominates everything; and the witness of Esdra proves this to be true" (250).

Masoretic Ezra-Nehemiah corpus. In the Rahlfs edition of the Septuagint, the exact texts Kassia refers to are 1 Esd 3:12, ὑπερισχύουσιν αἱ γυναῖκες, ὑπὲρ δὲ πάντα νικᾷ ἀλήθεια ("It is women who are surpassingly strong, but truth prevails over all"), and 4:13, περὶ τῶν γυναικῶν καὶ τῆς ἀληθείας ("concerning women and the truth").[42] The setting is found in 1 Esd 3–4. Three bodyguards debate before King Darius about what is the strongest. The third of them, Zerubbabel, asserts that women are, but since, like all else, they too are unrighteous, truth surpasses them too and endures forever: "Blessed be the God of truth!" He wins the contest and is rewarded with the rebuilding of the temple in Jerusalem. Kassia accommodates the text in order to say that yes, women do prevail over all—but only in alliance with truth, so to speak.

On the hazards of chastity, Kassia is clear-eyed, as she glosses a passage from Proverbs:

Better a fight than a furtive love (Prov 27:5),
for everyone is on guard against the one,
but strays beguiled into the other.[43]

To sum up Kassia's nonliturgical verse, what better way to capture her spirit than the following prayer, which collects several of her themes:

May Christ grant me rather to endure adversity with men [ἀνδράσι]
both thoughtful and most wise,
than to make merry with irrational fools.[44]

6. Conclusion

In conclusion, it can be seen that Kassia has profoundly interiorized the Word in Scripture to be able to express it the way she does in her theological poetry, liturgical doxology, and maxims of wisdom. In her thought world and in her writing, the remembrance of God's saving acts in Scripture is raised to its highest enactment in the liturgy. Her hermeneutic is typically shot through with a theology of woman in the economy of salvation, seen in terms of the Virgin Mary's role reversal of Eve, a typology

---

42. A. Rahlfs, *Septuaginta: Idest Vetus Testamentum graece iuxta LXX interpretes*, 2 vols. (Stuttgart: Württembergische Bibelanstalt, 1935).
43. Translated from the Greek in Tripolitis, *Kassia*, 134–35.
44. Translated from the Greek in Tripolitis, *Kassia*, 122–23.

long pondered in the Christian tradition and derived from the Adam/ Christ themes of the gospel and the Scriptures. It is a matter of wonder and gratitude that this godly feminist of ninth-century Constantinople survived in the Christian memory. Despite the obfuscations of misogyny, Kassia in her *Nachleben* gained the lasting respect of the Eastern churches and serves to inspire those of us today who hope to encourage the true good of women in society and in the church.

Bibliography

Bartholomew I of Constantinople, Patriarch. Address to the Synod of Bishops on the Word of God, Sistine Chapel, October 18, 2008. *L'Osservatore Romano*, weekly edition in English, October 22, 2008.

Beck, Hans-Georg. *Kirche und theologische Literatur im byzantinische Reich*. Munich: C. H. Beck, 1959.

Bentzen, Judith Anne. "A Study of the Liturgical and Secular Works of Blessed Kassia, Byzantine Nun and Poet." MA thesis, University of New England, 1994.

Charanis, Peter. "The Monk as an Element of Society." *DOP* 25 (1971): 61–84.

Catafygiotu Topping, Eva. "Women Hymnographers in Byzantium." *Dip* 3 (1982–1983): 98–111.

Eustratiades, Sophronius. "Κασιανὴ ἡ Μελωδός" [Kassia the Melodist]. Ἐκκλησιαστικὸς Φάρος 31 (1932): 92–112.

Fatouros, George, ed. *Theodori Studitae epistulae*. 2 vols. Berlin: de Gruyter, 1992.

Hatlie, Peter. *The Monks and Monasteries of Constantinople, ca. 350–850*. Cambridge: Cambridge University Press, 2007.

Herrin, Judith. "Theophano: Considerations on the Education of a Byzantine Princess." Pages 64–85 in *The Empress Theophano*. Edited by Adelbert Davids. Cambridge: Cambridge University Press, 1995.

———. "Women and the Faith in Icons in Early Christianity." Pages 38–79 in *Unrivalled Influence: Women and Empire in Byzantium*. Princeton: Princeton University Press, 2013.

Kazhdan, A. P., with the collaboration of Lee F. Sherry and Christine Angelidi. *A History of Byzantine Literature, 650–850*. Athens: National Hellenic Research Foundation Institute for Byzantine Research, 1999.

Kazhdan, A. P., and A. M. Talbot. "Women and Iconoclasm." *ByzZ* 84/85 (1991–1992): 391–408.

Krumbacher, Karl. "Kasia." Pages 305–70 in vol. 3.7 of *Sitzungsberichte der Bayerischen Akademie der Wissenshaften: Philosophisch-Philologische und Historische Klasse*. Munich: Verlag der Kaiserlichen Bayerischen Akademie, 1897.

Laiou, Angeliki E. "The Role of Women in Byzantine Society." *JÖB* 31 (1981): 233–60.

Lauxtermann, Marc. "Three Biographical Notes." *ByzZ* 91 (1998): 391–405.

Mango, Cyril. "Historical Introduction." Pages 1–6 in *Iconoclasm*. Edited by Anthony Bryer and Judith Herrin. Birmingham: University of Birmingham, 1977.

Moffatt, Ann. "Schooling in the Iconoclast Centuries." Pages 85–92 in *Iconoclasm*. Edited by Anthony Bryer and Judith Herrin. Birmingham: University of Birmingham, 1977.

Morris, Rosemary. *Monks and Laymen in Byzantium, 843–1118*. Cambridge: Cambridge University Press, 1995.

Rochow, Ilse. *Studien zu der Person, den Werken und dem Nachleben der Dicterin Kassia*. Berlin: Akademie-Verlag, 1967.

Sherry, Kurt. *Kassia the Nun in Context*. Piscataway, NJ: Gorgias, 2013.

Silvas, Anna M. "Kassia the Nun, c.810–c.865: An Appreciation." Pages 17–39 in *Byzantine Women: Varieties of Experience, AD 800–1200*. Edited by Lynda Garland. Aldershot: Ashgate, 2006.

Simić, Kosta. "Kassia's Hymnography in the Light of Patristic Sources and Earlier Hymnographical Works." *ZRVI* 48 (2011): 7–37.

Smythe, Dion, and J. R. Martindale. *Prosopography of the Byzantine Empire I (641–867)* Farnham: Ashgate, 2001.

Touliatos, Diane. "'Kassia' (c. 810–c. 343–867)." Pages 1–24 in vol. 1 of *Women Composers: Music through the Ages*. Edited by Martha Furman Schleifer and Sylvia Glickman. New York: Hall, 1996.

Treadgold, Warren T. "The Problem of the Marriage of the Emperor Theophilos." *GRBS* 16 (1975): 325–41.

Tripolitis, Antonia. *Kassia: The Legend, the Woman, and Her Work*. New York: Garland, 1992.

Trypanis, C. A. *The Penguin Book of Greek Verse*. Harmondsworth: Penguin, 1971.

Byzantine Reception of Biblical Revelation on the Virgin Mary

Mary B. Cunningham

The Virgin Mary, Theotokos ("God-bearer") or Meter Theou ("Mother of God") as she is variously described in texts, is a figure of central importance in Byzantine theology and spirituality.[1] In the course of the middle Byzantine period, which is normally defined as extending from about the seventh through the twelfth century, the cult of the Virgin Mary became firmly embedded in Byzantine society. Five feast days (her Nativity, Entrance into the Temple, Conception, Annunciation, and Dormition) were added to the liturgical calendar between about the sixth and early eighth centuries, along with other minor commemorations such as the honoring of her parents, Joachim and Anna, on the day after her nativity (September 9) and of relics such as her robe and belt (July 2 and August 31, respectively).[2] The

---

1. A great deal of work on the cult of the Virgin Mary in Byzantium has appeared in recent years. These include the collected articles in Sarah Jane Boss, ed., *Mary: The Complete Resource* (London: Burns & Oates, 2007); Chris Maunder, ed., *The Origins of the Cult of the Virgin Mary* (London: Burns & Oates, 2008); Maria Vassilaki, ed., *Mother of God: Representations of the Virgin in Byzantine Art* (Athens: Abbeville, 2000); Vassilaki, *Images of the Mother of God: Perceptions of the Theotokos in Byzantium* (Aldershot: Ashgate, 2004); Robert Norman Swanson, ed., *The Church and Mary*, SCH 39 (Woodbridge: Boydell, 2004); Bissera Pentcheva, *Icons and Power: The Mother of God in Byzantium* (University Park: Pennsylvania State University Press, 2006); Leslie Brubaker and Mary B. Cunningham, eds., *The Cult of the Mother of God in Byzantium: Texts and Images* (Farnham: Ashgate, 2011); Thomas Arentzen and Mary B. Cunningham, eds., *The Reception of the Virgin in Byzantium: Marian Narratives in Texts and Images* (Cambridge: Cambridge University Press, 2019).

2. For an overview, see Mary B. Cunningham, *Wider Than Heaven: Eighth-Century Homilies on the Mother of God* (Crestwood, NY: Saint Vladimir's Seminary Press, 2008), 19–28.

Feast of Christ's Meeting or Presentation in the Temple (February 2) began to acquire Marian significance, both because it represented her purification forty days after childbirth and because Symeon's prophecy that a "sword would pierce [Mary's] soul" (Luke 2:35) was understood to refer to her forthcoming pain at the foot of the cross.[3] Numerous churches dedicated to the Mother of God were founded in Constantinople, beginning in the late fifth century but especially from the sixth century onward.[4] Liturgical sermons and hymns honoring the Virgin proliferated, especially in connection with the feast days.[5] Miracle stories, as well as a few vitae of the Virgin Mary, also began to be composed in the middle Byzantine period.[6] All of this evidence testifies to the development of a thriving Marian cult, which, after slow beginnings in the fifth century in connection with the council of Ephesus (431), flourished especially from about the sixth century onward.[7]

---

3. Pauline Allen, "The Greek Homiletic Tradition of the Feast of the Hypapante: The Place of Sophronios of Jerusalem," in *Byzantina Mediterranea: Festschrift für Johannes Koder zum 65. Geburtstag*, ed. Klaus Belke et al. (Vienna: Böhlau, 2007), 1–12; Allen, "Portrayals of Mary in Greek Homiletic Literature (Sixth–Seventh Centuries)," in Brubaker and Cunningham, *Cult of the Mother of God*, 78–84.

4. Cyril Mango, "Constantinople as Theotokoupolis," in *Mother of God: Representations of the Virgin in Byzantine Art*, ed. Maria Vassilaki (Athens: Skira, 2000), 19–21.

5. Niki Tsironis, "The Mother of God in the Iconoclastic Controversy," in Vassilaki, *Mother of God*, 27–39.

6. A list can be found in François Halkin, ed., *Bibliotheca hagiographica graeca*, vol. 4 of *Auctarium* (Brussels: Société des Bollandistes, 1969), appendix 3: *Maria Deipara*, 256–73; many of these texts remain unedited. See Jane Baun, "Apocalyptic *Panagia*: Some Byways of Marian Revelation in Byzantium," in Brubaker and Cunningham, *Cult of the Mother of God*, 199–218.

7. For lively defense of the view that veneration of the Virgin Mary began much earlier, see Ally Kateusz, "Collyridian Déjà Vu: The Trajectory of Redaction of the Markers of Mary's Liturgical Leadership," *JFSR* 29.2 (2013): 75–92; Kateusz, "She Sacrificed Herself as the Priest: Early Christian Female and Male Co-priests," *JFSR* 33.1 (2017): 45–67; Stephen J. Shoemaker, *Mary in Early Christian Faith and Devotion* (New Haven: Yale University Press, 2016). More traditional—and still compelling—answers to this question can be found in Averil Cameron, "The Cult of the Virgin in Late Antiquity: Religious Development and Myth-Making," in Swanson, *Church and Mary*, 1–21; Cameron, "The Theotokos in Sixth-Century Constantinople: A City Finds Its Symbol," *JTS* 29 (1978): 79–108; Cameron, "The Virgin's Robe: An Episode in the History of Early Seventh-Century Constantinople," *Byzantion* 49 (1979): 42–56; Cameron, "Images of Authority: Élites and Icons in Late Sixth-Century Constantinople," *P&P* 84 (1979): 3–35; all reprinted in Cameron, *Continuity and Change in Sixth-Century Byzantium* (London: Variorum Reprints, 1981); Pentcheva, *Icons and Power*.

There are many aspects of Byzantine interpretation of the biblical figure of the Virgin Mary that could be covered in this essay, including not only architecture and texts but also art, numismatics, and sigillography, among others.[8] Partly for reasons of space, and partly because many of these subjects have received attention in other publications, this essay will focus only on liturgical and hagiographical texts from approximately the seventh through the tenth century. This period was particularly important in the development of ideas about the Virgin Mary. Liturgical texts, including especially festal sermons and hymns, began to portray Mary as a figure of importance in her own right. This is not to say that they underestimated her christological significance—in fact, this remained most preachers' chief preoccupation as they extolled Mary's importance as the Theotokos. Nevertheless, it is possible to trace a growing emphasis on the Virgin's intercessory power, as well as on her personal background, emotions, and role in the events of Christ's life in liturgical texts dating from about the seventh century onward. Such preoccupations are even more noticeable in the hagiographical texts that were being produced in this period, with a vita that is attributed to the seventh-century theologian, Maximos the Confessor (which survives, however, only in a later Georgian translation), providing a good example.[9]

---

8. For a preliminary orientation to these subjects, see the articles gathered in Vassilaki, *Mother of God*.

9. For a revised edition and English translation of the text, see Maximus the Confessor, *Life of the Virgin*, ed. and trans. Stephen J. Shoemaker (New Haven: Yale University Press, 2012); see also Michel van Esbroeck, ed., *Maxime le Confesseur: Vie de la Vierge*, CSCO 478–79, SI 21–22, 2 vols. (Leuven: Peeters, 1986). Van Esbroeck believed that this text is genuine and, following the opinion of Michael Tarchnisvili, argued that it was translated into Georgian by the monk Euthymios in the late tenth century. See van Esbroeck, *Maxime le Confesseur*, 2:vi–viii. Shoemaker, in a number of articles, accepts this attribution; see, for example, Shoemaker, "The Virgin Mary in the Ministry of Jesus and the Early Church according to the Earliest Life of the Virgin," *HTR* 98 (2005); Shoemaker, "The Georgian *Life* of the Virgin Attributed to Maximus the Confessor: Its Authenticity and Importance," in *Mémorial R. P. Michel van Esbroeck, S.J.*, ed. Alexey Muraviev and Basil Lourié (Saint Petersburg: Byzantinorossica, 1998), 67–84. In the introduction to his recent translation of the work, however, Shoemaker accepts the difficulty of proving Maximian authorship of the Greek prototype of the vita but still pushes for an early seventh-century date; see Maximus, *Life of the Virgin*, ed. Shoemaker, 21. A few scholars have disputed the authenticity of the work. See, for example, Ermanno M. Toniolo, "L'Akathistos nella Vita di Maria di Massimo il Confessore," in *Virgo Liber Dei: Miscellanea di stui in onore di P. Giuseppe*

One of the interesting features about the various genres of Marian literature in the Byzantine period is that they base themselves on quite different strands of tradition, according to their separate preoccupations. Festal sermons and hymns mostly follow the Old and New Testaments, gathering prophetic, typological, and narrative references to Mary into a rich, intertextual form of biblical exegesis. In addition to the canonical sources, these liturgical texts also began, especially after the seventh century, to employ apocryphal texts such as the second-century Protevangelium of James and later (mostly fifth- and sixth-century) accounts of Mary's dormition and assumption into heaven.[10] Hagiographical texts, however, including vitae and miracle stories about the Virgin as well as apocalypses, show a marked degree of independence from the biblical and even apocryphal sources.[11] Although the writers of these texts refer to the Old and New Testaments and may also draw on the apocryphal accounts for inspiration, they display a striking propensity to depart from these

---

M. Besutti, O. S. M., ed. Ignazio M. Calabuig (Rome: Edizioni Marianum, 1991), 209–28; and, most recently, Phil Booth, "On the *Life of the Virgin* Attributed to Maximus the Confessor," *JTS* 66 (2015): 149–203. Shoemaker responded to Booth's challenge in "The (Pseudo?-)Maximus *Life of the Virgin* and the Byzantine Marian Tradition," *JTS* 67 (2016): 115–42.

10. An edition of an early version of the Protevangelium of James may be found in Émile de Strycker, S.J., *La forme la plus ancienne du Protévangile de Jacques: Recherches sur le Papyrus Bodmer 5 avec une edition critique du texte grec et une traduction annotée*, SH 33 (Brussels: Societe des Bollandistes, 1961), 445–50. An English translation appears in J. K. Elliott, ed., *The Apocryphal New Testament: A Collection of Apocryphal Christian Literature in an English Translation Based on M. R. James* (Oxford: Clarendon, 1993), 57–67. For a discussion of eighth-century preachers' use of this apocryphal text, see Mary B. Cunningham, "The Use of the *Protevangelium of James* in Eighth-Century Homilies on the Mother of God," in Brubaker and Cunningham, *Cult of the Mother of God*, 163–78. On preachers' acceptance, from the seventh century onward, of apocryphal accounts of the dormition of the Virgin, see Brian E. Daley, S.J., *On the Dormition of Mary: Early Patristic Homilies* (Crestwood, NY: Saint Vladimir's Seminary Press, 1998), 9–35.

11. For the middle Byzantine lives of the Virgin, see notes 9, 61, 62. For a tenth-century collection of miracle stories associated with the Constantinopolitan shrine of the Pege, see Alice-Mary Talbot and Scott Fitzgerald Johnson, eds., *Miracle Tales from Byzantium* (Washington, DC: Dumbarton Oaks Medieval Library, 2012), 204–97. For the *Apocalypse of the Theotokos*, see M. R. James, ed., *Apocrypha anecdota*, TS 2.3 (Cambridge: Cambridge University Press, 1893), 109–26; Jane Baun, *Tales from Another Byzantium: Celestial Journey and Local Community in the Medieval Greek Apocrypha* (Cambridge: Cambridge University Press, 2007).

narratives and to add imaginative details of their own. Niki Tsironis has suggested, quite convincingly, the possibility of influence from one literary genre, or even medium, to another in the middle Byzantine period; specifically, she has argued that ideas about the Virgin Mary that were first expounded in poetry were transferred first to homilies, then to iconography, and finally to the liturgy, as they gradually gained acceptance by the body of Orthodox religious practice.[12] Hagiographical and apocalyptic texts seem to stand outside this circle of mutual influence. Jane Baun calls this a "paracanonical" tradition; it reflects the popular belief in Mary's power as divine mother and intercessor that emerged especially after the iconoclastic period.[13]

In this chapter, I shall divide the discussion into three main sections, focusing first on Marian festal sermons, then on hymnography, and finally on hagiography and apocalyptic texts. Owing to restrictions of space and to the size of the topic, it will be impossible to cover each of these topics in the detail that it deserves. I hope, however, to draw some conclusions concerning various authors' use of biblical revelation concerning the Virgin Mary, as well as to highlight the ways in which they choose to depart from this.[14]

A few more words of caution are necessary before we embark on this study. As in the case of most homiletic and hymnographic texts of the early Christian and Byzantine eras, many problems remain in the dating and attribution of this material. Although many texts can be attached to particular authors, others remain problematic, since the manuscript traditions frequently offer conflicting ascriptions. The lack of critical editions for both sermons and hymns also presents a problem: in most cases, we

---

12. Niki Tsironis, "From Poetry to Liturgy: The Cult of the Virgin in the Middle Byzantine Era," in Vassilaki, *Images of the Mother of God*, 91–92.

13. Jane Baun, "Discussing Mary's Humanity in Medieval Byzantium," in Swanson, *Church and Mary*, 66–67.

14. It should be noted here that, owing to a long delay in the publication of this essay, I have since written similar—or to some extent overlapping—studies of this subject matter. See, for example, Mary B. Cunningham, "Mary as Intercessor in Constantinople during the Iconoclast Period: The Textual Evidence," in *Presbeia Theotokou: The Intercessory Role of Mary across Times and Places in Byzantium*, ed. Pauline Allen, Andreas Külzer, and Leena Mari Peltomaa (Vienna: Österreichischen Akademie der Wissenschaften, 2015), 165–80; Cunningham, "The Life of the Virgin Mary according to Middle Byzantine Preachers and Hagiographers: Changing Contexts and Perspectives," *Apocrypha* 27 (2016): 137–59.

are dealing with texts that have been edited from individual manuscripts within diverse traditions. Hymnography remains the genre that is most in need of systematic study, with regard not only to the establishment of texts but also to questions of attribution and provenance. This genre belongs to a tradition that has been disseminated in a variety of service books that are still in use in modern Orthodox churches. Individual texts and writers fit seamlessly into liturgical services that are made up not only of hymnography but also of readings, responses, and prayers. Modern translations of most of the material that is to be discussed in this chapter remain scarce. It is to be hoped that essays such as the present one will highlight the need for further study and translation of many Marian texts belonging to the middle Byzantine period.

1. The Homiletic Tradition

The Marian sermons of the middle Byzantine period can be categorized mainly as festal orations. This tendency probably exists for two reasons. First, from about the sixth, but especially in the course of the seventh and eighth centuries, preachers felt the need to produce panegyrical sermons (often called *encomia* in the manuscripts) in honor of the recently established feasts celebrating events in the life of the Mother of God. It is not clear why this process took place slowly, with festal sermons appearing for the first time a number of years—in some cases, even a century—later than the date when a feast was added to the calendar. Some eighth-century Byzantine texts, such as John of Euboea's sermon on the conception of the Virgin Mary, reveal that even if Marian feasts had been officially instituted, they were not always widely celebrated by the middle of the eighth century.[15] Second, accidents in transmission have may have prevented earlier sermons produced by less acclaimed preachers from surviving. The transmission of festal sermons in manuscript collections that acted as digests of the most famous Greek fathers' writings for days or feasts of the liturgical year means that many homilies by earlier or less well-known preachers may have been lost.[16]

---

15. *CPG* 3:8135; John of Euboea, *In conceptionem* (PG 96:1473); see the discussion in Cunningham, *Wider Than Heaven*, 19–28, 182 nn. 45 and 51.

16. For lists and descriptions of the liturgical collections that transmit these homilies, see Albert Ehrhard, *Überlieferung und Bestand der hagiographischen und homiletischen Literatur der griechischen Kirche*, 3 vols (Leipzig: Hinrichs, 1936-1939). A

In the corpus that does survive, certain methods of biblical citation and interpretation predominate, although fresh engagement with Scripture also takes up considerable space. Most preachers who wrote on topics such as the Mary's nativity or entrance into the temple sought first to establish the prophetic basis for these themes. Explicit Old Testament testimony for the events in Mary's life was, of course, lacking; Byzantine exegetes, however, saw signs of her theological role in the incarnation of Christ as lurking ubiquitously beneath the literal meaning of Scripture. The implication here, according to Byzantine preachers such as Andrew of Crete, was that God planned for this virgin to give birth to his Son from the beginning of creation and that this represented a metaphysical renewal of that first creation. Andrew writes in his first homily on the nativity of the Virgin Mary, for example:

> Today the created precinct of the Creator of all things has been established, and the creature is newly prepared as a divine abode for the Creator. Today the nature that was formerly turned to dust takes on the beginning of deification, and the dust that has been exalted is urged to return to the glory that is on high. Today Adam, presenting her out of us and on our behalf as first-fruit to God, dedicates Mary, she indeed who was not mixed with the whole dough; through her is bread made for the remodelling of the race.[17]

This method of exegesis, which emphasizes the unity of the Old and New Testaments and sees Christ as the recapitulation or fulfillment of God's creation of the first man, Adam, owes much to the apostle Paul (e.g., 1 Cor 15:45–47), in the first place, and to early Christian theologians such as Irenaeus of Lyon who developed it further.[18] Byzantine preachers, including Andrew of Crete, also explored the concept in relation to the Virgin Mary,

---

discussion of the later uses and audiences for such liturgical collections may be found in Mary B. Cunningham, "Messages in Context: The Reading of Sermons in Byzantine Churches and Monasteries," in *Byzantium: Visions, Messages and Meanings; Festschrift for Prof Leslie Brubaker on Her Sixtieth Birthday*, ed. Angeliki Lymberopoulou (Farnham: Ashgate, 2011), 83–98.

17. *CPG* 3:8170; PG 97:808–12; Cunningham, *Wider Than Heaven*, 75.

18. Recent studies include Ysabel de Andia, *Homo vivens: Incorruptibilité et divinisation de l'homme chez Irénée de Lyon* (Paris: Etudes augustiniennes, 1994); John Behr, *Asceticism and Anthropology in Irenaeus and Clement* (Oxford: Oxford University Press, 2000); M. C. Steenberg, *Irenaeus on Creation: The Cosmic Christ and the Saga of Redemption*, VCSup 91 (Leiden: Brill, 2008).

describing her not only as the second Eve, who obeyed God rather than disobeying him, but also as the untouched (virginal) earth from which the second Adam, Christ, took his physical nature or as Eden, the paradise that contained the tree of life (Christ) or God himself.[19] The prophets, including Moses (who was believed to be the author of the Pentateuch, or first five books of the Old Testament), David, and Isaiah, preferred, according to Byzantine preachers, to refer to Mary in mysterious, coded ways. Those Christians who have enough theological discernment to perceive such signs are able to see allusions to her future role as the bearer, or container, of God throughout the Old Testament.

Although typology is not formally oracular, it is prophetic in the sense that it predicts the theological meaning of Mary's role as mother of Christ. Before exploring these various kinds of types, it is worth briefly defining typology as a method of textual exegesis. As Frances Young argues, typology is a modern concept; patristic and Byzantine commentators regarded it as one of many forms of allegory.[20] Whereas some modern scholars have distinguished typology from allegory, suggesting that whereas the former remains rooted in historical time, the latter sees an eternal meaning in the scriptural text.[21] Young, influenced by Sebastian Brock's work on Syriac hymnography, believes that typology serves to transfer us from a secular, and purely linear, time frame into an eternal state of existence in which the history of God's dispensation represents a unified and timeless reality.[22]

The types of the Virgin Mary that began to proliferate in Byzantine liturgical poetry seem to support this interpretation of their function.[23]

---

19. *CPG* 3:8170; Andrew of Crete, *Nat.* 1 (PG 97:816); Cunningham, *Wider Than Heaven*, 78–79.

20. Frances Young, *Biblical Exegesis and the Formation of Christian Culture* (Cambridge: Cambridge University Press, 1997), 152, 193; A. C. Charity, *Events and Their Afterlife: The Dialectics of Christian Typology in the Bible and Dante* (Cambridge: Cambridge University Press, 1996), 171, n. 2.

21. For example, Jean Daniélou, *From Shadows to Reality: Studies in the Biblical Typology of the Fathers* (London: Burns & Oates, 1960); G. W. H. Lampe and K. J. Woollcombe, *Essays in Typology*, SBT 22 (London: SCM, 1957).

22. Young, *Biblical Exegesis*, 151–57; S. P. Brock, *The Luminous Eye* (Rome: Centre for Indian and Inter-Religious Studies, 1985), 17.

23. For a preliminary study of this subject, see Mary B. Cunningham, "The Meeting of the Old and New: The Typology of Mary the Theotokos in Byzantine Homilies and Hymns," in Swanson, *Church and Mary*, 52–62. See also Paul Ladouceur, "Old Testament Prefigurations of the Mother of God," *SVTQ* 50 (2006): 5–57; Ephrem Lash,

Increasingly, such signs would be cited out of their textual context: it is clear that it is the meaning, not the historical background, of a type such as Jacob's ladder (Gen 28:10–17), the burning bush (Exod 3:1–8), or Gideon's fleece (Judg 6:37–40) that is important to Byzantine preachers and hymnographers. Such types can be grouped into categories that convey specific theological messages: for example, some types, such as Jacob's ladder (Gen 28:10–17), foreshadow Mary's role as a link between the created and divine worlds. Signs such as the burning bush and Gideon's fleece, meanwhile, indicate the way in which divinity can become immanent in creation. The fourth-century preacher John Chrysostom, commenting on the type of Gideon's fleece, remarks that God's quiet manifestation of dew on this material object prefigured his gentle and noiseless entrance into Mary's womb.[24] Other types, such as the unopened gate of the temple (Ezek 43:27–44), paradise (Gen 2:8–17), the locked garden, and the sealed spring (Song 4:12), signify Mary's virginity. In the case of paradise, or the garden of Eden, the type has a double resonance in that it also evokes the concept of Christ as the second Adam: just as God created the first man from untilled and unwatered soil, so also did he become incarnate out of Mary's untouched, virginal nature. Container types include the tabernacle (Exod 26; 35–36; 40) and its vessels, such as the jar containing manna (Exod 16:32–33), and the temple of Solomon (1 Kgs 6–8). Such signs signify unequivocally Mary's exalted role as one who contained God himself. The paradoxes that are inherent in this imagery were fully exploited by Byzantine preachers and hymnographers; in employing such types, they emphasized the physical nature of these objects, which could nevertheless contain, bring forth, or sustain a link with divinity.

The manner in which middle Byzantine preachers employed such typology could be creative or traditional. Whereas some writers provided new interpretations of well-established types, or occasionally even introduce new ones, others listed them in a string of acclamations that were often introduced by the greeting χαῖρε ("hail" or "rejoice"), known as the χαιρετισμός (Luke 1:28). The number of Old Testament types that signify the Virgin Mary was still expanding over the course of the eighth century; after this period, in which a number of sermons for recently introduced

---

"Mary in Eastern Church literature," in *Mary in Doctrine and Devotion*, ed. Alberic Stacpoole (Dublin: Columba, 1990), 58–80.

24. John Chrysostom, *Hom. Matt.* 26.39.3; Ladouceur, "Old Testament Prefigurations," 25.

feasts were composed for the first time, the genre became more conventional, at least in terms of Marian typology. Some of the most interesting eighth-century innovations, in the field of typology, were those that developed in connection with the Feast of Mary's Entrance into the Temple. As we see in the two sermons for this feast that are attributed to Germanus of Constantinople, a rich symbolism involving Mary as the living temple who brought to fulfillment the promise of the old, man-made Jewish temple was elaborated.[25]

Middle Byzantine preachers also used narrative in order to explore the Virgin Mary's character and role in the new dispensation. This exegetical technique is more literal in its approach to the subject, but it allowed preachers to explore the meaning of Scripture in a variety of innovative ways. Perhaps one of the most striking aspects of this method of exegesis is the way in which preachers felt free to retell the story of the Virgin Mary, employing not only the canonical gospels but also, especially after the beginning of the seventh century, the apocryphal sources.[26] The object of such narrative development was usually to explain or expand details that preachers and their audiences might see as ambiguous in Scripture, such as the period of mental turmoil that Mary experienced on hearing the archangel Gabriel's message at the annunciation or her true feelings on seeing her son die in agony on the cross. The laconic nature of the New Testament witness to the Virgin Mary is reflected to some extent in early Christian writings. Tina Beattie has suggested recently that this may reflect the importance of silence or a sense of mystery with regard to the Mother of God for writers of the postapostolic period.[27] This approach was gradually abandoned, however, as devotion toward Mary increased in the course of the fourth and fifth centuries. Later preachers appear to have felt increasingly free to elaborate on the gospel narratives, often with the help of apocryphal texts such as the Protevangelium of James.

---

25. *CPG* 3:8007–8; PG 98:292–320; Cunningham, *Wider Than Heaven*, 145–72. For a discussion of the homilies, along with doubts about the authenticity of the first, see Cunningham, *Wider Than Heaven*, 39–40. These doubts are echoed by Dirk Krausmüller in his "Making the Most of Mary: The Cult of the Virgin in the Chalkoprateia from Late Antiquity to the Tenth Century," in Brubaker and Cunningham, *Cult of the Mother of God*, 219–45. On the Feast of Mary's Entrance into the Temple, see now Jaakko Olkinuora, *Byzantine Hymnography for the Feast of the Entrance of the Theotokos*, SPF 4 (Helsinki: Suomen patristinen seura ry, 2015).

26. Cunningham, "Use of the *Protevangelium of James*," 167.

27. Tina Beattie, "Mary in Patristic Theology," in Boss, *Mary*, 77.

Examples of such narrative embellishment are easy to find in a number of middle Byzantine festal sermons. They include sermons for the Feast of the Annunciation, written by preachers including Germanus of Constantinople, Andrew of Crete, and the patriarch Photius.[28] Even within this genre, the variety of methods used to elaborate the narrative in Luke 1:26–38 (often conflated with Matt 1:18–25) is striking. Whereas Germanus composed two dramatic dialogues, first between Mary and Gabriel and then between Mary and Joseph, framed only by a narrative prologue and epilogue, Andrew of Crete placed his dialogic section within a more meditative, theological style of discourse.[29] It is striking that Photius, in comparison to his eighth-century predecessors, chose not to employ narrative or dramatic dialogue in his approach to the subject. His more sober treatment, which was characteristic of his mode of preaching, stood out in a narrative and dramatic tradition that had, from about the fifth century onward, become dominant in relation to the theme of the annunciation. Whether they used dialogue or not, preachers dealing with Mary's reception of the news of her impending conception of Christ, the Son of God, generally stressed her human emotions, including fear, doubt, wonder, and, eventually, trust in the angel's message.[30] In going further than Luke in their emphasis on Mary's initial anxiety, Byzantine preachers emphasized the paradox that lies at the heart of Christian doctrine: God himself chose to enter his creation as a man, using the body of an ordinary, albeit pure and virtuous, young woman for this purpose. Whereas some preachers also focused on the importance of Mary's free and considered acceptance

---

28. Germanus of Constantinople: *CPG* 3:8009; PG 98:320–40 (incomplete); Dumitru Fecioru, ed., "Un nou gen de predica in omiletica ortodoxa," *Biserica Ortodoxa Romana* 64 (1946): 65–91, 180–92, 386–96; Cunningham, *Wider Than Heaven*, 221–46 (on the basis of Fecioru's text). Andrew of Crete: *CPG* 3:8174; PG 97:881–913; Cunningham, *Wider Than Heaven*, 197–219. Photius: S. Aristarches, ed., Ἐκκλησιαστικὴ Ἀλήθεια [Ecclesiastical truth] (Constantinople: Démétrius Nicolaïdes, 1881–1882), 2:525–31; Cyril Mango, trans., *The Homilies of Photius, Patriarch of Constantinople* (Cambridge: Harvard University Press, 1958), 139–49.

29. See the analysis of both homilies in Aleksandr Petrovich Kazhdan, in collaboration with Lee Francis Sherry and Christina Angelidi, *A History of Byzantine Literature, 650–850* (Athens: National Hellenic Research Foundation, Institute for Byzantine Research, 1999), 61–64; Mary B. Cunningham, "Dramatic Device or Didactic Tool? The Function of Dialogue in Byzantine Preaching," in *Rhetoric in Byzantium*, ed. Elizabeth Jeffreys, SPBS 11 (Aldershot: Ashgate, 2003), 110–12.

30. Allen, "Portrayals of Mary," 69–88.

of God's will, others ignored this aspect of the story, occasionally even suggesting that the conception had taken place by the time she gave Gabriel her *fiat*.[31]

Middle Byzantine sermons on Mary's Entrance into the temple depended entirely on the apocryphal Protevangelium of James, since this subject did not appear in the canonical gospels at all. Homiletic elaboration of this theme could take a variety of forms, but narrative, as well as dramatic dialogue, was frequently an important element. Germanus of Constantinople's second sermon on the entrance into the temple, for example, constructs a dialogue between Mary's mother, Anna, and the high priest in the temple.[32] This interlude does not appear in the Protevangelium, which merely describes a formal reception in which the priest kisses and blesses the three-year-old child (7:2).[33] Germanus, however, invents an extensive monologue in which Anna explains her ancestral background, sterility, and wish to express thanks to God for this offspring by presenting the child to the temple. In the course of this statement, Anna explores the despair that led her, before her conception of Mary, to a state of Job-like penitence and dependence on God.[34] The high priest's response, meanwhile, foreshadows that of Symeon (Luke 2:28–35), as he blesses the child and extols the significance of her advent.[35] Throughout this sermon, Germanus reveals his acceptance of the apocryphal narrative, implying that it forms part of a seamless literary witness leading up to the good news of the New Testament. He emphasizes for the benefit of his congregation the biblical resonances (belonging to both the Old and New Testaments) of the text, but he also amplifies its narrative in a manner that had in previous centuries been confined to the canonical texts. In addition to exploiting the narrative and dramatic aspects of the Protevangelium, Germanus also displays its links with prophecy and typology. The procession of young girls with torches, which Joachim summons to accompany

---

31. As, for example, in Germanus's sermon on the annunciation, when the archangel Gabriel says, "I am amazed at the extent to which you have disbelieved my words, favored one, when you are so entirely pure and blameless. For behold, the King of Glory has come to dwell in you, the queen, I think, even as I speak" (Fecioru, "Un nou gen de predica," 83; Cunningham, *Wider Than Heaven*, 231).

32. *CPG* 3:8008; PG 98:312–16; Cunningham, *Wider Than Heaven*, 166–69.

33. Elliott, *Apocryphal New Testament*, 60.

34. *CPG* 3:8008; PG 98:313; Cunningham, *Wider Than Heaven*, 166–67.

35. *CPG* 3:8008; PG 98:316; Cunningham, *Wider Than Heaven*, 168–69.

the infant Mary to the temple, evokes Ps 44:15 LXX (45:15 MT).[36] The temple itself is a type for the Virgin who would later, like the holy of holies, contain God himself.[37] Festal sermons on the entrance of the Theotokos into the temple thus increasingly developed a rich typology and imagery involving the recapitulation of the old temple in the new, living body of the Virgin Mary.

Another interesting strand of narrative reflection on Mary can be found in sermons dealing with her lament at the foot of the cross. This theme seems to have appeared for the first time in the sixth century, in Romanos the Melode's kontakion on this subject, although its roots may be traced back even earlier to ancient Greek and Jewish traditions of lament, as well as to Syriac hymnography.[38] It is noteworthy that John, who is the only evangelist to describe Mary's presence at the foot of the cross, does not mention her sorrow or tears (John 19:25–27). In Byzantium, it is a post-sixth-century innovation to elaborate on this theme, and it was only after the period of iconoclasm that the idea appears to have taken hold, not only in liturgical texts but also in art. After Romanos's kontakion, sermons composed by eighth- and ninth-century preachers including Germanus of Constantinople and George of Nicomedia develop it further.[39] Germanus, echoing Romanos, has Mary address Christ as "my child and my God," as she seeks an answer to the mystery that she is watching unfold.[40] George of Nicomedia's sermon on Good Friday takes

---

36. PG 98:312; Cunningham, *Wider Than Heaven*, 164. For a more detailed elaboration of this scene, see *CPG* 3:8007; Germanus of Constantinople, *Hom. in Praes.* 1 (PG 98:297); Cunningham, *Wider Than Heaven*, 151–52.

37. *CPG* 3:8007; Germanus of Constantinople, *Hom. in Praes.* 1 (PG 98:293); Cunningham, *Wider Than Heaven*, 146: "For today she enters the temple of the law at the age of three, she who alone will be dedicated and called the spotless and highest temple of the Lord."

38. Paul Maas and C. A. Trypanis, eds., *Sancti Romani Melodi Cantica: Cantica Genuina* (Oxford: Clarendon, 1963), 142–49; Niki Tsironis, "The Lament of the Virgin Mary from Romanos the Melode to George of Nicomedia: An Aspect of the Development of the Marian Cult" (PhD diss., King's College London, 1998).

39. *CPG* 3:8031; Germanus of Constantinople, *Homilia in domini corporis sepulturam* (PG 98:244–90). Whereas Tsironis treats this sermon as genuine, J. Darrouzès attributes it to the early thirteenth-century patriarch Germanus II of Constantinople in Marcel Viller, ed., *Dictionnaire de Spiritualité ascétique et mystique: Doctrine et Histoire* (Paris: Beauchesne et ses fils, 1937–1995), 6:310. See Tsironis, *Lament of the Virgin Mary*, 223–28.

40. *CPG* 3:8031; PG 98:269C; Tsironis, *Lament of the Virgin*, 226.

this theme even further, however, influencing in turn a stream of later sermons and hymns on the same subject.[41] As Tsironis points out, George is concerned not only with providing a theological interpretation of Christ's passion but also with involving his audience in the event by means of his dramatic retelling of the story. Mary's distress serves not only to engage the congregation emotionally but also to emphasize the extent of Christ's sacrifice on behalf of humanity. The Virgin calls not only on the rest of humanity but on the whole of creation (sun, sky, earth, and meadows) to share in her lament. Christ's passion, like his incarnation, transforms creation, since he has entered it as God but has also experienced fully the human condition. Mary plays a powerful role in this sermon, as she orchestrates the lament for her son and is invoked as the "Mother of the Church" in whom the faithful may take refuge.[42]

Another aspect of the Virgin Mary's life, which is not elaborated in Scripture, is the story of her death and assumption into heaven. Martin Jugie, Antoine Wenger, Simon Mimouni, Michel van Esbroeck and, most recently, Stephen J. Shoemaker have studied the development of various groups of apocryphal writings that deal with this story.[43] According to Shoemaker, these did not begin to circulate before the late fifth century. They appeared first in the Near East (Syria, Palestine, and Egypt) but were subsequently disseminated throughout Christendom, being translated into numerous languages, during the next few centuries.[44] According to the fourteenth-century historian Nikephoros Kallistos Xanthopoulos, the emperor Maurice added the Feast of the Dormition ("falling asleep" or death) of the Virgin Mary (August 15) to the liturgical calendar at the end of the sixth century, having been influenced by

---

41. George of Nicomedia, *Oratio in illud:* "Stabant autem juxta crucem jesu Mater ejus, et soror Matris ejus" (PG 100:1457–89); Tsironis, *Lament of the Virgin*, 248–49, 279–89.

42. PG 100:1477.

43. Martin Jugie, *La mort et l'assomption de la sainte Vierge: Étude historico-doctrinale*, StT 114 (Vatican City: Biblioteca apostolica vaticana, 1944), 320–413; A. Wenger, *L'assomption de la très sainte Vierge dans la tradition byzantine du VIe au Xe siècle*, AOC 5 (Paris: Institut français d'études byzantines, 1955); Simon Claude Mimouni, *Dormition et assomption de Marie: Histoire des traditions anciennes*, ThH 98 (Paris: Beauchesne, 1995); Michel van Esbroeck, *Aux origines de la Dormition de la Vierge* (Aldershot: Variorum, 1995); Stephen J. Shoemaker, *Ancient Traditions of the Virgin Mary's Dormition and Assumption* (Oxford: Oxford University Press, 2002).

44. Shoemaker, *Ancient Traditions*, 25–77.

a tradition of commemoration that had existed in Palestine and Egypt from at least as early as the fifth century.[45]

The earliest surviving Byzantine homilies on Mary's dormition date from about the beginning of the seventh century.[46] It is likely that, as in the case of festal sermons on her nativity and entrance into the temple, these were composed specifically to adorn the newly established feast day. Brian Daley points out that these texts, like those composed for other Marian feasts, emphasized the liturgical context (often an all-night vigil honoring the feast) for which they were intended.[47] Their purpose was to engage contemporary congregations in the celebration of a mystery; as Andrew of Crete wrote in the early eighth century, "These are unknowable realities. But at least we can learn, as far as possible, the meaning of the rites that we attend today."[48] Preachers such as Andrew thus attempted both to teach the theological meaning of the event that was being celebrated and to extol its glory by means of high-flown rhetoric and imagery. It is noteworthy that Byzantine preachers tended to avoid explicit investigation of the events surrounding the Virgin's death and assumption. Although they did accept versions of the apocryphal accounts that were circulating in this period, these writers were reluctant to analyze exactly what occurred after the body disappeared from the tomb and ascended into heaven, preferring to describe this as a mystery beyond human understanding. Andrew of Crete implied that what happened to the Mother of God represented a foreshadowing of the resurrection that awaits all Christians after death; it also enabled her, however, to act as intercessor and protector for them during their lives here on earth.[49] Germanus of Constantinople, writing in about the same period, stressed the Virgin's mediating role, along with the requirement

---

45. Nicephoros Kallistos Xanthopoulos, *Hist. eccl.* 17.28 (PG 147:292).

46. For an excellent study and translations of selected texts, see Daley, *On the Dormition of Mary*.

47. Daley, *On the Dormition of Mary*, 28–29. Many of the surviving sermons on the dormition of the Mother of God were preached in all-night vigils on the eve of the feast. See C. Chevalier, "Les trilogies homilétiques dans l'élaboration des fêtes mariales, 650–850," *Greg* 18 (1937): 361–78.

48. *CPG* 3:8182; Andrew of Crete, *Dorm.* 2.3 (PG 97:1076C); Daley, *On the Dormition of Mary*, 29, 106. This sermon was erroneously published as the second in the trilogy; in fact, it was the first.

49. *CPG* 3:8183; Andrew of Crete, *Dorm.* 3.9 (PG 97:1100C); Daley, *On the Dormition of Mary*, 144–45.

for Christians to glorify her and to venerate her holy relics, to an even greater degree.[50]

In concluding this section on homiletics, it is worth asking whether it is possible to discern development in the treatment of the Virgin in Byzantine festal sermons between approximately the seventh and the tenth centuries. Some changes, as we have noted, are striking: from about the early seventh century onward, preachers began to make use of apocryphal texts concerning Mary's death and assumption into heaven in order to honor the Feast of the Dormition that had been established around the turn of the century. Extensive use of the Protevangelium of James, the second-century apocryphal gospel that dealt with Mary's conception and infancy, as well as with the events leading up to the nativity of Christ, became prevalent only at about the beginning of the eighth century, in connection with the Feasts of the Conception, Nativity, and Entrance into the Temple of the Mother of God. The employment of these apocryphal texts did not preclude, or supersede, that of the canonical Scriptures, including both Old and New Testaments. Middle Byzantine preachers continued to build on a tradition, which had begun in the early fifth century, of exegesis that explored the prophetic, typological, and narrative meaning of biblical references to the Virgin Mary. This process was characterized by a preference for intertextual citation that served to emphasize the unity of Scripture as a seamless expression of God's revelation. At the same time, Byzantine preachers were not afraid to add details of their own, such as imaginative dialogues, to narrative sections of the New Testament that dealt with Mary. By the eighth and ninth centuries, it is possible to detect variation in the ways that different preachers approached both Scripture and the Apocrypha. Whereas some preachers, such as the ninth-century patriarch Photius, were restrained in their treatment of the scriptural narrative and did not explicitly mention the apocryphal texts, others, such as George of Nicomedia, freely amplified the New Testament accounts with the help of the apocryphal and hagiographic traditions. It is also possible that variations in preaching techniques, along with some other aspects of Marian devotion, caused controversy in this period.[51]

---

50. *CPG* 3:8010; Germanus of Constantinople, *Dorm.* 1 (PG 98:340–8); Daley, *On the Dormition of Mary*, 19–20, 153–66.

51. Opposition to various aspects of the Virgin's cult, or to aspects of the apocryphal narrative, is suggested by preachers including Germanus of Constantinople and Theodore the Studite. See, for example, *CPG* 3:8008; Germanus of Constantinople,

2. Hymnography

The liturgical celebration of the feasts of Mary, the Mother of God, included not only the preaching of sermons but also the singing of hymns. Hymnography developed in parallel with homiletics, with the same writers (including Andrew of Crete, John of Damascus, Theodore the Studite, and Leo VI, among others) often composing works in both genres. As we saw above, Tsironis has argued that a transfer of ideas and imagery took place within Byzantine liturgical composition, so that "liturgical poetry" (by which she seems to mean early kontakia such as those written by the sixth-century poet Romanos the Melode and the famous Akathistos Hymn) influenced homilies, which in turn affected iconography and the liturgy itself.[52] By *liturgy*, Tsironis means the variety of hymnographic texts that provided most of the movable content of offices and occasional services in the Byzantine Orthodox Church. It is certainly likely that the more expansive and experimental nature of liturgical homilies, especially those that were composed for recently established feasts of the Mother of God, offered a fertile source of ideas for hymnographers. Marian hymns, including kanons and shorter texts such as theotokia and stavrotheotokia, appear to provide distillations of the most beautiful and compelling passages of earlier kontakia or sermons.[53]

One important feature that hymns share with sermons is an interest in intertextual exegesis and typology. The hymnographic genre of kanon is in fact based on a typological interpretation of Scripture, which explores the parallels between the Old Testament canticles and the event in the New Testament (or Apocrypha) that is being celebrated. To take one example, John of Damascus's kanon on the formition of the Mother

---

Praes. 1 (PG 98:312); Cunningham, *Wider Than Heaven*, 164; Photius, "Homily 9: The Birth of the Virgin," in *The Homilies of Photius*, trans. Cyril Mango, *On the Birth of the Virgin* 6 (Cambridge: Cambridge University Press, 1958), 168. Eirini Panou has discussed the question in an unpublished paper delivered to the 43rd Spring Symposium of Byzantine Studies, Birmingham, March 2010. I am grateful to Dr. Panou for sending me a copy of this paper.

52. Tsironis, "From Poetry to Liturgy," 91–92. The kontakia of Romanos are published in Maas and Trypanis, *Sancti Romani Melodi Cantica*; José Grosdidier de Matons, ed. and trans., *Romanos le Mélode: Hymnes*, 5 vols., SC 99, 110, 114, 128, 283 (Paris: Cerf, 1964–1981). For the Akathistos Hymn, see Leena Mari Peltomaa, *The Image of the Virgin Mary in the Akathistos Hymn*, MilM 35 (Leiden: Brill, 2001).

53. Tsirionis, "From Poetry to Liturgy," 97.

of God celebrates in each of its odes the foreshadowing of Mary's glorious assumption by reminding us of hymns uttered by Miriam, the prophet Habakkuk, and others, as we see in the following typical passage:

> Come, maidens and choristers,
> Join with the prophetess Miriam
> And raise up your voice in the song of her exodus;
> For this virgin now, God's Mother, who is peerless,
> Has come to the goal of her heavenward pilgrimage.[54]

Byzantine kanons resemble sermons in that they were composed for specific celebrations in the liturgical year and thus interpret particular events or holy figures. Their exegetical method, like that of many homilies, is intertextual and typological: in the case of Marian kanons, the hymnographer's main purpose is to show that her role in the incarnation was foreseen by prophets and foreshadowed by types and images throughout the Old Testament. Some kanons, however, employ narrative, dialogue, or acclamation in much the same way that sermons do. Not only cross-fertilization but also a blurring of the boundaries between the genres of festal sermons and kanons are evident throughout the middle Byzantine period.

The shorter types of hymns, such as theotokia and stavrotheotokia, as well as the strings of laudatory epithets that Christian Hannick calls simply "laudes marianae," however, do differ in important ways from homiletics.[55] These short hymns are scattered throughout the Byzantine service books and often cannot be assigned to any specific feast or celebration. Even more confusingly, such hymns may be inserted within the longer kanons, thus making it difficult to date them or assign them to particular hymnographers. To return to our earlier point about hymnography representing a distillation of themes and imagery that were first expounded in liturgical homilies, the shorter Marian hymns of the middle Byzantine period offer numerous examples of this tendency. Themes such as Mary's lament at the foot of the cross, which were first explored by preachers such as George of Nicomedia, appear in a condensed and refined form in the stavrotheotokia. Supplication to the Mother of God as intercessor, "guardian and powerful protector," and other epithets that appeared only slowly

---

54. Daley, *On the Dormition of Mary*, 241.
55. Christian Hannick, "The Theotokos in Byzantine Hymnography: Typology and Allegory," in Vassilaki, *Images of the Mother of God*, 69.

in Marian homilies is expressed repeatedly in middle Byzantine theotokia and other short hymns.⁵⁶

Much work remains to be done on Byzantine hymnography, although foundations do exist.⁵⁷ Issues such as various hymnographers' methods of exegesis, a development of ideas in relation to Mary's intercessory role in hymnography, and the precise relationship between sermons and hymns remain to be elucidated. What is undeniable is the continuous cross-fertilization and interchange between the two liturgical genres. Whereas sermons may, as Hannick argues, have served a more didactic and doctrinal function than did hymns, there can be no doubt that both literary genres served also—perhaps even primarily—as vehicles for praise and supplication to the Mother of God.⁵⁸

3. Hagiography

Writers of the middle Byzantine period also produced vitae and an apocalypse of the Virgin Mary. One of the interesting aspects of this group of texts is that it departs from the scriptural and even apocryphal traditions in striking ways, thus indicating the existence of a popular strand of Marian devotion that developed differently from the mainstream or official one. The use of terms such as *popular* and *official* in relation to the Marian cult in this period of course requires justification. Baun has suggested that popular beliefs and practices, while certainly not being confined to the less educated or official classes, were expressed mainly by anonymous authors in a variety of texts that take the form of hagiography, edifying and miracle stories, and apocalypses.⁵⁹ Such texts were widely

---

56. Tsironis, "From Poetry to Liturgy," 97–98.
57. Collected texts may be found in Jean-Baptiste Pitra, *Analecta sacra spicilegio Solesmensi parata*, 8 vols., repr. ed. (Farnborough: Gregg, 1967); Wilhelm von Christ and Matthaios Paranikas, eds., *Anthologia Graeca Carminum Christianorum*, repr. ed. (Hildesheim: Olms, 1963); Sophronios Eustratiades, Θεοτοκάριον (Chennevières-sur-Marne: L'Ermitage, 1931). Studies include Christian Hannick, "Exégèse, typologie et rhétorique dans l'hymnographie byzantine," *DOP* 53 (1999): 207–18.
58. Hannick, "Theotokos in Byzantine Hymnography," 69–70.
59. Baun, "Apocalyptic *Panagia*"; Baun, "Discussing Mary's Humanity"; Baun, *Tales from Another Byzantium*. For concepts of official and popular literature, see also Robert Browing, "The 'Low Level' Saint's *Life* in the Early Byzantine World," in *The Byzantine Saint*, ed. S. Hackel (London: Fellowship of Saint Alban and Saint Sergius, 1981), 117–27; Cyril Mango, "Discontinuity with the Classical Past in Byzantium," in

disseminated in Orthodox Christian society and monasteries, serving as private and public readings in mainly paraliturgical settings. Baun argues, however, that even if such literature circulated on the fringes of the official church, it influenced developments in Marian devotion and doctrine.[60] This theory is borne out if we consider the influence of so-called apocryphal texts on the Virgin's dormition on seventh- through tenth-century sermons for this feast.

Middle Byzantine vitae of the Virgin Mary include the Georgian translation of a Greek text that is attributed to Maximos, a life by Epiphanios, a monk of Monastery of Kallistratos in Constantinople (dated to between 783 and 813), and two that were composed by Symeon the Metaphrast and John Geometres in the tenth century.[61] These four vitae of Mary are related, either because they all employed an earlier narrative source or because they influenced each other. I have discussed elsewhere the scholarly controversy concerning the date of the Greek prototype of the Georgian *Life of the Virgin*; suffice it to say here that I concur with Phil Booth in placing the text in the tenth as opposed to the early seventh century.[62] The most striking feature of this tradition, for the purpose of this essay, is that it reveals a willingness to depart significantly from both the scriptural and apocryphal accounts in narrating the events in Mary's

---

Byzantium and the Classical Tradition, ed. Margaret Mullet and Roger Scott (Birmingham: Centre for Byzantine Studies, University of Birmingham, 1981), 48–57.

60. Baun, "Apocalyptic *Panagia*," 204.

61. Two editions of the vita by Epiphanios have been published, which are based on different manuscripts: PG 120:186–216; Albert Dressel, ed., *Epiphanii monachi edita et inedita* (Paris: Brockhaus et Avenarius, 1843), 13–44. See also Simon Claude Mimouni, "Les Vies de la Vierge: État du question," in *Les traditions anciennes sur la Dormition et l'Assomption de Marie: Études littéraires, historiques et doctrinales*, VCSup 104 (Leiden: Brill, 2011), 89. The *Metaphrastic Life* is edited in B. Latyshev, *Menologii anonymi Byzantini saeculi X quae supersunt*, 2 vols. (St. Petersburg: n.p., 1912), 2:345–83; the vita by John Geometres remains unedited, although the final part is published in Wenger, *Assomption de la très sainte Vierge*, 364–415. A new critical edition of the entire text is currently in preparation by Father Maximos Constas and Christos Simelides. They are basing their work on a text that was found in Wenger's archives but never published.

62. For bibliography, see above, note 9. On my own position, see Cunningham, "*Life of the Virgin Mary*"; Cunningham, "The *Life of the Theotokos* by Epiphanios of Kallistratou," in *The Reception of the Virgin in Byzantium: Marian Narratives in Texts and Images*, ed. Thomas Arentzen and Mary B. Cunningham (Cambridge: Cambridge University Press, 2019), 309–23.

legendary life, although these earlier texts provide the foundations for such elaboration. The Georgian vita includes some of the most striking deviations from the received narrative tradition (whether scriptural or apocryphal) in its account of Mary's life. The author reinterprets even the canonical gospel narratives, placing Mary at the center of Christ's ministry: according to the author, she accompanied her son wherever he went, guided his female followers, and remained at his side during the arrest, interrogation, and crucifixion.[63] Following an earlier tradition that is employed by some other patristic writers, the text suggests that Mary kept a vigil at Christ's tomb throughout the night after his burial, witnessing the opening of the tomb and her son's resurrection. She announced the good news to the disciples, thus preempting the myrrh-bearing women in this role. After this, the Virgin Mary is said to have overseen the work of the apostles after Christ's ascension, monitoring their fasting and prayer and sending them out on their missions.[64] This vita ends with accounts of the Virgin's death and assumption into heaven, based on an earlier apocryphal narrative, and of the translation of her relics to Constantinople during the reign of the emperor Leo I and his consort Verina (457–474).[65]

As Shoemaker has pointed out, the content of the Georgian *Life of the Virgin Mary* is nothing short of radical.[66] In placing Mary at the center of his narrative about the life of Jesus Christ, the author portrays her as a powerful matriarch. Not only does she direct her son in his decisions, but she takes over the leadership of his disciples after Christ's death and ascension into heaven. Taken in its entirety, it is clear that this vita presents a strikingly different message about the Virgin Mary—as Jesus's mother, disciple, and eventually leader of the earliest Christian church—from that presented in liturgical homilies and hymns. In addition to emphasizing Mary's importance in the life of Christ and his apostles, this vita also focuses attention on female figures, especially Mary Magdalene.[67]

Much work remains to be done on the relationship between the Georgian *Life of the Virgin* and the other three Byzantine hagiographical texts. Epiphanios's vita, which is the earliest of these, matches the

---

63. Maximus, *Life of the Virgin*, ed. Shoemaker, 101–18.
64. Maximus, *Life of the Virgin*, ed. Shoemaker, 122–26; Shoemaker, "Virgin Mary in the Ministry of Jesus," 454.
65. Maximus, *Life of the Virgin*, ed. Shoemaker, 130–48.
66. See esp. Shoemaker, "Virgin Mary in the Ministry of Jesus," 445–57.
67. Maximus, *Life of the Virgin*, ed. Shoemaker, 99, 117–18, 124.

narrative tradition found in the Georgian vita in many respects, with its inclusion of such scenes as Mary's childhood vision in the holy of holies of the Jewish temple, when God speaks to her and foretells her conception of Christ.[68] Details such as this are apparently unique to the middle Byzantine hagiographic tradition and have no foundation in apocryphal texts such as the Protevangelium of James. Epiphanios's vita also diverges in significant ways, however, from the narrative that appears in the Georgian vita. The Virgin Mary disappears from view in the section of the text that deals with Christ's ministry and miracles. The main purpose of Epiphanios's *Life of the Virgin*, which is written in a simple and unpretentious style, appears to be a harmonization of the apocryphal and biblical stories, beginning with Mary's conception and ending with her dormition. The author does not portray the Virgin Mary as a powerful leader of the early church, as the Georgian vita does, but he does stress her close maternal relationship with her son. Epiphanios also deviates from the other three texts in saying that Mary did *not* remain beside Christ's tomb all night and witness his resurrection; rather, she remained in the house in Jerusalem that she shared with the beloved disciple, John, because of her "unspeakable pain."[69] Christ, however, appeared to his mother in that setting so that he could put her mind at rest. The Virgin Mary is also described in this text as pursuing a strict ascetic life, especially after Christ's ascension into heaven. Epiphanios takes an interest in the sacred geography and the physical signs that remain of Mary's life in Palestine: he tells his readers that, according to Andrew of Crete, it is possible to this day to see dents in the marble of the holy house in Sion where the Mother of God performed genuflections in the course of her prayer.[70]

The other two vitae of the Virgin, both of which were composed in the second half of the tenth century, can be treated together. There has been some scholarly debate concerning their relationship: whereas Jugie argued for Symeon the Metaphrast's dependence on John Geometres, Wenger suggested the reverse.[71] Both Shoemaker and van Esbroeck believe that both texts are based on the Greek prototype of the surviving Georgian

---

68. Maximus, *Life of the Virgin*, ed. Shoemaker, 46; Epiphanis, "Vita deiparae," in *Epiphanii monachi*, ed. Albert Dressel (Paris: Brockhaus et Avenarius, 1843), 18.

69. Epiphanis, "Vita deiparae," 37.

70. Epiphanis, "Vita deiparae," 38.

71. M. Jugie, "Sur la vie et les procédés littéraires de Syméon Métaphraste: Son récit de la vie de la Sainte Vierge," *ÉO* 22 (1923): 5–10; Jugie, *Mort et l'assomption de*

Life of the Virgin, with each of the later authors working independently on their projects.[72] Symeon's *Metaphrastic Life* is the shorter of the two texts, representing a reworking of the narrative in the higher literary style that was popular in tenth-century literary circles. Symeon leaves out many details in Maximos's narrative, but he does emphasize the Virgin's closeness to Christ and her presence at his trial, crucifixion, burial, and resurrection. John Geometres's *Life of the Virgin* still awaits a full critical edition; although Wenger has published the last section of the text, the first half is accessible only in manuscripts.[73] One of the most interesting aspects of this text is that it stresses even more than the others Mary's important intercessory role for contemporary Christians. Not only does she play a central role in Christ's ministry, but she also participates directly in his healing and redemptive acts.[74] The level of Mariological devotion that characterizes this text has been noted not only by Shoemaker but also by scholars such as Jean Galot and Hilda Graef.[75]

Before concluding this section, it is necessary to consider briefly the ninth-century Apocalypse of the Theotokos, which describes the Virgin's journey to heaven and hell to view the various fates of the dead.[76] According to Baun, this text, along with other popular works such as the

---

la Sainte Vierge, 320; Wenger, *Assomption de la très sainte Vierge*, 193–95; Shoemaker, "Virgin Mary in the Ministry of Jesus," 460.

72. See van Esbroeck, *Maxime le Confesseur*, 19–29; Shoemaker, "Georgian *Life of the Virgin*"; Shoemaker, "Virgin Mary in the Ministry of Jesus," 460–61.

73. Wenger, *L'Assomption de la très sainte Vierge*, 364–415. Father Maximos Constas and Professor Christos Simelides are currently preparing a critical edition of the whole text, based on work that was completed by A. Wenger but never published. For the purposes of this essay, I have consulted a good manuscript in this tradition, Codex Vaticanus 504, fols. 172v–94v (1105).

74. See Shoemaker, "Virgin Mary in the Ministry of Jesus," 461.

75. According to Shoemaker, who does not underestimate the Mariological claims that are made in this text, "John explicitly links Mary's suffering with the process of human redemption, explaining that Mary suffered on our behalf, to achieve our salvation, and that Christ gave her as our ransom, while she, like the Father, gave him over to death on our behalf" ("Virgin Mary in the Ministry of Jesus," 462). See also Jean Galot, "La plus ancienne affirmation de la corédemption mariale: Le témoignage de Jean le Géomètre," *RSR* 45 (1957): 187–208; Hilda C. Graef, *Mary: A History of Doctrine and Devotion*, vol. 1 of *From the Beginnings to the Eve of Reformation*, rev. ed. (London: Sheed & Ward, 1985), 199–200.

76. The apocalypse, which survives in numerous manuscripts and various recensions, is edited in James, *Apocrypha Anecdota*, 109–26.

vitae of the Virgin that we have been examining, offers an alternative, and occasionally subversive, interpretation of the process of Christian redemption.[77] Mary functions in this text as a powerful matriarch who pleads with Christ, who is portrayed as righteous and remote, on behalf of Christian sinners who seek her mediation. Although the Apocalypse of the Theotokos stresses the Virgin's power as intercessor, along with her maternal and feminine characteristics, it never suggests that anyone but God is able to bring about redemption and salvation. In this respect, this apocalypse thus presents a less radical interpretation of Mary's role in the dispensation as that which is implied by the various middle Byzantine vitae of the Virgin.

Taken together, the hagiographical and apocalyptic sources present an interpretation of the Virgin Mary that differs markedly from that found in liturgical homilies and hymns. It appears that two distinct strands of Mariological writing existed in the middle Byzantine period, with one remaining faithful to biblical and patristic witnesses while the other was open to imaginative—and not always traditional—elaboration of her importance both as Christ's disciple and as intercessor. Whereas such a distinction between the two traditions is visible, it is also important to emphasize that they share certain features and that some overlap between the various literary genres also occurs. The Byzantine vitae of the Virgin Mary, for example, employ Scripture (including both Old and New Testaments) as much as do liturgical sermons and hymns; in addition, they occasionally launch into passages of Marian praise that include biblical types and poetic imagery that is similar to that employed in the homiletic and hymnographic traditions. It seems likely that lay and monastic Christians knew and enjoyed both genres; perhaps they were mindful of their respective liturgical or literary contexts and interpreted them accordingly.[78]

4. Conclusion

This essay has attempted to provide an overview of Marian exegesis in several genres of Byzantine texts dating roughly from the seventh through the tenth century. Although this large topic cannot be treated adequately in

---

77. Baun, *Tales from Another Byzantium*.

78. A modern, more extreme parallel might be the devout Christian who reads the New Testament at home and in church but can enjoy a film such as *Life of Brian* in a cinema without feeling that it challenges her understanding of the life and passion of Christ.

an essay of this length, it is possible to observe some general trends in this period and to draw a few conclusions. As we have seen, two distinct strands of Marian reflection emerged in this period, with liturgical texts such as festal sermons and hymns belonging to one, and hagiographical and apocalyptic texts belonging to the other. Related genres, such as edifying tales and miracle stories, have been omitted from the discussion altogether, but they can probably be assigned to the second of the two strands. Whereas official or liturgical material displays a tendency to conservatism, with exegetical methods such as typology or descriptive narrative becoming increasingly conventional in the work of preachers and hymnographers, popular texts reveal a striking willingness to elaborate Mary's history with imaginative and theologically daring details of their own.

In spite of these differences, some developments are detectable in both strands of the tradition. References to Mary's maternal tenderness, which are understood to be feminine qualities, become more frequent in posticonoclast texts, not only in the hagiographical but also in liturgical literary genres. Ioli Kalavrezou has noted the progression of such ideas from liturgical texts to religious art, especially icons.[79] A related, but slightly different, phenomenon is the growing emphasis in literature and art on Mary's intercessory powers.[80]

Middle Byzantine interpretation of the role of the Mother of God, with respect both to humanity and to God, was informed above all by the revelation that resides in Scripture. Because such revelation is scant and enigmatic with respect to Mary, however, this had to be supplemented by apocryphal texts, patristic witness, and eventually even the medieval imagination. The process as a whole, as Byzantine Marian texts bear witness, was motivated by growing interest in the Virgin, both as a human being and as intercessor and protector of Constantinople.

Bibliography

Allen, Pauline. "The Greek Homiletic Tradition of the Feast of the Hypapante: The Place of Sophronios of Jerusalem." Pages 1–12 in *Byzan-*

---

79. Ioli Kalavrezou, "Images of the Mother: When the Virgin Mary Became *Meter Theou*," *DOP* 44 (1990): 165–72.

80. For discussions of the development of this aspect of the Marian cult, see Cameron, "Virgin's Robe"; Vasiliki Limberis, *Divine Heiress: The Virgin Mary and the Creation of Christian Constantinople* (London: Routledge, 1994); Pentcheva, *Icons and Power*.

tina Mediterranea: Festschrift für Johannes Koder zum 65. Geburtstag. Edited by Klaus Belke, E. Kislinger, A. Külzer, and M. A. Stassinopoulou. Vienna: Böhlau, 2007.

———. "Portrayals of Mary in Greek Homiletic Literature (Sixth–Seventh Centuries)." Pages 69–90 in *The Cult of the Mother of God in Byzantium.* Edited by Leslie Brubaker and Mary Cunningham. Farnham: Ashgate, 2011.

Andia, Ysabel de. *Homo vivens: Incorruptibilité et divinisation de l'homme chez Irénée de Lyon.* Paris: Etudes augustiniennes, 1994.

Arentzen, Thomas, and Mary B. Cunningham, eds. *The Reception of the Virgin in Byzantium: Marian Narratives in Texts and Images.* Cambridge: Cambridge University Press, 2019.

Aristarches, S., ed. Ἐκκλησιαστικὴ Ἀλήθεια. [*Ecclesiastical Truth*] 2 vols. Constantinople: Démétrius Nicolaïdes, 1881–1882.

Baun, Jane. "Apocalyptic *Panagia*: Some Byways of Marian Revelation in Byzantium." Pages 199–218 in *The Cult of the Mother of God in Byzantium.* Edited by Leslie Brubaker and Mary Cunningham. Farnham: Ashgate, 2011.

———. "Discussing Mary's Humanity in Medieval Byzantium." Pages 63–72 in *The Church and Mary.* Edited by Robert Norman Swanson. SCH 39. Woodbridge: Boydell, 2004.

———. *Tales from Another Byzantium: Celestial Journey and Local Community in the Medieval Greek Apocrypha.* Cambridge: Cambridge University Press, 2007.

Beattie, Tina. "Mary in Patristic Theology." Pages 75–105 in *Mary: The Complete Resource.* Edited by Sarah Jane Boss. London: Burns & Oates, 2007.

Behr, John. *Asceticism and Anthropology in Irenaeus and Clement.* Oxford: Oxford University Press, 2000.

Booth, Phil. "On the *Life of the Virgin* Attributed to Maximus the Confessor." *JTS* 66 (2015): 149–203.

Boss, Sarah Jane, ed. *Mary: The Complete Resource.* London: Burns & Oates, 2007.

Brock, Sebastian P. *The Luminous Eye.* Rome: Centre for Indian and Inter-Religious Studies, 1985.

Browing, Robert. "The 'Low Level' Saint's *Life* in the Early Byzantine World." Pages 117–27 in *The Byzantine Saint.* Edited by Sergei Hackel. London: Fellowship of Saint Alban and Saint Sergius, 1981.

Brubaker, Leslie, and Mary B. Cunningham, eds. *The Cult of the Mother of God in Byzantium: Texts and Images*. Farnham: Ashgate, 2011.
Cameron, Averil. *Continuity and Change in Sixth-Century Byzantium*. London: Variorum Reprints, 1981.
———. "The Cult of the Virgin in Late Antiquity: Religious Development and Myth-Making." Pages 1–21 in *The Church and Mary*. Edited by Robert Norman Swanson. SCH 39. Woodbridge: Boydell, 2004.
———. "Images of Authority: Élites and Icons in Late Sixth-Century Constantinople." *P&P* 84 (1979): 3–35.
———. "The Theotokos in Sixth-Century Constantinople: A City Finds Its Symbol." *JTS* 29 (1978): 79–108.
———. "The Virgin's Robe: An Episode in the History of Early Seventh-Century Constantinople." *Byzantion* 49 (1979): 42–56.
Charity, A. C. *Events and Their Afterlife: The Dialectics of Christian Typology in the Bible and Dante*. Cambridge: Cambridge University Press, 1996.
Chevalier, C. "Les trilogies homilétiques dans l'élaboration des fêtes mariales, 650–850." *Greg* 18 (1937): 361–78.
Christ, Wilhelm von, and Matthaios Paranikas, eds. 1963. *Anthologia Graeca Carminum Christianorum*. Repr. ed. Hildesheim: Olms, 1963.
Cunningham, Mary. "Dramatic Device or Didactic Tool? The Function of Dialogue in Byzantine Preaching." Pages 101–13 in *Rhetoric in Byzantium*. Edited by Elizabeth Jeffreys. SPBS 11. Aldershot: Ashgate, 2003.
———. "The *Life of the Theotokos* by Epiphanios of Kallistratou." Pages 309–23 in *The Reception of the Virgin in Byzantium: Marian Narratives in Texts and Images*. Edited by Thomas Arentzen and Mary B. Cunningham. Cambridge: Cambridge University Press, 2019.
———. "The Life of the Virgin Mary according to Middle Byzantine Preachers and Hagiographers: Changing Contexts and Perspectives." *Apocrypha* 27 (2016): 137–59.
———. "Mary as Intercessor in Constantinople during the Iconoclast Period: The Textual Evidence." Pages 165–80 in *Presbeia Theotokou: The Intercessory Role of Mary across Times and Places in Byzantium*. Edited by Pauline Allen, Andreas Külzer, and Leena Mari Peltomaa. Vienna: Österreichischen Akademie der Wissenschaften, 2015.
———. "The Meeting of the Old and New: The Typology of Mary the Theotokos in Byzantine Homilies and Hymns." Pages 52–62 in *The Church and Mary*. Edited by Robert Norman Swanson. SCH 39. Woodbridge: Boydell, 2004.

———. "Messages in Context: The Reading of Sermons in Byzantine Churches and Monasteries." Pages 83–98 in *Byzantium: Visions, Messages and Meanings Meanings; Festschrift for Prof. Leslie Brubaker on Her Sixtieth Birthday*. Edited by Angeliki Lymberopoulou. Farnham: Ashgate, 2011.

———. "The Use of the Protevangelium of James in Eighth-Century Homilies on the Mother of God." Pages 163–78 in *The Cult of the Mother of God in Byzantium: Texts and Images*. Edited by Leslie Brubaker and Mary Cunningham. Farnham: Ashgate, 2011.

———. *Wider Than Heaven: Eighth-Century Homilies on the Mother of God*. Crestwood, NY: Saint Vladimir's Seminary Press, 2008.

Daley, Brian E., S.J. *On the Dormition of Mary: Early Patristic Homilies*. Crestwood, NY: Saint Vladimir's Seminary Press, 1998.

Daniélou, Jean. *From Shadows to Reality: Studies in the Biblical Typology of the Fathers*. London: Burns & Oates, 1960.

Dressel, Albert, ed. *Epiphanii monachi et presbyteri edita et inedita*. Paris: Brockhaus et Avenarius, 1843.

Ehrhard, Albert. *Überlieferung und Bestand der hagiographischen und homiletischen Literatur der griechischen Kirche*. 3 vols. Leipzig: Hinrichs, 1936–1939.

Elliott, J. K., ed. *The Apocryphal New Testament: A Collection of Apocryphal Christian Literature in an English Translation Based on M. R. James*. Oxford: Clarendon, 1993.

Esbroeck, Michel van. *Aux origines de la Dormition de la Vierge*. Aldershot: Variorum, 1995.

———, ed. *Maxime le Confesseur: Vie de la Vierge*. CSCO 478–79. SI 21–22. 2 vols. Leuven: Peeters, 1986.

Eustratiades, Sophronios. Θεοτοκάριον [*Collected Canons on the Theotokos*]. Chennevières-sur-Marne: L'Ermitage, 1931.

Fecioru, Dumitru, ed. "Un nou gen de predica in omiletica ortodoxa." *Biserica Ortodoxa Romana* 64 (1946): 65–396.

Galot, Jean. "La plus ancienne affirmation de la corédemption mariale: Le témoignage de Jean le Géomètre." *RSR* 45 (1957): 187–208.

Geerard, Maurice, ed. *Clavis patrum graecorum*. Vol. 3. Turnhout: Brepols, 2003.

Graef, Hilda C. *Mary: A History of Doctrine and Devotion*. Vol. 1 of *From the Beginnings to the Eve of Reformation*. Rev. ed. London: Sheed & Ward, 1985.

Halkin, François, ed. *Auctarium Bibliothecae hagiographicae graecae*. Brussels: Société des Bollandistes, 1969.
Hannick, Christian. "Exegèse, typologie et rhétorique dans l'hymnographie byzantine." *DOP* 53 (1999): 207–18.
———. "The Theotokos in Byzantine Hymnography: Typology and Allegory." Pages 69–76 in *Images of the Mother of God: Perceptions of the Theotokos in Byzantium*. Edited by Maria Vassilaki. Aldershot: Ashgate, 2004.
James, M. R., ed. *Apocrypha anecdota*. TS 2.3. Cambridge: Cambridge University Press, 1893.
Jugie, Martin. *La mort et l'assomption de la sainte Vierge: Étude historico-doctrinale*. StT 114. Vatican City: Biblioteca apostolica vaticana, 1944.
———. "Sur la vie et les procédés littéraires de Syméon Métaphraste: Son récit de la vie de la Sainte Vierge." *ÉO* 22 (1923): 5–10.
Kalavrezou, Ioli. "Images of the Mother: When the Virgin Mary Became Meter Theou." *DOP* 44 (1990): 165–72.
Kateusz, Ally. "Collyridian Déjà Vu: The Trajectory of Eedaction of the Markers of Mary's Liturgical Leadership." *JFSR* 29.2 (2013): 75–92.
———. *Mary and Early Christian Women: Hidden Leadership*. Cham, Switzerland: Palgrave Macmillan, 2019.
———. "She Sacrificed Herself as the Priest: Early Christian Female and Male Co-priests." *JFSR* 33.1 (2017): 45–67.
Kazhdan, Aleksandr Petrovich, in collaboration with Lee Francis Sherry and Christina Angelidi. *A History of Byzantine Literature, 650–850*. Athens: National Hellenic Research Foundation, Institute for Byzantine Research, 1999.
Krausmüller, Dirk. "Making the Most of Mary: The Cult of the Virgin in the Chalkoprateia from Late Antiquity to the Tenth Century." Pages 219–45 in *The Cult of the Mother of God in Byzantium: Texts and Images*. Edited by Leslie Brubaker and Mary Cunningham. Farnham: Ashgate, 2011.
Ladouceur, Paul. "Old Testament Prefigurations of the Mother of God." *SVTQ* 50 (2006): 5–57.
Lampe, G. W. H., and K. J. Woollcombe. *Essays in Typology*. SBT 22. London: SCM, 1957.
Lash, Ephrem. "Mary in Eastern Church Literature." Pages 58–80 in *Mary in Doctrine and Devotion*. Edited by Alberic Stacpoole. Dublin: Columba, 1990.

Latyshev, B. *Menologii anonymi Byzantini saceculi X quae supersunt.* 2 vols. St. Petersburg: n.p., 1912.

Limberis, Vasiliki. *Divine Heiress: The Virgin Mary and the Creation of Christian Constantinople.* London: Routledge, 1994.

Maas, Paul, and C. A. Trypanis, eds. *Sancti Romani Melodi Cantica: Cantica Genuina.* Oxford: Clarendon, 1963.

Mango, Cyril. "Constantinople as Theotokoupolis." Pages 19–21 in *Mother of God: Representations of the Virgin in Byzantine Art.* Edited by Maria Vassilaki. Athens: Abbeville, 2000.

———. "Discontinuity with the Classical Past in Byzantium." Pages 48–57 in *Byzantium and the Classical Tradition.* Edited by Margaret Mullet and Roger Scott. Birmingham: Centre for Byzantine Studies, University of Birmingham, 1981.

———, trans. *The Homilies of Photius, Patriarch of Constantinople.* Cambridge: Harvard University Press, 1958.

Matons, José Grosdidier de, ed. and trans. *Romanos le Mélode: Hymnes.* 5 vols. SC 99, 110, 114, 128, 283. Paris: Cerf, 1964–1981.

Maunder, Chris, ed. *The Origins of the Cult of the Virgin Mary.* London: Burns & Oates, 2008.

Maximus the Confessor. *Life of the Virgin.* Edited and translated by Stephen J. Shoemaker. New Haven: Yale University Press, 2012.

Mimouni, Simon Claude. *Dormition et assomption de Marie: Histoire des traditions anciennes.* ThH 98. Paris: Beauchesne, 1995.

———. "Les Vies de la Vierge: État du question." Page 75–115 in *Les traditions anciennes sur la Dormition et l'Assomption de Marie: Études littéraires, historiques et doctrinales.* VCSup 104. Leiden: Brill, 2011.

Olkinuora, Jaakko. *Byzantine Hymnography for the Feast of the Entrance of the Theotokos.* SPF 4. Helsinski: Suomen patristinen seura ry, 2015.

Peltomaa, Leena Mari. *The Image of the Virgin Mary in the Akathistos Hymn.* MilM 35. Leiden: Brill, 2001.

Pentcheva, Bissera. *Icons and Power: The Mother of God in Byzantium.* University Park: Pennsylvania State University Press, 2006.

Photius, Patriarch of Constantinople. "Homily 9: The Birth of the Virgin." Pages 164–76 in *The Homilies of Photius.* Translated by Cyril Mango. Cambridge: Cambridge University Press, 1958.

Pitra, Jean-Baptiste. *Analecta sacra spicilegio Solesmensi parata.* 8 vols. Repr. ed. Farnborough: Gregg, 1967.

Rahlfs, A. *Septuaginta: Idest Vetus Testamentum graece iuxta LXX interpretes.* 2 vols. Stuttgart: Württembergische Bibelanstalt, 1935.

Shoemaker, Stephen J. *Ancient Traditions of the Virgin Mary's Dormition and Assumption.* Oxford: Oxford University Press, 2002.

———. "The Georgian *Life* of the Virgin Attributed to Maximus the Confessor: Its Authenticity and Importance." Pages 67–84 in *Mémorial R. P. Michel van Esbroeck, S.J.* Edited by Alexey Muraviev and Basil Lourié. Saint Petersburg: Byzantinorossica, 1998.

———. *Life of the Virgin: Maximus the Confessor.* New Haven: Yale University Press, 2012.

———. *Mary in Early Christian Faith and Devotion.* New Haven: Yale University Press, 2016.

———. "The (Pseudo?-)Maximus *Life of the Virgin* and the Byzantine Marian Tradition." *JTS* 67 (2016): 115–42.

———. "The Virgin Mary in the Ministry of Jesus and the Early Church according to the Earliest Life of the Virgin." *HTR* 98 (2005): 441–67.

Steenberg, M. C. *Irenaeus on Creation: The Cosmic Christ and the Saga of Redemption.* VCSup 91. Leiden: Brill, 2008.

Strycker, Émile de, S.J. *La forme la plus ancienne du Protévangile de Jacques: Recherches sur le Papyrus Bodmer 5 avec une edition critique du texte grec et une traduction annotée.* SH 33. Brussels: Societe des Bollandistes, 1961.

Swanson, Robert Norman, ed. *The Church and Mary.* SCH 39. Woodbridge: Boydell, 2004.

Talbot, Alice-Mary, and Scott Fitzgerald Johnson, eds. *Miracle Tales from Byzantium.* Washington, DC: Dumbarton Oaks Medieval Library, 2012.

Toniolo, Ermanno M. "L'Akathistos nella Vita di Maria di Massimo il Confessore." Pages 209–28 in *Virgo Liber Dei: Miscellanea di stui in onore di P. Giuseppe M. Besutti, O. S. M.* Edited by Ignazio M. Calabuig. Rome: Edizioni Marianum, 1991.

Tsironis, Niki. "From Poetry to Liturgy: The Cult of the Virgin in the Middle Byzantine Era." Pages 91–92 in *Images of the Mother of God. Perceptions of the Theotokos in Byzantium.* Edited by Maria Vassilaki. Aldershot: Ashgate, 2004.

———. "The Lament of the Virgin Mary from Romanos the Melode to George of Nicomedia: An Aspect of the Development of the Marian Cult." PhD diss., King's College London, 1998.

———. "The Mother of God in the Iconoclastic Controversy." Pages 27–39 in *Mother of God: Representations of the Virgin in Byzantine Art.* Edited by Maria Vassilaki. Milan: Abbeville, 2000.

Vassilaki, Maria, ed. *Images of the Mother of God: Perceptions of the Theotokos in Byzantium*. Aldershot: Ashgate, 2004.

———, ed. *Mother of God: Representations of the Virgin in Byzantine Art*. Athens: Abbeville, 2000.

Viller, Marcel, ed. *Dictionnaire de Spiritualité ascétique et mystique: Doctrine et histoire*. 17 vols. Paris: Beauchesne, 1937–1995.

Wenger, A. *L'Assomption de la très sainte Vierge dans la tradition byzantine du VIe au Xe siècle*. AOC 5. Paris: Institut français d'études byzantines, 1955.

Young, Frances. *Biblical Exegesis and the Formation of Christian Culture*. Cambridge: Cambridge University Press, 1997.

The Virgin Mary and Ancient Jewish Literature

Martha Himmelfarb

Jews in antiquity were well aware of the significance of the Virgin Mary for Christians, as their occasional efforts at subversion of the Christian narrative indicate. According to the Babylonian Talmud, Jesus was the son not of a virgin but of a married woman and her lover and thus, by Jewish law, a bastard (b. Shab. 104b, b. San. 67a).[1] In the Toldot Yeshu (Life of Jesus) traditions, a linguistically and chronologically diverse group of texts of which the earliest appear to date to rabbinic times, Mary fares somewhat better.[2] Here, too, Jesus is a bastard, but Mary is a victim rather than a sinner: she becomes pregnant by a neighbor who passes himself off as her husband while her real husband is in the house of study.

In this essay, I consider three passages that reflect a different side of the response of ancient Jews to the figure of the Virgin: their appropriation of aspects of her role for Jewish purposes. Two of the heroines are mothers of the messiah; the other one is the mother of seven sons whose martyrdom is depicted as having redemptive significance. In addition, more than one passage in rabbinic literature represents a biblical heroine as embodying some aspect of the figure of the Virgin, and greater scholarly interest in the subject will surely uncover further instances of the impact of the Virgin in ancient Jewish texts.[3]

---

1. See Peter Schäfer, *Jesus in the Talmud* (Princeton: Princeton University Press, 2007), 16–18; Schäfer notes that the passage appears only in uncensored manuscripts and editions of the Talmud.

2. For texts and translation, see Michael Meerson and Peter Schäfer, eds. and trans., with the collaboration of Yaacov Deutsch et al., *Toldot Yeshu: The Life Story of Jesus*, 2 vols., TSAJ 159 (Tübingen: Mohr Siebeck, 2014). For the current state of the question, see Peter Schäfer, Michael Meerson, and Yaacov Deutsch, eds., *Toledot Yeshu (The Life Story of Jesus) Reconsidered*, TSAJ 143 (Tübingen: Mohr Siebeck, 2011).

3. I have argued that the figure of the Virgin also had an impact on the rabbis'

1. The Mother of the Disappearing Baby Messiah

The earliest of the passages to be considered here is a story found in the Jerusalem Talmud, a work completed in the fifth century; the story is attributed to a rabbi of the early fourth century.[4] The protagonist of the story is a Jew who is plowing his field when he hears his cow low. An Arab translates the sound: the Jew should stop plowing because the temple has been destroyed. A moment later the cow lows again. This time the Arab tells the Jew to take up the plow again: the messiah has been born in Bethlehem, and his name is Menahem son of Hezekiah. Having sold the cow and plow to become a peddler of babies' clothes, the Jew goes in search of the newborn messiah.

> He went from city to city until he came to that city. All the women made purchases except Menahem's mother. He heard the women calling, "Menahem's mother, Menahem's mother, come, buy something for your son." But she answered, "I would like to strangle him, the enemies of Israel, for on the day that he was born, the temple was destroyed." [The peddler] said, "We trust that as it was destroyed in his wake, in his wake it will be rebuilt." She said, "I have no money." "What does that matter to him?" he said. "Come and buy something for him. If you cannot pay today, I will come back another time and collect [the money]." After some time, he came to that city and asked her, "How is the baby doing?" She said, "After you saw me, winds and whirlwinds came and snatched him out my hands." (y. Ber. 2.4 [5a])[5]

---

representation of two of the biblical matriarchs, Sarah (Gen. Rab. 53:9) and Rachel (Lam. Rab. petihah 24), in Martha Himmelfarb, "The Mother of the Seven Sons in Lamentations Rabbah and the Virgin Mary," *JSQ* 22 (2015): 325–51.

4. I discuss this passage in greater detail in Martha Himmelfarb, "The Mother of the Messiah in the Talmud Yerushalmi and Sefer Zerubbabel," in *The Talmud Yerushalmi and Greco-Roman Culture*, ed. Peter Schäfer (Tübingen: Mohr Siebeck, 2002), 3:369–89. See also Himmelfarb, *Jewish Messiahs in a Christian Empire: A History of the Book of Zerubbabel* (Cambridge: Harvard University Press, 2017), 39–47, which takes into account two important discussions that appeared after the article: Hillel Newman, "The Birth of the Messiah on the Day of the Destruction: Historical and Anti-historical Notes," in *For Uriel: Studies in the History of Israel in Antiquity Presented to Professor Uriel Rappaport* [Hebrew], ed. Menahem Mor et al. (Jerusalem: Merkaz Zalman Shazar, 2006), 85–110; and Peter Schäfer, *The Jewish Jesus: How Judaism and Christianity Shaped Each Other* (Princeton: Princeton University Press, 2012), 214–35.

5. Unless otherwise indicated, translations are my own.

The story begins with good news: on the very day that the Second Temple was destroyed, the messiah was born. But at its conclusion, the messiah has disappeared, and there is no suggestion that he is coming back. Indeed, over the course of the story, the mother quite clearly expresses the desire to strangle her son: "I would like to strangle him, the enemies of Israel." The phrase "enemies of Israel," used euphemistically for the people of Israel or individual members of the people in negative contexts elsewhere in rabbinic literature, may be intended to tone down this unacceptable sentiment.[6] In light of the mother's shocking comment, the peddler's offer to return to collect from her should perhaps be read as a warning that he plans to check up on her behavior toward the baby. Furthermore, the mother's expressed wish to kill the child makes it difficult to know whether to believe her account of the unusual circumstances of the baby's disappearance at the end of the story. Perhaps we are to understand that she has invented the winds to cover up her own guilt.

Before I consider the significance of this story, I should note that most scholars have read it in more positive terms than I have suggested and have seen the mother as a more sympathetic character.[7] One point these readings emphasize is the story's use of the unusual word "whirlwind," which they take as an allusion to the wind that carried Elijah to heaven (2 Kgs 2:1, 11), according to the Aramaic translations of the Bible.[8] The allusion is understood to imply that like Elijah, the baby messiah has been taken up to heaven. But this understanding assumes that the mother is a reliable source, which, as I have just indicated, is by no means evident. Furthermore, even if the mother is reliable, in the absence of any further indications of interest in the Elijah narrative, it is far from certain that such an allusion is intended.

---

6. For the euphemistic use of the phrase, see, e.g., b. Ber. 4b. On the singular pronoun "him" with the plural "enemies of Israel," see Schäfer, *Jewish Jesus*, 228, 315–16, nn. 44–45.

7. See Yonah Frenkel, *Studies in the Spiritual World of the Aggadic Story* [Hebrew] (Tel Aviv: Hakibbutz Hameuchad, 1981), 160–63; Galit Hasan-Rokem, *Web of Life: Folklore and Midrash in Rabbinic Literature*, trans. Batya Stein (Stanford: Stanford University Press, 2000), 152–60 (originally published in Hebrew in 1996); Israel Knohl, *The Messiah before Jesus: The Suffering Servant of the Dead Sea Scrolls*, trans. David Maisel (Berkeley: University of California Press, 2000), 72–74. For a very different reading of the story that emphasizes the murderous desires of the mother, see Schäfer, *Jewish Jesus*, 214–35.

8. Frenkel, *Studies in the Spiritual World*, 163, n. 19; followed by Hasan-Rokem, *Web of Life*, 160; and Knohl, *Messiah before Jesus*, 132, n. 4.

The other factor that leads these scholars to a more optimistic reading is the version of the story in Lamentations Rabbah, a collection of homilies and interpretations of the book of Lamentations compiled in Palestine at about the same time as the Jerusalem Talmud. In this version of the story (Lam. Rab. 1:51), the mother explains her unwillingness to buy clothes for her son by saying, "I fear difficulties for my son." In other words, in contrast to the mother in the Jerusalem Talmud, she expresses anxiety for her son's future rather than the desire to strangle him. When the peddler asks about the child, she responds, "Did I not I tell you I feared difficulties for my son?," and goes on to recount the baby's disappearance. Even here there is no reason to understand the snatching of the baby by the winds to mean that he has been taken up to heaven to await the moment when he is called upon to manifest himself on earth, but the depiction of the mother makes it more likely that the baby's disappearance does not mean his demise. In any case, Lamentations Rabbah's revision of the story does not change the meaning of the story in the Jerusalem Talmud; rather, it testifies to how disturbing the reviser found the earlier story.

It is not surprising that stories about the Christian messiah exerted considerable attraction on Jewish inhabitants of the now Christian empire, and the story in the Jerusalem Talmud shows that the mother of the messiah was one feature of the story that they found compelling. But the story also shows that the rabbis of the Jerusalem Talmud did not share this popular enthusiasm. Their story, I suggest, pokes fun at a Jewish narrative that appropriated a central figure of the Christian narrative. It cannot be intended to make fun of the Christian narrative itself, since the messiah of the Jerusalem Talmud's story who never grew past infancy cannot possibly be confused with the Christian messiah. Rather, the story reflects the discomfort of the rabbinic elite with the popular Jewish desire for a story of the messiah that rivaled the Christian story. The disappearance of the messiah without any indication that he will one day return is one aspect of the mockery, and the depiction of the mother as a danger to her son is another.

2. The Mother of the Seven Sons

The second passage considered here appears in Lam. Rab. 1:50.[9] Lamentations Rabbah comes down to us in two recensions, reflected, on the one

---

9. I discuss this passage in greater detail in Himmelfarb, "Mother of the Seven Sons."

hand, in the *editio princeps*, which dates from the early sixteenth century, and the printed editions that followed and, on the other hand, in the edition of Salomon Buber.[10] Though the differences in content are small, the recensions differ considerably in their wording.[11] In what follows, I cite the Buber edition unless otherwise indicated. A shorter and less elaborate version of the story appears in the Babylonian Talmud (b. Git. 57b); there it is in Aramaic, while the story in Lamentations Rabbah is in Hebrew. Several later rabbinic texts also contain versions of the story. With the possible exception of the version in Pesiqta Rabbati, all are dependent on either Lamentations Rabbah or the Babylonian Talmud.[12]

Although the heroine of the story in Lamentations Rabbah, Miriam b. Tanhum, shares a name with the Virgin, she is the mother not of the messiah but of seven sons who die as martyrs at the hands of the Romans for refusing to worship an idol. An earlier version of the story appears in chapter 7 of 2 Maccabees, a work that dates back to perhaps the late second century BCE. Scholars have long noted that the language of chapter 7 is much simpler than the highly literary Greek of the rest of the work, which suggests that the story is a translation of a no-longer-extant Hebrew or Aramaic original. The story in 2 Maccabees was subsequently taken up and elaborated by the author of 4 Maccabees sometime after the turn of the era. The rabbis responsible for the passage in Lamentations Rabbah might well have known Greek, yet despite the availability of 2 and 4 Mac-

---

10. Salomon Buber, ed., *Midrasch Echa Rabbati* (Vilna: Romm, 1899). The Buber edition is based on a manuscript from the Casanata Library in Rome, with a manuscript from the British Museum providing the petihot, which are not found in the Casanata manuscript (p. 1 [introduction]); the passage discussed here appears on pp. 84–85. The *editio princeps* is reproduced in the standard printed editions of Midrash Rabbah.

11. See Paul Mandel, "Between Byzantium and Islam: The Transmission of a Jewish Book in the Byzantine and Early Islamic Periods," in *Transmitting Jewish Traditions: Orality, Textuality, and Cultural Diffusion*, ed. Yaakov Elman and Israel Gershoni (New Haven: Yale University Press, 2000), esp. 92–100. Mandel argues that the Buber edition reflects the original Palestinian version of the compilation, while the printed editions represent the Babylonian version and the changes that took place in the text in the course of its oral performance in Babylonia.

12. For references to the texts of the various versions and brief comments on their dates and relationships, see Gerson D. Cohen, "Hannah and Her Seven Sons in Hebrew Literature," in *Studies in the Variety of Rabbinic Cultures* (Philadelphia: Jewish Publication Society, 1991), 55–56, n. 3.

cabees and Christian homilies in praise of the Maccabean martyrs, the passage in Lamentations Rabbah shows no awareness of a connection to the Maccabees, nor does it show any literary connection to the story as it appears in 2 or 4 Maccabees. Thus it seems likely that it is a development of the Hebrew or Aramaic story on which 2 Maccabees drew.

Like the stories in 2 and 4 Maccabees, the story in Lamentations Rabbah depicts the persecuting empire as pagan, although use of the term "Caesar" for the emperor clearly identifies the empire as Rome rather than the Seleucid Empire of 2 and 4 Maccabees. Indeed, scholars have pointed out a number of parallels between Lamentations Rabbah and the literature of Christian martyrdom in the incidental details of their heroes' imprisonment and trials, and at least some of the details may reflect actual Roman practice.[13] Yet by the time Lamentations Rabbah was compiled, Rome had been Christian for some time, and, whatever the origins of the story, I shall argue that as it appears in Lamentations Rabbah, it can be fully understood only in relation to contemporary Christian veneration of the Virgin.

The story begins with the mother and her sons in captivity. One by one, the sons are brought before the emperor and ordered to worship an idol. Each son in turn refuses, citing a verse from the Torah to explain his refusal, and each in turn is condemned to death. Finally, the youngest son is brought out. He too refuses to commit idolatry and justifies his refusal with verses from the Torah and Psalms. But unlike his brothers, he is given a way to save himself without transgressing the Torah. The emperor offers to toss a ring in front of the idol. When the boy then bends to pick up the ring, onlookers will believe that he has fulfilled the emperor's command to worship the idol. The boy, however, rejects the emperor's plan and proceeds to taunt the emperor, citing biblical verses to demonstrate that, in contrast to the emperor's idol, the God of Israel is a living god and offering an insulting response to the emperor's question about why such a powerful god has permitted the brothers to meet such a terrible fate. The boy's courage and learning become even more impressive when we discover his age at the end of the account: six and a half years and two hours (Buber edition), or two years, six months, and six and a half hours (*editio princeps*).

Before the youngest son is taken to his death, the mother pleads with the emperor to be given the opportunity to embrace him. The emperor grants her request, and the mother offers her son her breasts and nurses

---

13. Cohen, "Hannah and Her Seven Sons," 43–49, and references there.

him. At least one modern reader has understood this act as a touching expression of maternal love.[14] But since in the ancient world the woman nursing a child was often not the child's mother, ancient readers were presumably less likely to associate nursing with maternal care.[15] Nor does such an interpretation fit well with the prooftext supplied by the Buber version: "Honey and milk are under your [fem. sing.] tongue" (Song 4:11).[16] The erotic tone of the verse from which the prooftext is drawn makes it an odd choice for an act of maternal tenderness: "Your lips distil nectar, my bride; honey and milk are under your tongue; the scent of your garments is like the scent of Lebanon." In addition, the feminine singular "your" does not fit the scene in Lamentations Rabbah, where the tongue in question is presumably the son's.

As far as I know, there is no precedent for a mother nursing her child before martyrdom in either Jewish or Christian literature. The passage in 2 Maccabees has the mother recall carrying her youngest son in her womb for nine months and nursing him for three years as she encourages him to choose death (2 Macc 7:26), but she does not engage in the act. In 4 Maccabees, the mother mentions pregnancy in her exhortation to her sons (4 Macc 15:6–7), but nursing appears only in the speech that the author imagines a less heroic mother might give (4 Macc 16:7). In the second half of the fourth century, Gregory of Nazianzus's *On the Maccabees* (Homily 15) has the mother show her grown sons her breasts as she urges them to martyrdom in a scene that echoes Hecuba's baring of her breasts in the *Iliad* (22.79–89) as she attempts to dissuade Hector from fighting Achilles.[17] Gregory certainly did not imagine the mother as a nursing mother,

---

14. Hasan-Rokem, *Web of Life*, 123.

15. For this point in relation to late antique Egyptian images of the Virgin nursing the Christ child, see Elizabeth S. Bolman, "The Enigmatic Coptic Galaktotrophousa and the Cult of the Virgin Mary in Egypt," in *Images of the Mother of God: Perceptions of the Theotokos in Byzantium*, ed. Maria Vassilaki (Aldershot: Ashgate, 2005), 13–22, esp. 15–16.

16. A later form of the story in Seder Eliyyahu Rabbah develops the idea even further: the milk and honey from the mother's breasts fill the son's mouth and fall to the ground before the quotation of the biblical text.

17. The homily appears as PG 35:916–17 (section 4); for a French translation, see Raphaëlle Ziadé, *Les martyrs Maccabées: De l'histoire juive au culte chrétien; Les homélies de Grégoire de Nazianze et de Jean Chrysostome*, VCSup 80 (Leiden: Brill, 2007), 301–11. For a date of 362 for this homily, when Julian's persecution of Christians made the Maccabean martyrs particularly relevant, see Martha Vinson, "Gregory Nazian-

however, for he also has her appeal to her hoary head to inspire her sons to obedience. Finally, it should be noted that despite their allusions to the physical aspects of motherhood, all three works praise the mother for transcending the limitations of being female. The passage in 2 Maccabees refers to her "masculine courage" (2 Macc 7:21), 4 Maccabees calls her "more noble than males in steadfastness, and more manly than men in endurance" (4 Macc 15:30, see also 16:14), and Gregory praises her as a "manly soul in a female body."

The only martyrdom account from antiquity to include the act of nursing, as opposed to its mere mention, is the Martyrdom of Perpetua and Felicitas, an account written in North Africa in the early third century. Yet here, too, the emphasis is on the heroine's transcendence of the limitations of the female body. Perpetua is a well-born Roman matron who has become a Christian and is imprisoned with her infant son as a member of a group of Christians awaiting their punishment. She is eager to die along with her fellow Christians, and she sees the baby's dependence on her for nourishment as an impediment to that goal. So after nursing the baby in prison for a time, she leaves him to the care of her father, whose pleas to renounce Christianity she has repeatedly rejected.[18] In a vision of the happy fate in store for her as a martyr, Perpetua sees herself triumphing in the arena over an Egyptian of frightening appearance; as she prepares for the fight, her clothes come off and she discovers that she has become a man.

Neither the literature of the mother of the Maccabean martyrs nor the Martyrdom of Perpetua and Felicitas, then, does much to illumine the scene in Lamentations Rabbah in which the mother nurses her youngest son. In order to make sense of the scene, I suggest turning to Christian veneration of the Virgin as nurse of the Christ child. The earliest sources do not display much enthusiasm for this theme. When in the Gospel of

---

zen's Homily 15 and the Genesis of the Christian Cult of the Maccabean Martyrs," *Byzantion* 64 (1994): 166–67. For an argument that at least the final form of the homily comes from later in Gregory's career during his time in Constantinople (379–381), see Ziadé, *Martyrs Maccabées*, 147–54, 174–75.

18. There is a large literature on Perpetua and gender. On Perpetua and motherhood, see, in particular, Elizabeth Castelli, "'I Will Make Mary Male': Pieties of the Body and Gender Transformation of Christian Women in Late Antiquity," in *Body Guards: The Cultural Politics of Gender Ambiguity*, ed. Julia Epstein and Kristina Straub (New York: Routledge, 1991), 33–43.

Luke, after Jesus has cast out a demon, a woman exclaims, "Blessed is the womb that bore you, and the breasts that you sucked!," Jesus responds, "Blessed rather are those who hear the word of God and keep it!" (Luke 11:27-28). By the fourth century the Virgin's role as nurse of the Christ child makes a more positive appearance in the Syriac liturgical poetry of Ephrem, and it plays a prominent role in the hymns of Romanos Melodos, the preeminent Greek liturgical poet of the sixth century.[19]

The most important hymn to the Virgin in Constantinople was the Akathistos Hymn. It dates to sometime from the fifth to the seventh century and consists of a series of acclamations of the Virgin. Of particular interest for the story of the mother and her sons is a passage at the end of a stanza that offers a typological reading of the Exodus: "Hail, promised land. / Hail, you from whom flow milk and honey" (11.16-17).[20] Read typologically, the promised land flowing with milk and honey is not a physical place, the last stage in the Exodus, but rather eternal life, with which the hymn also identifies the Virgin. The association of milk and honey with life after death is not unique to the Akathistos Hymn. The fourth- or fifth-century Apocalypse of Paul, one of the most popular apocalypses of antiquity, describes paradise, like Eden in Gen 2, with four rivers, of which one flows with milk and another with honey (Apoc. Paul 25-26).[21] The wide circulation of such a picture of paradise might have

---

19. For translations of Ephrem's hymns, see Kathleen E. McVey, *Ephrem the Syrian: Hymns*, CWS (New York: Paulist, 1989). For the Virgin as nurse of the Christ child, see Ephrem, *Nat.* 4.149-153, 184-185; 5.24; 11.4; 12.1; 18.12; Ephrem, *Virg.* 25.3. For the texts of Romanos's hymns, see Paul Maas and C. A. Trypanis, eds., *Sancti Romani Melodi Cantica: Cantica Genuina* (Oxford: Clarendon, 1963), 276-81; for English translation, see Marjorie Carpenter, trans. and annotator, *Kontakia of Romanos, Byzantine Melodist*, 2 vols. (Columbia: University of Missouri Press, 1970-1973). For the Virgin as nurse of the Christ child, see Kontakia "On the Nativity I" (1), strophes 2 and 23; "On the Nativity II" (2), strophe 13; "On the Presentation in the Temple" (4), strophe 4; "On the Marriage at Cana" (7), strophe 14; "On the Nativity of the Virgin Mary" (35), refrain; "On the Annunciation I" (36), strophe 1; "On the Annunciation II" (37), strophe 13. The numbers in parentheses refer to the edition of Maas and Trypanis.

20. For the typological reading of this strophe, see Leena Mari Peltomaa, *The Image of the Virgin Mary in the Akathistos Hymn*, MilM 35 (Leiden: Brill, 2001), 167-73; translation on 208. Peltomaa argues that the strophe's identification of the Virgin with elements usually taken as types of Christ himself is possible because of the hymn's focus on Mary's role in the incarnation.

21. The other two rivers flow with wine and oil (Apoc. Paul 27-28).

prepared a Christian listening to the Akathistos Hymn to understand the milk and honey flowing from the Virgin quite literally—as rivers.

A listener familiar with the praise of the Virgin as nurse of the Christ child could also have understood the milk and honey to flow from the Virgin's breasts, and it seems to me that the hymn may intend this double understanding. The invocation of the Virgin earlier in the strophe as the successor to the manna makes her a source of divine sustenance, and her identification with the promised land associates that divine sustenance with life after death.[22] Earlier Christian texts used the image of nursing, though not the Virgin as nurse, to describe the experience of the Christian, who drinks the milk of salvation offered by God or Christ.[23]

The association of the Virgin's milk with the milk and honey of the promised land and life after death helps to explain the act of nursing in Lamentations Rabbah and the use of the verse from Song of Songs as a prooftext for it. Before her son goes to his death, the mother offers him the milk (and honey) of immortality. The comparison of the mother of the seven sons to the Virgin Mary implicit in this scene is carried further in the mother's charge to her son as he is sent to his death: "Tell [Abraham] in my name: 'You built one altar, and you did not sacrifice your son. I built seven altars, and I did sacrifice my sons.'" The rabbis understood Abraham to have guaranteed the redemption of his descendants through his willingness to sacrifice his beloved son in response to God's request. The mother's words thus make a powerful claim: the martyrdom of her sons is an even more potent source of redemption than the near sacrifice of Isaac, since her sons did not simply face death but actually died—like the Christian savior. The mother's words also imply that she surpasses not only Abraham but the Virgin as well. Like the Virgin, she is a source of the milk of immortality, but she sacrificed seven sons to the Virgin's one.

After nursing her youngest son, the mother asks to be killed along with him. The mother in 2 Maccabees dies immediately after her sons, apparently as a martyr (7:41), while the martyrdom of the mother in 4

---

22. On the point about divine sustenance, see Vasiliki Limberis, *Divine Heiress: The Virgin Mary and the Creation of Christian Constantinople* (London: Routledge, 1994), 121–42, esp. 138, where she discusses part of strophe 11.

23. On 1 Peter and Clement of Alexandria, see Gail Paterson Corrington, "The Milk of Salvation: Redemption by the Mother in Late Antiquity and Early Christianity," *HTR* 82 (1989): 412–13; on Clement, see Bolman, "Enigmatic Coptic Galaktotrophousa," 17.

Maccabees is explicit (17:1). In Lamentations Rabbah, however, the emperor rejects the mother's request. After some time, we are told that she goes mad and throws herself from the roof. At her death, people recite the verse, "A joyous mother of children [or: sons]" (Ps 113:9), and the holy spirit responds with the verse from Lamentations to which the story is attached, "For these I weep" (Lam 1:16).[24] Thus after having implied that the mother is a source of immortality even greater than Abraham, Lamentations Rabbah assigns her a humiliating end that shows her unable to bear her sorrow. Even the biblical verses in the mother's honor do not do much to cushion the shock of disappointed expectations.

One way to makes sense of the mother's fate is to see it as a reflection of anxiety about the parallels to the figure of the Virgin. That is, having set up the mother to provide Jews with a heroine to rival the Virgin, Lamentations Rabbah wonders if such a figure is appropriate for Jews and proceeds to diminish her stature by showing her succumbing to her troubles. It is also possible that the fate of the mother reflects the association of the mother's sacrifice with the binding of Isaac. As we have seen, the mother compares herself to Abraham, but the terrible end Lamentations Rabbah assigns to her recalls the fate that Abraham and Isaac fear for Sarah in the Tanhuma, a midrash that dates from the eighth or ninth century. Upon receiving the command to sacrifice Isaac, Abraham worries that if he were to take Isaac away without giving Sarah an explanation, she might kill herself when she realized that the child was gone (Tanh. Vayera' 22). Later, as Isaac lies bound on the altar, he worries about how his mother will take the bad news: "Father, do not tell my mother when she is standing by a pit or when she is standing on the roof, lest she throw herself down and die" (Tanh. Vayera' 23). The description of the death that Isaac fears for his mother is very close to the death of the mother in Lamentations Rabbah.

In the Tanhuma's telling, the scenario that Isaac fears does not come to pass, but his near sacrifice is nonetheless the indirect cause of Sarah's death. After the successful completion of the test, with the ram substituted for Isaac on the altar, Satan, who had failed to tempt Abraham and Isaac to resist God's command, goes to Sarah disguised as Isaac and gives her an accurate account of the events that have just transpired, concluding, "If God had not told him: 'Do not raise your hand against the boy,' I would

---

24. The printed editions first quote Jer 15:9, "She who bore seven is forlorn," and attribute the verse from Psalms to a heavenly voice, as does the Babylonian Talmud, which cites only the verse from Psalms.

already be slaughtered." Upon hearing these words, Sarah dies, presumably of shock. Thus she, rather than Isaac, becomes a victim of Abraham's zeal to perform God's will.

Although the Tanhuma as a collection is too late to have had an impact on Lamentations Rabbah, the tradition just recounted could be earlier than the final editing of the collection. I find the possibility that Lamentations Rabbah alludes to this tradition attractive. As we have seen, Lamentations Rabbah makes an explicit comparison between the mother's sacrifice and Abraham's attempted sacrifice of Isaac in favor of the mother: she sacrificed seven sons to Abrahams's one, and Abraham's sacrifice was averted while hers actually took place. In light of the mother's insistence that her sacrifice was greater than Abraham's, it might have seemed appropriate to give her the very death Isaac feared for his own mother. In other words, the nature of the mother's death in Lamentations Rabbah may be intended to underline the fact that her sacrifices actually took place.

3. Hephzibah and the Beautiful Statue in Sefer Zerubbabel

Sefer Zerubbabel (the Book of Zerubbabel) is a Hebrew apocalyptic work composed early in the seventh century during the wars between the Byzantines and the Persians.[25] To some Jews, at least, these wars appeared to be the prelude to the messianic era. In particular, the brief period during which the Persians wrested Jerusalem from its Christian masters (614–628) seems to have encouraged the hope that God was about to return the holy city to its rightful rulers and establish the third temple. In response to these stirring events, Sefer Zerubbabel provides an elaborate eschatological scenario, presented as a revelation to Zerubbabel, a member of the Davidic line who was the Persian-appointed governor of Judea in the late sixth century BCE and who presided over the building of the Second Temple. The work is rather loosely organized, to put it gently, and contains a variety of originally freestanding sources. The plot

---

25. I discuss the mother of the messiah in Sefer Zerubbabel in greater detail in Himmelfarb, "Mother of the Messiah"; and Himmelfarb, *Jewish Messiahs*, 35–39, 48–52, 58–59. For the Hebrew text with French translation, see Israël Lévi, "L'Apocalypse de Zorobabel et le roi de Perse Siroès," in *Le ravissement du Messie à sa naissance et autres essais*, ed. Evelyne Patlagean (Louven: Peeters, 1994), 173–227. For an English translation, see Himmelfarb, *Jewish Messiahs*, 147–57.

summary that I am about to provide simplifies many of the difficulties in the text.

The work begins with God taking Zerubbabel to Rome, by which the author clearly means Constantinople, the new Rome, in response to his anguished prayer. In Rome, the archangel Michael appears to serve as the revealer for the rest of the work. Michael introduces Zerubbabel to the messiah descended from David, Menahem son of Ammiel, who is imprisoned there. Menahem is described in terms drawn from the suffering servant of Isa 53 (53:3–4) as "despised, severely wounded, and in pain."[26] The events of the eschaton begin to unfold, however, not with deeds performed by Menahem but with the exploits of his mother, Hephzibah, who kills the evil kings of Yemen and Antioch with the help of a wondrous staff. Five years after Hephzibah begins her campaign, the messiah descended from Joseph, Nehemiah son of Hushiel, arrives on the scene. He gathers the people together and resumes the offering of sacrifices, which had ceased with the destruction of the Second Temple in 70 CE, as Hephzibah slays Shiroi, king of Persia, who has come to do battle against them. But the messiah Nehemiah is soon killed by Armilos, the greatest of the eschatological opponents according to Sefer Zerubbabel.

Armilos, we learn, is the son of a beautiful stone statue of a virgin found in Rome in a "house of disgrace and scorn," apparently a church, that is impregnated by Satan.[27] Only after Armilos has slain Nehemiah does Menahem son of Ammiel take up his messianic mission. Together with Elijah the prophet, he brings Nehemiah back to life. Then he kills Armilos. Finally, God himself descends to fight the eschatological enemies, Gog and Magog and the forces of Armilos, and an enormous temple made in heaven descends to earth.

The identity of the beautiful statue of a virgin can hardly be in doubt, and it is also clear that the birth of Armilos is intended as a parody of the story of the virgin birth, with Satan as the father rather than God. Yet Sefer Zerubbabel's Byzantine contemporaries did not use sculpture in the round to depict the Virgin or Christ; their icons were two-dimensional. Sefer Zerubbabel's choice to depict the Virgin as a statue can perhaps be explained by an episode at the conclusion of the work in which Armilos takes the statue and sets it up for all the nations to worship. In other

---

26. Lévi, "Apocalypse de Zorobabel," 176; Himmelfarb, *Jewish Messiahs*, 149.

27. Lévi, "Apocalypse de Zorobabel," 180, and see n. 4 there; Himmelfarb, *Jewish Messiahs*, 152.

words, for Sefer Zerubbabel, veneration of the Virgin constitutes idolatry, and idols are three-dimensional.[28]

In contrast to the statue, Hephzibah is never described as beautiful, nor is her role as a warrior particularly motherly. Yet this role is clearly indebted to the contemporary Byzantine picture of Mary as protector of the faithful that led to the use of icons of the Virgin in battle. In 610, Heraklios, the emperor who was soon to lose and then regain Jerusalem, brought icons of the Virgin to his naval campaign against his predecessor Phokas. Later, during the siege of Constantinople by the Persians and Avars in 626, the patriarch Sergios had images of the Virgin and Christ child painted on the gates of the west side of the city, and contemporary accounts credited the Virgin and her son with protecting the city during Heraklios's absence.[29]

Furthermore, as Alexei Sivertsev has shown, just as the Virgin serves as the patron and protector of Constantinople, Hephzibah's military exploits are all in defense of Jerusalem: she defeats two kings who make war on the holy city, she participates in the battle against the king of Persia as he attacks Nehemiah and the children of Israel in Jerusalem, and she stands at the east gate of the city to prevent Armilos from entering after he has slain Nehemiah. Her association with Jerusalem is also reflected in her name, which means "I delight in her" and appears in Isaiah (62:4) as the new name that God will bestow on the restored Jerusalem.[30] By providing Jerusalem with its own guardian mother of the messiah, the author of Sefer Zerubbabel makes his holy city the equal of Constantinople.

Sefer Zerubbabel had a powerful impact on Jewish eschatology in the centuries that followed its composition, particularly with its picture of the relationship between the messiah son of Joseph and the messiah son of David. Yet while Armilos and his mother the statue show up along with the messiahs in some of these later works, Hephzibah enjoys a much more

---

28. See Himmelfarb, *Jewish Messiahs*, 56–58, where I correct the misunderstanding of Byzantine representation of the Virgin in my earlier discussion.

29. See Himmelfarb, "Mother of the Messiah," 384. For more extensive discussion and other instances, see Alexei M. Sivertsev, *Judaism and Imperial Ideology in Late Antiquity* (New York: Cambridge University Press, 2011), 93–101.

30. Sivertsev also suggests that Sefer Zerubbabel understands Hephzibah as Jerusalem's *tyche* (τύχη), the female personification of a city common in the Roman era, a role that also implies comparison to the Virgin, who had taken on the attributes of the *tyche* of Constantinople (*Judaism and Imperial Ideology*, 88–90, 101–4). On the Virgin as *tyche*, see also Limberis, *Divine Heiress*, 14–21, 124–33.

limited career. After Sefer Zerubbabel, she appears next in "That Very Day," a piyyut—or liturgical poem—written shortly after the Muslim conquest, a decade or two after the composition of Sefer Zerubbabel. Like Sefer Zerubbabel, "That Very Day" depicts Hephzibah as the mother of a messiah and as a warrior. But, as Sivertsev has shown, the piyyut adds an element to the picture of Hephzibah that does not appear in Sefer Zerubbabel, identifying her with her wondrous staff, which, like the staff of Aaron in the wilderness, blossoms (that is, gives birth to Menahem); contemporary Christians identified the Virgin with Aaron's blossoming staff.[31] Another difference between the piyyut and Sefer Zerubbabel is that for the piyyut, Hephzibah's son, though he bears the name Menahem son of Ammiel as in Sefer Zerubbabel, is not the Davidic messiah but the messiah descended from Joseph. In light of the combination of similarities and differences between the two works, Sivertsev argues that the piyyut reflects not dependence on Sefer Zerubbabel but independent development of the traditions on which Sefer Zerubbabel also drew.[32] But since the piyyut appears to allude to Sefer Zerubbabel, I would suggest instead that its identification of Menahem as messiah son of Joseph is an attempt to make sense of Sefer Zerubbabel's somewhat surprising picture of Hephzibah as more closely associated with the messiah son of Joseph than with her own son.[33]

After "That Very Day," Hephzibah appears, to the best of my knowledge, only twice more in Jewish texts: in a brief eschatological scenario in a twelfth-century manuscript from the Rhineland and in the Zohar, the classic work of Jewish mysticism from thirteenth-century Christian Spain. In the eschatological work, she is still a warrior, but in the Zohar, she is simply the mother of the Davidic messiah, Menahem son of Ammiel.[34] At one time, I understood Hephzibah's virtual disappearance in works that draw on other aspects of Sefer Zerubbabel as a reflection of anxiety about a mother for a Jewish messiah. But I have come to favor a different explanation. For Jews under Muslim rule, a mother of the messiah was less relevant than for Jews in Christian lands; thus it is not surprising that the two late appearances of Hephzibah are in works written in the Christian world. But even for Jews living among Christians, a mother of the messiah

---

31. Sivertsev, *Judaism and Imperial Ideology*, 119–22.
32. Sivertsev, *Judaism and Imperial Ideology*, 114–22.
33. Himmelfarb, *Jewish Messiahs*, 52–55.
34. Himmelfarb, *Jewish Messiahs*, 123–24.

who was a warrior made sense only in the context of comparable Christian claims for the Virgin. Thus Hephzibah would have lost her appeal as her deeds came to seem strange and unsettling rather than heroic. The mother of the seven sons, on the other hand, enjoyed considerable popularity in Western Europe in the Middle Ages.[35] She played a role that Christians continued to attribute to the Virgin, and in contrast to Hephzibah's role, it was one that medieval Jews found appropriate to a woman and mother.

Bibliography

Baumgarten, Elisheva, and Rella Kushelevsky. "From 'The Mother and Her Sons' to 'The Mother of the Sons' in Medieval Ashkenaz" [Hebrew]. *Zion* 71 (2006): 301–42.

Bolman, Elizabeth S. "The Enigmatic Coptic Galaktotrophousa and the Cult of the Virgin Mary in Egypt." Pages 13–22 in *Images of the Mother of God: Perceptions of the Theotokos in Byzantium*. Edited by Maria Vassilaki. Aldershot: Ashgate, 2005.

Buber, Salomon, ed. *Midrasch Echa Rabbati*. Vilna: Romm, 1899.

Carpenter, Marjorie, trans. and annotator. *Kontakia of Romanos, Byzantine Melodist*. 2 vols. Columbia: University of Missouri Press, 1970–1973.

Castelli, Elizabeth. "'I Will Make Mary Male': Pieties of the Body and Gender Transformation of Christian Women in Late Antiquity." Pages 29–49 in *Body Guards: The Cultural Politics of Gender Ambiguity*. Edited by Julia Epstein and Kristina Straub. New York: Routledge, 1991.

Cohen, Gerson D. "Hannah and Her Seven Sons in Hebrew Literature." Pages 39–60 in *Studies in the Variety of Rabbinic Cultures*. Philadelphia: Jewish Publication Society, 1991.

Corrington, Gail Paterson. "The Milk of Salvation: Redemption by the Mother in Late Antiquity and Early Christianity." *HTR* 82 (1989): 412–13.

Frenkel, Yonah. *Studies in the Spiritual World of the Aggadic Story* [Hebrew]. Tel Aviv: Hakibbutz Hameuchad, 1981.

---

35. Elisheva Baumgarten and Rella Kushelevsky, "From 'The Mother and Her Sons' to 'The Mother of the Sons' in Medieval Ashkenaz" [Hebrew], *Zion* 71 (2006): 301–42. See also Cohen, "Hannah and Her Seven Sons," 55–56, n. 3.

Hasan-Rokem, Galit. *Web of Life: Folklore and Midrash in Rabbinic Literature*. Translated by Batya Stein. Stanford: Stanford University Press, 2000.

Himmelfarb, Martha. *Jewish Messiahs in a Christian Empire: A History of the Book of Zerubbabel*. Cambridge: Harvard University Press, 2017.

———. "The Mother of the Messiah in the Talmud Yerushalmi and Sefer Zerubbabel." Pages 369–89 in vol. 3 of *The Talmud Yerushalmi and Greco-Roman Culture*. Edited by Peter Schäfer. Tübingen: Mohr Siebeck, 2002.

———. "The Mother of the Seven Sons in Lamentations Rabbah and the Virgin Mary." *JSQ* 22 (2015): 325–51.

Knohl, Israel. *The Messiah before Jesus: The Suffering Servant of the Dead Sea Scrolls*. Translated by David Maisel. Berkeley: University of California Press, 2000.

Lévi, Israël. "L'Apocalypse de Zorobabel et le roi de Perse Siroès." Pages 173–227 in *Le ravissement du Messie à sa naissance et autres essais*. Edited by Evelyne Patlagean. Louven: Peeters, 1994.

Limberis, Vasiliki. *Divine Heiress: The Virgin Mary and the Creation of Christian Constantinople*. London: Routledge, 1994.

Maas, Paul, and C. A. Trypanis, eds. *Sancti Romani Melodi Cantica: Cantica Genuina*. Oxford: Clarendon, 1963.

Mandel, Paul. "Between Byzantium and Islam: The Transmission of a Jewish Book in the Byzantine and Early Islamic Periods." Pages 74–106 in *Transmitting Jewish Traditions: Orality, Textuality, and Cultural Diffusion*. Edited by Yaakov Elman and Israel Gershoni. New Haven: Yale University Press, 2000.

McVey, Kathleen E. *Ephrem the Syrian: Hymns*. CWS. New York: Paulist, 1989.

Meerson, Michael, and Peter Schäfer, eds. and trans., with the collaboration of Yaacov Deutsch, David Grossberg, Avigail Manekin, and Adina Yoffie. *Toldot Yeshu: The Life Story of Jesus*. TSAJ 159. 2 vols. Tübingen: Mohr Siebeck, 2014.

Newman, Hillel. "The Birth of the Messiah on the Day of the Destruction: Historical and Anti-historical Notes." Pages 85–110 in *For Uriel: Studies in the History of Israel in Antiquity Presented to Professor Uriel Rappaport* [Hebrew]. Edited by Menahem Mor, Jack Pastor, Israel Ronen, and Yakov Ashkenazi. Jerusalem: Merkaz Zalman Shazar, 2006.

Peltomaa, Leena Mari. *The Image of the Virgin Mary in the Akathistos Hymn*. MilM 35. Leiden: Brill, 2001.

Schäfer, Peter. *Jesus in the Talmud*. Princeton: Princeton University Press, 2007.

———. *The Jewish Jesus: How Judaism and Christianity Shaped Each Other*. Princeton: Princeton University Press, 2012.

Schäfer, Peter, Michael Meerson, and Yaacov Deutsch, eds. *Toledot Yeshu (The Life Story of Jesus) Reconsidered*. TSAJ 143. Tübingen: Mohr Siebeck, 2011.

Sivertsev, Alexei M. *Judaism and Imperial Ideology in Late Antiquity*. New York: Cambridge University Press, 2011.

Vinson, Martha. "Gregory Nazianzen's Homily 15 and the Genesis of the Christian Cult of the Maccabean Martyrs." *Byzantion* 64 (1994): 166–92.

Ziadé, Raphaëlle. *Les martyrs Maccabées: De l'histoire juive au culte chrétien; Les homélies de Grégoire de Nazianze et de Jean Chrysostome*. VCSup 80. Leiden: Brill, 2007.

The Heavenly Guard of the Mother of God: Mary between the Angels in Early Byzantine Art

Maria Lidova

In recent decades, the question of the development of the cult of the Mother of God in Byzantium has gained particular scholarly attention, which has resulted in numerous publications, several research projects, a number of academic events, and specialized exhibitions.[1] Notwithstanding this great interest, the formation of Marian iconographies and the role that her images played in the dissemination of the veneration of the Mother of God still await further clarification, as well as proper and, one hopes,

---

I would like to thank the editors of this volume, Franca Ela Consolino and Judith Herrin, for their valuable comments and for inspiring me to look at the problem of women in relation to the Bible. I would also like to express my profound gratitude to John Mitchell, whose precious remarks helped improve the flow of this text.

1. To mention just a few: Maria Vassilaki, ed., *Mother of God: Representations of the Virgin in Byzantine Art* (Athens: Abbeville, 2000); Nicholas Constas, *Proclus of Constantinople and the Cult of the Virgin in Late Antiquity*, VCSup 66 (Leiden: Brill, 2003); Robert N. Swanson, ed., *The Church and Mary*, SCH 39 (Woodbridge: Boydell, 2004); Maria Vassilaki, ed., *Images of the Mother of God: Perceptions of the Theotokos in Byzantium* (Aldershot: Ashgate, 2005); Bissera V. Pentcheva, *Icons and Power: The Mother of God in Byzantium* (University Park: Pennsylvania State University Press, 2006); Chris Maunder, ed., *The Origins of the Cult of the Virgin Mary* (London: Burns & Oats, 2008); Leslie Brubaker and Mary B. Cunningham, eds., *The Cult of the Mother of God in Byzantium: Texts and Images* (Aldershot: Ashgate, 2011); Leena Mari Peltomaa, Andreas Külzer, and Pauline Allen, eds., *Presbeia Theotokou: The Intercessory Role of Mary across Times and Places in Byzantium (Fourth–Ninth Century)* (Vienna: Österreichischen Akademie der Wissenschaften, 2015); Thomas Arentzen and Mary B. Cunningham, eds., *The Reception of the Virgin in Byzantium: Marian Narratives in Texts and Images* (Cambridge: Cambridge University Press, 2019).

parallel systematization of both visual and textual material.[2] Paradoxically, scholars still debate whether the figure of Mary acquired importance and a certain independence in early Christian artwork right from the start or whether she was for a long time conditioned by and indissolubly linked to the figure of her Son, receiving visual embodiment only due to the instrumental role she played in the history of salvation.[3]

However problematic these questions might be, it is generally accepted that at least by the fifth or sixth century the image of the Virgin assumed a more or less defined form in art as well as in theology, establishing itself as the central phenomenon of Christian culture: the Theotokos became universally venerated in all territories of the Byzantine Empire.[4] The period in question was characterized by the appearance of numerous churches dedicated to the Virgin and, most of all, by the presence of her images in

---

2. For the most recent discussion of early medieval Marian iconography and its development, see Arne Effenberger, "Maria als Vermittlerin und Fürbitterin: Zum Marienbild in der spätantiken und frühbyzantinischen Kunst Ägyptens," in Peltomaa, Külzer, and Allen, *Presbeia Theotokou*, 49–108. See also Giuseppa Z. Zanichelli's contribution to this volume and the forthcoming publication by Mary B. Cunningham on the development of the cult of Mary.

3. This is in agreement with the ideas expressed by a number of Christian writers, such as John of Damascus, for example, who in "An Exact Exposition of the Orthodox Faith," particularly in the chapter dedicated to veneration of icons, writes: "It is the same way with the Mother of God, too, for the honor paid her is referred to Him who was incarnate of her" (John of Damascus, *An Exact Exposition of the Orthodox Faith*, trans. Frederic H. Chase [Washington, DC: Catholic University of America Press, 1958], 372). As Richard M. Price puts it, "Mary mattered precisely as the Theotokos, the one who gave birth to Christ, God and man. She was not yet a theme in her own right" (Price, "The Theotokos and the Council of Ephesus," in Maunder, *Origins of the Cult*, 89–103, quote at 96, see also 98). In the same volume, Antonia Atanassova provides a somewhat different vision of the same events: "It was his [Cyril of Alexandria's] victory at Ephesus, partial as it was, that would become the crucial element in facilitating the development of formal Marian theology as integral to Christian tradition" (Atanassova, "Did Cyril of Alexandria Invent Mariology?," in Maunder, *Origins of the Cult*, 105–25, esp. 105). On the early stages of Marian devotion, see also Stephen J. Shoemaker, *Mary in Early Christian Faith and Devotion* (New Haven: Yale University Press, 2016); Maria Lidova, "Embodied Word: Telling the Story of Mary in Early Christian Art," in Arentzen and Cunningham, *The Reception of the Mother of God*, 17–43.

4. For a detailed discussion of this development, see Averil Cameron, "The Early Cult of the Virgin," in Vassilaki, *Mother of God*, 3–15.

monumental decorations and on icons, miniatures, ivories, textiles, small-scale objects, seals, and even jewelry.

A general overview of the surviving monuments demonstrates that, from the very beginning, the image of the Mother of God surrounded by angels, flanking her figure and acting as her heavenly suite, was quite popular and widely used in a vast variety of cultural and social contexts. Symptomatic in this respect is the presence of this iconography on Byzantine private seals, with the earliest examples going back to the seventh century.[5] When studying these small tokens of personal authority—miniature but very detailed relief compositions—scholars presume their dependence on similar representations in monumental art. Indeed, it is in precisely this iconography of Mary between the angels that the figure of the Mother of God came to occupy the concave space of apse niches in the great majority of Byzantine churches.[6] Situated right above the main altar, this composition would acquire the function of the principle liturgical icon and central prayer image of the ecclesiastical space.[7]

Notwithstanding its importance, however, this iconography, though endlessly cited and amply referred to in literature, has barely ever been the subject of specific research, which may be the result of the apparently unproblematic meaning of this omnipresent image.[8] Hence this study was

---

5. Georgios Zacos and Alexander Veglery, *Byzantine Lead Seals*, 2 vols. in 6 parts (Basel: Augustin, 1972–1985), 1.2:722 no. 1125, 747 no. 1189, 765 no. 1236A, 1.3:1668 no. 2948; Valentina Shandrovskaya, "Kompositsia 'Bogomater s arkhanghelami' na vizantiyskikh pechatyakh" [Composition of the 'Mother of God with Archangels' on Byzantine seals], in *Vizantija v kontekste mirovoj kul'tury*, Trudy Gosudarstvennogo Ėrmitaža 42 (St. Petersburg: State Hermitage Museum, 2008), 238–51.

6. Robin Cormack, "Mother of God in the Apse Mosaics," in Vassilaki, *Mother of God*, 91–105.

7. On the question of the image in the apse: Maria Andaloro and Serena Romano, "L'immagine nell'apside," in *Arte e Iconografia a Roma da Constantino a Cola di Rienzo*, ed. Maria Andaloro and Serena Romano (Milan: Jaca, 2000), 93–132; Beat Brenk, *The Apse, the Image and the Icon: An Historical Perspective of the Apse as a Space for Images* (Wiesbaden: Reichert, 2010).

8. For the works treating this iconographic type, see Georg Stuhlfauth, *Die Engel in der altchristlichen Kunst* (Freiburg: Mohr, 1897), 54; Christa Ihm, *Die Programme der christlichen Apsismalerei vom 4. Jahrhundert bis zur Mitte des 8. Jahrhunderts* (Wiesbaden: Steiner, 1960), 52–61; Carlo Bertelli, *La Madonna di Santa Maria in Trastevere: Storia, iconografia, stile di un dipinto romano dell'ottavo secolo* (Rome: n.p., 1961), 45–47; Franz Rademacher, *Die Regina Angelorum in der Kunst des frühen Mittelalters* (Düsseldorf: Schwann, 1972); J. Barclay Lloyd, "Mary, Queen of the Angels:

determined, first, by the necessity of addressing that point of view and, second, and most of all, by the need to reconsider the development of Mary between the angels iconography in the early Byzantine period, something that must be done in order to understand the message and initial content of this central Christian image of female exultation.

1. Mary between the Angels: The Development of the Iconography

The rich artistic evidence demonstrates that the theme of Mary between the angels could receive quite different iconographic solutions in early Byzantine art. Nevertheless, within the great variety of forms and kinds, it is possible to single out several principle patterns. These patterns are not rigid, nor are they determined by the image of the Virgin, who could be represented either seated on the throne or standing, with or without the child. They primarily concern the way the winged messengers are shown on either side of the Theotokos. In each case, these specific modes display a number of peculiar and easily discernible features that might indicate probable common genetic links, as well as initial differences in geographic provenance or typology of utilized sources.

An attempt to look at the origins of any Marian iconography inevitably brings us back to the mosaic cycle of the infancy of Christ that decorates the triumphal arch of Santa Maria Maggiore church in Rome, usually dated to the times of Pope Sixtus III (432–440 CE).[9] Mary appears in the surviving decorations of the fifth century four times: in the annunciation, the ado-

---

Byzantine and Roman Images of the Virgin and Child Enthroned with Attendant Angels," *MAJ* 5 (2001): 5–24.

9. The church of Santa Maria Maggiore is one of the most discussed monuments in scholarly literature due to its unique character, early date, and, of course, the surviving fifth-century cycle, in which the image of the Mother of God acquires great significance for the first time. For one of the earliest thorough accounts of the program, see D. V. Ajnalov, "Mozaiki IV i V vekov: Issledovania v oblasti ikonographii i stilia drevnekhristianskogo iskusstva," *JMNP* 299 (1895): 94–155. For an overview of the existing historiography with a selection of the principal readings of the early Christian decoration of Santa Maria Maggiore, see Maria Raffaella Menna, "I mosaici della basilica di Santa Maria Maggiore," in *L'orizzonte tardoantico e le nuove immagini, 312–468*, vol. 1 of *La Pittura Medievale a Roma*, ed. Maria Andaloro (Rome: Jaca, 2006), 306–46. In very recent years, however, the program of imagery has once again become the focus of particular scholarly attention, with a series of articles and lengthy or abridged discussions in several PhD dissertations, as well as an important mono-

ration of the Magi, the presentation, and in the composition portraying the holy family at the gates of a city, which is, as a rule, interpreted as the encounter with Aphrodisius, governor of Soutinen in Egypt.[10] Besides the well-known chronological proximity of this cycle to the council of Ephesus of 431, at which Mary was proclaimed Theotokos (the God-bearer), great interest has been raised by the unusually rich costume of the Virgin, especially in relation to the much more modest garments with *maphorion* (μαφόριον) in which she is dressed in later depictions.[11]

In all four cases Mary was depicted in the attire of a high-ranking Roman woman, in a white tunic and a golden *dalmatica*.[12] The solemn nature of her costume is accentuated by the use of golden glass tesserae that determine the importance of the figure; it visually highlights her representation within the pictorial narrative and the general coloristic palette

---

graph: Gerhard Steigerwald, *Die frühchristlichen Mosaiken des Triumphbogens von St. Maria Maggiore in Rom* (Regensburg: Schnell & Steiner, 2016).

10. The encounter with Aphrodisius is an extremely rare subject in the history of Christian art that derives from apocryphal accounts. It is mainly known from the Gospel by Pseudo-Matthew (22–24), but it can also be found in the so-called Arabic Infancy Gospel. This identification of the scene was first proposed by Kondakov in the French edition of his history of Byzantine art: Nikodim Pavlovich Kondakov, *Histoire de l'art byzantine: Considéré principalement dans les miniatures* (Paris: Librairie de l'Art, 1886–1891), 105. For the detailed historiography on the subject and an alternative, though even less convincing, interpretation, see Suzanne Spain, "'The Promised Blessing': The Iconography of the Mosaics of S. Maria Maggiore," *ArtBul* 61 (1979): esp. 519 n. 7. For the most recent interpretation of the scene as a meeting between Christ and Emperor Augustus, see Steigerwald, *Die frühchristlichen Mosaiken*, 96–111.

11. On the Council of Ephesus, see Basil Studer, "Il Concilio di Efeso (431) nella luce della dottrina mariana di Cirillo di Alessandria," in *La mariologia nella catechesi dei Padri (età postnicena)* (Rome: Libreria Ateneo Salesiano, 1991), 49–67; John A. McGuckin, *St. Cyril of Alexandria and the Christological Controversy* (Crestwood, NY: Saint Vladimir's Seminary Press, 2004). On visual rendering of the figure of Mary in this decoration, see Maria Lidova, "The Imperial Theotokos: Revealing the Concept of Early Christian Imagery in Santa Maria Maggiore in Rome," *Conv.* 2 (2015): 60–81.

12. *Toga*, or *trabea picta*, according to Brenk; see Beat Brenk, *Die frühchristlichen Mosaiken in S. Maria Maggiore zu Rom* (Wiesbaden: Steiner, 1975), 50. Or *cyclas*, as was recently argued by Steigerwald; see Gerhard Steigerwald, "Die Rolle Mariens in den Triumphbogenmosaiken und in der Weiheinschrift der Basilika St. Maria Maggiore in Rom," *JAC* 51 (2008): 140. For a detailed discussion of this type of costume characteristic of a number of late antique female representations, see Kathrin Schade, *Frauen in der Spätantike—Status und Repräsentation: Eine Untersuchung zur römischen und frühbyzantinischen Bildniskunst* (Mainz: von Zabern, 2003), 107–12.

of the triumphal arch. The Virgin is the only one among the figures of the infancy cycle to be honored by precious sparkling robes, which not only refer clearly to the sacred/heavenly dimension of the golden background but also transmit a message of both divine and earthly royal power.

Another characteristic of the cycle that has attracted the particular attention of scholars is the presence of angels that always accompany the figure of Christ and his Mother on the triumphal arch of Santa Maria Maggiore. The appearance of such a heavenly retinue is quite unusual, as the angelic figures visually become participants engaged in the context of the scenes, on a par with the main protagonists, and assume particular importance in the narrative of the whole program. They stand beside the throne of the Virgin at the moment of the annunciation, while a further winged messenger descends from heaven, greeting Mary with the divine news of God's incarnation.[13] The composition of the adoration below, usually considered to be the most enigmatic scene of the whole cycle, is centered around the figure of the Christ child seated on an enormous and luxurious throne. Here the angels are visible behind the high back of the throne, looking at the star above, in this case, they are, clearly, more associated with Jesus himself than with Mary, seated on his right. In two other instances, dedicated to the encounters with Symeon at the temple and with Aphrodisius at the gates of Soutinen, the unearthly beings either follow or symmetrically flank the Mother of God and her Son, visually acting as their guards and courtly suite (fig. 1).

In the fifth-century decoration of the Roman basilica, the angels are represented standing full-length, almost frontally, wearing white tunics and *pallia*, and they are in most cases performing the gesture of *acclamatio*. Their attire and slightly larger proportions in relation to other figures, as well as their placement at some distance from the Virgin, create a visual impression of their functional role as official attendants silently accompanying the holy family.

Apparently this tradition and the desire to reproduce as many as four angels in the bodiless escort of the Virgin continues in the well-known composition of the Basilica of Sant'Apollinare Nuovo in Ravenna, which is

---

13. On the annunciation scene and its significance in this decoration, see G. de Spirito, "L'Annonciation de Sainte-Marie-Majeure: Image apocryphe?," *Apocrypha* 7 (1996): 273–92; Steigerwald, *Die frühchristlichen Mosaiken*, 33–52. See also the general discussion of this iconography in: Maria Lidova, "XAIPE MAPIA: Annunciation Imagery in the Making," *IKON* 10 (2017): 45–62.

Fig. 1. Rome, Santa Maria Maggiore, the decoration of the arch, right side. The presentation to the temple and encounter with Aphrodisius (?). Photograph by Maria Lidova.

often cited in connection with the fifth-century Roman cycle (fig. 2).[14] The early sixth-century scene, placed at the far eastern edge of the northern side of the nave, represents the Virgin enthroned with the Christ child and four heavenly beings that symmetrically frame the Mother of God.[15] The massive, winged figures beside Mary not only accentuate the importance of the two central figures but also mirror a similar composition across the nave, in which Jesus is rendered as an emperor on the throne also flanked by four angels. The four spiritual beings visually perform the role

---

14. E. Penni Iacco, *La basilica di St. Apollinare Nuovo di Ravenna attraverso i secoli* (Bologna: Ante quem, 2004); Deborah Deliyannis, *Ravenna in Late Antiquity* (Cambridge: Cambridge University Press, 2010), 146–74.

15. Many scholars assumed that the image could reproduce the composition of the Virgin enthroned commissioned by Emperor Leo I for the Blachernae Church in Constantinople; see Henri Stern, "Sur les influences byzantines dans les mosaïques ravennates du début du 6e siècle," in *Settimane di studi del Centro Italiano di Studi sull'Alto Medioevo* (Spoleto: CISAM, 1962), 9:526, 532; Friedrich Wilhelm Deichmann, *Kommentar*, vol. 2.1 of *Ravenna: Hauptstadt des spätantiken Abendlandes: Geschichte und Monumente* (Wiesbaden: Steiner, 1974), 148; Raffaella Ravenna Farioli Campanati, "Costantinopoli: Aspetti topografico-monumentali e iconografici," *Storia di Ravenna* 2.2 (1992): 147–48, n. 80; 137; 144. The question is purely hypothetical, however, and one may not speculate if the presence of the angels could have been determined by the same conjectural prototype.

Fig. 2. Ravenna, Sant'Apollinare Nuovo, The Mother of God enthroned flanked by four angels. Photograph by Maria Lidova.

of mediators between the Virgin and a long line of human figures along the nave; these figures assume the form of holy virgins and female martyrs preceded by the three Magi, carrying the gifts, after the modifications of the middle of the sixth century in this part of the program.[16] Taking into account the fact that Christ presides over the procession of male saints on the other side of the nave, the image of Mary here clearly serves as an exemplum and the most perfect embodiment of female sainthood.

Although the angelic figures in the mosaic program of Sant'Apollinare Nuovo suffered significantly from heavy restorations in the nineteenth century, the characteristically massive stature of the heavenly guards, as well as the nature of their original attire, seems to be faithfully reproduced. The latter is worth noticing, as it not only bears evident similarity to the Roman, white, toga-like robes of the angels in Santa Maria Maggiore but also clearly coincides with the garment of the Christ child on the lap of the Virgin. This might indicate the artist's intention to show these

---

16. On the modifications, see Giuseppe Bovini, "Antichi rifacimenti nei mosaici di S. Apollinare Nuovo a Ravenna," *CARB* 13 (1966): 51–81; Arthur Urbano, "Donation, Dedication, and *Damnatio Memoriae*: The Catholic Reconciliation of Ravenna and the Church of Sant'Apollinare," *JECS* 13 (2005): 77–110.

celestial beings and Jesus as having the same divine, immaterial nature in this scene.[17]

Angels that frame the figure of the Virgin in strictly frontal positions—"stiff and motionless," using Henry Maguire's terms—would become a constant leitmotif in later Byzantine art.[18] The mosaic decoration of the amphitheater chapel in Dürres (sixth to eighth century) serves as a good example. The heavenly beings are depicted in sumptuous courtly costumes, consisting of tunics and *paludamenta* fixed by fibulae on their shoulders; they hold staffs in their left hands with the palms of the right hands open before the chest.[19] They appear here in the full-fledged attire of royal guards at the side of the Virgin, who is represented without the child but wearing the regalia of a Byzantine empress (fig. 3). It may even be possible to see an echo of this early Byzantine mode of angelic representation in two other significant monuments, both related to the particular veneration that the images of the Mother of God regained after the end of the iconoclastic controversy. An evident parallel to the figure of the Virgin flanked by four angels, two on each side, is found in the decoration of the apse and the bema in the Church of the Dormition in Nicaea

---

17. For similar considerations, see: Liz James, "Matters of Materiality in Byzantium: The Archangel Gabriel in Hagia Sophia, Constantinople," *Journal of Art History* 86 (2017): 145–57, esp. 151, 154.

18. Henry Maguire, "Style and Ideology in Byzantine Imperial Art," *Gesta* 28 (1989): 223.

19. Maria Andaloro, "I mosaici parietali di Durazzo e dell'origine costantinopolitana del tema iconografico di Maria Regina," in *Studien zur spätantiken und byzantinischen Kunst: Festschrift Friedrich Wilhelm Deichmann*, ed. Otto Feld (Bonn: Habelt, 1986), 3:103–12; Dhorka Dhamo, "Les mosaïques paléochrétiennes en Albanie," *CARB* 40 (1993): 491–504; Reshat Gega, "L'architecture des monastères, byzantins et postbyzantins en Albanie," *CARB* 40 (1993): 505–25; Heide Buschhausen and Helmut Buschhausen, "Durazzo und die Anfänge des Christentums in Albanien," in *Steine Sprechen*, ZÖGDO 120 (Wien: Öster, 2001); Kim Bowes and Afri Hoti, "An Amphitheater and Its Afterlives: Survey and Excavation in the Dürres Amphitheatre," *JRA* 16 (2003): 381–94; Kim Bowes and John Mitchell, "The Main Chapel of the Durres Amphitheater: Decoration and Chronology," *MEFRA* 121 (2009): 569–95 (in this paper, the authors suggest that the mosaics should be dated later, to the ninth to eleventh century); Galina Fingarova, "Mary as an Intercessory in the Decoration of the Chapel in Durrës, Albania," in Peltomaa, Külzer, and Allen, *Presbeia Theotokou*, 203–18; Elisabetta Neri, Bernard Gratuze, and Nadine Schibille, "Dating the Mosaics of the Durres Amphitheater through Interdisciplinary Analysis," *JCH* 28 (2017) (supporting the early sixth-to-eighth century date).

Fig. 3. Durres, chapel in the amphitheater, Maria Regina between the angels. Photograph by Maria Lidova.

(fig. 4).²⁰ The winged attendants, wearing very rich garments with wide imperial *lōros* (λῶρος) bands and holding standards with the Trisagion, were placed frontally at the sides of the bema and identified by captions as Principalities, Virtues, Dominations, and Powers. Unfortunately, the monument does not survive today, as the church was destroyed in 1922; its decoration is known exclusively from black-and-white photographic reproductions taken not long before that date.

There is a great debate as to whether the church was decorated in the seventh century or whether it is an example of artistic activity in the region during the period of iconoclasm, an opinion that seems to find more and more supporters in recent scholarship.²¹ In this connection, several significant modifications, undertaken in the mosaic decoration of

---

20. On the angels in this program and further detailed bibliography, see Glenn Peers, *Subtle Bodies: Representing Angels in Byzantium* (Berkeley: University of California Press, 2001), 42–43, 82–88.

21. Marie-France Auzépy, "Liturgie et art sous les Isauriens: À propos de la Dormition de Nicée," in *Le saint, le moine et le paysan: Mélanges d'histoire byzantine offerts*

Fig. 4. Nicaea, Church of the Dormition, the Mother of God in the apse and angels in the bema. Source: P. Underwood, "The Evidence of Restorations in the Sanctuary Mosaics of the Church of the Dormition at Nicaea," *DOP* 13 (1959): fig. 3,7.

the sanctuary and clearly discernible even on the early twentieth-century photographs, leave room for varying interpretations.[22] The only clear fact is that at some point, most probably in the eighth century, a previous representation of the cross in the conch was replaced by the figure of the standing Virgin with the Christ child. However different their views might be, all scholars agree that even if the Virgin was not original and the heavenly beings predate it, the image of the Theotokos fits harmoniously into the preexisting program and would easily find theological substantiation and validity within that setting, regardless of when it was made.

Another great monument that continues the tradition of portraying the Mother of God with standing angelic figures on either side is the famous decoration of the altar space in the main church of the Byzantine

---

à Michel Kaplan, ed. Olivier Delouis, Sophie Métivier, and Paule Pagès (Paris: Sorbonne, 2016), 29–58.

22. Paul A. Underwood, "The Evidence of Restorations in the Sanctuary Mosaics of the Church of the Dormition at Nicaea," *DOP* 13 (1959): 235–43; Charles Barber, "The Koimesis Church, Nicaea: The Limits of Representation on the Eve of Iconoclasm," *JÖB* 41 (1991): 43–60; Barber, "Theotokos and Logos: The Interpretation and Reinterpretation of the Sanctuary Programme of the Koimesis Church, Nicaea," in Vassilaki, *Images of the Mother of God*, 51–59.

Empire—the Hagia Sophia in Constantinople (mid-ninth century).[23] In this case, the number of winged guards is limited to two instead of four, but their frontal poses, their solemn posture, and their elevated rank—transmitted through sumptuous garments and through the insignia of court officials—indicate that the same model could have been taken as the basis for this decoration. This hints at the idea of the restoration of the cult of icons and of the Theotokos.[24]

In both these complexes, the angelic figures do not flank the image of the Mother of God but are shifted to the sides of the bema space. Nevertheless, one may argue that the initial idea of their role and function as heavenly guards was maintained here. Hence, for a viewer, their presence was still strongly linked to the Virgin placed in the very center of the conch. Through the separation of the figures, the early Byzantine composition acquired additional spatial connotations as it enclosed the area of the sanctuary and assumed an outward orientation. This outward posture granted a more complex interaction with the ecclesiastics officiating at the altar and the congregation standing in the nave, as well as with other narrative compositions decorating the walls of the church.

A quite different rendering of angelic figures can be found on numerous Byzantine artworks from late antiquity to the Palaiologan period. The most characteristic features of this type consist of reverential poses of inclined figures, represented holding gifts (diadems or golden circular

---

23. Cyril Mango and Ernest J. W. Hawkins, "The Apse Mosaics of St. Sophia at Istanbul: Report on Work Carried Out in 1964," *DOP* 19 (1965): 115–51; Mango, "St. Michael and Attis," *DCAE* 12 (1984–1986): 39–45; Nikolas Oikonomidès, "Some Remarks on the Apse Mosaics of St. Sophia," *DOP* 39 (1985): 111–15 (suggesting an eighth-century dating); Robin Cormack, "The Mother of God in the Mosaics of Hagia Sophia at Constantinople," in Vassilaki, *Mother of God*, 111–12; James, "Matters of Materiality."

24. The monumental ninth-century program of the conch might not be the earliest representation of the Theotokos with angels in the main church of the empire. Attesting to that, among others, is the reference by Paul the Silentiary that describes four silver disks that once decorated the interior of Hagia Sophia Church. Three of them represented Christ, each time flanked either by angels, apostles, or prophets. The last *clipeus* was described by the sixth-century author as bearing the image of the Virgin. Considering the composition of the other three disks, it becomes probable that a similar setting was used for this representation, and angels appear to be the most suitable candidates for the attendants at the sides of the Mother of God; see Bertelli, *Madonna di Santa Maria in Trastevere*, 46–47; Cormack, "Mother of God in the Mosaics of Hagia Sophia," 108.

plates) or simply with their open hands raised as they turn toward the center and address the Mother of God.²⁵ The direction of the winged attendants, depicted as if from the side, and their particular engagement and active interaction with the Virgin became the most distinctive features of this type. It is this particular mode that distinguishes one of the earliest known representations of the Mother of God: the relief scene on the side of the silver reliquary of Nazarius in Milan, dating to the fourth century and thus predating the mosaic decoration of Santa Maria Maggiore in Rome (fig. 5).²⁶

Fig. 5. Milan, Diocesan Museum, silver reliquary of St. Nazarius. Mother of God enthroned with the Christ Child in her lap and attendants (angels?) at the sides. Photograph by Maria Lidova.

---

25. According to some scholars, this scheme most probably derives from the widely known composition of the *aurum coronarium*. This iconography was mainly used in Roman art to render the nuanced interrelation between the ruler and conquered peoples or vassals. Later on, it must have reproduced the real ceremonies of gift giving and the distribution of gold that formed an integral part of Byzantine imperial ceremonies. The popularity of this scene in the Eastern Roman Empire is best attested by the famous reliefs decorating the base of the obelisk of Theodosius I in the Hippodrome of Constantinople. See Theodor Klauser, "Aurum Coronarium," *MDAI* 59 (1944): 129–53; Roland Delmaire, *Largesses sacrées et res privata: L'aerarium impérial et son administration du IVᵉ au VIᵉ siècle* (Rome: École française de Rome, 1989), 377–400, esp. n. 1; Simon Hornblower and Antony Spawforth, eds., *The Oxford Classical Dictionary* (Oxford: Oxford University Press, 1996), 223.

26. See the following essays in Gemma Sena Chiesa, ed., *Il Tesoro di San Nazaro: Antichi argenti liturgici dalla basilica di San Nazaro al Museo Diocesano di Milano* (Milan: Silvana, 2009): Marco Navoni, "Per una storia della capsella argentea: Da Ambrogio a Carlo Borromeo fino ai nostri giorni," 17–26; Gemma Sena Chiesa, "La capsella e il suo decoro: Il linguaggio delle immagini fra devozione cristiana e tradizione imperiale," 27–54; Fabrizio Slavazzi, "La capsella di San Nazaro: Indagini sull'apparato figurativo," 55–62; and Elisabetta Gagetti, "Bibliografia storica. La fortuna nei secoli di un oggetto tra devozione e arte," 63–72.

This type of composition with angels offering gifts, addressing Christ and the Virgin Mary, receives further development in subsequent centuries. Beyond doubt, one of the most interesting early Byzantine examples of this kind survives on the palimpsest wall of Church of Santa Maria Antiqua and seems to go back to the first third of the sixth century (fig. 6).[27] The Virgin is represented as Maria Regina, vested in ceremonial attire on a sumptuous, lyre-backed throne. She wears a crown on top of a richly decorated cap, while a gorgeous *lōros*, a royal band, runs around her purple dress. The Christ child is seated in her lap while two angels at her sides, winged and wearing shining white robes, slightly bend toward her and offer her diadems. Only one, to the Virgin's left, is still preserved; the other was destroyed during the transformation of the original rectangular niche into a semicircular apse, most probably in the second half of the sixth century.

Fig. 6: Rome, Santa Maria Antiqua, "palimpsest" wall, reconstruction of the image of Maria Regina with angels. Source: W. de Grüneisen, *Sainte Marie Antique* (Rome: Breitschneider, 1911), 138, fig. 105.

---

27. Josef Wilpert, *Die römischen Mosaiken und Malereien der kirchlichen Bauten vom IV.-XIII. Jahrhundert*, 4 vols. (Freiburg: Herder, 1916), 2:658–60; 4:tables 133–34; Wladimir Grüneisen, *Sainte Marie Antique* (Rome: Bretschneider, 1911), 136–39; Nikodim Pavlovich Kondakov, *Ikonografia Bogomateri* (Saint Petersburg: Impera¬torskaia akademia nauk, 1914), 1:270, 276–80; Gerhard Steigerwald, "Das Königtum Mariens in Literatur und Kunst der ersten sechs Jahrhunderte" (PhD diss., Universität Freiburg, 1965), 185–93; Per Jonas Nordhagen, "The Earliest Decorations in Santa Maria Antiqua and Their Date," *AAAHP* 1 (1962): 56–57. As a rule, this mural is generally dated to the first half of the sixth century; a number of stylistic and iconographic peculiarities, however, as well as the history and sequence of power in early medieval Rome, permit this image to be attributed, in my view, to the time of Ostrogothic presence in Rome (i.e., the first third of the sixth century); for this, see Eva Tea, *La Basilica di Santa Maria Antiqua* (Milan: Pubblicazioni dell'Università Cattolica, 1937), 37, 171–73; Maria Lidova, "*Maria Regina* on the 'Palimpsest Wall' in S. Maria Antiqua Church in Rome: Historical Context and Imperial Connotations of the Early Byzantine Image," *Iconographica* 16 (2017): 9–25.

Another variation of this pattern, or possibly its equivalent, made the ceremonial nature of the composition more explicit, with angels represented holding censers and performing the role of deacons as they officiated before God's presence as if before the altar. These elements strengthened the scene's connotations of heavenly service and acquired particular liturgical meaning, in which the celestial beings, besides echoing the real church celebrations, served the purpose of unveiling the divine and sacred nature of the figures in the center. One of the most prominent examples of this type comes from Egypt and is found on a mural, decorating the apse of the XXVIII Chapel in Bawīt, in which angels are symptomatically indicated by the captions as ΑΓΓΕΛΟΣ ΘΕΟΥ and ΑΓΓΕΛΟΣ ΚΥΡΙΟΥ.[28] These names differ from more common identifications of the angels in Byzantium. Several surviving representations of the Virgin between the angels, such as the Cleveland tapestry (sixth century), the mosaic decoration in the apse of Gelati cathedral (1125–130) in Georgia, the church of the Mavriotissa in Kastoria (late twelfth century), are also accompanied by inscriptions. The Greek captions used in these monuments indicate that generally, though not exclusively, the two heavenly messengers were associated in Byzantium with the archangels Michael and Gabriel.

It seems legitimate to assume that through the spread of similar patterns, all subsequent compositions with angels represented from the side, either in inclined poses or making a step toward the center, continued the tradition set up in the early Byzantine period. This kind of dynamic interaction created a frozen moment in the ceremonial performance or the celestial liturgy, in which heavenly messengers presented Christ and his Mother to the viewer, fulfilling the intermediary link between worshippers and the deity. In these compositions, the concrete gifts are often missing or are substituted by the typical attributes of orb and scepter, as, for example, in the apse of the church of the Panaghia Angeloktistos in Cyprus (seventh century). The basic features, however, remain recognizable throughout the Byzantine period, as in the twelfth-century decorations at Kurbinovo in Macedonia and many others.

A possible connection of this iconography to the adoration of the Magi scenes has been amply discussed, as has a reference to the *aurum coronarium*. The offering of gifts to the newborn King received different interpretations in early Byzantine art. The most common was a horizontal development of

---

28. Ihm, *Die Programme*, 61, 203.

the composition in which the sages were standing in a row, one after the other, before the Virgin seated on the throne represented in profile. At quite an early stage, however, an alternative treatment of the theme became more prominent, with the figure of the Virgin put in the center and attendants shown symmetrically flanking Mary's throne on both sides.[29] The mural from the catacomb of Peter and Marcellinus in Rome (fourth century) is a good example of this solution, as even the number of Magi in this case is limited to two.[30]

Did the origin of this composition develop from the lost scene of the adoration, known to have decorated the façade of the Church of the Nativity in Bethlehem?[31] The importance of the site and the popularity of the scene in early Christian artworks, including pilgrims' tokens clearly associated with Palestine, have been seen as indicating possible genetic links between the enthroned Virgin and its placement in the apse and the decoration of the Bethlehem church.[32]

Several ivories, murals, and, most importantly, early Byzantine icons, however, bear a different type of composition of Mary between the angels. The heavenly beings in these cases appear behind the back of the throne, either flying above or standing in characteristic swirling poses, which transmit the idea of an inner dynamic movement and endow the scene with characteristic spatial—sometimes spherical—organization. The angels' immateriality is rendered through the instability of their postures.

---

29. Lloyd, "Mary, Queen of the Angels," 6.

30. Kondakov, *Ikonografia Bogomateri*, 30–34; Ihm, *Die Programme*, 52; Johannes G. Deckers, Hans Reinhard Seeliger, and Gabriele Mietke, *Die Katakombe "Santi Marcellino e Pietro": Repertorium der Malereien* (Vatican City: PIAC, 1987); Andaloro, *Orizzonte tardoantico*, 136–37; Jeffrey Spier, ed., *Picturing the Bible: The Earliest Christian Art* (New Haven: Yale University Press, 2007), 181, fig. 10 A–C: "Catacomb of Marcellinus and Peter: Frescoes from the 'Crypt of the Virgin.'"

31. Joseph A. Munitiz et al., *The Letter of the Three Patriarchs to the Emperor Theophilos and Related Texts*, (Camberley: Porphyrogenitus, 1997), 42. See also Dmitri V. Ainalov, *The Hellenistic Origins of Byzantine Art* (New Brunswick: Rutgers University Press, 1961), 233–37; André Grabar, *Martyrium: Recherches sur le culte des reliques et l'art chrétien antique*, 2 vols. (Paris: Collège de France, 1946), 2:163; Ihm, *Die Programme*, 52; Gerard A. Wellen, Theotokos: *Eine ikonographische Abhandlung über das Gottesmutterbild in frühchristlicher Zeit* (Utrecht: Het Spectrum, 1961), 147.

32. Maria Lidova, "The Adoration of the Magi: From Iconic Space to Icon in Space," in *Icons of Space: Studies in Hierotopy and Iconography; A Tribute to Alexei Lidov for His 60th Birthday* (forthcoming).

They are depicted bodiless, transparent, and almost flying or weightless, as if hanging in the air—the effect often created by the fact that their lower bodies are hidden behind the throne. A characteristic twist of the figures, in some cases discordant with the vertical axes and more in tune with the lyre-shaped back of the throne, or additional diagonal or irregular lines and inner directions, enrich the composition and often contrast with the rigid frontality and immobility of the Mother of God.

The most famous example of this kind is the Sinai icon of the Virgin flanked by two warrior saints (fig. 7).[33] The angels visible behind the throne differ significantly from other figures on the icon. The light colors of their robes and their dynamic poses make their bodies look almost transparent and immaterial. They direct their gazes upward to a segment of heaven that opens to let the divine light descend from the hand of God to Mary seated on the throne. This type of representation resembles a sixth-century ampulla from the Holy Land, now in Monza.[34] The pilgrim token bears depictions of the adoration of the Magi and the annunciation to the shepherds that respectively frame the Virgin enthroned, while two angels are represented flying behind the back of the throne. They flank the central figures and simultaneously perform the role of divine messengers to the kings and shepherds. At the same time, they stand for the heavenly realm, attested also by the star, placed strictly on the same vertical axis with the figures of Mary and the child.

A complex contrapposto twist of the angels, with the upper and lower parts of the body and the torso being oriented in opposite directions, marks numerous artworks of the early Byzantine period. This is seen in the icon of Maria Regina in the Basilica of Santa Maria in Trastevere in Rome (fig. 8), the mosaic representation of the Virgin in the northern aisle

---

33. Ernst Kitzinger, "Byzantine Art in the Period between Justinian and Iconoclasm," in *Berichte zum XI. Internationale Byzantinischen-Kongress* (Munich: Beck, 1958), 47; Kurt Weitzmann, *From the Sixth to the Tenth Century*, vol. 1 of *The Monastery of Saint Catherine at Mount Sinai: The Icons* (Princeton: Princeton University Press, 1976), 18–21 (B. 3); Peers, *Subtle Bodies*, 49–52; Robin Cormack, "Icon of the Virgin and Child between Archangels Accompanied by Two Saints," in Vassilaki, *Mother of God*, 262–63; Cormack, "The Eyes of the Virgin," in Vassilaki, *Images of the Mother of God*, 167–73.

34. André Grabar, *Ampoules de Terre Sainte (Monza-Bobbio)* (Paris: Klincksieck, 1958); Graziano Alfredo Vergani, "Ampolla-reliquiario con Adorazione del Bambino e Ascensione," in *La rivoluzione dell'immagine: Arte paleocristiana tra Roma e Bisanzio*, ed. Fabrizio Bisconti and Giovanni Gentili (Milan: Cinisello Balsamo, 2007), 202–3.

Fig. 7: Sinai, Monastery of Saint Catherine, icon of the Mother of God enthroned with saints. Photograph by Maria Lidova.

of Church of Saint Demetrius in Thessaloniki, the central plaques of ivory gospel covers, like the ones in Berlin and Paris (fig. 9), and in textiles, such as the great tapestry icon in Cleveland (fig. 10).[35] In the majority of these cases, the angels are represented in classical clothes of light whitish colors and holding scepters or orbs in one hand while keeping the open palm

---

35. On the Maria Regina icon, see Bertelli, *Madonna di Santa Maria in Trastevere*; Maria Andaloro, "La datazione della tavola di St. Maria in Trastevere," *RINASA* 19/20 (1972–1973): 139–215; Maria Lidova, "L'icona acheropita della Vergine di Santa Maria in Trastevere a Roma," in *Le arti a confronto con il sacro: Metodi di ricerca e nuove prospettive d'indagine interdisciplinare*, ed. Valentina Cantone and Silvia Fumian (Padova: Università degli Studi di Padova, 2009), 19–28; Lidova, "Empress, Virgin, *Ecclesia*: The Icon of Santa Maria in Trastevere in the Early Byzantine Context," *IKON* 9 (2016): 109–28. On the image in Thessaloniki, see Robin Cormack, *The Church of Saint Demetrios: The Watercolours and Drawings of W. S. George* (Thessaloniki: Municipality of Thessaloniki, 1985). On the ivory covers, see Christoph Stiegemann and Matthias Wemhoff, eds., "Diptychon mit thronendem Christus und thronender Maria mit Kind, No. X. 26," in *799: Kunst und Kultur der Karolingerzeit: Karl der Große und Papst Leo III in Paderborn*, 3 vols. (Mainz: P. von Zabern, 1999), 2:740–42 (with previous bibliography); John Lowden, "The Word Made Visible: The Exterior of the Early Christian Books as Visual Argument," in *The Early Christian Book*, ed. William E. Klingshirn and Linda Safran (Washington, DC: Catholic University of America Press, 2007), 13–47. On the tapestry icon in Cleveland, see Kurt Weitzmann, "Icon of the Virgin Enthroned, no. 477," in *Age of Spirituality: Late Antique and Early Christian Art, Third to Seventh Century* (New York: Metropolitan Museum, 1979), 532–33; Dorothy G. Shepherd, "An Icon of the Virgin," *BCM* 56.3 (1969): 90–120; Marie-Hélène Rutschowscaya, *Coptic Fabrics* (Paris: Biro, 1990), 134–35.

Fig. 8. Rome, Santa Maria in Trastevere, *Madonna della Clemenza*. Photograph by Maria Lidova.

Fig. 9. Berlin, Staatliche Museen zu Berlin, ivory diptych, Mother of God between the angels. Photograph by Maria Lidova.

Fig. 10. The Cleveland Museum of Art, tapestry, Mother of God between the angels. Photograph: The Cleveland Museum of Art (public domain).

of the other at chest level, creating in this mirrored gesture an additional bracket-like enclosure around the central figures.

The specificity of the curved, almost dancing, or slightly twisted posture of the angels in these works is so evident that it cannot be considered simply accidental. It would appear to indicate a characteristic artistic device often used by early medieval masters, and its popularity might suggest a particular prototype for the scheme, which is sometimes sought in Constantinople. Unfortunately, we do not know what the decoration of the Blachernae church, the principle Marian shrine of the city, looked like, although it is known to have included the scene of Mary between the angels.[36] It therefore remains extremely problematic to substantiate this as a possible origin, mainly because we are unable to reconstruct the missing intermediary links between different monuments, but also because the surviving visual material demonstrates an extremely wide range of forms and variations.

Finally, Mary appears flanked by angels in representations of a specific gospel event—the ascension of Christ into heaven. This composition is usually divided into two parts: the upper zone representing Christ surrounded by flying angels escorting him to the heavenly realms, the lower, earthly zone occupied by the apostles gathered around the Virgin, who is placed in the center. In this scene, Mary is regularly depicted flanked by two angels, which creates an effect of spatial interval, a kind of caesura, between the Virgin and the apostles. It is puzzling that the text of the gospel does not contain any indication or explanation of the presence of angels beside the Virgin, who is herself absent from the accounts of the ascension.[37] Their appearance must have been determined by the development of the iconography, by the homiletic tradition, and by the desire to emphasize the figure of Mary in order to grant her significance within the scene and to integrate her visually into the heavenly *apotheosis* of the celestial court above.[38]

---

36. Cyril Mango, *The Art of the Byzantine Empire, 312–1453: Sources and Documents* (Englewood Cliffs, NJ: Prentice-Hall, 1972), 34–35.

37. This lies behind Ally Kateusz's interpretation of the iconography as initially representing the ascension of Mary, with Christ depicted descending from heaven, and only subsequently being adopted for the image of the ascension of Christ: Kateusz, "Ascension of Christ or Ascension of Mary? Reconsidering a Popular Early Iconography," *JECS* 23 (2015): 273–303.

38. For some thoughts on this aspect, see Ioan Gotia, "L'Annunciazione/Incar-

The famous miniature in the sixth-century Rabbula Gospels is an outstanding example of this rendering. Interestingly, this image (Laurent. Plut. I. 56. fol. 13v) reunites several kinds of angelic representations discussed above, as pairs of angels had to be depicted three times in the scene (fig. 11).[39] First, they appear in the upper part, at the sides of the Savior holding the mandorla that frames his figure. Second, two more angels below offer golden diadems in their outstretched hands, as they prostrate themselves before the vision of Christ's ascension. Third, in the lower zone, winged attendants flank the Mother of God, as always in such instances actively communicating with the apostles, directing their attention to the theophany above. At the same time, these massive figures in white garments emphasize the importance of the Virgin within the group of Jesus's disciples. Performing a similar function as guards who both limit access to the divinity and also interact with approaching attendants, angels are represented in the apse of Eufrasius's church in Poreč (mid-sixth century) and in many other early Byzantine monumental decorations.[40]

The range of modes and treatments of Mary between the angels in early Byzantine art demonstrates its overwhelming popularity as well as its great variety. Significant differences and minor discrepancies in the iconography slightly alter the message conveyed by basically one and the same image. Hence on every occasion Marian compositions are endowed with subtle and more nuanced content, resulting in variations in emotional impact. As a consequence, in order to attempt an adequate reading of the scene, one has to approach various notions, texts, and ideas related to the Virgin that circulated widely at the time. In the end, these determined the understanding and spread of the theme of Mary between the angels in the early Byzantine period.

---

nazione come 'Porta della salvezza': Fondamenti teologici ed iconografici antichi," *SOC* 17 (2013): 73–166, esp. 87.

39. Carlo Cecchelli, Giuseppe Furlani, and Mario Salmi, eds., *The Rabbula Gospels: Facsimile Edition of the Miniatures of the Syriac Manuscript Plut. I,56 in the Medicaean-Laurentian Library* (Olten: Graf, 1959); Massimo Bernabò, ed., *Il tetravangelo di Rabbula: Firenze, Biblioteca Medicea Laurenziana, Plut. 1.56; L'illustrazione del nuovo testamento nella Siria del VI secolo* (Rome: Edizioni di storia e letteratura, 2008).

40. Henry Maguire and Ann Terry, *Dynamic Splendor: The Wall Mosaics in the Cathedral of Eufrasius at Poreč* (University Park: Pennsylvania State University Press, 2007).

Fig. 11. Florence, Biblioteca Medicea Laurenziana, Rabbula Gospels, Ascension of Christ (Laurent. Plut. I. 56. Fol. 13v). Photograph: Wikimedia Commons.

2. Mary between the Angels: The Concept behind the Image

The active presence of angels already in the fifth-century decoration of Santa Maria Maggiore, discussed in the previous section, inevitably raises questions and calls for explanation. First of all, it is important to understand whether and how such enrichment of the biblical account, unfolding in the mosaic registers of the arch, correlates with any textual tradition. Second, one must establish whether the appearance of angelic figures could have been determined by a motive unrelated to scriptural description, such as, for example, the necessity of conveying particular theological notions or the new status of the Virgin after the Council of Ephesus. A third alternative worth considering is that this iconographic solution could have been the result of artistic development and simple adaptation of an existing pagan or imperial visual repertoire for Christian use, a possibility that could find support in the numerous imperial connotations present in the cycle in general and in the princely figure of the Virgin in particular. Considering the fact that the pictorial cycle in Santa Maria Maggiore provides one of the first surviving instances of the Virgin Mary flanked by angelic figures in Christian monumental art, it might be seen as reflective of the early formative stages of this popular theme. Answers to these questions therefore acquire particular relevance for the general understanding of the whole subsequent artistic tradition.

Only partial justification for the angelic presence in Roman fifth-century mosaics can be found in religious texts usually associated with this imagery. As is well known, the pictorial cycles dedicated to the infancy of Christ and events before the nativity draw heavily on apocryphal sources.[41] This is due to the fact that the canonical narrative of Luke's Gospel, the only one in which Mary assumes particular importance, is not detailed or informative enough for the reconstruction of a coherent narrative of the life of the Virgin.[42] As a rule, scholars refer to two main apocryphal texts: the Gospel of Pseudo-Matthew (eighth to ninth century) and the Protevangelium of James (second century). The latter is not very helpful for the topic discussed here; the former, however, provides several interesting details. From chapter 6 of the Gospel of Pseudo-Matthew, we learn that while still at the temple and therefore before the incarnation, Mary was not only fed by angels but was also often seen in their presence: "She refreshed herself only with the food which she daily received from the hand of the angel.... The angels of God were often seen speaking with her, and they most diligently obeyed her" (Pseudo-Matt. 6 [ANF]). In connection with this text, it is worth noting that it contains a clear idea of reverence paid by heavenly beings to Mary even before she became the Mother of God. This attitude is significant, as it clearly relates with the way angels accompanying the Virgin are usually rendered in art.

The same text can also help to explain the angelic presence in the adoration scene of Santa Maria Maggiore. In recounting the arrival of the holy family in Bethlehem and their dwelling in the cave, the author writes: "And there she brought forth a son, and the angels surrounded Him when He was being born. And as soon as He was born, He stood upon His feet, and the angels adorned Him, saying: Glory to God in the highest, and on earth

---

41. On Marian and infancy cycles, see Jacqueline Lafontaine-Dosogne, "Iconography of the Cycle of the Infancy of Christ," in *The Kariye Djami*, ed. Paul A. Underwood, 4 vols. (London: Routledge, 1975), 4:163–241.

42. For general discussion, see J. K. Elliott, *The Apocryphal New Testament: A Collection of Apocryphal Christian Literature in an English Translation* (Oxford: Clarendon, 1994), 57–67; Savvas Agouridis, "The Virgin Mary in the Texts of the Gospels," in Vassilaki, *Mother of God*, 59–65; Ioannis Karavidopoulos, "On the Information Concerning the Virgin Mary Contained in the Apocryphal Gospels," in Vassilaki, *Mother of God*, 67–76; J. K. Elliott, "Mary in the Apocryphal New Testament," in Maunder, *Origins of the Cult*, 57–70.

peace to men of good will" (Pseudo-Matt. 13:2 [*ANF*]).⁴³ This event is further confirmed by another apocryphal text: the so-called Arabic, or Syriac, Gospel of the Infancy of the Savior (probably sixth century).⁴⁴ For some reason, this text is only sporadically discussed in connection with Byzantine Marian cycles. It provides a very interesting and much more detailed description of the story and is most likely based on the same sources as other infancy apocryphal writings. In relating the events at the cave of the nativity, the Syriac version also refers to the presence of angels at the site: "Then came shepherds; and when they had lighted a fire, and were rejoicing greatly, there appeared to them the hosts of heaven praising and celebrating God Most High" (4 [*ANF*]). The particular relevance of this source, however, is revealed in its account of the circumcision, which contains details unknown from other Apocrypha: "Then old Symeon saw Him shining like a pillar of light, when the Lady Mary, His virgin mother, rejoicing over Him, was carrying Him in her arms. And angels, praising Him, stood round Him in a circle, like life guards standing by a king" (6 [*ANF*]).

The mention of angels at the moment of the entrance of the holy family into the temple is striking and appears to complement the mosaic composition of the presentation scene in Santa Maria Maggiore, where two angels accompany the figure of Mary and a third is visible behind Joseph and the prophetess Anne. Besides attesting to the existence of heavenly creatures, seen by the penetrating gaze of Symeon, the angels are defined in the text as performing the role of guards to Christ, who is symptomatically compared here to an earthly king.

This passage of the Christian account is not only significant in itself and when analyzed within the broader textual tradition, but it appears especially relevant when compared with the extant artworks. It has been noted on numerous occasions that angels often acquired great importance in Byzantine art.⁴⁵ What interests us here is not so much the depictions of

---

43. This association is particularly interesting if compared with the liturgical interpretations of the spaces of a church. In the *Ecclesiastical History and Mystical Contemplation*, attributed to the patriarch Germanus, the apse "corresponds to the cave of Bethlehem where Christ was born," so the presence of angels assumes further justification; see Germanus of Constaninople, *On the Divine Liturgy*, trans. Paul Meyendorff (New York: Saint Vladimir's Seminary Press, 1999), 58–59; Cormack, "Mother of God in the Apse Mosaics," 95.

44. Elliott, *Apocryphal New Testament*, 100–107.

45. On angels and their representations, see Raffaele Garrucci, *Storia della arte cristiana nei primi otto secoli della chiesa*, 2 vols. (Prato: Guasti, 1877), 1:292–97; Stuhl-

narrative scenes in which angels perform specific roles—conditioned by the Old or New Testament—as heavenly messengers, mediators between God and humans, or transmitters of the divine will, but rather the inclusion of these higher beings in pictorial contexts that are not determined by any evident biblical account.

In addition to their solemn poses and their grand scale, the elevated status of angels, as we have seen, is regularly transmitted through various *insignia* that they hold in their hands, such as orbs and staffs, and sometimes through courtly costumes, such as the *divitision*, for example, often adorned by a luxurious imperial *lōros*.[46] As has been noted by Mango, however, "the imperial iconography of archangels never appears in narrative scenes" and manifests itself "only in static or 'iconic' images."[47] The early Christian roots of this tradition are attested in a famous passage of Severus of Antioch in which the sixth-century author criticizes the practice of depicting angels in imperial purple robes, "holding marks of universal power." Elsewhere he states that white vestments are more appropriate to them.[48] This passage interestingly correlates with the early,

---

fauth, *Die Engel in der altchristlichen Kunst*; Demetrios I. Pallas, "Himmelsmächte, Erzengel und Engel," in *Reallexicon zur Byzantinischen Kunst*, ed. Klaus Wessel and Marcell Restle (Stuttgart: Hiersemann, 1972), 3:14–119; Gerhard Podskalsky and A. Cutler, "Angel," in *The Oxford Dictionary of Byzantium*, ed. Alexander P. Kazhdan (Oxford: Oxford University Press, 1991), 97; Alexander P. Kazhdan and Nancy Patterson Ševčenko, "Archangel," in Kazhdan, *The Oxford Dictionary of Byzantium*, 155; M. Bussagli, *Storia degli angeli: Racconto di immagini e di idee* (Milan: Rusconi libri, 1995); Raffaella Giuliani, "Angelo," in *Temi di iconografia paleocristiana* (Vatican City: PIAC, 2000), 106–9; Marco Bussagli and Mario D'Onofrio, eds., *Le Ali di Dio: Messaggeri e guerrieri alati tra Oriente e Occidente* (Milan: Silvano, 2000); Peers, *Subtle Bodies*; Cecilia Proverbio, *La figura dell'angelo nella civiltà paleocristiana* (Todi: Tau Editrice, 2007); Elzbieta Jastrzebowska, "New Testament Angels in Early Christian Art: Origin and Sources," *MNEA* 8.49 (2009–2011): 153–64.

46. Colette Lamy-Lassalle, "Les archanges en costume impérial dans la peinture murale italienne," *Synthronon* (1968): 189–98; Mango, "St. Michael and Attis," 39–45; Maguire, "Style and Ideology"; Catherine Jolivet-Lévy, "Note sur la représéntation des archanges en costume impérial dans l'iconographie byzantine," *CahA* 46 (1998): 121–28.

47. Mango, "St. Michael and Attis," 44.

48. Giovan Domenico Mansi, *Sacrorum Conciliorum nova et amplissima collectio* (Paris: Welter, 1901–1927), 13:184; Mango, "St. Michael and Attis," 42–43; Peers, *Subtle Bodies*, 60, 74–75.

parallel tradition of representing angels in white tunics and *pallia* garments or in official, almost royal, attire.

The links between emperors and images of imperial power and angelic representations were very strong in Byzantium throughout its existence. Attempts to convey the courtly nature of heavenly guards in their mission to serve the almighty King and his Mother, for example in Santa Maria Maggiore, continue further in both Byzantine art and literature. Not only are angels systematically described and depicted in ways suitable for high imperial officials or military leaders, but vice versa: the emperors themselves are compared to angels in various panegyrics and official appellations.[49] The construction of the angelic image in terms of the reappropriation of official representations and the visual embodiment of real earthly power is particularly important. This indicates that from the very beginning, the image of the Mother of God between angels assumed characteristics of an official retinue, in which heavenly creatures found their closest visual and symbolic parallels with royal guards.

The assimilation was even more evident for medieval viewers since the iconography of Mary between the angels largely depended on compositions taken from purely secular contexts: the scheme behind it was primarily associated with official representations of consuls and emperors. Numerous ivory diptychs of the early Byzantine period attest to this, with consuls seated frontally and flanked by attendants, or allegories of Rome and Constantinople, or the clamorous example of the dedication page with Princess Anicia Juliana in the Vienna Dioscurides, made before 512 CE (cod. med. gr. 1. fol. 6v). Like images of the Virgin, the female ruler is represented enthroned, with two figures at her sides—not angels in this case but personifications (fig. 12).

Certain details in the garments of angels, and specifically the staves they are regularly depicted holding in their hands, justify their comparison and association with particular Byzantine imperial courtiers, such as *cubicularii*, *ostiarii*, or *silentarii*. The last rank is known to have been distinguished by the right to carry precious scepters (made of gold and decorated with pearls) as a distinctive attribute of the office.[50] It is

---

49. Maguire, "Style and Ideology," 222–24.

50. Kazhdan, *Oxford Dictionary of Byzantium*, 1896. The parallel between the *silentarii* and the angels was particularly emphasized by Gerhard Wolf in relation to the representation of heavenly beings on the icon from St. Maria in Trastevere; see Wolf, "Alexifarmaka: Aspetti del culto e della teoria delle immagini a Roma tra Bizan-

Fig. 12. Vienna Dioskurides, Princess Anicia Juliana (Cod. Med. Gr. 1, fol. 6v). Photograph: Wikimedia Commons.

particularly significant that several *silentarii* were appointed to serve and accompany the empress, which would have created a direct and emphatic parallel within court culture to representations of the Virgin escorted by celestial attendants. Another group of Byzantine courtiers has to be mentioned here, of course: eunuchs. They are known to have been regularly compared to angels in written accounts.[51] Eunuchs were largely engaged in the service of the imperial family and particularly in the care of imperial women.

Angels appear in Byzantine art in various contexts and situations and cannot be considered an exclusive characteristic of Marian iconography. Their presence beside Christ is quite logical and easily explained by the

---

zio e terra Santa nell'Alto Medioevo," in *Roma fra Oriente e Occidente: Settimane di Studio del Centro Italiano di Studi sull'Alto Medioevo XLIX*, 2 vols. (Spoleto: CISAM, 2002), 2:785.

51. Myrto Hatzaki, *Beauty and the Male Body in Byzantium: Perceptions and Representations in Art and Text* (Basingstoke: Palgrave Macmillan, 2009), 86–115; Maria Parani, "Look Like an Angel: The Attire of Eunuchs and Its Significance within the Context of Middle Byzantine Court Ceremonial," in *Court Ceremonies and Rituals of Power in Byzantium and the Medieval Mediterranean: Comparative Perspectives*, ed. Alexander Beihammer, Stavroula Constantinou, and Maria Parani (Leiden: Brill, 2013), 433–63; Georges Sidéris, "Sur l'origine des anges eunuques à Byzance," in *Constructing the Seventh Century*, ed. Constantin Zuckerman (Paris: Association des Amis du Centre d'histoire et civilisation de Byzance, 2013), 539–58.

religious texts, mainly by the Old Testament tradition and accounts of various epiphanies. This is important because the Christian understanding and interpretation of angels was deeply rooted in the preceding Jewish scriptural tradition.[52]

The appearance of heavenly beings at the side of God clearly functioned as a visual glorification of the divinity. It was partially predetermined by the Roman past and pertinent pagan iconographies of absolute triumphant victory and cosmic kingship, in which figures of victories and other winged creatures were abundantly used. Besides God himself, angels could also appear flanking the symbols of the cross, the ἑτοιμασία (throne of the second coming), and the altar.[53] Occasionally, they could be found flanking a particular saint, as in the case of Neophytos, who is represented between two angels in the chapel of his funerary cave and former place of seclusion (ἐγκλείστρα) at his monastery near Paphos, Cyprus (1182–1183). The mural clearly refers to the idea of the monk's sainthood and his prox-

---

52. See Lourdes Diego Barrado, "Le rôle des anges dans l'iconographie de la Rome byzantine," in *Les anges et les archanges dans l'art et la société à l'époque Préromane et Romane: Actes des XXIXe Journées Romanes de Cuixà, 8–16 juillet 1996*, CSMC 28 (Codalet: Association Culturelle de Cuixà, 1997), 133; Peers, *Subtle Bodies*, 13–60. For the problem of the adequate reconstruction of the early Christian understanding of angels and close links with the preceding scriptural tradition with a short overview of the related historiography, see Ellen Muehlberger, "Angels in the Religious Imagination of Late Antiquity" (PhD diss., Indiana University, 2008), 9–14. Muehlberger's dissertation provides more detailed discussion of these questions than her recent book, *Angels in Late Ancient Christianity* (New York: Oxford University Press, 2013). See also Garrucci, *Storia della arte cristiana*, n. 45.

53. The theme of angels flanking the altar is one of the central iconographies of the Byzantine world. An attentive analysis of the surviving monuments allows us to see the development of this theme from early examples, such as the mosaic decoration of Germigny-des-Prés (early ninth century), where the altar in question clearly alludes to the Old Testament ark of the covenant (Ann Freeman and Paul Meyvaert, "The Meaning of Theodulf's Apse Mosaic at Germigny-des-Prés," *Gesta* 40 [2001]: 125–39; Gillian Vallance Mackie, "Theodulf of Orléans and the Ark of the Covenant: A New Allegorical Interpretation at Germigny-des-Prés," *Racar* 32 [2007]: 45–58; Ivan Foletti, "Germigny-des-Prés, il Santo Sepolcro e la Gerusalemme celeste," *Conv.* 1 [2014]: 32–49), to the Middle Byzantine motif of angels standing beside the altar in the "communion of the apostles," a scene usually decorating the curved space of the apse. Archangels also regularly appear in Byzantine art flanking the sanctuary and decorating the iconostasis or framing the entrance to the church; see Georgi Gerov, "Angels—Entrance Guardians," *ZRVI* 46 (2009): 435–42.

imity to a heavenly being, attained through a pious earthly life.[54] Similar patterns were already in use in late antiquity for the representations of various saints, in particular Thecla and Simeon Stylites, both of whom are regularly portrayed accompanied by angels.[55]

Nevertheless, the overall analysis of the surviving artworks makes it absolutely clear that, with the exception of Christ, the Virgin is the only figure who is regularly and even primarily represented together with heavenly attendants. The question that arises is whether it is Mary who receives particular attention or the figure of the heavenly King who determines the official cortège. As Virgin and child usually appear indissolubly linked when depicted together, the issue is quite complicated. The iconographic development of this image, the fact that Jesus is absent from a number of such compositions, and certain literary sources, however, suggest that the theme of flanking angels possessed particular significance for the specific veneration of the Mother of God and acquired deep symbolic meaning for Christian viewers.[56]

---

54. Cyril Mango, "The Hermitage of St. Neophytos and Its Wall Paintings," *DOP* 20 (1966): 119–206. Interestingly, the idea that a perfect conduct of life can help one achieve a state similar to that of the angels is also present in Marian theology. In particular, this interpretation can be found in the works by Cyril of Jerusalem; see Cameron, "Early Cult of the Virgin," 7.

55. The Acts of Paul and Thecla provide the textual background for this kind of imagery; after describing Paul's appearance, the account states that "at one time he seemed like a man, at another time he seemed like an angel," suggesting that the parallel often drawn between holy men and the representations of the winged creatures must have strengthened this association (William Wright, *Apocryphal Acts of the Apostles* [London: Williams & Norgate, 1871], 2:237). See also John Chrysostom's eighth homily on Mathew, where he compares the numerous monks of the Egyptian desert to the "choirs of angels in human forms" (*Hom. Matt.* 2.2).

56. Attesting to this, for example, is a Coptic architrave of the early Byzantine period from the British Museum (EA1502), which carries an interesting inscription running in three rows. The sequence of text is interrupted by a shell-like palmette placed in the center of the upper line. Besides invoking the Holy Trinity at the beginning, the text goes on to address Michael, Mary, and Gabriel, in that order. Therefore, the names of two archangels both logically and visually flank the name Maria before the eyes of the reader, following what now seems to be the conventional if not archetypical notion of Mary between the angels. Symptomatically, the references to God, in terms of the Holy Trinity, occupying the primary position is somehow separated from the following tripartite structure, most of which fits the second (i.e., middle) row and in which the name of the Mother of God occupies the central position. On the whole,

In the Akathistos Hymn—one of the most important early Byzantine texts associated with the Virgin, generally attributed to Romanos Melodites but today often dated earlier—the reference to angels is made on several occasions.[57] The opening line of the first *ikos* (stanza) of this poetic glorification of the Theotokos contains a reference to the heavenly messenger of the annunciation. This creates the illusion that the hymn is an actualized dialogue between Mary and Gabriel and sets the pattern of multifarious acclamations of the Virgin, with "hail" or "rejoice" (χαῖρε). The epithets that follow are largely based on Old Testament figures whom Christians considered to be scriptural prefigurations of the Theotokos.

Interwoven with this poetic texture are several other instances that relate angels to gospel events, and more importantly to the Mother of God herself, proclaiming her to be the "depth invisible even to the eyes of angels," "miracle, much marveled of angels," one "who reflects the life of angels," and, finally, "most holy chariot of him who is above the cherubim, … most excellent abode of him who is above the seraphim."[58] The theme of angels features prominently also in the sixteenth kontakion: "All the orders of angels marveled at the great work of your incarnation; for they saw the God-inaccessible, as man, to all accessible, dwelling with us, and hearing from all: Halleluia." These epithets clearly indicate that it is the Virgin herself and not just her Son who is celebrated by the angels in the Akathistos Hymn.

The various pictorial contexts in which angels are used demonstrate that the addition of bodiless beings on either side of the central image, be it an altar or the figure of a saint, not only put particular emphasis on this representation but also underline the holiness of the motif and the superiority of the figure's divine nature within the heavenly hierarchies. Indeed, the idea of the Virgin, an earthly woman who became higher and more holy than the angels, superior to all heavenly beings and elevated

---

the rendering is very similar to the lintel with names of archangels and the Virgin on the tapestry at Cleveland (see online at https://tinyurl.com/SBL6011b).

57. Vasiliki Limberis, *Divine Heiress: The Virgin Mary and the Creation of Christian Constantinople* (London: Routledge, 1994); Luigi Gambero, *Mary and the Fathers of the Church: The Blessed Virgin Mary in Patristic Thought* (San Francisco: Ignatius, 1999); Ermanno M. Toniolo, *Akathistos: Saggi di critica e di teologia* (Rome: Centro di cultura mariana, 2000); Leena Mari Peltomaa, *The Image of the Virgin Mary in the Akathistos Hymn*, MilM 35 (Leiden: Brill, 2001).

58. For the Greek text and parallel translation, see Peltomaa, *The Image of the Virgin*, 1.

in the celestial court and in a position second only to God, is one of the principal concepts of Christian thought and a constant motif in liturgical prayers, hymns, homilies, and patristic writings. Suffice it to recall the lines of the very popular eastern Christian Marian prayer forming part of John Chrysostom's liturgy (fourth century): "More honorable than the cherubim, and beyond compare more glorious than the seraphim." As a consequence, this idea was systematically evoked in the minds of worshippers and at the same time visually attested in artistic representations of the Mother of God flanked by the angels.

In this connection, one has to question whether or not the composition of Mary between the angels would have had particular relevance for female members of the congregation. The involvement of women, especially empresses, in the development and formation of the early cult of the Virgin guaranteed a nuanced and engaging way for female worshippers to interact with representations of the Theotokos.[59] As a model of conduct and a didactic example, the figure of Mary, realized in artworks, not only served as a source of inspiration but also embodied the idea of the absolute spiritual triumph of female holiness, surpassing that of celestial beings.[60]

Due to her earthly origin, however, Mary always maintained an intermediary position in the heavenly realms, becoming an indispensable intercessor on behalf of humans before the Lord. Representations of the Mother of God between angels would therefore testify to her dwelling in paradise as well as to her role as Queen of Heaven and as divine authority for the celestial army. Last but not least, the bodiless guards would acquire particular significance for the central theme related to the Virgin: the incarnation.[61] The presence of angels would become fundamental for the transmission of the idea of two natures of Christ, whose humanity

---

59. Kate Cooper, "Empress and Theotokos: Gender and Patronage in the Christological Controversy," in Swanson, *Church and Mary*, 39–51; Jean-Michel Spieser, "Impératrices romaines et chrétiennes," *TM* 14 (2002): 593–604; Liz James, "The Empress and the Virgin in Early Byzantine Piety, Authority and Devotion," in Vassilaki, *Images of the Mother of God*, 145–52.

60. On the problem of female responses to images and their complex interactions with the figure of the Virgin in Byzantium, see Judith Herrin, *Unrivalled Influence: Women and Empire in Byzantium* (Princeton: Princeton University Press, 2013), esp. 28–29, 38–79, 131–93.

61. Peers rightly argues that the mystery of angelic nature formed a sort of counterpart in Byzantium to the complicated concept of God's incarnation (*Subtle Bodies*, 17, 106).

was granted by an earthly woman, while his divinity was attested by his celestial attendants.

Another aspect of the iconography in question relates to the necessity of visualizing Mary's glorification for the viewer, rendering explicit the celebration granted to her by the heavenly court. Numerous sources confirm that this regularly involves angels singing and performing ceremonies in honor of the Mother of God.[62] Already in a fourth-century homily dedicated to the Virgin, Epiphanius of Salamis describes a spiritual vision of heaven in which the Theotokos becomes the object of angelic προσκύνησις, or veneration.[63] Most importantly, however, this same idea is certified by the inscriptions that accompany and form an integral part of several representations of Mary between the angels.

One of these is the program of the Church of the Dormition in Nicaea, discussed above, that was complemented by a series of texts inlaid in the mosaic. The sentence above the image of the Mother of God was placed under the three rays of divine light descending from the hand of God placed in the segment of heaven at the top of the conch. Considering its location, the phrase was certainly of essential importance for the understanding of the program. It read: +ΕΓ ΓΑΣΤΡΟΣ ΠΡΟ ΕΩΣΦΟΡΟΥ ΕΓΕΝΗΚΑ ΣΕ ("From the womb before the morning star I begat Thee" (Ps 110:3 [109:3 LXX]). A verbal expression of the incarnation, this alludes here to God the Father, by whose will the Savior came into the world. The quotation commented on the image of the incarnation portrayed in the apse, where God the Father was depicted in the form of a hand, while Christ was unconventionally inscribed within Mary's figure. What particularly interests us here, however, is the line that was reproduced twice immediately below the figures of the angels in the bema: +ΚΑΙ ΠΡΟΣΚΥΝΗΣΑΤΩΣΑΝ ΑΥΤΩ(Ι) ΠΑΝΤΕΣ ΑΝΓΕΛΟΙ ("Worship him all the angels"). This is usually associated with Ps 97:7 (96:7 LXX), but it probably refers mainly

---

62. For example, the hymn "Χαῖρε Θεοτόκε ἀγαλλίαμα τῶν ἀγγέλων," preserved in the Greek papyrus 1029 at the British Museum, dated to the sixth century. See Anton Baumstark, "Ein frühchristliches Theotokion in mehrsprachiger Überlieferung und verwandte Texte des ambrosianischen Ritus," OC 7–8 (1918): 37–61.

63. "λέγω γὰρ ταύτην οὐρανὸν καὶ θρόνον ὁμοῦ τε καὶ σταυρόν· τὰς γὰρ ἁγίας ἀγκάλας ἐκτείνασα, τὸν δεσπότην ἐβάστασεν ὁ θρόνος χερουβικός, σταυροειδὴς, οὐράνιος, περὶ ἧς διὰ τῶν γραφῶν ἐν οὐρανοῖς παρακύπτω, καὶ βλέπω ταύτην ὑπὸ ἀγγέλων προσκυνουμένην" (PG 43:497). I would like to express my gratitude to Arkadiy Avdokhin for bringing this text to my attention.

to Paul's letter (Heb 1:6), as the latter is pertinent to the inscription in the conch as well as to the apse decoration in general (Heb 1:1–7).[64]

Spatially divided, these inscriptions united the entire program around the altar to form an unbroken text: From the womb before the morning star I begat Thee; worship him all angels." The first part referred to the incarnation, while the second responded with the call to all the angels to rejoice at the sublime miracle. As the space of the conch was in the end mainly occupied by the standing figure of the Virgin, the veneration of heavenly powers referred to in the inscriptions, in the first place, visually addressed and glorified the image of the Theotokos.

The decoration in Nicaea is not the only case of this kind. Coming from a completely different cultural milieu but again associated with the composition of Mary between the angels is the Latin inscription decorating the frame of the miraculous icon of Santa Maria in Trastevere in Rome (sixth to early eighth century). Only part of the text survives today. The text starts in the upper left corner with a cross, then proceeds horizontally and vertically on the frame. One line reads DS QYOD IPSE FACTYS EST, according to Bertelli's reconstruction, to be later continued by the words YTERO TYO, while the other part consists of ASTANT STYPENTES ANGELORYM PRINCIPES—GESTARE NATYM.[65] Neither of the lines is complete, but the surviving fragments allow us to make an approximate reconstruction and translation of the text: "The archangels stand in awe [at seeing you] holding the child ... since God has created himself [from thy womb?]."

It is evident that the inscription on the frame is not conventional and generalized but instead appears as a direct comment on the scene portrayed in the icon. Angels are referred to in the plural as standing immobile in silent adoration of the Mother of God, who gave the world Christ incarnate, closely corresponding with the artistic program of the

---

64. For this identification of the Nicaea text, see Cyril Mango, "The Chalkoprateia Annunciation and the Pre-eternal Logos," *DCAE* 17 (1993–1994): 165–70. Charles Barber, however, is critical of this view and sees the inscription as part of Odes Sol. 2.43 and Deut 32:43; see Barber, "Theotokos and Logos," esp. 51. The line also figures in the treatise *On the Divine Liturgy* by Germanus; see Germanus, *On the Divine Liturgy*, 74–75. This fact strengthens the attempt of some scholars to interpret the whole program, and figures of the angels in particular, within a liturgical context, in agreement with the parallelism of the earthly and heavenly church, characteristic of the Byzantine liturgical writings of the eighth and ninth centuries; see Auzépy, "Liturgie et art sous les Isauriens."

65. Bertelli, *Madonna di Santa Maria in Trastevere*, 34–42.

panel and its particular rendering of the angelic figures. In this, the second part of the sentence stresses the independence of God's prodigious act. It echoes liturgical and especially Christmas prayers that were widespread at the time, which singled out both the Theotokos, through whom the Savior came into the world, and Christ himself, who chose the Virgin Mary for his incarnation; at the same time, it emphasized the glorifying angels.[66]

The adoration of the Mother of God by angels is not merely an abstract custom of the otherworldly realm but serves as an expression of the appropriate attitude toward the Virgin Mary. The veneration paid by the heavenly beings assumes significance as the principle testimony to the sainthood of the Virgin, setting a model for worship and reverential conduct. Through the presence of heavenly guards at her side, the image of the Mother of God placed on the main axis of numerous Byzantine churches was visually glorified, endowed by imperial splendor, and liturgically celebrated before the eyes of the congregation.

This experience inspired viewers engaged in the liturgy, performed beneath the image, to ascend through their prayers to the Queen of Heaven and, by joining the angelic choir, to address their personal glorification to the Theotokos. Parallelism between the angelic hosts and earthly celebrants is commonplace in the Byzantine liturgical and theological tradition. Sometimes this parallelism led to the adoption of explicit manifestations related specifically to the Virgin.[67] Even sources that describe

---

66. "Vere dignum et justum est, aequum et salutare est, nos tibi gratias agere, Domine sancte, Pater omnipotens, aeterne Deus, quia hodie Dominus noster Jesus Christus dignatus est visitare mundum. processit de sacrario corporis virginalis, et descendit pietate de coelis. cecinerunt angeli, gloria in excelsis, cum humanitas claruit Salvatoris. omnis denique turba exultabat Angelorum: quia terra regem suscepit aeternum. Maria beata facta est templum pretiosum, portans Dominum dominorum. fenuit enim pro nostris delictis vitam praeclaram, ut mors pelleretur amara. illa enim viscera, quae humana non noverant macula, Deum portare meruerunt. Natus est in mundo, qui semper vixit et vivit in coelo, Jesus Christus, Filius tuus, Dominus noster. Per quem maiestatem tuam laudant angeli" (John Mason Neale and George Hay Forbes, *The Ancient Liturgies of the Gallican Church, Now First Collected, with an Introductory Dissertation, Notes, and Various Readings, Together with Parallel Passages from the Roman, Ambrosian, and Mozarabic* [Burntisland: Pitsligo, 1855], 36).

67. Germanus, *On the Divine Liturgy*; Rosemary Dubowchik, "Singing with the Angels: Foundation Documents as Evidence for Musical Life in Monasteries of the Byzantine Empire," *DOP* 56 (2002): 277–96, esp. 281–82; Muehlberger, *Angels in the Religious Imagination*, 114–28.

actual events tend to compare the congregation to the angels, as, for example, in a famous passage of Gregory of Nazianzus, who when describing the emperor Valens's entrance into a cathedral writes: "But when he came inside, he was thunderstruck by the psalm-singing that assailed his ears, and saw the ocean of people and the whole well-ordered array around the altar and nearby, which seemed to consist of angels rather than humans" (*Or.* 43.52). Texts like this indicate that similar ideas and associations must have been a standard topos already in the early Christian period.

The image of Mary between the angels beyond doubt constitutes one of the principle iconographic schemes in Byzantine art. Its origins are still uncertain and require further investigation. Nevertheless, it seems legitimate to assume that at quite an early stage, it was used not only for conveying a complex theological message but also, more importantly, for the promulgation and formation of the Marian cult. The pictorial structure defining this representation is multifaceted, for it depends on the parallel development of Christ's iconography, previous pagan imagery, and literary descriptions. Its popularity and long life speak of the efficacy and overall timeless significance of this early Byzantine visual formula.

Bibliography

Agouridis, Savvas. "The Virgin Mary in the Texts of the Gospels." Pages 59–65 in *Mother of God: Representations of the Virgin in Byzantine Art*. Edited by M. Vassilaki. Athens: Abbeville, 2000.

Ainalov, Dmitri V. *The Hellenistic Origins of Byzantine Art*. New Brunswick: Rutgers University Press, 1961.

———. "Mozaiki IV i V vekov: Issledovania v oblasti ikonographii i stilia drevnekhristianskogo iskusstva." *JMNP* 299 (1895): 94–155.

Andaloro, Maria. "I mosaici parietali di Durazzo e dell'origine costantinopolitana del tema iconografico di Maria Regina." Pages 103–12 in *Studien zur spätantiken und byzantinischen Kunst: Festschrift Friedrich Wilhelm Deichmann*. Edited by Otto Feld. Bonn: Habelt, 1986.

———. "La datazione della tavola di St. Maria in Trastevere." *RINASA* 19/20 (1972–1973): 139–215.

———, ed. *L'orizzonte tardoantico e le nuove immagini, 312–468*. Vol. 1 of *La pittura medievale a Roma*. Rome: Jaca, 2006.

Andaloro, Maria, and Serena Romano. "L'immagine nell'apside." Pages 93–132 in *Arte e Iconografia a Roma da Constantino a Cola di Rienzo*. Edited by Maria Andaloro and Serena Romano. Milan: Jaca, 2000.

Angelova, Diliana. *Sacred Founders: Women, Men, and Gods in the Discourse of Imperial Founding, Rome through Early Byzantium*. Berkeley: University of California Press, 2015.

Atanassova, Antonia. "Did Cyril of Alexandria Invent Mariology?" Pages 105–25 in *The Origins of the Cult of the Virgin Mary*. Edited by Chris Maunder. London: Burns & Oates, 2008.

Auzépy, Marie-France. "Liturgie et art sous les Isauriens: À propos de la Dormition de Nicée." Pages 29–58 in *Le saint, le moine et le paysan: Mélanges d'histoire byzantine offerts à Michel Kaplan*. Edited by Olivier Delouis, Sophie Métivier, Paule Pagès. Paris: Sorbonne, 2016.

Barber, Charles. "The Koimesis Church, Nicaea: The Limits of Representation on the Eve of Iconoclasm." *JÖB* 41 (1991): 43–60.

———. "Theotokos and Logos: The Interpretation and Reinterpretation of the Sanctuary Programme of the Koimesis Church, Nicaea." Pages 51–62 in *Images of the Mother of God*. Edited by Maria Vassilaki. Aldershot: Ashgate, 2005.

Barrado, Lourdes Diego. "Le rôle des anges dans l'iconographie de la Rome byzantine." Pages 133–44 in *Les anges et les archanges dans l'art et la société à l'époque Préromane et Romane: Actes des XXIXe Journées Romanes de Cuixà, 8–16 juillet 1996*. CSMC 28. Codalet: Association Culturelle de Cuixà, 1997.

Baumstark, Anton. "Ein frühchristliches Theotokion in mehrsprachiger Überlieferung und verwandte Texte des ambrosianischen Ritus." *OC* 7–8 (1918): 37–61.

Bernabò, Massimo, ed. *Il tetravangelo di Rabbula: Firenze, Biblioteca Medicea Laurenziana, Plut. 1.56; L'illustrazione del nuovo testamento nella Siria del VI secolo*. Rome: Edizioni di storia e letteratura, 2008.

Bertelli, Carlo. *La Madonna di Santa Maria in Trastevere: Storia, iconografia, stile di un dipinto romano dell'ottavo secolo*. Rome: n.p., 1961.

Bovini, Giuseppe. "Antichi rifacimenti nei mosaici di St. Apollinare Nuovo a Ravenna." *CARB* 13 (1966): 51–81.

Bowes, Kim, and Afri Hoti. "An Amphitheater and Its Afterlives: Survey and Excavation in the Dürres Amphitheatre." *JRA* 16 (2003): 381–94.

Bowes, Kim, and John Mitchell. "The Main Chapel of the Durres Amphitheater: Decoration and Chronology." *MEFRA* 121 (2009): 569–95.

Brenk, Beat. *The Apse, the Image and the Icon: An Historical Perspective of the Apse as a Space for Images*. Wiesbaden: Reichert, 2010.

———. *Die frühchristlichen Mosaiken in S. Maria Maggiore zu Rom*. Wiesbaden: Steiner, 1975.

Brubaker, Leslie. "The Vienna Dioskorides and Anicia Juliana." Pages 189–214 in *Byzantine Garden Culture*. Edited by Antony Robert Littlewood, Henry Maguire, and Joachim Wolschke-Bulmahn. Washington, DC: Dumbarton Oaks Research Library and Collection, 2002.

Brubaker, Leslie, and Mary B. Cunningham, eds. *The Cult of the Mother of God in Byzantium: Texts and Images*. Aldershot: Ashgate, 2011.

Buschhausen, Heide, and Helmut Buschhausen. "Durazzo und die Anfänge des Christentums in Albanien." Pages 1–19 in *Steine Sprechen*. ZÖGDO 120. Wien: Öster, 2001.

Bussagli, Marco. *Storia degli angeli: Racconto di immagini e di idee*. Milan: Rusconi libri, 1995.

Bussagli, Marco, and Mario D'Onofrio, eds. *Le Ali di Dio: Messaggeri e guerrieri alati tra Oriente e Occidente*. Milan: Silvana, 2000.

Cameron, Averil. "The Early Cult of the Virgin." Pages 3–15 in *Mother of God: Representations of the Virgin in Byzantine Art*. Edited by M. Vassilaki. Athens: Milan, 2000.

Cecchelli, Carlo, Giuseppe Furlani, and Mario Salmi, eds. *The Rabbula Gospels: Facsimile Edition of the Miniatures of the Syriac Manuscript Plut. I,56 in the Medicaean-Laurentian Library*. Olten: Graf, 1959.

Chiesa, Gemma Sena. "La capsella e il suo decoro: Il linguaggio delle immagini fra devozione cristiana e tradizione imperiale." Pages 27–54 in *Il Tesoro di San Nazaro: Antichi argenti liturgici dalla basilica di San Nazaro al Museo Diocesano di Milano*. Edited by Gemma Sena Chiesa. Milan: Silvana, 2009.

———, ed. *Il Tesoro di San Nazaro: Antichi argenti liturgici dalla basilica di San Nazaro al Museo Diocesano di Milano*. Milan: Silvana, 2009.

Constas, Nicholas. *Proclus of Constantinople and the Cult of the Virgin in Late Antiquity*. VCSup 66. Leiden: Brill, 2003.

Cooper, Kate. "Empress and Theotokos: Gender and Patronage in the Christological Controversy." Pages 39–51 in *The Church and Mary*. Edited by Robert N. Swanson. Woodbridge: Boydell, 2004.

Cormack, Robin. *The Church of Saint Demetrios: The Watercolours and Drawings of W. S. George*. Thessaloniki: Municipality of Thessaloniki, 1985.

———. "The Eyes of the Virgin." Pages 167–73 in *Images of the Mother of God*. Aldershot: Ashgate, 2005.

———. "Icon of the Virgin and Child between Archangels Accompanied by Two Saints." Pages 262–63 in *Mother of God: Representations of the*

Virgin in Byzantine Art. Edited by M. Vassilaki. Athens: Abbeville, 2000.

———. "Mother of God in the Apse Mosaics." Pages 91–105 in *Mother of God: Representations of the Virgin in Byzantine Art.* Edited by M. Vassilaki. Athens: Abbeville, 2000.

———. "The Mother of God in the Mosaics of Hagia Sophia at Constantinople." Pages 107–23 in *Mother of God: Representations of the Virgin in Byzantine Art.* Edited by M. Vassilaki. Athens: Abbeville, 2000.

Deckers, Johannes G., Hans Reinhard Seeliger, and Gabriele Mietke. *Die Katakombe "Santi Marcellino e Pietro": Repertorium der Malereien.* Vatican City: PIAC, 1987.

Deichmann, Friedrich Wilhelm. *Kommentar.* Vol. 2.1 of *Ravenna: Hauptstadt des spätantiken Abendlandes. Geschichte und Monumente.* Wiesbaden: Steiner, 1974.

Delbrück, Richard. *Die Consulardiptychen und verwandte Denkmäler.* Berlin: de Gruyter, 1929.

Deliyannis, Deborah. *Ravenna in Late Antiquity.* Cambridge: Cambridge University Press, 2010.

Delmaire, Roland. *Largesses sacrées et res privata: L'aerarium impérial et son administration du IVe au VIe siècle.* Rome: Ecole française de Rome, 1989.

Dhamo, Dhorka. "Les mosaïques paléochrétiennes en Albanie." *CARB* 40 (1993): 491–504.

Dubowchik, Rosemary. "Singing with the Angels: Foundation Documents as Evidence for Musical Life in Monasteries of the Byzantine Empire." *DOP* 56 (2002): 277–96.

Effenberger, Arne. "Maria als Vermittlerin und Fürbitterin: Zum Marienbild in der spätantiken und frühbyzantinischen Kunst Ägyptens." Pages 49–108 in *Presbeia Theotokou: The Intercessory Role of Mary across Times and Places in Byzantium, Fourth–Ninth Century.* Edited by Leena Mari Peltomaa, Andreas Külzer, and Pauline Allen. Vienna: Österreichischen Akademie der Wissenschaften, 2015.

Elliott, J. K. *The Apocryphal New Testament: A Collection of Apocryphal Christian Literature in an English Translation.* Oxford: Clarendon, 1994.

———. "Mary in the Apocryphal New Testament." Pages 57–70 in *The Origins of the Cult of the Virgin Mary.* Edited by Chris Maunder. London: Burns & Oats, 2008.

Farioli Campanati, Raffaella Ravenna. "Costantinopoli: Aspetti topografico-monumentali e iconografici." *Storia di Ravenna* 2.2 (1992): 127–57.

Fingarova, Galina. "Mary as an Intercessory in the Decoration of the Chapel in Durrës, Albania." Pages 203–18 in *Presbeia Theotokou: The Intercessory Role of Mary across Times and Places in Byzantium, Fourth–Ninth Century*. Edited by Leena Mari Peltomaa, Andreas Külzer, and Pauline Allen. Vienna: Österreichischen Akademie der Wissenschaften, 2015.

Foletti, Ivan. "Germigny-des-Prés, il Santo Sepolcro e la Gerusalemme celeste." *Conv.* 1 (2014): 32–49.

Freeman, Ann, and Paul Meyvaert. "The Meaning of Theodulf's Apse Mosaic at Germigny-des-Prés." *Gesta* 40 (2001): 125–39.

Gagetti, Elisabetta. "Bibliografia storica. La fortuna nei secoli di un oggetto tra devozione e arte." Pages 63–72 in *Il Tesoro di San Nazaro: Antichi argenti liturgici dalla basilica di San Nazaro al Museo Diocesano di Milano*. Edited by Gemma Sena Chiesa. Milan: Silvana, 2009.

Gambero, Luigi. *Mary and the Fathers of the Church: The Blessed Virgin Mary in Patristic Thought*. San Francisco: Ignatius, 1999.

Garrucci, Raffaele. *Storia della arte cristiana nei primi otto secoli della chiesa*. 2 vols. Prato: Guasti, 1877.

Gega, Reshat. "L'architecture des monastères, byzantins et postbyzantins en Albanie." *CARB* 40 (1993): 505–25.

Germanus of Constaninople. *On the Divine Liturgy*. Translated by Paul Meyendorff. New York: Saint Vladimir's Seminary Press, 1999.

Gerov, Georgi. "Angels—Entrance Guardians." *ZRVI* 46 (2009): 435–42.

Giuliani, Raffaella. "Angelo." Pages 106–9 in *Temi di iconografia paleocristiana*. Vatican City: PIAC, 2000.

Gotia, Ioan. "L'Annunciazione/Incarnazione come 'Porta della salvezza': Fondamenti teologici ed iconografici antichi." *SOC* 17 (2013): 73–166.

Grabar, André. *Ampoules de Terre Sainte (Monza-Bobbio)*. Paris: Klincksieck, 1958.

———. *Martyrium: Recherches sur le culte des reliques et l'art chrétien antique*. 2 vols. Paris: Collège de France, 1946.

Grüneisen, Wladimir. *Sainte Marie Antique*. Rome: Bretschneider, 1911.

Hatzaki, Myrto. *Beauty and the Male Body in Byzantium: Perceptions and Representations in Art and Text*. Basingstoke: Palgrave Macmillan, 2009.

Herrin, Judith. *Unrivalled Influence: Women and Empire in Byzantium*. Princeton: Princeton University Press, 2013.

Hornblower, Simon, and Antony Spawforth, eds. *The Oxford Classical Dictionary*. Oxford: Oxford University Press, 1996.

Iacco, E. Penni. *La basilica di St. Apollinare Nuovo di Ravenna attraverso i secoli*. Bologna: Ante quem, 2004.

Ihm, Christa. *Die Programme der christlichen Apsismalerei vom 4. Jahrhundert bis zur Mitte des 8. Jahrhunderts*. Wiesbaden: Steiner, 1960.

James, Liz. "The Empress and the Virgin in Early Byzantine Piety, Authority and Devotion." Pages 145–52 in *Images of the Mother of God*. Edited by M. Vassilaki. Aldershot: Ashgate, 2005.

———. "Matters of Materiality in Byzantium: The Archangel Gabriel in Hagia Sophia, Constantinople." *Journal of Art History* 86 (2017): 145–57.

Jastrzebowska, Elzbieta. "New Testament Angels in Early Christian Art: Origin and Sources." *MNEA* 8.49 (2009–2011): 153–64.

John of Damascus. *An Exact Exposition of the Orthodox Faith*. Translated by Frederic H. Chase. Washington, DC: Catholic University of America Press, 1958.

Jolivet-Lévy, Catherine. "Note sur la representátion des archanges en costume impérial dans l'iconographie byzantine." *CahA* 46 (1998): 121–28.

Karavidopoulos, Ioannis. "On the Information Concerning the Virgin Mary Contained in the Apocryphal Gospels." Pages 67–76 in *Mother of God: Representations of the Virgin in Byzantine Art*. Edited by M. Vassilaki. Athens: Abbeville, 2000.

Kateusz, Ally. "Ascension of Christ or Ascension of Mary? Reconsidering a Popular Early Iconography." *JECS* 23 (2015): 273–303.

Kazhdan, Alexander P., ed. *The Oxford Dictionary of Byzantium*. New York: Oxford University Press, 1991.

Kazhdan, Alexander P., and Nancy Patterson Ševčenko. "Archangel." Page 155 in *The Oxford Dictionary of Byzantium*. Edited by Alexander P. Kazhdan. Oxford: Oxford University Press, 1991.

Kiilerich, Bente. "The Image of Anicia Juliana in the Vienna Dioscurides: Flattery or Appropriation of Imperial Imagery." *SO* 76 (2001): 169–90.

Kitzinger, Ernst. "Byzantine Art in the Period between Justinian and Iconoclasm." Pages 1–50 in *Berichte zum XI. Internationale Byzantinischen Kongress*. Munich: Beck, 1958.

Klauser, Theodor. "Aurum Coronarium." *MDAI* 59 (1944): 129–53.

Kondakov, Nikodim Pavlovich. *Histoire de l'art byzantine: Considéré principalement dans les miniatures*. Paris: Librairie de l'Art, 1886–1891.

———. *Ikonografia Bogomateri*. Saint Petersburg: Imperatorskaia akademia nauk, 1914.
Lafontaine-Dosogne, Jacqueline. "Iconography of the Cycle of the Infancy of Christ." Pages 163–241 in vol. 4 of *The Kariye Djami*. Edited by Paul A. Underwood. 4 vols. London: Routledge, 1975.
Lamy-Lassalle, Colette. "Les archanges en costume impérial dans la peinture murale italienne." *Synthronon* (1968): 189–98.
Lidova, Maria. "The Adoration of the Magi: From Iconic Space to Icon in Space." In *Icons of Space: Studies in Hierotopy and Iconography; A Tribute to Alexei Lidov for His 60th Birthday*. Forthcoming.
———. "Embodied Word: Telling the Story of Mary in Early Christian Art." Pages 17–43 in *The Reception of the Virgin in Byzantium: Marian Narratives in Texts and Images*. Edited by Thomas Arentzen and Mary B. Cunningham. Cambridge: Cambridge University Press, 2019.
———. "Empress, Virgin, *Ecclesia*: The Icon of Santa Maria in Trastevere in the Early Byzantine Context." *IKON* 9 (2016): 109–28.
———. "L'icona acheropita della Vergine di Santa Maria in Trastevere a Roma." Pages 19–28 in *Le arti a confronto con il sacro: Metodi di ricerca e nuove prospettive d'indagine interdisciplinare*. Edited by Valentina Cantone and Silvia Fumian. Padova: Università degli Studi di Padova, 2009.
———. "The Imperial Theotokos: Revealing the Concept of Early Christian Imagery in Santa Maria Maggiore in Rome." *Conv.* 2 (2015): 60–81.
———. "*Maria Regina* on the 'Palimpsest Wall' in St. Maria Antiqua Church in Rome: Historical Context and Imperial Connotations of the Early Byzantine Image." *Iconographica* 16 (2017): 9–25.
———. "ΧΑΙΡΕ ΜΑΡΙΑ: Annunciation Imagery in the Making." *IKON* 10 (2017): 45–62.
Limberis, Vasiliki. *Divine Heiress: The Virgin Mary and the Creation of Christian Constantinople*. London: Routledge, 1994.
Lloyd, J. Barclay. "Mary, Queen of the Angels: Byzantine and Roman Images of the Virgin and Child Enthroned with Attendant Angels." *MAJ* 5 (2001): 5–24.
Lowden, John. "The Word Made Visible: The Exterior of the Early Christian Books as Visual Argument." Pages 13–47 in *The Early Christian Book*. Edited by William E. Klingshirn and Linda Safran. Washington, DC: Catholic University of America Press, 2007.

Mackie, Gillian Vallance. "Theodulf of Orléans and the Ark of the Covenant: A New Allegorical Interpretation at Germigny-des-Prés." *Racar* 32 (2007): 45–58.

Maguire, Henry. "Style and Ideology in Byzantine Imperial Art." *Gesta* 28 (1989): 217–31.

Maguire, Henry, and Ann Terry. *Dynamic Splendor: The Wall Mosaics in the Cathedral of Eufrasius at Poreč*. Pennsylvania: Pennsylvania State University Press, 2007.

Mango, Cyril. *The Art of the Byzantine Empire, 312–1453: Sources and Documents*. Englewood Cliffs, NJ: Prentice-Hall, 1972.

———. "The Chalkoprateia Annunciation and the Pre-eternal Logos." *DCAE* 17 (1993–1994): 165–70.

———. "The Hermitage of St. Neophytos and Its Wall Paintings." *DOP* 20 (1966): 119–206.

———. "St. Michael and Attis." *DCAE* 12 (1984–1986): 39–45.

Mango, Cyril, and Ernest J. W. Hawkins. "The Apse Mosaics of St. Sophia at Istanbul: Report on Work Carried Out in 1964." *DOP* 19 (1965): 115–51.

Mansi, Giovan Domenico. *Sacrorum Conciliorum nova et amplissima collectio*. Vol. 13. Paris: Welter, 1901–1927.

Maunder, Chris, ed. *Origins of the Cult of the Virgin Mary*. London: Burns & Oats, 2008.

McGuckin, John A. *St. Cyril of Alexandria and the Christological Controversy*. Crestwood, NY: Saint Vladimir's Seminary Press, 2004.

Menna, Maria Raffaella. "I mosaici della basilica di Santa Maria Maggiore." Pages 306–46 in *L'orizzonte tardoantico e le nuove immagini, 312–468*. Vol. 1 of *La Pittura Medievale a Roma*. Edited by Maria Andaloro. Rome: Jaca, 2006.

Muehlberger, Ellen. *Angels in Late Ancient Christianity*. New York: Oxford University Press, 2013.

———. "Angels in the Religious Imagination of Late Antiquity." PhD diss., Indiana University, 2008.

Munitiz, Joseph A., Julian Chrysostomides, Eirene Arvalia-Crook, and Charalambos Dendrinos, eds. *The Letter of the Three Patriarchs to the Emperor Theophilos and Related Texts*. Camberley: Porphyrogenitus, 1997.

Navoni, Marco. "Per una storia della capsella argentea: Da Ambrogio a Carlo Borromeo fino ai nostri giorni." Pages 17–26 in *Il Tesoro di San Nazaro: Antichi argenti liturgici dalla basilica di San Nazaro al Museo*

Diocesano di Milano. Edited by Gemma Sena Chiesa. Milan: Silvana, 2009.
Neale, John Mason, and George Hay Forbes. *The Ancient Liturgies of the Gallican Church, Now First Collected, with an Introductory Dissertation, Botes, and Various Readings, Together with Parallel Passages from the Roman, Ambrosian, and Mozarabic*. Burntisland: Pitsligo, 1855.
Neri, Elisabetta, Bernard Gratuze, and Nadine Schibille. "Dating the Mosaics of the Durres Amphitheater through Interdisciplinary Analysis." *JCH* 28 (2017): 27–36.
Nordhagen, Per Jonas. "The Earliest Decorations in Santa Maria Antiqua and Their Date." *AAAHP* 1 (1962): 56–57.
Oikonomidès, Nikolas. "Some Remarks on the Apse Mosaics of St. Sophia." *DOP* 39 (1985): 111–15.
Olovsdotter, Cecilia. *The Consular Image: An Iconological Study of the Consular Diptychs*. Oxford: Hadrian, 2005.
Pallas, Demetrios I. "Himmelsmächte, Erzengel und Engel." Pages 14–119 in vol. 3 of *Reallexicon zur Byzantinischen Kunst*. Edited by Klaus Wessel and Marcell Restle. Stuttgart: Hiersemann, 1972.
Parani, Maria. "Look Like an Angel: The Attire of Eunuchs and Its Significance within the Context of Middle Byzantine Court Ceremonial." Pages 433–63 in *Court Ceremonies and Rituals of Power in Byzantium and the Medieval Mediterranean: Comparative Perspectives*. Edited by Alexander Beihammer, Stavroula Constantinou, and Maria Parani. Leiden: Brill, 2013.
Peers, Glenn. *Subtle Bodies: Representing Angels in Byzantium*. Berkeley: University of California Press, 2001.
Peltomaa, Leena Mari. *The Image of the Virgin Mary in the Akathistos Hymn*. MilM 35. Leiden: Brill, 2001.
Peltomaa, Leena Mari, Andreas Külzer, and Pauline Allen, eds. *Presbeia Theotokou: The Intercessory Role of Mary across Times and Places in Byzantium (Fourth–Ninth Century)*. Vienna: Österreichischen Akademie der Wissenschaften, 2015.
Pentcheva, Bissera V. *Icons and Power: The Mother of God in Byzantium*. University Park: Pennsylvania State University Press, 2006.
Podskalsky, Gerhard, and Anthony Cutler. "Angel." Page 97 in *The Oxford Dictionary of Byzantium*. Edited by Alexander P. Kazhdan. Oxford: Oxford University Press, 1991.

Price, Richard M. "The Theotokos and the Council of Ephesus." Pages 89–103 in *The Origins of the Cult of the Virgin Mary*. Edited by Chris Maunder. London: Burns & Oates, 2008.

Proverbio, Cecilia. *La figura dell'angelo nella civiltà paleocristiana*. Todi: Tau Editrice, 2007.

Rademacher, Franz. *Die Regina Angelorum in der Kunst des frühen Mittelalters*. Düsseldorf: Schwann, 1972.

Rutschowscaya, Marie-Hélène. *Coptic Fabrics*. Paris: Biro, 1990.

Schade, Kathrin. *Frauen in der Spätantike—Status und Repräsentation: Eine Untersuchung zur römischen und frübyzantinischen Bildniskunst*. Mainz: von Zabern, 2003.

Sena Chiesa, Gemma. *Il Tesoro di San Nazaro: Antichi argenti liturgici dalla basilica di San Nazaro al Museo Diocesano di Milano*. Milan: Silvana, 2009.

Shandrovskaya, Valentina. "Kompositsia 'Bogomater s arkhanghelami' na vizantiyskikh pechatyakh" [Composition of the 'Mother of God with Archangels' on Byzantine seals]. Pages 238–51 in *Vizantija v kontekste mirovoj kul'tury*. Trudy Gosudarstvennogo Ėrmitaža 42. St. Petersburg: State Hermitage Museum, 2008.

Shepherd, Dorothy G. "An Icon of the Virgin." *BCM* 56.3 (1969): 90–120.

Shoemaker, Stephen J. *Mary in Early Christian Faith and Devotion*. New Haven: Yale University Press, 2016.

Sidéris, Georges. "Sur l'origine des anges eunuques à Byzance." Pages 539–58 in *Constructing the Seventh Century*. Edited by Constantin Zuckerman. Paris: Association des Amis du Centre d'histoire et civilisation de Byzance, 2013.

Slavazzi, Fabrizio. "La capsella di San Nazaro: Indagini sull'apparato figurativo." Pages 55–62 in *Il Tesoro di San Nazaro: Antichi argenti liturgici dalla basilica di San Nazaro al Museo Diocesano di Milano*. Edited by Gemma Sena Chiesa. Milan: Silvana, 2009.

Spain, Suzanne. "'The Promised Blessing': The Iconography of the Mosaics of St. Maria Maggiore." *ArtBul* 61 (1979): 519–25.

Spier, Jeffrey, ed. *Picturing the Bible: The Earliest Christian Art*. New Haven: Yale University Press, 2007.

Spieser, Jean-Michel. "Impératrices romaines et chrétiennes." *TM* 14 (2002): 593–604.

Spirito, Giuseppe de. "L'Annonciation de Sainte-Marie-Majeure: Image apocryphe?" *Apocrypha* 7 (1996): 273–92.

Steigerwald, Gerhard. *Die frühchristlichen Mosaiken des Triumphbogens von St. Maria Maggiore in Rom*. Regensburg: Schnell & Steiner, 2016.

———. "Das Königtum Mariens in Literatur und Kunst der ersten sechs Jahrhunderte." PhD diss., Universität Freiburg, 1965.

———. "Die Rolle Mariens in den Triumphbogenmosaiken und in der Weiheinschrift der Basilika St. Maria Maggiore in Rom." *JAC* 51 (2008): 140.

Stern, Henri. "Sur les influences byzantines dans les mosaïques ravennates du début du 6e siècle." Pages 526–32 in vol. 9 of *Settimane di studi del Centro Italiano di Studi sull'Alto Medioevo*. Spoleto: CISAM, 1962.

Stiegemann, Christoph, and Matthias Wemhoff, eds. "Diptychon mit thronendem Christus und thronender Maria mit Kind, No. X. 26." Pages 740–42 in vol. 2 of *799: Kunst und Kultur der Karolingerzeit; Karl der Große und Papst Leo III in Paderborn*. 3 vols. Mainz: von Zabern, 1999.

Studer, Basil. "Il Concilio di Efeso (431) nella luce della dottrina mariana di Cirillo di Alessandria." Pages 49–67 in *La mariologia nella catechesi dei Padri (età postnicena)*. Edited by Sergio Felici. Rome: Libreria Ateneo Salesiano, 1991.

Stuhlfauth, Georg. *Die Engel in der altchristlichen Kunst*. Freiburg: Mohr, 1897.

Swanson, Robert N., ed. *The Church and Mary*. SCH 39. Woodbridge: Boydell, 2004.

Tea, Eva. *La Basilica di Santa Maria Antiqua*. Milan: Pubblicazioni dell'Università Cattolica, 1937.

Toniolo, Ermanno M. *Akathistos: Saggi di critica e di teologia*. Rome: Centro di cultura mariana, 2000.

Underwood, Paul A. "The Evidence of Restorations in the Sanctuary Mosaics of the Church of the Dormition at Nicaea." *DOP* 13 (1959): 235–43.

Urbano, Arthur. "Donation, Dedication, and *Damnatio Memoriae*: The Catholic Reconciliation of Ravenna and the Church of Sant'Apollinare." *JECS* 13 (2005): 77–110.

Vassilaki, Maria, ed. *Images of the Mother of God: Perceptions of the Theotokos in Byzantium*. Aldershot: Ashgate, 2005.

———, ed. *Mother of God: Representations of the Virgin in Byzantine Art*. Athens: Abbeville, 2000.

Vergani, Graziano Alfredo. "Ampolla-reliquiario con Adorazione del Bambino e Ascensione." Pages 202–3 in *La rivoluzione dell'immagine:*

Arte paleocristiana tra Roma e Bisanzio. Edited by Fabrizio Bisconti and Giovanni Gentili. Milan: Cinisello Balsamo, 2007.

Weitzmann, Kurt. "Icon of the Virgin Enthroned, No. 477." Pages 532–33 in *Age of Spirituality: Late Antique and Early Christian Art, Third to Seventh Century*. New York: Metropolitan Museum, 1979.

———. *From the Sixth to the Tenth Century*. Vol. 1 of *The Monastery of Saint Catherine at Mount Sinai: The Icons*. Princeton: Princeton University Press, 1976.

Wellen, Gerard A. *Theotokos: Eine ikonographische Abhandlung über das Gottesmutterbild in frühchristlicher Zeit*. Utrecht: Het Spectrum, 1961.

Wilpert, Josef. *Die römischen Mosaiken und Malereien der kirchlichen Bauten vom IV.–XIII. Jahrhundert*. 4 vols. Freiburg: Herder, 1916.

Wolf, Gerhard. "Alexifarmaka: Aspetti del culto e della teoria delle immagini a Roma tra Bizanzio e terra Santa nell'Alto Medioevo." Pages 756–96 in vol. 2 of *Roma fra Oriente e Occidente: Settimane di Studio del Centro Italiano di Studi sull'Alto Medioevo XLIX*. Spoleto: CISAM, 2002.

Wright, William. *Apocryphal Acts of the Apostles*. Vol. 2. London: Williams & Norgate, 1871.

Zacos, Georgios, and Alexander Veglery. *Byzantine Lead Seals*. 2 vols. in 6 parts. Basel: Augustin, 1972–1985.

Early Medieval Iconography of the Virgin Mary between East and West

Giuseppa Z. Zanichelli

Over the centuries that witnessed the progressive but discontinuous shift from classical to Christian culture, a system of narrative and symbolic images established itself as one of the primary structures of communication. The centers where this system was planned and arranged coincide with the first four patriarchal sees: Rome, Antioch, Alexandria, and Constantinople. The preferred pilgrimage destination, Jerusalem, was added to these even before 451, the date of the Council of Chalcedon, which officially elevated the city to a patriarchal see.[1] Christian images first developed in the private sphere and were created chiefly for tombs and worship areas in homes, where women's presence was more felt. But after the Edict of Milan in 313, public images slowly gained ground as well. Their theological content was controlled by the priestly hierarchy, and in sacred buildings they were designed to illustrate the main doctrines that had emerged from the official exegesis and from the lively debate going on among the church fathers on the interpretation of the texts believed to have been revealed, especially regarding the dual nature of Christ.

Since the figure of the Virgin Mary appears only in a few episodes of the gospels, which are decidedly Christ-centered, her portrayal established itself slowly in the system of Christian images.[2] Initially, she appeared

---

1. Kurt Weitzmann, "*Loca Sancta* and the Representational Arts of Palestine," *DOP* 28 (1974): 31–55.

2. The episodes are the annunciation, visitation, nativity, annunciation to the shepherds, adoration of the Magi, flight into Egypt, and disputation among the doctors, to which we must add the crucifixion and the Pentecost. See Luigi Rosano, "Maria," in *Enciclopedia dell'arte medievale* (Rome: Istituto dell'Enciclopedia Italiana Treccani, 1997), 8:205.

only in connection with the story of Christ's infancy, especially the episode of the adoration of the Magi that records the earthly princes' tribute to the Messiah. The earliest documentation of Marian stories is found in the catacombs of Priscilla along the Via Salaria, with paintings that can be dated to between 230 and 270, a date that can narrowed to 250 for the area where the scenes in question were painted.³ The Virgin (fig. 1) appears there, following the iconography of the *mater*, with bared breast while nursing the Child (γαλακτοτροφούσα) and as a shortened type of the nativity.⁴ The classical image of the nursing goddess, such as Isis or Hera, however, is reinterpreted here with decidedly new semantics that derive from its combination with the theme of virginity. In fact, facing the seated mother is the figure of a prophet pointing to a star and identifiable as Isaiah or Balaam, whose texts were interpreted by the church fathers as a prophecy of Mary's virginity. Nearby, at the center of the vault over the cubiculum found adjacent to the large skylight, there appears the earliest surviving depiction of the annunciation (fig. 2), with Mary on the throne and the wingless angel in a subordinate position, like an earthly attendant. In this portrayal, as

Fig. 1: Rome, Catacombs of Priscilla, Virgin Nursing with Prophet. Source: Vincenzo Fiocchi Nicolai, Fabrizio Bisconti, and Danilo Mazzoleni, *Le catacombe cristiane di Roma* (Regensburg: Schnell & Steiner, 2002), 125, fig. 140.

---

3. Maria Giovanna Muzj, "La prima iconografia mariana," in *La Vergine Madre nella Chiesa delle origini*, ed. Ermanno Toniolo (Rome: Marianum, 1996), 209–43; Umberto Utro, "Maria nell'Iconografia cristiana dei primi secoli," in *Dal modello biblico al modello letterario*, vol. 1 of *Storia della mariologia*, ed. Enrico Dal Covolo and Aristide Serra (Rome: Città Nuova, 1998), 353–81.

4. Regarding the parallel spread of the γαλακτοτροφούσα theme in the Coptic world, see Victor Lasareff, "Studies in the Iconography of the Virgin," *ArtBul* 20 (1938): 27–36; Erica Cruikshank Dodd, "Christian Arab Sources of the Madonna Allattante in Italy," *AM* 2 (2003): 33–39.

Fig. 2: Rome, Catacombs of Priscilla, Annunciation. Source: P. Iacobone, *Maria a Roma: Teologia, culto e iconografia mariana a Roma, dalle origini all'Altomedioevo* (Todi: Tau 2009), 105, plate 1b.

in those of later centuries in Rome, Mary is dressed in keeping with the clothing standards of her illustrious patrons, aristocratic ladies like Priscilla *clarissima*, who belonged to the noble Acilii Glabriones family and was responsible for the tomb. The Virgin is here depicted on a stately seat, her head just barely veiled by a light fabric, a *rica*, while her body is covered by a tunic and *palla* falling in heavy folds, an expression of her high rank.[5] The angel, on the other hand, wears a short tunic without any distinctive mark, indicating a decidedly secondary role.

Another type of image was establishing itself in parallel, this one characterized by a nonnarrative structure: icons, ideal portraits not intended to evoke a single individual, as with the classical icons, but designed to depict the invisible. The frontal, static position of the figure portrayed achieves the effect of appealing to the viewer, provoking an emotional response of involvement. Of the oldest images documented by written sources that were intended for domestic use, none have survived.[6] But among these there must have been depictions of the Virgin, as we gather from the story of Pulcheria, who, in addition to founding the churches dedicated to Mary in Blachernae and Chalkoprateia, is said to have received (448–450) a portrait of the Virgin made by Luke from her sister-in-law Eudoxia, who

---

5. Beat Brenk, *Die Frühchristlichen Mosaiken in Santa Maria Maggiore zu Rom* (Wiesbaden: Steiner, 1975), 50–52.
6. Thomas F. Mathews, *Byzantium from the Antiquity to the Renaissance* (New York: Abrams 1998), 43–47.

was in Jerusalem.[7] Regardless of its veracity, this is a significant tale that emphasizes women's role in constructing Marian images. In fact, in this first phase, icons remained in the private sphere, preserving many formal characteristics of divine, imperial, and funerary images from which they are derived and without taking on any official liturgical function.[8] While we cannot attribute the praying figures in the catacombs to the category of images of the Virgin, given that none of them can be identified with certainty as Mary, clear inscriptions identify her in gold glass works produced in Rome, where she appears beside Agnes.[9] The link between the two female figures was so close that the liturgy of Mary was initially modeled on that of Agnes.[10]

Depictions of Christ's infancy were gradually enriched with details drawn from the latest apocryphal gospels, which provide most of the information on the Virgin. In particular, two texts exerted a strong influence: the Gospel of James, in Greek, to which we owe not only the names of Joachim and Anna but also the episodes of Mary's childhood and those connected to her marriage and childbirth in Bethlehem, and the Gospel of Pseudo-Matthew, in Latin, which not only expanded on the previous episodes but also dwelt on the miraculous events of Christ's infancy. With this expansion of source material, the annunciation is depicted as occurring while Mary is drawing water from the fountain or spinning purple wool for the temple curtains; we encounter the grotto with the ox and ass in the nativity or witness the extraordinary episodes of the flight into Egypt.[11]

---

7. Christine Angelidi, *Pulcheria: La castità al potere* (Milan: Jaca Book, 1996), 127–30; Anne L. McClanan, "The Empress Theodora and the Tradition of Women's Patronage in the Early Byzantine Empire," in *The Cultural Patronage of Medieval Women*, ed. June Hall McCash (Athens: University of Georgia Press, 1996), 52.

8. Hans Belting, *Likeness and Presence: A History of the Image before the Era of Art*, trans. Edmund Jephcott (Chicago: University of Chicago Press, 1994), 37.

9. On the issue of identifying the catacomb figures, see Fabrizio Bisconti, "L'orante, Maria e le acque: L'incontro dei temi," in *Deomene: L'immagine dell'orante tra Oriente e Occidente; Catalogo della mostra, Ravenna, Museo Nazionale, 25 marzo–24 giugno 2001*, ed. Angela Donati and Giovanni Gentili (Milan: Electa, 2001), 19–25.

10. Raffaele Garrucci, *Vetri ornati di figure in oro trovati nei cimiteri dei cristiani di Roma* (Rome: Tipografia delle Belle Arti, 1858), 73–77, pl. IX.

11. Jacqueline Lafontaine-Dosogne, *Iconographie de l'Enfance de la Vierge dans l'Empire byzantin et en Occident* (Brussels: Académie Royale de Belgique, 1964–1965); David R. Cartlidge and James Keith Elliott, *Art and the Christian Apocrypha* (London: Routledge, 2001), 21–46.

The fourth century was marked by the intensification of devotional images drawing on hagiography, among which the image of Mary clearly appears to be acting as an intercessor, as in the reliquaries of Nazarius (ca. 370–90; see fig. 5) and Brivio (late fourth or early fifth century).[12] The same pairing of Mary with the martyrs can be found in monuments, as documented by the *titulus* that stood below the lost apse of Santa Maria Maggiore in Rome, the basilica that Sixtus III (432–440) had built following the Council of Ephesus. This council had recognized the Virgin as Theotokos ("she who gave birth to God"), a title that underlined not only the direct emotional component of Mary's motherhood but also her role in the incarnation.[13] In the absence of this invaluable monument, which probably showed Mary enthroned with the Child on her lap, flanked by angels and martyrs, and perhaps with the pope who commissioned it standing on the left, scholars have found themselves at a loss to identify the two female figures depicted on the apsidal arch of the basilica. Yet both of them display characteristics that would feature in later images of Mary.[14] The figure weaving the purple thread in the first scene on the left (fig. 3) is almost always identified as Mary, and consequently the scene is interpreted as an annunciation.[15] Her clothing appears quite significant, given that she is wearing a fine golden garment with a *trabea* over a white tunic with sleeves ending in embroidered cuffs; beneath the hem of her tunic we can make out golden footwear. A sumptuous, rosette-shaped jewel embellishes the pearl belt marking the high waist of her dress, while pearls and precious stones adorn her hair, gathered up in braids. Although the fabric is precious, suggesting the desire to emulate the silk imported from Byzantium, which had quickly taken over the splendid court rituals

---

12. On Nazarius, see Gemma Sena Chiesa, ed., *Il Tesoro di San Nazaro: Antichi argenti liturgici della basilica di San Nazaro al Museo Diocesano di Milano* (Milan: Silvana, 2009). On Brivio, see Galit Noga-Banai, *The Trophies of the Martyrs: An Art Historical Study of Early Christian Silver Reliquaries* (Oxford: Oxford University Press, 2008), 38–61 and 122–23.

13. Ioli Kalavrezou, "Images of the Mother: When the Virgin Mary Became Meter Theou," *DOP* 44 (1990): 165–72; Averil Cameron, "The Cult of the Virgin in Late Antiquity: Religious Development and Myth-Making," in *The Church and Mary: Papers Read at the 2001 Summer Meeting and the 2002 Winter Meeting of the Ecclesiastical History Society*, ed. Robert N. Swanson (Woodbridge: Boydell, 2004), 1–21.

14. Brenk, *Die frühchristlichen Mosaiken*; Suzanne Spain, "'The Promised Blessing': The Iconography of the Mosaics of S. Maria Maggiore," *ArtBul* 61 (1979): 518–40.

15. Brenk, *Die frühchristlichen Mosaiken*.

Fig. 3. Rome, Santa Maria Maggiore, Triumphal arch, Annunciation.
Source: Maria Andaloro, *L'orizzonte tardoantico e le nuove immagini* (La pittura medievale a Roma I; Milan: Jaca Book, 2006), 334.

of the neighboring Sassanians, the style of the dress reflects once again the fashions of the Roman elite to which the work's patron, Pope Sixtus III, belonged. There are no elements that could suggest a direct derivation from the imperial tradition of Constantinople, and this is confirmed by a comparison with the panel on the nave of Santa Maria Maggiore depicting Moses rescued from the waters.[16]

In this episode, the pharaoh's daughter and her ladies are characterized by the same luxurious courtly attire; their hair, however, is not styled in the Roman way but hidden beneath jeweled bonnets, similar to those that would later adorn the heads of the ladies in Theodora's retinue in Ravenna.[17] The symbolic value of using these different hairstyles must have been quite noticeable to viewers of the time, as shown by the long procession of saints at Sant'Apollinare Nuovo (561–569): despite sporting a new, much

---

16. Ann M. Stout, "Jewelry as a Symbol of Status in the Roman Empire," in *The World of Roman Costume*, ed. Judith Lynn Sebesta and Larissa Bonfante (Madison: University of Wisconsin Press, 1994), 94; Mary Harlow, "Female Dress, Third-Sixth Century: The Message in the Media," *AntT* 12 (2004): 210.

17. Alexandra Croom, *Roman Clothing and Fashion* (Stroud: Amberley, 2010), 100.

more form-fitting kind of dress, they have significantly kept the classic traditional hairstyle, though the flowing *rica* must have acquired new meaning in light of Paul's exhortation to women to present themselves in public *capite velato* as a sign of submission and humility.[18]

On the arch of Santa Maria Maggiore, the second figure, sitting directly opposite the first near the throne of Christ in the scene of the adoration of the Magi, is wearing a long, dark mantle that covers her head but also gives a glimpse of the golden tunic beneath it. Two particularly interesting attributes appear to be the *mappa* (handkerchief) she is holding in her left hand and her red footwear.[19] Shortly before this, such features had characterized the two female figures, who, as the *tituli* indicate, personify the *Ecclesia ex circumcisione* and the *Ecclesia ex gentibus* in the counter-façade of Basilica of Santa Sabina (422–432). In this mosaic, the hairstyle of the two figures is completed by a white bonnet worn by women belonging to the middle classes starting in the mid-third century, and this attire would characterize many later images of Mary.

The impact that the recognition of the worship of the Virgin had on the production of images remains an unsolved problem, given that no documentation regarding the century following the mosaics at Santa Maria Maggiore has survived in the West. On the other hand, images of Mary began to pour in from the *loca sancta* of Palestine, brought by the pilgrims who had visited Nazareth and Bethlehem. What makes it more difficult to advance hypotheses on the formation of Marian images in Rome is the fact that the first surviving monument after this gap, which comes to us in a patchy state of preservation, presents some truly exceptional iconographic characteristics. It depicts Mary as Queen on the palimpsest wall of Santa Maria Antiqua, the oldest church dedicated to Mary in Rome, built at the foot of the Palatine Hill, in the Roman Forum (fig. 4).[20] Here the Virgin appears in a frontal position, seated on a jeweled throne, with the Child

---

18. Mary Rose D'Angelo, "Veil, Virgins and the Tongues of Men and Angels: Women's Heads in Early Christianity," in *Off with Her Head! The Denial of Women's Identity in Religion, Myth, and Culture*, ed. Howard Eilberg-Schwartz and Wendy Doniger (Berkeley: University of California Press, 1995), 131–66.

19. On the spread of red footwear in depictions of the fifth to sixth century, see Croom, *Roman Clothing and Fashion*, 131.

20. Concerning this problem, see Marion Lawrence, "Maria Regina," *ArtBul* 7 (1925): 150–61; Ursula Nilgen, "Maria Regina: Ein politischer Kultbildtypus," *RJK* 19 (1981): 3–35; Mary Stroll, "Maria Regina: Papal Symbol," in *Queens and Queenship in Medieval Europe*, ed. Anne J. Duggan (Woodbridge: Boydell, 1997), 173–203.

Fig. 4. Rome, Santa Maria Antiqua, Virgin Mary as Queen. Source: J. Rasmus Brandt, Giuseppe Morganti, and John Osborne, eds., *Santa Maria Antiqua al foro romano cent'anni dopo* (Rome: Campisano, 2005), fig. 13.

on her lap.[21] She wears a crown and is flanked by two angels who serve as standard-bearers: the role of the Virgin in the incarnation is now conveyed as queenship. The image has been interpreted as the first of a long series of Marian images, primarily commissioned by popes, equating the Mother of God with a figure of the Roman Church, though recent studies have demonstrated that the fresco was painted before the space was transformed into a church, thus highlighting the devotional and private nature of the depiction.[22] The highly imperial and Byzantine accentuation of her dress, characterized by the precious (*lōros*) λῶρος, provides an important element in support of the hypothesis that the work's iconography may have its origins in Constantinople.[23] This hypoth-

---

21. Christ holds the codex of the gospels and not the scroll of the law, as would be the case in sixth-century depictions.

22. Beat Brenk, *The Apse, the Image and the Icon: An Historical Perspective of the Apse as a Space for Images* (Wiesbaden: Reichart, 2010), 102–3.

23. The *loros* is a sumptuous stole measuring seven meters long and decorated with golden embroidery and precious stones, which in Byzantium was wrapped around the body of the emperor or empress, falling in a complex and formalized system of folds; it was worn exclusively for Easter ceremonies and alluded to the resurrection of Christ. The *mappa*, however, was not a strictly imperial attribute, as demonstrated by the fact that one appears in the mosaic of Theodora in San Vitale, Ravenna, in the hands of a lady and not the empress; see Gilbert Dagron, "From the *Mappa* to the *Akakia*: Symbolic Drift," in *From Rome to Constantinople: Studies in Honour of Averil Cameron*, ed. Hagit Amirav and Baster Haar Romeny (Leuven: Peeters, 2007), 203–20. It does

esis is further supported by the survival of numerous Byzantine theological sources that consider the Virgin a queen, chief among them the famous Akathistos Hymn.[24] It was somewhat weakened, however, not only by the iconoclasts' destruction of all contemporary ecclesiastical works but also by the lack of any descendants in Byzantine depictions after the ninth century, which instead characterized the Virgin as *Regina poli*—that is, Queen of Heaven—a symbol of imperial victory against the city's aggressors.[25] As John Osborne has correctly observed, in the absence of decisive elements, we may only hypothesize that this patchy fresco was commissioned privately by high-ranking Byzantine officers and soldiers who were in Rome in the years following the Gothic War.[26] They likely stayed in the guards' barracks on the Palatine Hill, and their place of worship would later be transformed into a church under Justin II (565–576). The private nature of the depiction—which in any case was no longer visible by 575, as it was painted over with a new devotional image portraying the more common annunciation—is underlined by the fact that this particularly imperial Byzantine version has no sequel, even in Rome, where from the eighth century on popes repeatedly commissioned the crowned Virgin, but without a *lōros*.

Over the course of the sixth century, worship of the Virgin spread dramatically, as indicated by the two new churches dedicated to her in Rome, Santa Maria in Trastevere and Santa Maria Antiqua; as a consequence, images of Mary proliferated and gave rise to private devotional depictions, theological portrayals in mosaics within churches, and icons. In all these cases, however, Mary appears dressed in an ample dark mantle covering her head over a white bonnet; the color of the mantle varies from purple to blue, brown or black, giving the image a more or less regal connotation. The spread of Marian images in diversified media suggests that her worship had penetrated every social sphere, becoming the preferred channel

---

not appear that the crown worn by the Virgin in Santa Maria Antiqua has *perpendulia* (golden chains of pearls and precious stones hanging at the sides of the face), an attribute that, on the other hand, is strictly connected to the imperial couple, like the buckle with the three hanging pearls; see Stout, "Jewelry as a Symbol of Status," 83.

24. Averil Cameron, "The Theotokos in Sixth-Century Constantinople," *JTS* n.s. 29 (1978): 79–108.

25. Bissera V. Pentcheva, *Icons and Power: The Mother of God in Byzantium* (University Park: Pennsylvania State University Press, 2006), 12–13.

26. John Osborne, "Images of the Mother of God in Early Medieval Rome," in *Icon and Word: The Power of Images in Byzantium; Studies Presented to Robin Cormack*, ed. Antony Eastmond and Liz James (Aldershot: Ashgate, 2003), 140.

Fig. 5. Rome, Catacombs of Commodilla, Virgin Enthroned between Saints Felix and Adauctus and the Deceased, Turtura. Source: Maria Antonietta Crippa and Mahmoud Zibawi, *L'arte paleocristiana. Visione e Spazio dalle origini a Bisanzio* (Milan: Jaca Book, 1998), 369, plate 165.

for communicating with the invisible, as indicated by Erik Thunø, who has emphasized how the Christian system of signs was established in the sixth century through the development of clearly defined hierarchical and symbolic structures.[27] It is no accident that at the beginning of the century, the fresco of Turtura, in the catacombs of Commodilla (fig. 5), clearly shows how the ritual of intercession inevitably leads to identification between the intercessor and the supplicant and how the spiritual model is reflected in visual reality.[28]

---

27. Erik Thunø, "The Cult of the Virgin, Icons and Relics in Early Medieval Rome: A Semiotic Approach," *AAAHP* 17 (2003): 79–141.

28. On the fresco of Turtura, see Eugenio Russo, "L'affresco di Turtura nel Cim-

Fig. 6. Croatia, Poreč, Euphrasian Basilica, *Apse*. Source: *Enciclopedia dell'arte medievale* 9 (Rome: Treccani, 1998), 176.

The spread of iconography featuring the Virgin enthroned, flanked by two angels serving as standard-bearers, was spurred by her appearance in monumental size in public places of worship, of which only sporadic traces remain today in Santa Maria Capua Vetere; the Blacherne in Constantinople; the Euphrasian Basilica in Parenzo (fig. 6); Sant'Apollinare Nuovo and Santa Maria Maggiore in Ravenna; Panagia Angeloktisti in Kiti (fig. 7a) and Panagia Kanakaria in Lythrankomi (fig. 7b), both in Cyprus; Saint Demetrius in Thessaloniki; Saint Sergius in Gaza; and the Church of the Nativity in Bethlehem.[29] But an important role in this spread must have been played by movable objects, such as icons, and especially textiles, given that weaving is the ultimate sacred art; the Apocrypha link it directly to the Virgin, who wove material that in this very period also began to be connected with the holy face of Christ, while in Constantinople the textile reliquaries of the Virgin—her dress, *maphorion* (mantle or veil), and belt—took on extraordinary importance.[30] An example of this produc-

---

itero di Commodilla, l'icona di S. Maria in Trastevere e le più antiche feste della Madonna a Roma," *BISIME* 59 (1980–1981): 71–150.

29. Christa Ihm, *Die Programme der christlichen Apsismalerei vom 4. Jahrhundert bis zur Mitte des 8. Jahrhunterts* (Stuttgart: Steiner, 1992).

30. Gerhard Wolf, "From Mandylion to Veronica: Picturing the 'Disembodied' Face and Disseminating the True Image of Christ in the Latin West," in *The Holy Face and the Paradox of Representation: Papers of a Colloquium Held at the Bibliotheca*

Fig. 7a. Cyprus, Kiti, Panagia Angeloktisti. Source: M. C. Crippa, M. Zibawi, *L'arte paleocristiana: Visione e Spazio dalle origini a Bisanzio* (Milan: Jaca Book, 1998), 398, fig. 354.

Fig. 7b. Cyprus, Nicosia, Archbishop Makarios Byzantine Museum, *Panagia Kanakaria*, from Lythrankomi. Source: M. C. Crippa, M. Zibawi, *L'arte paleocristiana: Visione e Spazio dalle origini a Bisanzio* (Milan: Jaca Book, 1998), 397, fig. 351.

Hertziana, Rome and The Villa Spelman in Florence, 1996, eds. Herbert L. Kessler and Gerhard Wolf; Bologna: Cluéb, 1998), 153–79; Annemarie Weyl Carr, "Threads of Authority: The Virgin Mary's Veil in the Middle Ages," in *Robes and Honor: the Medieval World of Investitures*, ed. Steward Gordon (New York: Palgrave, 2001), 63

tion can be found in the extraordinary Coptic tapestry at the Cleveland Museum of Art showing Mary enthroned, with the Child on her lap, in a space that is architecturally defined by two columns and surrounded by the shield-bearing busts of the twelve apostles, while Christ triumphant appears in the upper section.[31] The fact that the Child holds the scroll with the same gesture depicted in the Turtura panel in Rome (fig. 5) and in the apse of the Panagia Kanakaria in Lythrankomi (fig. 7b) bears witness not only to their common source but also to the circulation of these images in the Mediterranean basin.[32]

The Virgin enthroned also triumphs on another type of object: the bindings of liturgical codices, formed by diptychs with five compartments and made of ivory, a material that along with silk and precious metals was the preferred medium for diplomatic exchanges and official gifts, in both the political and the religious spheres.[33] Mary enthroned among the angels was represented on the front cover along with scenes from her childhood, while Christ enthroned between Peter and Paul occupied the back cover; all four surviving specimens have been attributed to an atelier in Constantinople active in the sixth century, though none of them was recorded there in either ancient or modern times.[34] This centralization of production, proven on an exclusively stylistic basis, tends to confirm Constantinople's fundamental role in designing sacred images, especially those of Mary, but it does not explain the iconographic variations that were primarily derived

---

31. Dorothy Shepherd, "An Icon of the Virgin: A Sixth-Century Tapestry Panel from Egypt," *BCM* 56 (1969): 90–120.

32. Shepherd, "Icon of the Virgin," 93–94. The Child holds the vertical scroll in his veiled left hand and rests his right hand atop it, in the gesture typical to the classical philosopher.

33. Anthony Cutler, *The Craft of Ivories: Sources, Techniques, and Uses in the Mediterranean World, A.D. 200–1400* (Washington, DC: Dumbarton Oaks Research Library and Collection, 1985).

34. On the attribution to Constantinople of the diptychs of the gospel book of Saint-Lupicin (Parigi, Bibliothèque nationale de France, MS lat. 9384), the gospel book of Ejmiatzin (Erevan, Matenandaran Library, MS 2374), and the gospel book of Andoche (Saulieu, Musée François-Pompon, with binding formed by two simple plates), see Jean-Pierre Caillet, "L'origine des derniers ivoires antiques," *RevA* 72 (1986): 7–15; see also John Lowden, "The Word Made Visible: The Exterior of the Early Christian Books as Visual Argument," in *The Early Christian Book*, ed. William E. Klingshirn and Linda Safran (Washington, DC: Catholic University of America Press, 2001), 13–47, which adds the fragmented diptych of Murano, the pieces of which are scattered among various collections.

from the Apocrypha and that characterize the scenes of Christ's infancy in the four surviving specimens. The fact that these diptychs were designed to embellish the bindings of gospel books containing the four canonical gospels renders the problem even more interesting, highlighting how the images could not have been exclusively instructional in purpose, as suggested by Pope Gregory I when arguing against the appeals for iconoclasm made by Serenus of Marseille.[35] Rather, their role appears fundamental to visualizing the invisible, and not solely for the *litteras nescientes*.[36]

It would be interesting to compare these bindings with the illustrations of the illuminated codices of this period, but unfortunately the one surviving Roman manuscript, the gospel book of Corpus Christi College in Cambridge, MS 286, only preserves miniatures depicting the scenes of the passion according to Luke.[37] Images in books from the Near East, however, are more numerous. In the contemporary Rabbula Gospels, laid out in the Syriac scriptorium of Saint John of Beth Zagba in 586, the Virgin appears (fol. 1v) as the ὁδηγήτρια, standing with the Child held on her left arm, dressed in purple and gold and framed by a ciborium made of marble, metal, and precious stones, and flanked by two peacocks, a Christological symbol as well as a symbol of royalty in the Middle Eastern tradition.[38] This aristocratic figure, which forms an *imago praefatoria*, contrasts with the Virgin as coprotagonist for the first time in the entire Christological cycle, from his infancy to the *post mortem* scenes. In these sequences, which, according to Kurt Weitzmann, were inspired by Jerusalemite models, the Virgin appears cloaked in her usual dark garments, with some exceptions, as demonstrated by the festive color of her mantle

---

35. George Henry Tavard, *The Thousand Faces of the Virgin Mary* (Collegeville, MN: Liturgical Press, 1996), 82–83.

36. Thunø, *Cult of the Virgin*, 90. See also Herbert L. Kessler, *Spiritual Seeing: Picturing God's Invisibility in Medieval Art* (Philadelphia: University of Philadelphia Press, 2000).

37. In the scene depicting the climb to Calvary (fol. 125r), only one female figure appears while rending her clothes and baring her breast, as an illustration of Luke 23:27. See Francis Wormald, *The Miniature in the Gospel of St Augustine (Corpus Christi College ms. 286)* (Cambridge: Cambridge University Press, 1954).

38. On the Rabbula Gospels, see Massimo Bernabò, ed., *Il Tetravangelo di Rabbula: Firenze, Biblioteca Medicea Laurenziana ms. Plut. 1.56; L'illustrazione del Nuovo Testamento nella Siria del VI secolo* (Rome: Edizioni di Storia e Letteratura, 2008). On the ὁδηγήτρια iconography, see Maria Vassilaki, ed., *Mother of God: Representations of the Virgin in Byzantine Art* (Athens: Abbeville, 2000).

in the episode of the wedding at Cana (fol. 5r).[39] In this extraordinary sequence, too, there is no lack of elements drawn from the Apocrypha, as easily seen in the annunciation to Zechariah, but especially in the annunciation to the Virgin, which clearly shows her spinning thread.

Two images of Mary from books of this period have also been preserved in Armenia, with the Virgin in the annunciation clad in a mantle with an abundant fringe, standing before a luxurious building, and in the adoration of the Magi enthroned in a rigidly frontal position, displaying a shield with an image of the Child.[40] Thus in the sixth century, while we note a rigorously formalized spread of Marian icons, there is a proliferation of variety in the narrative scenes, especially in the areas where Monophysitism was more hotly debated. This is shown in another series of ivories, made in Constantinople around 546 but intended for Bishop Maximianus of Ravenna (546–556).[41] The bishop's throne presents the sequence of the life of Christ with extraordinary scenes from his infancy; these include the panel showing the journey to Bethlehem, with Mary, suffering and weighed down by her pregnancy, supported by Joseph and balancing precariously on a donkey led by his stepson—a scene that would be rarely repeated, especially with this personal accentuation, in later centuries (fig. 8).[42]

The Marian images produced in Rome must also have included textiles, as the *Liber pontificalis* amply testifies, but those that survive from this period are paintings on panels or canvas and are simple portraits for public use in the *praesepia*—that is, the oratories built inside the main Marian basilicas.[43] The icons of Santa Maria Antiqua, Santa Maria Maggiore, and

---

39. Weitzmann, "*Loca Sancta* and the Representational Arts," 37–44.

40. These are the miniatures later added to the Gospels of Etchmiadzin (MS 2374 of Erevan) in 989; see Lilit Zakarian, "La miniature arménienne de la haute époque," in *La miniature arménienne: Collection du Maténandaran*, ed. Tamara Mazaéva (Erevan: Naïri, 2006), 11.

41. Clementina Rizzardi, "La cattedra eburnea di Massimiano a Ravenna: Rilettura stilistica," in *Hadriatica: Attorno a Venezia e al Medioevo tra arti, storia e storiografia; Scritti in onore di Wladimiro Dorigo*, ed. Ennio Concina, Giordana Trovabene, and Michela Agazzi (Padua: Il Poligrafo, 2002), 145–50.

42. One of the rare examples of this iconography is found in the binding of the gospel book of Saint-Lupicin.

43. On *Liber pontificalis*, see Maria Andaloro, "Immagine e immagini nel *Liber pontificalis* da Leone I a Adriano I," in *Il "Liber pontificalis" e la Storia Materiale: Atti del Convegno Internazionale, Roma, 21–22 febbraio 2002* (*Mededelingen van het Ned-*

Fig. 8. Paris, Bibliothèque nationale de France, MS Lat. 9384, Ivory binding: *Journey to Bethlehem*. Source: Jean-Pierre Caillet "L'origine des derniers ivoires antiques," *Revue de l'art* 72 (1986): 7–15.

the Pantheon, the three largest churches dedicated to the Virgin in the city of the popes, are all modeled on the iconography of the ὁδηγήτρια.[44]

While all these sacred images are thought to have been produced by the sixth century or the beginning of the seventh, the evidence throughout the seventh century appears quite limited; still production of Marian images did not slow down. In fact, another extraordinary image of the Mater Dei located in Santa Maria Antiqua has been assigned to this period, approximately around 650.[45] In it, a fragmentary fresco depicts the Virgin standing, leaning her face toward that of the Child; this might be early evidence of the iconography of the Eleousa (Virgin of Tenderness), which for a long time

---

erlands Institut te Rome, LX–LXI 2001–2002), ed. Herman Geertman (Assen: Van Gorcum, 2003), 45–103.

44. See catalogued works nos. 375–76 in Andaloro, *Aurea Rome: Dalla città pagana alla città Cristiana; Catalogo della mostra, Roma, Palazzo delle Esposizioni 20 dicembre 2000–24 aprile 2001*, ed. Serena Ensoli and Eugenio La Rocca (Rome: L'Erma di Bretschneider, 2000), 660–62. Regarding the Eastern origin of the icon in the *Monasterium tempuli*, see work no. 378 in Andaloro, *Aurea Rome*, 663.

45. Per Jonas Nordhagen, "La più antica Eleousa conosciuta: Una scoperta in S. Maria Antiqua," *BolA* 47 (1962): 351–53.

was believed to be an invention of the eleventh or twelfth century of Coptic or Byzantine origin.[46]

In any case, the presence of these images in Rome, whether they were of local or foreign origin, was the result of a specific project enacted under the supervision of the Roman curia. There was a genuine plan to export these images because of their effectiveness in the lengthy process by which Christianity spread to central and Northern Europe, and this plan was promoted by the Church of Rome even before the alliance with the Franks begun under Pope Zacharias (751). In fact, the venerable Bede testifies that when Benedict Biscop returned from his fourth journey to Rome in 679–680, he brought to the monasteries of Wearmouth and Jarrow, which he had just founded, not only reliquaries, books, the arch-cantor John, and a letter of privilege from Pope Agatho (678–681) but also *imagines* or *picturae imaginum* of the Virgin, saints, and the Old and New Testament stories.[47] An immediate reflection of these images can be found in the island's culture, as Ernst Kitzinger demonstrated in 1956 when he analyzed the iconography of the wooden chest that contained the relics of Cuthbert, crafted in Lindisfarne in 698, eleven years after the death of the sainted bishop and abbot.[48] Focusing his attention on the Virgin and Child carved on it, Kitzinger traced the new iconography, characterized by the position of the Virgin, back to Roman culture: the lower part of her body is in profile, but her face is in a frontal position. He highlighted how this iconography favored the expression of a more affectionate relationship between mother and child, as documented by other insular images deriving from this one, chief among them the Virgin and Child of the Book of Kells (Iona, ca. 800; fig. 9), in which the expression of this emotional bond

---

46. Robert P. Bergman suggests that this ivory, now in America, may be the first example of the Eleousa, agreeing that it dates to the sixth century ("The Earliest Eleousa: A Coptic Ivory in the Walters Art Gallery," *JWAG* 48 [1990]: 37–56).

47. Bede, *Vita sanct. abb.* 6: *picturas imaginum sanctarum quas ad ornandum ecclesiam beati Petri Apostoli quam construxerat detulit; imaginem videlicet beatae dei genitricis semperque virginis Mariae, simul et duodecim apostolorum.* See Ernst Kitzinger, "The Role of Miniature Painting in Mural Decoration," in *The Place of the Book Illumination in Byzantine Art*, ed. Kurt Weitzmann et al. (Princeton: Publications of the Art Museum of Princeton University, 1975), 118.

48. Ernst Kitzinger, "The Coffin-Reliquary," in *The Relics of St. Cuthbert*, ed. Christopher Francis Battiscombe (Oxford: Oxford University Press, 1956), 202–304; see also David H. Wright, review of *The Relics of St. Cuthbert*, ed. Christopher Francis Battiscombe, *ArtBul* 43 (1961): 141–60.

Fig. 9. Dublin, Trinity College Library, MS A. I (58), f. 7v: *Book of Kells, Virgin and Child*. Source: C. Farr, *The Book of Kells: Its Function and Audience* (London: The British Library, 1997), plate V.

achieves extraordinary intensity.[49]

In parallel, worship of Mary in Rome, which was favored by a strong presence of Greek monks, culminated during the papacy of Sergius I (687–701) with the institution of the last of the four Marian feast days recognized in the West: the assumption.[50] This more rigorous division of the Marian feast days, the result of more structured relations with the Byzantine world, led to a complex system of images in Rome, formed by assimilating, innovating, and transforming different iconographies that originated in theological and exegetical speculation but were also dictated by devotion. In this context, it is quite difficult to date the large encaustic panel preserved in Santa Maria in Trastevere (see fig. 8), which the restorations of the 1950s revealed in all its extraordinary complexity. The dates proposed vary between the sixth and early eighth centuries.[51] The image restates the iconography of Mary as queen, with her sumptuous crown enriched by *perpendulia*, her fine purple tunic embellished by a pearl-studded collar and

---

49. Martin Werner, "The Madonna and Child Miniature in the Book of Kells," *ArtBul* 54 (1972): 1–23 and 129–39; George Henderson, *From Durrow to Kells: The Insular Gospel-Books, 650–800* (London: Thames & Hudson, 1987), 154–55.

50. Andrew J. Ekonomou, *Byzantine Rome and the Greek Popes* (Lanham, MD: Lexington, 2007), 260–64.

51. Catalogued work no. 377 in Andaloro, *Aurea Roma*, 662–63.

rotae, but without a *lōros*, a crucial element in attributing the origins of this iconography to the imperial tradition of Constantinople. Comparisons and arguments raised by Carlo Bertelli at the time of the work's restoration suggest that Pope John VII (705–707) may have commissioned it, but it could be an older image reused/adapted by adding the figure of this pope in προσκύνησις.[52] His devotion to the worship of Mary is expressed not only in votive frescoes in Santa Maria Antiqua but also in the funerary chapel dedicated to the Virgin in Saint Peter's Basilica.[53] In the image, Mary was portrayed as a queen, with attributes entirely similar to those of the Madonna della Clemenza, but standing in the pose of prayer without the Child, while beside her the Pope, Johannes *indignus episcopus*, appeared once again, this time standing with a miniature of the oratory in his hands.[54] Surrounding the two main figures were depictions of episodes from the life of Christ up to the resurrection. The Virgin's role as mediator, indicated as *Sancta Dei Genitrix* in the *titulus*, is underlined by the fact that for the first time in Western tradition, the angelic greeting (Luke 1:28) appears to the side of the annunciation written in block capitals. As Ann Karin van Dijk has effectively suggested, this is a clear invitation to the faithful to repeat the invocation of the Mother of God for their own eternal salvation, as well as for that of the pope who commissioned the work.[55]

The rise of iconoclasm introduced by Leo III the Isaurian in 730 was immediately reflected in the handling of Western images, as demonstrated by the *Liber pontificalis*. It reports that when Pope Gregory III (731–741), who was of Syriac origin, consecrated an oratory in Saint Peter's dedicated to the Savior, Mary, and the saints in 731, he placed an image of the Virgin there, adorning it with a jeweled crown, necklace and earrings,

---

52. Carlo Bertelli, *La Madonna di Santa Maria in Trastevere: Storia—iconografia—mito di un dipinto romano dell'ottavo secolo* (Rome: Tipografia Eliograf, 1961). In fact, the figure of the donor is painted with tempera and not encaustic; see Osborne, "Images of the Mother of God," 149, n. 31.

53. Ann Karin van Dijk, "The Oratory of Pope John VII (705–7) in Old St Peter's" (PhD diss., Johns Hopkins University, 1995).

54. The mosaic fragment with the Virgin is currently found in the Dominican Church of San Marco in Florence; the fragment with the patron, however, is in Saint Peter's. See Ann Karin van Dijk, "Reading Medieval Mosaics in the Seventeenth Century: The Preserved Fragments from Pope John VII's Oratory in Old St Peter's," *W&I* 22 (2006): 285–91.

55. Ann K. van Dijk, "The Angelic Salutation in Early Byzantine and Medieval Annunciation Imagery," *ArtBul* 81 (1999): 420–36.

and a silver frame.⁵⁶ The image was transformed into an icon—that is, an object that imposes itself upon the collective consciousness by demanding respect and reverence. It interfaces directly with the divine archetype, not only becoming a direct channel of intercession, but taking on a concrete and fundamental role in liturgy. The last step was taken by Pope Stephen II (752–757), who, when faced with the threat of the Lombards, announced a litany, in the course of which he brought—*proprio umero*— the ἀχειροποίητον icon of Christ from the Sancta Sanctorum to Santa Maria Maggiore, which housed the icon of Mary.⁵⁷ This icon was destined to play a primary role when the procession of August 15 for the Feast of the Dormition would later be established.⁵⁸

Over the course of the eighth century, images of Mary proliferated, and a different type that had already become widespread in Coptic and Middle Eastern churches appeared in Rome: the image of the Virgin and Child in a niche. These images seem to take on particular connotations: being located outside the chancel, they are certainly not only an expression of piety on the part of laypeople but are probably also commissioned by women, given that they are often in the right nave—that is, on the side reserved for the female component of the religious community.⁵⁹ Both frequent repaintings and traces of candles and perfumes bear witness to the complex relationship between prayer and gift, between spiritual and physical, that characterizes devotional practice. And on this subject, we must remember that the panel of the Madonna della Clemenza originally bore witness to this practice in an extraordinary way. As Jonas Nordhagen has suggested, the Virgin depicted there probably held an actual golden processional cross, attached to the panel and offered by the building's patron.⁶⁰

---

56. Thomas F. X. Noble, *Images, Iconoclasm, and the Carolingians* (University Park: University of Pennsylvania Press, 2009), 127–28.

57. Enrico Parlato, "Le icone in processione," in *Arte e iconografia a Roma da Costantino a Cola di Rienzo*, ed. Maria Andaloro and Serena Romano (Milan: Jaca Book, 2000), 69–92, 74–75.

58. Hans Belting, *Bild und Kult: Eine Geschichte des Bildes vor dem Zeitalter der Kunst* (Munich: Beck, 1990), 363–68.

59. John Osborne, "Early Medieval Painting in San Clemente, Rome: The Madonna and Child in the Niche," *Gesta* 20 (1981): 299–310; Osborne, "Images of the Mother of God," 141–44.

60. Per Jonas Nordhagen, "Icon Designed for the Display of Sumptuous Votive

The West seems to have developed an increasingly complex relationship of use and exchange of images in general, and those of Mary in particular, in the very years when iconoclasm clearly interrupted these rituals in the East and when the iconophobic Islamic domination expanded to the areas around the Mediterranean. The frescoes of Santa Maria Antiqua indicate the importance of the model provided by papal patronage, which was very active throughout the eighth century, despite the repeated Lombard incursions against Rome and the later arrival of the Franks. Both Popes Zacharias (741–752) and Hadrian I (772–795) are portrayed beside the Virgin enthroned, who, in the latter case, is identified for the first time with the *titulus* of Maria Regina. To this last pope we also owe the gift to the basilica of Santa Maria Maggiore of a cloth *ex auro purissimo atque gemmis, habentem adsumptionem sanctae Dei genetricis*, the first ever example of this controversial iconography of the assumption.[61]

From this moment on, images of the Virgin were also documented in continental Europe, where there was no shortage of churches dedicated to her in previous centuries, such as the Daurade of Toulouse, which as late as the seventeenth century held considerable traces of its impressive mosaic decoration of Marian episodes and icons.[62] The first image of this new sequence is found in the Sacramentary of Gellone, which is one of the first works to document the new liturgical text developed at the court of Charlemagne after 784.[63]

The incipit page (fol. 1v) of this codex, made to be used by the diocese of Meaux in northeastern France, shows a standing female figure, identified by text as *SCA maria*, holding a processional cross from which an α and a ω hang in her left hand and holding a censer in her right. She appears dressed in a tunic of a cloth decorated with geometric patterns, while her head is covered by a hood, its lower edges falling on her shoulders. Elements clearly derived from Coptic sources lead us to think of examples of

---

Gifts," in *Studies of Art and Archaeology in Honour of Ernst Kitzinger* (Washington, DC: Dumbarton Oaks Research Library and Collection, 1987), 453–60.

61. Andaloro, "Immagine e immagini nel *Liber pontificalis*," 68.

62. Helen Woodruff, "The Iconography and Date of the Mosaics of La Daurade," *ArtBul* 13 (1931): 80–104.

63. Paris, Bibliothèque nationale de France, MS lat. 12048: catalogued work no. 7 in Marianne Besseyre, *Trésors carolingiens: Livres manuscrits de Charlemagn à Charles le Chauve; Catalogue de l'exposition, Paris, Bibliothèque nationale de France, Site Richelieu, 20 mars–14 juin 2007* (Paris: Bibliothèque nationale de France, 2007), 78–83.

books imported from the Mediterranean, though it is difficult to retrace the possible ways in which these elements spread, as they seem to have reached only outlying towns and cities.[64] In fact, the models in use in the court scriptorium at Aachen were derived from the tradition of the great imperial capitals: Ravenna, Rome, or Constantinople, and the Virgin had no place in the system of images developed to illustrate luxurious liturgical codices, except on the covers, which followed the examples of the previously mentioned diptychs with five sections produced in sixth-century Constantinople.[65] In each of these cases, the Virgin is dressed in a tunic and *maphorion*, but in an extraordinary purple manuscript, written in gold and silver and produced in Bavaria in the first quarter of the ninth century, the Virgin is again a *foemina clarissima*, dressed in the older, classical style and placed at the center of episodes that are very rarely depicted, such as Joseph doubting Mary's innocence or Mary entering her husband's home.[66] These diverse solutions bear witness to the presence and circulation in the Western Christian world of late antique codices of the New Testament of which only sporadic traces now remain, together with those that Kitzinger has defined as "iconographic guides"—that is, patterns of narrative sequences sent by Rome to support an orthodox portrayal of the gospels and lives of the saints.[67]

Starting with the papacy of Paschal I (795–823), we find the Virgin in Rome again as the protagonist of the mosaic decoration in the apse of Santa Maria in Domnica (fig. 10).[68] Restored between 817 and 822, it

---

64. Erwin Rosenthal, "Some Observations on Coptic Influence in Western Early Medieval Manuscripts," in *Homage to a Bookman: Essays on Manuscripts, Books and Printing; Written for Hans P. Kraus on His Sixtieth Birthday, Oct. 12 1967*, ed. Hellmut Lehmann-Haupt (Berlin: Mann, 1967), 51–74.

65. In particular, see the plate of the binding on the gospel book of Lorsch preserved in the Vatican Apostolic Library.

66. Catalogued work no. 5 in Béatrice Hernad, *Pracht auf Pergament: Schätze der Buchmalerei von 780 bis 1180; Katalog der Ausstellung, München, Kunsthalle der Hypo-Kulturstiftung vom 19. Oktober 2012 bis zum 13. Januar 2013* (Munich: Hirmer, 2012), 69.

67. Kitzinger, "Role of Miniature Painting," 117–20; Giuseppa Z. Zanichelli, "Les livres des modèles et les dessins préparatoires au Moyen Âge," *CSMC* 43 (2012): 61–70.

68. The only image earlier than this is the one in the chapel of Saint Venantius (625–650) in the Lateran Baptistery complex, where the Virgin, in a prayer pose, appears at the base of the apsidal recess, surrounded by saints and other prelates, whereas the vault of the apse is dominated by the bust of Christ between two angels;

Fig. 10. Rome, Santa Maria in Domnica, *Apse*. Source: *Enciclopedia dell'arte medieval* 4 (Rome: Treccani 1993), 315.

shows the Virgin enthroned with the Child among a choir of standing angels, with the pope kneeling before her, touching her holy foot while the Virgin blesses him. Paschal I bestowed images upon this church other objects with Marian, including a golden veil with the depiction of the nativity, which gives solid proof of the eminently Christ-centered meaning of these depictions.[69] But in the chapel that the pope had built in memory of his mother, *Theodora episcopa*, adjacent to the right nave of the building, there is a niche holding an image of the Virgin enthroned with the Child between two female saints, which, however restored, must have been an expression of the pope's personal, private devotion from the beginning, contrasting with the theological image in the larger church. In such a context, as Thunø has recently underlined, the reliquary enamel cross donated by this pope to the Sancta Sanctorum of the Lateran takes on extraordinary

---

see Gillian V. Mackie, *Early Christian Chapels in the West: Decoration, Function and Patronage* (Toronto: Toronto University Press, 2003), 212–30. On Santa Maria in Domnica, see Maria Andaloro and Serena Romano, "L'immagine nell'abside," in Andaloro and Romano, *Arte e iconografia a Roma*, 106–7.

69. Although the veil cited in the *Liber pontificalis* has disappeared, the cloth with the annunciation, now preserved in the Vatican Museums, remains to bear witness to the patronage of Paschal I.

Fig. 11: San Vincenzo al Volturno, Crypt of Epiphanius, *The Virgin Reading.* Source: Valentino Pace, "La pittura medievale nel Molise, in Basilicata e Calabria," in *La pittura in Italia: L'Altomedioevo*, ed. C. Bertelli (Milan: Electa, 1994), 271, fig. 346.

importance.[70] In fact, in the dedication, the pope offers the reliquary to the Virgin, whom he invokes as *REGINA MVNDI*, and defines the reliquary as *VEXILLUM CRVCIS*, emphasizing the unique role played by Mary not only in the incarnation, but also in humanity's path to salvation.[71]

In Paschal I's Rome, the Virgin appears at the center of theological speculation, which would directly impact her later representation, enriching it with new elements. The most important evidence in this regard is provided by the frescoes of the crypt that the abbot Epiphanius (824–842) had painted toward the end of his life in the monastery of San Vincenzo al Volturno. Here, the Virgin not only appears in the cycle on the infancy of Christ but two additional times, both in traditional iconography—enthroned with the Child in her lap—and on her own. In the latter image (fig. 11), she is portrayed seated on the throne, with her hair swept up in a sophisticated style of classical origin, partially covered by a veil and complete with a long *pendulia*, while showing a book propped up on her knees where we read *BEATAM ME DICENT*—that is, the passage of the Magnificat (Luke 1:46–55). The same text is quoted in the *Sermo de assumptione*

---

70. Erik Thunø, *Image and Relic: Mediating the Sacred in Early Medieval Rome* (Rome: L'Erma di Bretschneider, 2002).

71. For the interpretation of the reliquary's inscription and its consequent attribution to the patronage of Paschal I, see Charles Rufus Morey, "The Inscription on the Enameled Cross of Paschal I," *ArtBul* 19 (1937): 595–96.

Fig. 12. Sankt Gallen, Stiftsbibliothek, Cod. 53: *Ascension*. Source: W. Volger, ed., *La abbazia di San Gallo* (Milan: Jaca Book, 1990), 85, plate 13.

Mariae by Ambrose Autpert, who had been abbot of the monastery in 777–778. This very exegete was believed to be the source of inspiration for this new Marian iconography, as he had underlined the Virgin's spiritual maternity, even in connection with the human race, and her role as mediator, particularly significant in this crypt, which was built to serve a funerary purpose.[72] In this case, too, the writing on display serves to involve the faithful in devotion and prayer, as it does in the chapel of John VII in the Vatican.

The next step is represented by the ivory carving made by the monk Tuotilo in Saint Gall (fig. 12) as a decoration for the binding for the *Evangelium longum* (MS 53). On this cover, the assumption of the Virgin appears for the first time in the West (in 895), as undeniably indicated by the *titulus—Ascensio sce mariae—* set above Mary, who is portrayed standing with arms raised in a gesture of supplication and intercession, thus without the divine Child, and surrounded by angels.[73] In fact, although the Feast Day of the Assumption had enjoyed a stable place in Roman liturgy for over

---

72. John Mitchell, "The Crypt Reappraised," in *The 1980–1986 excavations*, vol. 1 of *San Vincenzo al Volturno*, part 1, ed. Richard Hodges, AMBSR 7 (London: British School at Rome, 1993), 75–114.

73. Marguerite Menz-von der Mühll, "Der St. Gallen Elfenbeine um 900," *FMSt* 15 (1981): 392–418; Henry Mayr-Harting, "The Idea of the Assumption of Mary in the

a century, the about her assumption was still lively and contradictory: while her assumption *in anima* was universally accepted, her assumption *in corpore* was still hotly debated.[74] It comes as no surprise that the monasteries played an important part in the creation of new iconographies, given that in the Carolingian era, monastic reform had restructured the types of sacred buildings within the monastic system. The main church, whose dedication might vary, and the church dedicated to Benedict were now joined by a third building dedicated to the Virgin, where the liturgy reserved for her was celebrated.

To some degree, this flowering of images in Rome and in the West must have influenced the revival of Marian images in Byzantium at the end of the iconoclastic period in 843. In fact, restoration was begun on the old apses, starting precisely with the Church of the Dormiton in Nicaea, where in 787 the council that readmitted images into the Byzantine liturgy had been held. The projects continued in Constantinople with the Chalkoprateia, and, in 867, with the Hagia Sophia.[75] In all of these monuments, the Virgin appears clad in fine blue or purple tunics, her mantle embellished with a sophisticated fringe and precious embroidery, while her presence multiplies in the Marian cycles, even in the passion and *post mortem* scenes. Starting around 900, the final image of these cycles became the κοίμησις—that is, the Virgin's "dormition into death"—a scene that normally unfolds over three panels, with the lower one showing the Virgin *gisante* among the apostles in prayer, the middle panel depicting Christ raising his mother's *animula* to the heavens, and the upper panel portraying her soul brought triumphantly to the heavens by the angels.[76] This new iconography spread in the West through textile and ivory pieces and was especially common in the Ottonian era, when the heavenly apotheosis of the Virgin became the archetype for the imperial apotheosis, granting her worship a noticeably political value in line with the directives of the *Reichskirche*. During this period, Germany and northern Italy

---

West, 800–1200," in *The Church and Mary*, ed. Robert Norman Swanson (Rochester, NY: Boydell, 2004), 86–111.

74. Stephen J. Shoemaker, *Ancient Traditions of the Virgin Mary's Dormition and Assumption* (Oxford: Oxford University Press, 2002).

75. Robin Cormack, "The Mother of God in Apse Mosaics," in Vassilaki, *Mother of God*, 91–105.

76. Rosalie Kachudas Baryames, *The Iconography of the Koimesis: Its Sources and Early Development* (East Lansing: Michigan State University Press, 1977).

became the source of major iconographic innovations that are primarily transmitted to us by the codices laid out in the scriptoria of the great imperial abbeys. In this context, the Virgin returns to her role as Theotokos, and the ceremonial complex of the court is reflected in the gospel scenes, where the image of Mary is included even when not explicitly cited in the text.[77] This was especially noticeable during the short reign of Otto III (996–1002), as demonstrated by his gospel book (Munich, Bayerische Staadsbibliothek, MS Clm 4453), which portrays the κοίμησις both on the Byzantine panel of the binding and in the text (fol. 161v). A direct comparison between the ivory crafted in Byzantium and the miniature created in the scriptorium of Reichenau instantly reveals how the model in the West was transformed and restructured, arranging the apostles in two groups of six and transforming the *elevatio animae* into the assumption.[78] The model of the imperial abbeys became a standard. Thus the Virgin, to whom nearly all the cathedrals would be progressively dedicated, with a profusion of altars consecrated to her, also became the official protectress of abbots, such as Witigowo, abbot of Reichenau (985–997), and bishops, such as Warmund of Ivrea (965–1011) and Bernward of Hildesheim (993–1022), her figure dominating the dedication scenes of the liturgical codices they commissioned.[79]

---

77. Daniel Russo, "Les représentations mariales dans l'art d'Occident: Essai sur la formation d'une tradition iconographique," in *Marie: Le culte de la Vierge dans la société médiévale*, ed. Dominique Iogna-Prat, Éric Palazzo, and Daniel Russo (Paris: Beauchesne, 1996), 209–32; see also Kristen Mary Collins, "Visualizing Mary: Innovation and Exegesis in Ottonian Manuscript Illumination" (PhD diss., University of Texas at Austin, 2007), 47–54.

78. Henry Mayr-Harting, *Themes*, vol. 1 of *Ottonian Book Illumination: An Historical Study* (London: Miller, 1991), 139–46.

79. Éric Palazzo, "Marie et une élaboration d'un espace ecclésial au haut Moyen Âge," in Iogna-Prat, Palazzo, and Russo, *Marie*, 313–25; Joachim Prochno, *Das Schreiber- und Dedikationbild in der Deutschen Buchmalerei, I, Bis zum Ende des 11. Jahrhunderts (800–1100) (Die Enwicklung des menschlichen Bildnisses*, hrsg. v. Walter Goetz, 2) (Leipzig: Teubner, 1929), 29; Adriano Peroni, "Il ruolo della committenza vescovile alle soglie del Mille: Il caso di Warmondo di Ivrea," in *Committenti e produzione artistico-letteraria nell'Alto Medioevo occidentale, Atti della XXXIX settimana di studio del CISAM, Spoleto, 4–10 aprile 1991* (Spoleto: CISAM, 1992), 247–74; Rainer Kahsnitz, "Inhalt und Aufbau der Handschrift: die Bilder," in *Das Kostbare Evangeliar des Heiligen Bernwald, Katalog der Ausstellung, Hildesheim, Dom- und Diozesanmuseum 6 Februar–21 marz 1993* (Munich: Prestel, 1993), 27–32.

Fig. 13: Essen, Münsterschatzmuseum, *Goldene Madonna* (*Enciclopedia dell'arte medievale* 6 [Rome: Treccani, 1998], 25).

One of the most extraordinary innovations of this period is the ever-growing presence of female patrons involved in the worship of Mary.[80] One need only cite the ciborium of Ambrose in Milan, one of the Ottonian capitals. Its northern side bears two female figures, identified as the empresses Adelaide and Theophanu, depicted praying on either side of the standing Virgin, who is holding an imperial crown while the dove of the Holy Spirit hovers above her.[81] Another example is the Golden Madonna of Essen (fig. 13), commissioned by the abbess Matilda (973–1011), cousin of Otto III. This precious sculpture depicts the Virgin enthroned with the Child as she holds the orb and cross in her right hand, rotating her body forward. This iconography has been connected with the new role held by women within the Ottonian dynasty, especially during the regency of Empress Theophanu (985–991).[82] Matilda of Essen also had herself portrayed with her brother Otto I, Duke of Swabia, the last representative of the Liudolf dynasty, in

---

80. Christina M. Nielsen warns against an interpretation overly conditioned by the gender history of the phenomenon, given the important role played by imperial patronage concerning the worship of Mary ("*Hoc opus eximium*: Artistic Patronage in the Ottonian Empire" [PhD diss., University of Chicago, 2002], 123). See also Collins, "Visualizing Mary," 11.

81. Patrick Corbet, "Les impératrices ottoniennes et le modèle marial," in Iogna-Prat, Palazzo, and Russo, *Marie*, 109–35.

82. Frank Fehrenbach, *Die Goldene Madonna im Essener Münster: Der Körper der Königin* (Essen: Tertium, 1996).

the enamel work adorning the lower part of the cross named after them, the Otto-Mathilden-Kreuz. The two siblings are shown grasping a processional cross that they hold up together, testifying to the two components of the Ottonian Empire, clergy and aristocracy.[83]

At the same time, manuscripts began to feature increasing numbers of female figures in connection with the Virgin, who became the model with which empresses, abbesses, and women belonging to the families of the highest nobility would identify.[84] The first and best-known codex is the one produced in Fulda in 975 containing the *Lives of Kilian and Margaret*, with a frontispiece showing the Virgin crowned and enthroned, crowning Saints Margaret and Regina, while the text identifies her as Theotokos, though the Child is absent.[85] In the same way, Mary was depicted in a lost codex—which is known from drawings—that showed Hadwig, abbess of Essen (910–951), and the nun Thiotera offering the book to the Virgin, who was shown enthroned among angels and holding a processional cross.[86] While these iconographies draw on elements from Roman and Byzantine tradition, they seem to enrich the Marian repertoire with direct references to Christological tradition.[87] Rather than being a simple illustration, they become an elaboration of exegesis, adding new elements, discussed in contemporary theological debate. This process is quite evident in the sacramentaries, where the image of the Virgin often becomes a figure associated with the church, especially when she appears in illustrations of the feast days of All Saints or Pentecost. But this process was also the foundation for the miniature that was at the center of a lively debate, the image at folio 40v of the Sacramentary of Peterhausen, which

---

83. Catalogued work no. 152 in Brigitta Falk, *Krone und Schleier: Kunst aus mittelalterlichen Frauenklöstern; Katalog der Ausstellung, Essen, Ruhrlandmuseum—Bonn, Kunst- und Austellungshalle vom 19. März bis 3. Juli 2005* (Munich: Hirmer, 2005), 273.

84. Rosamond McKitterick, "Women in the Ottonian Church: An Iconographic Perspective," in *Women in the Church: Papers Read at the 1989 Summer Meeting and the 1990 Winter Meeting of the Ecclesiastical History Society* (Oxford: Blackwell, 1990), 79–100.

85. Cynthia J. Hahn and Hans Immel, eds., *Passio Kiliani, Ps-Theotimus, Passio Margaretae, Orationes: Niedersäcsische Landesbibliothek Hannover Ms. I 189* (Gratz: Akademische Druck, 1988).

86. Katrin Graf, *Bildnisse schreibender Frauen im Mittelalter 9. bis Anfang 13. Jahrhundert* (Basel: Schwabe, 2002), 34–37.

87. Collins, "Visualizing Mary," 95–98.

seems to combine iconographic elements from the most dissimilar traditions.[88] It depicts a female figure on the throne, clad in a pink tunic with an embroidered collar and a mantle of precious fabric edged in gold, her haloed head encircled by a crown with *perpendulia*, while she holds a processional cross in her right hand and a book in her left; the throne is a simple parallelepiped with a long cushion. Alongside the more immediately recognizable Byzantine elements, there is no lack of Roman touches that lead us to identify her with the church—not the papal church, but rather an extraordinary expression of the *Reichskirche*, which looked to Byzantium in order to dominate the West. In fact, she is the ideal bride, as suggested by the figure of Christ enthroned facing her from the adjacent page in the manuscript, thus symbolizing the couple from the Song of Songs. This image has no direct descendants, given that shortly after the beginning of the second millennium, the imperial and Roman churches would break the truce that until then had been maintained with difficulty, and the figure of Mary and thus her iconography would take on a different role within the reform movement. Shortly after the Concordat of Worms (1122), she would be depicted as Sponsa-Ecclesia in the mosaic-decorated apse of Santa Maria Trastevere, in a skillful, layered reference to the oldest Roman tradition.[89]

An expression of authority or piety, of exegesis or devotion, the Virgin gradually became an autonomous figure in the first millennium, and through a myriad of nuances and a variety of depictions, she took on the role of mediator between individuals and Christ, between holders of political power and the Roman church. And whether as Theotokos in the East or as Mater Dei in the West, she acquired a dominant and legitimate role of high symbolic value, one capable of responding with extraordinary adaptability to the diverse needs of different Christian cultures.

Bibliography

Andaloro, Maria. *Aurea Rome: Dalla città pagana alla città Cristiana; Catalogo della mostra, Roma, Palazzo delle Esposizioni 20 dicembre 2000–24 aprile 2001*. Edited by Serena Ensoli and Eugenio La Rocca. Rome: L'Erma di Bretschneider, 2000.

---

88. Heidelberg, Cod. Sal. IXb; see also Collins, "Visualizing Mary," 152–57.
89. Ernst Kitzinger, "A Virgin's Face: Antiquarianism in the Twelfth Century," *ArtBul* 62 (1980): 6–19.

———. "Immagine e immagini nel *Liber pontificalis* da Leone I a Adriano I." Pages 45–103 in *Il "Liber pontificalis" e la Storia Materiale: Atti del Convegno Internazionale, Roma, 21–22 febbraio 2002 (Mededelingen van het Nederlands Institut te Rome, LX–LXI 2001–2002).* Edited by Herman Geertman. Assen: Van Gorcum, 2003.

———. *L'orizzonte tardoantico e le nuove immagini, 312–468.* Vol. 1 of *La pittura medievale a Roma*. Milan: Jaca Book, 2006.

Andaloro, Maria, and Serena Romano. "L'immagine nell'abside." Pages 95–130 in *Arte e iconografia a Roma: Da Costantino a Cola di Rienzo.* Edited by Maria Andaloro and Serena Romano. Milan: Jaca Book, 2000.

Angelidi, Christine. *Pulcheria: La castità al potere.* Milan: Jaca Book, 1996.

Baryames, Rosalie Kachudas. *The Iconography of the Koimesis: Its Sources and Early Development.* East Lansing: Michigan State University Press, 1977.

Belting, Hans. *Bild und Kult: Eine Geschichte des Bildes vor dem Zeitalter der Kunst.* Munich: Beck, 1990.

———. *Likeness and Presence: A History of the Image before the Era of Art.* Translated by Edmund Jephcott. Chicago: University of Chicago Press, 1994.

Bergman, Robert P. "The Earliest Eleousa: A Coptic Ivory in the Walters Art Gallery." *JWAG* 48 (1990): 37–56.

Bernabò, Massimo, ed. *Il Tetravangelo di Rabbula: Firenze, Biblioteca Medicea Laurenziana ms. Plut. 1.56; L'illustrazione del Nuovo Testamento nella Siria del VI secolo.* Rome: Edizioni di Storia e Letteratura, 2008.

Bertelli, Carlo. *La Madonna di Santa Maria in Trastevere: Storia—iconografia—mito di un dipinto romano dell'ottavo secolo.* Rome: Tipografia Eliograf, 1961.

Besseyre, Marianne. *Trésors carolingiens: Livres manuscrits de Charlemagn à Charles le Chauve; Catalogue de l'exposition, Paris, Bibliothèque nationale de France, Site Richelieu, 20 mars–14 juin 2007.* Paris: Bibliothèque nationale de France, 2007.

Bisconti, Fabrizio. "L'orante, Maria e le acque: L'incontro dei temi." Pages 19–25 in *Deomene: L'immagine dell'orante tra Oriente e Occidente; Catalogo della mostra, Ravenna, Museo Nazionale, 25 marzo–24 giugno 2001.* Edited by Angela Donati and Giovanni Gentili. Milan: Electa, 2001.

Brandt, J. Rasmus, Giuseppe Morganti, and John Osborne, eds. *Santa Maria Antiqua al foro romano cent'anni dopo.* Rome: Campisano, 2005.

Brenk, Beat. *Die Frühchristlichen Mosaiken in Santa Maria Maggiore zu Rom*. Wiesbaden: Steiner, 1975.

Brenk, Beat. *The Apse, the Image and the Icon: An Historical Perspective of the Apse as a Space for Images*. Wiesbaden: Reichart, 2010.

Caillet, Jean-Pierre. "L'origine des derniers ivoires antiques." *RevA* 72 (1986): 7–15.

Cameron, Averil. "The Cult of the Virgin in Late Antiquity: Religious Development and Myth-Making." Pages 1–21 in *The Church and Mary: Papers Read at the 2001 Summer Meeting and the 2002 Winter Meeting of the Ecclesiastical History Society*. Edited by Robert N. Swanson. Woodbridge: Boydell, 2004.

Cameron, Averil. "The Theotokos in Sixth-Century Constantinople." *JTS* n.s. 29 (1978): 79–108.

Carr, Annemarie Weyl. "Threads of Authority: The Virgin Mary's Veil in the Middle Ages." Pages 59–93 in *Robes and Honor: The Medieval World of Investitures*. Edited by Steward Gordon. New York: Palgrave, 2001.

Cartlidge, David R., and James Keith Elliott. *Art and the Christian Apocrypha*. London: Routledge, 2001.

Chiesa, Gemma Sena, ed. *Il Tesoro di San Nazaro: Antichi argenti liturgici della basilica di San Nazaro al Museo Diocesano di Milano*. Milan: Silvana, 2009.

Collins, Kristen Mary. "Visualizing Mary: Innovation and Exegesis in Ottonian Manuscript Illumination." PhD diss., University of Texas at Austin, 2007.

Corbet, Patrick. "Les impératrices ottoniennes et le modèle marial." Pages 109–35 in *Marie: Le culte de la Vierge dans la société médiévale*. Edited by Dominique Iogna Prat, Éric Palazzo, and Daniel Russo. Paris: Beauchesne, 1996.

Cormack, Robin. "The Mother of God in Apse Mosaics." Pages 91–105 in *Mother of God: Representations of the Virgin in Byzantine Art*. Edited by Maria Vasilake. New York: Abbeville, 2000.

Crippa, Maria Antonietta, and Mahmoud Zibawi. *L'arte paleocristiana: Visione e Spazio dalle origini a Bisanzio*. Milan: Jaca Book, 1998.

Croom, Alexandra. *Roman Clothing and Fashion*. Stroud: Amberley, 2010.

Cutler, Anthony. *The Craft of Ivories: Sources, Techniques, and Uses in the Mediterranean World, A.D. 200–1400*. Washington, DC: Dumbarton Oaks Research Library and Collection, 1985.

D'Angelo, Mary Rose. "Veil, Virgins and the Tongues of Men and Angels: Women's Heads in Early Christianity." Pages 131–66 in *Off with Her Head! The Denial of Women's Identity in Religion, Myth, and Culture*. Edited by Howard Eilberg-Schwartz and Wendy Doniger. Berkeley: University of California Press 1995.

Dagron, Gilbert. "From the *Mappa* to the *Akakia*: Symbolic Drift." Pages 203–20 in *From Rome to Constantinople: Studies in Honour of Averil Cameron*. Edited by Hagit Amirav and Baster Haar Romeny. Leuven: Peeters, 2007.

Dijk, Ann Karin van. "The Angelic Salutation in Early Byzantine and Medieval Annunciation Imagery." *ArtBul* 81 (1999): 420–36.

———. "The Oratory of Pope John VII (705–7) in Old St Peter's." PhD diss., Johns Hopkins University, 1995.

———. "Reading Medieval Mosaics in the Seventeenth Century: The Preserved Fragments from Pope John VII's Oratory in Old St Peter's." *W&I* 22 (2006): 285–91.

Dodd, Erica Cruikshank. "Christian Arab Sources of the Madonna Allattante in Italy." *AM* 2 (2003): 33–39.

Ekonomou, Andrew J. *Byzantine Rome and the Greek Popes*. Lanham, MD: Lexington, 2007.

Falk, Brigitta. *Krone und Schleier: Kunst aus mittelalterlichen Frauenklöstern; Katalog der Ausstellung, Essen, Ruhrlandmuseum—Bonn, Kunst- und Austellungshalle vom 19. März bis 3. Juli 2005*. Munich: Hirmer, 2005.

Farr, C. *The Book of Kells: Its Function and Audience*. London: British Library, 1997.

Fehrenbach, Frank. *Die Goldene Madonna im Essener Münster: Der Körper der Königin*. Essen: Tertium, 1996.

Garrucci, Raffaele. *Vetri ornati di figure in oro trovati nei cimiteri dei cristiani di Roma*. Rome: Tipografia delle Belle Arti, 1858.

Graf, Katrin. *Bildnisse schreibender Frauen im Mittelalter 9. bis Anfang 13. Jahrhundert*. Basel: Schwabe, 2002.

Hahn, Cynthia J., and Hans Immel, eds. *Passio Kiliani, Ps-Theotimus, Passio Margaretae, Orationes: Niedersäcsische Landesbibliothek Hannover Ms. I 189*. Gratz: Akademische Druck, 1988.

Harlow, Mary. "Female Dress, Third-Sixth Century: The Message in the Media." *AntT* 12 (2004): 203–15.

Henderson, George. *From Durrow to Kells: The Insular Gospel-Books, 650–800*. London: Thames & Hudson, 1987.

Hernad, Béatrice. *Pracht auf Pergament: Schätze der Buchmalerei von 780 bis 1180; Katalog der Ausstellung, München, Kunsthalle der Hypo-Kulturstiftung vom 19. Oktober 2012 bis zum 13. Januar 2013*. Munich: Hirmer, 2012.

Iacobone, P. *Maria a Roma: Teologia, culto e iconografia mariana a Roma, dalle origini all'Altomedioevo*. Todi: Tau, 2009.

Ihm, Christa. *Die Programme der christlichen Apsismalerei vom 4. Jahrhundert bis zur Mitte des 8. Jahrhunterts*. Stuttgart: Steiner, 1992.

Kalavrezou, Ioli. "Images of the Mother: When the Virgin Mary Became Meter Theou." *DOP* 44 (1990): 165–72.

Kahsnitz, Rainer. "Inhalt und Aufbau der Handschrift: Die Bilder." Pages 18–55 in *Das Kostbare Evangeliar des Heiligen Bernwald: Katalog der Ausstellung, Hildesheim, Dom- und Diozesanmuseum 6 Februar–21 marz 1993*. Munich: Prestel, 1993.

Kessler, Herbert L. *Spiritual Seeing: Picturing God's Invisibility in Medieval Art*. Philadelphia: University of Philadelphia Press, 2000.

Kitzinger, Ernst. "The Coffin-Reliquary." Pages 202–304 in *The Relics of St. Cuthbert*. Edited by Christopher Francis Battiscombe. Oxford: Oxford University Press, 1956.

———. "The Role of Miniature Painting in Mural Decoration." Pages 99–142 in *The Place of the Book Illumination in Byzantine Art*. Edited by Kurt Weitzmann, William C. Loerke, Ernst Kitzinger, and Hugo Buchthal. Princeton: Publications of the Art Museum of Princeton University, 1975.

———. "A Virgin's Face: Antiquarianism in the Twelfth Century." *ArtBul* 62 (1980): 6–19.

Lafontaine-Dosogne, Jacqueline. *Iconographie de l'Enfance de la Vierge dans l'Empire byzantin et en Occident*. Brussels: Académie Royale de Belgique, 1964–1965.

Lasareff, Victor. "Studies in the Iconography of the Virgin." *ArtBul* 20 (1938): 26–65.

Lawrence, Marion. "Maria Regina." *ArtBul* 7 (1925): 150–61.

Lowden, John. "The Word Made Visible: The Exterior of the Early Christian Books as Visual Argument." Pages 13–47 in *The Early Christian Book*. Edited by William E. Klingshirn and Linda Safran. Washington, DC: Catholic University of America Press, 2001.

Mackie, Gillian V. *Early Christian Chapels in the West: Decoration, Function and Patronage*. Toronto: Toronto University Press, 2003.

Mathews, Thomas F. *Byzantium from the Antiquity to the Renaissance.* New York: Abrams, 1998.
Mayr-Harting, Henry. "The Idea of the Assumption of Mary in the West, 800–1200." Pages 86–111 in *The Church and Mary.* Edited by Robert Norman Swanson. Rochester, NY: Boydell, 2004.
———. *Themes.* Vol. 1 of *Ottonian Book Illumination: An Historical Study.* London: Miller, 1991.
McClanan, Anne L. "The Empress Theodora and the Tradition of Women's Patronage in the Early Byzantine Empire." Pages 50–72 in *The Cultural Patronage of Medieval Women.* Edited by June Hall McCash. Athens: University of Georgia Press, 1996.
McKitterick, Rosamond. "Women in the Ottonian Church: An Iconographic Perspective." Pages 79–100 in *Women in the Church: Papers Read at the 1989 Summer Meeting and the 1990 Winter Meeting of the Ecclesiastical History Society.* Oxford: Blackwell, 1990.
Mitchell, John. "The Crypt Reappraised." Pages 75–114 in part 1 of *The 1980–1986 Excavations.* Vol. 1 of *San Vincenzo al Volturno.* Edited by Richard Hodges. AMBSR 7. London: British School at Rome, 1993.
Morey, Charles Rufus. "The Inscription on the Enameled Cross of Paschal I." *ArtBul* 19 (1937): 595–96.
Menz-von der Mühll, Marguerite. "Der St. Gallen Elfenbeine um 900." *FMSt* 15 (1981): 392–418.
Muzj, Maria Giovanna. "La prima iconografia mariana." Pages 209–43 in *La Vergine Madre nella Chiesa delle origini.* Edited by Ermanno Toniolo. Rome: Marianum, 1996.
Nicolai, Vincenzo Fiocchi, Fabrizio Bisconti, and Danilo Mazzoleni. *Le catacombe cristiane di Roma.* Regensburg: Schnell & Steiner, 2002.
Nielsen, Christina M. "*Hoc opus eximium*: Artistic Patronage in the Ottonian Empire." PhD diss., University of Chicago, 2002.
Nilgen, Ursula. "Maria Regina: Ein politischer Kultbildtypus." *RJK* 19 (1981): 3–35.
Noble, Thomas F. X. *Images, Iconoclasm, and the Carolingians.* University Park: Pennsylvania State University Press, 2009.
Noga-Banai, Galit. *The Trophies of the Martyrs: An Art Historical Study of Early Christian Silver Reliquaries.* Oxford: Oxford University Press, 2008.
Nordhagen, Per Jonas. "Icon Designed for the Display of Sumptuous Votive Gifts." Pages 453–60 in *Studies of Art and Archaeology in Honour of*

Ernst Kitzinger. Washington, DC: Dumbarton Oaks Research Library and Collection, 1987.

———. "La più antica Eleousa conosciuta: Una scoperta in S. Maria Antiqua." *BolA* 47 (1962): 351–53.

Osborne, John. "Early Medieval Painting in San Clemente, Rome: The Madonna and Child in the Niche." *Gesta* 20 (1981): 299–310.

———. "Images of the Mother of God in Early Medieval Rome." Pages 135–51 in *Icon and Word: The Power of Images in Byzantium; Studies Presented to Robin Cormack*. Edited by Antony Eastmond and Liz James. Aldershot: Ashgate, 2003.

Pace, Valentino. "La pittura medievale nel Molise, in Basilicata e Calabria." Pages 270–88 in *La pittura in Italia: L'altomedioevo*. Edited by C. Bertelli. Milan: Electa, 1994.

Palazzo, Éric. "Marie et une élaboration d'un espace ecclésial au haut Moyen Âge." Pages 313–25 in *Marie: Le culte de la Vierge*. Edited by Dominique Iogna-Prat, Eric Palazzo, and Daniel Russo. Paris: Beauchesne, 1996.

Parlato, Enrico. "Le icone in processione." Pages 69–92 in *Arte e iconografia a Roma da Costantino a Cola di Rienzo*. Edited by Maria Andaloro and Serena Romano. Milan: Jaca Book, 2000.

Pentcheva, Bissera V. *Icons and Power: The Mother of God in Byzantium*. University Park: Pennsylvania State University Press: 2006.

Peroni, Adriano. "Il ruolo della committenza vescovile alle soglie del Mille: Il caso di Warmondo di Ivrea." Pages 247–74 in *Committenti e produzione artistico-letteraria nell'Alto Medioevo occidentale: Atti della XXXIX settimana di studio del CISAM, Spoleto, 4–10 aprile 1991*. Spoleto: CISAM, 1992.

Prochno, Joachim. *Bis zum Ende des 11. Jahrhunderts (800–1100)*. Vol. 1 of *Das Schreiber- und Dedikationbild in der Deutschen Buchmalerei*. Leipzig: Teubner, 1929.

Rizzardi, Clementina. "La cattedra eburnea di Massimiano a Ravenna: rilettura stilistica." Pages 145–50 in *Hadriatica: Attorno a Venezia e al Medioevo tra arti, storia e storiografia; Scritti in onore di Wladimiro Dorigo*. Edited by Ennio Concina, Giordana Trovabene, and Michela Agazzi. Padua: Il Poligrafo, 2002.

Rosano, Luigi. "Maria." Pages 205–6 in vol. 8 of *Enciclopedia dell'arte medievale*. Rome: Istituto dell'Enciclopedia Italiana Treccani, 1997.

Rosenthal, Erwin. "Some Observations on Coptic Influence in Western Early Medieval Manuscripts." Pages 51–74 in *Homage to a Bookman:*

Essays on Manuscripts, Books and Printing; Written for Hans P. Kraus on His Sixtieth Birthday, Oct. 12 1967. Edited by Hellmut Lehmann-Haupt. Berlin: Mann, 1967.

Russo, Daniel. "Les représentations mariales dans l'art d'Occident: Essai sur la formation d'une tradition iconographique." Pages 173–291 in *Marie: Le culte de la Vierge dans la société medieval.* Edited by Dominique Iogna-Prat, Éric Palazzo, and Daniel Russo. Paris: Beauchesne, 1996.

Russo, Eugenio. "L'affresco di Turtura nel Cimitero di Commodilla, l'icona di S. Maria in Trastevere e le più antiche feste della Madonna a Roma." *BISIME* 59 (1980–1981): 71–150.

Shepherd, Dorothy. "An Icon of the Virgin: A Sixth-Century Tapestry Panel from Egypt." *BCM* 56 (1969): 90–120.

Shoemaker, Stephen J. *Ancient Traditions of the Virgin Mary's Dormition and Assumption.* Oxford: Oxford University Press, 2002.

Spain, Suzanne. "'The Promised Blessing': The Iconography of the Mosaics of S. Maria Maggiore." *ArtBul* 61 (1979): 518–40.

Stout, Ann M. "Jewelry as a Symbol of Status in the Roman Empire." Pages 77–100 in *The World of Roman Costume.* Edited by Judith Lynn Sebesta and Larissa Bonfante. Madison: University of Wisconsin Press, 1994.

Stroll, Mary. "Maria Regina: Papal Symbol." Pages 173–203 in *Queens and Queenship in Medieval Europe.* Edited by Anne J. Duggan. Woodbridge: Boydell, 1997.

Tavard, George Henry. *The Thousand Faces of the Virgin Mary.* Collegeville, MN: Liturgical Press, 1996.

Thunø, Erik. "The Cult of the Virgin, Icons and Relics in Early Medieval Rome: A Semiotic Approach." *AAAHP* 17 (2003): 79–141.

———. *Image and Relic: Mediating the Sacred in Early Medieval Rome.* Rome: L'Erma di Bretschneider, 2002.

Utro, Umberto. "Maria nell'Iconografia cristiana dei primi secoli." Pages 353–81 in *Dal modello biblico al modello letterario.* Vol. 1 of *Storia della mariologia.* Edited by Enrico Dal Covolo and Aristide Serra. Rome: Città Nuova, 1998.

Vassilaki, Maria, ed. *Mother of God: Representations of the Virgin in Byzantine Art.* Athens: Abbeville, 2000.

Volger, W., ed. *La abbazia di San Gallo.* Milan: Jaca Book, 1990.

Weitzmann, Kurt. "*Loca Sancta* and the Representational Arts of Palestine." *DOP* 28 (1974): 31–55.

Werner, Martin. "The Madonna and Child Miniature in the Book of Kells." *ArtBul* 54 (1972): 1–23 and 129–39.
Wolf, Gerhard. "From Mandylion to Veronica: Picturing the 'Disembodied' Face and Disseminating the True Image of Christ in the Latin West." Pages 153–79 in *The Holy Face and the Paradox of Representation: Papers of a Colloquium held at the Bibliotheca Hertziana, Rome and The Villa Spelman in Florence, 1996*. Edited by Herbert L. Kessler and Gerhard Wolf. Bologna: Clueb, 1998.
Woodruff, Helen. "The Iconography and Date of the Mosaics of La Daurade." *ArtBul* 13 (1931): 80–104.
Wormald, Francis. *The Miniature in the Gospel of St Augustine (Corpus Christi College ms. 286)*. Cambridge: Cambridge University Press, 1954.
Wright, David H. Review of *The Relics of St. Cuthbert*, ed. Christopher Francis Battiscombe. *ArtBul* 43 (1961): 141–60.
Zakarian, Lilit. "La miniature arménienne de la haute époque." Pages 11–19 in *La miniature arménienne: Collection du Maténandaran*. Edited by Tamara Mazaéva. Erevan: Naïri, 2006.
Zanichelli, Giuseppa Z. "Les livres des modèles et les dessins préparatoires au Moyen Âge." *CSMC* 43 (2012): 61–70.

Women, Wine, and the Apostasy of the Wise: Sirach 19:2 in Medieval Latin Literature

Giuseppe Cremascoli

Anyone approaching a study of biblical texts, especially the wisdom books, cannot help but be fascinated and at times surprised by the stream of aphorisms defining the characteristic traits, both complex and fleeting, of the human condition. In terms of style, we note that, especially in Proverbs, these traits are invoked in a series of parallelisms and comparisons, which aim to shed light on the world and on reality, organized into categories of wisdom and seen from different perspectives. One common theme of the sententious elements running through the whole body of texts is women, whose power and force of attraction over men and their lives is described, for better and—more frequently—for worse. Of all the passages, that found in the ninth section is quite well known, in part because it is used in the liturgy: set at the conclusion of the work as an "Ode to a Capable Wife," it celebrates woman as a source of security and happiness to her husband.[1] Hence one of the aphorisms proclaims: "He who finds a wife finds a goodness and will draw delight from the Lord" (*qui invenit mulierem invenit bonum et hauriet jucundiatem a Domino*). Thus reads the critical edition of the Vulgate, which, within its apparatus of variations, sets the teaching *bonam* beside *muli-*

---

1. See Robertus Weber and Bonifatius Fischer, eds., *Biblia sacra iuxta vulgatam versionem* (Stuttgart: Deutsche Bibelgesellschaft, 1994), henceforth *Biblia sacra*; cf. Prov 31:10–31: Gianfranco Ravasi and Bruno Maggioni, eds., *La Bibbia: Via, verità e vita; Nuova versione ufficiale della Conferenza episcopale italiana* (Cinisello Balsamo: San Paolo, 2009), henceforth *La Bibbia*. For its use in liturgy, see *Missale Romanum: Commune non Virginum; Pro nec virgine nec martyre; Lectio epistolae*, juxta typicam ed. (Regensburg: Pustet, 1932).

erem[2] and provides a text with a slight differences of meaning compared to what we find in the form established by the new, official version of the Italian Episcopal Conference: "He who finds a wife finds a fortune and obtains the favor of the Lord" (*chi trova una moglie trova una fortuna e ottiene il favore del Signore*).[3]

Naturally, problematic and unfortunate situations are also provided for and described with vivid realism, as in this aphorism: "It is better to live in a desert land than with a contentious and fretful wife."[4] Men are perceived as vulnerable and defenseless before women, especially when the overall effect is made yet stronger and more alluring by the artfulness of prostitutes, who can make even the seemingly strong and unshakable succumb.[5] Regardless, men are urged to be ever vigilant and on their guard, as there is no end to the dangers of these affairs.[6]

When looking at these themes elsewhere in the wisdom books, which this essay will explore in particular, we note first of all the difference in atmosphere created by the pessimism seen in Qoheleth. In the few aphorisms regarding women, its judgments are dire and sweeping, defining women as "more bitter than death," a tangle of nets and snares from which man may be spared only by the mercy of God.[7] Lengthy sections of the

---

2. *Biblia sacra*, Prov 18:22. In the apparatus, we read the variations *bonam mulierem / mulierem bonam* and the following addition to our verse: *qui expellit mulierem bonam expellit bonum, qui autem tenet adulteram stultus est et impius*.

3. *La Bibbia*, Prov 18:22.

4. NRSV, Prov 21:19.

5. *La Bibbia*, Prov 7:25–26: "Il tuo cuore non si volga verso le sue vie, non vagare per i suoi sentieri, perché molti ne ha fatti cadere trafitti ed erano vigorose tutte le sue vittime" (NRSV: "Do not let your hearts turn aside to her ways; do not stray into her paths. For many are those she has laid low, and numerous are her victims"). In the notes to *La Bibbia*, as a comment on the entire excerpt, we read: "The chapter again involves two female figures, before whom the young disciple must choose: 'lady wisdom' (verses 1–5) or the lustful adulteress (verses 6–27), who is depicted in a highly effective sequence with a lively narrative."

6. *La Bibbia*, Prov 31:3: "Non concedere alle donne il tuo vigore, né i tuoi fianchi a quelle che corrompono i re" (NRSV: "Do not give your strength to women, your ways to those who destroy kings"). This, on the other hand, is the text handed down by the Vulgate: *Ne dederis mulieribus substantiam tuam et vias (divitias: varia lectio) tuas ad delendos reges*.

7. *La Bibbia*, Eccl 7:26, 28: "Trovo che amara più della morte è la donna: essa è tutta lacci, una rete il suo cuore, catene le sue braccia. Chi è gradito a Dio la sfugge, ma chi fallisce ne resta preso…. Quello che io ancora sto cercando e non ho trovato

book of Sirach take on the theme of male-female relationships, extolling the qualities of the ideal wife but also using expressions of grim pessimism when describing the misfortune of men whose wives are not equal to their domestic duties. It is essential to read Sir 25:17–36, in which the wicked woman is portrayed in somber tones,[8] and the first twenty-four verses of the following chapter, where a comparison is made between the good wife and the bad wife.[9] The former is celebrated with tenderness and affection, given the happiness that she provides her husband: in this case, he is the recipient of a special, divine benevolence, such that he spends his days in peace.[10] However, the sacred author seems to focus more on opposing situations, caused by a tendency to evil, which he indicates are particularly intense and devastating in women, as it gives rise to sin and death;[11] we must not forget that "any iniquity is small compared to

---

è questo: un uomo fra mille l'ho trovato, ma una donna fra tutte non l'ho trovata" (NRSV: "I found more bitter than death the woman who is a trap, whose heart is snares and nets, whose hands are fetters; one who pleases God escapes her, but the sinner is taken by her.... See this is what my mind has sought repeatedly, but I have not found. One man among a thousand I found, but a woman among all these I have not found"). The critical apparatus to *La Bibbia* specifies: "It must, however, be noted that in 9:9 Ecclesiastes invites the reader to 'enjoy life with the woman whom you love,' that is, with one's wife, identifying in married love one of the few positive aspects of existence." The *fallisce* ("[he who] fails") of the above-cited Prov 7:26 corresponds to *peccator est* in the Vulgate.

8. See *Biblia sacra*, in a pericope that, in the various editions of the *Biblia iuxta vulgatam Clementinam*, is titled *De muliere nequam*.

9. See *Biblia sacra* in the pericope titled *De muliere nequam et de muliere proba*. Note that the biblical text to which we refer in this note and in the previous note has undergone corrections and modifications in its structure and interpretation in the new official version of the Italian Episcopal Conference (see note 1, above).

10. *La Bibbia*, Sir 26:2–3: "Una donna valorosa è la gioia del marito, egli passerà in pace i suoi anni. Una brava moglie è davvero una fortuna, viene assegnata a chi teme il Signore" (NRSV: "A loyal wife brings joy to her husband, and he will complete his years in peace. A good wife is a great blessing; she will be granted among the blessings of the man who fears the Lord"). *Biblia sacra*, Sir 26:2–3: *mulier fortis oblectat virum suum et annos vitae illius in pace implebit; pars bona mulier bona, in parte bona* [in parte: *varia lectio*] *timentium Deum dabitur viro pro factis bonis*.

11. *La Bibbia*, Sir 25:24: "Dalla donna ha inizio il peccato e per causa sua tutti moriamo" (NRSV: "From a woman sin had its beginning, and because of her we all die"). *Biblia sacra*, Sir 25:33: *a muliere initium factum est peccati et per illam omnes morimur*. In the apparatus of the notes to the Italian version, on p. 1457 we read: "The theorization of original sin [is] ... significant: it is caused by woman, who becomes a

a woman's iniquity."[12] Defenseless and ever in danger of falling helplessly for her charms,[13] men must remember that "many have been seduced by a woman's beauty" because "by it passion is kindled like a fire" (NRSV Sir 9:9). Thus, it is a mistake to give oneself completely to a woman,[14] and it is wise not to linger in those places where one might enjoy her company.[15]

It is against the background described here that we must read and interpret the short verse in which Sirach proclaims that wine and women have the power to lead the wise to apostasy.[16] The saying is well known in Western history and spirituality, and, in a certain sense, it summarizes the messages set out in the parallel texts cited above. Let us now turn to documenting its presence and use in late antique and medieval Latin literature, identifying themes and peculiarities of discourse. The first result from an examination of the texts is the idea, considered a given, that the

---

vehicle for death. The perspective is decidedly sexist. The theory would be taken up again by the fathers and the later catechesis of the Church."

12. NRSV: Sir 25:19. *Biblia sacra*, Sir 25:33: *brevis malitia* [*omnis malitia: varia lectio*] *supra malitiam mulieris; sors peccatorum cadat super eam*.

13. *La Bibbia*, Sir 9:8: "Distogli lo sguardo da una donna avvenente, non fissare una bellezza che non ti appartiene" (NRSV: "Turn away your eyes from a shapely woman, and do not gaze at beauty belonging to another"); Sir 25:21: "Non soccombere al fascino di una donna, per una donna non ardere di passione" (NRSV: "Do not be ensnared by a woman's beauty, and do not desire a woman for her possessions"). *Biblia sacra*, Sir 9:8: *averte faciem tuam a muliere compta et non circumspicias speciem alienam*; Sir 25:28: *ne respicias in mulieris speciem et non concupiscas mulierem in specie*.

14. *La Bibbia*, Sir 9:2: "Non darti interamente a una donna sì che essa s'imponga sulla tua forza" (NRSV: "Do not give yourself to a woman and let her trample down your strength"). *Biblia sacra*, Sir 9:2: *non des mulieri potestatem animae tuae ne ingrediatur in virtute tua et confundaris*.

15. *La Bibbia*, Sir 42:12–14: "E non sederti insieme con le donne, perché dagli abiti esce la tignola e dalla donna malizia di donna. Meglio la cattiveria di un uomo che la compiacenza di una donna; una donna impudente è un obbrobrio" (NRSV: "Do not let her ... spend her time among married women; for from garments comes the moth, and from a woman comes woman's wickedness. Better is the wickedness of a man than a woman who does good; it is woman who brings shame and disgrace"). *Biblia sacra*, Sir 42:12–14: *et in medio mulierum noli commorari; de vestimentis enim procedit tinea et a muliere iniquitas viri* [*viro: varia lectio*]. *melior est iniquitas viri quam benefaciens mulier et mulier confundens in obprobrium*.

16. *La Bibbia*, Sir 19:2: "Vino e donne fanno deviare anche i saggi" (NRSV: "Wine and women lead intelligent men astray"). *Biblia sacra*, Sir 19:2: *vinum et mulieres apostatare faciunt sapientes*.

apostasy of which the wise man is a victim due to women coincides *tout court* with lust in its physical and carnal aspects, of which greed, especially with regard to wine, is the immediate and concrete cause.

Around this verse from Sirach on the apostasy mentioned above, what often emerges, especially in treatises *De cavendis vitiis*, is the apostle's warning to guard against drunkenness, because wine leads to lust[17] and causes disorder, especially for those called to the quiet of the religious and monastic life. In particular, this last point is discussed in a passage from the correspondence between Abelard and Heloise, which recalls that drunkenness dims the divine gift of reason within us and is the source of much ruin, as Scripture often reminds us.[18] In fact, the passage cites many biblical verses on the matter, including those that blame wine, together with women, for being the cause of apostasy in the wise.[19] The mischievous reader wonders whether Heloise herself ought to have been included among such women, but the context offers no information in that regard.

Other texts claim that it is the sin of gluttony as such and its effects—some of which are repugnant and despicable—that induces one to lust, a claim made in discussions studded with biblical texts, including the verse in Sirach on wine and women. Alan of Lille, for example, in his *De arte praedicatoria* has a chapter against gluttony (*Contra gulam*), which, after the ritual list of the usual scriptural passages on wine as an incentive to lustfulness, condemns overindulgence in food as "a grave of the mind, a heap of dung, a source of extravagance, a mother of sickness" (*mentis sepulcrum, acervus stercorum, origo luxuriae, mater nauseae*).[20] Even more realistic is the passage by Jerome quoted by Alard Gazet in

---

17. For an example characterizing wine as leading to lust, see Hincmarus Remensis, *De cavendis vitiis et virtutibus exercendis*, ed. Doris Nachtmann, QGM 16 (Munich: MGH, 1998), 150, in which, in the long list of biblical passages warning against the sin of gluttony, we first have Eph 5:18 (*nolite inebriari vino in quo est luxuria*) and, in conclusion, Sir 19:2 (*vinum et mulieres apostatare faciunt sapientes*).

18. Abelard, *Ep.* 6.17; Ileana Pagani, ed., *Epistolario di Abelardo ed Eloisa* (Turin: UTET, 2004), 354: *quid etiam tam religioni quietique monasticae contrarium est quam quod luxuriae fomentum maxime praestat et tumultus excitat, atque ipsam Dei in nobis imaginem, qua praestamus ceteris, id est rationem, delet? hoc autem vinum est, quod supra omnia victui pertinentia plurimum scriptura damnosum asserit, et caveri admonet.*

19. See the list of biblical passages, including Sir 19:2, in Abelard, *Ep.* 16.17; Pagani, *Epistolario di Abelardo ed Eloisa*, 354.

20. Alanus de Insulis, *Arte praed.* 6 (PL 210:119–20).

his commentary on Cassian's *De institutis coenobiorum*, in which he discusses the spirit of fornication (*De spiritu fornicationis*) in relation to the verse from Sirach that now occupies our attention. Writing to the presbyter Amand, Jerome poses a close and concrete connection between overindulgence in food and lust, due to the explosion of "sexual pleasure" (*voluptas genitalium*) when the belly is full of food washed down with excessive quantities of wine.[21]

Drunkenness and dependence on wine would be most serious in those called to minister to souls. In a sermon by an unknown author published in the Patrologia Latina as an appendix to the works by John, archbishop of Rouen, discussing the pastoral office (*De officio pastorali*), the accent is placed on the apostle's entreaty that no drunkards be promoted to bishop.[22] The reason is expressed in these terms: "Do not be full of wine. For it is most shameful for a priest to be addicted to the bottle. Drunkenness makes reason blind, thus Solomon: 'Wine and women lead men astray'" (*Non vinolentum, turpissimum enim presbyterum vino deditum esse. Ebrietas excaecat rationem, unde Salomon: Vinum et mulieres apostatare faciunt hominem* [al., *sapientes*]).[23] Thus apostasy would be the result of a dimmed reason, the unfortunate fate one risks when succumbing to the power of wine and women.

There are, however, authors and texts that do not insist on this connection between wine—or overindulgence in food, in general—and yielding

---

21. On Cassian's text, see note 66 below. For Alard Gazet's comment, see PL 49:265C: *teste D. Hieronymo ep. 146, "gula fomes sit et mater libidinis, ventremque cibo distentum et vini potionibus irrigatum voluptas genitalium sequatur, et pro ordine membrorum ordo sit vitiorum." ... hinc scriptura passim haec duo vitia conjungit. Ose. IV: fornicatio, vinum et ebrietas auferunt cor. Ecclus 19:2 vinum et mulieres apostatare faciunt sapientes.* Slight variations in Jerome's text (*Ep.* 45.2) are noted in the critical edition by Isidor Hilberg (*Sancti Eusebii Hieronymi Epistulae*, 3 vols., CSEL 54–56 [Vindobonae: Tempsky, 1910–1918], 3:488, lines 15–18).

22. John of Rouen, "Incerti auctoris Sermones sex ad populum," *Serm.* 2 (PL 147:224A): *qualis autem debeat presbyter esse describit apostolus cum dicit: oportet episcopum sine crimine esse, tamquam Dei dispensatorem, non protervum, non iracundum, non vinolentum, non percussorem, non turpis lucri appetitorem* [Titus 1:7] ("How the priest should be is described by the apostle when he says: 'a bishop, as God's steward, must be blameless; he must not be arrogant or quick-tempered or a drunkard or violent or greedy for gain'").

23. John of Rouen, "Incerti auctoris Sermones sex ad populum," *Serm.* 2 (PL 147:224C).

to the temptations of the flesh, as may be suggested by the verse in Sirach. In these cases, the verse is quoted partially, speaking of the harm of wine without dwelling on any responsibility women bear for the apostasy of the wise. The enemy, then, is only gluttony, an inclination to be controlled, as we read in Benedict's *Rule* in the chapter dealing with the measure of drinking (*De mensura potus*). There the ideal solution, we read, would be to give drinking up entirely, in keeping with the perfection of the monastic life and so gain special merit.[24] However, the times are not considered favorable for such a radical renunciation, and the lawmaker limits himself to hoping for a use of wine that is "not to the point of saturation … but sparingly" (*non-usque ad satietatem … sed parcius*).[25] The *auctoritas* is provided by the verse in Sirach, quoted, however, with some alterations to keep remain focused. In fact, we read: "because wine leads even wise men astray" (*quia vinum apostatare facit etiam sapientes*).[26]

It should be noted that the shortened form of the verse in Sirach referred to in Benedict's *Rule*—that is, excluding the reference to women as the cause of apostasy in the wise—was used in the most important medieval Latin glossaries to explain the term *apostatare*. Since Isidore of Seville, who had formed a prior collection, this word has been handed down in the sense in which it is used even today, and it is found in this meaning in the best-known collections of Latin glossaries. The apostate is one who rejects the Christian faith after baptism and goes back to infecting himself with the lies and rituals of idolatry.[27] However, in addition to the meaning now illustrated, in the glossaries a judgment with broader implications was already making its way into the explanation of the term, because there the apostate is both one who abandons the faith and one who, on a whim,

---

24. Benedict, *Reg.* 40.3–4; Benedict, *Regula: De mensura potus*, ed. Giorgio Picasso (Cinisello Balsamo: San Paolo, 1996), 132–34: *credimus eminam vini per singulos sufficere per diem. quibus autem donat Deus tolerantiam abstinentiae, propriam se habituros mercedem sciant* ("we believe that a *hemina* of wine a day is sufficient for each. But those to whom God gives the strength to abstain should know that they will receive a special reward").

25. Benedict, *Reg.* 40.6.

26. Benedict, *Reg.* 40.7.

27. Isidorus of Seville, *Etym.* 8.10.5; Isidorus of Seville, *Etymologiarum sive Originum libri XX*, ed. Wallace M. Lindsay (Oxford: Clarendon, 1911): *Apostatae dicuntur qui post baptismum Christi susceptum ad idolorum cultum et sacrificiorum contaminationem revertuntur* (*Etym.* 8.10.5).

leaves the path of good and takes up that of evil.[28] Papias blends the two situations in a single term, feeling that they are connected, in the sense that the one gives rise to the other.[29]

Osbern and Huguccio Pisanus refer to this particular verse from Sirach in their glossaries, composed after that of Papias; however, they cite the biblical verse in the form provided in Benedict's *Rule*, thus indicating wine alone as the cause of apostasy in the wise, without saying that women also have their role in it, as we read in the text of the Scriptures. Osbern accepts the two components in the concept of apostasy, with reference to a passage by Pope Siricius in which he condemns the Christian who forswears his faith.[30] The verse in Sirach is quoted in the definition explaining *apostatare*, with reference only to wine, as a synonym of *pervertere*.[31]

Huguccio Pisanus also gives great attention to these terms, but he downplays the reference to rejecting the Christian faith and insists on the idea of the fall from honesty to perversion, from good to evil. One of the *derivationes* is, as in Osbern, "from the opposite of *apostolus*" (*ab apostolus per contrarium*),[32] thus giving rise to the following definition: "The

---

28. For an example, see "Glossarium Ansileubi" in *Glossaria Latina iussu Academiae Britannicae edita*, ed. Wallace M. Lindsay et al. (repr., Hildesheim: Olms, 1965), 58: "AP 153 (Isid. 8,10,5); 154: apostatare: retro ire, prevaricare." For further information to bring the concept of apostasy into greater focus, especially in the early Middle Ages, see the entries for *apostata* and *apostatare* in the indexes of Gustavus Loewe and Georgius Goetz, eds., *Corpus glossariorum Latinorum* (repr., Amsterdam: Hakkert, 1965), 6:82a.

29. Papias, *Elem. lit.* 90–91; Papias, *Elementarium littera A*, ed. Violetta de Angelis (Milan, Cisalpino-Gogliardica, 1977–1980), 304: *apostata qui recedit de via iusta, post baptismum ad idola convertitur—apostatare retroire, praevaricari, et post baptismum ad idola verti* ("Apostate: he who turns back from the straight and narrow path and turns to idols after his baptism. Apostatize: turn back, transgress, and turn to idols after baptism").

30. Osbern, *Deriv.* A.32.5–7; Ferruccio Bertini and Vincenzo Ussani Jr., eds., *Derivazioni*, 2 vols. (Spoleto: CISAM, 1996): *et per antifrasin apostata te .i. renuntiatus vel perversus, unde apostaticus a um .i. perversus, et hec apostasia renuntiatio, in decretis Sirici pape "adiectum est et quosdam Christianos ad apostasiam transeuntes,"* with a reference in the note to Siricius, *Ep. pontif.* 225 (PL 13:1136A).

31. Osbern, *Deriv.* A.32.8; Bertini and Ussani, *Osberni derivations: et apostatare .i. pervertere, unde in libro sapientie: vinum apostatare facit etiam sapientes*.

32. Uguccione da Pisa, *Derivationes*, ed. Enzo Cecchini et al. (Florence: SISMEL Edizioni del Galluzzo, 2004), S322 [11]:1179: "Thus it seems formed by *apo* and *stans*, as if it were *retro stans* (turned backward) or, as they say, derived from the opposite of

apostate is called this or that—distorted one, renouncer, fugitive, most backward one; in particular he is said to be an apostate who first does well but then is perverted and acting badly goes backwards" (*et dicitur hic et hec apostata -e, perversus, renuntiatus, refuga, retromissus; proprie ille dicitur apostata qui primo bene agit, sed postea pervertitur et male agendo retro abit*).³³ Huguccio quotes the verse in Sirach under the term *apostato -as*, accompanied by this explanation: "To move back from good, to become perverse, to act perversely, thus in the Book of Wisdom: 'wine leads even wise men astray" (*retro abire a bono, perverti* [in the apparatus: *scripsi*: pervertere *codd.*], *perverse agere, unde in Libro Sapientiae "vinum apostatare facit etiam sapientes"*).³⁴ However, the verse is quoted without cuts—that is, with the full list of the causes of perversion, which are wine and women— in John of Genoa's *Catholicon*. In fact, in conclusion to the information gathered by Huguccio Pisanus and pointing out exactly the biblical book from which the verse is cited, he writes: "Thus Sir 19: wine and women lead even wise men astray" (*unde Ecclesiastici XIX: vinum et mulieres apostatare* [*apostotare* in the cited edition] *faciunt etiam sapientes*).³⁵

Beyond lexicographical inventories, the two components of apostasy— that is, the loss of faith and the plunge into total ruin, imprisoned in the abyss of evil—accompany the reference to the verse in Sirach in different shades and hues; the authors use it to urge readers to attain even complete chastity or to warn them not to yield to the delusions and charms of those specters that accompany the seduction of lust. An infrequent yet present idea in discussions of chastity is that the failure to uphold this virtue either points to a lack of faith or it leads to its rejection—that is, to apostasy. The theme is dealt with in the *Sermo de castitate*, by an unknown author, and given as an appendix to the works of Augustine in Patrologia Latina. At its beginning, the discussion cites the verse in Sirach,³⁶ later proclaiming that

---

apostolus, or from *appostus, -a, -um*, which means distorted and contrary and comes from *appono*" (*unde videtur componi ab apo et stans, quasi retro stans, vel, ut dicunt, derivatur ab apostolus per contrarium, vel ab appostus -a -um, quod est perversus et contrarius, et fit ab appono*).

33. Uguccione da Pisa, *Derivationes*, with the idea reiterated in S322 [12]:1180: *unde apostaticus –a -um, perversus, et apostasia -e, renuntiatio, retro ad malum itio.*

34. Uguccione, *Derivationes*.

35. Johannes de Balbis, *Catholicon*, repr. ed. (Westmead: Gregg, 1971), s.v. *apostota* [corr.: *apostata*].

36. *Sermo de castitate* 1 (PL 39:2291): *quandocumque castitatem, fratres carissimi, secundum quod decet et expedit, commendamus ... et illud Salomonis: Vinum et mulieres*

adultery is an irrefutable sign of a lack of faith in God because the adulterer, heedless of God's law, commits an act which he seeks to hide from men. In fact, the verse of the psalm in which we read that it is "foolish" (*insipiens*) to state that God does not exist is here applied to adulterers.[37]

Apostasy from the Christian faith, resulting in the ruin of peoples and civilizations, is the explicit subject of Salvian's commentary to the verse in Sirach in reference to both of the causes of apostasy in the wise: wine and women. Many are familiar with the pages of the *De gubernatione Dei* in which Salvian describes the ever-spreading immorality in lands converted to Christianity that by then had become guilty of apostasy and had become worse than the barbarians, whose subjects they were fatally destined to become. In a world, then, in unstoppable decline, young and old[38] "drink, gamble, commit adultery, and act mad" (*bibunt, ludunt, moechantur, insaniunt*), going so far, for this very reason, as to reject the Christian faith.[39] Solomon is naturally the personification of this apostasy from the proper faith for having yielded to the allure of foreign women until he was finally dragged into idolatry. Rabanus Maurus invokes the story, after citing the passage in Sirach,[40] in his anguish at the thought that such a wise king,

---

apostatare faciunt etiam sapientes et arguunt sensatos [Eccl 19:2] ("In every circumstance, dearest brothers, we recommend chastity … and that saying on Solomon: 'Wine and women lead even the wise to apostasy, and bring blame upon the sensible'" [Eccl 19:2]).

37. *Sermo de castitate* 6 (PL 39:2293): *sed de talibus clamat per prophetam Spiritus sanctus. Dixit, iniquit, insipiens in corde suo: non est Deus* [Ps 13:1].

38. Salvian of Marseilles, *Gub. Dei* 6.78 (*De gubernatione Dei*, ed. Georges Lagarrigue, SC 220 [Paris: Cerf., 1975], 412,49–54): "There I saw pitiable things—that is, that there was no difference between elders and the young. They shared the same coarseness, the same frivolity: lust, drinking, forms of perdition; all of them equally did the same things: gambling, becoming inebriated, fornicating, giving themselves up to liberties at banquets" (*vidi ego illic res lacrymabiles: nihil scilicet inter pueros differre et senes. una erat scurrilitas, una levitas; simul omnia, luxus, potationes, perditiones; cuncta omnes pariter agebant, ludebant, ebriabantur, moechabantur, lasciviebant in conviviis*)

39. *Gub. Dei* 6.79 (ed. Lagarrigue, 142,58–62): "And what else? Through all these behaviors we have mentioned, they tumbled down, so that in them that famous saying of the holy word came to pass: wine and women lead to apostasy from God" (*et quid plura? In hoc per cuncta illa, quae diximus, devoluti sunt ut compleretur in eis dictum illud sermonis sacri: vinum et mulieres apostatare faciunt a Deo. nam dum bibunt, ludunt, moechantur, insaniunt, Christum negare coeperunt*). Note the biblical quotation, in this text adapted to support its stated argument.

40. Rabanus Maurus, *Comm. in Eccl.* 4.10 (PL 109:888CD): *vinum et mulieres apostatare faciunt sapientes … quod bene expertus est Salomon*.

"ignominiously imprisoned" (*turpiter detentus*) by the love of foreign women, may have worshiped their idols, thus having to be listed among the apostates.⁴¹ The story of Solomon also inspired the speech that Gregory VII made to Alfonso, king of Castille, whom he warned to put an end to the "illicit union" (*illicitum conubium*) begun with a blood relative of his wife's,⁴² approved by a false monk collaborating with a fallen woman, at the service of Satan.⁴³ When quoting the verse in Sirach—from which any mention of wine is omitted—he comments on it by recalling the story of the very wise King Solomon, (shamefully) destroyed as a man and as a king by the "unchaste love of women" (*incestus mulierum turpiter amor*).⁴⁴ The false monk was said to have been forced into seclusion within the walls of Cluny.⁴⁵

---

41. Rabanus Maurus, *Comm. in Eccl.* 4.10 (PL 109:889A): "who, after receiving much wisdom—almost a river of it—from God, abandoned the God of his fathers and joined with foreign women and, an ignominious prisoner of their love, had profane temples and various idols made for them. For this reason he both lost the honor of his greatest glory and deserved to be listed among the apostates" (*qui postquam accepit a Deo multam sapientiam quasi flumen, deseruit Deum patrum suorum, et junctus est mulieribus alienigenis, quarum amore turpiter detentus, fana profana et idola diversa eis fabricavit. unde et laudem gloriae maximae perdidit et non inter electos sed inter apostatas computari promeruit* [1 Kgs 11]).

42. Gregory VII, *Reg.* 8.3 (Erich Gaspar, ed. Epistolae Selectae, MGH [Berlin: Weidmann, 1967], 520,9–11): *Vires resume, illicitum conubium, quod cum uxoris tuę consanguinea inisti, penitus respue* ("Gather together your strength, and fully reject the illicit union that you have undertaken with the blood relative of your wife");

43. "But now acknowledge that the devil, envious as usual of your salvation and that of all those who should have been saved through you, has driven your virile soul from the straight and narrow path using one of his followers, a certain Robert, a false monk, and his old accomplice, a fallen woman" (*at nunc comperto, quod diabolus tuę saluti et omnium qui per te salvandi erant more suo invidens per membrum suum, quemdam Rodbertum pseudomonachum, et per antiquam adiutricem suam, perditam feminam, viriles animos tuos a recto itinere deturbavit* [ed. Gaspar, 519,24–28]).

44. "Let not the love of an unchaste woman tear you away from the warnings of salvation and our rules, because women lead the wise to apostasy. In fact, the unchaste love of women brought that very wise King Solomon dishonorably to ruin, and by the judgment of God he tore the most flourishing kingdom of Israel nearly entirely from the hands of his posterity" (*non te a salutaribus monitis atque institutis nostris inceste mulieris amor abripiat, quia mulieres apostatare faciunt sapientes. ipsum quippe regem sapientissimum Salomonem incestus mulierum turpiter amor dejecit et florentissimum regnum Israel Dei judicio pene totum de manu posteritatis eius abrupit* [ed. Gaspar, 519–20]).

45. *Prędictum sane nefandissimum Rodbertum monachum, seductorem tui et per-*

Innocent III also mentions the events narrated by Scripture, with an extensive list designed to illustrate how many came to ruin "by the beauty of a woman" (*propter speciem mulieris*), as the verse in Sirach proclaims, which he quotes in its entirety, including the "blame upon the sensible" (*arguent sensatos*), which concludes the text provided in the Vulgate.[46] The pope makes many references to events in the Bible in order to document the various forms of lust and the punishments meted out for it. The picture is very broad and also invokes events for which the reference to the verse in Sirach cannot be called appropriate because, in the cases cited, it is neither wine nor women that triggers the disaster. The first events to be recalled are those narrated in Gen 19 regarding Sodom, destroyed due to the sins that stained its inhabitants.[47] Again, in Genesis, he recalls the massacre of the Shechemites by the two sons of Jacob, Simon and Levi, implacable even against their father's will in avenging the wrong inflicted on their sister Dinah, who was dishonored by Shechem, son of Hamor the Hivite, prince of that land.[48]

The list of those ruined by sexual behaviors condemned by divine law continues by recalling Er and Onan, sons of Judah, who are guilty—especially the latter—of doing what was "displeasing in the sight of the Lord" and are therefore punished such that they lost their lives.[49] The book of Numbers tells of the apostasy of Israel for the worship of Baal-Peor, when "the people began

---

turbatorem regni, ab introitu ecclesie separatum intra claustra monasterii Cluniacensis in penitentiam retrudi decernimus (ed. Gaspar, 520,15–18).

46. Innocent III, *Cont. mundi* 2.23 (Innocent III, *De contemptu mundi sive de miseria humane conditionis*, ed. Renato d'Antiga [Parma: Nuova Pratiche Editrice, 1994], 112,2): "Thus, what we read is true: 'Many have been lost by the beauty of a woman.' In fact, 'Wine and women lead the wise to apostasy and bring blame upon the sensible'" (*verum est ergo quod legitur: "propter speciem mulieris multi perierunt." nam: "vinum et mulieres apostatare faciunt sapientes et arguunt sensatos"*). For the first of the sayings quoted, see Sir 9:9. For the other, note that there is no trace of the second part of the formula in the version of *La Bibbia: Via, verità e vita*, Sir 19:2: "Vino e donne fanno deviare anche i saggi" (NRSV: "Wine and women lead intelligent men astray").

47. *Quis eius* [*sc. luxuriae*] *multiplices species sufficienter valeat explicare? hec enim Pentapolim cum adiacenti regione subvertit* (ed. d'Antiga, 112,1). See *La Bibbia* and NRSV, Gen 19:12–29 (Sodom and Gomorrah destroyed).

48. *Sichem cum populo interemit* (ed. d'Antiga, 112,1). See *La Bibbia* and NRSV, Gen 34:1–5 (the rape of Dinah), 6–24 (the marriage agreement between the sons of Jacob and the Sechemites), 25–31 (Dinah's brothers avenge their sister).

49. *Her et Onan filios Iuda percussit* (ed. d'Antiga, 112,1). Cf. *La Bibbia* and NRSV, Gen 38:6–92, in conclusion to verse 10 regarding Onan: "Ciò che egli faceva era male

to have sexual relations with the women of Moab," and of the scourge that followed as divine punishment until Phinehas, son of Eleazar, avenged himself, stabbing the Israelite and the Midianite woman.[50] The offense that the Benjaminites of Gibeah committed against the Levite concubine in Ephraim triggered the war that led to the undoing and ruin of that tribe of Israel.[51] Hophni and Phinehas, sons of the priest Eli, "lay with women who served at the entrance to the tent of the meeting" (1 Sam 2:22 NRSV), rejecting the warnings of their meek, pious father who was too soft with them. Thus divine judgment fell upon them, leading to their death, when Israel was defeated by the Philistines, and the ark of the covenant of the Lord was seized.[52]

The list of those ruined by the sins of lust goes on to consider similarly painful and dramatic cases. Uriah lost his life due to the plotting of King David, who was smitten with the man's wife, Bathsheba.[53] Tamar, dishonored by Amnon, was avenged by her brother Absalom, who had the guilty man killed during a banquet.[54] Consumed by lust, the two elder judges of Israel slandered chaste Susannah, and, for this reason, when they were unmasked, they were put to death.[55] Lust was also the cause when Reuben was denied the blessing of his father, whose nuptial bed he had violated;[56]

---

agli occhi del Signore, il quale fece morire anche lui" (NRSV: "What he did was displeasing in the sight of the Lord, and he put him to death also").

50. *Judaeum et Madianitidem pugione transfodit* (ed. d'Antiga, 112,1). See *La Bibbia* and NRSV, Num 25:1–17 (worship of Baal of Peor).

51. *Tribus Beniamin pro uxore levitae delevit* (ed. d'Antiga, 112,1). See *La Bibbia* and NRSV, Judg 19–20, for the story of the crime of Gibeah and the war against the Benjaminites.

52. *Filios Eli sacerdotis in bello prostravit*. See *La Bibbia* and NRSV, 1 Sam 2:12–17 (Eli's wicked sons); 4:1–11 (the ark of God captured).

53. *Haec Uriam occidit* (ed. d'Antiga, 112,1). See *La Bibbia* and NRSV, 2 Sam 11:1–27.

54. *Ammon interfecit* (ed. d'Antiga, 112,1). See *La Bibbia* and NRSV, 2 Sam 13:1–22 (Amnon and Tamar), 23–39 (Absalom avenges the violation of his sister).

55. *Presbyteros lapidavit* (ed. d'Antiga, 112,1). For the rather vague suggestion in PL 217:726A, the reference is to Dan 13, where we read the tale of the chaste Susannah and the two elder judges of Israel put to death for the scheme they had hatched against her.

56. *Ruben maledixit* (ed. d'Antiga, 112,1). See *La Bibbia* and NRSV, Gen 35:22: "Mentre Israele abitava in quel territorio, Ruben andò a unirsi con Bila, concubina del padre, e Israele lo venne a sapere" (NRSV: "While Israel lived in that land, Reuben went and lay with Bilhah his father's concubine, and Israel heard of it"), and Gen 49:3–4: "Ruben ... tu non avrai la preminenza, perché sei salito sul talamo di tuo padre, hai

Samson fell victim to the seductions of Delilah;[57] Solomon was dragged into infamy and idolatry.[58] The pope's style is dry and stony, pressing the reader with his incessant list of tragic events and figures led to extreme ruin for having yielded to the allure of womanly beauty and sensual desire. In fact, in commenting on all the events he has evoked, the pope concludes, as we have seen, stating, "Thus what we read is true: 'Many have been lost by the beauty of a woman'" (*verum est ergo quod legitur: "propter speciem mulieris multi perierunt"*). Immediately thereafter, in confirmation, we read the verse from Sirach, introduced by a weighty *nam*.[59]

To Jonas of Orléans, this biblical formulation serves as a link in the progression of thoughts regarding the deadly consequences of the sins of gluttony and lust.[60] Concerning gluttony, he cites the passage of Jerome that would also be used by Alard Gazet—as we have seen—to describe the "insane pleasure" (*insana voluptas*) that defeats those who succumb to this vice.[61] The discussion immediately falls on the devastating effects of fornication, among which we must note those that distance people from

---

profanato così il mio giaciglio" (NRSV: "Reuben ... you shall no longer excel because you went up onto your father's bed; then you defiled it—you went up to my couch!").

57. *Sansonem seduxit* (ed. d'Antiga, 112,1). See *La Bibbia* and NRSV, Judg 16:4–21 (Samson and Delilah).

58. *Salomonem pervertit* (ed. d'Antiga, 112,1). See *La Bibbia* and NRSV, 1 Kgs 11:1–2: "Il re Salomone amò molte donne straniere, oltre la figlia del faraone: moabite, ammonite, edomite, sidonie e ittite, provenienti dai popoli di cui aveva detto il Signore agli Israeliti: non andate da loro ed essi non vengano da voi, perché certo faranno deviare i vostri cuori dietro i loro dei" (NRSV: "King Solomon loved many foreign women along with the daughter of Pharaoh: Moabite, Ammonite, Edomite, Sidonian, and Hittite women, from the nations concerning which the Lord had said to the Israelites, 'You shall not enter into marriage with them, neither shall they with you; for they will surely incline your heart to follow their gods'").

59. See note 46, above.

60. John of Orléans, *Inst. laic.* 3.6 (PL 106:244D): *de octo vitiis principalibus*. Toward the end of the long list of biblical passages on gluttony, and after citing Sir 19:2, the text concludes: "In fact, gluttony gives rise to foolish gaiety, coarseness, frivolity, empty talk, bodily filth, mental instability, drunkenness, and lustfulness" (*ex gula quippe nascitur inepta laetitia, scurrilitas, levitas, vaniloquium, immunditia corporis, instabilitas mentis, ebrietas, libido*).

61. John of Orléans, *Inst. laic.* 3.6 (PL 106:244D): "As the blessed Jerome in fact says, sexual desire immediately follows a belly full of food washed down with many drinks" (*ut enim beatus Hieronymus ait, ventrem cibo distentum et diversis potionibus irrigatum statim voluptas genitalis sequitur*). See note 21, above.

God, leading to apostasy. One's entire psychological and physical state is subverted,[62] but above all it is faith that is impacted because the sinner ends up feeling hatred toward divine law, forgetful of his future life and eternal fate, heeding only the allure of earthly pleasures.[63]

As part of these thoughts commenting on the verse from Sirach, the authors also proceed to compare complete chastity and the choice to marry. Their judgment is always in favor of the former of the two states, seen as an irrefutable sign of having given priority to God and thus achieving the height of Christian perfection. One of the sermons attributed to Hildebert of Lavardin in the Patrolgia Latina first gives a list, with the verse from Sirach, of other biblical passages with similar meaning and events related to figures swept away by lust[64] and then praises the choice of those who consequently practice continuous and complete abstinence, thus making God a perpetual offering, an uninterrupted "sacrifice" (*sacrificium*) this is the act of perfect piety, out of reach to those subject to conjugal servitude.[65]

When dealing with the theme of sexual abstinence, some authors, within the radical emphasis of their own discourse, have at times used expressions revealing a sort of anguish at the thought of the long, dreadful struggle demanded of those who, due to their status in life, must maintain complete chastity. We need only read the first chapter of the sixth book of Cassian's *De institutis coenobiorum*, where he speaks of "the spirit of fornication" (*de spiritu fornicationis*). Alard of Gazet commented on the short text, gathering passages by other writers and biblical texts on the theme, including the verse in Sirach. Cassian's text is peppered with expressions inspired by his belief in the extreme difficulty and the fierce struggle faced by those aiming for the ideal of Christian perfection through complete chastity. He even declares, in no uncertain terms, that few succeed at

---

62. John of Orléans, *Inst. laic.* 3.6 (PL 106:245A): "Fornication then gives rise to blindness of the mind, fickleness of the eyes and all the body, uncontrolled love, often even at the risk of one's life, wantonness, jesting, impudence, and a lack of any restraint" (*nascitur vero ex fornicatione caecitas mentis, inconstantia oculorum vel totius corporis, amor immoderatus, saepe periculum vitae, lascivia, joca, petulantia et omnis incontinentia*).

63. John of Orléans, *Inst. laic.* 3.6 (PL 106:245A): *odium mandatorum Dei, mentis enervatio et iniustae cupiditates, negligentia vitae futurae et praesentis delectatio.*

64. Hildebert of Lavardin, *Serm.* 76.617 (PL 171:711BCD).

65. Hildebert of Lavardin, *Serm.* 76.618 (PL 171:711D–12A): *Quis his exemplis et monitis instructus assidue continenter vivit, juge sacrificium Deo reddit, quod non offerunt qui conjugio serviunt, sed illi qui perpetuae devoti sunt castitati.*

achieving full victory. Such is the "immense war" (*immane bellum*) without a truce: it accompanies a man's life from the ardors of early puberty and is destined to vanish only with victory over all other vices.[66] He thus theorizes on sources of interference within the disorderliness of human nature, wounded and disfigured by vice, among which lust would be the most resistant, as it may only be defeated by a victory achieved in every sphere of virtue.

In any case, Cassian's text seems dictated by touches of anguish and suffering, and it is no coincidence that in his commentary Alard Gazet cites the well-known passage in which Jerome describes the specters of temptation that reached him even in his hermitage, while he repented bitterly. This anguish caused tears and moans, but even in his wracked and disheveled body, the memory of dancing maidens, of days spent in Rome, called to him ever powerfully.[67] Today's reader gets the impression that at one time this entire sphere of the human condition was approached largely through axioms, without allowing too many questions, or, in any case, under the belief that everything had been settled once and for all. Despite all this, questions and dilemmas sprang up everywhere (as they do today), and it is always interesting to see the themes that emerged and to catch a glimpse of any solutions.

---

66. See John Cassian, "De institutis coenobiorum," in *Institutions cénobitiques*, ed. Jean-Claude Guy and Jean Cassien, SC 109 (Paris: Cerf, 1965), 262,1–6: *secundum nobis traditione patrum adversus spiritum fornicationis certamen est, longum prae caeteris ac diuturnum et perpaucis ad purum devictum, inmane bellum et quod, cum a primo tempore pubertatis impugnare incipiat hominum genus, non nisi prius cetera vitia superentur extinguitur* (*Inst. coen.* 6.1).

67. See the comment on Cassian by Alard Gazet (PL 49:268B): "Oh, how many times—he [Jerome] says—while I was in the hermitage and in that desolate desert that, scorched by the burning sun, offers monks a most harsh shelter, I had the impression that I was among the pleasures of Rome!... Each day tears, each day groans: and if ever I was overcome by drowsiness hanging over me, I would hurl upon the bare earth my bones, which barely held themselves together. And thus even I, who out of fear of Gehenna had condemned myself to such a prison, with only scorpions and wild beasts for company, would often take part in the dances of maidens" (*O quoties, inquit [Hieronymus], in eremo constitutus, et in illa vasta solitudine quae solis exusta ardoribus horridum monachis praestat habitaculum, putabam me Romanis interesse deliciis!... quotidie lacrymae, quotidie gemitus: et si quando repugnantem somnus imminens oppressisset, nuda humo vix ossa haerentia collidebam. Ille igitur ego, qui ob gehennae metum tali me carcere ipse damnaveram, scorpionum tantum socius et ferarum, saepe choris intereram puellarum*) This refers to Jerome's letter to Eustochius (*Ep.* 22.7).

Among the commentaries on the Sirach passage, we must note that in the above-quoted *Sermo de castitate* (*Sermon on Chastity*), set as an appendix to the writings of Augustine in Patrologia Latina,[68] the discussion touches on some problems of sexual ethics with enlightened reflections dictated by good sense. Above all, it condemns men's insistence on requiring faithfulness from their wives while effectively denying that husbands have the same obligations. The author wonders, "Why do they not keep faith with their wives, who desire their wives to be faithful?" (*quare non servant fidem uxoribus suis, quam sibi ab eis servari desiderant?*).[69] The text then uses the *derivatio nominis* of "man from strength" (*vir a virtute*) and "woman from softness, that is, fragility" (*mulier a mollitie, id est fragilitate*), to point out the ridiculousness that befalls the man who wants his wife to be victorious over the beast of lust, while he—the strong one—is defeated at the very start of the battle.[70] The discussion concludes with a declaration: "In the Catholic faith, all that is forbidden to women is absolutely forbidden to men as well" (*in fide catholica quidquid mulieribus non licet, omnino nec viris licet*).[71]

The author of our *Sermo* then shifts his attention to especially difficult situations, which he knows and describes but which he does not seem inclined to view with particular compassion. These involve husbands forced to be away from home at length "compelled by business or the command of the king" (*compellente negotio aut jubente rege*)—that is, due to business or military commitments. To those finding themselves in such situations, he asks this question: "how can I preserve chastity?" (*quomodo castitatem servare possim?*).[72] The answer, given with extreme firmness, is based only on motivation and matters of faith. Conjugal fidelity must be maintained, even in these cases, "because of God and for the salvation of his own soul" (*propter Deum et animam suam*).[73] Transgres-

---

68. See note 36, above.

69. *Serm. cast.* 1 (PL 39:2292B).

70. *Serm. cast.* 1 (PL 39:2292B): *cum enim vir a virtute nomen acceperit, et mulier a mollitie, id est fragilitate; quare contra crudelissimam bestiam libidinem vult unusquisque uxorem suam victricem esse, cum ipse ad primum libidinis ictum victus cadat?*

71. *Serm. cast.* 3 (PL 39:2292C).

72. See *Serm. cast.* 7 (PL 39:2293A): *sed forte dicet aliquis: ecce compellente negotio aut jubente rege ab uxore tot mensibus aut annis separatus, quomodo castitatem servare possim?*

73. *Serm. cast.* 7 (PL 39:2294B): *rogo vos, fratres charissimi, si propter negotii necessitatem et regis jussionem unusquique ab uxore sua interdum etiam longo tem-*

sors ought to seek refuge in repentance at the thought of final judgment and eternal torment.[74]

In the *Moralis philosophia* attributed to Hildebert of Lavardin, the doctrine expressed in Sir 19:2 is held to be in perfect harmony with the teachings of the classics, as found in the citations to which he refers—from Sallust, Seneca, and Cicero.[75] Especially significant is the parallelism between the Bible verse and the hexameter of Ovid's *Fasti*, in which Venus and wine are named as the cause of ruin for noble spirits. Ovid's verse is adapted to the thought that Hildebert wishes to express, but it is clear that the pairing of *Venus* and *vinum*, even in the *Fasti*, becomes a hendiadys to indicate a deadly force: indeed, "it broke even the lofty breasts" (*sublimia pectora fregit*).[76]

The Christian authors who comment on the verse from Sirach expand on the discussion to show that the apostasy of which the biblical text speaks is to be identified with the loss of wisdom or even the total ruin that devastates lives. To Rabanus Maurus, wine and women "lead against and away from true knowledge" (*faciunt adversos et alienos a sapientia*),[77]

---

pore separatur; quare propter Deum et animam suam tam longo spatio temporis castitas non servatur?

74. *Serm. cast.* 7 (PL 39:2294B): *sciant qui talia agunt, quod si eis non poenitentia subvenerit, cum ante tribunal Christi stare coeperint, ab auditu malo liberari non poterunt: sed dicetur illis: Discedite a me, maledicti, in ignem aeternum* (Matt 25:41).

75. See Hildebert of Lavardin, *Mor. phil.* 1.49 (PL 171:1041B–42B); the chapter titled *De pudicitia* is a cento from passages of Sallust, *Bel. Cat.* 54, *paucis mutatis*, as we read in the notes; Seneca, *Ben.* 7.2; and Cicero, *Off.* 1.30. The references should be corrected and completed thus: *Bel. Cat.* 51.3; *Ben.* 7.2.2; and *Off.* 1.30.106.

76. Hildebert of Lavardin, *Mor. phil.* 1.49 (PL 171:1042B): *nam venus et vinum sublimia pectora fregit. item "vinum et mulieres apostatare faciunt sapientes."* In Ovid, *Fasti* 1.301, the hexameter begins with *non*, which Hildebert changes to *nam*. The thought of the classical poet is, in any case, substantially in line with the verse from Sirach. In fact, while weaving his praise of ancient astronomers, Ovid recalls that neither Venus nor wine weakened their sublime hearts (*non Venus et vinum sublimia pectora fregit*).

77. Rabani Maurus, *Comm. in Eccl.* 1.10 (PL 109:888D): *vinum, inquit, et mulieres apostatare faciunt sapientes et arguunt sensatos, ac si diceret, ebrietas et fornicatio illos qui se sapientes in acumine ingenii et in subtilitate sensus aestimant faciunt adversos et alienos a vera sapientia, et reprehensibiles esse ostendunt, eo quod praeter donum praecipuum sapientiae in stultitiam maximam devoluti sunt* ("Wine, it says, and women lead wise men to apostasy and cast blame on the sensible; it is as if it said: drunkenness and fornication render those who believe themselves wise—due to a sharp intellect

as the tragic epilogue to Solomon's glorious reign shows.[78] After quoting Sirach, Innocent III leaves the theme of wine in the shadow and concentrates his discussion on women—or, rather, on the "beauty" (*species*) they represent[79]—to say that woman "weakens strength, diminishes sense, consumes day, wastes wealth" (*vires enervat, sensus diminuit, dies consumit, opes effundit*).[80] The story of Solomon is, however, generally evoked to mean apostasy in Christian terms—that is, as a distancing from the proper faith and a return to idolatry or even as a rejection of one's bond to God. In fact, carried away by his passion for foreign women, Solomon built places of worship to idols, and for this reason "deserved to be listed among the apostates" (*inter apostatas computari promeruit*).[81] After all, as the texts cited above have shown, the adulterer's offense also drags him into rejecting God—that is, into the ignorance of he who says "there is no God" (*non est Deus*), as we read in the Psalm verse quoted as a comment on this transgression against divine law.[82] To Salvian, the wine and women referred to in the verse from Sirach invoke the pitiful spectacle of cities that had by then fallen prey to disorder and vice, where immorality and licentiousness carried Christians away to the apostasy of their faith. Indeed, he quotes the biblical passage with a modification to the text, saying that the result of transgressions is the rejection of God.[83]

There are also positive interpretations, so to speak, of the verse from Sirach, quoted to praise the values connected to a temperate and wise use of sexual activity in marriage or to the privileges of virginity, as it is understood in the Christian message. Ambrose pairs the quotation from Sirach with a reference to the teachings of Paul on marriage and virginity in order to sing the merits of "temperance" (*temperantia*) even in married life—naturally, to ward off what might be caused by excess or abuse to the detriment of the weaker party. In marriage, too, the values of equilibrium and moderation inspired by wisdom and by mutual respect are to

---

and fine sense—contrary and averse to true knowledge and show them to be reprehensible because regardless of their special gift of knowledge, they have plummeted to the greatest idiocy").

78. Rabani Maurus, *Comm. in Eccl.* 1.10 (PL 109:888D): *quod bene expertus est Salomon.*
79. See note 46, above.
80. Innocent III, *Cont. mundi* 2.23 (ed. d'Antiga, 112,2).
81. See note 41, above.
82. Ps 13:1; see note 37, above, and its context.
83. See note 39, above, and its context.

be honored, such that to violate them is a kind of adultery, as the apostle rightly teaches.[84]

This line of thinking leads Ambrose to discuss virginity, a theme beloved by him and present in many of his works. Celebrated examples and biblical texts are cited, but the basic idea is emphasized in these phrases: "The Virgin bore the safety of the world" (*Virgo genuit mundi salutem*) and "the Virgin bore universal life" (*Virgo peperit vitam universorum*).[85] Thus the greatness of virginity lies in its having been chosen for the mystery of the incarnation in the gift of universal salvation.[86] Hence, the verse from Sirach which we are discussing leads us to reflect both on the harm caused by yielding to intemperance and passion as well as on the impossibility of fully participating in the plan designed by God to redeem humanity from sin.

This gives rise to the effort spent in warning readers to be vigilant and cautious so as not to be swept away by the sirens of sensual pleasure. In Hugh of Saint Victor's *Appendix ad opera dogmatica* in Patrologia Latina, we read a peculiar adjustment (*accomodatio*), commenting on this biblical verse so as to convince the wise man to stay away from wine and women.[87] After defining man and woman as "two flint stones" (*duo lapides igniferi*), the author warns the wise man to realize that many have been lost "due to wine, like a poison, and to women—that is, pleasures" (*propter vinum tamquam virum et propter feminas, id est voluptates*).[88] The author's zeal

---

84. Ambrose, *Ep. extra coll.* 14.32 (Ambrose, *S. Sancti Ambrosii episcopi Mediolanensis opera 21: Discorsi e lettere*, ed. Michaela Zelzer and Gabriele Banterle [Milan: Biblioteca Ambrosiana, 1988], 278): *vinum et mulieres apostatare faciunt etiam prudentes. unde Paulus etiam in ipsis coniugiis temperantiam docet; est enim velut quidam adulter incontinens in matrimonio qui legem apostolicam praevaricatur.*

85. Ambrose, *Ep. extra coll.* 14.33 (ed. Zelzer and Banterle, 278).

86. Ambrose, *Ep. extra coll.* 14.33 (ed. Zelzer and Banterle, 278): *Quid autem loquar quanta sit virginitatis gratia, quae meruit a Christo eligi ut esset etiam corporale Dei templum, in qua corporaliter, ut legimus, habitavit plenitudo divinitatis?*

87. *De bestiis et aliis rebus*, in Hugh of Saint Victor, *Append.* 2.2 (PL 177:58A): *vinum et mulieres apostatare faciunt homines sapientes* [Sir 19]. *Verum vir sapiens et prudens a vino et a muliere se avertet.*

88. Hugh of Saint Victor, *Append.* 2.2 (PL 177:58B): *sunt autem duo lapides igniferi, masculus et femina. Tu igitur professor prudentiae, intellige multos periisse propter vinum tanquam virum* [sic], *et propter feminas, id est voluptates, et cautus esto ut salvus evadas* ("They are in fact two flint stones, male and female. Thus you who profess wisdom, understand that many have been lost due to wine, like a poison, and to women—that is, pleasures—and be on your guard to avoid them").

in such warnings therefore becomes constant, based on a framework in which one rather unchangeable component is man, who is fragile, restless, and condemned to a perennial struggle so as not to fall for the allure of women, which he has always felt but has been compelled to resist its appeal. The discourse is always in generic and universal terms, but we sense that the recipient of the admonishment is always the "man of God" (*homo Dei*), whose vocation—whether priestly or monastic—would make any yielding an apostasy, a fall into the deadly clutches of the evil one. The warnings can take on different accents, but the content is unchanging: everyone—chief among them the man of God—is said to be imprudent and foolish in seeking danger, whose intensity cannot be doubted and which, therefore, must always be avoided.[89]

The *Sermo de castitate* cited above is especially addressed to the young, who tend to deny that practicing these virtues is possible. The author indicates the remedies to be used: sobriety in eating and the careful avoidance of dangers, which arise in relationships with women, when one falls into "familiarity" (*familiaritas*) or in "suspect company" (*suspecta societas*).[90] To confirm this, he immediately quotes three biblical passages, including the verse from Sirach. A collection of scriptural texts on this theme is found in the *testimonia* given between the appendices to the works of Isidore of Seville in the Patrologia Latina. The lists are set out in the chapters that condemn fornication and intemperance in drinking.[91] We must note that the specter of the "beauty of women" (*species mulieris*) is also insistently invoked, especially if she is "foreign" (*aliena*), when the lists conclude with

---

89. Hugh of Saint Victor, *Append.* 2.2 (PL 177:58A), before citing the verse from Sirach (see note 88, above): *cave ergo, homo Dei, ebrietatem, nec obligeris luxuriae voluptate, ut non interficiaris a diabolo.*

90. *Serm. cast.* 1 (PL 39:2291): *forte adolescentes et adhuc in viridi aetate positi dicunt: juvenes homines sumus, continere non valemus. quibus nos respondere et possumus et debemus, ne forte ideo castitatem custodire non possint, quia amplius manducant quam expedit, et vinum amplius accipiunt quam oportet, familiaritatem mulierum vitare nolunt atque earum suspectam societatem habere nec metuunt nec erubescunt* ("Adolescents and those who are in the bloom of their youth may say: we are young, and we cannot be restrained. To those we can and must respond if by chance they are unable to guard their chastity because they eat more than needed and take more wine than is necessary, they do not wish to avoid familiarity with women, and they do not fear nor are ashamed of having their suspect company").

91. See Isidore of Seville, appendix 11, *Testimonia divinae scripturae et patrum* (PL 83:1208): ch. 16: *non fornicandum*; ch. 17: *fugiendam ebrietatem*.

the verses, again from Sirach, that recommend staying on one's guard, because there is always a fire lurking, waiting to devour its victims.[92]

These biblical texts—or others of similar meaning—are also quoted by Abelard, who accepts their message fully, all the while extolling the splendors of chastity proposed by Christianity, which, he writes, is more in line with certain philosophical doctrines than with traditions of Judaism.[93] The long list of biblical texts which he immediately quotes—especially from Sirach, but also Eccl 7:26, "I found more bitter than death the woman" (*inveni amariorem morte mulierem*)—shows, he observes, how dangerous and problematic it is to cultivate friendships and familiarity with women.[94] We hope it does not seem disagreeable to say that today's readers would like to catch some hint of a personal, concrete tone in this discourse of Abelard's and not merely traces of what are, all told, stereotypes. Yet this is not so, and we, terribly curious and even pitiless, have a nagging desire to hear from Héloïse's husband, even simply as a person familiar with the problem.

When writing on these subjects, other authors address very specific categories of readers, generally priests or monastics. Chrodegang of Metz wrote a *Regula canicorum* in which the verse from Sirach is used above all to dissuade readers from intemperance in drinking, the cause of evil and ruin.[95] In the same line of thinking, and with highly emphatic phras-

---

92. PL 83:1209C: *speciem alienae mulieris multi mirati reprobati sunt. colloquium enim ejus quasi ignis exardet. cum aliena muliere non accumbas supra cubitum, et non alterceris cum illa in vino, ne forte declinet cor tuum ad illam, et sanguine labaris in perditione.* The passage, with modifications to the text, comes from the *Biblia sacra*, Sir 9:11-13.

93. Abelard, *Theol. Chr.* 2.87 (Eligio M. Buytaert, ed., *Petri Abaelardi Theologia Christiana*, CCCM 12.2 [Turnhout: Brepols, 1969], 170,1264-68): "That, if after considering the philosophers' abstinence and greatness of mind we also consider their restraint, we will find that many have addressed our confusion and that that beauty of Christian chastity that the Judeans did not understand had its origins in them" (*quod si post abstinentiam et magnanimitatem philosophorum eorum quoque continentiam consideremus, multa in confusionem nostram de eis et ab eis scripta reperiemus et in eis Christianae castimoniae, quam Judaei non intellexerunt, incepisse pulchritudinem*).

94. Abelard, *Theol. Chr.* 2.91 (ed. Buytaert, 172,1338-1340): *His et illa consonant de Ecclesiastico, de molestiis et periculoso feminarum consortio, tam propriarum quam extranearum.*

95. Chrodegang of Metz, (PL 89:1085-86), in the chapter *de ebrietate a clero devitanda atque detestanda*. In PL 89:1083-1084 (*Reg. can.* 61), we find the chapter *de familiaritate a clericis mulierum extranearum devitanda*.

ing, he condemns familiarity with women, seeing it as incompatible with serving at the altar[96] and a violation of the "orders of the faith" (*depositum fidei*).[97] As for the danger, it arises from the fact that cohabitation leads to involvement with the devil.[98] Canons are also warned not to believe themselves to be more saintly than David or wiser than Solomon.[99] The other point that must not be forgotten, concludes Chrodegang, regards the story of our ancestor, driven out of paradise for having listened to a woman.[100] In monastic tradition, solitude and the hermit's life are always recommended as means for defeating those temptations set against chastity; that is, against the pernicious inducer of lustful craving, as Cassian says, so as to free the mind from the specters of seduction when communicating with God.[101] In commenting on this passage from Cassian, Alard Gazet specifies that he writes of the distance that a monk must keep between himself and those living in the world—especially women.[102]

The texts quoted to this point—and others we could draw on—refer to a substantially unchanged framework formed by certainties arising not

---

96. Chrodegang of Metz, *Reg. can.* 56 (PL 89:1083C): "In fact, frequent contact with women is the first temptation, and it shows the clergymen to be reprehensible. Indeed, you who at the altar speak with the Lord, what have you to speak of with women?" (*prima quidem tentamenta sunt feminarum frequentes accessus, et reprehensibiles exhibent clericos. quid tibi revera cum feminis qui ad altare cum Domino fabularis?*)

97. Chrodegang of Metz, *Reg. can.* 56 (PL 89:1083C): "Everyone in public, and the farmers in the fields, and the plowmen and the winegrowers will criticize you harshly every day if, against the orders of the faith, you presume to live with women" (*Te cuncti in publico, te in agro rustici, aratores ac vinitores quotidie graviter lacerabunt si contra depositum fidei cum feminis habitare contendis*).

98. Chrodegang of Metz, *Reg. can.* 56 (PL 89:1083D): "If women live with men, the devil's snare shall not be wanting" (*si cum viris feminae habitaverint, viscarium diaboli non deerit*).

99. Chrodegang of Metz, *Reg. can.* 56 (PL 89:1084A): *meminere debent canonici quod nec Davide sanctiores, nec Salomone sapientiores possunt esse.*

100. Chrodegang of Metz, *Reg. can.* 56 (PL 89:1084B): *meminere debent quod paradisi colonum de possessione sua mulier ejecit.*

101. John Cassian, *Inst. coen.* 6.3 (266,14–18): *ita plurimum confert ad depellendum hunc specialiter morbum quies ac solitudo, ut mens aegra minime diversis figuris interpellata ad puriorem perveniens contemplationis intuitum facilius pestiferum concupiscentiae fomitem radicitus possit eruere.*

102. See the commentary on Cassian by Alard Gazet (PL 49:270, note d): *id est fuga hominum saecularium et maxime mulierum.*

from ignorance of the problems but from the conviction that they are to be overcome by an asceticism constantly supported by the criteria of "resisting" (*age contra*). We know—these texts seem to say—what the apostasy of the wise is, as described in Sirach; the means to avoid succumbing to it are well known and need only be applied. It is entirely clear, then, and there is no point troubling oneself with questions. But permit us a few thoughts in the margins. We are separated from the period when the texts quoted in this essay were written by structural differences in thought and lifestyle that are well known to all, not to mention the vast developments that the sciences have made in our culture, seeking to probe the depths of the psyche. In light of this elementary thought, we can certainly suppose that beyond our texts on the apostasy of the wise, other documents from the same centuries might lead to discovering secret throbbings of the soul, repressed but not blotted out—not even after the ascetic, keeper of the wisdom, invoked by the passage from Sirach we have been discussing, has achieved victory.

I have touched on this theme in an essay on the relationship between abstinence from sex and Christian perfection,[103] adding, as an *auctoritas*, a text by Atto of Vercelli, drawn from a letter addressed to priests advising them to keep themselves "from the companionship of women" (*a contubernio mulierum*).[104] The elegantly crafted passage has an ascetic context of renunciation and struggle, where womanly beauty is invoked "as a disgrace" (*ad flagitium*). However, in the background, we note an atmosphere, though repressed, of mirage and enchantment, and the alluring situations from which one must be on one's guard are listed; the remarkable detail of the choice of fascinating realities to be guarded against is impressive.

> Well-styled hair, a beautiful face, batting eyelashes, that which flows from the eyes, amiable conversation, modulation of voice, a pleasant appearance, gentle persuasiveness, pretty jewels, elegant dress, perfumes, a light gait, and a body in full bloom.[105]

---

103. Giuseppe Cremascoli, "Astinenza dal sesso e perfezione cristiana," in *Comportamenti e immaginario della sessualità nell'alto medioevo* (Spoleto: CISAM, 2005), 649–74.

104. Atto of Vercelli, *Ep.* 9 (*Ad omnes sacerdotes dioecesis Vercellensis*) (PL 134:118C): *custodite ergo vos, fratres carissimi, a contubernio mulierum, ne membra Christi membra faciatis meretricum* [1 Cor 6:15]: *unde difficile evadere potestis, nisi ab earum consortio declinetis.*

105. Atto of Vercelli, *Ep.* 9 (PL 134:118D): *Compti crines, venusta facies, nictatio*

In commenting on the letter of Atto in my previous essay, I concluded: "These are rhetorical *topoi*, without a doubt, but if Atto of Vercelli employed them, there must have been a reason for it."[106]

Bibliography

Ambrose. *Sancti Ambrosii episcopi Mediolanensis opera 21: Discorsi e lettere*. Edited by Michaela Zelzer and Gabriele Banterle. Milan: Biblioteca Ambrosiana, 1988.
Balbis, Johannes de. *Catholicon*. Repr., Westmead: Gregg, 1971.
Benedict. *Regula: De mensura potus*. Edited by Giorgio Picasso. Cinisello Balsamo: San Paolo, 1996.
Bertini, Ferruccio, and Vincenzo Ussani Jr., eds. *Osberni derivationes*. Spoleto: Centro italiano di studi sull'alto medioevo, 1996.
Buytaert, Eligio M., ed. *Petri Abaelardi Theologia Christiana*. CCCM 12.2. Turnhout: Brepols, 1969.
Cassian, John. "De institutis coenobiorum." Pages 1–6 in *Institutions cénobitiques*. Edited by Jean-Claude Guy. SC 109. Paris: Cerf, 1965.
Cremascoli, Giuseppe. "Astinenza dal sesso e perfezione Cristiana." Pages 649–74 in *Comportamenti e immaginario della sessualità nell'alto medioevo*. Spoleto: CISAM, 2005.
Gaspar, Erich, ed. *Epistolae Selectae*. MGH. Berlin: Weidmann, 1967.
Hilberg, Isidor, ed. *Sancti Eusebii Hieronymi Epistulae*. 3 vols. CSEL 54–56. Vindobonae: Tempsky, 1910–1918.
Hincmarus, Remensis. *De cavendis vitiis et virtutibus exercendis*. Edited by Doris Nachtmann. QGM 16. Munich: MGH, 1998.
Innocent III. *De contemptu mundi sive de miseria humane conditionis*. Edited by Renato d'Antiga. Parma: Nuova Pratiche Editrice, 1994.
Isidore of Seville. *Etymologiarum sive Originum libri XX*. Edited by Wallace M. Lindsay. Vol. 8. Oxford: Clarendon, 1941.
Lindsay, Wallace M. "Glossarium Ansileubi." In *Glossaria Latina iussu Academiae Britannicae edita*. Edited by Wallace M. Lindsay et al. Repr. ed. Hildesheim: Olms, 1965.

---

palpebrarum, elisio oculorum, affabilitas sermonum, garrula modulatio, visus facilis, blanda suasio, praeclara monilia, schemata vestium, olfactio unguentorum, mollis incessus ac totus corporis luxus.
106. Cremascoli, "Astinenza," 669.

Loewe, Gustavus, and Georgius Goetz, eds. *Corpus glossariorum Latinorum*. Vol. 6. Repr., Amsterdam: Hakkert, 1965.
Missale Romanum: Commune non Virginum; Pro nec virgine nec martyre; Lectio epistolae. Juxta typicam ed. Regensburg: Pustet, 1932.
Pagani, Ileana, ed. *Epistolario di Abelardo ed Eloisa*. Turin: UTET, 2004.
Papias. *Elementarium littera*. Edited by Violetta de Angelis. Milan: Cisalpino-Gogliardica, 1977–1980.
Ravasi, Gianfranco, and Bruno Maggioni, eds. *La Bibbia: Via, verità e vita; Nuova versione ufficiale della Conferenza episcopale italiana*. Cinisello Balsamo: San Paolo, 2009.
Salvian of Marseilles. *De gubernatione Dei*. SC 220. Paris: Cerf., 1975.
Uguccione, da Pisa. *Derivationes*. Edited by Enzo Cecchini and Guido Arbizzoni. Florence: SISMEL Edizioni del Galluzzo, 2004.
Weber, Robertus, and Bonifatius Fischer, eds. *Biblia sacra iuxta vulgatam versionem*. Stuttgart: Deutsche Bibelgesellschaft, 1994.

The Women of the Old Testament in Early Medieval Poetry: Judith and the Others

Francesco Stella

1. The Canon of the Biblical Heroines in One Verse

Medieval Christian culture, as will certainly emerge from the contributions to this volume, was much less reluctant to place value on women than classical culture was, but it strictly selected the contexts and values in which women would become symbols and representations. That selection was based on the needs of the social system in which cultural expressions gradually came to operate—above all, those of the moral world, which was considered the carrier of such expressions.

The canon of exemplary biblical women, who were a model for virtuous behaviors or symbols of religious life, was established rather early in the patristic tradition. We find a trace of it in Jerome's *Ep.* 65, written for the virgin Principia in the form of an explanation of Ps 44, interpreted as an epithalamium for Christ and the church. In it, Jerome emphasizes the indispensability of a series of female figures in the success of the sacred people throughout history, and Augustine returns to the list in a condensed form in *Nat. grat.* 26, writing on the women who, like Mary, not only lived without sin but also lived in accordance with justice. In the poetic tradition, this canon, which is mentioned in other documentary sources, is condensed into a brief list quoted in a verse of the short poem *De virginitate* by Venantius Fortunatus (530–607), which came to enjoy a certain success.[1] Composed in Poitiers in 567, when Agnes, the adopted daughter

---

1. In fact, we find it again cited as a famous reference in the text of the blessing of Judith, daughter of Charles the Bald and wife of Aedhelwulf, king of Wessex, as quoted by Hincmar of Rheims in his *Incoronationes Regiae* (PL 125:811): *Despondeo te uni viro virginem castam, atque pudicam futuram conjugem, ut sanctae mulieres fuere viris*

of Queen Radegund, was named abbess, it has been described by Maria I. Campanale as a "mystic epithalamium," in that it blends the *de virginitate* genre (praise and encouragement for virginal living), previously tackled by Ambrose and Jerome, and the epithalamium (wedding poem) genre, adapted to the theme of the mystical marriage between consecrated virgins and Christ.[2] According to Campanale, the four-hundred-hexameter poem is organized into an *exordium* (introduction), based on the description of the blessed souls in heaven, a *perì gamou* (celebration of marriage), a *laus sponsae* (praise of the bride), and an epilogue, and each part includes a series of exempla. Among these, within the praise of the bride, there is an emphasis on the *felix virginitas* ("happy" or "fecund" virginity) of Mary, who was honored with the generation of her Lord, a condition that cannot be equaled even by the most famous women of the Bible: "Though Sarah, Rebecca, Rachel, Esther, Judith, Anna, and Naomi rise up to the stars, they were not worthy of generating the father of the world" (*Sarra Rebecca Rachel Hester Judith Anna Noemi / quamvis praecipue culmen ad astra levent, / nulla tamen meruit mundi generare parentem*; Virg. 99–101). The biblical women, listed with the *accumulatio* or *articulus*, which we know to be one of Venantius's most beloved rhetorical figures, are presented as a sort of *a minori* example, which Campanale defines as "a model of non-preferability."[3] This position is later corrected or integrated into other sections, where some of the women cited are invoked as positive individual examples.[4]

Venantius's verse, however, presented a list of excellent women inferior only to Mary, a list that the poet's stylistic authority establishes as a model of expression for later writers. The first of these is found in the work of the monk Agius of Corvey, who composed a dialogue-based *consolatio* for the death of the abbess Hathumoda in 876, drawing widely on the bib-

---

suis, Sara, Rebecca, Rachel, Esther, Judith, Anna, Noemi, favente auctore et sanctificatore nuptiarum, Jesu Christo Domino nostro.

2. Maria I. Campanale, "Il *De Virginitate* di Venanzio Fortunato (*carm*. 8, 3 Leo): Un epitalamio mistico," *IL* 2 (1980): 75–128. In addition to Ambrose's *De virginitate* and *De virginibus*, Campanale recalls Jerome's *Ep.* 22 and 130; Augustine's *De sancta virginitate*; Gregory of Nazianzus's *Partenìes épainos* and *Hypothékai parthénois* (PG 37:521–78, 578–632); and Gregory of Nyssa's *Perì parthenías*; see Campanale, "De Virginitate," 75, n. 1.

3. Campanale, "*De virginitate*," 122.

4. Judith, for instance, in Venantius Fortunatus, *Virg*. 304: *hoc etiam recolens, quid possit parcior usus: / sobrietas Judith vincere sola facit.*

lical exemplum, which he unimaginatively understood as a list of famous figures who were also dead.[5] After a series of prophets and fathers, he adds female names for the sake of equality (*Virg.* 299–300): Sarah, Rebecca, Rachel, Deborah, Naomi, Ruth, Anna, Huldah, Susanna, Judith, and Esther.[6] Agius's list closely follows that of Venantius for the first hemistich of verse 299, but he varies the second—Esther, Judith, Anna, Naomi— moving the first two heroines to the following verse and replacing them with Ruth and Deborah, and adding Huldah, prophetess of 2 Kgs 22, and Susanna, the beautiful wife of Joakim, who was harassed by two elders while bathing in her garden and was later defended against their accusations by Daniel (Dan 13). This variation may demonstrate that Agius's source was not directly Venantius, or not just him, but that Venantius was helpful to Agius, lending his source a brilliant and widely accepted poetic arrangement. In the history of medieval Latin poetry, it seems that Huldah is cited by only one other poet, another Carolingian, a few decades prior to Agius: Walafrid Strabo of Reichenau. His work, *De imagine Tetrici*, an enigmatic, short, allegorical poem in 268 verses on the court of Louis the Pious, was written when the statue of Theoderic was transported from Ravenna to Aachen.[7] In his poem, he pauses to praise the queen and empress Judith, who had been Louis's second wife since 818, comparing her to the fair Rachel who loved Benjamin just as Judith loved little Charles, later the emperor Charles the Bald, who appears to have been Walafrid's pupil. The poet emphasizes the significance of her name, matching her "valor and religious spirit" (*at Judith virtute refert et religione*; *Virg.* 193) with that of the biblical heroine, who beheaded the Assyrian invader, freeing and saving her fellow citizens. He also recalls an unusual characteristic of the queen: the ability to play an instrument ("Judith strummed the instrument with the sweet-sounding plectrum"; *organa dulcisono percurrit pectine Judith*; *Virg.* 198).[8] This aspect allows the poet a comparison

---

5. On Agius, see Francesco Stella, *La poesia carolingia* (Florence: Le Lettere, 1995), 93–94, 310–21, 479–81.

6. Ernst Dümmler et al., eds., *Poetae Latini aevi Carolini*, 4 vols., MGH (Berlin: Weidmann, 1896), 3:378.

7. See Michael Herren, "The *De imagine Tetrici* of Walahfrid Strabo: Edition and Translation," *JML* 1 (1991): 118–39.

8. The editor Dümmler connects this *Virg.* 198 to Jdt 16:1–2—the Song of Praise— *cantate Domino meo in cymbalis*, but this may perhaps refer to Judith the empress and not to the biblical heroine. Unless otherwise noted, all translations are my own.

with the prophetess Miriam, who in Exod 15:20 plays the drums ("a timbrel in her hand"; *tympanum in manu sua*; see *Imag. Tetr.* 197: "Miriam beat the rough-sounding skin of the timbrels" [*tympana raucisona pulsavit pelle Maria*]). He seizes the chance for further hyperbole in writing that, if Sappho and Huldah were there (2 Kgs 22:14), Judith would even be able to compose metric poetry and issue prophecies, adding the habitual praise for a woman "despite" being a woman—"In fact, whatever the limits of your sex may have detracted has been compensated by a life dedicated to spiritual practice" (*quicquid enim tibimet sexus subtraxit egestas / reddidit ingeniis culta atque exercita vita*)—followed by praise in the form of a list (fruitfulness, learning, kindness, strength of spirit, eloquence) and good wishes for her life and afterlife.

This poetic list of biblical women was taken up again three centuries later by the poet Marbod of Rennes (1035–1123), schoolmaster at Angers, who, in his famed *Liber decem capitulorum* on the ten subjects of Christian culture, dedicated the fourth chapter to women (*De matrona*). In it, he overturns all the anti-female prejudice common to the misogynist literature of the Middle Ages, although he also contributes to it in other texts. He, too, emphasizes that Mary was not the only one to raise the prestige and importance of women, but in addition to her, we read that many women were endowed with manly merit at times superior to that of men, and through their strength they received due glory. He lists Sarah, Rebecca, Rachel, Esther, Judith, Anna, and Naomi, comparing them to the seven stars. He pauses to praise Judith, Esther, and Ruth individually, dedicating a few verses to each of them.[9] This time, the form of the verse

---

9. Marbod of Rennes, *Lib. dec. cap.* 79–97: "And however, with this exception, since the conception of Mary appears a unique event, we read that more than a few women have had a manly mind, or have even exceeded men, and with a strong spirit have received the just reward together with the glory that they deserved. We read that Sarah, Rebecca, Rachel, Esther, Judith, Anna, and Naomi, whom the generations of old held to be like the seven stars, were equal to men or exceeded them. For Judith achieved an excellent endeavor, which none of the men had dared undertake, returning after having killed Holofernes, and the salvation granted to the city of Bethulia by a woman kept away the enemy, driven out from every other city, out of fear. Everlasting fame honors Queen Esther, who, married to the tyrant like a lamb to a cruel wolf, risking her life, was unafraid of crossing that threshold from which none who passed through it without permission returned, and in defense of her people put her own safety at stake, and turned the edict of death intended for her people against the enemy. I speak not of Ruth, who, accompanying alone her chaste mother-in-law,

repeats Venantius's model without variations, and Marbod's contribution is limited to the *amplificatio* of information on three of the main figures, later finishing this portrait of female virtues with saintly or pagan exempla such as Lucretia, Thrasea, and Alcestis.

2. The Model of Avitus

While Venantius provided a model in verse for the canon of biblical heroines, the poetic text model for *De virginitate* is the eponymous book by Alcimus Avitus, archbishop of Vienne from 494 to 523; he also wrote the poem *De spiritalis historiae gestis*, five books on sacred history from the creation to the crossing of the Red Sea, which soon became a textbook in medieval schools. After writing the poem, and thus after 506–507, Avitus sent Bishop Apollinare, upon the latter's request, a short book on the "religion of our relatives" or "on the virgins in our family," written for his sister Fuscina, who had become a nun. The topic employed by Avitus is not structured according to the exempla, as in Venantius, but follows the reasoning found in the treatises of the church fathers, especially Augustine. The main comparison is, of course, with Mary, offering the opportunity for an extensive description. After this excerpt, Avitus urges the reader to combat, quoting as examples the famed women he had come across in his readings: "On fact, for some time now the glory of your sex has often been known through reading" (*nam gloria dudum / sexus ista tui nota est tibi saepe legendo*; vv. 340–341).

He begins with Deborah, who spurred the Israelite army on against the Canaanites led by the general Sisera—whose gigantic body he describes,

---

deserved to give royal blood to her children, while she fled her country and parents because of her faith" (*hoc tamen excepto quoniam res unica constat, / non paucas legimus mentes gessisse virorum, / aut etiam superare viros, et pectore forti / dignam mercedem merita cum laude tulisse. / Sara, Rebecca, Rachel, Esther, Judith, Anna, Noemi, / sidera ceu septem quas saecula prisca tulerunt, / aequiparasse viros, aut exsuperasse leguntur. / nam Judith egregium facinus, quod nemo virorum / ausus erat, gessit, caeso rediens Holoferne, / Bethuliaeque salus urbi data per mulierem, / urbibus a reliquis pulsum deterruit hostem. / Esther reginam commendat fama perennis, / quae velut agna lupo crudeli nupta tyranno / non timuit, capitis discrimine, limen inire, / quod non exibat quisquis non jussus inisset, / opposuitque suam propria pro gente salutem, / edictumque necis populi conuertit in hostes. / ruth taceo quae sola socrum comitata pudicam, / ad regale genus meruit transfundere prolem, / dum fidei causa patriam fugit atque parentes*).

a fact extraneous to the Bible and perhaps derived from the *conflatio* with Goliath—and predicted their defeat. He continues with Jael, who is not named and who stabs Sisera in her tent, thus celebrating a "female ... victory" (*femineus ... triumphus*; v. 362). He then digresses on the personified representation of virginity as described by Prudentius, explicitly cited, and how it is glorified throughout the Holy Scriptures; he rapidly retraces this theme from Ruth through the prophetic books to Esther and Judith, briefly summarizing Judith's undertaking of false seduction and murder: "How could one forget Esther and the lies of the chaste Judith, in which the satrap is aroused by the trickery of her painted face and the woman continues to avoid his obscene bed and suppresses his furious gaze by cutting off his head?" (vv. 391–394).[10] After this consideration of the heroine, the biblical *percursio* continues to the end of the New Testament, culminating in praise of reading sacred texts and its effect on individual behavior, repeating the tale of the wise and the foolish virgins (Matt 25) and its commentaries in an already varied thematic context.

Another example surfaces only in verses 513–514, and it concerns a martyr: the well-known legend of Eugenia of Rome, who refused to be married and thus hid in a monastery disguised as a man, where she was discovered when a woman fell in love with her, believing her to be a man. When rejected, the woman denounced Eugenia, forcing her to reveal herself. Immediately thereafter, Avitus identifies exemplary virginity in the story of Joseph, who is sold by his brothers and who resists the advances of Potiphar's wife: Potiphar's wife is not even named as a character in a story known to all.

The next reference is to Susanna (vv. 549–551), who fled from attacks by two elders: "After him, who will ever celebrate with sufficient praise Susannah, who, at a delicate age, defeated the desires and mad conspiracy?" (*Susannam post hunc dignis quis laudibus umquam / excolat, infirmis quondam quae vicit in annis / improba vota senum coniuratosque furores?*). Her story, like that of Judith, is not passed down in the Hebrew Bible but only in Greek (Dan 13 LXX), and it is told with a certain narrative flavor owing to differentiation of the characters and psychological analysis otherwise absent or only roughly sketched in other exempla. One can easily imagine the episode of the two judges who walk away but then soon find

---

10. Alcimus Avitus, *Virg.*: *Hester quid memorem et castae mendacia Judith, / ornati cum fraude Satraps accenditur oris, / cum manet illudens obscenum femina lectum / desectoque feros compescit vertice visus?*

themselves in the same place, both consumed by the desire to see Susanna, the one having already declared it, the other until then unsuspected of it. Avitus also dramatizes the dissent of Susanna, who is uncertain as to how to respond to the harassment of the two. Daniel's intervention to save her, by consulting the two elders separately and thus discovering the truth, is an opportunity for a further digression on the history that awaited the prophet after his emergence onto the sacred stage. The short poem closes with the glorification of virgins, first to enter the kingdom of heaven, and the final example of Martha and Mary, the later of whom keeps the best part for herself, as Avitus's sister had done by choosing to enter a convent.[11]

3. The Intercultural Foresight of Dracontius: Biblical and Pagan Heroines

Dracontius of Carthage was the first poet to make extensive use of female exempla, an aspect of his work that until now has been little observed by scholars.[12] He authored a collection of *Romulea* (short poems on "Roman" subjects) recounting episodes of myth; a Christian poem, *De laudibus Dei*, largely composed of biblical paraphrases and doctrinal and moral exposition; and a *Satisfactio* to the Vandal king, which requested the author's release from prison.

---

11. This contribution had already been written (2010) when Avitus's *De virginitate* (or, rather, the *De consolatoria castitatis laude*) was published in the edition Alcimus Avitus, *Éloge consolatoire de la chasteté (sur la virginité)*, ed. Nicole Hecquet-Noti (Paris: Cerf, 2011), which I was unable to use.

12. The bibliography on Dracontius through 1996 has been collected and discussed by Luigi Castagna in *Studi draconziani (1912-1996)* (Naples: Loffredo, 1997). A number of works have been published in recent years (up to 2011), of which two also examine the *De laudibus Dei*: Myriam De Gaetano, *Scuola e potere in Draconzio* (Alessandria: Edizioni dell'Orso, 2009); Giovanni Santini, *Inter iura poeta: Ricerche sul lessico giuridico in Draconzio* (Rome: Herder, 2006). I have written on Dracontius several times, particularly in articles; see Stella, "Fra retorica e innografia: Sul genere letterario delle 'Laudes Dei' di Draconzio," *Phil* 132 (1988): 213–45; Stella, "Ristrutturazione topica ed estensione metaforica nella poesia cristiana: Da spunti draconziani," *WS* 102 (1989): 1–17; Stella, "Per una teoria dell'imitazione poetica cristiana: Saggio di analisi sulle *Laudes Dei* di Draconzio," *IL* 7–8 (1985–1986): 193–224; Stella, "Innovazioni lessicali dell *Laudes Dei* di Draconzio fra latinità tardo-antica e medievale," *IL* 21 (1999): 417–44; Stella, "Epiteti di Dio in Draconzio fra tradizione classica e cristiana," *CCC* 8 (1987): 601–33; Stella, "Variazioni stemmatiche e note testuali alle *Laudes Dei* di Draconzio: Con edizione del florilegio Paris, *B.N.*, Lat. 8093, f. 15ᵛ (sec. VIII–IX)," *FM* 3 (1996): 1–34.

The third book of *De laudibus Dei* begins with a laudatory hymn to omnipotence and divine generosity, which are contrasted with human greed, represented by the episode in the gospels of the rich man and Lazarus. Its central part (*Laud. Dei* 76–530), symbolically addressed to non-Christian readers, includes a series of examples of moral behavior, closing with a second hymn followed by a confession of individual sins and a concluding prayer. The exempla thus have a demonstrative function as examples of morality even in pagan history, following the pattern of Tertullian's *Ad martyras* (4.2–3) and, above all, Augustine's *De civitate Dei* (5.12–13). The first part of the poem features stories of personal or family sacrifices, to be compared with that of Abraham for Isaac, such as Menoeceus; Codrus; Leonidas; the Philaeni; Lucius Junius Brutus; Verginius (though he is not named explicitly), who killed his daughter Verginia to prevent her from being dishonored by Appius Claudius; Manlius Torquatus, who had his son killed for disobeying military orders; Scaevola; Curtius, and Regulus. These are followed by the stories of the sacrificial loyalty of two cities, Saguntum and Numantia, after which Dracontius announces with his usual wordiness—but also with the ideological openness that we have recognized in other aspects of his poem—his wish to balance his survey with a series of female exempla:[13]

> Lest anyone by chance believe that these words are dedicated only to men, and that woman is as an inert sex, weak with her fragile body, terrified by the weight of fame, and fearful of pursuing it beyond life at the cost of heroic suffering, having refused the countless eternal gifts of God, I will add that even a wicked woman can offer material for the highest consideration: nothing in the world is bolder than she when caught at fault; they draw courage from their very crime, and wrath provides women with an unstoppable force. Thus from that very place whence are they capable of drawing inspiration for their mad wickedness may they

---

13. In an unpublished chapter of my undergraduate thesis, "L'epica di Draconzio fra tradizione classica e Cristiana" (PhD diss., Università di Firenze, 1986), supervised by Rosa La Macchia and Rita Pierini, I dedicated a few dozen pages to observations on the ideology of harmony between the natural elements and social classes; to Dracontius's celebration of the role of women in marriage and in the community; to his theory on the overthrowing of the classes and the new relationship between Romans and Barbarians; and to his theology of forgiveness, the grace/free will dialectic, and his idea of evil, which reveal a nonchalantly modern Augustinianism capable of engaging in dialogue with the classical poetic tradition so as to resemanticize it in the face of completely new problems and ideals.

gather honest feelings around their heart and do what befits their dignity, what the reputation of their modesty demands, and what may aid them in attaining the glory of their future life. (*Laud. Dei* 3.468–479)[14]

The introduction to the female exempla thus paints an anthropological picture true to the misogyny at the heart of ancient culture and in fact based on the verses of Juvenal: "Nothing is bolder than they when they are discovered: they draw courage and wrath from their own guilt" (*nihil est audacius illis / deprensis: iram atque animos de crimine sumunt*; *Sat.* 6.284–285); "They show courage in the foul deeds they dare to commit" (*fortem animum praestant rebus quas turpiter audent*; 6.97). Women are capable of grand gestures, and it is right to attribute the proper importance to them, but—the poet would seem to say—the energy they employ in these undertakings is simply the underside of the violence that they ordinarily express in committing evil (*mala femina*). Reading between the lines of this excerpt of *De laudibus Dei* in light of Juvenal, but also in light of the fact that nearly all the (male) examples adopted to this point are *exempla scelerum*, enables us, however, to propose the hypothesis that here Dracontius is actually attempting to correct the negative topos inherited from Juvenal, whose terms he reuses but reverses their sense, though without arriving at a purely positive or neutral connotation of women's nature.[15]

The first example adopted in *Laud. Dei* 3.480–495 is that of the very chaste Judith, who "pretended to love Holofernes, and, penetrating the general's camp, a fearful place even for men, generated true glory from a simulated crime [the betrayal of her people]."[16] The term used by Dracon-

---

14. Dracontius, *Laud. Dei* 3.468–479: *sed ne forte viris tantum data verba putentur / et quasi sexus iners, fragili sub corpore mollis / laudis onus metuens, ne sit sibi fama superstes / tormentis quaesita suis, aeterna recuset / plurima dona Dei, laudis mala femina summae / materiem retinere potest: audacius illis / deprensis nihil est, animos de crimine sumunt / datque nimis grandem mulieribus ira furorem. / unde igitur furiale nefas assumere possunt, inde pios animi rapiant sub pectore motus / et faciant quod honesta decet, quod fama pudoris / exigit et vitae prodest sub laude futurae.* Reproduced here, with some changes, is the translation by Francesco Corsaro, ed., *Blossii Aemili Dracontii, De laudibus Dei libri tres*, CISAM (Catania: Università di Catania, 1962), 159.

15. The observation that the examples are all *exempla scelerum* belongs to Claude Moussy; see the comment in his edition of Dracontius: *Réparation*, part 3 of *Louanges de Dieu*, vol. 2 of *Oeuvres* (Paris: Les Belles Lettres, 1988), 102.

16. *Judith Holofernem castissima finxit amare / et sibimet peperit de ficto crimine laudem / castra ducis metuenda viris ingressa virago.*

tius to define her character is *virago*, which, according to Claude Moussy, takes on the meaning here of "heroine" or, more literally, "woman warrior," as Ovid had done in reference to Minerva in *Metam.* 2.765 ("a formidable woman in war"; *huc ubi pervenit belli metuenda virago*) and as Dracontius would do when referring to Clytemnestra in *Orest. trag.* 752 or to Medea in *Rom.* 10, 12, and 62. Judith thus takes on a specifically warlike connotation. There follows a depiction of the military camp, which constitutes a work of compositional skill marked by references to Statius, *Theb.* 4.321 and by expressions extolling female courage as superior to that of men: "the assault of men is not so great a force" (*et quod tanta manus non est aggressa virorum*; *Laud. Dei* 3.486) or "woman alone" (*femina sola*; 3.487); then comes the tale of the decapitation and display of the head to the Hebrew notables and to her city, which gave Judith both freedom and victory. The episode concludes with a hymnodic ending that reiterates the femininity of her undertaking against a courageous male commander: "The bold and courageous commander dies at the dagger of a woman" (*femineo mucrone perit dux fortis et audax*; v. 478). He was crushed not by battle but by the hope of pleasure (*promissa voluptas*; v. 492), but "the pleasure was hoped for but not consummated" (*sperata licet, non est perfecta libido*; v. 493); typical of Dracontius, he does not resist the temptation of the paradox, emphasizing the punishment for a crime of adultery not yet committed. Also typical of Dracontius is the sophisticated reuse of a thematic intertext such as Paulinus of Nola's (355–431) poem *Carm.* 26, in which Judith was cited within a series of examples of victory achieved without weapons but through the protection of God: "The wily Judith with her chaste cunning deceived and mocked Holofernes, who had terrorized mighty people far and wide. She remained inviolate in that lewd bed, and then fled from the barbarians' camp victorious after slaughtering their leader" (*terrentem magnos late populos Holofernem / arte pudicitiae deceptum callida Judith / risit, in impuro quae non polluta cubili / barbara truncato victrix duce castra fugavit*; 26.165).[17] Paulinus, however, brings out the derisory aspect of the episode, leading to the contrast *impuro/polluta* later exploited by Dracontius and emphasizing the heroine's warrior-like virtues less than her cunning, which finds no importance in Dracontius's portrayal.[18]

---

17. Translation from *The Poems of St. Paulinus of Nola*, trans. P. G. Walsh (New York: Newman, 1975), 259–60.

18. Paulinus of Nola also cites Judith in *Carm.* 28, another *natalicium* for Felix, which, describing the paintings in the basilica of Nola, mentions the depiction of the

The other examples adopted in the *De laudibus Dei*, however, are drawn from Roman history and pagan mythology: Semiramis, Tomyris, Evadne, Dido, and Lucretia, women who vary greatly and are exponents of virtues or abilities that are often contradictory but who are equally courageous and determined. The moral that the poet draws from them in verses 524–530 is that "a thousand types [*exempla*] of crimes everywhere are attributed to this or that woman: they committed them either because they were influenced by the mirage of a bit of glory, or certainly out of devotion, but to a vain deity" (*Milia femineis numerantur ubique catervis / exempla scelerum: modicae vel laudis amore / aut certe fecere pie pro numine vano*). Following this is a comparison between legendary gods and the true God, who is later praised with another lengthy hymnodic discourse. This conclusion/transition seems to confirm that Dracontius bases his material on a rhetorical inventory and treats it as such—namely, an inventory of crimes perpetrated for glory. This perpetration of crimes for glorious purposes has positive connotations because it is presented in the anthropological preface as one of the objectives to which women must not feel inadequate; they are, in any case (*certe*), crimes for a good cause (*pie*), committed for a noble aim, though at times—in all cases except for Judith—in the name of a pagan deity. The biblical narratives become intertwined with the exemplary materials of the rhetoricians and poets in the wake of Augustine's *De civitate Dei*, but without any further cultural contrast.

4. The Other Judiths, from Aldhelm to Milo

Naturally, Paulinus of Nola, Dracontius, and Avitus were not the first to write poetry about Judith. Before them, Prudentius had mentioned her in *Psychomachia*:

> "Shalt thou, O troubler of mankind, have been able to resume thy strength and grow warm again with the breath of life that was extinguished in thee, after the severed head of Holofernes soaked his Assyrian chamber with his lustful blood, and the unbending Judith, spurning the lecherous captain's jeweled couch, checked his unclean passion with the sword, and woman as she was, won a famous victory over the foe with no trembling hand, maintaining my cause with boldness heaven-inspired?"

---

heroine in a tableau dedicated to women: *ast aliam sexus minor obtinet, inclita Judith, / qua simul et regina potens depingitur Esther* (28.26–27).

> But perhaps a woman still fighting under the shade of the law had not force enough, though in so doing she prefigured our times, in which the real power [Christ] has passed into earthly bodies to sever the great head by the hands of feeble agents? (58–69)[19]

The episode is recalled within a discussion on *Pudicitia* toward the *Libido* that she defeated, and the context leads the poet, in a passage of concentrated strength, to force or constrain the meaning of the episode into a particular area. It is shifted onto the level of sexual mores, raising Judith to a symbol of virtue, avenger of the attempted adultery, rather than a symbol of courage, and makes her into a typological figure that hints at the present time, in which the authentic virtue (of Christ) has been made flesh in an earthly body to cut off the great head of the enemy through the work of feeble servants (*infirmos*).

Sidonius Apollinaris (430–486) had also spoken of her in his *Carm.* 16, in which he invites his zither and his spirit to sing no longer of pagan deities but of the God who penetrated the breast of Miriam and helped "the hand of Judith as it smote the neck of Holophernes, when the trunk was laid prostrate with the throat cut through and the strong blow gloriously disguised the weak sex" (*quique manum Judith ferientem colla Olophernis Iuuisti, exciso iacuit cum gutture truncus / et fragilis valido latuit bene sexus in ictu*; 16.11–13).[20] Thus the episode is one of the elements of a biblical aretalogy, which includes other episodes, but it is noted not just for its usual contrast between strength and femininity but for its emphasis on divine intervention rather than the heroine's initiative. This aspect is imposed by the hymnodic context, in which the subject must topically remain the "you" of that God who is being celebrated, and thus each event must be presented in light of the external agent.

---

19. Prudentius, *Psych.* 58–69: *tene, o vexatrix hominum, potuisse resumptis / viribus extincti capitis recalescere flatu, / Assyrium postquam thalamum ceruix Olofernis / caesa cupidineo madefactum sanguine lauit / gemmantemque torum moechi ducis aspera Judith / spreuit et incestos compescuit ense furores, / famosum mulier referens ex hoste tropaeum / non trepidante manu, vindex mea caelitus audax. / at fortasse parum fortis matrona sub umbra / legis adhuc pugnans, dum tempora nostra figurat, / vera quibus virtus terrena in corpora fluxit, / grande per infirmos caput excisura ministros.* Translation from H. J. Thomson, trans., *Prudentius*, vol. 1, LCL (Cambridge: Harvard University Press, 1949).

20. Translation from Sidonius, *Poems and Letters*, trans. W. B Anderson (Cambridge: Harvard University Press, 1936), 1:243.

The next appearance—besides Venantius, who, in addition to the mnemonic verse of the female canon, quickly cites Judith in verse 304 of the same poem, *De virginitate*—is found in the third poetic *De virginitate* of the Latin tradition, that of Aldhelm of Malmesbury (639–709), excluding simple mentions in lists of biblical books, which are not considered in this essay. This metric reduction of the prose *De laude virginitatis* is dedicated to the monastic community of Barking and is, in any case, much more extensive than the precedents of Avitus and Venantius.[21] In fact, it occupies 2,904 hexameters dedicated to explaining the doctrine on the matter (i.e., virginity), composing a sort of themed bibliography in verse and a history of martyrial and institutional virginity, especially in monastic and church institutions. It is also replete with biblical references and exempla; those drawn from the Bible are explained in the last part of the text within a sort of *psychomachia* from Nabal to Joseph to Judith. To the latter, in the Anglo-Latin poet's redundant and rather empty style, he dedicates a brief narrative and exegetical elaboration:

> What can be said of Judith, born of noble stock, who with her pure body disdained the king's brothel and with her heart trod on unholy, lustful relations with the pagan? Through this endeavor her chaste satchel brought the bloodied trophy to her fellow citizens who had run the risk of death, keeping her modesty intact with a devout mind, and thus chaste purity triumphantly disdained the vice of the flesh, guilty of immoral stain, and she resisted the attack with the arrows of combatant virginity to prevent the filthy poison of the brothel from creeping into her delicate members, reaching her innermost organs. (*Laud. virg.* 2560–2570)[22]

---

21. For the comprehensive edition, see Rudolf Ehwald, *Aldhelmi opera*, MGH (Berlin: Weidmann, 1913–1919). For a critical review of the prose treatise (with an edition of the glosses), see Aldhelm of Malmesbury, *Prosa de virginitate cum glosa Latina atque Anglosaxonica*, ed. Scott Gwara, CCSL 124 (Turnhout: Brepols, 2001). For an English translation, see Michael Lapidge and James L. Rosier, eds., *Aldhelm: The Poetic Works* (Cambridge: Brewer, 1985). The most significant study of Aldhelm as a poet (up to 2011) remains Andy Orchard, *The Poetic Art of Aldhelm* (Cambridge: Cambridge University Press, 1994), while on the *De virginitate*, see George T. Dempsey, "Aldhelm of Malmesbury's Social Theology: The Barbaric Heroic Ideal Christianised," *Peritia* 15 (2001): 58–80; Emma Pettit, "Holiness and Masculinity in Aldhelm's Opus Geminatum De Virginitate," in *Holiness and Masculinity in the Middle Ages*, ed. Patricia H. Cullum and Katherine Jane Lewis (Cardiff: University of Wales Press, 2004), 8–23.

22. Aldhelm of Malmesbury, *Laud. verg.* 2560–2570: *quid referam Judith generosa*

Aldhelm employs strong terms to glorify her rejection of relations with the pagan king and the display of the severed, bloody head as the triumph of chastity, and he portrays the battle as spiritual combat (*virgineis ... sagittis*) and highlights the contrast between the woman and the poison of a corrupt sexuality (*postribulum*, used twice). Here we sense the influence of Prudentius's model, with the allegorization and radical abstraction of Judith's character, whose feminine aspect becomes secondary, though there is some allusion to it in the *fibras fragiles* of line 2570, almost as if to echo the expressions of Sidonius or Dracontius.

5. Instances in the Carolingian Age

The popularity of Prudentius is confirmed in part by the reuse of his expression *castae mendacia*, from the above-cited *Psychomachia*. We find it again in the *titulus* of Wigbodus, *Esther quid memorem et castae mendacia Judith?* (1:8:2,23), within a summary of biblical books composed in the proto-Carolingian era, late eighth century, by recovering passages from Eugenius and Avitus.[23] Even in the fully Carolingian era, the heroine is mentioned above all in biblical *percursiones* (today, we might say parades), such as that in *Carm.* 41 by Theodulf, bishop of Orléans (d. ca. 821). this was transmitted in the early Middle Ages as a metric introduction to complete scriptural codices—"We find then the story of a woman famed for her undertaking, Judith, under whose blows fell unchaste madness" (*scribitur insignis Judith mox femina facti / incestus cecidit qua feriente furor*)—and in very similar terms in *Carm.* 21—"With her sword Judith drove back unchaste madness, but she did not succeed in driving back you, unjust scourge of death" (*incestos Judith compescuit ense furores, / te non compescit, mortis iniqua lues*; 21.71–72). These occur within a series of examples of famous figures who did not escape death, whose consoling

---

stirpe creatam / prostibulum regis temnentem corpore puro / et stuprum sceleris calcantem corde profanum? / civibus idcirco mortis discrimina passis / casta cruentatum gestauit bulga tropeum / seruans integrum deuota mente pudorem. / sic vitium carnis polluta sorde nocentis / integritas almo contemnit casta triumpho / aemula virgineis proturbans bella sagittis, / lurida prostibuli ne possit serpere virus / in fibras fragiles succensis torre medullis.

23. Dümmler et al., *Poetae Latini aevi Carolini*, 1:96; later updated by Luigi Munzi, ed., "Compilazione e riuso in età carolingia: Il prologo poetico di Wigbodo," *RomanoBarbarica* 12 (1992–1993): 189–210.

topic we have already seen in previous examples. Here, a faint allusion to female characterization reemerges and accompanies the praise of chastity, or rather the punishment of lust. In the next generation, Walafrid Strabo, as we have seen, would again invoke the biblical Judith to celebrate the imperial Judith, praised for her *virtus* and *religio* as was her namesake.

The other instances in this era come from the monk and schoolmaster Milo of Saint-Amand (d. 871/872), author of a poem in two books, *De sobrietate*, which has been studied little in relation to its value and originality. This poem adapts the distant model of Prudentius's *Psychomachia* to deal with moral subjects using an exegetical method—that is, by commenting on biblical references. In the first book, he dedicates a long passage to Judith, which is the most extensive in Latin poetry (Milo, *Sobr.* 16.331–393 [sixty-three verses]).[24] It is dominated by psychological matters as much as moral ones, carefully describing the details of the scene, absolutely unusual in a doctrinal work, which the author presents as a chronicle of the *historica ratio*—that is, the narration rather than the spiritual, typological, or tropological meaning—trusting that this order of the events is governed by divine providence. Certainly, the heroine is repeatedly described as *casta*, as would occur when he refers to her in another episode, verse 476: "your pure acting praises you, Judith, and makes you blessed" (*acta pudicitiae te, Judith, laude bearunt*). We are also reminded of the *sobrietas* that permits her to be included in the gallery of examples in the poem, for after her husband's death, she kept to her room alone (or, rather, "with her sister, moderation"; *cum sobrietate sorore*), fasting in her beauty and her propriety and thus becoming, in an innovation of religious imagination, a model of salvation for widows. Declaring that he will skip over the details of her story, which the poet knows is familiar to all, he focuses on the simulated offer of adultery made by the *castissima foemina* and imagines the expression of Holofernes upon seeing the woman, a vision of dignity before his coarse, surly eyes, the expression of a shaken soul and of lust set ablaze. Death enters through the large windows and takes him prisoner; the luxury and pleasures of the banquet only hasten the end, and the wine that has been drunk will only serve to soften the pain of the blows.[25] The incipit

---

24. Milo, *Sobr.* 16.331–393 (ed. Dümmler et al., 3:625–27).

25. The reference to entering through large windows might cause one to think of Judith's eyes, but this is actually a reference, correctly identified by the editor Ludwig Traube, to the image in Jer 9:21: *quia ascendit mors per fenestras nostras, ingressa est domos nostras*. A characteristic of Milo's craft is cross-referencing biblical passages

of the epilogue, which makes use of Virgilian expressions, requalifies the protagonist as an example of moral virtue, but immediately after the epithet *bellatrix*, in an accumulation of virtues (*virtutibus associatis*), it brings out once more the warrior aspect that had been obscured by the writers after Dracontius. The passage lingers at length on colorful details: the refined clothing, the luxurious backdrop of the Assyrian banquet, the chronology of Judith's stay at court (here five days, as opposed to four in the biblical account), the trunk without a head or a name, its display to the Hebrews and the Assyrians on the walls at dawn. The episode is immediately followed by that of Jael, introduced in the form of a comparison.[26] Her moderation (the *sobrietas* recalled in verse 391), which is the constant theme of each of the poem's stories, perhaps lay in her serving milk instead of water to the general Sisera, who had fled to her tent, and in the strength with which she succeeded in stabbing his temple with a sharp nail, demonstrating courage, combativeness, and boldness. Behind the characters, the Moderation that had offered the milk armed the woman with a hammer, punishing the sacrilegious commander for his offense.

The next story (*Sobr.* 17) is that of Esther, in a sequence that apparently calls up Venantius's exempla of female heroism, here forcibly adapted to fit examples of moderation.[27] Esther is one such example due to her fasting, probably a reference to a detail just barely hinted at in the Bible: Esth 2:15, the moderation with which Esther had preferred not to use all the

---

(through reciprocal intrascriptural references) to deepen the meaning of the text further while strengthening its expressiveness in an unexpected manner.

26. Milo, *Sobr.* 16.386–393: *sic Iahel, uxor Aber, Sisaram post bella fugacem, / quae male nongentis falcatis curribus egit / qui dum poscit aquas, lac accipit—hospita amico / asperior solito clauo terebrauit acuto / pertractans in fronte locum; mors iuncta sopori est. / sobrietas ductrix lac praebuit atque reatum / sacrilegi pugnax audaci perculit ulna / femineasque manus fabrorum malleus auxit.*

27. Milo, *Sobr.* 17.394–410: *Hester reginam jejunia sobria regi / fecerunt gratam, quam non sua forma suasit / terribili feritate suo se offerre marito: / lamentum gemitus luctus suspiria saccus / verterunt urnam cunctasque ex ordine sortes. / haec humilis deiecit Aman regina superbum, / sub rege Asuero populus quem cunctus honorans / orabat genibus telluris in aequore flexis, / extulit et ligno iam spe meliore leuatum, / quod quinquagenis cubitis altum ipse pararat / Mardocheo humili; finis fuit iste superbo. / spectauere decem pendentem in stipite nati, / quod genitor passus, passuri sorte reatus. / sic cadit in foueam commenti fraudibus instans; / inlaqueatur enim, nodos qui nectit iniquos. / sic ruit ascendens ventosa superbia fastum; / invidia occumbit, genitrix quae facta diabli est.*

resources that the king had provided to those seeking to be queen or the fast that she had undertaken when she decided to go before King Xerxes and beg for mercy for the Jews, whom Haman had wished to persecute. The source is probably Ambrose, who in the *Hel.* 9 had specified that "with her fast Judith beheaded Holofernes, and by the same method Esther freed her people, to whom the drunken Haman paid the penalty for his wrongdoing" (*Judith ieiunans Holophernem obtruncat, iisdem artibus populum suum liberat Esther, cui poenas ebrius Aman exsolvit*). Here the interpretation is so forced as to deny that her beauty was the reason for the king's choice (*non sua forma suasit*). But most of the verses dedicated to this character focus on the conspiracy of Haman, whose fate on the fifty-cubit-high gallows (Esth 5:14) is depicted as a reversal, to his detriment, of the fate that he had initiated for the Jews and is dramatized by the detail of his ten sons witnessing his death, sons who are actually only named in the Bible much later on as victims of the Jews' retaliation (Esth 9:12). Here the moral crux of the story is presented as the reversal of arrogance and treachery, which turn against those guilty of such sins, and the starting point of *sobrietas* is nothing more than a narrative pretense. In fact, Milo resumes the story of Judith in the second book ("we mocked the infamous Holofernes, whom the chaste Judith beheaded"; *risimus infandum quem Judith casta Holofernem / truncavit*; *Sobr.* 2.200–201) to contrast it—by setting it in the role of a monument to chastity—against the dramatic nature of another severed head, that of John the Baptist, beheaded by the "monkey dancer of the prophet" (*saltatrix simia vatis*), which in turn sets off a tirade against carnal lust, richly embellished with biblical exempla.

In the same period, Judith appears several times as a character in the rhythmic version of the *Cena Cypriani*, drafted by the deacon Johannes Hymonides around 876 for the festivities connected to the emperor Charles the Bald's visit to Rome and the object of recent critical attention.[28] As we know, in this scriptural masquerade composed in prose between the end of the fourth and the beginning of the fifth centuries, each of the characters appears as an invitee to the wedding banquet of King Joel in Cana and is portrayed with an adjective or a gesture recalling his or her role in the Bible. Judith is here presented as a "victor" and as "chaste," combining the two most frequent connotations with which she was associated in late

---

28. Among many titles, see, for example, Rabanus Maurus and Giovanni Immonide, *La Cena di Cipriano*, ed. Elio Rosati and Francesco Mosetti Casaretto (Alessandria: Edizioni dell'Orso, 2002).

antique literature, but also as the lead dancer and as an example of beauty and elegance in her hair and clothing.[29]

A few decades earlier in rhythmic literature, however, Judith had received the honor of a short poem dedicated entirely to the events of her life, evidence of the popularity of her story, of which the rhythmic text was probably a recited version. This is the Strecker III rhythmic poem, passed down in its entirety, alongside many other examples of this genre, in the manuscript in Verona, Biblioteca Capitolare XC (85), and in part in other contemporary manuscripts (ninth to tenth century)—Paris lat. 1154, Bruxellensis 8860-67, Verona 88 [83]—fifty stanzas of three catalectic trochaic septenarius or fifteen-syllable lines. Unfortunately, most of these (stanzas 13-44) are illegible given the Veronese scrawl in which the most complete version was written. Here, as far as one can decipher, Judith—in any case, also celebrated as a woman—is above all a symbol of the victory over pagan peoples, as the text closes with a wish for victory similar to that in the Bible story: "But they praised Judith of all women: may that God that then defeated the Assyrian troops through the strength of her courage and her heroic arm bring the pagan peoples who do not believe in the Lord to ruin" (*Judith vero inter omnes laudauerunt feminas. / ille deus, qui percussit tunc castra Assyrii / in virtute preualenti et in forti brachio, / perdat gentes paganorum incredulas domino*). At the time, it was thought that the text could be placed in the context of the Carolingian wars against the Saxons, or rather—given its probable northern Italian origins—the Muslims (793) or the Avars (796). Another clue is the exegetic interest in the book of Judith, favored by the presence of an empress by that name, to whom Rabanus Maurus dedicated his commentary of the Bible text in the 830s. But the warlike atmosphere renders the first dating more likely. The course of the tale retraces that of the biblical book, recalled in quick strokes for a readership already familiar with the story, but with the desire to contextualize it in chronological terms ("it was in the thirteenth year of the reign"; *anno tertio in regno cum esset et decimo*) instead of portraying a character and to stay as true as possible to the source, which is just barely adapted to rhythmic requirements. The story is transformed indirectly into a sort of epic, with

---

29. Johannes Hymonides, *Cena Cypr.* 2.34: *Judith victrix Oloferni offert opertorium*; 2.150: *Lazarus sepultus umbram, Judit casta soleam*; 2.259: *Judith sericum seruabat casta coopertorium*; 2.199: *choreas Judith ducebat et Jubal psalterium*; 2.247: *Bersabeth crines decoros et Judith conopeum*.

the repetition of epithets for the same characters (such as "Holefernes ... head of the army"; *Olofernus ... princeps militiae*) or recurring words and phrases such as "many nations" (*multas gentes*), "against the nations" (*contras gentes*), "with his God" (*deo suo*), and "sword" (*gladius*), with a patina of clericalization that emerges when compared with the source: in stanza 48, the rhythmic poem uses "churches" (*ecclesiis*) while the original text has "people" (*populous*).[30] The result is the equivalent of a fifteenth-century *cantare* on knights or paladins, concentrating on essential elements and select scenes of the story and almost completely closed to any chance of exegesis or symbolism other than a superficial contrast between Christians and unbelievers, and it is probably a Latin precursor of this folkloristic and literary genre.

6. Exegetical Success and Later Developments

The figure of Judith is presented in different ways in the forms of early medieval cultural expression beyond Latin poetry: the thesis of Cécile Coussy documents her above all in iconography, but Old English literature presents another, unfortunately mutilated poem on Judith, preserved in the famous Cotton Vitellius A. XV of the British Library that also holds *Beowulf*.[31] The most significant trace is without a doubt the commentary—the first ever dedicated in the Latin West to this book of the Bible—that Rabanus Maurus, abbot of Fulda and later archbishop of Mainz (d. 856), devoted to it and that has been discussed in a recent critical edition.[32] The commentary was composed around 834, when Rabanus Maurus was still abbot of Fulda, and is dedicated to the empress Judith, as attested by the preface in verse and the *carmen figuratum* accompanying it. Along with the commentary to the book of Esther, with which it is

---

30. For an analysis of these recurring terms, see Stella, *Poesia carolingia latina a tema biblico* (Spoleto: CISAM, 1993), 332–35.

31. Céline Coussy, *La figure de Judith dans l'Occident médiéval (V–XV siècles)*, 2 vols. (Limoges: Université de Limoges, 2004). Unfortunately, it appears that the book, published in two volumes (with additional iconography), is not available in Italian libraries and is absent from the Bibliothèque Nationale in Paris and the Bodleian Library at Oxford University. Stacy S. Klein analyzes the context of the Old English poem in a chapter of her *Ruling Women: Queenship and Gender in Anglo-Saxon Literature* (Notre Dame: University of Notre Dame Press, 2006).

32. Rabanus Maurus, *Commentario al Libro di Giuditta*, ed. Adele Simonetti, MM 73, Testi 19 (Florence: SISMEL-Edizioni del Galluzzo, 2008).

usually associated in the numerous manuscripts preserving it, the poem was revised and rededicated to the empress Ermengarde, wife of Lothair, a few years later (around 840).[33] As Adele Simonetti has noted, this commentary is not terribly systematic, owing to the lack of direct sources on which to base it, and it is founded on two fundamental meanings: literal and allegorical. The exegete explains this in the double preface published as poem no. 4 by Ernst Dümmler in *Poetae Latini aevi Carolini*. In his prose dedication (PL 109:539), Rabanus Maurus clearly presents his comments on Judith and Esther, associated with the gift for the queen as a model of behavior to imitate for "virtue and study in good works" (*virtutes ac studium in bono opere*), all the more so because the empress shares the name of one and the regal dignity of the other. He specifies, however, that both characters are allegorical figures (although further on he uses the term "type," *typus*) of the church, even though Judith is in any case a *castitatis exemplar*. The qualifying point of their exemplary nature lies—as in the rhythmic poem and only there—in the fact that both defeated spiritual enemies with strength and physical enemies with the maturity of wisdom. In the same way, if the empress Judith, who had already proven her ability to conquer her enemies, had persevered in this behavior, she would have easily overcome all her opponents.[34] Thus what emerges is a purely war-related and antipagan interpretation, which seems peculiar to the second generation of Carolingians.

The dedication in verse, which is composed of thirty-five mesostic hexameters in hymnodic style and ends in a generic, long-winded prayer

---

33. On the interpretative success of the book of Esther, see Elisabetta Limardo Daturi, *Représentations d'Esther entre écritures et images* (Bern: Lang, 2004), which, however, does not consider the Latin poetic sources.

34. PL 109:539: *sanctarum mulierum quas sacra Scriptura commemorat, virtutes ac studium in bono opere imitari, non frustra arbitratus sum quarumdam illarum historiam, allegorico sensu ad sanctae Ecclesiae mysterium a nobis translatam, vestro nomini dicare atque transmittere, Judith videlicet, atque Esther: quarum unam coaequatis nomine, alteram dignitate. quae quidem ob insigne meritum virtutis, tam viris, quam etiam feminis sunt imitabiles, eo quod spiritales hostes animi vigore, et corporales consilii maturitate vicerunt. Sic et vestra nunc laudabilis prudentia, quae jam hostes suos non parva ex parte vicerat, si in bono coepto perseverare atque semetipsam semper meliorare contenderit, cunctos adversarios suos feliciter superabit*. Isidore of Seville presents the same interpretation, which was standard throughout the Middle Ages: *Judith et Esther typum Ecclesiae gestant, hostes fidei puniunt, ac populum Dei ab interitu eruunt* (*Alleg.* 122 [PL 83:116A]).

requesting that God protect the queen, was published as the first, but was actually composed as the second (for Ermengarde). The second, in twenty hexameters, addresses Ermengarde directly, urging her not to disdain the "commissioned work" (*opus commissum*) and the "sent song" (*carmen missum*) of her devoted servant. It then praises the recipient and proposes to her the noble example of the heroine Judith ("pray, accept Judith as a noble model for all: in fact, you will imitate her at the same time in your mind and by your hand" [*accipe, quaeso, Judith exemplar nobile cunctis, / mente manuque simul atque hanc imitabere rite*; vv. 10–11). He thus acknowledges the moral and political aspect of the biblical model because it will render her welcome to Christ in heaven and prevent the enemy (a sign that seems to coincide with that of the rhythmic poem) from saying so much as *puppup*, an onomatopoeic word perhaps referring to children's talk. This word seems to be found exclusively in Aldhelm (*regales vastans caulas bis dicere puppup*; *De virg.* 20), and Rabanus Maurus reuses it in his *Laud. cruc.* 2.21. The content of this dedication is similar to the one for Ermengarde in his commentary on the book of Esther, a "queen whose wisdom and steadiness of mind and victory over her enemies offer all Christians a most noble model, so that they may follow divine law and, maintaining a firm hope in the goodness of God, have faith in the possibility of being freed from all enemies."[35] The similarity of both topic and expressions confirms the parallelism and the near equivalence that the two biblical figures enjoyed in this period. Rabanus Maurus adds in the verse preface that the queen, like Esther, is urged to take care of her people, raising them up in every manner. Indeed, beauty and strength fade, and as day becomes night and the leaves and flowers fall, so Ermengarde—whom the poet salutes from his bed, where he lies ill—will be "a guest for a short time" (*parvi temporis hospes*; guest of a short time). In this dedication, of a more personal and reasoned kind, in which Rabanus Maurus reuses expressions such as "O, powerful queen" (*o regina potens*), which Venantius Fortunatus had dedicated to Radegund, Esther is set forth as an example of wisdom, tenacity, and success in her hope in God and obedience to the law. These qualities ensure her effectiveness in the fight against

---

35. Rabanus Maurus, *Carm.* 4 (ed. Dümmler et al., 2:167–68): *expositionem libri Hester reginae ... cuius prudentia et constantia mentis victoriaque de hostibus nobilissimum quibusque fidelibus praebet exemplum, ut divinam legem servantes et spem firmam in dei bonitate habentes confidant se de universis inimicis liberandos.*

her enemies, but above all, unlike Judith, she is a model queen, a woman to whom power offered the condition and the opportunity to do good.[36]

Mentions of Judith after the ninth century are relatively few, but they seem to emphasize a specific typification of the figure: the strong and victorious woman, a model for other women in power, treated in an identical way as Esther, who, however, was much less popular in poetry.[37]

In tenth- to thirteenth-century poetry, Judith returns as an example in *Scolasticus* by Walter of Speyer (ca. 963–1027), who dedicated verses to her that sung of military undertakings but placed them in a passage devoted to controlling one's instincts, thus indirectly praising her for her chastity.[38] Similarly, the twelfth-century *Vita Eduardi* dedicates some verses to the wedding of Edward the Confessor and his queen Edith, celebrating the king's piety, writing that he had entrusted himself to God, who inspired the victories of Joseph, Judith, and Susannah in

---

36. Rabanus Maurus's relationship with these empresses has been studied through biblical models by Mayke B. de Jong, "The Empire as Ecclesia: Hrabanus Maurus and biblical *Historia* for Rulers," in *The Uses of the Past in the Early Middle Ages*, ed. Yitzhak Hen and Matthew Innes (Cambridge: Cambridge University Press, 2000), 191–226.

37. If we exclude mentions of Esther in lists of biblical books, she is only quoted in two passages by Paulinus of Nola (*Carm.* 26.95 and 28.27), which later surface together with other biblical heroines in Marbod's *Liber decem capitolorum*, and obviously in Petrus Riga's *Aurora* and John of Garland's *Epithalamium virginis*. Aelfric had produced an English version of the book of *Esther*; see Mary Clayton, "Aelfric's *Esther*: A *speculum reginae*?," in *Text and Gloss: Studies in Insular Learning and Literature Presented to Joseph Donovan Pheifer*, ed. Helen Conrad-O'Briain, Vincent John Scattergood, and Anne Marie D'Arcy (Dublin: Four Courts, 1999), 89–101. Carolingian political treatises had made her a paradigm of equality in royalty, as documented by Franz-Reiner Erkens in "*Sicut Esther Regina*: Die westfränkische Königin als *consors regni*," *Francia* 20 (1993): 15–38, and this tendency revealed a continuity in the post-Carolingian period, becoming a topos, as documented by Louis L. Huneycutt in "Intercession and the High-Medieval Queen: The Esther Topos," in *Power of the Weak: Studies on Medieval Women*, ed. Jennifer Carpenter and Sally-Beth MacLean (Urbana: University of Illinois Press, 1995), 126–46. Discussion of Esther in later periods is found in Birgit Franke, *Assuerus und Esther am Burgunderhof: Zur Rezeption des Buches Esther in den Niederlanden (1450–1530)* (Berlin: Mann, 1998), while reinterpretations of her in late medieval mysticism have been gathered in Louise Gnädinger, "Esther: Eine Skizze," *ZDP* 113 (1994): 31–62.

38. Walter of Speyer, *Scol.* 4.87–88: *Anne oblita tibi pudibundae foedera Judith / non hoc pacta modo? quae postquam legis in umbra / marcida sopiti transfixit colla tyranni, / cartallum festina suum ceruice recisa / te pereunte domum victrix reditura grauauit / incolumisque suam duce me repedauit in urbem.*

chastity, resuming the exemplary sequence that we have seen at work in the poets of late antiquity. But the relationship to the model becomes more pertinent in the *Vita Mathildis* by Donizo of Canossa as a model of virile opposition to the kings (2.798-799). After the eleventh century, the exemplum emerges again, primarily in specifically biblical poems such as the *De ordine mundi* attributed to Hildebert of Lavardin (1056-1133), who broadly elaborated on Judith, or the excerpt already mentioned in the *Liber decem capitulorum* by Marbod of Rennes (1035-1123). The citations remain rather numerous (Bernard of Morlaix, Walter of Châtillon, John of Garland and others), proving the popularity of the figure, who would later dominate Renaissance and Baroque iconography. Perhaps more varied is her success in exegesis, which saw the emergence of interpretations only hinted at in the early Middle Ages: the devotion to Mary sustained by Cistercian culture, for example, led Helinand of Froidmont (ca. 1160-1230) to consider Judith a type of the Virgin rather than the church, while John of Salisbury (1120-1180) in his *Policraticus* makes her an example of *pia simulatio*—that which the early medieval poets had defined *castae mandacia Judith*—within a debate on ethical/political methodology.[39] The etymological interpretations of the figures' names, however, do not seem to have had cultural impacts: based on Jerome, they are reproposed Rabanus Maurus's *De natura rerum*, in which Judith is associated with "praise or confessing" (*laudans vel confitens*) and Esther "hiding" (*absconsa*) (3.1).

7. Other Biblical Heroines

The example of Judith—and, in part, Esther and other Old Testament heroines—has provided us with a guide for exploring the presence of biblical women in Latin and other poetry of the early Middle Ages, including moral interpretations and political adaptations, but above all in the contextualizations that as the various poetic frameworks required, each time

---

39. On Judith as a type of the Virgin, see Anne T. Thayer, "Judith and Mary: Hélinand's Sermon for the Assumption," in *Medieval Sermon and Society: Cloister, City, University; Proceedings of International Symposia at Kalamazoo and New York*, ed. Jacqueline Hamesse et al. (Louvain-la-Neuve: FIDEM, 1998), 63-75. Judith has been discussed as an example of *pia simulatio* by Marcia Lillian Colish, "Rethinking Lying in the Twelfth Century," in *Virtue and Ethics in the Twelfth Century*, ed. István Pieter Bejczy and Richard G. Newhauser (Leiden: Brill, 2005), 155-73.

producing a new variation on the meaning attributed to the figure. These instances should be compared with the hundreds of mentions in exegesis, letters, chronicles, and hagiography in order to obtain a reliable picture of the cultural meaning and social impact of figures who are so forcefully projected into mythology. But even limiting our study to poetic literature, what emerges vividly are both the constants of a moral and ideological exemplariness and the wealth of human nuances and adaptations for the intended readers; the poets skillfully bring these out in different frameworks and contexts, starting with the biblical tale, along with its less visible details, some even reconstructed by narrating their verisimilitude.

And Judith is clearly not the only case, though perhaps she is the one that offers the greatest continuity and variety of reuses. A more extensive but never exhaustive analysis would require us to retrace the poetic rewritings of episodes regarding Sarah's late fertility, celebrated in the so-called biblical epic by Marius Victor and Cyprianus Gallus, before the revivals of the tenth century brought back the late Carolingian era and Matthew of Vendôme (late twelfth century) made her one of the characters in his *Tobias*. The prophetess Anna, mother of Samuel, makes a shy appearance in some poems by Walafrid Strabo and Milo of Saint-Amand, but she would only later take on an important role, in the paraphrases of the book of Kings that proliferated in the twelfth century (especially the *In libros Regum* by Hildebert of Lavardin) and in other biblical poetry of the same period and of the following century (such as, again, *Tobias* and the *Epithalamium Virginis*). Naomi is cited just three times before the twelfth century. Rachel (and her counterpart Leah) was widely celebrated by the poet Cyprianus in *Genesis* and in the best Carolingian hymns, and she was also present in much poetry of the twelfth century, well beyond the religious sphere. Rebecca, mother of Isaac, is perhaps the first biblical woman of the Old Testament documented in Latin poetry (in Commodian, Hilarius, Ambrose, and Paulinus of Nola, then in Cyprianus the poet and Arator). Deborah only just surfaced in the Carolingian age and under Matilda.

Limits of space prevent such an investigation, but it could produce important information on the representation of biblical women in an early Middle Ages, in which the written documentation, especially if sung in liturgy or rhythmic poetry, often had a much greater actual circulation than the iconography that influences us so deeply today. Our impression, which we hope may serve as an entreaty for a monograph, is that these instances are structured around a few but very specific theoretical and political core ideas: trust in God, even beyond the limits of nature and one's strengths; ability to exceed males despite their uncertainty and fearfulness; warrior-like and regal exemplariness; chastity for the purposes of achieving success as well as fertility despite all expectations—in other words, exceptional qualities serving as the distinctive mark of short narrative or lyrical cycles that are soon firmly established around select exegetical/ideological motifs. Beauty is limited to being an instrument for achievement, as with Esther or Judith, or an element that can only be interpreted on an allegorical level, as with Rachel. The bride of the Song of Solomon is entirely absent in early medieval Latin poetry, and poems dedicated solely to Susannah and Jezebel only appear in the twelfth century. The picture clearly needs to be completed, including an investigation of femininity in the New Testament, which brings qualities of gentleness, tenderness, even sensuality, and emotional and spiritual union with a person or a message, all of which are extraneous or marginal to the Old Testament (except the Song of the Songs) and, in part, to the early Middle Ages. The early centuries evidently favor sharp hues and simple contrasts and extol women's abilities in sexual self-control, combativeness, and the empowerment of communities. These abilities are better suited to the needs and therefore the values of the intellectual class, with its ecclesiastical background and its political points of reference. But every text of any depth manages to soften the unyielding, monumental quality of these models, shedding a different light on them and thus providing us with some glimmer of alternative and complementary interpretations awaiting our attention.

Bibliography

Aldhelm of Malmesbury. *Prosa de virginitate cum glosa Latina atque Anglosaxonica*. Edited by Scott Gwara. Turnhout: Brepols, 2001.
Avitus, Alcimus. *Éloge consolatoire de la chasteté (sur la virginité)*. Edited by Nicole Hecquet-Noti. Paris: Cerf, 2011.
Campanale, Maria I. "Il *De Virginitate* di Venanzio Fortunato (*carm*. 8, 3 Leo): Un epitalamio mistico." *IL* 2 (1980): 75–128.
Castagna, Luigi. *Studi draconziani (1912–1996)*. Naples: Loffredo, 1997.
Clayton, Mary. "Aelfric's *Esther*: A *speculum reginae*?" Pages 89–101 in *Text and Gloss: Studies in Insular Learning and Literature Presented to Joseph Donovan Pheifer*. Edited by Helen Conrad-O'Briain, Vincent John Scattergood, and Anne Marie D'Arcy. Dublin: Four Courts, 1999.

Colish, Marcia Lillian. "Rethinking Lying in the Twelfth Century." Pages 155–74 in *Virtue and Ethics in the Twelfth Century*. Edited by István Pieter Bejczy and Richard G. Newhauser. Leiden: Brill, 2005.

Corsaro, Francesco, ed. *Blossii Aemili Dracontii, De laudibus Dei libri tres*. Catania: Università di Catania, 1962.

Coussy, Céline. *La figure de Judith dans l'Occident médiéval (V–XV siècles)*. 2 vols. Limoges: Université de Limoges, 2004.

Daturi, Elisabetta Limardo. *Représentations d'Esther entre écritures et images*. Bern: Lang, 2004.

Dempsey, George T. "Aldhelm of Malmesbury's Social Theology: The Barbaric Heroic Ideal Christianised." *Peritia* 15 (2001): 58–80.

Dümmler, Ernst, Ludwig Traube, Paul Winterfeld, and Karl Strecker, eds. *Poetae Latini aevi Carolini*. 4 vols. MGH. Munich: Weidmann, 1978.

Ehwald, Rudolf. *Aldhelmi opera*. MGH. Berlin: Weidmann, 1913–1919.

Erkens, Franz-Reiner. "*Sicut Esther Regina*: Die westfränkische Königin als *consors regni*." *Francia* 20 (1993): 15–38.

Franke, Birgit. *Assuerus und Esther am Burgunderhof: Zur Rezeption des Buches Esther in den Niederlanden (1450–1530)*. Berlin: Mann, 1998.

Gaetano, Myriam de. *Scuola e potere in Draconzio*. Alessandria: Edizioni dell'Orso, 2009.

Gnädinger, Louise. "Esther: Eine Skizze." *ZDP* 113 (1994): 31–62.

Herren, Michael. "The *De imagine Tetrici* of Walahfrid Strabo: Edition and Translation." *JML* 1 (1991): 118–39.

Huneycutt, Louis L. "Intercession and the High-Medieval Queen: The Esther Topos." Pages 126–46 in *Power of the Weak: Studies on Medieval Women*. Edited by Jennifer Carpenter and Sally-Beth MacLean. Urbana: University of Illinois Press, 1995.

Jong, Mayke B. de. "The Empire as Ecclesia: Hrabanus Maurus and Biblical *Historia* for Rulers." Pages 191–226 in *The Uses of the Past in the Early Middle Ages*. Edited by Yitzhak Hen and Matthew Innes. Cambridge: Cambridge University Press, 2000.

Klein, Stacy S. *Ruling Women: Queenship and Gender in Anglo-Saxon Literature*. Notre Dame: University of Notre Dame Press, 2006.

Lapidge, Michael, and James L. Rosier, eds. *Aldhelm: The Poetic Works*. Cambridge: Brewer, 1985.

Maurus, Rabanus. *Commentario al Libro di Giuditta*. Edited by Adele Simonetti. MM 73, Testi 19. Florence: SISMEL-Edizioni del Galluzzo, 2008.

Maurus, Rabanus, and Giovanni Immonide. *La Cena di Cipriano*. Edited by Elio Rosati and Francesco Mosetti Casaretto. Alessandria: Edizioni dell'Orso, 2002.
Moussy, Claude. *Réparation*. Part 3 of *Louanges de Dieu*. Vol. 2 of *Oeuvres*. Paris: Les Belles Lettres, 1988.
Munzi, Luigi, ed., "Compilazione e riuso in età carolingia: Il prologo poetico di Wigbodo." *RomanoBarbarica* 12 (1992–1993): 189–210.
Orchard, Andy. *The Poetic Art of Aldhelm*. Cambridge: Cambridge University Press, 1994.
Paulinus. *The Poems of St. Paulinus of Nola*. Translated by P. G. Walsh. New York: Newman, 1975.
Pettit, Emma. "Holiness and Masculinity in Aldhelm's Opus Geminatum De Virginitate." Pages 8–23 in *Holiness and Masculinity in the Middle Ages*. Edited by Patricia H. Cullum and Katherine Jane Lewis. Cardiff: University of Wales Press, 2004.
Santini, Giovanni. *Inter iura poeta: Ricerche sul lessico giuridico in Draconzio*. Rome: Herder, 2006.
Sidonius. *Poems and Letters*. Translated by W. B Anderson. Cambridge: Harvard University Press, 1936.
Stella, Francesco. "L'epica di Draconzio fra tradizione classica e Cristiana." PhD diss., Università di Firenze, 1986.
———. "Epiteti di Dio in Draconzio fra tradizione classica e cristiana." *CCC* 8 (1987): 601–33.
———. "Fra retorica e innografia: Sul genere letterario delle 'Laudes Dei' di Draconzio." *Phil* 132 (1988): 213–45.
———. "Innovazioni lessicali dell *Laudes Dei* di Draconzio fra latinità tardo-antica e medieval." *IL* 21 (1999): 417–44.
———. *La poesia carolingia*. Florence: Le Lettere, 1995.
———. *Poesia carolingia latina a tema biblico*. Spoleto: CISAM, 1993.
———. "Per una teoria dell'imitazione poetica cristiana: Saggio di analisi sulle *Laudes Dei* di Draconzio." *IL* 7–8 (1985–1986): 193–224.
———. "Ristrutturazione topica ed estensione metaforica nella poesia cristiana: Da spunti draconziani." *WS* 102 (1989): 1–17.
———. "Variazioni stemmatiche e note testuali alle *Laudes Dei* di Draconzio: Con edizione del florilegio Paris, *B.N.*, Lat. 8093, f. 15^v (sec. VIII–IX)." *FM* 3 (1996): 1–34.
Thayer, Anne T. "Judith and Mary: Hélinand's Sermon for the Assumption." Pages 63–75 in *Medieval Sermon and Society: Cloister, City, University; Proceedings of International Symposia at Kalamazoo and New*

York. Edited by Jacqueline Hamesse, Beverly Mayne Kienzle, Anne T. Thayer, and Debra L. Stoudt. Louvain-la-Neuve: Fédération Internationale des Instituts d'Etudes Médiévales, 1998.

Thomson, H. J., trans. *Prudentius*. Vol. 1. LCL. Cambridge: Harvard University Press, 1949.

Women and the Bible in Latin Letter Collections of the Early Middle Ages (Sixth to Ninth Century)

Christiane Veyrard-Cosme

In an era such as the early Middle Ages, governed by predominantly patriarchal ideological models, women seem to have rarely occupied a prominent position in cultural and exegetical fields. From the little girl to the young woman, from the wife to the older woman, what is immediately clear from the evidence are the social functions they fulfill, both the function of the woman-womb inherited from antiquity and the domestic roles they assumed—namely, that of the good spinner and the servant devoted to the well-being of the household in the broadest sense. Maternity and domestic authority are, moreover, the areas in which points of comparison between representatives of the feminine side of society can often be made. Education—the ability to master book culture, to write and to formulate ideas, and to grasp the meaning of Holy Scripture through a hermeneutic-based interpretation—these are not the regular parameters that guided the evaluation of a woman worthy of the name, at least in the vast majority of cases.[1]

But even so, there are women who seem to have been exceptions while also being exceptional in their femininity—for example, consecrated virgins living on the edge of the world of women. They held a privileged place, especially in the early period, and this is demonstrated most particularly in the epistolary field, notably in the letters addressed by male authors to women. But what sort of place is this? In this essay, we will investigate the ambiguity of relationships that women maintained with the Bible, directly

---

1. On this subject, see Jane Stevenson, *Women Latin Poets: Language, Gender, and Authority from Antiquity to the Eighteenth Century* (Oxford: Oxford University Press, 2005), 108–12. See also Régine Le Jan, *La Société du haut Moyen Age (VIe-IXe s.)* (Paris: Colin, 2006–2011), ch. 9: "Masculin/féminin," 211–32.

or indirectly; ask ourselves if they were initiators and/or targets of written texts; and, finally, define the ultimate perspective of such texts.[2]

1. The Bible, Reservoir of Models of Behavior for Women

Women's relations with the Bible in medieval letter collections may be envisaged initially through the lens of intradiscursive presence. In epistolary discourse, when male writers of the church addressed female correspondents, they set up an analogical and metaphorical relationship in which they did not hesitate to make unclear distinctions between the sexes in order to offer better paradigms of behavior for their female addressees. Speaking from the high position of authority conferred on them by their ministry and patriarchal culture, they could legitimize their chosen examples. In the case of Fulgentius of Ruspe, this gave them an etymological base for shifting the traditional limits imposed by the strict separation of men and women.

1.1. The Bible and the Metamorphosis of the *Virago*

In a long letter, Bishop Fulgentius of Ruspe, who died in 533, responds to his correspondent Proba, a servant of God designated by the formula *sancta Christi virgo*, in reply to her questions about how notions of humility and chastity should be understood.[3] This letter-treatise, which dates from the beginning of the sixth century CE, offers an instructive reading of etymological-ethical reasoning. Fulgentius grounds his argument on the etymon *vir-* in order to demonstrate equality between women and men as far as spiritual virtues are concerned, basing this on an extract from the first book of the Bible (Gen 2:21–23):[4]

> In effect, God wanted to make the goodness of virginity so great that he did not shrink from calling it by a term other than virtue. Whoever

---

2. See Jane Stevenson, "Anglo-Latin Women Poets," in *Latin Learning and English Lore: Studies in Anglo-Saxon Literature for Michael Lapidge*, ed. Katherine O'Brien O'Keefe and Andy Ochard (Toronto: University of Toronto Press, 2005), 2:86–107.

3. On this text and author, see Joan M. Ferrante, *To the Glory of Her Sex: Women's Roles in the Composition of Medieval Texts* (Bloomington: Indiana University Press, 1997), 42. We owe the examples of Fulgentius and Nicholas I to this work (here 14–17; see also the examples from Alcuin, 54–55). See also Fulgentius of Ruspe, *Lettres ascétiques et morales*, ed. Jean Fraipont, trans. Daniel Bachelet, SC 487 (Paris: Cerf, 2004).

4. Unless otherwise indicated, all translations are my own.

wants to investigate the term *virgin* attentively will find that it derives from virtue. Virgin, young woman, is used for *virago*, a virile woman; for woman was so called by Holy Scripture because she had been made from man [*vir*]. In addition, this is what the translation made by Saint Jerome teaches, following the particularities of the Hebrew of the book of Genesis. The translation contains the following terms:

The Lord God cast Adam into sleep, and while he was asleep, he took one of his ribs, dressed it in flesh, and from the rib that he had taken from Adam, the Lord God made woman and led her to Adam, and Adam said, "Here is the bone of my bones and the flesh of my flesh. She will be called *virago* because she was taken from man [*vir*]." (Fulgentius, *Ep.* 3.7 [CCSL 91:215])[5]

Thus if the name of woman, *virago*, derives from the word man, *vir*, who could doubt the fact that man [*vir*] was so called from the word virtue? And because, according to the teaching of Paul, all these things were done to serve as examples [*figura*] for us [1 Cor 10:6], in the woman, *virgo*, who came from the rib of man, *vir*, it is certainly the church that was prefigured; she is taken from a man and, once taken from him, united with him, and from that moment she has in truth the virtue from which the true name of woman, *virago*, comes. That is why Paul does not hesitate to name this woman *virago*, otherwise known as virgin, who was taken from man, as not only virgin but also man. He says to the faithful, "I have engaged you to one man alone as a pure virgin to present herself to Christ." Christ is the man from which the virgin was taken [2 Cor 11:2]. To the same faithful, the apostle says: "until we all may arrive at the unity of faith and the knowledge of the Son of God, at the perfection of the age of man, at the full measure of the age of Christ" [Eph 4:13]. And this is also what David's spiritual exhortation sets forth, to both men and women together: work in a manly way and may your heart be comforted, all of you who have hope in the Lord [Ps 30:25]. (Fulgentius, *Ep.* 3.8 [CCSL 91:215])[6]

---

5. *Tam magnum quippe Deus voluit esse bonum virginitatis, ut illud non aliunde, sed ex vocabulo dignaretur nominare virtutis. virginis itaque si quis velit diligenter considerare vocabulum, ex virtutis inveniet nomine derivatum; virgo enim dicitur, quasi virago; virginem vero scriptura sancta non ob aliud vocatam dicit, nisi quia de viro sumpta est. hoc autem a sancto Hieronimo secundum Hebraicam proprietatem libri Geneseos docet expressa translatio, in qua sic habetur: immisit ergo Dominus Deus soporem in Adam; cumque obdormisset, tulit unam de costis eius, et replevit carnem pro ea, et aedificavit Dominus Deus costam quam tulerat de Adam in mulierem, et adduxit eam ad Adam. dixitque Adam: hoc nunc os ex ossibus meis, et caro de carne mea. haec vocabitur Virago, quoniam de viro sumpta est.*

6. *Itaque cum viraginis nomen ex nomine viri descenderit, quis dubitet quod vir a*

In this way, with a play on the terminology—*vir/virtus/virago/virgo*—the bishop manages to establish a virtual entity, the virile woman, based on interwoven biblical citations, drawn from the letters of Paul or biblical translations proposed by Jerome. And far from the sarcastic use of this term *virago*, to which readers of profane Latin literature had become accustomed, this word would henceforth become esteemed through its own hybridity. It is interesting to realize that it is the book of Genesis, once translated and interpreted, that in some way gives rise to the birth of a different evaluation of femininity.

1.2. Women/Masculine Models

The voluminous correspondence of Pope Nicholas I (800–867), also known as Nicholas the Great, provides a privileged place from which to observe the way women may have been appreciated in the light of the Bible. In *Ep.* 28 addressed to Queen Ermentrude, the pontiff compares his correspondent, who has sent him numerous gifts, to a celebrated sovereign, the queen of Sheba, well known from 1 Kings, whose gifts gave King Solomon such pleasure: "To see the great variety of gifts you have offered us, we have judged your devotion to us even greater than that of the queen of Sheba" (Nicholas I, *Ep.* 28).[7] In his twilight years, Nicholas I, famous for his wish to establish the superiority of pontifical power over imperial power, also took part in a conflict in the East between the supporters of Photius, who had been elected to the patriarchate even though he was a layman, and the supporters of his predecessor, Ignatius, who had been deposed by Emperor Michael III

---

virtute vocatus sit? et quia, sicut Paulus docet, illa omnia in figura facta sunt nostri [1 Cor 10:6], *profecto in illa virgine quae ex viri fiebat costa, futura iam tunc praefigurabatur Ecclesia, quae vere de viro sumpta, et de quo sumpta illi coniuncta, inde habet in veritate virtutem, unde habet verum viraginis nomen. propter quod hanc viraginem, id est virginem, quae de viro sumpta est, non solum virginis, sed etiam viri nomine Paulus non dubitat appellare; dicit enim fidelibus despondi enim vos uni viro virginem castam exhibere Christo* [2 Cor 11:2]. *Christus est quippe vir de quo haec virgo sumpta est. ipsis denuo fidelibus idem apostolus dicit: donec occurramus omnes in unitatem fidei et agnitionis Filii Dei, in virum perfectum, in mensuram aetatis plenitudinis Christi* [Eph 4:13]. *per sanctum quoque David, tam viris quam mulieribus in commune spiritalis huiuscemodi promulgatur hortatio: viriliter agite et confortetur cor vestrum, omnes qui speratis in Domino* [Ps 30:25].

7. See Ernst Dümmler and Ernst Perels, eds., *Epistolae Karolini aeui IV*, MGH (Berlin: Weidmann 1925), 294: *nam et munerum vestrorum diversis speciebus oblatis, ... reginae Austri industriam tuam praetulimus* [cf. Matt 12:42; Luke 11:31].

in 858. As a supporter of Ignatios, the pope deposed Photius in 863, who then broke off relations with Rome. In 866—one year before the condemnation and exile of Photius—Nicholas wrote two letters, one addressed to Theodora, mother of Michael III and previously regent, and the other to the Empress Eudokia Dekapolitissa, wife of the same ruler.

In these two letters, the pope employs a series of formulas that echo the principal prejudices voiced about women in a universe governed by a patriarchal mentality. The letter sent to Theodora is an eloquent composition that brackets the addressee between two masculine figures at the opening of the letter, placing her among the cohort of august empresses that hold a preeminent position in relation to that of her husband, who opposed the position defended by the papacy. At the end, he compares her to Moses and Aaron, then Samuel and Zacharias, and finally to Jesus himself:

> We recall in detail and with great care the virtues that are yours and with which you are endowed and that in these days that you live through have not led you to appear to fall below any of the august empresses and do not even find you inferior to any of them in matters of piety. And we do not cease endlessly to thank all-powerful God for these virtues that he has given to you and to whom you owe them, and we do not cease to bless his holy name, and very often we cite the example of your piety and your devotion in our sermons to the faithful so that they can imitate it. Even when the prince your husband expressed views contrary to the laws of the church, you were not frightened to think correctly and to defend what was right. You, I repeat, you remained to the end in the true faith in teaching your only son to follow the path of his father—not his earthly father but his celestial Father. Who could adequately express the quality of your morals, the courage of your acts and your corrections? When you held the imperial position alone, with the help of the Lord you protected the church of the Lord not only from the visible enemy, but also, and as firmly as a man, you protected the church of the Lord from the invisible enemy— that is to say, from error—and like a ray of sunshine, you chased the clouds of perverse opinions from the face of the church. The heretics perceived a virile force in you, and, astonished by your robust and invincible character, they doubted your womanly condition. (Nicholas I, *Ep.* 95)[8]

---

8. See Dümmler and Perels, *Epistolae Karolini aeui IV*, 547: *virtutes vestras, quibus praeditae antecedentium vos Augustarum nulli diebus istis apparuistis secundae, quibus etiam, et praecipue in causa pietatis, earum nemini estis inferiores inventae, subtiliter atque sollicite recolentes, Deo cunctipotenti, cuius munere has percepistis, grates inmensas referre et eius sancto nomini benedicere non cessamus atque piorum studiorum*

The discourse addressed by the writer to the empress is full of epideictic formulations based on rhetorical questions, exclamations that are either assertions or affirmations disguised in order to arrive at this proclamation: your virtues are indescribable. Taking care to enclose the eulogy of a woman in divine praise (*Deo cunctipotenti, Domino cooperante*), Nicholas I places his correspondent on a pedestal, while all the time celebrating her high achievements (*facta fortia*), whose teleological dimension is firmly underlined: the imitation of the believers and the glory of God who bestows on them the world. All the same, it is the semantic field of epic that is here utilized to sing (*enarrare, narrare*) the praise of a woman who has a virile force (*virile pectus*) and shows an invincible character (*insuperabile robur*). The verb *mirari*, used to define the common reaction to this anomaly (*quod femina fueris ambiguum habuerunt*), clearly serves as a fireguard, a barrier controlling the exaltation of the case, in the final analysis. The political power exercised in an unprecedented situation (*cum sola principabaris*) is enough to explain this extraordinary portrait of a woman celebrated for an epic hero's virility (*virile pectus* being the qualification for the hero of an epic).

Now to give formative examples of endurance to his addressee, the pope proposes models for the empress to follow, not the least of which is the following:

> Moses the legislator and Aaron the saint of the Lord put up with the rancor, rude offences, and revolt of those whom Moses had taken into his bosom as sons and loved so much that when the Lord wanted to exterminate them and make a great nation of him alone, he said: "Either forgive their sin or remove me from the book that you have written." The blessed Samuel was displaced from power by those who had received many benefits from him. Similarly, the prophet Zacharias was stoned on

---

vestrorum praeconia pro imitatione audientium inter fidelium colloquia iugiter enarramus. tu quippe etiam principe marito tuo contra leges ecclesiae sentiente superstite sana sapere et recta defendere non formidasti. tu, inquam, in horthodoxa religione perseverans unicum filium non terreni patris, sed supercaelestis iter aggredi docuisti. quis autem morum insignia, quis correctionum tuarum facta fortia narrare sufficiat? cum enim sola principabaris, Domino cooperante non solum ab hoste visibili, verum etiam nullo mare infirmior ecclesiam Domini ab hoste invisibili, hoc est ab errore, texisti et perversorum dogmatum nebulam tamquam solis radius ab ecclesiae facie depulisti [cf. Job 13:4; Wis 2:3]. *senserunt in te heretici virile pectus et mirantes insuperabile robur, quod femina fueris, ambiguum habuerunt.*

the order of the one who had regained the kingdom through the help of Zacharias's own father, and when Zacharias was showing him the correct way to salvation. But why should we delay among the human race when the mediator between God and men, our Lord Jesus Christ himself, had to sustain disgrace, spitting, flagellation, and death on the cross, even from those among whom he had restored sight to the blind, recalled many to health from an untold number of ills, and revived the dead to life? (Nicholas I, *Ep.* 95)[9]

These figures of lawgivers, priests, and prophets associated with the person of Christ himself bestow a martyr-like aura on the woman addressed, which raises her to the rank of a saintly figure and a persecuted sage. Through this epistolary discourse, the pope offers not just a rereading of his correspondent's situation but also an ethical program based on masculine *virtus*. There are, however, cases in which women of the Bible are used as examples for masculine recipients of papal correspondence.

1.3. Men and the Feminine Model

In *Ep.* 96, the pope invites his correspondent Empress Eudokia Dekapolitissa, wife of Michael III, to intervene with her husband in favor of the return of Ignatios. At the beginning of his letter, the sovereign pontiff underlines the role played by justice among royal virtues and praises feminine force (*fortitudo*), which reprises the elements we found in the previous letter.

> Nothing is more suitable for royal power than the love of Justice; nothing is more honorable for womanly weakness than mental force. What could be more praiseworthy, more vigorous, than a woman who takes on

---

9. See Dümmler and Perels, *Epistolae Karolini aeui IV*, 548: *nam legifer Moyses et Aaron, sanctus Domini, murmur et duras contumelias atque seditionem patiuntur ab his, quos velut filios in sinu portabat et adeo diligebat, ut Domino volenti eos perdere et facere eum in gentem magnam diceret* [cf. Exod 32:10]: *aut dimitte eis hanc noxam aut dele me de libro quem scripsisti* [cf. Exod 32:31–32]. *sic beatus Samuhel ab his, quibus multa praestiterat beneficia, de principatu propellitur; sic propheta Zaccharias ab eo, cui pater suus regnum vindicaverat et ipse viam salutis ostendebat, lapidibus impetitur* [cf. 2 Chr 24:21–22]. *sed quid per hominum genus diutius immoremur, quando ipse mediator Dei et hominum dominus noster Iesus Christus* [cf. 1 Tim 2:5] *ab his, quibus caecos inluminavit, languidos plurimos pristinae sanitati restituit, mortuos excitavit, probra, sputa, flagella et mortem crucis sustinuit?*

a manly force and triumphs over the will of men in a pious undertaking? (Nicholas I, *Ep.* 96)[10]

Encouraging the addressee with these words—*precamur ... ita ut feminae infirmitatis oblitae viriliter agere studeatis*—the pope paints a picture of the principal tasks of the wife of an emperor.

> It is not in vain that Christ our God made you consort of your husband's imperial power: he put you in that position for one sole purpose—to aid his church, to look after its activities, to bring help to its servants, to console those who suffer, to raise up the exiled and banished, and to put back in order everything that was twisted, confused, untidy, and destroyed and to give it back its previous force, so that you bring your help as a manly and strong woman, a precious assistant to your husband, who has so much to do, so many innumerable tasks, to hold out a helping hand, to prevent him from falling from the pinnacle of justice in all his diverse and varied jobs. For this reason, at the beginning of the world, the Lord offered the first created being of the human race a similar help to prevent a solitary man from falling too easily from the summit and having great difficulty in getting up again after his fall, without the advice of another. (Nicholas I, *Ep.* 96)[11]

The end of the passage displays a clear reference to the biblical Eve, companion of the first created (πρωτόπλαστος), as an example proposed to Eudokia. But this figure, a model for the empress, is manifestly reversible, in the arsenal of feminine paradigms; susceptible of inciting imitation by

---

10. See Dümmler and Perels, *Epistolae Karolini aeui IV*, 549: *nihil in regia sublimitate iustitiae dilectione decentius, nihil in infirmitate muliebri fortitudine mentis honestius. quid autem laudabilius vel robustius, quam si femina virile pectus induat et adhuc in causa pietatis virorum studia superet?*

11. See Dümmler and Perels, *Epistolae Karolini aeui IV*, 549: *non enim frustra nobilitatem vestram Christus Deus noster imperii coniugis vestri fecit consortem nec posuit vos, nisi ut ecclesiam eius adiuvetis, erga statum eius vigiletis, famulis ipsius auxiliemini, maerentes consolemini, oppressos et elisos erigatis* [cf. Pss 144:14; 145:8], *pulsos et exiliatos revocetis et cuncta depravata, confusa, inordinata et destructa vigori pristino reformetis, nihilominus etiam, ut tamquam fortis virago et insignis adiutrix viro vestro ad multa intendenti et innumera disponenti adiutorium inpendatis, et, ne inter tot varietates a iustitiae culmine decidat, manum solatii quodammodo porrigatis. sic Dominus in principio condicionis humanae protoplasto mulieris adiutorium sibi simile tribuit, ne videlicet vir solitarius alterius forte consilio destitutus facilius ad ima decideret difficiliusque post casum resurgeret* [cf. Gen 2:20ff.].

her qualities as a partner, she plays a role of resistance, becoming an element of comparison in order to destroy and condemn Photius's conduct, which the pope considers a usurpation. In the following extract, taken from the same letter, Photius is presented as "new Eve," a pejorative formula that shows that he is seduced by the serpent, the ancient enemy: "Believe us; in these times in which we live, the expulsion of venerable Ignatios [and] the promotion of presumptuous Photius are an evil for your empire on the same level as the temptation of Eve" (Nicholas I, *Ep.* 96).[12] The pope assures her, "The serpent of old, the ancient enemy, does not cease to torment the church of the Lord, composed of men and women, with a variety of plots" (Nicholas I, *Ep.* 96).[13] In this contest, Eudokia is invited to behave like a new Esther, "Keeping your faith intact while continuing along the right road for the people of God, which is the church, act in the style of holy Queen Esther of this people, and enflame your husband with the fear and the love of God, and, while knowing how to retain reason, make him burn with zeal for the restoration of the holy church of Constantinople" (Nicholas I, *Ep.* 96).[14] While labeling Photius *moechus* ("adulterous," "debauched"), the pope concludes his admonition/advice with this phrase: "So leave aside all womanly weakness and put every effort into obtaining from your husband what is holy and what is best for the holy church" (Nicholas I, *Ep.* 96).[15] Thus the biblical Eve can become an ambivalent model, a carrier of praiseworthy but also condemnable elements, depending on the context in which she is called to insert herself. As the outstanding example of woman in the Bible, Eve can perform a double role in masculine discourse and may challenge a male or female addressee depending on the case.

---

12. See Dümmler and Perels, *Epistolae Karolini aeui IV*, 550: *nam, nobis credite: non minus his temporibus venerabilis Ignatii repulsio seu temeratoris Photii promotio imperio vestro quam Evae suggestio nocuit.*

13. See Dümmler and Perels, *Epistolae Karolini aeui IV*, 550: *ille namque priscus serpens et antiquus adversarius non cessat ecclesiam Domini, quae de utroque sexu componitur, diversis vexare machinamentis.*

14. See Dümmler and Perels, *Epistolae Karolini aeui IV*, 550: *... ut vos in integritate fidei et in tramite rectitudinis populo Dei, qui est ecclesia, more sanctae illius Hester reginae perseverantes virum quoque vestrum circa Dei timorem amoremque succendatis et erga sanctae ecclesiae Constantinopolitanae recuperationem prudenter inflammetis.*

15. See Dümmler and Perels, *Epistolae Karolini aeui IV*, 550: *deponite ergo cunctam muliebrem infirmitatem et erga eum ea, quae pia sunt, quae sanctae ecclesiae congruunt, impetrare satagite.*

2. Women and the Bible: A Motif of Epistolatory Discourse— the Example of the Correspondence of Alcuin

2.1. Presentation of the Documentation

At the beginning of the ninth century, the anonymous author of the Vita Alcuini, dedicated to the historical and spiritual journey of Alcuin, also called Albinus, the Anglo-Saxon cleric and adviser of Charlemagne, makes the following point:

> At Emperor Charles's request, Albinus wrote a very useful book on the Holy Trinity, as well as books on rhetoric, dialectic, and music. For Gundrad, he wrote a book on the nature of the soul. At the request of the women, Gisela and Rotrud, he composed in a very suitable manner, an admirable work on the Gospel of John, based partly on Saint Augustine and partly on his own analysis. (Vita Alc. 21)[16]

So Alcuin is going to dedicate his *Commentary on the Gospel of John* to his female correspondents. It is worth noting the importance that the text of this gospel clearly held in the insular world of which Alcuin was a product. For example, at the very beginning of the eighth century, a copy of the Gospel of John accompanied the very important insular figure of Cuthbert right into his coffin. In addition, this gospel is the element that in chapter 7 of the Vita Alcuini occasions a description of mystical rapture (ἔκστασις), attributed to the eponymous hero, Alcuin.

Among Alcuin's many correspondents there are noble women from the entourage of kings, with whom the counselor of the Frankish sovereign is in contact, and many women dedicated to the religious life. Several

---

16. *Postulante namque imperatore Karolo, scripsit librum de sancta Trinitate utilissimum, necnon de rethorica, dialectica et musica. scripsit ad Gundradam de animae ratione. postulantibus feminis Gisla et Richtrude honestissime super evangelium Iohannis partim de suo, partim de sancto Augustino mirabile opus composuit.* Text in Christiane Veyrard-Cosme, *La Vita beati Alcuini (IXe s.): Les inflexions d'un discours de sainteté; Introduction, édition et traduction annotée du texte d'après Reims, BM 1395 (K 784)*, EAMA 54 (Paris: Institut d'Etudes Augustiniennes, 2017), 296–97 (and 117–29); On the Vita Alcuini, see also Walter Berschin, *Karolingische Biographie, 750–920*, vol. 3 of *Biographie und Epochenstil im lateinischen Mittelalter* (Stuttgart: Hiersemann, 1991), 175–82. On Alcuin, see esp. Donald A. Bullough, *Alcuin: Achievement and Reputation*, ESMAR 16 (Leiden, Brill, 2004).

of these also come from the aristocracy and even from royal families, as is the case with Gisela, sister of Charlemagne, and Rotrud, his daughter, or Æthelburg, daughter of the king of Mercia. Gisela, Rotrud's aunt, and Rotrud, her niece, are both nuns at the monastery of Chelles that Gisela directs. They are in the first rank of female correspondents of the cleric, as is clear at least from one collection of epistolary correspondence.[17]

A paragraph of the letter written by the two women highlights the Jeromian dimension of this corpus. Both of them address the one they identify as their teacher/master (*magister*), the abbot of Saint Martin at Tours, and beg him to deliver what they have been requesting for a long time, an exegetical commentary on the Gospel of John, in these terms:

> Remember that the most illustrious doctor of divine Scripture of the holy church, the blessed Jerome, far from scorning the prayers of noble women, dedicated to them several works on the interpretation of the Prophets and very often, also at their request, sent off letters and messages from the stronghold of Bethlehem, consecrated by the birth of Christ our God, toward the heights of Rome, without fearing the distance from earth or the tumultuous waves of the Adriatic Sea, seeing in them elements capable of preventing him from meeting the demands of the holy virgins. There is less danger in navigating on the river of the Loire, provided with a solid bed, than on the very deep Tyrrhenian Sea. And it will be easier to find a carrier for your letters from Tours to Paris than to find a porter for his from Bethlehem to Rome! (Alcuin, *Ep.* 196)[18]

Clearly, here, for the correspondents, it is a particular side of the Stridonian native that is put forward: Jerome, the author of commentaries on

---

17. This collection includes numbers 195, 196, 213, and 214 in the MGH edition (Dümmler, *Epistolae Karolini aeui II*).

18. See Ernst Dümmler, ed., *Epistolae Karolini aeui II*, MGH (Berlin: Weidmann, 1895), 324–25: *memento clarissimum in sancta ecclesia divinae scripturae doctorem, beatissimum siquidem Hieronimum, nobilium nullatenus spernere feminarum preces, sed plurima illarum nominibus in propheticas obscuritates dedicasse opuscula; saepiusque de Bethleem castello, Christi dei nostri nativitate consecrato, ad Romanas arces epistolares iisdem petentibus volare cartulas, nec terrarum longinquitate vel procellosis Adriatici maris fluctibus territum, quin minus sanctarum virginum petitionibus adnueret. minore vadosum Ligeri flumen quam Tyrreni maris latitudo periculo navigatur. et multo facilius cartarum portitor tuarum de Turonis Parisiacam civitatem, quam illius de Bethleem Romam, pervenire poterit.*

Isaiah and Ezekiel destined for Paula and her daughter Eustochium, who is also the addressee of a famous letter in which the doctor of the church engaged her to find a teacher capable of making the best exposition of Holy Scripture. For women like Gisela and Rotrud, immersed in a typological culture, in the exegetical sense of the term, such a presentation could only have the corollary of presenting them as a validating antitype, that of noble women and studious companions of the translator and commentator of the Vulgate, all the more so because Alcuin had for his part undertaken a revision of the biblical text. Thus as letter writers they seek to appear as worthy heirs of the late antique female patricians, who had adopted a lifestyle founded on the knowledge of Scripture and study.

Now, as we have recently demonstrated, the manuscript tradition of Alcuin's works shows that this letter is transmitted immediately before the Alcuinian commentary, while the dedicatory letter of Alcuin's *explanatio* circulates on its own.[19] The arrangement is not the result of the vagaries of transmission—it stems from a wish emphatically expressed by the author. In the letter that accompanies the long-awaited commentary, the writer is careful to add a precise detail, which is in no way an aside:

> I have preceded this work by the letter containing your request, so that future readers will be able to see the eagerness of your devotion and a witness to my obedience. I also added the letter in which I agreed to your wish, and I put it there as a prologue to our little work. (Alcuin, *Ep.* 214)[20]

The construction of a Jeromian ethos is clearly illuminated by these remarks. At the heart of a *renovatio* desired by the Frankish Empire, Alcuin puts on a Stridonian stature, which finally takes form in the collection of characteristics incorporated into the group of twenty-six letters of Alcuin's correspondence addressed to his female respondents. These texts, letters of direction, are based on a large number of citations borrowed directly from Jerome's letters

---

19. See Christiane Veyrard-Cosme, "Les soeur, filles, et cousine de Charlemagne dans le monde culturel carolingien," in *Les Réseaux Familiaux: Antiquité Tardive et Moyen Age; In memoriam A. Laiou et E. Patlagean*, ed. Béatrice Caseau, CRHCBM 37 (Paris: Association des Amis du Centre d'Histoire, 2012), 163–73.

20. See Dümmler, *Epistolae Karolini aeui II*, 357–58: *quod legebam ... protuli; praeponens etiam huic operi epistolam petitionis vestrae, ut in posterum agnoscerent legentes vestrae devotionis studium et meae oboedientiae occasionem. adiunxi quoque epistolam annuentem voluntati vestrae. quam etiam quasi prologum anteposui opusculo nostro....*

of direction sent to Heliodorus and also to Eustochium or to Paula. From this moment on, through the theme of women and the Bible, the importance of another complementary coupling arises, that of master and disciples.

2.2. The Paradigm of the *Magister* in the Examination of Exegetical Correspondences

Whether they were actually sent or not, because the letters are discourse addressed to the absent one, they share in a literary fiction, so that their content, the message they deliver to the addressees, corresponds both to a historical content and to a virtual given.[21] In such a context, the place of the master and his disciples draws not only on a real and historical fact but also on a complex ensemble of mental representations. From this point on, the evocation of the magisterial relationship in this body of material could be understood as the result and reflection of a collection of determining elements that root themselves in an anthropological-religious tradition.[22] Here the configuration desired by Alcuin, so as to leave a Jeromian image to posterity, implies an understanding of the magisterial relationship as engaging *magister* and disciples in an exchange based on a predominantly speculative reciprocity. The interaction of the poles of this fundamental binomial finds its expression in the historical reasoning proposed by the *magister* in the composition of his *explanatio*. If, as Françoise Waquet has shown, we can identify in the Alcuinian letters features that often take into account the relations between *magister* and disciples—intellectual, social, and didactic features—the dominant one in the exchange between Gisela and Rotrud, on one side, and Alcuin, on the other, underlines that they both wish to state that their relationship built on exegetical teaching, through formulas that rest on analogy, metaphor, and paraphrase.[23] The

---

21. On this theme, see Geneviève Haroche-Bouzinac, *L'épistolaire* (Paris: Hachette, 1995), esp. 70–80.

22. See the reflections of Frédéric Guidon in the introduction (esp. 8–15) of his thesis on French literature, "La dialectique du maître et du disciple en littérature: L'exemple du roman fin de siècle (Bourget, Barrès, Gide)" (PhD diss., Université Paul Verlaine-Metz, 2011), NNT : 2011METZ002L . tel-01748814; see also, on this subject, George Steiner, *Lessons of the Masters* (Cambridge: Harvard University Press, 2003), quoted by Guidon, "La dialectique du maître," 9–12, esp. 7–46.

23. Françoise Waquet, *Les Enfants de Socrate: Filiation intellectuelle et transmission du savoir, XVIIe–XXIe siècle* (Paris: Albin Michel, 2008), quoted by Guidon, "La dialectique du maître," 13.

two women willingly use images designed to display their *libido sciendi*. Their letter opens with terms that exude ardor, desire, and hunger:

> When your wisdom, venerable magister, exposed this knowledge of Holy Scripture to us and we had absorbed a little of it, knowledge as sweet as honey, afterwards the desire for a very holy instruction burned in us more and more every day because we wanted an instruction that contains the purification of the soul, relief from our mortal condition, the hope of eternal blessedness.... It is the manna that satiates without sickening, nourishes without ceasing. These are the fruits of the divine harvest, the ears [of corn] ground by the hands of the apostles and offered by them to nourish believing souls. (Alcuin, *Ep.* 196)[24]

Employing Old Testament allusions and formulations repeated during late antiquity, and rewriting Luke 6:1, Gisela and Rotrud call also for the establishment of an interaction based on instruction, delivered in the form of letters and writing, in order to quench an inextinguishable thirst:

> Very dear master, we beg your piety not to neglect us by forgetting to send us the consolation of your letters. You may show yourself to us, who ask this of you by the intermediary of a letter, so that our heart's desire may understand your voice in the depths of our hearts. For in the same way that the tongue of the speaker is profitable to the ears of the listener, the pen of the writer benefits the eye of the reader, and the ideas of the one who sends the letter enter the depths of the heart in the same way as words of the instructor. This is why, most holy father, we ask you not to refuse this request. Irrigate our humble withered hearts with water from the source of salvation. We most definitely do not want what Solomon said about those who hide their wisdom to happen to you—what is the point of hidden treasure, of concealed wisdom? We prefer that what the Lord said through the mouth of the prophet should apply to you: open your mouth, and I will fill it. Open your mouth to explain to us with the inspiration of the Holy Spirit the *Commentary of Saint John the Evangelist*, and reveal to us the venerable ideas of the holy fathers on this

---

24. See Dümmler, *Epistolae Karolini aeui II*, 323–24: *postquam, venerande magister, aliquid de melliflua sanctae scripturae cognitione, vestra sagacitate exponente, hausimus, ardebat nobis, ut fatemur, de die in diem desiderium huius sacratissimae lectionis, in qua purificatio est animae, solatium mortalitatis nostrae et spes perpetuae beatitudinis ... haec est manna, quae sine fastidio satiat, sine defectu pascit. haec sunt divinae segetis grana, apostolicis fricata manibus atque per eos fidelium epulis animarum apposita.*

subject. Do not leave us without food, lest we fall from the road. (Alcuin, *Ep.* 196)²⁵

The *magister* replies with a letter of syntactic parallelisms (*quantum ... tantum, tanta ... facultas, quanta ... voluntas*) associated with sonorous echoes (*facultas/voluntas*), which allow him to set up a circular form at the heart of the correspondence and mimic the interaction, which results in the creation of the commentary:

> As much as I praise your outstanding attention to the very holy solicitude of wisdom, so much I mourn my incapacity and I know it; I find myself very far from being at the height of your praiseworthy devotion. If only I had in my breast the capacity to write at the level of your wish to read! (Alcuin, *Ep.* 213)²⁶

The dramatization of the pedagogical relationship is given material form by the indications left by the letter writer for posterity, so that the different letters that make up the corpus preserve it forever in the order he intended. A spatial as well as a temporal organization is thus put in place by the letter-writing *magister*—the discovery of the Bible is not given in a rigid personal exchange but step by step in a biblical itinerary designed for all potential readers beyond Gisela and Rotrud. Returning to the reproach they sent him, for not having time to write a commentary, Alcuin replies by interlacing the adjectival personal pronouns of the second and first per-

---

25. See Dümmler, *Epistolae Karolini aeui II*, 324: *sed vestram, carissime doctor, deprecamur pietatem, ne nos litterarum tuarum solatio deseras. poteris te ipsum nobis quaerentibus per litterarum officia ostendere, ut intellegatur vox tua in archano cordis nostri desiderio. nam, sicut loquentis lingua in aure audientis, ita scribentis calamus proficit in oculo legentis; et ad interiora cordis pervenit sensus dirigentis sicut verba instruentis. quapropter, beatissime pater, noli te ipsum nobis negare. inriga salutiferi fontis unda pectora nostrae paruitatis arentia ... nolumus, ad te pertineat quod Salomon ait de eis, qui suam solent celare sapientiam: thesaurus occultatus et sapientia abscondita, quae utilitas in utrisque?* [cf. Sir 41:17] *sed magis Domino dicente per prophetam: aperi os tuum et ego adimplebo illud* [cf. Ps 80:11]. *aperi os tuum in sacratissimam, Spiritu sancto inspirante, beati Iohannis evangelistae expositionem, et venerabiles sanctorum patrum pande nobis sensus. ... noli nos ieiunias dimittere, ne deficiamus in via* [cf. Matt 15:32].

26. See Dümmler, *Epistolae Karolini aeui II*, 354: *quantum in sanctissimo sapientiae studio optimam in vobis laudo devotionem, tantum mei ipsius plango imperitiam; meque ipsum longe inparem vestrae laudabili devotioni agnosco. atque utinam tanta esset in meo pectore facultas scribendi, quanta est in vobis voluntas legendi.*

sons (my/your) in an exchange that represents the agreement between the two elements of the binomial relationship (*binôme*):

> Therefore I see that one could perhaps find a certain balance between my refusal and your request, so that your love might not be scorned by my silence, or that my temerity in following your request might not be criticized. (Alcuin, *Ep.* 213)[27]

Beyond this metadiscourse, set up for the direction of conscience in order to give it a real existence, we note that the *magister* feels the need to preserve a trace of his disciples' request. It is clearly because he also needs these disciples to establish him as *venerandus magister* for all posterity. In their relationship with the Bible, the women here serve also as alibis for the master's identity, and the letters' function is to describe ethos of Alcuin in words that become narratival at certain moments and no longer simply discourse. This is an image of the *magister* of the Carolingian Renaissance, an image to which posterity would add in order to maintain it with an equal strength. As we see, however, in the reflection of the letter writer on his exegetical productions and the methods by which he creates his *explanationes*, the binary model of author/addressees seems to be a delusion, unless it is understood as a simple circular system of ideas and suggestions. In fact, the composition of the commentary is the final outcome of elements both diverse and complementary: the request (*voluntas*) of the women, who present themselves as wishing to study in the school of Master Alcuin, thus finds a way to combine with the capacity (*facultas*) of the Master, to broach the creation of an exegetical text on the Gospel of John, even though Alcuin, in formulae that also associate diverse and complementary images, often oxymoronic, considers John himself as the Evangelist *in divinorum profunditate mysteriorum eminentiorum* and praises his gospel *in quo sunt altiora mysteria divinitatis*.[28] Here we have, in some way, the illustration of what Jennifer Summit tried to demonstrate in a recent article: women here collaborate in the authorial dimension of the biblical commentary edited by Alcuin, in the ways they

---

27. See Dümmler, *Epistolae Karolini aeui II*, 356: *quapropter forsan temperamentum quoddam inter meam negationem vestramque petitionem inveniri posse video, ne omnino vel caritas vestra taciturnitate mea spernatur, vel temeritas mea in vestrae petitionis obsequio reprehendatur.*

28. See Alcuin, *Ep.* 213 (Dümmler, *Epistolae Karolini aeui II* 354); Alcuin, *Ep.* 195 (ed. Dümmler, *Epistolae Karolini aeui II*, 323).

provoke and maintain his wish to set out a hermeneutical introduction to Holy Scripture.[29]

The relations between the Bible and women in the correspondence of the early Middle Ages are thus very complex. Mastery of Latin, learned and practiced as a nonmaternal tongue by women of the nobility, allowed the medieval aristocracy to establish a boundary of social and political influence within which patriarchal models were reproduced, and not an area that would be a free space for the feminine elements of this society. Once educated, a woman might sometimes be used to support the valorization of a man. If through Scripture Nicholas I offered a range of paradigms to women who held power or women close to this imperial power, Charlemagne found in his sister Gisela, abbess of Chelles, trained in sacred study, a counterpart that allowed him to complete his ethos as emperor, lover of wisdom, and author of a *renovatio* highly desired by his advisers and by himself.

Similarly, Alcuin, *magister* of Gisela and Rotrud, found the way to enhance his own *memoria* through his disciples. Thus Holy Scripture, despite itself, sometimes serves as a lettered/sophisticated writing, which tries to affirm itself at the expense of women, even while it appears to illuminate them.

Bibliography

Berschin, Walter. *Karolingische Biographie, 750–920*. Vol. 3 of *Biographie und Epochenstil im lateinischen Mittelalter*. Stuttgart: Hiersemann, 1991.

Bullough, Donald A. *Alcuin: Achievement and Reputation*. ESMAR 16. Leiden, Brill, 2004.

Dümmler, Ernst, ed. *Epistolae Karolini aeui II*. MGH. Berlin: Weidmann, 1895.

Dümmler, Ernst, and Ernst Perels, eds. *Epistolae Karolini aeui IV*. MGH. Berlin: Weidmann 1925.

Ferrante, Joan M. *To the Glory of Her Sex: Women's Roles in the Composition of Medieval Texts*. Bloomington: Indiana University Press, 1997.

---

29. See Jennifer Summit, "Women and Authorship," in *The Cambridge Companion to Medieval Women's Writing*, ed. Carolyn Dinshaw and David Wallace (Cambridge: Cambridge University Press, 2003), 91–108. See also June Hall McCash, "The Cultural Patronage of Medieval Women: An Overview," in *The Cultural Patronage of Medieval Women*, ed. June Hall McCash (Athens: University of Georgia Press, 1996).

Fulgentius of Ruspe. *Sancti Fulgentii episcopi Ruspensis Opera.* Edited by Jean Fraipont. CCSL 91. Turnhout: Brepols, 1968.

———. *Lettres ascétiques et morales.* Edited by Jean Fraipont. Translated by Daniel Bachelet. SC 487. Paris: Cerf, 2004.

Guidon, Frédéric. "La dialectique du maître et du disciple en littérature: L'exemple du roman fin de siècle (Bourget, Barrès, Gide)." PhD diss., Université Paul Verlaine-Metz, 2011. NNT : 2011METZ002L . tel-01748814.

Haroche-Bouzinac, Geneviève. *L'épistolaire.* Paris: Hachette, 1995.

Le Jan, Régine. *La société du haut Moyen Age (VIe–IXe s.).* Paris: Colin, 2006–2011.

McCash, June Hall. "The Cultural Patronage of Medieval Women: An Overview." Pages 1–49 in *The Cultural Patronage of Medieval Women.* Edited by June Hall McCash. Athens: University of Georgia Press, 1996.

Steiner, George. *Lessons of the Masters.* Cambridge: Harvard University Press, 2003.

Stevenson, Jane. "Anglo-Latin Women Poets." Pages 86–107 in vol. 2 of *Latin Learning and English Lore: Studies in Anglo-Saxon Literature for Michael Lapidge.* Edited by Katherine O'Brien O'Keefe and Andy Ochard. Toronto: University of Toronto Press, 2005.

———. *Women Latin Poets: Language, Gender, and Authority from Antiquity to the Eighteenth Century.* Oxford: Oxford University Press, 2005.

Summit, Jennifer. "Women and Authorship." Pages 91–108 in *The Cambridge Companion to Medieval Women's Writing.* Edited by Carolyn Dinshaw and David Wallace. Cambridge: Cambridge University Press, 2003.

Veyrard-Cosme, Christiane. "Les soeur, filles, et cousine de Charlemagne dans le monde culturel carolingien." Pages 163–73 in *Les Réseaux Familiaux: Antiquité Tardive et Moyen Age; In memoriam A. Laiou et E. Patlagean.* Edited by Béatrice Caseau. CRHCBM 37. Paris: Association des amis du Centre d'histoire et civilisation de Byzance, 2012.

———. *La Vita beati Alcuini (IXe s.): Les inflexions d'un discours de sainteté; Introduction, édition et traduction annotée du texte d'après Reims, BM 1395 (K 784).* EAMA 54. Paris: Institut d'Etudes Augustiniennes, 2017.

Waquet, Françoise. *Les Enfants de Socrate: Filiation intellectuelle et transmission du savoir, XVIIe–XXIe siècle.* Paris: Albin Michel, 2008.

Women Writers and Holy Writ in the Latin Early Middle Ages: The Bible in Dhuoda and Hrotsvit

Franca Ela Consolino

Very few women's voices have reached us from the Latin early Middle Ages, and not all of them speak about the Bible. The earliest text belongs to Baudonivia, a Merovingian nun at Sainte-Croix in Poitiers, and the early seventh-century author of the life of Radegund, the queen and saint who founded the convent.[1] Her biography, which seeks to integrate the one that Venantius Fortunatus had composed a few years earlier, is of little interest to our inquiry because its references to Scripture are limited and not particularly meaningful: several expressions of biblical origin do not refer to their original contexts; some citations are borrowed, as they were included in passages from the Vita Caesarii that Baudonivia draws on; and others hold no surprises because—as in some references to episodes from the gospels—they serve to illustrate the spirituality of the protagonist and her *imitatio Christi*.[2] Similarly, the work of the other early medieval female

---

1. My references are to the edition published by Bruno Krusch, *Scriptorum rerum Merovingicarum*, MGH (Hannover: Hahn, 1888), 2:377–95; the text of the *Vita Radegundis* has now been published with annotations and translation by Paola Santorelli, ed., *La Vita Radegundis di Baudonivia* (Naples: D'Auria, 1999). See also the English translation in Jo Ann McNamara, E. Gordon Whatley, and John E. Halborg, eds., *Sainted Women of the Dark Ages* (Durham: Duke University Press, 1992), 70–105.

2. For examples of a biblical expressions put to different use, see *cum gladiis et fustibus* (Baudonivia, *Vita Rad.* 2.380, line 18), which in the gospels (Matt 26:47, 55; Luke 22:52) refers to the squad that went to capture Christ, and which in Baudonivia refers to the pagans who fought against the queen's attempt to set fire to their temple; and *respexit Dominus humilitatem ancillae suae* (16.389.6) from the Magnificat (Luke 1:48) and later *exultavit in gaudio* (16.389.11) spoken by Elizabeth to Mary (Luke 1:44) are used by Radegund when she obtains the reliquaries of the cross from the emperor Justin. A good example of borrowed citations is the concentration of references found

hagiographer we know of, the nun Hygeburg, is not a significant document. It deals with the brothers and saints Wynnebald, abbot of Heidenheim (d. 761), whose life she wrote, and Willibald, bishop of Eichstätt (d. 786 or 787), who dictated some notes to Hygeburg on his journey to the East.[3] In fact, references to the Bible are quite rare in Hygeburg's work; they serve primarily to recall the events that had taken place in the Holy Land sites that Willibald had visited. Finally, the Bible is not cited in the three letters that the mother, Herchenefreda, sent to the future bishop of Cahors, Didier (d. ca. 655) and that his biographer included in the life of the saint.[4]

Only two women writers, the Carolingian noblewoman Dhuoda and the Saxon nun Hrotsvit, reserve space for the Bible, to which they refer in ways that differ from each other but that were not entirely new in the Latin West. Like the martyr Perpetua of Carthage (d. 203), whose diary occupies the greater part of the *passio* named after her, Dhuoda is the author of a single text written in dramatic circumstances.[5] For both writers, Scripture is the book of reference, but it does not entirely or even partly form the theme of their discussion. We might, however, identify a precedent for Hrotsvit in the Roman aristocrat Proba, who had composed a Virgilian cento to sing the story of salvation using the words of Rome's greatest poet.[6] The Saxon

---

in 9.384.10–15, on which the analysis by Santorelli, *Vita Radegundis*, 131–32.208–19. For some examples using biblical references to illustrate *imitation Christi*, see 8.383.20–21 (*pro persequentibus se semper oravit et orare docuit*), which is the application of Matt 5:44 (*orate pro persequentibus et calumniantibus vos*); 10.384.27–28, where she recalls the multiplication of the loaves and fish (Matt 14:19–21) to comment on the miracle of the wine vessel that never empties; and the two contiguous citations in 16.388.1–2 (Ps 83:13 and Matt 22:37 = Deut 6:5), that introduce and give reasons for her desire to obtain the reliquary of the cross.

3. O. Holder-Egger, *Vita SS. Willibaldi et Wynniebaldi*, MGH (Hannover: Hahn, 1887), 1:80–117 (*Vita Willibaldi episcopi Eichstetensis*, 86–106, and *Vita Wynniebaldi abbatis Heidenhemensis*, 106–17).

4. Krusch, *Scriptorum rerum Merovingicarum*, 4:569–70.

5. The Passio Perpetuae et Felicitatis also includes a vision by the catechist Satirus (chs. 11–12) and interventions by the unknown editor, who introduces the story (chs. 1–2) and wrote the final section regarding the martyrdom of its protagonists (ch. 14–21).

6. Proba, *Cent.* 23: *Vergilium cecinisse loquar pia munera Christi*. On the short poem and its author, see the recent Proba, *Il Centone*, ed. Antonia Badini and Antonia Rizzi (Bologna: Dehoniane, 2011); for *Cent.* 23, see 151–52. For an English translation, see Sigrid Schottenius Cullhed, ed. and trans., *Proba the Prophet: The Christian Virginilian Cento of Faltonia Betitia Proba* (Leiden: Brill, 2015).

nun shares with the Roman *clarissima* her literary ambitions, her remarkable ability in verse, and her skillful experience in composition, even on subjects unrelated to the Bible.

The similarities, however, between the two ancient authors and their colleagues in the early Middle Ages are not striking, both due to the distinctive personality of each writer and to the developments in Christian culture and literature that took place in the long stretch of time separating Perpetua from Hrotsvit. These changes are connected above all to the establishment of biblical exegesis and the ascetic ideal that arose in the *pars orientis* and were later passed on to the Latin West. Here both mediation with the Greek world and the autonomous quest for hermeneutical and behavioral parameters can be traced back to the initiative of illustrious men of the church between the fourth and fifth centuries. This included bishops such as Ambrose and Augustine, or monks such as Rufinus and Jerome. Confined to their role as recipients of exegesis and parenesis, laypeople were more actively involved only as dedicatees or patrons of individual works.

Some leading female exponents of the Roman senatorial aristocracy emerged as sponsors and/or dedicatees of exegetical writings, or, more frequently, of their translations from Greek, commissioned from Jerome or Rufinus. They remain, however, at the margins of the process of interpretation, never speaking in their own name (out of modesty, Marcella attributed her interpretations to Jerome) and in the best case (as with Fabiola and Marcella) going only so far as to raise questions on Scripture. As Christiane Veyrard-Cosme shows us in this volume, their role would be no different from that of the correspondents of Alcuin. Like the Roman noblewomen of the late fourth and early fifth centuries, these ladies of the elite who chose the way of the cloister revealed their interest in Scripture by requesting an expert opinion without getting involved in a true comparison of views. Also in the late fourth and early fifth centuries, the intensive propaganda of the ascetic ideal, aimed primarily at a female readership, had found a repository of figures and behaviors in the Bible to which women who had taken vows of chastity could conform.[7] The exempla of biblical heroines previously proposed by authors such as

---

7. On the use of the Bible in ascetic propaganda, see Paola Francesca Moretti, "La Bibbia e il discorso dei Padri latini sulle donne: Da Tertulliano a Girolamo," in *Le donne nello sguardo degli antichi autori cristiani*, ed. Kari Elisabeth Børresen and Emanuela Prinzivalli (Trapani: Il Pozzo di Giacobbe, 2013), 5.1:137–73.

Ambrose or Jerome would enjoy long-lasting, constant popularity in the early Middle Ages. Francesco Stella's analysis in this volume bears significant witness to their success in poetry.

When they turn to Scripture, Dhuoda and Hrotsvit deal with a well-established exegetical and parenetic tradition under the exclusive control of men of the church. Therefore, the fact that both authors drew on the Bible without having sought the prior assent of ecclesiastical hierarchies appears all the more significant.

1. Dhuoda

> Holy Writ is set before the eyes of the mind like a kind of mirror, that we may see our inward face in it; for therein we learn the deformities, therein we learn the beauties that we possess; there we are made sensible what progress we are making, there too how far we are from proficiency. (Gregory the Great, *Moral.* 2.1.1)[8]

Thus had Gregory the Great summarized the educational role of the Bible. The Bible, however, is not the only mirror possible: a different mirror, though one steeped in the word of God, is the little book that an attentive mother composed from afar for her adolescent son between November 30, 841, and February 2, 843 CE:

> I, Dhuoda, though of weak intellect and living unworthily among worthy women, am, however, your mother, my son William, and now the subject of my manual turns to you, so that ... you, though pressed upon by throngs of worldly and secular activities, might not neglect to read often this little book addressed from me to you.... In it, you will find all matters on which you may wish to quickly inform yourself, and you will also find in it a mirror [*speculum*] in which you can without hesitation

---

8. Gregory the Great, *Moral.* 2.1.1: *scriptura sacra mentis oculis quasi quoddam speculum opponitur, ut interna nostra facies in ipsa videatur. ibi etenim foeda, ibi pulchra nostra cognoscimus. ibi sentimus, quantum proficimus, ibi a prouectu quam longe distamus.* Gregory the Great, *Morales sur Job: Livres I et II*, ed. and trans. Robert Gillet and André De Gaudemaris, SC 32, repr. ed. (Paris: Cerf, 1975), 252. Translation from John Henry Parker, J. G. F. Rivington, and J. Rivington, trans., *Morals on the Book of Job by St. Gregory the Great*, 3 vols. (London: Parker, 1844). On the derivation of this image from Augustine, see I Deug-Su, "Gli specula," in *Lo spazio letterario del Medioevo, Il Medioevo latino*, ed. Guglielmo Cavallo, Claudio Leonardi, Enrico Menestò (Rome: Salerno, 1993), 1.2:515–34; esp. 516–18.

contemplate the health of your soul, so that you may be pleasing not only in this world but to Him who shaped you "from mud" [Gen 1:7]: this, my son William, is absolutely necessary for you, so that in both things you may show yourself capable of being useful to the world and always pleasing to God in everything. (*Lib. man.* prol. 5–27)⁹

The author is Dhuoda, a lady of the high Carolingian aristocracy and a member of the reigning family after her marriage in 824 CE to Bernard, count of Girona and Barcelona, duke of Septimania, and son of Charlemagne's cousin, William of Toulouse, the celebrated hero of the fight against the Saracens and a future saint.¹⁰ What made her a writer was

---

9. Dhuoda, *Lib. man.* prol. 5–27: *Dhuoda quanquam in fragili sensu, inter dignas uiuens indigne, tamen genitrix tua, fili Wilhelme, ad te nunc meus sermo dirigitur manualis, ut…, inter mundanas et saeculares actionum turmas oppressus, hunc libellum a me tibi directum frequenter legere … non negligas, … inuenies in eo quidquid in brevi cognoscere malis; inuenies etiam et speculum in quo salutem animae tuae indubitanter possis conspicere, ut non solum saeculo, sed ei per omnia possis placere qui te formavit ex limo* (Gen 1:7): *quod tibi per omnia necesse est, fili Wilhelme, ut in utroque negotio talis te exibeas, qualiter possis utilis esse saeculo, et Deo per omnia placere valeas semper.* I cite and translate the text established by Pierre Riché, *Dhuoda, Manuel pour mon fils,* trans. Bernard de Vregille and Claude Mondésert, SC 225 (Paris: Cerf, 1997), 225. See also the English translation by Carol Neel, *Handbook for William: A Carolingian Woman's Counsel for Her Son* (Washington, DC: Catholic University of America Press, 1991).

10. Having risen to the height of power under Louis the Pious, Bernard had become the tutor of Charles the Bald, whose rights against his half-brothers he had defended, in agreement with the empress Judith. Due to his close friendship with the empress, Bernard attracted the accusation, we know not how well founded, of adultery, of which he publicly cleared himself in 831, when he was already married to Dhuoda. On the vicissitudes of Bernard and their political, social, and family context, see Marcelle Thiébaux, ed., *Dhuoda, Handbook for Her Warrior Son: Liber manualis* (Cambridge: Cambridge University Press, 1998), 13–18, 35. For an initial presentation on Dhuoda, in addition to Thiébaux's historical contextualization (*Dhuoda*, 6–13), see Peter Dronke, *Women Writers of the Middle Ages: A Critical Study of Texts from Perpetua (d. 203) to Marguerite Porete (d. 1310)* (Cambridge: Cambridge University Press 1984), 36–54; Régine Le Jan, "The Multiple Identities of Dhuoda," in *Ego Trouble: Authors and Their Identities in the Early Middles Ages,* ed. Richard Corradini et al. (Vienna: Österreichische Akademie der Wissenschaften, 2010), 211–19. On William, see Robert Auty et al., eds., *Lexikon des Mittelalters,* 10 vols. (Munich: Artemis-Verlag, 1977–1999), s.v. "Wilhelm," 9:15152, no. 45 *W. I. d. Hl.*, 151–52. William is the protagonist of a series of *chansons de gestes* (known as the *Cycle de Guillaume*) and of

the enforced separation from her son, as Dhuoda herself declares before beginning her treatise:

> Seeing many women in this world enjoy closeness to their children, and perceiving myself, Dhuoda, as separated and set at such a great distance from you, my son William, for this reason, prey to anguish and full of the desire to be of use to you, I send you this booklet that I have had transcribed in my name, so that you may read it and use it as a model, and I rejoice at the thought that, while I am absent in body, the presence of this little book will bring back to your mind, when you read it, that which you must do out of respect for me. (*Lib. man.* epigr. 4–10)[11]

What Dhuoda does not say is that their forced separation is the direct consequence of her husband's political choices during the dynastic struggles among the descendants of Louis the Pius. Having first sided with Pepin II of Aquitaine, Bernard had not supported his godson and former pupil Charles the Bald against his half-brother Lothair. After the victory of the former at Fontenoy (June 25, 841 CE), however, Bernard had shifted to his side, and as a token of his loyalty he had to leave his firstborn son William, who was not yet fifteen, at court. Dhuoda, who at her husband's request was then living in Uzès, where she looked after the family's interests, decided to dictate and have transcribed a short treatise for her son that would provide him with all the necessary guidelines for living and behavior. The age of fifteen—he would be sixteen when Dhuoda finished her text—was not considered young at the time (Charles the Bald was just a bit older than William) and would not seem to require such a detailed guide as that which his mother decided to produce for him. Its composition was inspired, rather, by the fear—probably dictated by a direct experience in that environment—of the possible risks to which the boy would be exposed at the court of a sovereign who could make him pay for any of his father's mistakes.[12] Hence Dhuoda

---

Willehalm by Wolfram von Eschenbach; see Auty et al., *Lexikon des Mittelalters*, s.v. "Wilhelmsepen," 9:198–201.

11. Dhuoda, *Lib. man.* epigr. 4–10: *cernens plurimas cum suis in saeculo gaudere proles, et me Dhuodanam, o fili Wilhelme, a te elongatam conspiciens procul, ob id quasi anxia et utilitatis desiderio plena, hoc opusculum ex nomine meo scriptum in tuam specietenus formam legendi dirigo, gaudens quod, si absens sum corpore, iste praesens libellus tibi ad mentem reducat quid erga me, cum legeris, debeas agere.*

12. It is likely that Dhuoda had already experienced courtly life in the palace at Aachen, where she had celebrated her wedding (*Lib. man.* praef. 4–6); see Janet L. Nelson, "Dhuoda," in *Lay Intellectuals in the Carolingian World*, ed. Patrick Wormald

chose to give this writing the form of a *liber manualis* ("handbook," the Latin equivalent of the Greek ἐγχειρίδιον)—that is, a text of limited length that William could keep at hand and always carry with him.¹³

The work's definition as a *liber manualis*, as with that of a *speculum* ("mirror"), points to a specific type of writings, the *specula*: short guides to moral principles that aimed to give readers concrete instructions for living, their authority based on Scripture and the church fathers.¹⁴ In Carolingian times, beginning in the late eighth century, five further *specula* had been written for laypeople before Dhuoda's manual: the treatise written by Paulinus of Aquileia for Duke Eric of Friuli, those by Alcuin for count Wido of Brittany, and by Jonas of Orléans for count Matfrid, and two for kings, Louis the Pious and Pepin I of Aquitaine.¹⁵ In the ideal models

---

and Janet L. Nelson (Cambridge: Cambridge University Press, 2007), 106–20, esp. 118–19; for the identification of the *domus magna* of 3.9.6-7 with Louis the Pious's palace at Aachen, see also Nelson, "Gendering Courts in the Early Medieval West," in *Gender in the Early Medieval World: East and West*, ed. Leslie Brubaker and Julia M. H. Smith (Cambridge: Cambridge University Press, 2004), 185–97, esp. 195.

13. Dhuoda, *Lib. man.* incip. 42–45: *quod volo ut cum ex manu mea tibi fuerit directus, in manu tua libenter facias amplecti eum opus, et tenens, volvens, legensque stude opere compleri dignissime.*

14. For general information, see Alain Dubreucq, "La littérature des *specula*: Délimitation du genre, contenu, destinataires et réception," in *Guerriers et moines: Conversion et sainteté aristocratique dans l'occident médiéval (IXᵉ-XIIᵉ siècle)*, ed. Michel Lauwers, Antibes 2002 (Turnhout: Brepols, 2002), 17–39; on Dhuoda, 31–33. For the Carolingian era, see Raffaele Savigni, "Gli 'specula' carolingi," in *Un ponte fra le culture: Studi medievistici di e per I Deug-su*, ed. Claudio Leonardi, Francesco Stella, and Patrizia Stoppacci (Florence: SISMEL Edizioni del Galluzzo, 2009), 23–48, esp. 46.

15. The first three *specula* are the *Liber exhortationis ad Henricum comitem seu ducem Forojuliensem* (PL 99:197–282), written by Paulinus of Aquileia in 796-97; the *Liber de virtutibus et vitiis* (PL 101:613–38), written by Alcuin for the count Guido; and the *De institutione laicali* by Jonas of Orléans (PL 106:121–278, and now Jonas of Orléans, *Instruction des laïcs*, ed. Odile Dubreucq, 2 vols., SC 549–50 [Paris: Cerf, 2012–2013]). *De institutione laicali* has survived in two drafts: the first version, dedicated to count Matfrid of Orléans, composed immediately after 818, now edited by Francesco Veronese (Giona di Orléans, *Istruzioni di vita per i laici* [Pisa: Pacini, 2018]), and a more extensive version following his misfortune in February 828; see Alain Dubreucq, introduction to *Le métier de roi*, by Jonas of Orléans, ed. Alain Dubreucq, SC 407 (Paris: Cerf, 1995), 28–31. The *specula* for the two kings are, respectively, the *Via regia*, composed by Smaragdus of Saint Mihiel between 819 and 839 (PL 102:935–70), and the *De institutione regia*, which Jonas of Orléans sent in 831 to king Pepin of Aquitaine (Jonas of Orléans, *Le métier de roi*, ed. Dubreucq). For general information

they proposed, these men of the church put on display "portraits of kings, clergymen, and pious laymen who resembled the authors more than the dedicatees" (except, perhaps, in the case of Louis the Pious).[16]

The same cannot be said of Dhuoda because her social status coincided with that of her son, and the behavioral model that the *Liber manualis* proposes reflects her awareness of the privileges of the high aristocracy to which her family belonged. This difference in purpose as compared to other *specula* appears evident even in the way in which Dhuoda discusses the metaphor of the mirror itself. Alcuin had intended that the dedicatee of *De virtutibus et vitiis*, when peering into the mirror of that book, would only see how to act in the ups and downs of life in order to reach eternal beatitude.[17] This was not the case for Dhuoda, in whose mirror William would see the instructions required not only to be pleasing to God but also to be of use to the world; the teachings of the Bible to which she referred were chosen to help him attain this dual purpose. Thus we ought to ask ourselves how much Dhuoda's intentions and the particular circumstances in which she wrote may have influenced both her choice of scriptural passages and their interpretation.

It would be much easier to find the answer if we were better informed about the author and her education. Unfortunately, Dhuoda tells us nothing about her family of origin nor of the environment in which she lived before marriage, though it is reasonable to suppose that she lived at the court of Louis the Pious. The only source that mentions her is the *Liber manualis*, from which we infer that she had received a serious *institutio* (training) and had a good library at her disposal, but we have no way of determining whether and to what extent education, mentality, and knowledge of the Bible on par with Dhuoda's were common outside of the cloister.[18] On the specifics of her approach to the sacred text, however, we

---

on the *specula principis*, see Auty et al., *Lexikon des Mittelalters*, s.v. "Fürstenspiegel," 4:1040–49; for the Carolingian era, see Anton, *Fürstenspiegel und Herrscherethos in der Karolingerzeit* (Bonn: Rohrscheid, 1968).

16. Michel Rouche, "Miroir des princes ou miroir du clergé?," in *Committenti e produzione artistico-letteraria nell'alto Medioevo occidentale, 4–10 aprile 1991*, SSAM 39 (Spoleto: Centro italiano di studi sull' Alto Medioevo 1992), 341–64, quote at 364.

17. PL 101:613C.

18. On the books that Dhuoda may have had access to as a laywoman, see the reconstruction by Pierre Riché, "Les bibliothèques de trois aristocrates latins carolingiens," *Le Moyen Âge* 69 (1963): 87–104.

may gather some insight from a comparison with the three previous Carolingian treatises dedicated to figures belonging to the nobility.[19]

Though Dhuoda was not unlettered, her Latin—while passionate and effective—is far from flawless. The debatable literary quality of her text is not the only element differentiating her from the Carolingian authors of *specula* that preceded her. Rather, what decisively sets her apart from them is her condition as a woman, even more so as a laywoman and a wife, as well as her motivations, which are much stronger. In writing their manuals, the three ecclesiastics were also spurred by the close bond between author and dedicatee: Alcuin takes on a paternal attitude (*paternae admonitionis*), an insistent brotherly relationship (*Frater mi, karissime frater*) ties Paulinus of Aquileia to Eric of Friuli, and Jonas says his writing is moved by charity.[20] Dhuoda, however, is the mother of the recipient, and given his young age and lack of worldly experience, he must be initiated into both the spiritual life and the public life, where he is required to behave in ways appropriate to his rank. This dual undertaking and the quite different strength of motherly love characterize Dhuoda's task and give it a considerably superior weight to that of the mere transmission of doctrine that we expect from men of the church:

> Son, Dhuoda is always beside you to instruct you, and if I may fail you by dying (as must happen), you have here this little moral treatise to warn you, and—reading me with the spirit and the body, and praying to God—you will be able to see as if in the image of a mirror and find therein the full description of your duties toward me. Son, you will have learnéd men who will give you a rich and broad education, but not in the same way, with the spirit that burns in their breast, as I who am your mother, my firstborn. (*Lib. man.* 1.7.15–23)[21]

---

19. I have preferred to leave out of the comparison the *De institutione regia* by Jonas of Orléans and *Via regia* by Smaragdus due to the greater accentuation of the moral responsibilities that characterizes the *specula* intended for a king; see Rachel Stone, "Kings Are Different: Carolingian Mirrors for Princes and Lay Morality," in *Le Prince au miroir de la littérature politique de l'Antiquité aux Lumières*, ed. Frédérique Lachaud and Lydwine Scordia (Rouen-Le Havre: Publications des Universités de Rouen et du Havre, 2007), 69–86.

20. PL 106:123B.

21. Dhuoda, *Lib. man.* 1.7.15–23: *Hortatrix tua Dhuoda semper adest, fili, et si defuerim deficiens, quod futurum est, habes hic memoriale libellum moralis, et quasi in picturam speculi, me mente et corpore legendo et Deum deprecando intueri possis, et quid erga me obsequi debeas pleniter inveniri potes. fili, habebis doctores qui te plura*

As René Wasselynck notes, "Three essential elements characterize the moral principles of the early Middle Ages: the teaching is concrete, priority is given to the study of sin, and the philosophical point of view is all but nonexistent."[22] Dhuoda's manual also shies away from philosophical speculation and is primarily of a practical nature. In it, however, the study of sin is not dominant, both because the author is a laywoman and, above all, because her fears for her son's eternal salvation are augmented by the thought of his physical survival in a court and at the side of a king, when both could become hostile to him in retaliation against his father, a situation that causes her anguish. This intense emotional involvement, which runs through the entire *Liber manualis*, gives it an absolutely unique character.

2. The Presence of the Bible

The main reference text for all authors of *specula* is the Bible, supplemented to a varying degree by quotes from other texts, especially those of the church fathers. Dhuoda is no exception.[23] About two thirds of her biblical citations derive from the Old Testament, with a marked preference for the Psalms (about 200 instances out of a total of 650 scriptural citations noted by Pierre Riché). The prevalence of this book was due to its use in liturgy and inclusion in prayer books, and it was furthered by the partial transcription of a treatise attributed to Alcuin on the choice and recitation of the Psalms.[24] The inclusion of this treatise is a good reflection of Dhuoda's personality as a writer, always seeking to enrich her text with external contributions pertaining to the themes discussed and to show her skills and the breadth of her reading, wherever possible.[25]

---

et ampliora doceant documenta, sed non aequali conditione, animo ardentis in pectore, sicut ego genitrix tua, fili primogenite.

22. René Wasselynck, "Les 'Moralia in Job' dans les ouvrages de morale du haut moyen âge latin," *RTAM* 31 (1964): 5–31, quote from 30.

23. On the presence and use of the Bible in Dhuoda's work, see Franca Ela Consolino, "Dhuoda, la Bibbia e l'educazione dei figli," in *La Bibbia nell'interpretazione delle donne*, ed. Claudio Leonardi, Francesco Santi, and Adriana Valerio (Florence: Atti di Convegni, 2002), 49–68.

24. The *De psalmorum usu liber* (PL 101:465B–68A), to which Dhuoda refers in *Lib. man.* 11.1: *qualiter ordinem psalmorum ex parte compones*; see Riché, *Dhuoda*, 35. Riché notes how, in regard to the Psalms, she has a distinct preference for nos. 36, 50, and 118 ("La Bible de Dhuoda," *RAug* 33 [2003]: 209–13).

25. By quoting Prudentius (*Cath.* 9.52–53, 57 and 4.1.33–35, but just before that,

By and large, Dhuoda extracts instructions of a practical nature from the Bible based on an exegesis attentive to the moral meaning and less to allegory. This approach is revealed in her ability to adapt biblical exempla to the situation in which her son finds himself. Essentially concrete implications derive from her reflections on the good and bad advisers recorded in Scripture, showing William how important it is to surround oneself with the right people.[26] These implications arise as she refers to a precise hierarchy of moral and social values in the exempla used to illustrate what honors are due to one's father (*Lib. man.* 3.1–3). Thus the two opposing behaviors of Isaac and Absalom toward their respective fathers take on special importance when applied to William's specific situation and to the central place of the father and paternal family in the system of values outlined by Dhuoda, in which love and respect for one's father are second only to those for God—a lesson learned by William, who paid for it with his life.[27]

Also underlining the need to obey one's father is the moral lesson—differing from the usual one—that the author draws from the episode of the sons of Eli.[28] In the Bible story, they are punished for not having listened

---

she had echoed *Cath.* 9.55 and 6.147–48), citing unidentifiable works of poetry (*Lib. man.* 3.10.130–146; 4.7.6–9, 25–30; and 4.8.225–227) and including four rhythmic poems she had composed herself (the epigram, an acrostic poem of seventy-six verses; 10.1 and 10.2, dedicated to William, the second of which is an acrostic; and 10.6.15–38, which is her epitaph). In addition to mentioning authors such as Augustine or Isidore and making citations (see Riché, *Dhuoda*, 383–85), she also exhibits her skills in numerology (6.4) and in the calculation and meaning of letters and numbers (9), a broad debate on the meaning of *quasi* (5.1.25–99), and the last section on reciting psalms, drawing on a work attributed to Alcuin (see note 24, above).

26. Divided, respectively, into good advisers (Samuel, Daniel, Joseph, Jethro, and Achior; *Lib. man.* 3.5) and bad advisers (Ahithophel and Haman; 3.7), whom Dhuoda contrasts with Doeg the Idumean and the humble Mordechai.

27. Dhuoda, *Lib. man.* 3.2.15–17 (*ego autem admoneo te..., ut in primis diligas Deum ... deinde ama, time et dilige patrem tuum*): 3.1 and 3.2 are dedicated to duties toward one's father. To avenge the death of his father, who was accused of treason and condemned by Charles the Bald (844), and regain possession of Toulouse, William made war against the king, seeking the support of the Muslims of Cordoba. In 850, the failure of this attempt cost him his life; see Thiébaux, *Dhuoda*, 35–37.

28. Dhuoda, *Lib. man.* 3.1.24–27; further details in Consolino, "Dhuoda," 60. A preliminary investigation into the variations, which were not necessarily voluntary, compared to the biblical text is found in Bernadette Janssens, "L'étude de la langue et les citations latines dans le *Liber manualis* de Dhuoda: Un sondage," in *Aevum inter*

to their father's last command, but it is God himself who made them disobey, for he had decided to slay them (1 Sam 2:25). The Bible also gives importance, however, to the responsibilities of Eli, a father who was too lenient and had tolerated his sons' wicked behavior; it is no accident that his story became an example of the risks brought on by laxity in childrearing.[29] Dhuoda, who had witnessed the revolt of the sons of Louis the Pious against their father (having just alluded to it) and who is keen to instill in William total respect for his father, recalls only the sons' guilt, transformed into an exemplum of the punishment awaiting those who fail to heed fatherly warnings.[30]

Dhuoda contrasts the punishment of the disobedient sons with the reward—both earthly and heavenly—that God grants pious and obedient children:

> In fact, "blessing" and "upholding" God and obeying their fathers and fulfilling their orders to a good degree, "they will inherit the earth" [Ps 36:9 and 22]. And if, by listening to my previous recommendations, you apply them through worthy acts, not only will you have a part in some of the good things on this earth, but you will also deserve to possess, along with the saints, that land of which the Psalmist says: "I believe that I will see the good things of the Lord in the land of the living" [Ps 26:13]. (*Lib. man.* 3.1.68–75)[31]

An extensive series of examples proves the validity of this statement: Shem and Japheth, Isaac, Jacob, and Joseph, who due to their filial devotion obtained divine benevolence while still alive (3.3). The exemplum of Joseph is of particular interest because his story shows how even an obedient son can encounter dangers and difficulties, but it gives reassur-

---

utrumque: Mélanges offerts à Gabriel Sanders, ed. Marc van Uytfanghe and Roland Demeulenaere (The Hague: Nijhoff Steenbrugis, 1991), 259–75.

29. See Pierre Riché, *Éducation et culture dans l'Occident barbare*, 3rd ed. (Paris: Seuil, 1973), 501.

30. Dhuoda, *Lib. man.* 3.1.23–24: *in multis, non tui similes, audivimus opus patratum*. See Riché, *Dhuoda*, 136–37, n. 3.

31. Dhuoda, *Lib. man.* 3.1.68–75: *nam benedicentes et sustinentes Deum atque Patribus obedientes et illorum jussa animo libenti complentes, ipsi hereditabunt terram* [Ps 36:9 and 22]. *quod si tu audiens, facti quos supra tibi commemoro impleveris dignis, non solum in hanc terram habebis in aliquibus sortem, sed etiam illam cum sanctis mereberis possidere, de qua ait Psalmista: credo videre bona Domini in terra viventium* [Ps 26:13].

ance that in each case the divine reward will arrive while we are yet living. Dhuoda's faith in a dual reward—earthly and heavenly—and her conviction that certain behaviors guarantee both are confirmed much more in the Old Testament than in the New, which is loath to give reassurance on earthly prosperity as a reward for those who act properly. This may help to explain the greater frequency of the Old Testament citations in the *Liber manualis*.[32]

Dhuoda also turns to the Bible to underline the importance of her writing, referring to the evangelizing work of Paul:

> May this book, which must provide you with a model, be thus called *Manualis*: the words come from me, but it is up to you to put them into practice, and—as someone says [*ut ait quidam*]—"I planted, Apollos watered, but God gave the growth" [1 Cor 3:6]. At this point, my son, what more can I say except that, through your previous merits, in this work "I have fought with zeal for a good outcome, and keeping the faith, I have brought my journey to successful completion?" [2 Tim 4:7]. And in whom could all this have value, if not in him who has said: "it is finished"? [John 19:30]. In fact, all that I have developed from the beginning in this volume.... I have put to work and brought to completion in him who is called God. (*Lib. man.* incip. 45–56)[33]

The last citation, taken from John, uses the words of Christ to sanction Dhuoda's work as a parent, which she had just set under the aegis of Paul. The comparison of Dhuoda's initiative to the apostle's evangelization efforts is suggested by her references to 1 Cor 3:6 and 2 Tim 4:7. The latter maintains the concept of taking final stock, which in the original context was underlined by the certainty of the author's near death ("for I am already poured out like a drink offering and the time of my release

---

32. We must not, however, necessarily hypothesize, along with Marie Anne Mayeski (*Dhuoda: Ninth Century Mother and Theologian* [Scranton: University of Scranton Press, 1995], 123–24), that Dhuoda saw any congruence between her times and those of the Old Testament.

33. Dhuoda, *Lib. man.* incip. 45–56: *dicatur enim iste formatus libellus manualis, hoc est sermo ex me, opus in te, et ut ait quidam: ego plantavi, Apollo rigavit, Deus autem incrementum dedit.* [1 Cor 3:6] *quid hic aliud possum dicere, fili, nisi quod ex meritis precedentibus tuis in hoc labore cum studio operis* boni certavi. fidem servans cursu consumavi felici? [2 Tim 4:7] *et in quo haec vigeant, nisi in illum qui dixit: consumatum est?* [John 19:30]. *quicquid enim in hoc Manuali incohans deduxi volumine ... usque in finem in illum consumavi opere qui dicitur Deus.*

begins"; *ego enim iam delibor et tempus meae resolutionis instat*; 2 Tim 4:6) in order to give prominence to his successfully completed mission. What is even more significant in defining Dhuoda's role is the reference to 1 Cor 3:6, by virtue of which she proposes herself as an intermediary between her son and God. Distancing herself from the *specula* of her ecclesiastical predecessors, Dhuoda boldly compares herself to the apostle, perhaps because she is unconnected to the church hierarchies or perhaps because, as Paul does with the Corinthians, she claims her own responsibility for William's religious upbringing.

Further on, the third chapter of 1 Corinthians also provides the motherly metaphor of nourishment ("like children in Christ, I gave you milk to drink, not food"; *Tamquam parvulis in Christo, lac vobis potum dedi, non escam*; 1 Cor 3:1–2), which Paul had adapted for himself and which Dhuoda appropriates, underlining—with the polyptoton *parvula* and *parvulum*—her own humility: "A little woman, I gave you, little in Christ, milk to drink, not food" (*tanquam parvula parvulum in Christo lac potum dedi, non escam*; *Lib. man.* 6.1.17–18). In its metaphorical meaning, this image of nourishing primarily refers to the spiritual fatherhood performed by men of the church.[34] Applying it to herself, Dhuoda places herself on par with them, and she attributes to herself a role not dissimilar from that given to godfathers at baptism during the Carolingian era.[35]

Unlike the men of the church, who become mothers to the spirit, Dhuoda is such even in the flesh, as she herself observes shortly thereafter, distinguishing physical from spiritual motherhood so as to claim both of them.[36]

> Regarding the quality of worldly things and the consideration of your rank, within the limits of my abilities I have assisted you in setting everything in order [*ordinatrix astiti in cunctis*], so that while you provide your current service you may proceed without blame, free and untrou-

---

34. See Katrien Heene, *The Legacy of Paradise: Marriage, Motherhood and Women in Carolingian Edifying Literature* (New York: Lang, 1997), 180–81, which underlines how Dhuoda's testimony is one of a kind (180).

35. See Pauline Stafford, "Parents and Children in the Early Middle Ages," *EME* 10 (2001): 257–71, esp. 267.

36. Dhuoda, *Lib. man.* 7.1.10–12: *secundum dicta namque doctorum, duo nativitates in uno homine esse noscuntur, una carnalis, altera spiritualis, sed nobilior spiritualis quam carnalis.* On the Augustinian origin of this distinction, see Riché, *Dhuoda*, 299, n. 2.

bled. But now, starting anew as a mother for the second time, of the spirit as of the flesh, I will never cease to advise you on the way in which, with the help of God, you may perfect the service of your spirit, so that each day you may be born again in Christ. (*Lib. man.* 7.1.1–9)[37]

The expression *ordinatrix ... in cunctis*, which also occurs elsewhere, clarifies the remarkably practical character of Dhuoda's teaching, which in the course of the same chapter again underlines the duality of her motherhood toward William.[38] Again referring to Paul, she recognizes in fact that one may have many spiritual fathers, but she also recalls the mothers of the martyrs Celsus and Symphorian, who were twice mothers to their sons (*primae et secundae nativitatis genitrices in Christo suis extiterunt prolibus*; *Lib. man.* 7.3.7–15).[39]

Naturally, not all of Dhuoda's biblical references are the result of an equally original insight, nor are they all equally significant. Thus while such references confirm the author's rhetorical studies, her approach to the Bible is not made distinctive by her allusion to God opening the mouths of the dumb and giving eloquence to those who cannot speak, which she writes in the prologue, nor by her nod to the famous episode of Balaam's donkey, to whom God granted the gift of speech—a reference that often occurs in poems to underline the author's modesty.[40] Rather, what seems

---

37. Dhuoda, *Lib. man.* 7.1.1–9: *qualitas temporalium, ut, absque reprehensione, tempore dum vivis in militia actuali, sive dignitatis contemplationum, secure et quiete valeas incedere, prout valui ordinatrix tibi astiti in cunctis. nunc vero deinceps militiam animae tuae qualiter, auxiliante Deo, ad summum usque perducas, velut genitrix secunda mente et corpore ut in Christo cotidie renascaris ammonere non cesso.*

38. Dhuoda, *Lib. man.* 1.1.4–5: *ordinatrix tibi in cunctis adsisto*, regarding the criteria for choosing psalms to recite.

39. Containing a citation of Gal 4:19 (*filioli mei, quos iterum parturio, donec Christus in vobis firmius formetur*) and 1 Cor 4:15 (*per evangelium ego vos genui*). On the importance of mothers of the saints due to their influence on their children, see Heene, *Legacy of Paradise*, 167–71.

40. On opening the mouths of the dumb, see Dhuoda, *Lib. man.* prol. 4–5: *Adest semper ille qui ora aperit mutorum et infantium linguas facit disertas*, a reference to Wis 10:21: *Sapientia aperuit os mutorum et linguas infantium fecit disertas.* The same reference also appears, in a similar context, in Jonas of Orléans, *De institutione laicali* (*Instruction des laics*, ed. Dubreucq, 1:1–27). On the Balaam episode, see Ernst Robert Curtius, *Europäische Literatur und lateinisches Mittelalter* (Bern: Francke, 1948), 263; see also the English edition, Ernst Robert Curtius, *European Literature and the Latin Middle Ages* (repr., Princeton: Princeton University Press, 1990), 236–37.

to me more interesting in terms of originality is the way that the allusion to this famous Old Testament episode is set between two references to the same verse in the gospels, that of Christ's reply to the Canaanite woman who asked him to free her daughter from the devil, "Yet even the dogs under the table eat the children's crumbs" (*nam et catelli comedunt sub mensa de micis puerorum*; Mark 7:28; cf. 15:27):

> And, in fact, it may sometimes happen that a bothersome little dog under her lord's table, among the other dogs, manages to seize upon and eat the crumbs that fall from above [Mark 7:28; cf. Matt 15:27]. For he who made the mouth of a dumb animal speak [Num 22:28] is able, by his ancient mercy, to open up my spirit and grant me understanding, and he who prepares the table for his faithful in the desert ... can, even in my case, willingly grant the wish of his maidservant by his desire, so that, at least under his table—that is, under the holy church—I may from afar see the dogs—that is, the ministers of holy altars—and from the crumbs of spiritual understanding for me and for you, my fine son William, may I put together a discourse that is fine and brilliant and worthy and appropriate. (*Lib. man.* 1.2.7–20)[41]

The passage, used to show William that both of them must seek out God (*quaerendus est Deus, fili, mihi et tibi*), is remarkable, given Dhuoda's self-identification with the Canaanite woman, and even more so in terms of the novelty of her exegesis, which makes a distinction unknown elsewhere between the dogs near the table, who would be the priests, and she herself, who—despite being farther from them—manages to gather up the crumbs of divine wisdom. With this interpretation, Dhuoda not only reformulates the biblical exegesis for a new, practical use, but she also grants herself the power to draw on divine teachings without the mediation of the clergy, whose position she recognizes as preeminent but not exclusive.[42]

---

41. Dhuoda, *Lib. man.* 1.2.7–20: *nam solet fieri ut aliquotiens importuna catula, sub mensa Domini sui, inter catulos alteros, micas cadentes valeat carpere et mandere. potens est enim ille qui os animalis muti loqui fecit, mihi secundum suam priscam clementiam aperire sensum et dare intellectum; et qui parat fidelibus suis in deserto mensam ... potest et me ancillae suae ex suo desiderio compleri voluntatem, [p]saltim ut sub mensam illius, infra sanctam videlicet ecclesiam, possim procul conspicere catulos, hoc est sanctis altaribus ministros, et de micis intellectu spirituali mihi et tibi, o pulcher fili Wilhelme, pulchrum et lucidum dignumque et abtum colligi valerem sermonem.*

42. On this passage and its relationship to the previous exegesis, see the accurate and thorough analysis by Mayeski, *Dhuoda*, 72–92 and 145–54.

Biblical quotations can be handled in a highly personal way, even without an original exegesis. To clarify the meaning of this claim, I will start with two books in the Old Testament: the Song of Solomon, which was commented upon many times between late antiquity and the early Middle Ages, and the book of Job, the subject of Gregory the Great's famous treatise. The two books are at opposite poles in terms of how often they are quoted: the Song is nearly absent, while the book of Job is quoted as much as the Gospel of John.[43] Among the books of the New Testament, its frequency is inferior only to that of Matthew; among those of the Old Testament, it is second only to the Psalms and Sirach, which gained a place of importance due to its sententious nature. While the Song is also infrequently cited by other *specula*, the remarkable occurrence of verses from the book of Job, however, is peculiar to Dhuoda.

Of the three instances of the Song noted by Riché, the first consists of the reuse of an expression taken entirely out of its original context; the second is anything but certain.[44] The third, however, is certain, where the verse (Song 2:6 and 8:3) is quoted within a discussion on using two hands when counting on one's fingers:

> Regarding this calculation made with both hands, you will find it written: "his left hand is under my head and his right will embrace me." What must we take for the left hand, my son, if not the present life, in which each of us is tossed about in toiling? And what is shown in the right hand, if not the holy and worthy heavenly fatherland? (*Lib. man.* 6.4.51–56)[45]

In the allegorical meaning attributed to the verse here, it has been seen an autonomous attempt on the part of Dhuoda, who—left to her own

---

43. Along with the thirty instances of Job noted by Riché, at least one more must be added, at 1.1.30. See note 56, below.

44. The first, Song 4:11—"Your lips distill nectar, my bride" (*favus distillans labia tua, sponsa*)—is used in 3.5.23–24 to describe the words of a great man (*favum distillant labia eius*). The second, in 7.6.7, is most certainly a modified reference to Hag 2:24 (*et ponam te quasi signaculum*), with which she shares the reference to the divine reward; it is therefore unnecessary to recall Song 8:6 (*pone me ut signaculum super cor tuum, ut signaculum super brachium tuum, quia fortis est ut mors dilectio*), as it is quite different, even in context.

45. Dhuoda, *Lib. man.* 6.4.51–56: *de qua subputatione ambarum inuenies scriptum: laeua eius sub capite meo et dextera illius amplexabitur me. quid in sinistra, fili, nisi praesens intelligitur vita, in qua unusquisque elaborando voluitur nostrum? et quid in dextera, nisi sancta et digna coelestis ostenditur patria?*

devices—would have offered a "particularly arbitrary and flat" interpretation.[46] This is not exactly the case, because the exegesis proposed here has two precedents (not hitherto noted, as far as I know), which appear unlikely to be debated: the commentaries of Bede and Alcuin.[47] Thus we have here a further confirmation of Dhuoda's readings and of their targeted use because this allegorical interpretation of the two hands embraces both this life and the next, in line with the dual perspectives of the *Liber manualis*, whose instructions are aimed at the achievement of recognition in this and the other world.

Moreover, the absence of the Song is easily explained by its usual connection to the ascetic life and the love between God and the soul (or the virgin) consecrated to him. It is no coincidence that the Song is absent in the treatises of Alcuin and Jonas while present in Paulinus of Aquileia, whose *speculum* traces a spiritual pathway for Eric of Friuli that does not take into consideration marriage and is difficult to distinguish from that of a monk. In Paulinus's *exhortatio*, the few passages mentioned concern the mysticism of the soul, seeking to unite with the groom.[48]

We now come to the book of Job, which—due above all to the exegesis of Gregory the Great—enjoyed great success in the Middle Ages, and its interpretation by the Carolingian age pointed to the protagonist as a model for the perfect father, who in his prosperity had protected the poor, orphans, and widows, and in his tribulations had successfully overcome his trials.[49] In the *specula* written just before Dhuoda's, the presence of the book of Job varies. Absent in Alcuin's *De virtutibus* and infrequent in Paulinus of Aquileia, it is, however, cited several times in Jonas's *De instructione laicali*, especially in the second volume dealing with married life, of which he and the prophet Tobias are considered exponents.[50] Dhuoda, too, finds

---

46. Mayeski, *Dhuoda*, 46 ("particularly arbitrary and flat").

47. Bede, *In cant.* 6.119: *sinistram Dei ecclesia prosperitatem videlicet vitae praesentis quasi sub capite posuit quam intentione summi amoris premit, dextera vero Dei eam amplectitur quia sub aeterna eius beatitudine tota deuotione continetur;* Alcuin, *Comp. in Cant.* 8.4: *leva incarnationis Christi dona designat, et dextera futura sanctorum cum Christo gaudia esprimit.*

48. Paulinus, *Lib. exhort.* 28.70 (Song 3:4); 34.87 (Song 2:1); 66.211 (Song 3:4).

49. See Pierre Riché, "La Bible et la vie politique dans le haut Moyen Age," in *Le Moyen Age et la Bible*, ed. Pierre Riché and Guy Lobrichon (Paris: Beauchesne, 1984), 385–400; on Job as an exemplary father who passed from prosperity to trials, see 397.

50. Paulinus of Aquileia cites Job 2:6–7 and 42:7–8 at *Lib. exhort* 56.170; Job 1:12 and 2:6 at *Lib. exhort* 64.203, and Job 10:22 at *Lib. exhort* 66.222, also in connection

a model for good behavior in Job but does not associate him with Tobias, nor does she connect him with married life.[51]

Dhuoda's quotations from Job favor certain chapters and passages in particular, and their presence bears witness to an active approach to Holy Writ, at times mediated by other readings. Thus the affirmation that no one on this earth is innocent, not even a day-old child (*non enim est homo qui non peccet, ne si unius diei sit vita eius*; *Lib. man.* 3.11.138–139), refers to Job 14:4–5, according not to the Vulgate, which does not contain it, but to the *Vetus latina* version, the same one used in *Moralia in Job*. Gregory had used it to demonstrate the existence of original sin and the impossibility of salvation without baptism,[52] while Dhuoda cites it to urge William to make confession.

Dhuoda's affinity with the sentiments expressed by the prophet justifies the double reference to Job 30:16: "And now my soul is poured out within me" (*in memet ipso marcescit anima mea*). In the preface (which does not coincide with the beginning of the work, as it is preceded by the incipit, an epigram, and a prologue), Dhuoda first underlines her burning desire to see her son again and the pain caused her by the enforced separation, concluding thus: "I would have wished it, had God given me the possibility, but since salvation is far from me, a sinner, I continue to wish for it and in this desire *my soul is poured out within me*" (*Lib. man.* praef. 31–33).[53] Shortly thereafter, Dhuoda returns to the same verse to express her suffering because she is denied the chance to behold God: "In being denied any sight of him, so much is *my soul poured out within me* that my desire burns" (*Lib. man.* 1.1.300).[54]

---

with Job's trials. On Jonas, see Raffaele Savigni, "Les laïcs dans l'écclésiologie carolingienne: Normes statutaires et idéal de 'conversion,'" in *Guerriers et moines: Conversion et sainteté aristocratique dans l'occident médiéval (IXe–XIIe siècle)*, ed. Michel Lauwers (Turnhout: Brepols, 2002), 41–92; on Job as a model for married laypeople, see 46–47.

51. See Dhuoda, *Lib. man.* 4.6.30–31, with a citation of Job 31:1, and 4.8.42–45, with citations of Job 31:32 and 29:16.

52. Gregory the Great, *Moral.* 9.21.32: *perpetua quippe tormenta percipiunt et qui nihil ex propria voluntate peccauerunt. hinc namque scriptum est: non est mundus in conspectu eius nec unius diei infans super terram. hinc per semetipsam veritas dicit: nisi quis renatus fuerit ex aqua et spiritu, non potest introire in regnum dei* [John 3:5].

53. Dhuoda, *Lib. man.* praef. 31–33: *volueram quidem, si daretur mihi virtus de Deo; sed quia longe est a me peccatrice salus, volo, et in hac voluntate meus valde marcessit animus* [cf. Job 30:16 *in memet ipso marcescit anima mea*].

54. Dhuoda, *Lib. man.* 1.1.30: *In hac denegatione conspicuitatis valde* meus marcescit animus: *aestuat enim sensus*.

This second reference, not noted by Riché, shows how Dhuoda uses the same expression to indicate her two greatest desires and to lament the emptiness of two distances: the earthly distance of her son and the spiritual distance of God. In his *Moralia in Job*, Gregory the Great used the verse in reference to the condition of the chosen, who are wracked with pain on earth to rejoice later in heaven.[55] We do not know whether Dhuoda had read this passage and therefore consciously deviated from it. In any case, she gives voice to her double discomfort through the words of Job, stricken with suffering: "And now my soul is poured out within me, and days of affliction seize me" (*nunc autem in memet ipso marcescit anima mea, et possident me dies afflictionis*; Job 30:16).

The string of references found in 1.5.48–52, however, can be simply explained by her excellent knowledge of this book. These phrases return to Dhuoda's memory more easily than others:

> He himself is the immeasurable, he, as Scripture says, is the one for whom "the morning stars sing together, and all the sons of God shout for joy" [Job 38:7]. It is he who "laid the foundation of the earth and stretched the line upon it" [Job 38:4–5], "shut in the sea with doors and made clouds its garment" [Job 38:8–9] (*Lib. man.* 1.5.48–52)[56]

We might expect that Dhuoda would turn to Genesis to describe the work of God the creator, and not—as she actually does—to the first reply that God gives Job, addressing him from the whirlwind. Dhuoda recalls this passage, which begins with *accinge sicut vir* ("gird up your loins like a man"), to instruct William shortly thereafter on the proper attitude toward God:

> William, my fine and lovable son, I also urge you not to hesitate to procure, among the worldly cares of this life, many volumes in which you may perceive and learn through the teaching of the holiest learned men, in greater quantity and importance than what is written above, something about God as creator of your people. Pray to him, hold him dear and love him. If you do this, he will be your guardian, companion, and

---

55. Gregory the Great, *Moral.* 20.27.56: *Electorum quippe anima nunc marcescit, quia in illa postmodum aeterna exsultatione viridescit. Modo eos dies afflictionis possident, quia dies laetitiae post sequuntur.*

56. Dhuoda, *Lib. man.* 1.5.48–52: *Ipse est quem nullus aestimare potest; ipse est, ut ait scriptura, quem laudant simul astra matutina et cui omnes jubilant filii Dei* [Job 38:7]. *Ipse est qui posuit fundamenta terrae et extendit super eam lineam* [Job 38:4–5], *conclusit mare terminis, posuitque nubem vestimenta eius* [Job 38:8–9].

home, way, truth, and life, giving you the prosperity of the world in great abundance, and he will turn your enemies toward peace. But as it is written in the book of Job, "gird up your loins like a man" [Job 38:3 and 40:7], be humble of heart and also chaste in the body, and, turning heavenward, "clothe yourself with glory and splendor" [Job 40:10]. (*Lib. man.* 1.7.2–120)[57]

The context from which the two quotes were drawn is that of the confrontation with God, who—accused by Job—replies to him from the whirlwind and challenges Job to engage in dialogue with him (Job 40:1–10). Latin exegetical tradition had interpreted the first of the two verses as an invitation to material and spiritual chastity,[58] as the loins are the seat of lust, and Dhuoda subscribes to this interpretation.

Things change when God issues Job an impossible challenge: to be like him (Job 40:9–14). In the Bible, the glory and beautiful garments with which Job is asked to compete belong to God, the magnificence of which— Gregory the Great explains—is due to the radiance of the just in death (*Moral.* 32.6.8). In Dhuoda's text, there is no trace of such an interpretation; rather, splendor and beautiful garments, with which she boldly refers to William, do not implicate on her part a "foolish attempt to rival God."[59] In fact, the context clarifies the glory of William and the brilliance of his dress as that which God expects from him: if he prays to and loves God, God will reward William by giving him worldly prosperity and reconciling his enemies; William (*tu autem*) must strive, however, to be chaste and glorious.

---

57. Dhuoda, *Lib. man.* 1.7.2–12: *Admoneo te etiam, o mi fili Wilhelme pulchre et amabilis, ut inter mundanas huius saeculi curas, plurima volumina librorum tibi adquiri non pigeas, ubi de deo creatori tuorum per sacratissimos doctorum magistros aliquid sentire et discere debeas, plura atque maiora quam supra scriptum est. Ipsum obsecra, dilige et ama. Quod si feceris, erit tibi custos, dux, comes et patria, via, veritas et vita, tribuens tibi prospera in mundo largissime, et omnes inimicos tuos conuertet ad pacem. Tu autem, ut scriptum est in Iob, accinge sicut vir lumbos tuos; sis humilis corde castusque et corpore, atque erectus in sublime esto gloriosus valde et speciosis induere vestibus.*

58. See Isidore, *Etym.* 11.1.98. *unde et ad Iob in exordio sermonis dictum est: "Accinge sicut vir lumbos tuos": ut in his esset resistendi praeparatio, in quibus libidinis est usitata dominandi occasio.* Gregory expanded on this the most in *Moral.* 28.3.12; to him, *luxuria* also indicates, in a figurative sense, the pride of chastity.

59. Dronke, *Women Writers*, 44.

We are thus led back to one of the foundations of Dhuoda's use of biblical citations: she draws on Scripture for behavioral guidelines that aim at procuring success even in this world, among the difficulties of life at court. In fact, the author expected that the manual would also be read by her other son, who at the time was very small and whose name she did not even know, and in the meantime it would also be of use to William's young *commilitones* ("comrades").[60] Dhuoda offers both him and them a picture of the society and the lay elite to which she belongs, carefully placing her son's present and future actions within the framework holding both her husband's vicissitudes and the respect due to him, as well as the history and continuity of his family, made evident even in William's duty to pray for his father's deceased relatives, of whom a list is provided (*Lib. man.* 10.5.1–5; see also 8.14). In the *Liber manualis*, whose teachings could also be used by the young king, the use of Scripture thus contributes to the construction of a lay spirituality, for it is set in a worldly perspective in which the church is not given a central place nor is any contrast made between the world and God.[61] William's steps in the world would be guided not by the Virgin mother, who is never mentioned, but by the tenacious will of his earthly mother, the "weak" Dhuoda.[62]

---

60. On the birth of William's brother, see Dhuoda, *Lib. man.* praef. 15–17. The boy ought to have been called Bernard like his father and should perhaps be identified as that Bernard Plantevelue whose son—William the Pious, duke of Aquitaine—would found the abbey of Cluny; see Riché, *Dhuoda*, 21 and n. 3; *Lexikon des Mittelalters*, s.v. "Bernhardt, 3 B. Plantapilosa," 1:1983–84.

61. See the interesting observations made on this subject by Martin A. Claussen, "God and Man in Dhuoda's Liber Manualis," in *Women in the Church*, ed. William J. Sheils and Diana Wood (Oxford: Blackwell, 1990), 43–52. On the possibility of the teachings being used by the young king, see Régine Le Jan, "Dhuoda ou l'opportunité du discours féminin," in *Agire da donna: Modelli e pratiche di rappresentazione (secoli VI–X)*, ed. Cristina La Rocca (Turnhout: Brepols, 2007), 109–28.

62. This aspect is well illustrated by Robert Luff, "Schreiben im Exil: Der 'Liber manualis' der frankischen Adeligen Dhuoda," *MJ* 35 (2000): 249–66, which perceives the *Liber manualis*'s originality in the very tension between the traditional topoi of modesty and the overwhelming desire to compose a literary work that fully reflected her personality. Mary is never referenced in the *Liber manualis*, unless there is an allusion to the Virgin in epigr. 30–31, but it would still be an isolated mention. Dhuoda's silence on the Virgin finds a partial explanation in the fact that the worship of Mary emerged gradually during the reign of Charles the Bald, but shortly after the drafting of the *Liber manualis* (see Dominique Iogna-Prat, "Le culte de la Vierge sous le règne de Charles le Chauve," in *Marie: Le culte de la Vierge dans la société médiévale*, ed. Domi-

3. Hrotsvit

Though absent from Dhuoda's Manual, the Virgin is of fundamental importance to Hrotsvit, a Saxon noblewoman who was born around 935 CE and died around 973 CE; she was raised and lived in the Benedictine abbey at Gandersheim, founded in 852 by Duke Liudolf, progenitor of the Ottonian dynasty. Intended for young women of noble lineage, this foundation enjoyed the special favor of Otto I, who in 947 had annulled its original dependence on royal control, giving the abbess the right to serve justice, mint coins, keep an army, and have a seat in the diet. Possibly a relative of the ruling family, and in any case of noble origins (as proven by her presence at Gandersheim), Hrotsvit owed her education to two women: Rikkardis, who is otherwise unknown, and the abbess Gerberga II (940–1001 CE), daughter of Henry of Bavaria (thus niece of Otto I the Great), who led the convent beginning in 959. The freedom of contact (in particular with the court, where she may have stayed) and movement that are gathered from Hrotsvit's writings do not fit with the monastic profession and are rather suited to the condition of a canoness, a role generally attributed to her today.[63]

Hrotsvit's works have been organized into three books, the order of which reflects the chronology of their composition and the literary genre to which they belong. The first, composed in two stages and published no earlier than 962, comprises eight sacred legends (*Maria, Ascensio, Gongol-*

---

nique Iogna-Prat, Éric Palazzo, and Daniel Russo [Paris: Beauchesne, 1996], 65–98), while under Charlemagne it initially grew only to a limited extent in response to the anti-adoptionist controversy and with Christological intent; see Gabriela Signori, *Maria zwischen Kathedrale, Kloster und Welt* (Sigmaringen: Thorbecke, 1995), 63–65; Irene Scaravelli, "Per una mariologia carolingia: Autori, opere e linee di ricerca," in *Gli studi di mariologia medievale: Bilancio storiografico*, ed. Clelia Maria Piastra (Florence: SISMEL Edizioni del Galluzzo, 2001), 65–85, esp. 77–78.

63. Of the many works on Hrotsvit, I shall limit myself to highlighting Katharina M. Wilson, ed., *Hrotsvit of Gandersheim: Rara avis in Saxonia?* (Ann Arbor: Marc, 1987); Ferruccio Bertini, "Rosvita, la poetessa," in *Medioevo al femminile*, ed. Ferruccio Bertini et al. (Rome: Laterza, 1993), 63–95; Peter Dronke, "Hrotsvitha," in *Women Writers of the Middle Ages*, 55–83; Armando Bisanti, *Un ventennio di studi su Rosvita di Gandersheim* (Spoleto: CISAM, 2005); Phyllis R. Brown and Stephen L. Wailes, eds., *A Companion to Hrotsvit of Gandersheim (fl. 960): Contextual and Interpretative Approaches*, CCT 34 (Leiden: Brill, 2013). For an essentially informational work, see Carla Del Zotto, *Rosvita: La poetessa degli imperatori sassoni* (Milan: Jaca Book, 2009).

phus, Pelagius, Theophilus, Basilius, Dionysius, and *Agnes*), all in leonine hexameters except for one in elegiac couplets, which is the only one to deal with an actual event: the martyrdom of young Pelagius (d. 925), killed for having refused the advances of the Caliph of Cordova. The second book, also written in two stages and published by 965, contains six plays in rhyming prose on stories of martyrdom (*Dulcitius* and *Sapientia*), the redemption of courtesans (*Abraham* and *Paphnutius*), and conversions to the true faith (*Calimachus* and *Gallicanus*). After the plays, the manuscript provides thirty-five hexameters consisting of the captions (*tituli*) to fourteen scenes of the Apocalypse. The third book, more connected in subject matter to the court, contains two epic historic poems: the first is on Otto I (the *Gesta Ottonis*, in 1,517 hexameters, composed at the request of Gerberga II and the archbishop of Mainz, William) and was finished before 968, while the second regards the origins of the convent at Gandersheim (*Primordia coenobii Gandeshemensis*, in 600 hexameters) and is her last work, completed no earlier than 973.

In the case of the first two books, it was Hrotsvit who chose the subject, initially proceeding in secret and with many uncertainties (praef. 1.6), but she later gained confidence to the point where she wished to submit her writings to the judgment of her scholarly contemporaries and requested their opinions. Her decision to write moral plays, however unworthy, in opposition to the morally questionable but very much admired plays of Terence shows us a woman aware of her literary abilities and determined to make them known. This awareness, which shines through in spite of her repeated and conventional declarations of inability, is evident even in the way the author defines herself: *clamor validus*, "vigorous voice" (praef. 2.3). As Jacob Grimm first noted, through this New Testament connection, Hrotsvit translates the meaning of her name into Latin, and the translation can be understood as "powerful witness" for God or as "vigorous affirmation" of Christian truth.[64] As Peter Dronke observes, however, for a reader of the time, *clamor validus* would have brought to mind the *ego vox*

---

64. Jacob Grimm, *Lateinische Gedichte des 10. und 11. Jahrhunderts* (Göttingen: Dieterich, 1838), 9. For the New Testament origin of the connection, see Walter Berschin, in his edition of Hrotsvit, *Opera omnia* (Munich: Teubner, 2001), vii (this is the latest critical edition of Hrotsvit's oeuvre) recalls Heb 5:7: *cum clamore valido et lacrimis offerens et exauditus pro sua reverentia*. On the two possible meanings of the Latin translation, see Katharina M. Wilson, *Hrotsvit of Gandersheim: A Florilegium of Her Works* (Cambridge: Boydell and Brewer, 1998), 4.

clamantis ("I am the voice of the one calling") with which John the Baptist identifies (John 1:23) and at the same time would have alluded to the uproar caused by a work presenting itself as a Christian attempt to counter Terence.[65]

Among the many writings on Christian subjects occupying the first two books, the Bible is directly referenced only in the thirty-five verses commenting on the fourteen scenes of a figurative cycle on the Apocalypse, thus placing the author in symbolic continuity with the *Dittochaeum* by Prudentius, the Christian author she most often recalls.[66] Having been asked to provide the captions for an iconographic subject determined by others, the author had minimal ability to interpret. Although the depictions regard themes dear to her (the struggle between heaven and hell, the rewarding of saints and martyrs, the tribute that the heavenly host pays to divine majesty), Hrotsvit's favorite subjects that are most emphasized are: the testimony of faith and, even more so, the glorification of chastity and virginity in particular.[67] Therefore, it is significant that her only personal contribution is, at line 1, the characterization of John as a "virgin" (*virgo*). This is not required to explain the images, but it underlines the apostle's adherence to that which the author believes is the most perfect way of life.

The importance that Hrotsvit attaches to martyrdom and chastity emerges clearly from the hagiographical subjects forming the base of her writings. The passions and legends she puts into verse or plays take on varying themes that are not always obvious: the theme of the pact with the devil (in the short poems *Theophilus* and *Basilius*), destined to have a great success; the tale of the martyr Dionysius, who after his own decapitation picks up his head and brings it with him to his burial site; and the story of Gongulphus, a lay protagonist more like a knight than a martyr. While the series of short poems ends with praising Agnes, who brings together the dual merits of virginity and martyrdom, the pious canoness has no qualms about discussing two legends of repentant women sinners in the plays *Abraham* and *Paphnutius*.

In a work thus characterized that gives ample space to women (positive figures, with the sole exception of the Gongulphus's wife), Hrotsvit's knowledge of the Bible can be clearly seen in her lexical choices (for which

---

65. Dronke, *Women Writers*, 70.
66. Helene Homeyer, ed., *Hrotsvite opera* (Munich: Schöningh, 1970), 494–95.
67. Homeyer, *Hrotsvite opera*, 378.

her familiarity with liturgical practice is also of importance), in some citations that are of an authoritative value and in reference exempla and episodes that she often finds in her models. She maintains a relationship with these models that is not always easy to define. We do not always know the prose text on which her rewriting was based, and any possible changes could be entirely or partly dependent on her further readings and, above all, on the need for a more effective expression.[68]

Only two short poems out of eight (*Maria* and the *De ascensione Domini*) and one play out of six (*Calimachus*) deal with biblical figures, specifically the Virgin Mary and the apostle John, but the events regarding them do not derive from the New Testament; this is because the author preferred apocryphal stories to the canonical books.

The last of the three in chronological order of composition, the play *Calimachus* (the complete title is *Resuscitatio Drusianae et Calimachi*, "The Resurrection of Drusianae and Calimachus") retells an episode from the apocryphal Acts of John. The tale is set in the city of Ephesus, where the young Callimachus falls madly in love with Drusiana, the wife of Andronicus, with whom she lives in chastity. Though his friends try to dissuade him, Callimachus makes his amorous advances to the woman, who prays to God to let her die so as not to bring about the young man's damnation. Her request is fulfilled, and after the funeral, John learns of the reason for her death from Andronicus. In the meantime, Callimachus, who cannot rid himself of his lust, corrupts Fortunatus, Andronicus's steward, so that he can enter Drusiana's tomb and possess her while dead, as he could not do when she was alive. Having penetrated the tomb, the two have already unwrapped her shroud, the body now covered by a single veil, when a snake slithers out, killing Fortunatus and causing Callimachus to fall to the ground, where the snake lies upon his body. The next day, the third day after Drusiana's death, John and Andronicus go to the tomb, where a handsome, smiling young man tells them that he has come for Drusiana—who has just barely escaped violence and whom the apostle will resuscitate—and for him who lies next to her tomb. John then sees Callimachus, on his back and with an enormous snake lying atop him, and Fortunatus, dead. John drives out the snake and resuscitates first Callimachus, who confesses his offense and converts, and then Drusiana, who asks John for permission

---

68. On Hrotsvit's sources and readings, see Katrinette Bodarwé, "*Sanctimoniales Litteratae*," in *Schriftlichkeit und Bildung in den ottonischen Frauenkommunitäten Gandersheim, Essen und Quedlinburg* (Münster: Aschendorff, 2004), 309–15.

to resuscitate Fortunatus. Fortunatus has no desire to return to life among such virtuous people, however, so he flees. After celebrating the Eucharist, John has the revelation that Fortunatus is about to die from the snake's poison, and the events confirm his prediction.

The innovation that Hrotsvit produces when compared to the Acts of John mainly concerns the characterization and interaction of the figures. Callimachus's letter is replaced with a direct conversation with the woman. Drusiana is worried about the ruin that her beauty may cause in that tender young man (*delicato juveni*), but her suffering could also be due to her fear of yielding.[69] Callimachus appears moved by sincere affection and not just by lust. Fortunatus is utterly wicked, as he invites Callimachus to violate the deceased woman ("There's the body—she looks asleep, / Her face is not that of a corpse, / Nor are her limbs corrupt— / Use her as you will"; 7.1).[70] After Fortunatus's resurrection, he has difficulty accepting what has happened and wishes to die so as not to witness the good of others ("If, as you maintain, / Drusiana brought me back to life, / And Callimachus believes in Christ, / I, of my own free will, choose death over life— / I prefer not to exist at all, / Than to see him so overfull with the Power of Grace"; 9.28), and the instant death that seizes him is consistent with this radicalization.[71]

In comparison with the Latin model, besides this emphasis on the completely evil character of Fortunatus, the most remarkable element may be the lesser role given to the apostle. John makes some sententious comments, but on the whole he is given less space than in the Apocrypha. This is not only because he is also the protagonist of other events, but also because he speaks at greater length there. In the Acts of John, he dedicates a sermon to the death of Drusiana, of which there is no trace in *Calimachus*. The tone of his speech is also different when he prays for Callimachus's resurrection in *Calimachus*. His convoluted speech does not occur in the Apocrypha ("O Inscrutable and wondrous God, / Thou alone art what Thou art, / Thou canst mix the elements, and create man, / And,

---

69. This has been suggested by Ferruccio Bertini, *Il "teatro" di Rosvita: Con un saggio di traduzione del "Calimachus"* (Genua: Tilgher, 1979), 129–36, chap. 4 (interpretation of *Calimachus*); and, previously, by Gustavo Vinay, *Alto medioevo latino: Conversazioni e no* (Naples: Guida, 1978), 512–32.

70. Translation from Larissa Bonfante, trans., *The Plays of Hrotswitha of Gandersheim: Bilingual Edition*, ed. Robert Chipok (Mundelein, IL: Bolchazy-Carducci, 2013), 156–57 (Latin and English on facing pages).

71. Translation from Bonfante, *Plays of Hrotswitha of Gandersheim*, 180–81.

separating the elements, dissolve him. / Grant this Callimachus breath and make him whole again").[72] It is difficult to ascertain whether Hrotsvit is motivated by the wish to instruct or the desire to demonstrate her skill (and I would tend toward the second hypothesis).

In any case, what appears important is that Hrotsvit's choice does not involve a text of particular theological or didactic weight but is rather oriented toward a model that lends itself to dramatic, surprising developments. It is true that Drusiana is a champion of chastity, but her story might attract the interest of readers and listeners, although it is unlikely that the plays were performed, due to its two sinful themes: the courtship of a Christian, married woman and, above all, necrophilia, which is only avoided at the last moment. The values proclaimed by this text are always the same, as is the final triumph of faith and chastity. The suspicion remains, however, that the author's choice had settled on the Apocrypha because it offered a particularly well-suited plot for constructing a play of remarkable, dramatic strength, rich in suspense.

The importance of Hrotsvit's choice of models also stands out in the short poem on the ascension (*De ascensione Domini*), which draws its material from the canonical texts but presents a different version of the events; it also contains the annunciation to Mary of her future heavenly glory. Hrotsvit says that she based her work on the translation of a Greek text that has not survived and was attributed to an otherwise unidentified bishop John. There are 150 hexameters in total, about half of which are devoted to speeches made by the resurrected Christ. The first is the investiture of the apostles (*Ascens. Dom.* 23–74); the second, shorter speech (vv. 77–93), is his taking leave of his mother; the third, finally, is his farewell to his disciples (vv. 109–112), who are immediately afterward reassured by *duo viri* who predict the return of Christ during the judgment (vv. 122–126). In the meantime, with his lyre in heaven, David sings of Christ's arrival (vv. 101–102 and 104–106), and, finally, God the Father expresses his satisfaction with his Son (vv. 134–140).

Both the speeches and the narrative sections lean considerably toward instruction from the very beginning, which summarizes Christ's earthly vicissitudes, specifying how the absence of original sin prevented him from being caught in the tight snares of death.[73] The didactic tone is maintained

---

72. Translation from Bonfante, *Plays of Hrotswitha of Gandersheim*, 164–65.
73. The absence of original sin had already been stated in Hrotsvit, vv. 17–18: *nec*

in Jesus's first speech, in which—between two broadsides against the wicked Judeans—he recalls having created man and the world with his own hands (*Ascens. Dom.* 44–45). The importance of virginity stands out in his speech when he takes leave of his mother, through the remark on entrusting the Virgin—the most chaste among women and the only one worthy of generating him (*inveni solam prae cunctis te quia castam / condignamque meum corpus generasse sacratum*; vv. 82–83)—to the care of John, the disciple who shines with the jewels of virginity (v. 91). The divine status of the resurrected Christ is authenticated by the voice of God the Father, who is pleased with him (vv. 134–135). The voice uses words that recall the episode of the baptism of Christ and that refer to the image—taken from Ps 110:1—of the enemies made to serve as God's footstool (vv. 139–140).

The entrusting of Mary to John, which occurred during the crucifixion in the gospels (John 19:26), is here shifted to the moment of the ascension: the Son promises the Virgin that when she leaves this world, not only will he send her to the heavenly host, but he will also personally come to gather her blessed soul and place it in the kingdom of heaven. In the fate reserved for Mary—a fate of which nothing is said in the canonical gospels—we have seen the influence of that apocryphal tale that circulated in the West from a Latin translation under the title *Liber de transitu beatae Mariae Virginis*. It seems to me that Hrotsvit's text does not authorize this interpretation, for what is being emphasized here is only the special welcome that the soul of the mother of God receives in heaven immediately after death; there is no mention of the passage of her body. On the other hand, the ambiguity of the expression *de mundo discedere* ("leave the world"; v. 84) could refer to a normal death, to the ascension of the body after death, or to its being transferred to heaven without passing through death.[74]

Unfortunately, our ignorance of Hrotsvit's source makes it impossible to define the character and breadth of her personal contribution, but it remains true that—both in the absence and presence of substantial changes—the author alone is responsible for her text. Compared to the assumption of the Virgin, which had been proclaimed by Pope Sergius

---

mortis vinclis se posse tenerier artis, / qui solus culpae fuerat sine sordibus Adae; and even earlier in verse 4: *qui solus maculis potuit sine vivere cunctis*.

74. On the Apocrypha relating to the assumption and the difference between the assumption (occurring by passing through death) or the passage (*transitus*) of Mary to heaven, see Enrico Norelli, "Maria negli apocrifi," in Piastra, *Studi di mariologia medievale*, 19–63, esp. 35–61.

I (687–701 CE) and was also supported by Ambrose Autpert (d. 784) in his *Sermo de assumptione*, Hrotsvit has maintained a cautious attitude, whether by choice or because she agreed to follow the model. The poet, who was not yet thirty when writing her second poetic essay, composed a *summa* on the meaning of the ascension, the central role of the Virgin, and the importance of virginity, which was to be submitted to the nuns and canonesses of Gandersheim but also to its learned readers outside the cloister. The poem's conclusion singles out the readers when the author addresses them to ask for intercession with that God whom she has praised: "Whoever may read these verses, say with a compassionate spirit: 'Merciful King, pardon and have mercy on the humble Hrotsvit and enable her to continue to raise odes in your honor even to heaven, she, who, weaving your praises into verse, sung of your admirable deeds'" (*Ascens. Dom.* 147–150).

Mentioned several times in Hrotsvit's work, Mary is the protagonist of her earliest composition, which opens the collection of short poems: the "Story of the Birth and the Praiseworthy Life of the Intact Mother of God," which she attributed to James, brother of the Lord (*historia nativitatis laudabilisque conversationis intactae Dei genitricis quam scriptam repperi sub nomine sancti Iacobi fratris Domini*).[75] Actually, as Karl Strecker demonstrated in the early twentieth century, her source is not the Gospel of James but a Latin reworking of the Gospel of Pseudo-Matthew, which starts with the conception of Anna and ends with the infancy of Jesus, and which presumably dates to the first quarter of the seventh century.[76] Hrotsvit was the first to put it into verse, and, indeed, her poem is among the earliest testimonies to the developments within this apocryphal story.[77]

---

75. See Ferruccio Bertini, "La figura di Maria nell'opera di Rosvita," in *Maria di Nazaret nell'antica letteratura cristiana* (Genoa: D.AR.FI.CLET, 1993), 79–87; Monique Goullet, "Hrosvita de Gandersheim, *Maria*," in Iogna-Prat, Palazzo, and Russo, *Marie*, 441–70.

76. Karl Strecker, "Hrotsvits Maria und Pseudo-Matthaeus," in *Jahresbericht des Gymnasium zu Dortmund* (Grüwell: Crüwell, 1902), 3–23. Jan Gijsel shows that this is the most likely date within a chronological range going from the mid-sixth century to the end of the eighth (*Libri de Nativitate Mariae: Pseudo-Matthaei Evangelium* [Turnhout: Brepols, 1997], 59–67).

77. Around 800, this text must have circulated in two different editions, the original one (A) and a second, more carefully edited one (P): Hrotsvit's text descends from one of the two branches of the latter, and hers is the third oldest in the tradition, as it

In this long composition (891 verses, the longest of her short poems), we can identify not only some minor changes, often dictated by literary and stylistic motivations, but also a definite tendency toward narration and direct interventions on the part of the author. In recalling the events, Hrotsvit accentuates the special bond tying Mary to Christ and distancing Mary from Joseph. This is a leitmotif of the entire poem, characterized by a close connection between the power of the child Jesus and his mother, who shares with him a position at the forefront.[78]

Among her more significant personal interventions, we especially recall the poem in elegiac couplets (vv. 13–44), in which the young poet asks the virgin to assist her (v. 17, *adesse*) in composing the poem. Another of Hrotsvit's contributions is the symbolic value inherent in her characterization of Joachim, future father of the Virgin, as a good shepherd (vv. 58–63); it is one of those exegetical expansions that have characterized the Christian epic from its beginnings. There are also some reflections, which are absent in Pseudo-Matthew, on the Virgin as intermediary of the redemption and the return of humanity to its status before original sin (vv. 209–225) and on Mary as mother of the Savior (vv. 299–311). Finally, there is the declaration (vv. 527–542) of omitting certain events (included, moreover, in Pseudo-Matthew) that are recalled only through apophasis: the conversation between Mary and the angel, Joseph's sadness when he discovers Mary to be pregnant, and the manner in which he is consoled.[79]

Two changes aimed at eliminating inconsistencies in the prose text must be added to this list. Pseudo-Matthew (9:1) has two distinct annunciations: the first at a fountain and the other two days later, while the Virgin is spinning scarlet thread. Hrotsvit keeps only the second. The other revision, a delicate one from a theological viewpoint, concerns the pregnancy of Anne, the long-barren wife of the priest Joachim (the entire story is inspired by that of Elizabeth and Zechariah, parents of John the Baptist).

---

derives from a prose text very close to that of the Vatican Palatine Latin Codex 430, which dates to the first half of the ninth century; see Jan Gijsel, "Zu welcher Textfamilie des Pseudo-Matthäus gehört die Quelle von Hrosvits Maria?," *CM* 32 (1980): 279–88, esp. 282–83.

78. This aspect is thoroughly explained by Helene Scheck, *Reform and Resistance: Formations of Female Subjectivity in Early Medieval Ecclesiastical Culture* (Albany: State University of New York Press, 2008), 144–47.

79. Rijkel Ten Kate, "Hrosvits *Maria* und das Evangelium des Pseudo-Matthäus," *CM* 22 (1961): 195–204, esp. 203–4.

The Gospel of James gave a rough sketch of a miraculous conception *in absentia* (4:2); Pseudo-Matt. 3 implicitly corrects this by stating that Anne was already pregnant when Joachim left the city, disheartened by the accusation of not being pleasing to God, who had denied him descendants.[80] It does not, however, leave out the claim of barrenness that the slave makes to Anne at the moment when—on the very foundation of the story in Pseudo-Matthew—the latter must be aware that she is expecting a child. Hrotsvit eliminates the inconsistency, shifting the conception to after Joachim's return: his wife's pregnancy, which the angel announces to him, is set in the immediate future (*mox praenobilis Anna / concipiet*; vv. 180–181), and when Anne sees her husband again, she expresses her happiness at the possibility of conceiving a son (who in fact will be born nine months later).[81]

The contributions most significant to us are those of the author, which clarify, on the one hand, the role that she attributes to the Virgin in relation to Christ and, on the other, that which she grants herself. Besides the obvious mentions of Mary as a new Eve who redeems humanity and the allusions to her virginal conception, in its first two verses, the poem affirms the Virgin's power and majesty as the sole hope of the world, "glorious lady of the heavens" (*dominatrix inclita caeli*; v. 13), "holy mother of the heavenly king" (*sancta parens regis*; v. 14), and shining star of the sea. We have here a preview of some themes that recur in the poem but also in later texts. The royalty and power of the Virgin would in fact form the basis of her action in *Teophilus*, in which Mary's mediation would permit the repentant culprit to break his pact with the devil. In it, Mary is granted sovereignty over heaven and the world with expressions very similar to those of this first short poem: "mother of the eternal one, lady of the world" (*aeterni genitrix, eadem mundi dominatrix*; v. 208) and "powerful lady of the heavens"

---

80. See Ps.-Matt. 3:2, versions A and P, in which the angel says to Joachim *quam* [scil. Annam] *scias ex semine tuo concepisse filium*.

81. The inconsistency in Pseudo-Matthew, which Hrotsvit appears to have resolved, has already been brought to light by Strecker, *Hrosvits Maria*, 8–9, who is uncertain whether to attribute its correction to her or to one of her sources. But *concepi gaudia prolis* in verse 261, referring to a future pregnancy, has all the appearance of being a correction of a simple *concepi* that Hrotsvit must have read in her source; see Gijsel, "Zu welcher Textfamilie," 286–87. The same solution is adopted in the apocryphal *De nativitate Mariae*, a reworking of Pseudo-Matthew after 868–869; see Rita Beyers, ed., *Libri de nativitate Mariae: Libellus de nativitate sanctae mariae*, CCSA 10 (Turnhout: Brepols, 1997), 221–22 and 228. See also Gijsel, "Zu welcher Textfamilie," 286–87.

(*potens dominatrix / caelorum*; vv. 333-334). In *Teophilus*, Hrotsvit takes a bold step further and associates the Virgin with one or more figures in the Trinity: she is mentioned along with the Father and the Son (vv. 165-166) and with the Holy Spirit (vv. 179-180). As in the prose source, Theophilus is guilty of having turned away from the Son and the Mother (vv. 214-215).

Another element that recurs not only in the poem on the Virgin is the definition of Mary as a "star of the sea" (*stella maris*), previously mentioned by Isidore of Seville (*Maria inluminatrix, sive stella maris*; *Etym.* 7.10.1), who here comments on the pronunciation of the name chosen for her and communicated by God himself (*Maria* 275-276).[82] This definition would return in the play *Abraham* when the old hermit Ephrem explains to the protagonist, Mary, the meaning of her name: "Mary means 'star of the sea,' because the world moves around her and the celestial axis turns on her" (2.3).

Given the dominant position she assigns the Virgin, Hrotsvit appears to be in keeping with a trend that may not yet have been shared by the majority, but it certainly had precedents. Alcuin had defined the Virgin as the Queen of Heaven and Mother of God, invoking her intercession.[83] After all, the controversy of the late eighth and early ninth centuries against adoptionism to prove Christ's original divinity had insisted on the power of intercession that Mary enjoys as mother of God (Theotokos). This same power of intercession was attested to between the tenth and eleventh centuries in Reichenau, in a miniature with captions, and in a hymn mentioning both Christ's descent to earth so as to lead his Mother to heaven (this is the promise made to her in Hrotsvit's *Ascensio*, but with the added, explicit reference to the Virgin's *transitus*) and the salvation of Theophilus by her hand.[84]

---

82. In *Maria* 276, it is the voice of God who orders that the newborn girl be called Mary: *"stella maris" lingua quod consonat ergo latina.*

83. Alcuin, *Inscriptiones in monasterio S. Petri Salisburgensi* 16.2 (*regina polorum*); 18.2 (*Christi mater*); *Inscriptiones locorum sacrorum* 110.4.1 (*regina, dei genitrix, virgo Maria*); 12.6 (*regina poli*). See, respectively, Ernst Dümmler, Ludwig Traube, Paul Winterfeld, and Karl Strecker, eds, *Poetae Latini aevi Carolini*, 4 vols, MGH (Munich: Weidmann, 1978), 1:338, 339, 341, and 355.

84. *Anal. hymn.* 51, 211, stanza 22 (descent of Christ) and stanzas 32 and 35 (Theophilus); see Homeyer, *Hrotsvite opera*, 153. Éric Palazzo, however, points to a manuscript from the second half of the tenth century (Paris Bibl. de l'Arsenal 610 fol. 25v) from Reichenau-Mittelzell, containing a miniature of a rare iconography that depicts the Virgin interceding with the Lord, with the following verses above the

Thus, in this, Hrotsvit is not original, and she had perhaps been commissioned to write it. In fact, it is likely that the short poem on the Virgin was composed at the same time as the founding of a Benedictine community at Gandersheim that was subordinate to Hrotsvit's abbey and referred to a church dedicated to Mary. In any case, she retains the merit for having anticipated through her writings that development of the devotion to the Virgin that would only be brought about at the Ottonian court some years later, with the arrival of the Byzantine princess Theophanu, wife of Otto II; she would bring up her daughters at Gandersheim, which from 973 on would be exclusively for canonesses.[85]

The poem is also of interest due to the logical transition in which Hrotsvit goes so far as to associate the Virgin with God in her request for inspiration. Since Mary has carried the King of the universe in her womb (vv. 29–30), the poet hopes that he who ordered Balaam's donkey to speak and who made the Mother of his Son different from all others due to her merits may loosen her tongue and permit her to sing of him and the Virgin. Thus Hrotsvit would avoid being condemned for laziness and would one day join the wise virgins through the merit acquired in composing the poem (vv. 39–44). In this somewhat contorted way, the author sets up a kind of collaboration between the Virgin and God for her own benefit: the former is called upon to assist her, the latter to inspire her. While the reference to Balaam's donkey is rather common (we saw it in Dhuoda as well), the use of the parable of the foolish virgins to justify the decision to compose poetry—indeed, to present it as a duty—is entirely original. Arming herself with the gospel, Hrotsvit thus manages to transform her unauthorized gesture of self-affirmation into an act of duty, one that would be a serious guilt to neglect.

---

image: *aurea stella maris, regalis virgula floris / supplicat hic genito virgo Maria suo. / ut clemens famulis gratissima dona salutis / dignetur ferre matris honore suae.* See Palazzo, "Marie et l'élaboration d'un espace ecclésial au haut Moyen Âge," in Iogna-Prat, Palazzo, and Russo, *Marie*, 313–25, esp. 319 and the reproduction of the folio on 325.

85. Patrick Corbet, "Les impératrices ottoniennes et le modèle marial: Autour de l'ivoire du château Sforza de Milan," in Iogna-Prat, Palazzo, and Russo, *Marie*, 109–35. The transformation of the church dedicated to Mary into a Benedictine convent dates to before 973 ("Impératrices ottoniennes," 112). The possibility, raised by Wilson (*Hrotsvit of Gandersheim: A Florilegium*, 9), that the choice of themes of Greek origin was due to Hrostvit having frequented the empress Theophanu is unacceptable for chronological reasons, as she had arrived in Germany only in 973—that is, well after the composition of Hrotsvit's first two books.

Another indication of her poetic intentions is the declaration that she would leave out some episodes that need no mention because they are all found in the canonical gospels (v. 538) and exceed her meager strength (v. 539).[86] In omitting these well-known stories, she reveals her preference for the episodes that appear to have been recalled in church less frequently (verses 540–542). Considerations of this kind often appear in the Apocrypha,[87] but here the topos also serves to motivate the criteria for the author's choice and her preference for noncanonical texts.

Hrotsvit had previously justified her use of apocryphal sources in the preface to the poems:

> If, then, I am rebuked for having drawn some poems of this book from apocryphal works, *as some believe* [emphasis added], this is not the result of bold presumption but rather is an error due to my ignorance, because when I began to weave the plot of this series of compositions, I was unaware that some of the texts on which I had decided to work were of dubious authenticity. But when I learned of it, I wished not to destroy them, because that which today seems false perhaps one day will be proven and recognized as true. (praef. 2s)[88]

Hrotsvit offers two justifications, one after the other. In the first, she points the finger at her own initial ignorance, which led her to consider the noncanonical texts valid. In the second, she explains that, having learned of the dubious authenticity of her sources, she decided not to destroy her poems because one day the truthfulness of the texts she had used might be proven.

Evaluating the weight and meaning of these statements is no simple task, but one fact is evident: though she was still a beginner, and despite her repeated professions of modesty, Hrotsvit was convinced of the value of her writings, such that she decided to have them circulated and to submit

---

86. Verse 538: *haec evangelici demonstrant cuncta libelli*. Actually, with respect to her source, Hrotsvit also leaves out the trial of the bitter water, missing from the canonical texts but included in Pseudo-Matt. 12, and does so without advising her readers.

87. Their appearance in the Apocrypha has already been noted by Strecker, *Hrosvits Maria*, 5–6, in relation to verses 538–42.

88. Praef. 2s.: *si autem obicitur, quod quaedam huius operis juxta quorundam aestimationem sumpta sint ex apocrifis, non est crimen praesumptionis iniquae, sed error ignorantiae, quia, quando huius stamen seriei coeperam ordiri, ignoravi dubia esse in quibus disposui laborare. at ubi recognovi, pessumdare detrectavi, quia, quod videtur falsitas, forsan probabitur esse veritas.*

them for the evaluation of scholars.[89] It is for them that she must justify her use of the Apocrypha, and she does so by relativizing their unreliability ("as some believe"), which in the future could be disproved ("because that which today seems false, perhaps one day will be proven and recognized as true"). It has been said that in this statement the truth would be affirmed in rhetorical rather than empirical terms, in that Hrotsvit—being unable to guarantee the reliability of her sources—appears to substitute objective truth for the truth of her intentions.[90] Perhaps, however, there is a simpler explanation.

In addition to being supported by a skillful use of rhetoric, Hrotsvit's thoughts reflect opinions present within the church, in which debate was raging on the Apocrypha and the legitimacy of their use in the liturgy, with special attention given to texts on Mary.[91] Not only was the church divided on the need to exclude the Apocrypha from the list of permitted readings, but it had also encouraged their use even in iconography, whether in individual depictions or figurative cycles. Certain episodes, such as the angel feeding the child Mary at the annunciation by the well and the Virgin spinning scarlet thread for the incredulous midwife, had already been documented between the fifth and sixth centuries.[92] In times closer to Hrotsvit, the interest in apocryphal stories on the Virgin is dem-

---

89. Concerning this point, in addition to Dronke, *Women Writers*, 65–68, see the recent Scheck, *Reform and Resistance*, 134–35.

90. Katharina M. Wilson, *Hrotsvit of Gandersheim: The Ethics of Authorial Stance*, DMTS 7 (Leiden: Brill, 1988), 5.

91. Antonio Acerbi, "Gli apocrifi tra 'auctoritas' e 'veritas,'" in *La Bibbia nel Medio Evo*, ed. Giuseppe Cremascoli and Claudio Leonardi (Bologna: Edizioni Dehoniane, 1996), 109–39; on the controversy that pitted Hincmar of Reims (who was in favor of the liturgical use of Pseudo-Matthew and of the *Transitus Mariae*) against Ratramnus in the mid-ninth century, and regarding the import of the Pseudo-Gelasian Decree, which placed the Apocrypha among the *non recepti* books, see esp. 121–29.

92. Louis Réau, in *Nouveau Testament*, part 2 of *Iconographie de la bible*, vol. 2 of *Iconographie de l'art chrétien* (Paris: Presses Universitaires de France, 1956), points out a marble tablet in Saint-Maximin in Provence carved with the depiction of Mary being fed by an angel (fifth century) (167); in Milan, a sixth-century Byzantine ivory carving with the Virgin at the well (178); the Virgin spinning thread portrayed in the fifth-century mosaic in Santa Maria Maggiore, in the sixth-century mosaic in Ravenna, and on the ivory Throne of Maximian (179). Of the two midwives, the incredulous Salome began to be depicted in the sixth century (again on the Throne of Maximian), while Zelomi was only portrayed starting in the second half of the eleventh; see Hélène Toubert, "La Vierge et les sages-femmes: Un jeu iconographique entre les évangiles

onstrated by both the figurative cycle on the entire story of Joachim and of Anne, which Leo III (795–816) had ordered to be depicted on the walls of Saint Paul's in the early ninth century; by the Marian cycle at San Vincenzo al Volturno; and finally by the frescoes of Santa Maria a Castelseprio, painted no later than the first half of the tenth century, which gave the Virgin a central role and are partly dedicated to her infancy.[93]

Therefore, we ought not be surprised by the use of apocryphal sources, nor wonder why Hrotsvit had chosen precisely and only those, favoring them over canonical texts. An explanation for this preference could certainly come from the prominent role of the hagiographical *lectiones* in the Benedictine office.[94] In the case of *Maria*, we could add the concordance of the Benedictine model with the life that the Virgin led in the temple, and we could add the possibility of a broader and more detailed illustration of the requirements for a life serving God.[95] It has also been suggested, not incorrectly, that the image of the Virgin weaving purple thread (vv. 362–363) might evoke the weaving of purple and gold silk in the splendor of the Ottonian court.[96] Thus there is a glimmer of a further reason, one less pious and more profane, that may have guided Hrotsvit's choice of the theme and sources as early as *Maria*, the first work of a young author, who nonetheless had a well-defined literary personality: a *Lust zu fabulieren*, a fondness for narrating and entertaining that is not fulfilled by creating works for instruction. Encouraged by a learned abbess and having a foreseeable audience in both the noblewomen of Gandersheim and in a court that hosted for varying lengths of time figures such as Archbishop Bruno of Cologne (brother and chancellor of Otto I and a fervent admirer of Terence), Ratherius of

---

apocryphes et le drame liturgique," in Iogna-Prat, Palazzo, and Russo, *Marie*, 327–60, esp. 335.

93. On the depiction in Saint Paul's, see Gijsel, *Die Quelle*, 288. For the centrality of the Virgin in the frescoes of Santa Maria a Castelseprio, see the reconstruction by Paula D. Leveto, "The Marian Theme of the Frescoes in S. Maria at Castelseprio," *ArtBul* 72 (1990): 393–413.

94. Wilson, *Hrotsvit of Gandersheim: A Florilegium*, 1.

95. See Scheck, *Reform and Resistance*, 144: "Mary provides a model for monastic women." See also Stephen L. Wailes, "The Sacred Stories in Verse," in Brown and Wailes, *A Companion to Hrotsvit of Gandersheim*, 85–120, esp. 95–103.

96. Jane Stevenson, "Hrotsvit in Context: Convents and Culture in Ottonian Germany," in Brown and Wailes, *A Companion to Hrotsvit of Gandersheim*, 47.

Verona, or Liutprand of Cremona, Hrotsvit found in literary activity not just a way to educate but also a chance to assert her own gifts as a writer.[97]

This is a trait that Hrotsvit shared with Dhuoda, and it is not the only one. These two noblewomen, who were always ready to reiterate their inferiority as women, never gave up the right—which is also a privilege—to personally choose the texts to be considered and the moral lessons to be drawn from them. In this sense, there is a strong suspicion that canonical and apocryphal Scripture might also have been a lofty pretense to them, although we know not how consciously it was adopted. While the Bible served as a seal of authority for Dhuoda's instructional precepts, Hrotsvit found in biblical Apocrypha—no more and no less than in the legends of the saints—edifying subjects (at times not lacking in some objectionable traits), which enabled her to offer moral lessons without having to sacrifice the exhibition of her own talents through writings that pique the readers' interest while providing enjoyable entertainment.

Bibliography

Acerbi, Antonio. "Gli apocrifi tra 'auctoritas' e 'veritas.'" Pages 109–39 in *La Bibbia nel Medio Evo*. Edited by Giuseppe Cremascoli and Claudio Leonardi. Bologna: Edizioni Dehoniane, 1996.

Anton, Hans Hubert. *Fürstenspiegel und Herrscherethos in der Karolingerzeit*. Bonn: Rohrscheid, 1968.

Auty, Robert, et al., eds. *Lexikon des Mittelalters*. 10 vols. Munich: Artemis-Verlag, 1977–1999.

Bertini, Ferruccio. *Il "teatro" di Rosvita: Con un saggio di traduzione del "Calimachus."* Genua: Tilgher, 1979.

Bertini, Ferruccio. "La figura di Maria nell'opera di Rosvita." Pages 79–87 in *Maria di Nazaret nell'antica letteratura cristiana*. Genoa: D.AR.FI.CLET, 1993.

———. "Rosvita, la poetessa." Pages 63–95 in *Medioevo al femminile*. Edited by Ferruccio Bertini, Franco Cardini, Claudio Leonardi, and Mariateresa Fumagalli Beonio Brocchieri. Rome: Laterza, 1993.

Beyers, Rita, ed. *Libri de nativitate Mariae: Libellus de nativitate sanctae Mariae*. CCSA 10. Turnhout: Brepols, 1997.

---

97. On Hrotsvit and her audience, see the most recent Linda A. McMillin, "The Audiences of Hrotsvit," in Brown and Wailes, *A Companion to Hrotsvit of Gandersheim*, 311–27.

Bisanti, Armando. *Un ventennio di studi su Rosvita di Gandersheim*. Spoleto: CISAM, 2005.
Bodarwé, Katrinette. "*Sanctimoniales Litteratae.*" Pages 309–15 in *Schriftlichkeit und Bildung in den ottonischen Frauenkommunitäten Gandersheim, Essen und Quedlinburg*. Münster: Aschendorff, 2004.
Bonfante, Larissa, trans. *The Plays of Hrotswitha of Gandersheim: Bilingual Edition*. Edited by Robert Chipok. Mundelein, IL: Bolchazy-Carducci, 2013.
Brown, Phyllis R., and Stephen L. Wailes, eds. *A Companion to Hrotsvit of Gandersheim (fl. 960): Contextual and Interpretative Approaches*. CCT 34. Leiden: Brill, 2013.
Claussen, Martin A. "God and Man in Dhuoda's Liber Manualis." Pages 43–52 in *Women in the Church*. Edited by William J. Sheils and Diana Wood. Oxford: Blackwell, 1990.
Consolino, Franca Ela. "Dhuoda, la Bibbia e l'educazione dei figli." Pages 49–68 in *La Bibbia nell'interpretazione delle donne*. Edited by Claudio Leonardi, Francesco Santi, and Adriana Valerio. Florence: SISMEL, 2002.
Corbet, Patrick. "Les impératrices ottoniennes et le modèle marial: Autour de l'ivoire du château Sforza de Milan." Pages 109–35 in *Marie: Le culte de la Vierge dans la société médiévale*. Edited by Dominique Iogna-Prat, Éric Palazzo, and Daniel Russo. Paris: Beauchesne 1996.
Cullhed, Sigrid Schottenius, ed. *Proba the Prophet: The Christian Virginlian Cento of Faltonia Betitia Proba*. Translated by Sigrid Schottenius Cullhed. Leiden: Brill, 2015.
Curtius, Ernst Robert. *Europäische Literatur und lateinisches Mittelalter*. Bern: Francke, 1948.
———. *European Literature and the Latin Middle Ages*. Repr. ed. Princeton: Princeton University Press, 1990.
Deug-Su, I. "Gli specula." Pages 515–34 in vol. 1.2 of *Lo spazio letterario del Medioevo, Il Medioevo latino*. Edited by Guglielmo Cavallo, Claudio Leonardi and Enrico Menestò. Rome: Salerno, 1993.
Dronke, Peter. "Dhuoda," Pages 36–54 in in *Women Writers of the Middle Ages: A Critical Study of Texts from Perpetua (d. 203) to Marguerite Porete (d. 1310)*. Cambridge: Cambridge University Press, 1984.
———. "Hrotsvitha," Pages 55–83 in *Women Writers of the Middle Ages: A Critical Study of Texts from Perpetua (d. 203) to Marguerite Porete (d. 1310)*. Cambridge: Cambridge University Press, 1984.

———. *Women Writers of the Middle Ages: A Critical Study of Texts from Perpetua (d. 203) to Marguerite Porete (d. 1310)*. Cambridge: Cambridge University Press, 1984.

Dubreucq, Alain. "La littérature des *specula*: Délimitation du genre, contenu, destinataires et réception." Pages 17–39 in *Guerriers et moines: Conversion et sainteté aristocratique dans l'occident médiéval (IXe–XIIe siècle), Antibes 2002*. Edited by Michel Lauwers. Turnhout: Brepols, 2002.

Dümmler, Ernst, Ludwig Traube, Paul Winterfeld, and Karl Strecker, eds. *Poetae Latini aevi Carolini*. 4 vols. MGH. Munich: Weidmann, 1978.

Gijsel, Jan. *Libri de Nativitate Mariae: Pseudo-Matthaei Evangelium*. Turnhout: Brepols, 1997.

———. "Zu welcher Textfamilie des Pseudo-Matthäus gehört die Quelle von Hrosvits Maria?" *CM* 32 (1980): 279–88.

Goullet, Monique. "Hrosvita de Gandersheim, Maria." Pages 441–70 in *Marie: Le culte de la Vierge dans la société médiévale*. Edited by Dominique Iogna-Prat, Éric Palazzo, and Daniel Russo. Paris: Beauchesne 1996.

Gregory the Great. *Morales sur Job: Livres I et II*. Edited and translated by Robert Gillet and André De Gaudemaris. SC 32. Repr. ed. Paris: Cerf, 1975.

Grimm, Jacob, and Andreas Schmeller, eds. *Lateinische Gedichte des 10. und 11. Jahrhunderts*. Göttingen: Dieterich, 1838.

Heene, Katrien. *The Legacy of Paradise: Marriage, Motherhood and Women in Carolingian Edifying Literature*. New York: Lang, 1997.

Holder-Egger, O., ed. *Vita SS. Willibaldi et Wynniebaldi*. MGH SS 15. Hannover: Hahn, 1887.

Homeyer, Helene, ed. *Hrotsvite opera*. Munich: Schöningh, 1970.

Hrotsvit. *Opera Omnia*. Edited by Walter Berschin. Munich: Teubner, 2001.

Iogna-Prat, Dominique. "Le culte de la Vierge sous le règne de Charles le Chauve." Pages 65–98 in *Marie: Le culte de la Vierge dans la société médiévale*. Edited by Dominique Iogna-Prat, Éric Palazzo, and Daniel Russo. Paris: Beauchesne, 1996.

Jan, Régine Le. "Dhuoda ou l'opportunité du discours féminin." Pages 109–28 in *Agire da donna: Modelli e pratiche di rappresentazione (secoli VI–X)*. Edited by Cristina La Rocca. Turnhout: Brepols, 2007.

———. "The Multiple Identities of Dhuoda." Pages 211–19 in *Ego Trouble: Authors and Their Identities in the Early Middles Ages*, ed. Richard Cor-

radini, Matthew Gillis, Rosamund McKitterick, and Irene van Renswoude. Vienna: Österreichische Akademie der Wissenschaften, 2010.
Janssens, Bernadette. "L'étude de la langue et les citations latines dans le *Liber manualis* de Dhuoda: Un sondage." Pages 259–75 in *Aevum inter utrumque: Mélanges offerts à Gabriel Sanders*. Edited by Marc van Uytfanghe and Roland Demeulenaere. The Hague: Nijhoff Steenbrugis, 1991.
Kate, Rijkel Ten. "Hrosvits *Maria* und das Evangelium des Pseudo-Matthäus." *CM* 22 (1961): 195–204.
Krusch, Bruno, ed. *Scriptorum rerum Merovingicarum*. Vol. 2. MGH. Hannover: Hahn, 1888.
———, ed. *Scriptorum rerum Merovingicarum*. Vol. 4. MGH. Repr. Turnhout: Brepols, 2010.
Leveto, Paula D. "The Marian Theme of the Frescoes in S. Maria at Castelseprio." *ArtBul* 72 (1990): 393–413.
Luff, Robert. "Schreiben im Exil: Der 'Liber manualis' der frankischen Adeligen Dhuoda." *MJ* 35 (2000): 249–66.
Mayeski, Marie Anne. *Dhuoda: Ninth Century Mother and Theologian*. Scranton: University of Scranton Press, 1995.
McMillin, Linda A. "The Audiences of Hrotsvit." Pages 311–27 in *A Companion to Hrotsvit of Gandersheim (fl. 960): Contextual and Interpretative Approaches*. Edited by Phyllis R. Brown and Stephen L. Wailes. Leiden: Brill, 2013.
McNamara, Jo Ann, E. Gordon Whatley, and John E. Halborg, eds. *Sainted Women of the Dark Ages*. Durham: Duke University Press, 1992.
Moretti, Paola Francesca. "La Bibbia e il discorso dei Padri latini sulle donne: Da Tertulliano a Girolamo." Pages 137–73 in *Le donne nello sguardo degli antichi autori cristiani*. Edited by Kari Elisabeth Børresen and Emanuela Prinzivalli. Vol. 5.1 of *La Biblia e le donne*. Trapani: Il Pozzo di Giacobbe, 2013.
Neel, Carol. *Handbook for William: A Carolingian Woman's Counsel for Her Son*. Washington, DC: CUA Press, 1991.
Nelson, Janet L. "Dhuoda." Pages 106–20 in *Lay Intellectuals in the Carolingian World*. Edited by Patrick Wormald and Janet L. Nelson. Cambridge: Cambridge University Press, 2007.
———. "Gendering Courts in the Early Medieval West." Pages 185–97 in *Gender in the Early Medieval World: East and West*. Edited by Leslie Brubaker and Julia M. H. Smith. Cambridge: Cambridge University Press, 2004.

Norelli, Enrico. "Maria negli apocrifi." Pages 19–63 in *Gli studi di mariologia medievale: Bilancio storiografico*. Edited by Clelia Maria Piastra. Florence: SISMEL Edizioni del Galluzzo, 2001.

Orléans, Jonas d'. *Instruction des laics*. Edited by Odile Dubreucq. 2 vols. Translated by Odile Dubreucq. Sources Chrétiennes. SC 549–50. Paris: Cerf, 2012–2013.

———. *Le métier de roi*. Edited by Alain Dubreucq. SC 407. Paris: Cerf, 1995.

Palazzo, Éric. "Marie et l'élaboration d'un espace ecclésial au haut Moyen Âge." Pages 313–25 in *Marie: Le culte de la Vierge dans la société médiévale*. Edited by Dominique Iogna-Prat, Éric Palazzo, and Daniel Russo. Paris: Beauchesne, 1996.

Paola, Santorelli, ed. *La Vita Radegundis di Baudonivia*. Naples: D'Auria, 1999.

Parker, John Henry, J. G. F. Rivington, and J. Rivington, trans. *Morals on the Book of Job by St. Gregory the Great*. 3 vols. London: Parker, 1844.

Proba. *Il Centone*. Edited by Antonia Badini and Antonia Rizzi. Bologna: Dehoniane, 2011.

Réau, Louis. *Nouveau Testament*. Part 2 of *Iconographie de la bible*. Vol. 2 of *Iconographie de l'art chrétien*. Paris: Presses Universitaires de France, 1956.

Riché, Pierre. "La Bible de Dhuoda." *RAug* 33 (2003): 209–13.

———. "La Bible et la vie politique dans le haut Moyen Age." *Le Moyen Age et la Bible*. Edited by Pierre Riché and Guy Lobrichon. Paris: Beauchesne, 1984.

———. "Les bibliothèques de trois aristocrates latins carolingiens." *Le Moyen Âge* 69 (1963): 87–104.

———. *Dhuoda, Manuel pour mon fils*. Translated by Bernard de Vregille and Claude Mondésert. SC 225. Paris: Cerf, 1997.

———. *Éducation et culture dans l'Occident barbare*. 3rd ed. Paris: Seuil 1973.

Rouche, Michel. "Miroir des princes ou miroir du clergé?" Pages 341–64 in *Committenti e produzione artistico-letteraria nell'alto Medioevo occidentale, 4–10 aprile 1991*. SSAM 39. Spoleto: Centro italiano di studi sull' Alto Medioevo, 1992.

Savigni, Raffaele. "Gli 'specula' carolingi." Pages 23–48 in *Un ponte fra le culture: Studi medievistici di e per I Deug-su*. Edited by Claudio Leonardi, Francesco Stella, and Patrizia Stoppacci. Florence: SISMEL Edizioni del Galluzzo, 2009.

———. "Les laïcs dans l'écclésiologie carolingienne: Normes statutaires et idéal de 'conversion.'" Pages 41–92 in *Guerriers et moines: Conversion et sainteté aristocratique dans l'occident médiéval (IXe–XIIe siècle)*. Edited by Michel Lauwers. Turnhout: Brepols, 2002.

Scaravelli, Irene. "Per una mariologia carolingia: Autori, opere e linee di ricerca." Pages 65–85 in *Gli studi di mariologia medievale: Bilancio storiografico*. Edited by Clelia Maria Piastra. Florence: SISMEL Edizioni del Galluzzo, 2001.

Scheck, Helene. *Reform and Resistance: Formations of Female Subjectivity in Early Medieval Ecclesiastical Culture*. Albany: State University of New York Press, 2008.

Signori, Gabriela. *Maria zwischen Kathedrale, Kloster und Welt*. Sigmaringen: Thorbecke, 1995.

Stafford, Pauline. "Parents and Children in the Early Middle Ages." *EME* 10 (2001): 257–71.

Stevenson, Jane. "Hrotsvit in Context: Convents and Culture in Ottonian Germany." Pages 35–62 in *A Companion to Hrotsvit of Gandersheim (fl. 960): Contextual and Interpretative Approaches*. Edited by Phyllis R. Brown and Stephen L. Wailes. Leiden: Brill, 2013.

Stone, Rachel. "Kings Are Different: Carolingian Mirrors for Princes and Lay Morality." Pages 69–86 in *Le Prince au miroir de la littérature politique de l'Antiquité aux Lumières*. Edited by Frédérique Lachaud and Lydwine Scordia. Rouen-Le Havre: Publications des Universités de Rouen et du Havre, 2007.

Strecker, Karl. "Hrotsvits Maria und Pseudo-Matthaeus." Pages 3–23 in *Jahresbericht des Gymnasium zu Dortmund*. Grüwell: Crüwell, 1902.

Thiébaux, Marcelle, ed. *Dhuoda, Handbook for Her Warrior Son: Liber manualis*. Cambridge: Cambridge University Press, 1998.

Toubert, Hélène. "La Vierge et les sages-femmes: Un jeu iconographique entre les évangiles apocryphes et le drame liturgique." Pages 327–60 in *Marie: Le culte de la Vierge dans la société médiévale*. Edited by Dominique Iogna-Prat, Éric Palazzo, and Daniel Russo. Paris: Beauchesne 1996.

Veronese, Francesco, ed. Giona di Orléans, *Istruzioni di vita per i laici*. Pisa: Pacini, 2018.

Vinay, Gustavo. *Alto medioevo latino: Conversazioni e no*. Naples: Guida, 1978.

Wailes, Stephen L. "The Sacred Stories in Verse" Pages 85–120 in *A Companion to Hrotsvit of Gandersheim (fl. 960): Contextual and Interpreta-*

tive Approaches. Edited by Phyllis R. Brown and Stephen L. Wailes. Leiden: Brill, 2013.

Wasselynck, René. "Les 'Moralia in Job' dans les ouvrages de morale du haut moyen âge latin." *RTAM* 31 (1964): 5–31.

Wilson, Katharina M. *Hrotsvit of Gandersheim: A Florilegium of Her Works*. Cambridge: Boydell and Brewer, 1998.

———, ed. *Hrotsvit of Gandersheim: Rara avis in Saxonia?* Ann Arbor: Marc, 1987.

———. *Hrotsvit of Gandersheim: The Ethics of Authorial Stance*. DMTS 7. Leiden: Brill, 1988.

Zotto, Carla Del. *Rosvita: La poetessa degli imperatori sassoni*. Milan: Jaca Book, 2009.

The Reception of Biblical Texts and Their Normative Effect upon Marriage, Adultery, and Divorce from the Seventh to the Eleventh Century

Ines Weber

1. The Sinfulness of Man

In the following formula of endowment from the ninth century, the groom signed over the dowry, or matrimonial gift, to his bride so that they both could benefit from it:

> The supreme and ineffable Father, whose being prevails over all and permeates even the atoms themselves and the void through the originality of his nature, ... this higher being through the character of all good inhering in him, ... and through his likewise eternal and consubstantial wisdom, opens a resplendent living space of heavenly transcendence to five double rows of spiritual hosts that are created for the praise and glory of his name. These angelic choirs of the most subtle nature are each assigned their own special service and are honored with testimonials in accord with the will of their Creator.... Truly, that choir that, because of the illustriousness it had received at its creation thanks to divine generosity, had assumed the name of Lucifer, puffed itself up in self-adulation by forgetting to look upon the exquisiteness of its Creator and to feel awe before his transcendence. Deprived of its luminous aspect and black with every sin, it immediately plummeted into the depths of hell.... So, as one reads, the remaining hosts of heaven—horror-stricken by the ruin and demise of the wicked because they feared to fall in a similar manner—turned away from the crossroad of freedom to the incomplete and simple keeping of the good so that in no way could they be touched by the inclination to sin. This is why it is said that the human race had its beginning in such a manner that it may progress through obedience to glory, which the haughty one [that is, Lucifer] had lost because of irreparable guilt. Here, however, it is not to be understood that the good arbiter of all creatures wanted to fashion the increase of the human race in such

a way that the men might licentiously abuse all the women they might desire, but rather that the fidelity of marriage be preserved between man and woman, since he had betrothed the first created [that is, Adam] not to several women but only to one; for he said through the same saint and wise man: "A man will leave his father and mother and bind himself to his wife, and they will be two in one flesh." [Gen 2:24] Consequently, that one—who betroths a man to a virgin and decides that they should be two in one flesh—forbids the encroachment by a third person, man or woman, and fights against him or he, that is because of the discord that he [that is, the third person] has brought about between the two. This is supported by such explicit declarations from the New and Old Testament that it no longer needs to be corroborated through our arguments. (*Form. extr.* 1.13)[1]

Various aspects here draw the attention of the reader who is interested in questions concerning the reception of the Bible in the context of norma-

---

1. All translations are my own unless otherwise noted. For the Latin, see Karl Zeumer, ed., *Formulae Merowingici et Karolini aevi*, MGH (Turnhout: Brepols, 2010), 541–42: *summus et ineffabilis pater, cuius super essentia ipsas etiam athomos et inane principalitate naturae percurrit ... per insitam sibi, quamvis non temporaliter, totius boni formam, per coeternam videlicet ac consubstantialem sapientiam, bis quinis spiritualium catervarum ordinibus ad laudem et gloriam nominis sui conditis, caelicae sublimitatis splendifluum prestitit habitaculum. illi vero subtilissimae naturae angelici chori secundum beneplacitum Creatoris sui, aliis alii dispositi ministeriis et honorum decorati donariis.... verum chorus ille, qui ob claritatem, quam ex divina munificentia creando susceperat, nomen accepit Luciferi, dum sui conditoris excellentiam respicere maiestatemque revereri non meminit, sese mirans intumuit. nec mora, luculento habitu viduatus, in voraginem baratri omni turpitudine defuscatus corruit. tunc caetera celicorum agmina discrimine ac ruina scelestorum perculsa, dum similem casum timuerunt incurrere, de bivio libertatis imperfectum et simplicem bonitatis habitum sic leguntur evasisse, ut nequaquam amplius affeccio peccandi posset eos attingere. ea igitur causa genus humanum sumpsisse perhibetur originem, ut obediendo proficisceretur ad gloriam, quam superbus amiserat ob inremediabilem culpam. cuius generis propaginem non sic intelligitur amplificari voluisse bonus omnis creaturae dispositor, ut licenter quibuslibet viri mulieribus abuterentur, sed inter marem ac feminam fides servaretur coniugii, cum protoplasto non plures, sed unam desponsaverit; cum per eundem sanctum adhuc et sapientem dixerit: "relinquet homo patrem suum et matrem et adherebit uxori suae, et erunt duo in carne una." qui ergo uni viro virginem unam despondit quique duos in carne una constituit, subtiliter interventionem tercii vel terciae propter duorum discidium arguens interdicit. verum istud tantis nove legis et vetustae nititur assertionibus, ut nostris argumentis firmari non indigeat.*

tive texts of the early Middle Ages.[2] First of all, the narrative about the creation of man is itself astonishing. In contrast to various other formulae, which draw the narrative only from the stories of Genesis (1:27–28, as well as 2:18–24), the starting point here is sought in the myth of the fallen angels.[3] In this representation, God first created the angels. Some of these were not obedient to him but rather raised themselves above God's goodness and, for this reason, were cast down by him into hell. The other choirs of angels therefore thought better of their conduct and decided to remain loyal to God. But still, God apparently did not want to let his creation be so incomplete and decided to create the human race. This creation was intended—differently from the fallen angels!—to come to glory through obedience. The writer of the formula knows exactly how such an obedience should look. God did not want "to fashion the increase of the human race in such a way that the men might licentiously abuse all the women they might desire, but rather that the fidelity of marriage be preserved between man and woman, since he had betrothed the first created [that is, Adam] not to several women but only to one" (*Form. extr.* 1.13.541–542).

Behind these descriptions stood that conception of marriage in which a man and a woman were dependent upon one another as creatures of equal value and rank and succeeded in becoming the "completion of God's intention in creation" only "when they united in marriage, were true to each other, and showed love for one another."[4] After all—so the formula continues—man had left father and mother in order to bind himself to his wife, so that the two became one flesh. This one flesh, however, may under no circumstances be destroyed. Consequently, God forbade "the encroachment by a third person, man or woman, and [fought] against him or her because of the discord that he [that is, the third person] has brought about between the two." Accordingly, the man as well as the woman was explicitly obliged to maintain marital loyalty on the basis of the "declarations from the New and Old Testament" (*Form. extr.* 1.13.541–542).

Thus this formula, just like other normative texts of the early Middle Ages, had at its disposal an extremely positive image of marriage, as well as

---

2. In addition to the formulas, councils, capitularies, books of penance, and laws.
3. See Ines Weber, "Die Bibel als Norm! Eheschließung und Geschlechterverhältnis im frühen Mittelalter zwischen biblischer Tradition und weltlichem Recht," in *Geschlechterverhältnisse und Macht: Lebensformen in der Zeit des frühen Christentums*, ed. Irmtraud Fischer and Christoph Heil, EUZ 21 (Berlin: LIT, 2010), 257–304.
4. See Weber, "Die Bibel als Norm!," 301.

of the sexes. For one also can read repeatedly in the works of other authors that marriage was the highest good because it had been instituted and blessed by God himself.[5] In this formula, though, man and woman also appear in an extremely positive light because God basically had trusted the first human couple, as well as the angels, to choose the good.

How the understanding of adultery was rooted in such a system, and how this understanding was substantiated through a massive conglomeration of biblical arguments, is only just beginning to be noticed in research to the present.[6] The basics of marriage theology in the ninth century have been discussed, and various references have been made to the reception of the chastity clauses in Matthew, the πορνεία ideas of Paul, and the cultic purity concept in the Old Testament.[7] The connection to adultery, divorce, and separation, partially gleaned from the New Testament, has also been mentioned.[8] And it is also the case that the multifarious nature of such an

---

5. See Hans-Werner Goetz, *Frauen im frühen Mittelalter* (Weimar: Böhlau, 1995), 168–96, esp. 168, 178, 191.

6. See Philip L. Reynolds, *Marriage in the Western Church: The Christianization of Marriage during the Patristic and Early Medieval Periods*, VCSup 24 (Leiden: Brill, 1994), 315–419.

7. On marriage theology, see Goetz, *Frauen*, 168–96; see also Philip L. Reynolds, "Marrying and Its Documentation in Pre-modern Europe: Consent, Celebration, and Property," in *To Have and to Hold: Marrying and Its Documentation in Western Christendom, 400–1600*, ed. Philipp L. Reynolds and John Witte (Cambridge: Cambridge University Press, 2007), 1–42, esp. 16; Reynolds, "Dotal Charters in the Frankish Tradition," in Reynolds and Witte, *To Have and to Hold*, 114–64, esp. 114–32; Reynolds, *Marriage in the Western Church*, 315–419. On *porneia*, see Hubertus Lutterbach, *Sexualität im Mittelalter: Eine Kulturstudie anhand von Bußbüchern des 6. bis 12. Jahrhunderts*, BAK 43 (Cologne: Böhlau, 1999), 96–106, 122–49; see also Ines Weber, *Ein Gesetz für Männer und Frauen: Die frühmittelalterliche Ehe zwischen Religion, Gesellschaft und Kultur*, 2 vols., MF 24.1–2 (Ostfildern: Thorbecke, 2007), 1:151–91.

8. See Goetz, *Frauen*, 168–96; see also Lutterbach, *Sexualität*, 96–106, 122–49; Weber, *Ein Gesetz*, 151–91; Karl Ubl, *Inzestverbot und Gesetzgebung: Die Konstruktion eines Verbrechens (300–1100)*, MSKG 20 (Berlin: de Gruyter, 2008); Ubl, "Doppelmoral im karolingischen Kirchenrecht? Ehe und Inzest bei Regino von Prüm," in *Recht und Gericht in Kirche und Welt um 900*, ed. Wilfried Hartmann, SHK 69 (Munich: Oldenbourg, 2007), 95–102; Hinkmar von Reims, *De divortio Lotharii regis et Theutbergae reginae*, ed. Letha Böhringer, MGH (Hannover: Hahn, 1992); Letha Böhringer, "Gewaltverzicht, Gerichtswahrung und Befriedung durch Öffentlichkeit: Beobachtungen zur Entstehung des kirchlichen Eherechts im 9. Jahrhundert am Beispiel Hinkmars von Reims," in *Rechtsverständnis und Konfliktbewältigung: Gerichtliche und außergerichtliche Strategien im Mittelalter*, ed. Stefan Esders (Cologne: Böhlau, 2007), 255–89.

offense, seen against the background of the special social situation of the early Middle Ages, as well as the fundamental legal possibilities of action on the part of those concerned, has already been explained elsewhere in the context of specific communicative situations raised by the corresponding texts.[9] But to what extent biblical texts were taken up within the arguments concerning adultery, to what purpose they were employed, and in which way a complete framework of standards could be established have remained unexamined to the present.

Thus the prohibition of the entire spectrum of adultery within the knowledge of a broad biblical legacy is illuminated in the following essay, against the background of the image of marriage portrayed above. Both secular and biblical lines of argument will be made accessible and placed in relation to each other. In order to do this, a short survey of the marriage regulations themselves is first necessary.

2. The Understanding of Adultery in the Normative Texts of the Seventh to the Twelfth Century

2.1. Standards in the Conclusion of a Marriage

The marriage regulations that had developed in accordance with specific group relationships in the early Middle Ages included four essential elements, without which—apart from some exceptions—the marriage was not considered to be legally concluded and which also corresponded to the understanding of marriage cited above. First of all, the consent of all those concerned, which meant the agreement of the bride and bridegroom as well as that of the parents or relatives in each case. Then—at least in the well-to-do classes—a dowry or matrimonial gift was conferred, which provided for the widow after the death of her husband, but which was also intended to make the newly founded marital couple financially independent. Finally, the marriage had to take place publicly and to satisfy certain formal regulations, including that written endowment agreement cited at the beginning of this essay.[10] All these elements were, on the one hand, justified through formal secular regulations but, on the other hand, were

---

9. See Weber, *Ein Gesetz*, 151–91; see also Wolfgang Graf, "Der Ehebruch im fränkischen und deutschen Mittelalter unter besonderer Berücksichtigung des weltlichen Rechts" (PhD diss., Universität Würzburg, 1982).

10. See Weber, *Ein Gesetz*, 47–63, 83–150.

placed decidedly in the biblical tradition and justified first and foremost by the two creation stories in Genesis, as well as by statements in the book of Tobit.[11] Consequently, all the persons taking part in the marriage ceremony were, on the one hand, treated equally, and, on the other hand, the woman, to whom initially no public, legally effective action had been conceded in early medieval society, was also included in it and was provided with security by it.

2.2. Adultery

Against the background of this specific method of concluding a marriage, a quite particular definition of what had to be considered adultery developed in the early Middle Ages. Adultery was much more than just an extramarital sexual relationship, because basically every action that infringed upon the lawful event of concluding a marriage was stigmatized as a forbidden sexual relationship, *adulterium* or *fornicatio*. The starting point was the issue of marital consent. With the use of legal categorizations and theological arguments from the Bible—more precisely, selected passages from the Old and New Testaments—a consistent image of what was considered to be a forbidden extramarital sexual relationship emerged in early medieval society, for "not only the law condemns" adultery—that is, the secular law—"but also the authority of the gospel completely forbids that it happens."[12] Let us follow, first of all, the trail of legal argument.

From the beginning, basically all the persons who were involved in the business of concluding a marriage and who infringed upon the consensual agreement were considered to be adulterers in the early Middle Ages:

(1) The bridal couple that initiated a marriage, or even a sexual relationship, without having first obtained the necessary agreement of all parties was characterized as adulterous because no one was allowed to marry a wife "against the will of the parents/relatives" (*contra parentum voluntatem*) and no one was permitted to enter a sexual relationship without previously having "been bound in marriage by the parents/relatives" (*a parentibus sociata*).[13] This conduct—as Burchard of Worms also argued at

---

11. See Weber, "Die Bibel als Norm!," 284–304.

12. Rabanus Maurus, *Poen. lib.* 3 (PL 112:1406A): *adulterium autem non solum lex damnat, sed etiam evangelica auctoritas omnino fieri vetat.*

13. See *Fori Jud.* 3.4.7 (Karl Zeumer, ed., *Leges Visigothorum*, MGH [Hannover: Hahn, 1902], 150): *si puella vel vidua ad domum alterius pro adulterio venerit, eamque*

the beginning of the eleventh century—must be seen as adultery because whoever had done this had "violated a virgin" (*corrupisti virginem*) and thereby "violated [the lawful] wedding" (*nuptias violasti*), regardless of whether he "later married the same woman" (*eamdem suscepisti uxorem*; *Decr. lib.* 19 [PL 140:958C]).

(2) Above and beyond this—and this is astonishing, but also consistent with the process of concluding a marriage in the early Middle Ages—all those persons who, without the support of the rest of the relatives, had agreed (*consentire*) either to an extramarital sexual relationship, or even to a marriage, were considered adulterers, for "the relatives who were present at the resolution shall suffer the same judgment" (*et cognati, qui illi consilio interfuerit, patiantur eandem sententiam*) as the bridal couple itself.[14] Accordingly, as a rule, the relatives were required to perform the same or only a marginally different type of penance as the man and woman themselves.

(3) Following on from this understanding of marriage, engaged, married, and even widowed persons who had dismissed their partners and joined themselves to another without legally annulling the existing agreements were likewise considered adulterers.[15] If a marriage could be

---

vir ipse habere coniugem vellit. si puella ingenua sive vidua ad domum alienam adulterii perpetratione convenerit, et ipsam ille uxorem habere voluerit, et parentes, ut se habeant, adquiescant: ille pretium det parentibus, quantum parentes puelle vellint, vel quantum ei cum ipsa muliere convenire potuerit. mulier vero de parentum rebus nullam inter fratres suos, nisi parentes voluerint, habeat portionem. See also, *Fori Jud.* 3.4.15 (ed. Zeumer, 156); *Ed. Roth.* 189 (Friedrich Bluhme, ed., *Leges Langobardorum*, MGH [Hannover: Hahn, 1868], 39); Rob Meens, ed., *The Penitential of Finnian and the Textual Witness of the Paenitentiale Vindobonense "B"* (Toronto: Pontifical Institute of Mediaeval Studies, 1993), 400. On *contra parentum voluntatem*, see Ghärbald of Luttich, *Capitulary* 2.4 (Peter Brommer, Rudolf Pokorny, and Martina Stratmann, eds., *Capitula episcoporum*, 4 vols., MGH [Hannover: Hahn, 1995], 1:27); *Capit. Silv.* 1–2 (ed. Brommer, Pokorny, and Stratmann, 3:81). On *a parentibus sociata*, see *Lex Baiuv.* 8.8 (Ernst Maria Augustin Schwind, ed., *Lex Baiuvariorum*, MGH [Hannover: Hahn, 1926], 357).

14. See *Paen. Ps.-Egb.* 2.8 (F. W. H. Wasserschleben, ed. *Die Bussordnungen der abendländischen Kirche* [Halle: Graeger, 1851], 325); see also *Paenitentiale Hubertense* (Raymund Kottje, ed. *Paenitentialia minora Franciae et Italiae saeculi VIII–IX*, CCSL 156 [Turnhout: Brepols, 1994], 16, 20); *Paen. Mers.* 23 (ed. Kottje, 175–76); Rabanus Maurus, *Poen. lib.* 3 (PL 112:1406C–D); *Fori Jud.* 3.3.11 (ed. Zeumer, 144–45).

15. See *Paen. Sil.* c. 157 (Ludger Körntgen and Francis Bezler, eds., *Paenitentialia Hispaniae*. Vol. 2 of *Paenitentialia Franciae, Italiae et Hispaniae saeculi VIII–XI*, CCSL 156A [Turnhout: Brepols, 1998], 32): *qui dimiserit uxorem suam et duxerit aliam ... a*

dissolved at all, then as a rule this could occur only with the consent of all those involved. One of the few exceptions was the case of fornication, discussed below.[16]

(4) Inevitably, the same persons were called adulterers if they conducted an extramarital sexual relationship.[17] The name was applied even to engaged partners, for the agreement to conclude a marriage made the marriage obligatory; with an agreement, the marriage was concluded.[18] This meant that the "daughter of a free Burgundian" (*Burgundionis ingenii filia*), for example, was to be condemned according to the *Lex Burgundionum*, because "before she [had been] given to a husband" (*priusquam marito tradatur*) she had "in secret bound herself" to a man of her choice "through the shamefulness of adultery" (*occulte adulterii se foeditate coniuncxerit*).[19] But at the same time, all those persons who maintained a sexual relationship to an engaged, married, or widowed

---

communione fidelium abstinendus. See also *Conf. Ps.-Egb.* c. 19 (ed. Wasserschleben, 308–9); *Paen. Sil.* 155 (Turnhout: Brepols, 1998), 31; *Decr. Verm.* 756 8 (A. Boretius and V. Krause, eds., *Capitularia regum Francorum*, 2 vols., MGH [Hannover: Hahn, 1883–1897], 40–41; see also the texts in note 34.

16. See below; on further cases of the separation of married couples, see Weber, *Ein Gesetz*, 47–85.

17. See *Paen. Ps.-Egb.* 2.7 (ed. Wasserschleben, 324): in the case at issue, the man and the woman receive exactly the same penitential sentence. See also *Paen. Mers.* W10.12 (ed. Kottje, 129); *Paen. Vall.* 6.20 (Hermann Joseph Schmitz, ed., *Die Bussbücher und die Bussdisciplin der Kirche* [Mainz: Kirchheim, 1883], 360); *Paen. Finn.* 51 (Ludwig Bieler, ed., *The Irish Penitentials*, SLH 5 [Dublin: Dublin Institute for Advanced Studies, 1963], 92); Columban, *Paen. Columb.* C16 (G. S. M. Walker, *Sancti Columbani opera*, SLH 2 [Dublin: Dublin Institute for Advanced Study, 1957], 176); *Paen. Oxon.* 1.10 (ed. Kottje, 23); *Paen. Vall.* 1.15 (ed. Schmitz, 267); *Paen. Cas.* 17 (ed. Schmitz, 404); *Paen. Sil.* 165 (ed. Körntgen and Bezler, 32); *Fori Jud.* 3.4.12 (ed. Zeumer, 151–52); Wilfried Hartmann, ed., *Konzil von Worms 868: Überlieferung und Bedeutung*, AAWG 105 (Göttingen: Vandenhoeck & Ruprecht, 1977), 279; *Paen. Ps.-Rom.* 14 (ed. Schmitz, 476); *Fori Jud.* 3,4,3 (ed. Zeumer, 148); *Paen. Ps.-Greg.* 4 (Franz Kerff, ed., "Das Paenitentiale Pseudo-Gregorii: Eine kritische Edition," in *Aus Archiven und Bibliotheken: Festschrift für Raymund Kottje zum 65. Geburtstag*, ed. Hubert Mordek [Frankfurt am Main: Lang, 1992], 161–88, esp. 169–70); *Paen. Sil.* 165 (ed. Körntgen and Bezler, 32).

18. Weber, *Ein Gesetz*, 86–92; see also Ines Weber, "'Wachset und mehret euch': Die Eheschließung im frühen Mittelalter als soziale Fürsorge," in *Ehe—Familie—Verwandtschaft: Vergesellschaftung in Religion und sozialer Lebenswelt*, ed. Andreas Holzem and Ines Weber (Paderborn: Schöningh, 2008), 145–80, esp. 150–52.

19. See *Lib. const.* 44.1 (Ludwig Rudolf von Salis, ed., *Leges Burgundionum*, MGH

The Reception of Biblical Texts and Marriage, Adultery, and Divorce   329

person, regardless of whether they themselves were married or not, were considered adulterers.[20] All of these acts were considered equal to an extramarital offense, for which atonement had to be made. The only difference was in the extent of the penance, for this was dependent, among other things, on the status of the persons concerned.[21] These are precisely the arguments that had already played a role in the formula from the ninth century cited at the beginning of this essay, which Burchard of Worms also cites here: If the partner relationship between the two married people is broken apart by another person, then adultery has occurred. If this person himself or herself is married, then another case of adultery is added to this—namely, the breach of the partner relationship between the adulterer and his or her marital partner. But double adultery requires a doubly severe atonement.

(5) In accordance with this argumentation, then, every marital partner who, along with the relationship to the marriage partner, also maintained

---

[Hannover: Hahn, 1892], 74); see also *Ed. Roth.* 179 (ed. Bluhme, 37); *Fori Jud.* 3,4,2 (ed. Zeumer, 147–48).

20. See *Cap. Jud.* 7.3 (Rob Meens, ed., *Het tripartite boeteboek: Overlevering en betekenis van vroegmiddeleeuwse biechtvoorschriften (met editie en vertaling van vier tripartita)*, MSB 41 [Hilversum: Verloren, 1994], 442): *si quis cum uxore alterius adulteraverit ... laicus V ann. paenit., II ex his i.p.e.a.; hii supra scribti a communione priventur. post actam paenit. reconcilientur ad communionem*; see also *Paen. Ps.-Greg.* 4 (ed. Kerff, 169–70); *Paen. Ps.-Egb.* 2.10 (ed. Wasserschleben, 325); *Paen. Vig.* 77 (ed. Körntgen and Bezler, 10); *Paenitentiale Silense* (ed. Körntgen and Bezler, 29); *Paen. Vall.* 6 (ed. Schmitz, 357); *Can. Wall.* A:17 P 27 (ed. Bieler, 138); *Cap. Jud.* 7.4 (ed. Meens, 442); *Paen. Sang.* 4, 5 (ed. Meens, 330); *Fori Jud.* 3.4.9 (ed. Zeumer, 150–51); *Ed. Roth.* 212, 213 (ed. Bluhme, 44); *Lex Baiuv.* 8.10 (ed. Schwind, 358); *Capit. Olon.* 822/823.3 (ed. Ubl, 317); Columban, *Paen Columb.* 14 (ed. Walker, 174); *Paen. Mers.* 8, 9, 23 (ed. Kottje, 128, 175–76); *Paen. Flor.* 8 (ed. Kottje, 15, 19); *Paen. Sang.* 29.1 (ed. Meens, 396); *Paen. Vall.* I.14 (ed. Schmitz, 266); *Paen. Par.* 7 (ed. Kottje, 14, 18); *Conc. Trib.* 895.5 (A. Boretius and V. Krause, eds., *Capitularia regum Francorum*, 2 vols., MGH [Hannover: Hahn, 1883–1897], 2:207); *Fori Jud.* 3.4.1 (ed. Zeumer, 147); *Paen. Vall.* 6.20 (ed. Schmitz, 360); *Fori Jud.* 3.4.14 (ed. Zeumer, 155); *Decr. Verm.* 756.8 (ed. Ubl, 40–41); Columban, *Paen. Columb.* 16 (ed. Walker, 176).

21. Worms, *Decr. lib.* 19, Sp. 957D: *moechatus es cum uxore alterius, tu non habens uxorem? XL dies in pane et aqua ... cum septem sequentibus annis poeniteas. si moechatus es tu uxoratus cum alterius uxore, quia habuisti quodmodo impleres tuam libidinem, duas carinas, cum quatuordecim sequentibus annis poenitere debes, unam quia super uxorem tuam alteram habuisti, ecce unum adulterium: habuisti etiam alterius uxorem, ecce aliud adulterium, et nunquam debes esse sine poenitentia.*

a permanent relationship to another woman, or even to a concubine, also had to be considered an adulterer.[22]

All of these offenses were accompanied by biblical justifications:

(1) In this sense, the engaged or married partner violated the standard when he left his wife and married another spouse because he—also according to biblical law—"is an adulterer" (*adulter est*).[23] After all—so argued Rabanus Maurus—one could read in the gospel: "Whoever has dismissed his wife and led home another breaks the marriage" (*qui dimiserit uxorem suam, et aliam duxerit, moechatur*; Poen. lib. 3 [PL 112:1406A–B; cf. 1406C–D]). The saying attributed to Jesus in the argument with the Pharisees is used here to establish the offense of adultery and to brand it as sinful conduct. This saying, which is handed down differently in the different gospel traditions, was received in two variants in the texts at hand.[24] Rabanus Maurus is clearly likely to have had the Lucan version, which is considered the original one, in view.[25] The *Paenitentiale Pseudo-Egberti*, however, took up the Marcan form, for the offense here is played out equally for both sexes, just as in Mark: if the "woman has left her lawful husband and chosen another, then she should be worthy of the same judgment" (*si mulier virum suum legitimum deseruerit et alium elegerit, sit eadem sentential digna*), so that not only was the wife forbidden to leave her husband, but the husband also was forbidden to leave his wife (2.8). Both were considered to be adulterers and "the same judgment" (*eadem sentential*; 2.8) was pronounced over both.[26] Mark had accommodated

---

22. *Capit. Ital. episc.* c. 5 (ed. Boretius and Krause, 1:202): *et hoc etiam scribimus, ut cunctis diligentes inquirat: ut si est homo uxorem habens, et supra ipsa cum alia adulterans et concubinam habuerint, a tali igitur inlicita perpetratione faciat eos cum omni sollicitudine separari*; see also Rodulf of Bourges, *Capit. episc.* 1.42 (R. Pokorny and M. Stratmann, eds., *Capitula episcoporum*, 2 vols., MGH [Hannover: Hahn, 1995], 2:265); *Paen. Sil.* 149 (ed. Körntgen and Bezler, 31); *Liut. Leg.* 104 (ed. Bluhme, 125); *Paen. Cas.* 17 (ed. Schmitz, 404).

23. See *Paen. Ps.-Egb.* 2.8 (ed. Wasserschleben, 325).

24. See Mark 10:11–12: *et dicit illis quicumque dimiserit uxorem suam et aliam duxerit adulterium committit super eam et si uxor dimiserit virum suum et alii nupserit moechat*; Luke 16:18a: *omnis qui dimittit uxorem suam et ducit alteram moechatur*. See also Michael Theobald, "Jesu Wort von der Ehescheidung," *TQ* 175 (1995): 109–24, esp. 114–15, 117.

25. See Dieter Zeller, *Der erste Brief an die Korinther*, KEK 5 (Göttingen: Vandenhoek & Ruprecht, 2010), 244.

26. See *Paen. Ps.-Egb.* 2.8 (ed. Wasserschleben, 325).

Jesus's words to the practice prevailing in his Jewish-Hellenistic congregations, in which the woman could also initiate divorce.[27] The fact that the *Poenitentiale* employed the Marcan and not the Lucan variant could indicate that in the social practice of this region, a divorce brought from the woman's side was also possible.

(2) Continuing in the application of the gospel passages, the conduct of people who married a divorced spouse was also against the norm because—in reference to Matt 5:32b; 19:9b, as well as Luke 16:18b—"The Lord himself said, 'Whoever marries a divorced woman commits adultery [*qui dimissam duxerit, adulterat*].'"[28] The argument behind this was made in these terms: with such conduct, the already unlawful adultery that had arisen with the divorce was extended still further.

(3) The same applied to the woman who had married a man honorably but had then separated herself from him and later had committed herself to another in adultery.[29] Whether or not the man to whom she had subsequently committed herself had also for his part become guilty of an adulterous offense, and if so what offense, was not explained in more detail at the Irish synod. The council texts from the ninth century, however, express themselves very clearly in this regard. Thus it was forbidden for a man after the death of his spouse to marry the woman with whom he in his lifetime had already committed adultery. Such an "execrable thing" (*rem execrabilem*) had "to be detested by all Catholics" (*catholicis omnibus detestandam*), for such a relationship may not "rightly be called a marriage when through it arise the evils that the apostle enumerates—namely, fornication, impurity, licentiousness, and the others, the last of these being poisoning and homicide" (*iure dici matrimonium potest, per quod oriuntur, quae apostolus numerat mala, quae sunt fornicatio, inmunditia, luxuria et*

---

27. See Theobald, "Jesu Wort," 114.

28. See *Paen. Hub.* 46 (ed. Kottje, 113); see also *Paen. Mers.* b 4 (ed. Kottje, 173); *Paen. Sil.* 157 (ed. Körntgen and Bezler, 32); Ghärbald of Lüttich, *Capitulary* 2 (ed. Brommer, Pokorny, and Stratmann, 1:27); *Capit. Silv.* 1–2 (ed. Brommer, Pokorny, and Stratmann, 3:81); *Paen. Oxon.* 2.2 (ed. Kottje, 191); Maurus, *Poenitentium liber*, 1406A–B; *Capit. Trev.* c. 9" (ed. Brommer, Pokorny, and Stratmann, 1:56). See Matt 5:32b: *et qui dimissam duxerit adulterat*; Matt 19:9b: *qui dimissam duxerit moechatur*; Luke 16:18b: *et qui dimissam a viro ducit moechatur*.

29. *Syn. prim.* 19 (ed. Bieler, 56): *mulier Christiana quae acciperit virum honestis nuptis [-iis?] et postmodum discesserit a primo et junxerit se adulter[i,]o, quae haec fecit[,] excommonis sit.*

cetera, ad ultimum vero veneficia et homicidia).[30] Quoting word for word the catalogue of vices in Gal 5:19, which also is found in a similar form in 1 Cor 6:9-10; Eph 5:5; and 1 Cor 5:11, the council fathers condemned such a union with acute precision, even to the extent of maintaining that the death of the first spouse could not lead to any lawful marriage between the earlier adulterers.[31] But what was so abhorrent about such a union? It is once again that understanding of marriage explained at the beginning of this essay that is likely to be the basis of the argumentation here as well. Recall: if a man and woman married, they became one flesh, after which the union fundamentally became inseparable. Every person who now intruded into this union broke it apart and polluted it. Such an "intrusion of a third party" was, in any case, forbidden.[32] But if a marriage was later attached to this forbidden relationship, then such a union could only be the mixing of poison.

(4) Even "those who lead other women home after they have sent away their wives because of fornication" (*quod hi, qui causa fornicationis dimissus uxoribus*) had "to be seen as adulterers according to the word of the Lord" (*Domini sentential adulteri esse notentur*).[33] As a rule, the innocent spouse was allowed to leave his or her partner when the latter had committed adultery.[34] This was also ensured biblically with

---

30. *Conc. Trib.* 895.40 (ed. Boretius and Krause, 236-37); see also Synode de Beauvais, *Conc. Meld-Par.* 69 (ed. Boretius and Krause, 117); *Fori Jud.* 3.4.12 (ed. Zeumer, 151-52); *Conc. Trib.* 895.51 (ed. Boretius and Krause, 241).

31. See Gal 5:19, 21c: *manifesta autem sunt opera carnis quae sunt fornicatio inmunditia luxuria.... quoniam qui talia agunt regnum Dei non consequentur*; 1 Cor 6:9-10: *an nescitis quia iniqui regnum Dei non possidebunt? nolite errare: neque fornicarii neque idolis servientes neque adulteri neque molles neque masculorum concubitores neque fures neque avari neque ebriosi neque maledici neque rapaces regnum Dei possidebunt*; Eph 5:5: *hoc enim scitote intellegentes: quod omnis fornicator aut inmundus aut avarus quod est idolorum servitus non habet hereditatem in regno Christi et Dei*; 1 Cor 5:11: *nunc autem scripsi vobis non commisceri si is qui frater nominatur est fornicator aut avarus aut idolis serviens aut maledicus aut ebriosus aut rapax, cum eiusmodi nec cibum sumere.*

32. See *Form. extr.* 1.13 (ed. Zeumer, 541-42).

33. *Conc. Par.* 69.2 (A. Werminghoff, ed., *Concilia*, MGM [Hanover: Hahn, 1908], 2.2:671).

34. See *Conc. Par.* 69.2 (ed. Werminghoff, 2.2:670-71); see also Paul Willem Finsterwalder, ed., "Judicia Theodori," in *Die Canones Theodori Cantuariensis und ihre Uberlieferungsformen*, UB 1 (Weimar: Böhlaus, 1929), 270; Meens, *Penitential of Finnian*, 428; *Paen. Mart.* 40 (Walther von Hörmann, ed., *Bussbücherstudien VI*

the citation of Matt 19:9.[35] Individual traditions, then, even allowed a subsequent marriage to the betrayed partner.[36] Other traditions, on the other hand, prohibited precisely this remarriage, so that those persons who acted in a manner contrary to it were characterized as *adulteri* in individual texts.[37] What was the justification for this? The fathers of the council at Friaul wrote,

> For even if it is read in the text of the gospel that the Lord said that the man is permitted to send away his wife only in the case of adultery, one nevertheless cannot read there that he [that is, the Lord] has allowed him to bind another woman to himself in marriage while his former wife still lives; it is much more the case that no doubt can exist that he has forbidden it. He says, namely: "Whoever has sent his wife away, except for the case of adultery, and has led another woman home, commits adultery."

In order to gain clarity about this gospel passage, the council fathers performed a word-for-word exegesis on the corresponding passage from the Gospel of Matthew and then justified their decision with the position assumed by the passage "except in the case of adultery" inserted into the sentence structure:

[Weimar: Böhlau, 1914], 378); *Conc. Suess.* 744.9 (ed. Werminghoff, **2.1:35**); Bourges, *Capit. episc.* 1.42 (Pokorny and Stratmann, 2:265). The following texts, however, decide that even in the case of adultery the spouse may not be dismissed; see Franz Bernd Asbach, "Judicia Theodori," in "Das Poenitentiale Remense und der sogen. Excarpsus Cummeani: Überlieferung, Quellen und Entwicklung zweier kontinentaler Bußbücher aus der 1. Hälfte des 8. Jahrhunderts" (PhD diss., Universität Regensburg, 1975), 83; Finsterwalder, "Judicia Theodori," 260.

35. See Matt 5:32a: *ego autem dico vobis quia omnis qui dimiserit uxorem suam excepta fornicationis causa facit eam moechari et qui dimissam duxerit adulterat*; Matt 19:9a: *dico autem vobis quia quicumque dimiserit uxorem suam nisi ob fornicationem et aliam duxerit moechatur.*

36. See *Paen. Ps.-Theod.* 4.19.18 (ed. Wasserschleben, 582; Carine van Rhijn, ed., *Paenitentiale Pseudo-Theodori*, CCSL 156B [Turnhout: Brepols, 2009], 28); see also *Conf. Ps.-Egb.* 19 (ed. Wasserschleben, 308–9); Finsterwalder, "Judicia Theodori," 251, 277; Asbach, "Judicia Theodori," 83; *Paen. Sil.* 145 (ed. Körntgen and Bezler, 30); *Paen. Mers.* b 31 (ed. Kottje, 176); *Cap. Jud.* 9.1c (ed. Meens, 446); Finsterwalder, "Judicia Theodori," 261; Meens, *Penitential of Finnian*, 426; *Paen. Oxon.* 2.2 (ed. Kottje, 191); *Conc. Rom.* 826.36 (ed. Boretius and Krause, 582).

37. See *Conc. For.* a. 796 vel 797 (ed. Werminghoff, 2.1:192–93); see also *Capit. Trev.* 9 (ed. Brommer, Pokorny, and Stratmann, 56); *Paen. Mart.* 24, 37 (ed. von Hörmann, 370, 377).

Because, as one sees, the equivocal expression "except in the case of adultery" stands in the middle, it can, of course, be asked whether the dictum "whoever has dismissed his wife except in the case of adultery" refers only to permission for the dismissal of the wife or to both—that is, to take another woman as a wife while the former still lives, as though He had said: "Whoever has dismissed his wife and accepted another, except in the case of adultery, commits adultery."

They finally sought advice in the "commentary of the highly experienced blessed Jerome" and there "carefully" and "attentively" investigated his "interpretation." The result: the insertion "can refer only to the permission to dismiss the wife," for, according to Jerome's justification, the initially innocent spouse also "is not permitted—namely, to replicate the misdeed of the adulterous wife." Even when that wife

> has split the two, [who] certainly [are] still one flesh, through the offense of adultery that divides them into three, the husband is not allowed to recklessly divide the three into four through his action. For this reason, it is openly explained that it is to be understood that as long as the adulteress lives, the husband is not allowed to enter into a second marriage, and he cannot remain unpunished when he does so.[38]

---

38. *Conc. For.* a. 796/797 10 (ed. Werminghoff, 2.1:193): *nam etsi legatur in sacris evangelicis paginis sola fornicationis causa dixisse Dominum dimittere virum uxorem suam, non tamen legitur concessisse aliam vivente illa in coniugio sibi sociare, prohibuisse quidem modis omnibus non ambigitur. ait enim: "quicumque dimiserit uxorem suam nisi ob fornicationem et aliam duxerit, moechatur." qua de re ita diffinire prospeximus, ut juxta eiusdem Domini mellifluam vocem nemo haec interdicta violator inculcare praesumat. sed quoniam in medio ambiguus interponitur sermo, id est "nisi ob fornicationemm, quaeri nimirum potest, utrum ad solam licentiam dimittendi uxorem "qui dimiserit uxorem suam nisi ob fornicationem" an etiam ad utrumque dictum referatur, hoc est ad aliam vivente illa accipiendam, quasi dixerit: "qui dimiserit uxorem suam et aliam nisi ob fornicationem duxerit, moechatur." et idcirco peritissimi viri beati Hieronimi libellum commentariorum recenseri nobis studiose mandavimus, anxiae [sic] utique cognoscere festinantes, qualiter hisdem famosissimus doctor haec sacrata dominica verba juxta capatioris ingenii sui subtilitatem sensisse monstraretur. cuius nimirum sensum, sagaciter explorantes, in promptum nichilominus patuit ad solam dimittendi uxorem licentiam pertinere. nam cum more suo vir sanctus ad huius capituli summatim seriem exponendam transcurreret, inter cetera et post pauca sic ait: et quia poterat, inquit, accidere, ut aliquis calumniam faceret innocenti et ob secundam copulam nuptiarum veteri crimen inpingeret, sic prior dimitti jubetur uxor, ut secundam prima vivente non habeat. non enim debet imitari malum adultere uxoris, et si illa duo, immo unam carnem per*

Once again, we come full circle to the formula already repeatedly mentioned: the relationship between a man and a woman, who had become inseparable on the basis of the marriage, may not be broken apart by anyone. The idea of the one flesh of the married couple, along with Matthew's clauses on adultery, also laid the foundations here for establishing the offense.

(5) Accordingly, it had to be seen as especially injurious "to have two wives at the same time, or concubines ... for while it is of no advantage in the household, it will bring damage to the soul." With reference to Eph 5:9 and surrounding verses, which had been employed in a different way within other marriage regulations, precisely on behalf of the equal treatment of the married couple, and not in the sense of the subordination of the wife under the authority of the husband, it was also argued here that "just as Christ has preserved the church as pure, so must the husband preserve his marriage as pure."[39] Once again, the image of the one flesh stood behind these reflections. Just as every human being nourishes and tends his or her own flesh (Eph 5:29), so also the husband ought to preserve the purity of the flesh that he shared with his wife since the conclusion of marriage.[40] And so in this case, it was in fact the husband—not just first and foremost, but he alone—who was urged to maintain marital fidelity.

2.3. The Consequence: Loss of the Kingdom of God

But what happened to those who, in spite of these prohibitions, infringed on the norm? Both men and women had to reckon with severe punishment. Among such penitential requirements were long periods of fasting, as well as denial of a Christian burial.[41] And then there is the argument that—in

---

scissuras fornicationum divisit in tres, non decet, ut maritus nequius exsequendo tres dividat in quattuor. unde patenter datur intellegi: quamdiu vivit adultera, non licet viro nec potest inpune secundas contrahere nuptias.

39. *Conc. Rom.* 826 37 (ed. Boretius and Krause, 582): *ut non liceat uno tempore duas habere uxores sive concubinas. nulli liceat uno tempore duas habere uxores, quia, cum domui non sit lucrum, animae fit detrimentum. nam sicut Christus castam observat eclesiam, ita vir castum debet custodire coniugium*; cf. *Conc. Par.* 69.2 (ed. Werminghoff, 2.2:670–71). See Weber, "Die Bibel als Norm!," 274–76, 290.

40. Eph 5:29: *nemo enim umquam carnem suam odio habuit sed nutrit et fovet eam sicut et Christus ecclesiam.*

41. See *Paen. Ps.-Egb.* 2.8 (ed. Wasserschleben, 325): *qui uxorem suam legitimam deseruerit et aliam mulierem ceperit, adulter est; ne det ei ullus presbyter eucharistiam,*

reference to 1 Cor 5:11—as the apostle Paul "himself writes, [believers] shall not eat" (*nec cibus sumendus est*) with such persons.[42] In addition, the adulterer could also be condemned to repay the dowry or matrimonial gift several times over.[43] In all cases, however, the same penitential requirements awaited the man as well as the woman.[44] It was Rabanus Maurus who drew special attention to the fact that "the Christian religion [condemns] the adultery of both sexes on the same scale." Nevertheless, he saw problems precisely here that were rooted in the legal situation of the early Middle Ages. Because women in early medieval legal practice were, as a rule, capable of only limited action in the public realm, they could "not easily accuse their husbands of adultery," so that there was "no punishment for sins committed in secret" by the men. Husbands, however, were able "with greater ease to bring charges against their adulterous wives before the priests.... Thus although the case for men and women is quite similar, the criminal proceedings are suspended sometimes for lack of evidence."[45] But that was to be avoided, precisely upon the basis of the principle of equality mentioned at the beginning.

---

neque ullum eorum rituum, qui Christianum hominem decent; et si eum obire contigerit, ne ponatur cum Christianis hominibus. et si mulier virum suum legitimum deseruerit et alium elegerit, sit eadem sententia digna, ut supra dictum est; et cognati, qui illi consilio interfuerint, patiantur eandem sententiam, nisi prius ad emendationem se convertere velint, prout confessarius eorum eis

42. 1 Cor 5:11: *nunc autem scripsi vobis non commisceri si is qui frater nominatur est fornicator aut avarus aut idolis serviens aut maledicus aut ebriosus aut rapax cum eiusmodi nec cibum.* For the quote, see Felix, *Counc. Sav.* a. 859 c. 16 (Wilfried Hartmann, ed., *Concilia*, MGM [Hanover: Hahn, 1984], 3:479); see also, for example, *Paen. Cas.* o.c. (ed. Schmitz, 430).

43. See *Fori Jud.* 3.4.7 (ed. Zeumer, 150); see also Columban, *Paen. Columb.* 16 (ed. Walker, 176); *Ed. Roth.* 179 (ed. Bluhme, 37); *Fori Jud.* 3.4.2 (ed. Zeumer, 147–48); *Paen. Ambr.* 2.2 (Ludger Körntgen, ed., *Studien zu den Quellen der frühmittelalterlichen Bussbücher*, QFRM 7 [Sigmaringen: Thorbecke, 1993]); Salis, *Leges Burgundionum: Liber Constitutionum* 61, 93.

44. See, for example, *Paen. Finn.* 51 (ed. Bieler, 92); see also *Paen. Ps.-Egb.* 2.8 (ed. Wasserschleben, 325); *Capit. Trev.* 9 (ed. Brommer, Pokorny, and Stratmann, 56); *Paen. Ps.-Egb.* 2.7 (ed. Wasserschleben, 324); *Paen. Ps.-Egb.* 2.10 (ed. Wasserschleben, 325); 4 (ed. Kerff, 169–70); *Paenitentiale Hubertense* (ed. Kottje, 16, 20); *Paen. Mers.* 23 (ed. Kottje, 175–76).

45. Maurus, *Poen. lib.* 3 (PL 112:1406B–C): *item in decretis Innocentii papae, cap. 24, scriptum est quod viri cum adulteris non conveniant. et illud desideratum est sciri cur communicantes viri cum adulteris uxoribus non conveniant, cum contra uxores in*

The councils and capitularies, which, true to type, often recognized no penitential punishments, often forbade a remarriage after a separation.[46] Above and beyond this, permission for the spouse to kill the adulterer and adulteress, if he had caught both in the act, is found in isolated cases in the *leges*.[47] Even if Hans-Werner Goertz assumes that this punishment was seldom put into practice or not at all, these are nonetheless hard sanctions that require explanation.[48] Upon closer examination, the texts show that the authors here, too, could have used Old Testament passages as their models, which then, along with Roman law, would have acted as a precedent for the corresponding regulations, for exactly such a case is dealt with in Lev 20:10 as well as in Deut 22:22.[49] There, the law insisted upon punishment, but only if the adulterers were caught *in flagranti*. Adultery was considered to be an offense within private law and for this reason could be sanctioned personally by the individual concerned.[50] The fact that in the Old Testament texts there is no passage that shows that the same right was conceded to the wife as that enjoyed by her husband can be explained quickly. In the ancient Near East, adultery was seen as an injustice committed against the husband. Extramarital sexual relationships on

---

consortio adulterorum virorum manere videantur. super hoc Christiana religio adulterium in utroque sexu pari ratione condemnat. sed viros suos mulieres non facile de adulterio accusant, et non habent latentia peccata vindictam. viri autem liberius uxores adulteras apud sacerdotes deferre consueverunt: et ideo mulieribus, prodito earum crimine, communio denegatur. virorum autem latente commisso, non facile quisquam ex suspicionibus abstinetur. qui utique submovebitur, si ejus flagitium detegatur. cum ergo par causa sit, interdum probatione cessante, vindictae ratio conquiescit.

46. See, for example, *Capit. Trev.* c. 9 (ed. Brommer, Pokorny, and Stratmann, 56): *si alicuius uxor adulterata fuerit vel si ipse adulterium commiserit, quia neque dimissus ab uxore neque dimissa a marito alteri coniungatur;* see also *Concilium Foroiuliense*, 192–93; *Conc. Suess.* 744.9 (ed. Werminghoff, 2.1:35).

47. See *Ed. Roth.* 212 (ed. Bluhme, 44): "Antiqua. Si adulter cum adultera occidatur. Si adulterum cum adultera maritus occiderit, pro homicidio non teneatur"; see also *Fori Jud.* 3.4.4 (ed. Zeumer, 149); *Lib. const.* 35.2; 68.1, 2 (ed. von Salis, 9, 95); *Fori Jud.* 3.2.2 (ed. Zeumer, 133–34); *Fori Jud.* 3.4.5 (ed. Zeumer, 149).

48. Goetz, *Frauen*, 238.

49. Lev 20:10: *si moechatus quis fuerit cum uxore alterius et adulterium perpetrarit cum coniuge proximi sui morte moriantur et moechus et adultera.* Deut 22:22: *si dormierit vir cum uxore alterius uterque morientur id est adulter et adultera et auferes malum de Israhel.*

50. Georg Braulik, *Deuteronomium II: 16,18–34,12,* NEB 5, KATE 28 (Würzburg: Echter, 1992), 167.

the part of the man were considered adultery only when he intruded into the marital community of another man. Then, again, the right to indemnification rested upon the latter. But the wife had no recourse in the case of her husband's adultery. This understanding of adultery, however, no longer lay at the basis of the texts of the seventh to the eleventh century. The fact, though, that one nowhere reads of the wife's right to kill, and only once about the surrender of the adulterers to the wife, may be due to the social practice of the time and the lack of possibilities for legal action conceded to the woman connected with it. Thus it should be emphasized all the more that in the cases already mentioned both partners in adultery were always killed and that in no way was it the woman alone who met this fate. On the contrary, according to some texts, only the husband was put to death, above all when he was not able to clear himself of the charge of adultery by swearing an oath.[51] By the middle of the ninth century, however, resistance to this practice seems to have increased. At the Council of Mainz (861–863), the question—namely, whether the husband "is allowed according to secular law to kill her" if his "wife has committed adultery"—was answered in the following way: "The holy church of God is never bound by secular laws. It does not possess the sword, except for the spiritual and the divine ones; he shall not kill her but rather let her live; she does not kill but rather gives life."[52] The council fathers thus countered secular law with an alternative action because they did not want themselves to be bound by the former.

Along with these punishments, all of which—whether with biblical foundation or not—were to be performed in the here and now and which always served the purpose of peace within the congregations and the world, the offense of adultery was also discussed in the context of the Christian message of salvation and thus within reflections upon the kingdom of God.[53] Such discussions and reflections took place in the various council and capitulary texts, as well as in the penitential books. There were

---

51. See *Lex Baiuv.* 8.1 (ed. Schwind, 353–54); *Can. Wall.* [A] 17 (P XXVII) (ed. Bieler, 138); *Ed. Roth.* 213 (ed. Bluhme, 44).

52. *Council of Mainz* a. 861–863 (Wilfried Hartmann, ed., *Die Konzilien der karolingischen Teilreiche, 860–874*, MGH Concilia 4 [Hannover: Hahnsche Buchhandlung, 1998], 131): *si cuius uxor adulterium perpetraverit, utrum marito ipsius liceat secundum mundanam legem eam interficere. Sancta dei ecclesia mundanis numquam constringitur legibus; gladium non habet nisi spiritalem atque divinum; non occidit, sed vivificat.*

53. Weber, *Ein Gesetz*, 380–81.

urgent warnings about the offense, because adulterers "as the apostle says, will not gain the kingdom of God" (*sicut ait apostolus, regnum dei non consequentur*).[54]

> For because of such an illicit love, some have been destroyed through poison, others by means of the sword or through other evil deeds. Therefore, those evils, through which the kingdom of God must be closed to human beings, must be cut out with the sharpest knife and with all the medical arts, "since of course," as the same apostle says, "those who act in this way will not gain the kingdom of God."[55]

It cannot be clarified without further investigations of exegesis in the early Middle Ages whether the writers of the texts in their considerations always had only the Pauline expressions in mind, which state that the unrighteous will not possess the kingdom of God (1 Cor 6:9–10; Gal 5:19–21; Eph 5:5) or whether such texts are to be read in the larger context of the proclamation of the kingdom of God—that "core of Jesus's work"—that, as is known, runs through all the gospel texts.[56] For it is not possible, on the basis of the present state of research, to say in what way the biblical texts were interpreted in the context of knowledge about the other texts, what cross references were possible, and how reference was made among them. Relevant investigations are lacking. The fact that reflections on the kingdom of God in the gospels are at no place brought into connection with adultery or fornication speaks in favor of the possibility that the authors draw exclusively upon Paul in the texts examined here.

In this way, the circle comes around again to the formula cited at the beginning of this essay, so that we can at least state the following: all of the offenses named here were considered sinful conduct. Just as in that formula, which had connected the act of creation with the fall of the angels and so for the very first time had integrated adultery into the context of the

---

54. Felix, *Counc. Sav.* 16 (ed. Hartmann, 3:479).

55. *Conc. Trib.* 895.40 (ed. Boretius and Krause, 236–37): *quia pro tam inlicito amore alii veneno, alii gladio vel aliis diversis sunt perempti maleficiis. Idcirco acutissimo ferro et totius generis artificio sunt resecanda, per quae caelestia regna sunt obcludenda;* "*quoniam*," *ut idem apostolus ait,* "*qui talia agunt, regnum Dei non consequentur*"; cf. *Paen. Mart.* 37 (ed. von Hörmann, 377).

56. For the text of the Pauline citations, see note 31. See Hermann-Josef Venetz, "Jesus von Nazaret: Prophet der angebrochenen Gottesherrschaft; Grundlegende Reich Gottes-Texte der synoptischen Evangelien," *BK* 62 (2007): 78–88, quote at 78.

sinful offenses committed by human beings and had banished Lucifer to hell, it is likely that this context of evil was implied in all the texts in which the loss of the kingdom of heaven was mentioned.

3. Marriage, Adultery, and the Decision between Secular Law and Biblical Foundation—A Conclusion

The following can be stated as a result: The notion of marriage as a consensual contractual event among four legally equal parties is just as much the basis of the early medieval understanding of adultery as are the ideas on adultery presented in the New Testament or derived from the gospels or the letters of Paul. These ideas, which differ in detail in various passages, were synchronized in the early medieval texts and combined there to form a consistent doctrine. Secular legal regulations concerning marriage were combined with biblical ideas in such a way that, even in the sphere of marital offenses, the conclusion of a marriage was consistently formulated and, at the same time, the entire spectrum of New Testament thought was considered. But the entire array of offenses was also anchored in Christian thought about sin and in Christian anthropology, which similarly was based upon an equality of the sexes.

With regard to the relationship between groups and between the sexes, this had the result that the man and the woman, but also the respective relatives, were treated equally. Just as all the partners in the consensual event of concluding a marriage were placed on the same level, all violations of the norm entailed the same consequences for all those participating. Those punishments that were applied to the bride and groom, or to the married couple as a whole, and that, in accord with the New Testament model, in most cases prohibited a remarriage were, in an agrarian society, extremely hard and therefore a deterrent, because survival was possible only within intact family relationships. And these were focused on three factors: the indissolubility of the marital union, the woman's need for protection, and the need for peace within the community, because adultery contains in itself an extreme potential for destroying the group.[57] The woman—who, as a rule, could not act effectively in the public realm and thus could not act independently and, as a result, was clearly more endangered in the

---

57. On the entire theme of remarriage, see Weber, *Ein Gesetz*, 60–63 (remarriage of widows), 177–82, 189, 191.

face of wrongful accusation from the man's side—was to be protected.[58] In addition, the woman was not to be forced to live without protection outside the familial community after the dissolution of the marriage.[59]

Bibliography

Asbach, Franz Bernd. "Das Poenitentiale Remense und der sogen. Excarpsus Cummeani: Überlieferung, Quellen und Entwicklung zweier kontinentaler Bußbücher aus der 1. Hälfte des 8. Jahrhunderts." Ph.D. diss., Universität Regensburg, 1975.

Beyerle, Franz, ed. *Leges langobardorum, 643–866*. GWR NS 8. Witzenhausen: Deutschrechtlicher Instituts-Verlag, 1962.

Bieler, Ludwig, ed. *The Irish Penitentials*. SLH 5. Dublin: Dublin Institute for Advanced Studies, 1963.

Bluhme, Friedrich, ed. *Leges Langobardorum*. MGH. Hannover: Hahn, 1868

Böhringer, Letha. "Gewaltverzicht, Gerichtswahrung und Befriedung durch Öffentlichkeit: Beobachtungen zur Entstehung des kirchlichen Eherechts im 9. Jahrhundert am Beispiel Hinkmars von Reims." Pages 255–89 in *Rechtsverständnis und Konfliktbewältigung: Gerichtliche und außergerichtliche Strategien im Mittelalter*. Edited by Stefan Esders. Cologne: Böhlau, 2007.

Boretius, A., and V. Krause, eds. *Capitularia regum Francorum*. 2 vols. MGH. Hannover: Hahn, 1883–1897.

Brommer, Peter, Rudolf Pokorny, and Martina Stratmann, eds. *Capitula episcoporum*. 4 vols. MGH. Hannover: Hahn, 1995.

Braulik, Georg. *Deuteronomium II: 16,18–34,12*. NEB 5. KATE 28. Würzburg: Echter, 1992.

Brommer, Peter, ed. "Capitula Silvanectensia 1–2." Page 81 in vol. 3 of *Capitula Episcoporum*. 4 vols. MGH. Hannover: Hahn, 1984.

———, ed. "Ghärbald of Luttich II." Page 27 in vol. 1 of *Capitula Episcoporum*. 4 vols. MGH. Hannover: Hahn, 1984.

Finsterwalder, Paul Willem. Die Canones Theodori Cantuariensis und ihre Überlieferungsformen. UB 1. Weimar: Böhlau, 1929.

---

58. For a further example for an unjustified accusation, see *Grim. leg.* 7 (Franz Beyerle, ed., *Leges langobardorum, 643–866*, GWR n.s. 8 [Witzenhausen: Deutschrechtlicher Instituts-Verlag, 1962], 75–76).

59. On the theme of the separation of a marriage, see the literature in note 8.

Goetz, Hans-Werner. *Frauen im frühen Mittelalter*. Weimar: Böhlau, 1995.
Graf, Wolfgang. "Der Ehebruch im fränkischen und deutschen Mittelalter unter besonderer Berücksichtigung des weltlichen Rechts." Ph.D. diss., Universität Würzburg, 1982.
Hartmann, Wilfried, ed. *Concilia*, vol. 3. MGM. Hanover: Hahn, 1984.
———, ed. *Konzil von Worms 868: Überlieferung und Bedeutung*. AAWG 105. Göttingen: Vandenhoeck & Ruprecht, 1977.
———, ed. *Die Konzilien der karolingischen Teilreiche, 860–874*. MGH Concilia 4. Hannover: Hahnsche Buchhandlung, 1998.
Hörmann, Walther von, ed. *Bussbücherstudien VI*, Weimar: Böhlau, 1914.
Kerff, Franz, ed. "Das Paenitentiale Pseudo-Gregorii: Eine kritische Edition." Pages 161–88 in *Aus Archiven und Bibliotheken: Festschrift für Raymund Kottje zum 65. Geburtstag*. Edited by Hubert Mordek. Frankfurt am Main: Lang, 1992.
Körntgen, Ludger, ed. *Studien zu den Quellen der frühmittelalterlichen Bussbücher*. QFRM 7. Sigmaringen: Thorbecke, 1993.
Körntgen, Ludger, and Francis Bezler, eds. *Paenitentialia Hispaniae*. Vol. 2 of *Paenitentialia Franciae, Italiae et Hispaniae saeculi VIII–XI*. CCSL 156A. Turnhout: Brepols, 1998.
Kottje, Raymund, ed. *Paenitentialia minora Franciae et Italiae saeculi VIII–IX*. CCSL 156. Turnhout: Brepols, 1994.
Lutterbach, Hubertus. *Sexualität im Mittelalter: Eine Kulturstudie anhand von Bußbüchern des 6. bis 12. Jahrhunderts*. BAK 43. Cologne: Böhlau, 1999.
Meens, Rob, ed. *Het tripartite boeteboek: Overlevering en betekenis van vroegmiddeleeuwse biechtvoorschriften (met editie en vertaling van vier tripartita)*. MSB 41. Hilversum: Verloren, 1994.
———, ed. *The Penitential of Finnian and the Textual Witness of the Paenitentiale Vindobonense "B."* Toronto: Pontifical Institute of Mediaeval Studies, 1993.
Rhijn, Carine van, ed. *Paenitentiale Pseudo-Theodori*. CCSL 156B. Turnhout: Brepols, 2009.
Reims, Hinkmar von. *De divortio Lotharii regis et Theutberga reginae*. Edited by Letha Böhringer. MGH. Hannover: Hahn, 1992.
Reynolds, Philip L. "Dotal Charters in the Frankish Tradition." Pages 114–64 in *To Have and to Hold: Marrying and Its Documentation in Western Christendom, 400–1600*. Edited by Philip L. Reynolds and John Witte. Cambridge: Cambridge University Press, 2007.

---. *Marriage in the Western Church: The Christianization of Marriage during the Patristic and Early Medieval Periods.* VCSup 24. Leiden: Brill, 1994.

---. "Marrying and Its Documentation in Pre-modern Europe: Consent, Celebration, and Property." Pages 1–42 in *To Have and to Hold: Marrying and Its Documentation in Western Christendom, 400–1600.* Edited by Philip L. Reynolds and John Witte. Cambridge: Cambridge University Press, 2007.

Salis, Ludwig Rudolf von, ed. *Leges Burgundionum.* MGH. Hannover: Hahn, 1892.

Schmitz, Hermann Joseph, ed., *Die Bussbücher und die Bussdisciplin der Kirche.* Mainz: Kirchheim, 1883.

Schwind, Ernst Maria Augustin, ed. *Lex Baiuvariorum.* MGH. Hannover: Hahn, 1926.

Theobald, Michael. "Jesu Wort von der Ehescheidung." *TQ* 175 (1995): 109–24.

Ubl, Karl, ed. *Inzestverbot und Gesetzgebung: Die Konstruktion eines Verbrechens (300–1100).* MSKG 20. Berlin: de Gruyter, 2008.

---, ed. "Doppelmoral im karolingischen Kirchenrecht? Ehe und Inzest bei Regino von Prüm." Pages 91–124 in *Recht und Gericht in Kirche und Welt um 900.* Edited by Wilfried Hartmann. SHK 69. Munich: Oldenbourg, 2007.

---. *Inzestverbot und Gesetzgebung: Die Konstruktion eines Verbrechens (300–1100).* MSKG 20. Berlin: de Gruyter, 2008.

Venetz, Hermann-Josef. "Jesus von Nazaret: Prophet der angebrochenen Gottesherrschaft; Grundlegende Reich Gottes-Texte der synoptischen Evangelien." *BK* 62 (2007): 78–88.

Walker, G. S. M. *Sancti Columbani opera.* SLH 2. Dublin: Dublin Institute for Advanced Study, 1957.

Wasserschleben, F. W. H., ed. *Die Bussordnungen der abendländischen Kirche.* Halle: Graeger, 1851.

Weber, Ines. "Die Bibel als Norm! Eheschließung und Geschlechterverhältnis im frühen Mittelalter zwischen biblischer Tradition und weltlichem Recht." Pages 257–304 in *Geschlechterverhältnisse und Macht: Lebensformen in der Zeit des frühen Christentums.* Edited by Irmtraud Fischer and Christoph Heil. EUZ 21. Berlin: LIT, 2010.

---. *Ein Gesetz für Männer und Frauen: Die frühmittelalterliche Ehe zwischen Religion, Gesellschaft und Kultur.* 2 vols. MF 24.1–2. Ostfildern: Thorbecke, 2007.

———. "'Wachset und mehret euch': Die Eheschließung im frühen Mittelalter als soziale Fürsorge." Page 145–80 in *Ehe—Familie—Verwandtschaft: Vergesellschaftung in Religion und sozialer Lebenswelt*. Edited by Andreas Holzem and Ines Weber. Paderborn: Schöningh, 2008.

Werminghoff, A., ed. *Concilia*, vol. 2. 2 parts. MGM. Hanover: Hahn, 1908.

Zeller, Dieter. *Der erste Brief an die Korinther*. KEK 5. Göttingen: Vandenhoeck & Ruprecht, 2010.

Zeumer, Karl, ed. *Formulae Merowingici et Karolini aevi*. MGH. Turnhout: Brepols, 2010.

———, ed. *Leges Visigothorum*. MGH. Hannover: Hahn, 1902.

Biblical Figures of Women in the Qur'an

Ulrike Bechmann

The issue of the reception of biblical figures of women in the Qur'an raises profound, basic questions about the reception and intertextuality of biblical texts, extrabiblical traditions, and the Qur'an, for the Qur'an accepts not only the Bible but also the Bible and its reception. This can only be indicated here through brief reflections on the hermeneutical stances inherent in a religious studies approach that makes reference to current discussion on the origins of the Qur'an.

Biblical figures of women are relatively rare in the Qur'an. It is not that women played no role in it but that they appear relatively seldom and, except for Maryam (Mary), are never mentioned by name. In contrast to the Bible, elaborate narratives about women are lacking in the Qur'an, although various verses do refer to them. The reason for this absence is the fact that the Qur'an contains few narratives at all; its texts are to be recited and heard. They are partly of a liturgical nature, and much is in rhyme and is full of poetry that can hardly be reproduced in most of the translations (except for the one by Friedrich Rückert).[1] The Qur'an frequently relates direct speech, conversations between God and Muhammad as the arbiter of revelation. The "you" spoken by God, however, is directed at all who hear or read the text. If wisdom texts, prophetic speech, and narrative *grosso modo* are spread over various books in the Bible, then the Qur'an combines the most varied sorts of texts in the new genre 'sura,' as it alone is represented in the Qur'an.[2] Many of the biblical and extrabiblical allusions

---

For Marie-Theres Wacker on her sixtieth birthday.

1. See Navid Kermani, *Gott ist schön: Das ästhetische Erleben des Koran* (Munich: Beck, 1999).

2. See Angelika Neuwirth, *Der Koran als Text der Spätantike: Ein europäischer Zugang* (Berlin: Insel, 2010), 561. Unless otherwise indicated, all translations from German sources are my own.

support the narrative less than they serve a certain exegetical or paraenetical interest.³ The motifs of old Arabian, Jewish, or Christian-Arabian origin that lay behind them are obviously assumed to be well known. The qur'anic reception of biblical feminine figures seen from the perspective of the study of religions cannot, for this reason, be treated in isolation as a relationship strictly between the Bible and the Qur'an but rather must consider the relationship of these revelatory texts to other literature from the traditions of late antiquity. The controversial and current debate about the origins of the Qur'an can be pursued in regard to feminine figures only by using examples; the other references must follow in summary.⁴

1. The Relationship between the Bible and the Qur'an

1.1. The Religious Studies Perspective on the Reception of the Bible in the Qur'an

The Qur'an's own understanding of the relationship between biblical and qur'anic texts starts from a single revelation inscribed upon heavenly tablets preserved only in the Qur'an.⁵ The originally homonymous torah and gospel had been corrupted over the course of time, so a new revelation, this time in the Arabic language, became necessary.⁶ Still, the previous revelations remained valid for each community.

---

3. See Neuwirth, *Der Koran*, 565: "verschiedenste Textsorten zu der neuen, vom Koran allein Repräsentierten Gattung 'Sure.'" On self-referentiality, see *Der Koran*, 137–45; Nicolai Sinai, *Fortschreibung und Auslegung: Studien zur frühen Koraninterpretation*, DisAr 16 (Wiesbaden: Harrassowitz, 2009).

4. The Qur'an translation used in the original German version of this essay is: Hartmut Bobzin, *Der Koran: Aus dem Arabischen neu übertragen von Hartmut Bobzin unter Mitarbeit von Katharina Bobzin*, NOB (Munich: Beck, 2010). The translation used in this English version, with slight modifications, is: Abdullah Yusuf Ali, *The Holy Qur'an* (Ware, UK: Wordsworth, 2000).

5. The Jewish concept of the revelation upon heavenly tablets is developed, for example, in the book of Jubilees; see Lynn Liddonici and Andrea Lieber, eds., *Heavenly Tablets. Interpretation, Identity and Tradition in Ancient Judaism*, JSJSup 119 (Leiden: Brill, 2007).

6. See Stefan Schreiner, "Der Koran als Auslegung der Bibel—die Bibel als Verstehenshilfe des Korans," in *"Nahe ist dir das Wort...": Schriftauslegung in Christentum und Islam*, ed. Hansjörg Schmid, Andreas Renz, and Bülent Ucar, TFCI (Regensburg: Pustet, 2010), 167–83.

This understanding of revelation in qur'anic theology differs from the reconstruction of the historical processes at work in the origin of the Qur'an offered by religious studies or literary criticism. In the latter, the matter at issue is the new identity of the text of the Qur'an formed through the reception of biblical texts, motifs, and other materials; its reshaping in the context of the texts and traditions in late antiquity; and the formulation of completely new content. That there is a reception of biblical texts is stated in the Qur'an itself. In the Muslim tradition, the biblical material is called the *Isrā'īlīyāt*. The similarity in content is shown by the fact that, at the beginning, the debate was whether the Islamic message was a Jewish or a Christian heresy.[7]

In the nineteenth century, interest in Islam and the East grew along with the colonization of Islamic areas.[8] Similarities and differences between the Bible and the Qur'an, as well as the extrabiblical tradition, prompted Jewish and Christian research on the Qur'an.[9] Such work, however, was often conducted under the hermeneutical assumption that the qur'anic reception (through Muhammad's authorship) was wrong, incomplete, or divergent. The Bible was accepted unquestioningly as a normative master text against which the reception was measured. The theological autonomy of the Qur'an and its validity as a text on its own rarely came into view. Only a more intensive preoccupation with the Deuterocanon and the texts found at Qumran expanded the view to encompass further extrabiblical Christian and Jewish text collections as a basis for the reception of biblical motifs in the Qur'an. Newer approaches to reception and intertextuality, as well as the perception of Muslim research on the Qur'an, led to a nuanced perspective on the relationship between the Bible and the Qur'an, even if apologetic works are still to

---

7. See Stefan Schreiner, "Die 'Häresie der Ismaeliten': Der Islam als politisches und theologisches Problem der Christen und die Anfänge christlich-antiislamischer Polemik," in *Identität durch Differenz? Wechselseitige Abgrenzungen in Christentum und Islam*, ed. Hansjörg Schmid, TFCI (Regensburg: Pustet, 2009), 119–38.

8. See Edward W. Said, *Orientalism* (London: Routledge & Kegan Paul, 1978).

9. See Wilhelm Rudolph, *Die Abhängigkeit des Qorans von Judentum und Christentum* (Stuttgart: Kohlhammer, 1929); Theodor Nöldeke, *Geschichte des Qorāns*, 3 vols. (Leipzig: Dieterich'sche Verlagsbuchhandlung, 1938); Abraham Geiger, *Was hat Mohammed aus dem Judenthume aufgenommen? Eine von der Königl. Preussischen Rheinuniversität gekrönte Preisschrift* (Leipzig: Kaufmann, 1902); Heinrich Speyer, *Die biblischen Erzählungen im Qoran* (Hildesheim: Olms, 1988).

be found today.[10] The question whether or not the Qur'an must be read against the background of Eastern Christian (Syro-Aramaic) language and liturgy sparked a lively debate beginning in 2000.[11] The research team of the Corpus Coranicum project led by Angelika Neuwirth in Berlin understands the Qur'an as a text from late antiquity that already reflects upon the Jewish and Christian exegesis of biblical material (and thereby does not simply take over material from the Bible). Such reflection must thus be integrated into the hermeneutical discourse on texts from late antiquity, including the Qur'an. Christian and Jewish congregations in Arabia and elsewhere in the broader sphere of the later Roman Empire lived not only with the texts of the Bible but also with the interpretation and continued written reception of those texts.

The discussion of the reception of biblical figures of women in the Qur'an must be embedded in this broader academic discourse. Texts from the Jewish-Hellenistic corpus of the texts classified as rewritten Bible, or other independent traditions, were sometimes more influential than the Bible text itself. The following comparison of the Bible and the Qur'an does not place the Bible in a hierarchy but rather lays down a basis for working out an independent qur'anic theology.

1.2. Biblical Figures of Women in the Qur'anic Reception

In the following, the biblical narrative thread in the Old and New Testaments guides the treatment of the biblical-qur'anic figures of women and sums up the content that frequently appears in several *sūrah*s. In this way, the relative chronology of the Qur'an passages, which is sometimes disputed, is also taken into account. The feminine figures cannot simply be identified by name. There is no Eve in the Qur'an as such because the first woman of humankind in the Qur'an is not called Eve; consequently, all the connotations attached to the name Eve should not be applied. The use of biblical names also suggests that the biblical figures served as normative models and

---

10. See, for example, Marilyn R. Waldman, "New Approaches to 'Biblical' Materials in the Qur'ān," *MW* 75 (1985): 1–16; Franz V. Greifenhagen, "Cooperating Revelations? Qur'an, Bible and Intertextuality," *Arc* 33 (2005): 302–17.

11. See Christoph Burgmer, ed., *Streit um den Koran: Die Luxenberg-Debatte; Standpunkte und Hintergründe* (Berlin: Schiler, 32007); see also Mitri Raheb, "Contextualising the Scripture: Towards a New Understanding of the Qur'an—An Arab-Christian Perspective," *SWC* 3 (1997): 180–201.

endangers a more objective view that recognizes that the Qur'an assumes knowledge of the biblical and extrabiblical traditions but interprets them anew.

2. The Reception of Feminine Figures from the Hebrew Bible

2.1. The First Created: The Wife of Adām

2.1.1. Man and Woman: One Creation

The knowledge and acknowledgment of God's power as Creator is one of the theological starting points for the origin of Islam. Statements on creation are "a consistent benchmark of qur'anic preaching," since such statements provide proof of God's exclusive power and sovereignty.[12] Sūrat al-'Alaq (The Clinging Clot) is considered to be one of the earliest *sūrahs*, and the creation of humans is its focus.

> In the name of Allah, most gracious, most merciful
> Proclaim in the name of your Lord and cherisher, who created—
> Created the human being out of a (mere) clot of congealed blood. (Q al-'Alaq 96:1–2)

Sūrat al-'Alaq already contains *in nuce* the relationship between humans and God. The creation of human beings stands at the beginning of the world; therefore, there are no differences between the sexes. Before the division of humanity into different sexes, there was a being who consisted of two sexes or was without sex. Only through the separation of the woman from this being did the two sexes originate. Central is God's exclusive and sovereign activity as Creator, who makes all human beings out of clay, drops of blood, or drops of semen: something special comes out of something negligible. Both sexes come from God out of one being. Therefore, the calls to knowledge and acknowledgment of God are also directed

---

12. Friedmann Eissler, "Adam und Eva in Islam," in *Adam und Eva in Judentum, Christentum und Islam*, ed. Christfried Böttrich, Beate Ego, and Friedmann Eissler, JCI (Göttingen: Vandenhoeck & Ruprecht, 2011), 138–199; statements on creation are "ein beständiger Bezugspunkt der koranischen Predigt" (139). See also Jolanda Guardi, "Eva e la creazione nel Corano, nella tradizione musulmana e nella teologia feminista," *AScR* 11 (2006): 281–90; Amina Wadud, *Qur'an and Woman: Rereading the Sacred Text from a Woman's Perspective* (New York: Oxford University Press, 1999).

at both human beings, and this establishes the direct relationship of both to God. Both are able to recognize through what is taught by the pen (Q al-'Alaq 96:4–5) how they can turn to God and that this is their goal. Both are given righteous guidance; both are therefore responsible for their actions. Whoever deviates from the right path can ask for forgiveness in order to restore relationship with God. This fundamental equality of humans runs through the entire Qur'an (see, e.g., Q an-Nisā' 4:1). When human beings as the *children of adām* are addressed, both sexes are meant, for "Adam is always at the same time both a proper name and a generic term."[13]

2.1.2. The Role of the First Woman

The first woman remains nameless: it is said that she is "part of a pair."[14] The qur'anic tradition makes use of the biblical motif (Gen 2:21–22) in its own theological proclamation of the righteous guidance and responsibility of both humans. It is not the Qur'an but Islamic tradition that first developed the motif of Adam's rib, from which the woman was created, to the disadvantage of women in general.

As in the Bible, the Qur'an's texts dealing with paradise stand in the context of the creation texts. Paradise, to be sure, is also the starting point of creation in the circle of the angels, but it is also repeatedly described as the goal after death and is imagined in magnificent word pictures, mosaics, or images as a place of hope. The motif of the tree of life in paradise is assumed to be well known. Which elements are especially taken up and recomposed as new material depends upon the context of the *sūrah* and the purposes of its message. Only the Muslim tradition refers to the name, taken from the polyphonic tradition, of Hawa (*ḥawwâ* in Gen 3:20; 4:1) for the first woman. The Qur'an itself does not mention the name.

The scene describing the temptation of the humans in paradise quite clearly shows that the basis of the reception is not restricted to Gen 2–3; the story is interwoven with other traditions about the heavenly court of the angels, the fall of the angels, the challenge to God through Iblis, and the permission given to him to be allowed to tempt humans (see Job 1–2). Other motifs suggest additional extrabiblical Jewish and Christian traditions. Q Ṭā Hā 20:115–124 is cited here as an example:

---

13. Eissler, "Adam und Eva," 152: "Adam ist immer Eigenname und Gattungsbegriff zugleich."
14. Eissler, "Adam und Eva," 155: "Teil eines Paares."

We had already, beforehand, taken the covenant of Adam, but he forgot; and we found on his part no firm resolve. When we said to the angels, "Prostrate yourselves to Adam," they prostrated themselves, but not Iblis; he refused. Then we said, "Oh Adam! Verily this is an enemy to you and to your wife; so let him not get you both out of the garden, so that you land in misery. There is therein (enough provision) for you not to go hungry nor to go naked, nor to suffer from thirst, nor from the sun's heat."

But Satan whispered evil to him: he said, "Oh Adam! Shall I lead you to the Tree of Eternal Life and to a kingdom that never decays?" In the result, they both ate of the tree, and so their nakedness appeared to them. They began to sew together, for their covering, leaves from the garden; thus did Adam disobey his Lord and allow himself to be seduced. But the Lord chose him (for his grace); He turned to him and gave him guidance. He said, "Get down, both of you—all together, from the garden, with enmity one to another. But if, as is sure, there comes to you guidance from me, whosoever follows my guidance will not lose his way nor fall into misery. But whosoever turns away from my message, verily for him is a life narrowed down, and we shall raise him up blind on the day of judgment."

In contrast to the Hebrew Bible, the woman here plays no independent (negative) role against Adam. Satan seduces *both* human beings, and the action of both is presented as a duality: both eat together. In the end, the goal of the paradise texts, too, is to show that all people are themselves responsible for their transgressions. God's compassion, however, transcends even the transgression of listening to the blandishments of Iblis. This is illustrated by the similar passage about the first pair of human beings.

2.2. The Mother of Isḥāq: Ibrāhīm's Wife

Neither Sarah nor Hagar is mentioned by name in the Qur'an. If it is nevertheless possible to apply these names to Ibrāhīm's wives in the Qur'an, it is because they are mentioned by name in the tradition of Qur'an commentaries, in the stories about the prophets, and in the Hadith, the narrative traditions outside the Qur'an.

From the long Sarah tradition (Gen 11:27–23:20), the Qur'an takes up, in three *sūrahs*, the announcement of Isaac's birth made to Sarah and Abraham, together with the subsequent judgment upon Sodom and Gomorrah (Gen 18–19), so that not only the motifs but also the narrative context of

Gen 18–19 is absorbed into the Qur'an. These *sūrah*s also assume Jewish and (Eastern) Christian exegetical traditions connected with Gen 18–19.[15] In the different *sūrah*s, the portrayal of Ibrāhīm's wife varies considerably, from no mention of her at all (e.g., Q Ḥijr 15:51–57) to a central role (e.g., Q Hūd 11).

> Has the story reached you, of the honored guests of Abraham?… (When they did not eat), he conceived a fear of them. They said, "Fear not," and they gave glad tidings of a son endowed with knowledge. But his wife came forward (laughing) aloud; she smote her forehead and said, "A barren old woman!" They said, "Even so has your Lord spoken; and he is full of wisdom and knowledge." (Q Adh-Dhāriyāt 51:24, 28–30)

In Q Adh-Dhāriyāt 51:24–30, Ibrāhīm's wife reacts with a gesture of disbelief in the proclamation made to Ibrāhīm and argues her objection. Her reaction assumes that she has heard the conversation. In the Bible, Sarah is discovered and states her argument only upon request. Here, however, she challenges the messengers on her own initiative. She herself has a voice; she herself formulates the objection of her age; she receives her own corroborating pledge through the messengers. Yes, it is a miracle, but God's wisdom and knowledge of the situation makes the birth of the child possible.

The most complete reception of the story of Sarah follows in Q Hūd 11:69–74:

> There came our messengers to Abraham with glad tidings. They said, "Peace!" He answered, "Peace!" and hastened to entertain them with a roasted calf. But when he saw their hands went not towards the (meal), he felt some mistrust of them and conceived a fear of them. They said, "Fear not: We have been sent against the people of Lūṭ." And his wife was standing (there), and she laughed; but we gave her glad tidings of Isaac and, after him, of Jacob. She said, "Alas for me! Shall I bear a child, seeing I am an old woman, and my husband here is an old man? That would indeed be a strange thing!" They said, "Do you wonder at Allah's decree? The grace of Allah and his blessings on you, oh you people of the house! For he is indeed worthy of all praise, and full of all glory!" When fear had

---

15. See Andrew E. Arterbury, "Abraham's Hospitality among Jewish and Early Christian Writers: A Tradition History of Gen 18:1–16 and Its Relevance for the Study of the New Testament," *PRSt* 30 (2003): 359–76; see also Edward Noort, ed., *Sodom's Sin. Genesis 18–19 and Its Interpretations*, TBN 7 (Leiden: Brill, 2004).

passed from (the mind of) Abraham and the glad tidings had reached him, he began to plead with us for Lūt's people.

Ibrāhīm's encounter with God's messengers frames the central scene of proclamation, which is completely directed toward the woman as the recipient of the promise. Sarah's famous laugh from Gen 18:12 is introduced more abruptly in Hūd 11; it is obviously a fixed element of the tradition. Ibrāhīm's wife is a woman who has been called; the structure of the scene contains formal elements such as those in the calling of biblical prophets. Ibrāhīm's wife receives the revelation of Isḥāq and his son Ya'qūb. She formulates the decisive hindrance of her age as the objection she presents to God's messengers. In response to her objection, she receives as corroboration the message of God's blessing and compassion, to which age is no hindrance. God's messengers emphasize that Ibrāhīm's wife will bear Isḥāq and will have Yaq'ūb as his descendant. Praise of God is the appropriate reaction to God's miracles. The mother of Isḥāq shifts here much more clearly into the center of the story, in comparison with Ibrāhīm, than is the case in Gen 18. Only after the proclamation is made to his wife does Ibrāhīm emerge from his state of shock.

In Q al-Ḥijr 15:51–57, on the other hand, Ibrāhīm's wife plays no role at all. The birth of a wise boy is proclaimed only to Ibrāhīm. The objection of advanced age is applied only to him, and it is rebutted through the confession of a God who is not to be doubted. Ibrāhīm's wife as a bearer of meaning is absent here; this void stands in sharp contrast not only to the traditional material but also to other *sūrah*s within the Qur'an.

The qur'anic reception of the Sarah traditions thus varies the motif and relies on different traditions according to the theological accent desired. Thus, for example, the lack of anthropomorphism in Q Hūd 11, in contrast to the Bible, corresponds strongly with the Jewish interpretation of Gen 18 in Genesis Rabbah.[16] But other early Jewish and Christian traditions about Sarah's royal or noble origins and the fact that she, like Ibrāhīm, left her home were also widespread and were developed anew in the Muslim tradition. Sarah's beauty, her endangerment by a tyrant, Ibrāhīm's passing her off as his sister, Pharaoh's attempt to seize her, Pharaoh's punishment and subsequent gift to her of Hagar as a slave—all

---

16. See Michael E. Lodahl, *Claiming Abraham: Reading the Bible and the Qur'an Side by Side* (Grand Rapids: Brazos, 2010), esp. 9–24; Gisela Egler, "Sarah and Hagar in islamischer Tradition," *Cibedo* 6 (1992): 182–86.

of this was in circulation. The motif of Ibrāhīm as the first Muslim is transferred to Sarah as the first Muslima, a motif that in Mecca is also connected with Hājar.

2.3. Hājar (Hagar), the Mother of Ismāʿīl (Ishmael)

Hagar is not mentioned in the Qur'an, nor is she identified as the mother of Ismāʿīl, although the latter plays an important role. "Islamic scholars … will be struck by the paucity of sources when compared with what may be found in the Judeo-Christian traditions."[17] It was later tradition that inserted Hājar into the exegesis of Q Ibrāhīm 14:37, which says:

> Oh, our Lord! I have made some of my offspring to dwell in a valley without cultivation, by your sacred house, in order, oh our Lord, that they may establish regular prayer. So fill the hearts of some among men with love towards them, and feed them with fruits, so that they may give thanks.

The context of the *sūrah* provides no clues that the subject here might be Hājar and Ismāʿīl, but the empty spaces, such as "some of my offspring," were easy to fill later on when one connected Ismāʿīl and Hājar with the Kaʿba. The Hadith collection by Sahih al-Bukhari was the first to record Hājar, together with Ismāʿīl, as the founder, or one of the founders, of the rites in Mecca.[18]

---

17. Hibba Abugideiri, "Hagar: A Historical Model for Gender Jihad," in *Daughters of Abraham: Feminist Thought in Judaism, Christianity and Islam*, ed. Yvonne Yazbeck Haddad and John L. Esposito (Gainesville: University Press of Florida, 2001), 81–107, esp. 81.

18. There, Ibrāhīm brings Hājar with Ismāʿīl to a waterless place, which Ibrāhīm, in response to Hājar's reproaches, reveals as a command of God. Hājar piously trusts in God's sustenance. When the water runs out and the child is threatened by death, she runs in despair back and forth between the mountains al-Safa and al-Marwa until she finds, through the aid of an angel, the Zam Zam springs and then encloses them. The act of running between the two mountains belongs to the rite of the hajj. Only Q al-Baqarah 2:158 could possibly be interpreted in the sense of this running, but it, too, does not mention Hājar. Only later was the rite clarified, either in a transformation of an older meaning or through a new interpretation. The memory of Hājar as the ancestral mother of the Arabs (see Gen 25:12–18) continues to live in the collective memory of the pilgrimage. The pilgrims not only follow in the footsteps of Ibrāhīm and Ismāʿīl, but they also relive the fate and salvation of Hājar. Hājar's grave is vener-

2.4. The Women around Mūsā

The Qur'an also incorporates the exodus narrative and the story of Moses's childhood as one of the elements in it (Exod 1–2). Mūsā is the prophet mentioned most frequently in the Qur'an.[19] In this context, Moses's mother, his sister, and his wife Zipporah are also mentioned in Sūrat Ṭā Hā (20) and Sūrat al-Qaṣaṣ (28), albeit without being named. The few sentences and allusions assume that the story of the child Moses is well known. In both passages, the subject is how Mūsā is first abandoned and then given back to his mother through the action of his sister.

The main focus is on the guidance and preservation of the prophet Mūsā in the midst of all dangers and in the face of his enemies (Pharaoh and Pharaoh's wife). On the occasion of Mūsā's preservation as a small boy, God speaks directly with his mother: she receives a revelation. God promises her that Mūsā will remain unscathed; nevertheless, the mother is portrayed as agitated and inconsolable, so that God restores her child to her through the aid of his sister, "that her eye might be cooled and she should not grieve" (Q Ṭā Hā 20:40).

Thus Mūsā's mother receives a sign so that she trusts in God's proclamations. Interesting is the fact that God is moved to pity by the mother's sadness and grief at the loss of her—even if saved—son. God's wish that she might not be sad contributes not only to her joy but also to the goal "that she might know that the promise of Allah is true" (Q al-Qaṣaṣ 28:13). Thus the concern is once again the proclamation of God's properties, not

---

ated in Mecca at the Ka'ba; see Riffat Hassan, "Feast of Sacrifice in Islam: Abraham, Hagar and Ishmael," in *Commitment and Commemoration: Jews, Christians, Muslims in Dialogue*, ed. André Lacoque (Chicago: Exploration, 1994), 131–50; Fred Leemhuis, "Hājar in the Qur'ān and Its Early Commentaries," in *Abraham, the Nations, and the Hagarites: Jewish, Christian, and Islamic Perspectives on Kinship with Abraham*, ed. Martin Goodman, George H. Van Kooten, and Jacques Van Ruiten, TBN 13 (Leiden: Brill, 2010), 503–8; Alan M. Cooper, "Hagar In and Out of Context," *USQR* 55 (2001): 35–46; Thomas Michel, "Hagar: Mother of Faith in the Compassionate God," *ICMR* 30 (2004): 47–54; Jessica Grimes, "Reinterpreting Hagar's Story," *Lect* 1 (2004): https://tinyurl.com/SBL6011a.

19. On Mūsā in the Qur'an, see, by way of example, Karl Prenner, *Muhammad und Musa: Strukturanalyse und theologiegeschichtliche Untersuchungen zu den mekkanischen Musa-Perikopen des Qur'an*, Studien (Christlich-Islamisches Schrifttum) 6 (Altenberge: Christlich-Islamisches Schrifttum, 1986); Brannon M. Wheeler, *Moses in the Qur'an and Islamic Exegesis* (London: Routledge, 2002).

the portrayal of the feminine figure. By way of example, the story of Mūsā's childhood is cited here from Sūrat al-Qaṣaṣ.

> So we sent this inspiration to the mother of Moses: "Suckle (your child), but when you have fears about him, cast him into the river, but fear not nor grieve; for we shall restore him to you, and we shall make him one of our messengers." Then the people of Pharaoh picked him up (from the river); (it was intended) that (Moses) should be to them an adversary and a cause for sorrow, for Pharaoh and Hāmān and (all) their hosts were men of sin. The wife of Pharaoh said, "(Here is) joy of the eye, for me and for you; slay him not. It may be that he will be of use to us, or we may adopt him as a son." And they perceived not (what they were doing)! But there came to be a void in the heart of the mother of Moses. She was going almost to disclose his (case), had we not strengthened her heart (with faith), so that she might remain a (firm) believer. And she said to the sister of (Moses), "Follow him." So she (the sister) watched him in the character of a stranger. And they knew not. And we ordained that he refused to suck at first, until (his sister came up and) said, "Shall I point out to you the people of a house that will nourish and bring him up for you and be sincerely attached to him?" Thus did we restore him to his mother, that her eye might be comforted, that she might not grieve, and that she might know that the promise of Allah is true. But most of them do not understand. (Q al-Qaṣaṣ 28:7–13)

This episode is followed by the migration to Midian. Q al-Qaṣaṣ 28:23 takes up elements from Exod 2:15–22, where Moses helps Zipporah and her sisters water their herds and then receives Zipporah as his wife. The Bible, however, speaks of seven sisters; here there are only two. It is possible that here, as in the following *sūrah*, motifs from the scene at the well with Jacob and Rachel (Gen 29) enter the narrative, since the biblical Moses does not have to work to receive Zipporah, but the biblical Jacob must do so for the sake of the two daughters. In contrast to the Bible, one of the daughters in the Moses story seizes the initiative and suggests that the father keep him on as a servant. This woman appears as an independent conversation partner.

> And when he arrived at the watering (place) in Madyan, he found there a group of men watering (their flocks), and besides them he found two women who were keeping back (their flocks). He said, "What is the matter with you?" They said, "We cannot water (our flocks) until the shepherds take back (their flocks); and our father is a very old man." So he watered (their flocks) for them; then he turned back to the shade

and said, "Oh my Lord! Truly am I in (desperate) need of any good that you do send me" Afterwards one of the (women) came (back) to him, walking bashfully. She said, "My father invites you so that he may reward you for having watered (our flocks) for us." So when he came to him and narrated the story, he said, "Fear you not; you have escaped (well) from unjust people." Said one of the (women), "Oh my (dear) father! Engage him on wages; truly the best of men for you to employ is the (man) who is strong and trusty." He said, "I intend to wed one of these my daughters to you, on condition that you serve me for eight years; but if you complete ten years, it will be (grace) from you. But I intend not to place you under a difficulty; you will find me, indeed, if Allah wills, one of the righteous." He said, "Be that (the agreement) between me and you; whichever of the two terms I fulfill, let there be no ill will to me. Allah be a witness to what we say." (Q al-Qaṣaṣ 28:23–28)

Then, at verse 29, the subject turns to the calling of Moses (cf. Exod 3).

2.5. The Seductress of Yūsuf and the Cunning of Women

The Joseph novella (Gen 37–50) is interpreted in Sūrat Yūsuf (12), that is, Joseph. Whereas the biblical narrative appears to value narrative tension, the *sūrah* aims to demonstrate by means of examples God's guidance and preservation of the prophet Yūsuf. The *sūrah* is formed as a speech by God. The assessments of the acting persons govern proper understanding of the action. "Instead of the reader reliving the *plot*, the reader is expected to take note of the sayings of higher wisdom."[20] In this way, the *sūrah* is not a retelling of the story but rather an independent composition incorporating further extrabiblical motifs. Yūsuf is sold, comes to Egypt, and is bestowed by God with all wisdom. Here begins the conflict with the wife of an Egyptian. Her negative moral characterization makes it clear from the beginning that the woman is the classic seductress of the innocent and believing. Verse 24 already anticipates the positive outcome of the story; all that remains unresolved is how Yūsuf will be preserved, not that he will be preserved.

---

20. Harald Schweizer, "Die Josefsgeschichte im Koran und in der hebräischen Bibel: Synoptischer Vergleich," *BN* n.s. 144 (2010): 15–39, esp. 21: "Anstatt den plot mitzuerleben, ist vom Leser gefordert, dass er die höheren Weisheiten zur Kenntnis nimmt." See also Schweizer, "Koranische Fortschreibung eines hebräischen Textes: Hermeneutische Überlegungen anhand der Gestalt Josefs," *BN* n.s. 143 (2009): 69–79.

But she in whose house he was sought to seduce him from his (true) self. She fastened the door and said, "Now come, you (dear one)!" He said, "Allah forbid! Truly (your husband) is my lord! He made my sojourn agreeable! Truly to no good come those who do wrong!" And (with passion) did she desire him, and he would have desired her, but that he saw the evidence of his Lord; thus (did we order) that we might turn away (all) evil and shameful deeds from him, for he was one of our servants, sincere and purified. So they both raced each other to the door, and she tore the shirt from his back. They both found her lord near the door. She said, "What is the (fitting) punishment for one who formed an evil design against your wife but prison or a grievous chastisement?" He said, "It was she who sought to seduce me—from my (true) self." And one of her household saw (this) and bore witness (thus)—"If it be that his shirt is rent from the front, then is her tale true, and he is a liar! But if it be that his shirt is torn from the back, then she is the liar, and he is telling the truth!" So when he saw his shirt—that it was torn at the back—(her husband) said, "Behold, it is a snare of you women! Truly, mighty is your snare! Oh Joseph, pass over this! (Oh wife), ask forgiveness for your sin, for truly you have been at fault!" (Q Yūsuf 12:23–29)

Without God's preservation, Yūsuf would have succumbed to Egyptian's wife's attempts at seduction. Thus does the woman's attempt at seduction and defamation fail; she is found guilty. The Egyptian characterizes her conduct as the usual cunning conduct of all women (12:28). The scene is interrupted before the conclusion (12:33–34), in which the wife answers the defamation of her character.

Ladies in the city said, "The wife of the (great) 'Aziz is seeking to seduce her slave from his (true) self; truly he has inspired her with violent love. We see she is evidently going astray." When she heard their malicious talk, she sent for them and prepared a banquet for them. She gave each of them a knife, and she said (to Joseph), "Come out before them." When they saw him, they did extol him, and (in their amazement) cut their hands. They said, "Allah preserve us! This is no mortal! This is none other than a noble angel!" She said, "There before you is the man about whom you did blame me! I did seek to seduce him from his (true) self, but he did firmly save himself guiltless!… And now, if he does not do my bidding, he shall certainly be cast into prison, and (what is more) be of the company of the vilest!" He said, "Oh my Lord! The prison is more to my liking than that to which they invite me; unless You turn away their snare from me, I should (in my youthful folly) feel inclined towards them and join the ranks of the ignorant." So his Lord hearkened to him (in his prayer) and turned away from him their snare; verily, he hears and knows (all things). (Q Yūsuf 12:30–34)

In the Bible, Joseph's beauty prompts Potiphar's wife to want to seduce him again and again (Gen 39:6–10); these attempts are given no explanation or understanding. The Qur'an deepens and expands this motif, but it also expresses understanding for Pharaoh's wife, who, through the "ladies of the city," is in a certain way rehabilitated because of Yūsuf's extraordinary beauty (like a "noble angel"). Since the motif is also found in Jewish midrash, it is true here as well that the characterization of the seductive Egyptian woman draws from a larger stock of texts and stories than just the biblical account. Yet in spite of all this justification, in the end the woman remains at fault in the face of God, and Yūsuf is preserved.

Thus only God's help saves Yūsuf from the woman's cunning. The story illustrates the necessity, but also the possibility, of holding fast to faith even under adverse circumstances and of imploring God for help in such situations. The tradition, as well as later literature, developed this scene into a love story between Joseph and Suleika.[21]

2.6. The Queen of Sheba

The queen of Sheba, already legendary in the Bible (1 Kgs 10:1–13), is given her own fabulous character in the Qur'an (Q an-Naml 27:22–44), with motifs that lie outside the Bible. Legends about this queen and her southern Arabian kingdom exist in Jewish, Ethiopian, and southern Arabian traditions.[22] In the Qur'an, the story stands in the series of narratives about the prophets who were signs for humans: Mūsā, Sālih (the prophet for the Thamūd), and Lūt. Solomon gathers his host of men, djinns, and birds, but he misses the hoopoe and intends to punish it for staying away. However, the hoopoe brings news that the queen of the Sabaeans is rich and powerful; however, her people, through Satan's work, do not worship God but rather the sun (Q an-Naml 27:22–28). Solomon sends a letter via the hoopoe and calls on the people to repent: "Be not arrogant against me,

---

21. See Erika Glassen, "Die Josephsgeschichte im Koran und in der persischen und türkischen Literatur," in *Paradeigmata: Literarische Typologie des Alten Testaments*, ed. Franz Link, 2 vols., SL 5 (Berlin: Duncker & Humblot, 1989), 1:169–79.

22. See the thematic volume of the journal *Graphé* 11 (2002), Jacob Lassner, *Demonizing the Queen of Sheba: Boundaries of Gender and Culture in Postbiblical Judaism and Medieval Islam*, CSHJ (Chicago: University of Chicago Press, 1993).

but come to me in submission (to the true religion)" (27:31). While the Bible still sees the queen of Sheba as a ruler who puts Solomon to the test and then recognizes his superiority, the roles here are reversed from the outset: the queen of Sheba is put to the test. Here further additional legendary material enters the story. The queen decides against a war that her advisors recommend and offers gifts instead. Since the issue in question is her conversion to the right faith, Solomon refuses them and challenges his subjects to see who can be the first to bring him the throne of the queen.

> Said one who had knowledge of the book, "I will bring it to you within the twinkling of an eye!" Then when (Solomon) saw it placed firmly before him, he said, "This is by the grace of my Lord!—to test me whether I am grateful or ungrateful! And if any is grateful, truly his gratitude is (again) for his own soul; but if any is ungrateful, truly my Lord is free of all needs, supreme in honor!" He said, "Transform her throne out of all recognition by her; let us see whether she is guided (to the truth) or is one of those who receive no guidance." So when she arrived, she was asked, "Is this your throne?" She said, "It was just like this." (And Solomon said,) "We were given the knowledge before her and we had surrendered (to Allah)." And (all) that she was wont to worship instead of Allah hindered her, for she came of unbelieving folk. She was asked to enter the lofty palace. But when she saw it, she thought it was a lake of water, and she (tucked up her skirts), uncovering her legs. He said, "This is but a palace paved with slabs of glass." She said, "Oh my Lord! I have indeed wronged my soul. I do (now) submit (in Islam), with Solomon, to the Lord of the worlds." (Q an-Naml 27:40–44)

The queen of Sheba is brought by a djinn to Solomon, is put to the test, and becomes a convert. She confesses her sin and places herself under God's will. In this treatment of the queen of Sheba, she becomes the model for those who convert from polytheism to the confession of the one God. The Islamic tradition gives the queen the name Bilqis.

2.7. Lūt's Wife and Daughters

As in the biblical context, the passage recounting the affliction and salvation of Lūt and his family (Q Hūd 11:77–81) follows directly after the announcement made to Ibrāhīm's wife.[23] The Qur'an takes up only a few

---

23. See Michael E. Lodahl, "Disputing over Abraham Disputing with God: An Exercise in Intertextual Reasoning," *CSR* 34 (2005): 487–504.

of the elements of Gen 19, among them Lūt and his daughters. Lūt offers his daughters to those from the city pressing upon him, but they refuse the offer. The longer biblical passage in which Lot offers up his daughters in order to spare his guests is condensed into a single sentence.

> When our messengers came to Lūt, he was grieved on their account and felt himself powerless (to protect) them. He said, "This is a distressful day." And his people came rushing towards him, and they had been long in the habit of practicing abominations. He said, "Oh my people! Here are my daughters; they are purer for you (if you marry)! Now fear Allah and cover me not with shame about my guests! Is there not among you a single right-minded man?" They said, "Well, you know we have no need of your daughters; indeed, you know quite well what we want!" He said, "Would that I had power to suppress you, or that I could betake myself to some powerful support." (The messengers) said, "Oh Lūt! We are messengers from your Lord! By no means shall they reach you! Now travel with your family while yet a part of the night remains, and let not any of you look back. But your wife (will remain behind); to her will happen what happens to the people. Morning is their time appointed; is not the morning nigh?" (Q Hūd 11:77–81)

In Gen 19:26, Lot's wife is turned into a pillar of salt because she disobeys the command not to look back, but here Lūt's wife has no choice. She must look back because her fate is foreordained, and she is destroyed like the others. On the other hand, the fate of the daughters is so foreordained that nothing happens to them. The fate of the feminine figures in Lūt's household shows that the will of God happens irrevocably, positively as well as negatively. God's messengers save the prophet Lūt from a most difficult predicament, which is a hopeful prospect for believers in the present.

2.8. Women as Examples of Faith and Disbelief (Q at-Taḥrīm 66:10–12)

The Qur'an mentions Lūt's wife a second time, together with Nūh's (Noah's) wife; they appear in Q at-Taḥrīm 66:10 as examples for unbelievers. Once again, the main concern is not the personality of the women but rather the example that they provide for the faithful today. In the Bible there is nothing in particular and certainly nothing negative to be read about Noah's wife; Lot's wife, by contrast, is turned into a pillar of salt (Gen 19:26). This *sūrah*, however, assumes knowledge about the women that presumably goes beyond the biblical texts. Only in this way can one explain that the women, without any further context, are presented as examples of disbelief. Again it is the case that everyone, including the women themselves, must answer to God. These examples emphasize the independence of women in religious decisions.

> Allah sets for an example to the unbelievers, the wife of Nūh and the wife of Lūt; they were (respectively) under two of our righteous servants, but they were false to their (husbands), and they profited nothing before Allah on their account but were told, "Enter the fire along with (others) that enter!" (Q at-Taḥrīm 66:10)

Added to them in verses 11–12 are two more women as examples of faith: the wife of Pharaoh and Maryam:

> And Allah sets forth as an example to those who believe, the wife of Pharaoh: behold, she said, "Oh my Lord! Build for me, in nearness to you, a mansion in the garden, and save me from Pharaoh and his doings, and save me from those that do wrong; and Maryam the daughter of ʿImrān, who guarded her chastity, and we breathed into (her body) of our spirit, and she testified to the truth of the words of her Lord and of his revelations, and she was one of the devout (servants). (Q at-Taḥrīm 66:11–12)

The wife of Pharaoh, however, also appears as the opponent of Mūsā when she is allied with the hostile Pharaoh (Q al-Qaṣaṣ 28:9). She herself is well disposed to the child and gives the command to let the boy live, but her affiliation with Pharaoh will prove to be a calamity for her.

3. The Reception of New Testament and Apocryphal Traditions about Women

3.1. The Protevangelium of James and Christian Marian Traditions

The reception of New Testament traditions in Sūrat Maryam (19) and Sūrat Āl ʿImrān (3) concentrates especially on the Lukan childhood stories about Jesus (Luke 1–2). However, these qur'anic traditions make clear that the broad field of apocryphal literature, including the varied early Christian Marian traditions in the Eastern churches, belongs to the sphere of reception. The Protevangelium of James especially influenced the Qur'an's texts on Maryam.²⁴ The manifold relationships of qur'anic texts to other texts confirm what the concept of intertextuality determines: the immense possibilities of textual relationships. Tryggve Kronholm observes: "We are faced with a flood of influence with almost innumerable branches."²⁵

From the large number of possible intertextual references, the Protevangelium of James is singled out here due to the clear references to the Maryam tradition. Presumably written in the second century, the Protevangelium of James was not accepted as part of the New Testament canon, but the many attestations of this gospel testify to its wide dissemination; today 140 Greek manuscripts still exist. It is likely to have belonged to the stock of texts and traditions about Christian life in the Arabian Peninsula. In the earliest preserved version, from the fourth century, the Protevangelium of James carries the heading "Birth of Mary" and, in the subtitle, the name of James. "As a characterization of the overall intention of this work..., the key words 'praise of Mary' offer themselves."²⁶ It fills in the blank narrative spaces in the life of Mary in the gospels so as to underscore Mary's particular saintliness. For the development of the Mariological tradition as a whole, it was of great significance.

3.2. Sequence of Scenes in the Maryam *Sūrahs* in Comparison with Luke 1–2 and the Protevangelium of James

A direct comparison of the individual scenes reveals the specific goals of the text as well as the commonalities and differences in the use of the tradition. The two Maryam *sūrahs* incorporate elements of Protevangelium of James and the Lukan tradition in significanly different ways.

An overview of the individual motifs of the narratives in all four important traditions dealing with the childhood stories about Mary and Jesus shows that in the Qur'an only Sūrat Āl 'Imrān has the prayer of 'Imran's wife (the mother of Maryam); further, this prayer has only one parallel: in the Protevangelium of James. The Protevangelium first

---

24. See Ulrike Bechmann, "Apokryphe Evangelientradition im Koran," *BK* 60 (2005): 108–11.

25. Tryggve Kronholm, "Dependence and Prophetic Originality in the Koran," *OS* 31–32 (1982–1983): 47–70, esp. 60; Greifenhagen, "Cooperating Revelations?"

26. Hans-Josef Klauck, *Apokryphe Evangelien: Eine Einführung* (Stuttgart: Katholisches Bibelwerk, 2002), 90: "Als Charakterisierung der Gesamtintention dieses Werkes ... Bietet sich das Stichwort 'Marienlob' an."

describes Joachim and Anna, Mary's parents, then discusses the events beginning with the miraculous birth of Mary, her life in the temple as a virgin, her purity, the virgin birth, and her flight to Egypt. Mary's exceptionality is shown by the heavenly proclamation of the birth of Jesus. When the angel Gabriel announces to Mary the miraculous birth, she must hide herself in the temple to escape unfounded accusations. She is examined and conceives and finally gives birth as a virgin to Jesus, which a midwife confirms. The motifs in the verses about Maryam in Q Āl ʿImrān 3:33–48 suggest a relationship between its content and the Protevangelium of James. By contrast, the John/Zechariah tradition (Yahya/ Zakariyyā) with the miraculous conception and birth to old and barren parents exists in both *sūrah*s and in Luke's Gospel but not in Protevangelium of James.

In the Mary/Maryam passages, the parallels alternate. There is only one element that serves as a common core in all four traditions: the proclamation made to Mary/Maryam that she, as a virgin, will give birth to a son, Jesus, or ʿIsa. Thereupon, Mary/Maryam answers the heavenly messenger with an only slightly varied question in return: "How can that occur, seeing as I know no man?" Each of the different narrative traditions, however, creates its own special theological perspective.

Q 19:1–33	Q 3:33–51	Luke 1–2	Prot. Jas. 1–16
	Prayer of the wife of ʿImran		Prayer of Joachim/Anna
	Pregnancy of the wife of ʿImran		Proclamation of Mary's pregnancy
	Maryam in the temple		Mary in the temple
	Sustenance through God		Sustenance through God
Prayer of Zakariyyā	Prayer of Zakariyyā	Prayer of Zakariyyā	
Proclamation of Yahya	Proclamation of Yahya	Proclamation of John	
Proclamation to Maryam	Proclamation to Maryam	Proclamation to Maryam	Proclamation to Maryam

Maryam hides	Maryam hides		Maryam hides
			Accusation in the temple; examination of Joseph/Mary
Birth 'Isa (palm)		Birth Jesus (stall)	Birth Jesus (stall)
Sign: Speech of 'Isa	Sign of 'Isa	Sign: cloths	Sign: virgin birth
'Isa as a child	Acts of 'Isa		
Accusation in the temple		Presentation in the temple	
'Isa defends Maryam			

3.3. The Wife of 'Imran, the Mother of Maryam, in Q Āl 'Imrān 3:33–37

Of course, there is no biblical mention of the mother of Maryam, 'Imran's wife, but the Protevangelium of James knows of Mary's parents. Since the wife of 'Imran is so closely connected with Maryam in the *sūrah*s, she may be mentioned here at least briefly. The high esteem enjoyed by Maryam depends upon her; she is the one who consecrates her daughter Maryam to God.

The wife of 'Imran and her child Maryam stand in a series of the elect that begins with Adam. What Protevangelium of James narrates in broad strokes is concentrated in the few verses of Q Āl 'Imrān 3:33–37. Nothing is said about 'Imran himself other than that he lends his name. Two passages of direct speech from the wife of 'Imran, however, are passed down. Her prayer promises Maryam to God even before her birth and asks for the acceptance of her child; Maryam's childhood in the temple and her miraculous sustenance through God's help are praised as miracles. The wife of 'Imran repeats this request after Maryam's birth, and she herself gives Maryam her name. She also articulates two divine predictions: God hears and knows everything, and she and her child can find refuge with God. The wife of 'Imran is heard by God, and Maryam is accepted by God in a special way.

3.4. The Wife of Zechariah

In the Lukan childhood stories, the proclamation of John's birth to Elizabeth and Zechariah (Luke 1) precedes the proclamation of Jesus's birth to Mary. Both traditions are connected in a similar way in Sūrat Maryam (19) and Sūrat Āl ʿImrān (3). In the Protevangelium of James, this material is not included.

According to the classic dating of the text, Sūrat Maryam (19) belongs among the Meccan *sūrah*s; that is, it originated earlier than Sūrat Āl ʿImrān (3). During this period, Muhammad's proclamation was largely rejected by polytheistic Mecca, and his followers were a minority there. In a comparison of both *sūrah*s, the different accents also become clear, although they cannot be detailed here. The Qur'an's proclamation of Yahya closely resembles the proclamation of ʿIsa to Maryam and in places even has the same wording.

Q 19:2–11	Q 3:37–41
	37 Right graciously did her Lord accept her: he made her grow in purity and beauty; to the care of Zakariyyā was she assigned. Every time that he entered (her) chamber to see her, he found her supplied with sustenance. He said, "Oh Mary! Whence (comes) this to you?" She said, "From Allah, for Allah provides sustenance to whom he pleases without measure."
2 (This is) a recital of the mercy of your Lord to his servant Zakariyyā.	
3 Behold, he cried to his Lord in secret,	38 There did Zakariyyā pray to his Lord,
4 praying, "Oh my Lord! Infirm indeed are my bones, and the hair of my head glistens with gray. But I am never unblessed, oh my Lord, in my prayer to you! 5 Now I fear (what) my relatives (and colleagues) (will do) after me, but my wife is barren.	saying,

So give me an heir from yourself—(one that) will (truly) represent me, and represent the posterity of Jacob, and make him, oh my Lord, one with whom you are well pleased!"	"Oh my Lord! Grant unto me a progeny from you that is pure; for you are he who hears prayer!"
	39 While he was standing in prayer in the chamber, the angels called unto him:
7 "Oh Zakariyyā, we give you good news of a son: his name shall be Yahyā; on none by that name have we conferred distinction before."	"Allah gives you glad tidings of Yahyā, witnessing the truth of a word from Allah, and (besides) noble, chaste, and a prophet—of the goodly company of the righteous."
8 He said, "Oh my Lord, how shall I have a son when my wife is barren and I have grown quite decrepit from old age?"	40 He said, "Oh my Lord! How shall I have a son, seeing I am very old and my wife is barren?"
9 He said, "So (it will be); your Lord says, 'That is easy for me; I did indeed create you before, when you had been nothing!'"	"Thus," was the answer, "does Allah accomplish what he wills."
10 (Zakariyyā) said, "Oh my Lord! Give me a sign."	41 He said, "Oh my Lord! Give me a sign!"
"Your sign," was the answer, "shall be that you shall speak to no man for three nights, although you are not dumb."	"Your sign," was the answer, "shall be that you shall speak to no man for three days but with signals.
11 So Zakariyyā came out to his people from his chamber. He told them by signs to celebrate Allah's praises in the morning and in the evening.	Then celebrate the praises of your Lord again and again and glorify him in the evening and in the morning."

The prayer of Zakariyyā and the proclamation of the miraculous birth of Yahya stand in the foreground in both *sūrah*s. In comparison with the Lukan childhood story, the wife of Zakariyyā here recedes into the background. She is only indirectly introduced through Zakariyyā's objection to the angel. In both *sūrah*s, the infertility of both stands equally against the prospect of a descendant. As in the subsequent proclamation to Maryam, this scene is shaped as a prophetic calling (of Yahya as well as of 'Isa) with an objection and an affirming sign. This wondrous birth of the prophet proclaims God's will and the possibility of creating a child even for an old, barren married couple. The creation of humans serves as proof that this is nothing special for God.

The wife of Zakariyyā, known in the Bible as Elizabeth (Luke 1:13, 24), bears no name in the Qur'an. Her only distinguishing mark is that she is barren and will give birth to a son. As such, she is characterized in parallel with the mother of Isḥāq (Sarah)—and in a special way quite differently— and also in parallel with Maryam. In the qur'anic message, the accent is not so much on the salvation of the individual feminine figures as much as on the sign of a miraculous birth of a prophet who repeatedly heralds the greatness and the creative power of the one God throughout history.

3.5. Maryam

The Zakariyyā episode stands in both *sūrahs* before the proclamation to Maryam as the virgin bearer of 'Isa. *Sūrah* 19 is even titled "Maryam," and *sūrah* 3 bears the heading "The Family of 'Imran," that is, the family of Maryam. Both *sūrahs* make reference especially to Maryam and the birth and significance of 'Isa. Maryam is the only woman from the Bible who is mentioned by name in the Qur'an. Approximately seventy verses make reference to Maryam, and her name stands alone or, in most cases, together with 'Isa (Jesus), who is characterized as "'Isa, the son of Maryam." Outside of the Qur'an, this title appears especially in apocryphal texts. As Martin Bauschke argues, "This title for Jesus probably comes originally from the Ethiopian Church and was brought to Mecca by the Muslim exiles when they returned there."[27] The Qur'an's esteem for Maryam presumably reflects the veneration of Mary that was widespread in the Christian Arab sphere in the seventh century.[28]

---

27. Martin Bauschke, *Jesus im Koran* (Cologne: Böhlau, 2001), 184, n. 41: "Wahrscheinlich stammt dieser Titel Jesu ursprünglich aus der Äthiopischen Kirche und wurde von den muslimischen Exulanten bei ihrer Rückkehr nach Mekka dorthin gebracht."

28. See Arent J. Wensinck and P. Johnstone, "Maryam," in *Encyclopedia of Islam*, ed. C. E. Bosworth et al., 2nd ed. (Leiden: Brill, 1991), 628–32.

Each of the two *sūrah*s, in comparison with one another, has its own theological accent.

3.5.1. Maryam in Q Maryam 19:16–36

Verse 16 opens a new section in the *sūrah* with the words: "Relate in the book (the story of) Mary!," though it is unclear what this "book (of) Mary" refers to. Sūrat Maryam recalls the calling of the prophets throughout time in order to proclaim faith in the one God; Muhammad stands in this line. Yahya (the biblical John the Baptist) and ʿIsa, who will return at the end of time, also belong to these prophets. After the Zakariyyā episode (Q Maryam 19:1–11) and the announcement of the birth of Yahya (19:12–15), there follows the proclamation made to Maryam (19:16–21), the birth of ʿIsa under the palm tree (19:22–26), and the confirming miracle signaling ʿIsa as the new prophet (19:27–33).

At the center of the Maryam episode stands the proclamation of ʿIsa's virgin conception and birth. Maryam's conception is the exact opposite of that of the old, infertile married couple in the preceding verses. She is a virgin, young, single, in the temple, and without a man! But neither extreme poses a difficulty for God the Creator of the world and of human beings. The pregnancies bear witness to divine compassion and God's omnipotence and uniqueness, and they lead prophetically into the concept of faith in the one God.

The location of the proclamation made to Maryam remains vague; it is a "place in the East" where there is a screen (Q Maryam 19:16–17). This motif could come from the Protevangelium of James. Sūrat Maryam only hints at this, while Sūrat Āl ʿImrān amplifies it.

Maryam plays an outstanding role in these prophetic events: she herself receives a divine revelation, believes, and gives birth as a virgin to the prophet ʿIsa. She proves to be the true believer because she, in contrast to Zakariyyā, does not doubt the word of the divine messenger. The question of how she can give birth without having a man is again answered by the angel with a reference to God's creative power. Maryam's question is less a doubt than it is the question about *in what way* God will act. The motifs of fright, the messenger from God, the proclamation, and Maryam's query are also found in Luke.

Independent traditions are followed in the birth scene. The birth of ʿIsa under a palm tree is without clear antecedent; only the Pseudo-Gospel of Matthew, which is difficult to date and of uncertain origin, has this motif.[29] Maryam feels herself alone and abandoned at the birth and wishes to die, but the newborn child 'Isa speaks, comforts Maryam, and, as an affirmative miracle, points out God's provision of sustenance through fresh water and fresh dates. 'Isa proclaims himself as a sign through which God desires to guide human beings.

3.5.2. Maryam in Q Āl 'Imrān 3:42–51

As in Sūrat Maryam (19), Sūrat Āl 'Imrān (3) first recalls the prophets from Adam to 'Isa who were sent to the people of Israel. Q Āl 'Imrān 3:33–47 is assigned to the Medina period. Here the conflict with earlier theologies dominates, and the authenticity of the qur'anic proclamation is placed in opposition to them. The *sūrah* reminds us that the righteous guidance of earlier times, the torah, was rejected by the previous recipients of the revelation. Yahya and 'Isa continue this righteous guidance by means of their prophecy—but also without lasting success—so the Qur'an renews the proclamation of God's righteous guidance.

The chief element of the Maryam episode in Sūrat Āl 'Imrān is once again the announcement of 'Isa's birth (Q Āl 'Imrān 3:41–47). But preceding this is now what was only implied in Sūrat Maryam: Maryam's earlier history (3:33–38) and the announcement of Yahya's birth (3:39–40). At the beginning of the proclamation scene, Maryam responds to God's election of her by being humble, bowing down, and prostrating herself, as she was instructed (3:43). These three acts correspond to the postures taken during Muslim prayer: the internal attitude, the bowing of the body, and the bowing by the community as the expression of the deepest devotion. Maryam worships God in the Muslim form.

Verse 44 interrupts the scene. God reveals to Muhammad that Maryam has acquired enemies and that the lot has fallen on her, an indication that she is endangered as many prophets had been before her and as it was foretold about Mary in the Protevangelium of James. Only then does the proclamation continue with verse 45.

In Sūrat Maryam (19), Mary has a vision; in Sūrat Āl 'Imrān (3), she hears a message (an audition). The name of her future child is revealed to

---

29. See Klauck, *Apokryphe Evangelien*. This gospel, written in Latin, originated presumably in the West only ca. 600–625 CE. On parallels in the Arabic childhood gospel, see Martin Bauschke, "Der koranische Jesus und die christliche Theologie," *MThZ* 52 (2001): 26–33; see also Neuwirth, *Der Koran*, 484–89.

her: "Christ Jesus, the son of Mary" (Q Āl 'Imrān 3:45). The child is held in honor in this world and in the world beyond; he moves into proximity to God. These characteristics mark 'Isa as a special prophet, because he is born of Maryam. The descent from her is thus placed on the same level as his acceptance in this world and the world beyond. To be the son of Maryam thus means closer definition in terms of content, a definition that derives from Maryam's special nature. Maryam's question about how she as a virgin is to give birth is answered by the creative power of God.

As in the gospels, Sūrat Maryam and Sūrat Āl 'Imrān also establish their own theological accents in their different reception of the childhood stories. Structurally, there appears to have been a similar process in regard to the childhood stories as that in the gospels. The early proclamation (here Sūrat Maryam, there Mark) displays no interest in the childhood of Jesus/'Isa but is interested in his prophetic being. Only the later proclamation fills this gap (Q Āl 'Imrān 3:33–47; Luke 1–2; Matt 1–2).

3.5.3. Maryam as a Prophetess in the Qur'an?

Whether and to what extent Maryam might be a prophetess has been answered in most cases in the Islamic tradition with a no, but the debate already shows that this is not so clear. A particular characterization of Maryam as a prophetess is consistent with the entire context of Sūrat Āl 'Imrān. Much points to the fact that, in this function, Maryam belongs to the chain of the prophets sent by God. Through the preceding presentation of the election and the childhood of Maryam, the later proclamation scene in Q Āl 'Imrān 3:42–47 shifts Maryam into the central characterization indigenous to the Qur'an as a woman with a special prophetic quality.[30] Everything that distinguishes masculine prophets is fulfilled by Maryam through her special function. Thus Sūrat Āl 'Imrān makes Maryam's theological significance more precise in comparison with Sūrat Maryam. The clan of 'Imran, with Maryam's mother and Maryam herself, represents the female element in the prophetic tradition and so provides a balance to the patriarchal Ibrāhīm tradition.[31] The following texts speak in favor of seeing Maryam as a prophetess:

---

30. See Loren D. Lybarger, "Gender and Prophetic Authority in the Qur'anic Story of Maryam: A Literary Approach," *JR* 80 (2000): 240–70.
31. See Angelika Neuwirth, "Mary and Jesus—Counterbalancing the Biblical

- Whatever Q Maryam 19:16a means by the book of Maryam, the fact that any kind of book is ascribed to Maryam already assigns her to the higher ranks of those to whom a divine revelation is given.
- Zakariyyā's portrayal as a prophet contains echoes of Maryam's similar case; for example, the prayer of Maryam's mother for a child corresponds to the prayer of Zakariyyā.
- Q Āl 'Imrān 3:33 counts 'Imrān's clan with Maryam as the daughter of 'Imrān, Zakariyyā, Yahya (John), and 'Isa (Jesus), among the previous prophets.
- Through literary parallelism, Maryam's birth is given the same weight as that given to the birth of 'Isa.
- Her mother proclaims Maryam's birth after a prayer, she dedicates Maryam to God, and Maryam is accepted by God through the care given to her in the temple. She is thus esteemed just as highly in this world and the world beyond as 'Isa.
- A direct revelation from God is bestowed on Maryam twice, when the virgin conception and birth of 'Isa and his significance as a sign for humanity is proclaimed to her.
- Maryam herself twice becomes the prophetess of the message of God's compassion (Q Āl 'Imrān 3:37) through her own actions and speech, in the same way as 'Isa is a prophet and a sign of God's compassion through his actions and speech.
- Maryam conceives 'Isa exclusively through the Spirit (see Q Al-Anbiya 21:91; at-Taḥrīm 66:12), blown into her by Gabriel, breathed in through the creation of his spirit.

3.5.4. Maryam as *Siddiqa* (the Truthful)

The high value placed upon Maryam in the Qur'an is evidenced by the title *siddiqa* ("the righteous, truthful one") in Q al-Mā'idah 5:75: "Christ, the son of Mary, was no more than a Messenger; many were the messengers that passed away before him. His mother was a woman of truth." The hon-

---

Patriarchs: A Re-reading of sūrat Maryam in sūrat Āl 'Imrān (Q 3:1–62)," *ParOr* 30 (2005): 231–60.

orary title is used otherwise only for patriarchs and the pious.[32] Maryam is especially venerated in Islamic mysticism and popular piety.[33]

4. Conclusion

The foregoing examples of biblical feminine figures and their incorporation into the Qur'an show that a simple comparison of the Bible and the Qur'an falls short of what one might expect. The Qur'an interprets not merely the Bible but also other receptions of the Bible. Insofar as this is true, every comparison must, on the one hand, take into consideration not only the biblical texts but also their paths of reception up to the time of the Qur'an and, on the other hand, consider the literary and theological objective of each of the *sūrah*s.

The narrative interest in the shaping of feminine figures comes to the fore, also shown by the fact that they—except in Maryam's case—are nameless. These biblical women are a part of the history of revelation; they are prophetic antecedents who, in their function as models of faith as well as in the failure to believe, are treated just like male biblical figures. The Qur'an uses their stories, which are often assumed to be well known (including the widespread popular traditions and received texts about them), in order to proclaim something about God's action. This guiding rationale determined which elements were taken up from the large sphere of received texts. Hājar in the hajj and Maryam in the mysticism and popular piety of Islam command an outstanding role, even if it is different from the one in the biblical tradition.

Bibliography

Abugideiri, Hibba. "Hagar: A Historical Model for Gender Jihad." Pages 81–107 in *Daughters of Abraham: Feminist Thought in Judaism, Christianity and Islam*. Edited by Yvonne Yazbeck Haddad and John L. Esposito. Gainesville: University Press of Florida, 2001.

Ali, Abdullah Yusuf. *The Holy Qur'an*. Ware, UK: Wordsworth, 2000.

---

32. See Heribert Busse, *Die theologischen Beziehungen des Islams zu Judentum und Christentum: Grundlagen des Dialogs im Koran und die gegenwärtige Situation*, Grundzüge 72 (Darmstadt: Wissenschaftliche Buchgesellschaft, 1988), 54.

33. See Annemarie Schimmel, *Jesus und Maria in der islamischen Mystik* (Munich: Kösel, 1996), esp. 141–58.

Arterbury, Andrew E. "Abraham's Hospitality among Jewish and Early Christian Writers: A Tradition History of Gen 18:1–16 and Its Relevance for the Study of the New Testament." *PRSt* 30 (2003): 359–76.

Bauschke, Martin. *Jesus im Koran*. Cologne: Böhlau, 2001.

———. "Der koranische Jesus und die christliche Theologie." *MThZ* 52 (2001): 26–33.

Bechmann, Ulrike. "Apokryphe Evangelientradition im Koran." *BK* 60 (2005): 108–11.

Bobzin, Hartmut. *Der Koran: Aus dem Arabischen neu übertragen von Hartmut Bobzin unter Mitarbeit von Katharina Bobzin*. NOB. Munich: Beck, 2010.

Burgmer, Christoph, ed. *Streit um den Koran: Die Luxenberg-Debatte; Standpunkte und Hintergründe*. Berlin: Schiler, 2007.

Busse, Heribert. *Die theologischen Beziehungen des Islams zu Judentum und Christentum: Grundlagen des Dialogs im Koran und die gegenwärtige Situation*. Grundzüge 72. Darmstadt: Wissenschaftliche Buchgesellschaft, 1988.

Cooper, Alan M. "Hagar in and out of Context." *USQR* 55 (2001): 35–46.

Egler, Gisela. "Sarah and Hagar in islamischer Tradition." *Cibedo* 6 (1992): 182–86.

Eissler, Friedmann. "Adam und Eva in Islam." Pages 138–99 in *Adam und Eva in Judentum, Christentum und Islam*. Edited by Christfried Böttrich, Beate Ego and Friedmann Eissler. JCI. Göttingen: Vandenhoeck & Ruprecht, 2011.

Geiger, Abraham. *Was hat Mohammed aus dem Judenthume aufgenommen? Eine von der Königl. Preussischen Rheinuniversität gekrönte Preisschrift*. Leipzig: Kaufmann, 1902.

Glassen, Erika. "Die Josephsgeschichte im Koran und in der persischen und türkischen Literatur." Pages 169–79 in vol. 1 of *Paradeigmata: Literarische Typologie des Alten Testaments*. Edited by Franz Link. 2 vols. SL 5. Berlin: Duncker & Humblot, 1989.

Greifenhagen, Franz V. "Cooperating Revelations? Qur'an, Bible and Intertextuality." *Arc* 33 (2005): 302–17.

Grimes, Jessica. "Reinterpreting Hagar's Story." *Lect* 1 (2004): https://tinyurl.com/SBL6011a.

Guardi, Jolanda. "Eva e la creazione nel Corano, nella tradizione musulmana e nella teologia feminista." *AScR* 11 (2006): 281–90.

Hassan, Riffat. "Feast of Sacrifice in Islam: Abraham, Hagar and Ishmael." Pages 131–50 in *Commitment and Commemoration: Jews, Christians,*

Muslims in Dialogue. Edited by André Lacoque. Chicago: Exploration, 1994.

Kermani, Navid. *Gott ist schön: Das ästhetische Erleben des Koran.* Munich: Beck, 1999.

Klauck, Hans-Josef. *Apokryphe Evangelien: Eine Einführung.* Stuttgart: Katholisches Bibelwerk, 2002.

Kronholm, Tryggve. "Dependence and Prophetic Originality in the Koran." *OS* 31–32 (1982–1983): 47–70.

Lassner, Jacob. *Demonizing the Queen of Sheba: Boundaries of Gender and Culture in Postbiblical Judaism and Medieval Islam.* CSHJ. Chicago: University of Chicago Press, 1993.

Leemhuis, Fred. "Hājar in the Qurʾān and Its Early Commentaries." Pages 503–8 in *Abraham, the Nations, and the Hagarites: Jewish, Christian, and Islamic Perspectives on Kinship with Abraham.* Edited by Martin Goodman, George H. Van Kooten, and Jacques Van Ruiten. TBN 13. Leiden: Brill, 2010.

Liddonici, Lynn, and Andrea Lieber, eds. *Heavenly Tablets: Interpretation, Identity and Tradition in Ancient Judaism.* JSJSup 119. Leiden: Brill, 2007.

Lodahl, Michael E. *Claiming Abraham: Reading the Bible and the Qurʾan Side by Side.* Grand Rapids: Brazos, 2010.

———. "Disputing over Abraham Disputing with God: An Exercise in Intertextual Reasoning." *CSR* 34 (2005): 487–504.

Lybarger, Loren D. "Gender and Prophetic Authority in the Qurʾanic Story of Maryam: A Literary Approach." *JR* 80 (2000): 240–70.

Michel, Thomas. "Hagar: Mother of Faith in the Compassionate God." *ICMR* 30 (2004): 47–54.

Neuwirth, Angelika. *Der Koran als Text der Spätantike: Ein europäischer Zugang.* Berlin: Insel, 2010.

———. "Mary and Jesus—Counterbalancing the Biblical Patriarchs: A Rereading of sūrat Maryam in sūrat Āl ʿImrān (Q 3:1–62)." *ParOr* 30 (2005): 231–60.

Nöldeke, Theodor. *Geschichte des Qorāns.* 3 vols. Leipzig: Dieterich'sche Verlagsbuchhandlung, 1938.

Noort, Edward, ed. *Sodom's Sin. Genesis 18–19 and Its Interpretations.* TBN 7. Leiden: Brill, 2004.

Prenner, Karl. *Muhammad und Musa: Strukturanalyse und theologiegeschichtliche Untersuchungen zu den mekkanischen Musa- Perikopen des Qur'an*. Studien (Christlich-Islamisches Schrifttum) 6. Altenberge: Christlich-Islamisches Schrifttum, 1986.

Raheb, Mitri. "Contextualising the Scripture: Towards a New Understanding of the Qur'an—an Arab-Christian Perspective." *SWC* 3 (1997): 180–201.

Rudolph, Wilhelm. *Die Abhängigkeit des Qorans von Judentum und Christentum*. Stuttgart: Kohlhammer, 1929.

Said, Edward W. *Orientalism*. London: Routledge & Kegan Paul, 1978.

Schimmel, Annemarie. *Jesus und Maria in der islamischen Mystik*. Munich: Kösel, 1996.

Schreiner, Stefan. "Die 'Häresie der Ismaeliten': Der Islam als politisches und theologisches Problem der Christen und die Anfänge christlich-antiislamischer Polemik." Pages 119–38 in *Identität durch Differenz? Wechselseitige Abgrenzungen in Christentum und Islam*. Edited by Hansjörg Schmid. TFCI. Regensburg: Pustet, 2009.

———. "Der Koran als Auslegung der Bibel—die Bibel als Verstehenshilfe des Korans." Pages 167–83 in *"Nahe ist dir das Wort...": Schriftauslegung in Christentum und Islam*. Edited by Hansjörg Schmid, Andreas Renz, and Bülent Ucar. TFCI. Regensburg: Pustet, 2010.

Schweizer, Harald. "Die Josefsgeschichte im Koran und in der hebräischen Bibel: Synoptischer Vergleich." *BN*, n.F., 144 (2010): 15–39.

———. "Koranische Fortschreibung eines hebräischen Textes: Hermeneutische Überlegungen anhand der Gestalt Josefs." *BN* n.s. 143 (2009): 69–79.

Sinai, Nicolai. *Fortschreibung und Auslegung: Studien zur frühen Koraninterpretation*. DisAr 16. Wiesbaden: Harrassowitz, 2009.

Speyer, Heinrich. *Die biblischen Erzählungen im Qoran*. Hildesheim: Olms, 1988.

Wadud, Amina. *Qur'an and Woman: Rereading the Sacred Text from a Woman's Perspective*. New York: Oxford University Press, 1999.

Waldman, Marilyn R. "New Approaches to 'Biblical' Materials in the Qur'ān." *MW* 75 (1985): 1–16.

Wensinck, Arent J., and P. Johnstone. "Maryam." Pages 628–32 in *Encyclopedia of Islam*. Edited by C. E. Bosworth, E. van Donzel, W. P. Heinrichs, and C. Pellat. 2nd ed. Leiden: Brill, 1991.

Wheeler, Brannon M. *Moses in the Qur'an and Islamic Exegesis*. London: Routledge, 2002.

Contributors

Ulrike Bechmann, MA, has held the position of Professor for Religious Studies and Head of the Department of Religious Sciences at Karl-Franzens-University of Graz, Austria, since 2007.

Franca Ela Consolino studied at the Scuola Normale of Pisa and taught at the University of Siena and University of Calabria. She is currently Professor of Latin Language and Literature at the University of l'Aquila, where she also teaches medieval Latin literature. The author of numerous studies of late antique writing, both Christian and pagan, in their philological as well as historical aspects, her research interests include models of episcopal and feminine sanctity as well as the role of women in the Christianization of the western aristocracy.

Stavroula Constantinou is Associate Professor in Byzantine Studies at the University of Cyprus. Her research focuses on Byzantine hagiography, gender, and ritual, and her publications include *Female Corporeal Performances: Reading the Body in Byzantine Passions and Lives of Holy Women* (2005) and *Byzantine Thaumaturgic Narratives: The Art of Miracle Story Collection* (forthcoming).

Giuseppe Cremascoli is Professor Emeritus of the History of Medieval Latin Literature at the University of Bologna and the author of over six hundred works on medieval spirituality and culture, including specialist studies of Uguccione da Pisa (Bishop of Ferrara), Rolando da Cremona, Gregory the Great, and Durando di San Porziano.

Mary B. Cunningham is Honorary Associate Professor of Historical Theology in the Department of Theology and Religious Studies at the University of Nottingham. She has published books and articles on the cult of the Virgin Mary in Byzantium, early Christian and Byzantine homiletics, and hagiography.

Judith Herrin is Professor Emerita and Constantine Leventis Visiting Fellow of King's College London and author of *Byzantium: The Surprising Life of a Medieval Empire* (2007). In 2016 she was awarded the Heineken Prize for History.

Martha Himmelfarb is the William H. Danforth Professor of Religion and Director of the Program in Judaic Studies at Princeton University.

Maria Lidova is an art historian who studied in Russia (Moscow State University), Italy (Scuola Normale Superiore di Pisa), Paris (École normale supérieure), and Florence (Max-Planck Kunsthistorisches Institut). She has published several papers on early Byzantine and medieval art and is preparing a book on the early Roman icons of the Virgin. She was a Junior Research Fellow at Wolfson College, Oxford University, was a member of the "Empires of Faith" project, and was a cocurator of the exhibition "Imagining the Divine" at the Ashmolean Museum in Oxford.

Rosa Maria Parrinello is a high school teacher of Italian Literature and History and a researcher in Byzantine Studies. She has published extensively on early monasticism in Gaza and Palestine, including a broader study, *Il monachesimo bizantino* (2012). She also contributed a chapter on Theodora Palaiologina to *Donne e Bibbia nel Medioevo, sec. XII–XV: Tra ricezione e interpretazione* (2011).

Anna M. Silvas is Senior Research Fellow at the University of New England, Australia, author of many studies and translations of the Cappadocian fathers, including Macrina the Younger, *Philosopher of God* (2008), *The Rule of St. Basil in Latin and English* (2013), and Basil of Caesarea, *Questions of the Brothers: Syriac Text and English Translation* (2014).

Francesco Stella, University of Siena, is full professor of Medieval Latin Literature and coordinator of some international projects of digital philology. His books include *La poesia carolingia* (1995), *Poesia e teologia: Occidente latino dal IV all'VII secolo* (2001), *Hagiographica Coreana* (2007–), *Walahfridus Strabo Visio Wettini* (2009), and, most recently, *Analisi letteraria e testo digitale* (2017).

Christiane Veyrard-Cosme was a student of the École normale supérieure, Fontenay-aux-Roses and gained her PhD and HDR at the Université Sorbonne Nouvelle-Paris 3. She is currently Professor of Latin language and literature at Université Sorbonne Nouvelle-Paris 3 and Director of the Centre d'Etudes et de Recherches Antiques et Médiévales. Her research interests focus on Latin literature of the early Middle Ages, especially hagiography and letter writing.

Ines Weber is Professor of Church History and Patristics at the Catholic Private University of Linz in Austria. Her research focuses on medieval church history, nineteenth- and twentieth-century church history, the history of piety and theology (including anthropology, the end of time, and gender), the diocese of Linz, and Christian education in general.

Giuseppa Z. Zanichelli is Full Professor of the History of Medieval Art at Salerno University, Italy. Her primary fields of research are illuminated manuscripts of the Middle Ages produced in Italy and the problems connected with patronage, readers, and the meaning of the images selected, within their context. Most of her publications are on the North Italian scriptoria, not only in monastic communities (as analyzed in *La sapienza degli angeli* [2003] and *Catalogo dei manoscritti polironiani* [3 vols., 1998–]) but also among lay scholars, particularly female ones, such as Matilda, countess of Tuscany.

Primary Sources Index

Hebrew Bible/Old Testament		37–50	357
		38:6–92	216
Genesis	216, 261–62, 296, 326	39:6–10	359
1:7	281	49:3	217
1:27–28	323	50:1	44
2	111		
2–3	350	Exodus	111
2:8–17	79	1–2	355
2:9	42	2:15–22	356
2:18–24	323	3	357
2:20	266	3:1–8	79
2:21–22	350	15:20	234
2:21–23	260	16:32–33	79
2:24	322	26	79
3:19	43	32:10	265
3:20	350	32:31–32	265
4:1	350	35–36	79
6–24	216	40	79
11:27–23:20	351		
18	353	Levitcus	
18–19	351–52, 375	20:10	337
18:12	353		
18:1–16	352, 374	Numbers	216
19	216, 361	22:28	292
19:12–29	216	23:3	46
19:26	361	25:1–17	217
25–31	216		
25:8	41	Deuteronomy	
25:12–18	354	6:5	278
28:10–17	79	22:22	337
29	356	32:43	153
33:11	41	34:8	44
34:1–5	216		
35:20	44	Judges	
35:22	217	6:37–40	79

Judges (cont.)		13:4	264
16:4–21	218	14:4–5	295
19–20	217	29:16	295
		30:16	295–96
Ruth	236	31:1	295
		31:32	295
1 Samuel		38:3	297
2:12–17	217	38:4–5	296
2:22	217	38:7	296
2:25	288	38:8–9	296
		40:1–10	297
2 Samuel		40:7	297
11:1–27	217	40:9–14	297
13:1–22	217	40:10	297
		42:7–8	294
1 Kings	262		
6–8	79	Psalms	34, 36–37, 47, 108, 286, 293
10:1–13	359	13:1	214, 223
11	215	22	288
11:1–2	218	26:13	288
		30:25	261–62
2 Kings		33:20	44
2:1	105	35:9	61
2:11	105	36:9	288
22	233	44	231
22:14	234	44:15	83
		45:3	45
2 Chronicles		49:14	43
24:21–22	265	80:11	273
		83:13	278
Ezra	66	88:49	43
		89:5	61
Esther	236, 249–53	97:7	152
2:15	246	102:15	43, 45, 61
5:14	247	110:1	305
9:12	247	110:3	152
		113:9	113
Job	293–95	114:7	43
1–2	350	117:6	43
1:12	294	132:1	46
1:21	43, 47	144:14	266
2:6	294	145:8	266
2:6–7	294		
5:9	47	Proverbs	205
10:22	294	2:5	59

Primary Sources Index 383

7:25–26	206	Daniel	
7:26	207	13	217, 233, 236
18:22	206		
21:19	206	Habakkuk	88
27:5	67	3:1–19	64
31:3	206	3:14	64
31:10–31	205		
		Haggai	
Ecclesiastes		2:24	293
7:26	206, 226		
9:9	207	Deuterocanonical Books	
19:2	214		
28	206	Tobit	326
Song of Songs	112, 196, 255, 293	Sirach	207, 223, 226, 293
2:1	294	9:2	208
2:6	293	9:8	208
3:4	294	9:9	208, 216
4:11	109, 293	9:11–13	226
4:12	42, 79	10:19	43
8:3	293	19	213, 224
8:6	293	19:2	vi, 205, 208–16, 218–19, 221–25, 228
Isaiah	78, 168, 270	25:17–36	207
6:6–7	64	25:19	208
8:18	42, 44	25:21	208
53	115	25:24	207
53:3–4	115	25:28	208
58:6	41	25:33	207–8
62:4	116	26:2–3	207
		41:17	273
Jeremiah		42:12–14	208
9:21	245		
15:9	113	2 Maccabees	107–8
15:19	41	7	107
38:15	41	7:21	110
		7:26	109
Lamentations	106	7:41	112
1:16	113		
		1 Esdras	66
Ezekiel	270	3–4	67
7:3	46	3:12	67
22:15	61	4:13	67
43:27–44	79		

4 Maccabees	107–8	Luke	42, 44, 81, 111, 143, 169, 180, 364, 369
15:6–7	109	1	366
15:30	110	1–2	362–64, 371
16:7	109	1:13	368
16:14	110	1:24	368
17:1	113	1:26–38	81
		1:28	79, 185
3 Esdras	66	1:42	44
		1:44	277
Old Testament Pseudepigrapha		1:46–55	190
		1:48	277
Odes of Solomon		1:75	42
2.43	153	2:22–38	64
		2:28–35	82
New Testament		2:35	72
Matthew	293, 324, 335	6:1	272
1–2	371	6:30	45
1:18–25	81	6:44	47
2:10	41	7:36–50	64
3:13–15	61	11:27–28	111
3:14	61	11:31	262
5:12	44	16:18	330–31
5:32	331, 333	22:52	277
5:44	278	23:27	180
7:14	41		
10:38	42	John	268–69, 274, 293
12:42	262	1:23	301
14:19–21	278	1:29	46
15:27	292	3:5	295
15:32	273	8:41	42
19:9	331, 333	12:1–8	64
21:18	44	14:23	44, 47
22:37	278	19:25–27	83
25	236	19:26	305
25:41	222	19:30	289
26:47	277		
26:55	277	Acts	
		4:32	44–45, 47
Mark	330	15:30	43
7:28	292		
9:23	43	Romans	
10:11–12	330	5:14	56
		8:17	42
		8:35	42, 45

Primary Sources Index

11:33	41	5:18	209		
		5:28	21		
1 Corinthians	16	5:29	335		
3:1–2	290	6:12	44		
3:6	289–90				
4:15	291	Philippians			
5:11	332, 336	1:28	45		
6:9–10	332, 339	1:29	46		
6:15	228	2:7	63		
6:20	42	2:12	44		
7:4	18, 20	2:15	43		
7:16	45	3:3	44		
7:32	44	3:8	42, 46		
9:27	42	4:4	42		
10:6	261–62				
10:29	47	Colossians			
11:3	14–15	2:9	61		
11:9	17				
12:21–22	15	1 Thessalonians			
12:25	15	2:4	46		
14:34–35	39	2:8	44		
15:22–45	56	4:13	43		
15:45–47	77	4:14	43		
15:52	43				
		2 Thessalonians			
2 Corinthians		1:7	44		
5:8	41, 43	3:18	42		
6:14	45				
8:9	63	1 Timothy			
9:7	44	1:28	45		
11:2	44, 261–62	2:5	47, 265		
11:23	41	3:15	43		
12:20	45	6:12	44		
Galatians		2 Timothy			
2:6	45	2:5	42		
4:19	291	2:15	46		
5:19	332	2:19	46		
5:19–21	339	4:6	290		
		4:7	41, 289		
Ephesians		4:10	41		
4:1	42				
4:13	261–62	Titus			
5:5	332, 339	1:7	210		
5:9	335				

Primary Sources Index

Hebrews
- 1:1–7 — 153
- 1:6 — 153
- 5:7 — 300
- 11:38 — 47
- 12:29 — 61

James — 170, 306, 308

1 Peter — 26, 112
- 1:5 — 47
- 1:8 — 43
- 2:3 — 26
- 2:18–24 — 26
- 5:4 — 44

Qur'anic Texts

Q al-Baqarah
- 2:158 — 354

Q Āl ʿImrān — 363, 369, 371
- 3 — 362, 366, 370
- 3:1–62 — 372, 375
- 3:33 — 372
- 3:33–37 — 365
- 3:33–38 — 370
- 3:33–47 — 370–71
- 3:33–48 — 364
- 3:33–51 — 364
- 3:37 — 372
- 3:37–41 — 366
- 3:39–40 — 370
- 3:41–47 — 370
- 3:42–47 — 371
- 3:42–51 — 370
- 3:43 — 370
- 3:45 — 371

Q an-Nisāʾ
- 4:1 — 350

Q al-Māʾidah
- 5:75 — 372

Q Hūd
- 11 — 352–53
- 11:69–74 — 352
- 11:77–81 — 360–61

Q Yūsuf
- 12 — 357
- 12:23–29 — 358
- 12:30–34 — 359

Q Ibrāhīm
- 14:37 — 354

Q al-Ḥijr
- 15:51–57 — 352–53

Q Maryam — 369, 371
- 19 — 362, 366, 370
- 19:1–11 — 369
- 19:1–33 — 364
- 19:2–11 — 366
- 19:12–15 — 369
- 19:16a — 372
- 19:16–17 — 369
- 19:16–21 — 369
- 19:16–36 — 369
- 19:22–26 — 369
- 19:27–33 — 369

Q Ṭā Hā
- 20 — 355
- 20:40 — 355
- 20:115–124 — 350

Q Al-Anbiya
- 21:91 — 372

Q an-Naml
- 27:22–28 — 359
- 27:22–44 — 359
- 27:40–44 — 360

Q al-Qaṣaṣ
- 28 — 355
- 28:7–13 — 356

Primary Sources Index

28:9	362	21	244
28:13	355	26	240
28:23	356	26.95	252
28:23–28	357	28	240
		28.27	252
Q Adh-Dhāriyāt		41	244
51:24	352		
51:24–30	352	Cicero, *De officiis*	
51: 28–30	352	1.30	222
		1.30.106	222
Q at-Taḥrīm			
66:10	361–62	Juvenal, *Saturae*	
66:10–12	361	6.284–285	239
66:11–12	362		
66:12	372	Ovid, *Metamorphoses*	
		2.765	240
Q al-ʿAlaq	349		
96:1–2	349	Procopius, *Historia arcane*	
96:4–5	350	1.14	27
		10.3–4	27

Rabbinic Sources

Prudentius, *Psychomachia*

b. Berakhot		58–69	242
4b	105		
		Sallust, *Bellum Catilinae*	
y. Berakhot		51.3	222
2.4	104	54	222
Genesis Rabbah	353		
53:9	104	Seneca, *De Beneficiis*	
		7.2	222
Lamentations Rabbah		7.2.2	222
1:50	106	Statius, *Thebaid*	
1:51	106	4.321	240
24	104		

Early and Medieval Christian Writings

Greek and Latin Works

Abelard, *Epistulae*

Aristaenetus, *Epistulae*		6.17	209
1.13	45	16.17	209
Catullus, *Carmina*		Abelard, *Theologia Christiana*	
4	251	2.87	226
8	232	2.91	226
16	242		

Aldhelm of Malmesbury, *De laude virginitatis*
2560–2570 — 243

Alanus de Insulis, *De arte praedicatoria*
6 — 209

Alcimus Avitus, *De virginitate* — 236

Alcuin, *Compendium in Cantica Canticorum*
8.4 — 294

Alcuin, *Epistulae*
195 — 274
196 — 269, 272–73
214 — 270
213 — 273–74

Ambrose, *Helia et Jejunio*
9 — 247

Ambrose, *Epistulae extra collectionem*
14.32 — 224
14.33 — 224

Andrew of Crete, *In dormitionem*
2.3 — 85
3.9 — 85

Andrew of Crete, *In nativitatem*
1 — 78

Apocalypse of Paul
25–26 — 111
27–28 — 111

Atto of Vercelli, *Epistolae*
9 — 9
262.2 — 45

Augustine, *De civitate*
5.12–13 — 241, 238

Augustine, *De natura et gratia*
26 — 231

Augustine, *Sermones*
51.2–3 — 56

Basil, *Regulae brevius tractatae*
8.1 — 45

Basil of Caesarea, *Homiliae*
19.6 — 43

Bede, *In Cantica Canticorum*
6.119 — 294
8.4 — 294

Bede, *Vita sanctorum abbatum*
6 — 183

Benedict, *Regula*
40.3–4 — 211
40.6 — 211
40.7 — 211

Buchard of Worms, *Decretorum libri*
19 — 327, 329

Chrodegang of Metz, *Regula canonicorum*
56 — 227
61 — 226

Columban, *Paenitentiale Columbani*
16 — 328–29, 336

Confessionale Pseudo-Egberti
19 — 328, 333

Dhuoda, *Liber manualis*
1.1.4–5 — 291
1.1.30 — 295
1.1.300 — 295
1.2.7–20 — 292
1.5.48–52 — 296
1.7.2–12 — 297

1.7.2–120	297	11.4		111
1.7.15–23	285	12.1		111
3.1–3	287	18.12		111
3.1.23–24	288	184–185		111
3.1.24–27	287			
3.1.68–75	288	Ephrem, *De virginitate*		
3.2.15–17	287	25.3		111
3.5	287	99–101		232
3.10.130–146	287	193		233
3.11.138–139	295	198		233
4–5	291	299–300		300
4–6	282	304		232
4–10	282			
4.6.30–31	295	*Formulae extravagantes*		
4.7.6–9	287	1.13		322, 332
4.8.225–227	287	1.13.541–542		323
4.25–30	287			
5–27	281	Fulgentius, *Epistulae*		
6.1.17–18	290	3.7		261
6.4.51–56	293	3.8		261
7.1.1–9	291			
7.1.10–12	290	Germanus of Constantinople, *Homilia in*		
7.3.7–15	291	*praesentationem*		
8.14	298	1		83
10.5.1–5	298			
11.1	286	Germanus of Constantinople, *In dormi-*		
15–17	298	*tionem*		
31–33	295	1		86
42–45	283			
45–56	289	Germanus of Constantinople, *In praesen-*		
		tationem		
Dracontius of Carthage, *De laudibus Dei*		1		87
3.468–479	239			
3.480–495	239	Gregory, *Vita Theodorae Thessalonicae*		
3.486	240	8		15
76–530	238			
		Gregory VII, *Registrum*		
Dracontius of Carthage, *Romuleum*		8.3		215
10	240			
12	240	Gregory the Great, *Moralia*		
62	240	2.1.1		280
		9.21.32		295
Ephrem, *De nativitate*	56	20.27.56		296
4.149–153	111	28.3.12		297
5.24	111	32.6.8		297

Hildebert of Lavardin, *Moralis philosophia*
1.49   222

Hildebert of Lavardin, *Sermones*
76.617   219
76.618   219

Hrotsvit, *De ascensione Domini*
23–74   304
44–45   305
147–150   306

Hugh of Saint Victor, *Appendix ad opera dogmatic*
2.2   224–25

Innocent III, *De contemptu mundi*
2.23   216, 223

Irenaeus, *Adversus haereses*
3.22.4   56
5.19.1   56

Isidore of Seville, *Allegoriae quaedam Sacrae Scripturae*
122   250

Isidore of Seville, *Etymologiae*
7.10.1   309
8.10.5   211
11.1.98   297

Jerome, *Epistulae*
22   232
22.7   220
22.21   56
45.2   210
130   232

Johannes Hymonides, *Cena Cypriani*
2.34   248
2.150   248
2.199   248
2.247   248
2.259   248

John Cassian, *De institutis coenobiorum*
6.1   220
6.3   227

John Chrysostom, *Homiliae in Matthaeum*
2.2   149
26.39.3   79

John Chrysostom, *Homiliae in Psalmos*
44.7   56

John of Orléans, *De institutione laicali*
3.6   218–19

John of Rouen, *Sermones*
2   210

Justin, *Dialogus cum Tryphone*
100   56

Marbod of Rennes, *Liber decem capitulorum*
79–97   234

Maximus the Confessor, *Alexiad*
5.9.2–3   36

Milo of Saint-Amand, *De sobrietate*
2.200–201   247
16.331–393   245
16.386–393   246
17   246
17.394–410   246

Nicephoros Kallistos Xanthopoulos, *Historia ecclesiastica*
17.28   85

Nicholas I, *Epistulae*
28   262
95   263, 265
96   265–67

Osbern, *Derivationes*
A.32.5–7   212

A.32.8	212	*Paenitentiale Pseudo-Romanum*	
Paenitentiale Ambrosianum		14	328
2.2	336	*Paenitentiale Pseudo-Theodori*	
		4.19.18	333
Paenitentiale Casinense	336		
17	328, 330	*Paenitentiale Sangallense tripartitum*	
		4	329
Paenitentiale Finniani		5	329
51	328, 336	29.1	329
Paenitentiale Floriacense		*Paenitentiale Silense*	
8	329	145	333
		149	330
Paenitentiale Hubertense		155	328
46	331	157	327, 331
		165	
Paenitentiale Martenianum		328	
24	333		
37	333, 339	*Paenitentiale Vallicellanum*	
40	332	1.14	329
		1.15	328
Paenitentiale Merseburgense		6	329
b 4	331	6.20	328–29
8	329	*Paenitentiale Vigilanum*	
9	329	77	329
W10.12	328		
23	327, 329, 336	Papias, *Elementarium littera*	
b 31	334	90–91	212
Paenitentiale Oxoniense		Proba, *Centone*	
1.10	328	23	278
2.2	331, 333	151–52	278
Paenitentiale Parisiense simplex		Protevangelium of James 74, 80, 82, 86,	
7	329	92, 98, 143, 362–66, 369–70	
		1–16	364
Paenitentiale Pseudo-Egberti			
2.7	328, 336	Prudentius, *Cathemerinon*	
2.8	327, 330, 335–36	4.1.33–35	286
2.10	329, 336	6.147–48	287
		9.52–53	286
Paenitentiale Pseudo-Gregorii		9.55	287
4	328–29	9.57	286

Pseudo-Matthew 143, 170, 306–8, 312, 369
3   308
3:2   308
6   143
9:1   307
12   311
13:2   144
22–24   125

Rabanus Maurus, *Commentarius in Ecclesiasticum*
1.10   222–23
4.10   214–15

Rabanus Maurus, *De laudibus crucis*
2.21   251

Rabanus Maurus, *Poenitentium liber*
3   326–27, 330, 336

Salvianus Massiliensis, *De gubernatione Dei*
6.78   214
6.79   214

Sermo de castitate
1   221, 225
3   221
7   221–22

Siricius, *Epistolae Romanorum pontificum*
225   212

Tertullian, *Ad martyras*
4.2–3   238

Tertullian, *De carne Christi*
17   56

Theodore the Studite, *Epistulae*
142.19–21   53

Theodore the Studite, *Orationes*
13.3   35

43.52   155

Walafrid Strabo of Reichenau, *De imagine Tetrici*
197   234

Walter of Speyer, *Scolasticus*
4.87–88   252

Lives of the Saints

Baudonivia, *Vita Radegundis*   277
2.380.18   277
131–32.208–19   278

Vita Alcuini
21   268

Vita Caesarii   277

Vita Eduardi   252

Vita Mariae junioris
7   25
8   26

Vita Mathildis   253

Vita Matronae
5   29
36   29
50   29

Vita Thomaïs
7   25–26
9   25
15   25

Conciliar and Synodal Documents

Concilium Foroiuliense
a. 796 vel 797   333–34

Concilium Meldense-Parisiense
69   332

Concilium Parisiense
   69.2   332, 335

Concilium Romanum
   826.36   333
   826.37   335

Concilium Suessionense
   744.9   333, 337

Concilium Triburiense
   895.5   329
   895.40   332, 339
   895.51   332

Synodus primus S. Patricii
   19   331

Modern Authors Index

Abugideiri, Hibba 354, 373
Acerbi, Antonio 312, 314
Agouridis, Savvas 143, 155
Ainalov, Dmitri V. 136, 155
Ali, Abdullah Yusuf 346, 373
Allen, Pauline 72, 75, 81, 95, 97, 121–22, 129, 158–59, 163
Andaloro, Maria 123–24, 129, 136, 138, 155, 162, 172, 181–82, 184, 186–87, 189, 196–97, 202
Andia, Ysabel de 77, 96
Angelidi, Christine 53, 68, 81, 99, 170, 197
Angelova, Diliana 156
Angold, Michael 13, 22, 30–31
Anton, Hans Hubert 284, 314
Arentzen, Thomas 71, 90, 96–97, 121–22, 161
Aristarches, S. 81, 96
Arterbury, Andrew E. 353, 374
Arvalia-Crook, Eirene 162
Asbach, Franz Bernd 333, 341
Atanassova, Antonia 122, 156
Auty, Robert 281–82, 284, 314
Auzépy, Marie-France 130, 153, 156
Balbis, Johannes de 213, 229
Barber, Charles 131, 153, 156
Barrado, Lourdes Diego 148, 156
Baryames, Rosalie Kachudas 192, 197
Baumgarten, Elisheva 118
Baumstark, Anton 152, 156
Baun, Jane 72, 74–75, 89–90, 93–94, 96
Bauschke, Martin 368, 370, 374
Beattie, Tina 80, 96
Beaucamp, Joelle 33, 47
Bechmann, Ulrike vi, 6, 345, 363, 374, 377
Beck, Hans-Georg 46–47, 55, 68
Behr, John 77, 96
Belting, Hans 170, 186, 197
Bentzen, Judith Anne 51, 55–56, 58, 66, 68
Bergman, Robert P. 183, 197
Bernabò, Massimo 141, 156, 180, 197
Berschin, Walter 268, 275, 300, 316
Bertelli, Carlo 123, 132, 138, 153, 156, 185, 190, 197, 202
Bertini, Ferruccio 212, 229, 299, 303, 306, 314
Besseyre, Marianne 187, 197
Beyerle, Franz 341
Beyers, Rita 308, 314
Bezler, Francis 327–31, 333, 342
Bieler, Ludwig 328–29, 331, 336, 338, 341
Bisanti, Armando 299, 315
Bisconti, Fabrizio 137, 166, 168, 170, 197, 201
Blamires, Alcuin 16–17, 30
Bluhme, Friedrich 327, 329–30, 336–38, 341
Bobzin, Hartmut 346, 374
Bodarwé, Katrinette 302, 315
Böhringer, Letha 324, 341–42
Bolman, Elizabeth S. 109, 112, 118
Bonfante, Larissa 172, 203, 303–4, 315
Booth, Phil 74, 90, 96
Boretius, A. 328–30, 332–33, 335, 339, 341
Boss, Sarah Jane 71, 80, 96

Bovini, Giuseppe 128, 156
Bowes, Kim 129, 156
Brandt, J. Rasmus 174, 197
Braulik, Georg 337, 341
Brenk, Beat 123, 125, 156, 169, 171, 174, 198
Brock, Sebastian P. 78, 96
Brommer, Peter 327, 331, 333, 336–37, 341
Browing, Robert 89, 96
Brown, Peter 22, 30
Brown, Phyllis R. 299, 313–15, 317, 319–20
Brubaker, Leslie 71–72, 74, 77, 80, 96–99, 121, 157, 283, 317
Buber, Salomon 107–9, 118
Bullough, Donald A. 268, 275
Burgmer, Christoph 348, 374
Buschhausen, Heide 129, 157
Buschhausen, Helmut 129, 157
Bussagli, Marco 145, 157
Busse, Heribert 373–74
Buytaert, Eligio M. 226, 229
Caillet, Jean-Pierre 179, 182, 198
Cameron, Averil 72, 95, 97, 122, 149, 157, 171, 174–75, 198–99
Campanale, Maria I. 232, 255
Carpenter, Marjorie 111, 118
Carr, Annemarie Weyl 178, 198
Cartlidge, David R. 170, 198
Castagna, Luigi 237, 255
Castelli, Elizabeth 110, 118
Catafygiotu Topping, Eva 46, 48, 51, 66, 68
Cecchelli, Carlo 141, 157
Charanis, Peter 57, 68
Charity, A. C. 78, 97
Chevalier, C. 85, 97
Chiesa, Gemma Sena 133, 157, 159, 163–64, 171, 198
Christ, Wilhelm von 89, 97
Chrysostomides, Julian 162
Clark, Elizabeth A. 17, 30
Claussen, Martin A. 298, 315
Clayton, Mary 252, 255

Cohen, Gerson D. 107–8, 118
Colish, Marcia Lillian 253, 256
Collins, Kristen Mary 193–96, 198
Connor, Carolyn L. 33, 48
Consolino, Franca Ela iii, iv–vii, 1, 7, 121, 277, 286–87, 315, 377
Constantinou, Stavroula v, 3–4, 13, 24, 31, 147, 163, 377
Constas, Nicholas 121, 157
Cooper, Alan M. 355, 374
Cooper, Kate 151, 157
Corbet, Patrick 194, 198, 310, 315
Cormack, Robin 123, 132, 137–38, 144, 157, 175, 192, 198, 202
Corrington, Gail Paterson 112, 118
Corsaro, Francesco 239, 256
Coussy, Céline 249, 256
Cremascoli, Giuseppe vi, 3, 205, 228–29, 312, 314, 377
Crippa, Maria Antonietta 176, 178, 198
Croom, Alexandra 172–73, 198
Cullhed, Sigrid Schottenius 278, 315
Cunningham, Mary B. v, 5, 42, 71–72, 74–78, 80–83, 87, 90, 96–99, 121–22, 157, 161, 377
Curtius, Ernst Robert 291, 315
Cutler, Anthony 145, 164, 179, 198
D'Angelo, Mary Rose 173, 199
D'Onofrio, Mario 145, 157
Dagron, Gilbert 13, 31, 41, 48, 174, 199
Daley, Brian E. 74, 85–86, 88, 98
Daniélou, Jean 78, 98
Daturi, Elisabetta Limardo 250, 256
Deckers, Johannes G. 136, 158
Deichmann, Friedrich Wilhelm 127, 129, 155, 158
Delbrück, Richard 158
Deliyannis, Deborah 127, 158
Delmaire, Roland 133, 158
Dempsey, George T. 243, 256
Dendrinos, Charalambos 162
Deug-Su, I. 280, 283, 315, 318
Dewing, H. B. 27, 31
Dhamo, Dhorka 129, 158
Dijk, Ann Karin van 185, 199

Dodd, Erica Cruikshank 168, 199
Dressel, Albert 90, 92, 98
Dronke, Peter 281, 297, 299–301, 312, 315
Dubowchik, Rosemary 154, 158
Dubreucq, Alain 283, 291, 316, 318
Dümmler, Ernst 233, 244–45, 250–51, 256, 262–63, 265–67, 269–70, 272–75, 309, 316
Effenberger, Arne 122, 158
Egler, Gisela 353, 374
Ehrhard, Albert 76, 98
Ehwald, Rudolf 243, 256
Eissler, Friedmann 349–50, 374
Ekonomou, Andrew J. 184, 199
Elliott, James Keith 74, 82, 98, 143–44, 159, 170, 198
Erkens, Franz-Reiner 252, 256
Esbroeck, Michel van 73, 84, 92–93, 98, 101
Eustratiades, Sophronios 58, 63, 68, 89, 98
Falk, Brigitta 195, 199
Farioli Campanati, Raffaella Ravenna 127, 159
Farr, C. 184, 199
Fatouros, George/Georgios 41–48, 51, 68
Featherstone, Jeffrey 29, 31
Featherstone, Michael 39–40, 48
Fecioru, Dumitru 81–82, 98
Fehrenbach, Frank 194, 199
Ferrante, Joan M. 260, 275
Fingarova, Galina 129, 159
Finsterwalder, Paul Willem 332–33, 341
Fischer, Bonifatius 205, 230
Foletti, Ivan 148, 159
Forbes, George Hay 154, 163
Franke, Birgit 252, 256
Freeman, Ann 148, 159
Frenkel, Yonah 105, 118
Fulgentius of Ruspe 260, 276
Furlani, Giuseppe 141, 157
Gaetano, Myriam de 237, 256

Gagetti, Elisabetta 133, 159
Galatariotou, Catia 28, 31
Galot, Jean 93, 98
Gambero, Luigi 150, 159
Garrucci, Raffaele 144, 148, 159, 170, 199
Gaspar, Erich 215–16, 229
Geerard, Maurice xi, 98
Gega, Reshat 129, 159
Geiger, Abraham 347, 374
Germanus of Constaninople 144, 159
Gerov, Georgi 148, 159
Giannarelli, Elena 35, 48
Gijsel, Jan 306–8, 313, 316
Giuliani, Raffaella 145, 159
Glassen, Erika 359, 374
Gnädinger, Louise 252, 256
Goetz, Georgius 212, 230
Goetz, Hans-Werner 324, 337, 342
Gotia, Ioan 140, 159
Goullet, Monique 306, 316
Grabar, André 136–37, 159
Graef, Hilda C. 93, 98
Graf, Katrin 195, 199
Graf, Wolfgang 325, 342
Gratuze, Bernard 129, 163
Greifenhagen, Franz V. 348, 363, 374
Grimes, Jessica 355, 374
Grimm, Jacob 300, 316
Grüneisen, Wladimir 134, 160
Guardi, Jolanda 349, 374
Guidon, Frédéric 271, 276
Hahn, Cynthia J. 195, 199
Halborg, John E. 277, 317
Halkin, François 72, 99
Halsall, Paul 25–26, 31
Hannick, Christian 88–89, 99
Harlow, Mary 172, 199
Haroche-Bouzinac, Geneviève 271, 276
Hartmann, Wilfried 324, 328, 336, 338–39, 342–43
Hasan-Rokem, Galit 105, 109, 119
Hassan, Riffat 355, 374
Hatlie, Peter 34, 40, 48, 51, 53, 57, 68
Hatzaki, Myrto 147, 160

Hawkins, Ernest J. W. 132, 162
Heene, Katrien 290–91, 316
Henderson, George 184, 199
Hernad, Béatrice 188, 200
Herren, Michael 233, 256
Herrin, Judith iii–v, vii, 1, 14, 31, 33–34, 36–39, 48, 52–53, 68–69, 121, 151, 160, 378
Hilberg, Isidor 210, 229
Himmelfarb, Martha v, 6, 103–4, 106, 114–17, 119, 378
Hincmarus, Remensis 209, 229
Holder-Egger, O. 278, 316
Homeyer, Helene 301, 309, 316
Hörmann, Walther von 332–33, 339, 342
Hornblower, Simon 133, 160
Hoti, Afri 129, 156
Huneycutt, Louis L. 252, 256
Iacco, E. Penni 127, 160
Iacobone, P. 169, 200
Ihm, Christa 123, 135–36, 160, 177, 200
Immel, Hans 195, 199
Immonide, Giovanni 247, 257
Iogna-Prat, Dominique 193–94, 202–3, 298–99, 306, 310, 313, 315–16, 318–19
James, Liz 129, 132, 151, 160, 175, 202
James, M. R. 74, 93, 98–99
Jan, Régine Le 259, 276, 281, 298, 316
Janssens, Bernadette 287, 317
Jastrzebowska, Elzbieta 145, 160
Johnson, Scott Fitzgerald 74, 101
Johnstone, P. 368, 376
Jolivet-Lévy, Catherine 145, 160
Jong, Mayke B. de 252, 256
Jugie, Martin 39, 49, 84, 92, 99
Kahsnitz, Rainer 193, 200
Kalavrezou, Ioli 33, 49, 95, 99, 171, 200
Kaldellis, Anthony 23, 31
Karavidopoulos, Ioannis 143, 160
Kate, Rijkel Ten 307, 317
Kateusz, Ally 72, 99, 140, 160
Kazhdan, Aleksandr Petrovich 52–53, 55, 68, 81, 99, 145–46, 160, 164
Kerff, Franz 328–29, 336, 342

Kermani, Navid 345, 375
Kessler, Herbert L. 178, 180, 200, 204
Kiilerich, Bente 160
Kitzinger, Ernst 137, 161, 183, 187–88, 196, 200, 202
Klauck, Hans-Josef 363, 370, 375
Klauser, Theodor 133, 161
Klein, Stacy S. 249, 256
Knohl, Israel 105, 119
Kondakov, Nikodim Pavlovich 125, 134, 136, 161
Körntgen, Ludger 327–31, 333, 336, 342
Kottje, Raymund 327–29, 331, 333, 336, 342
Krause, V. 328–30, 332–33, 335, 339, 341
Krausmüller, Dirk 80, 99
Kronholm, Tryggve 363, 375
Krumbacher, Karl 55, 58, 69
Krusch, Bruno 277–78, 317
Külzer, Andreas 75, 96–97, 121–22, 129, 158–59, 163
Kushelevsky, Rella 118
Ladouceur, Paul 78–79, 99
Lafontaine-Dosogne, Jacqueline 143, 161, 170, 200
Laiou, Angeliki E. 25–26, 31, 33, 49, 56, 69, 270, 276
Lampe, G. W. H. 78, 99
Lamy-Lassalle, Colette 145, 161
Lapidge, Michael 243, 256, 260, 276
Lasareff, Victor 168, 200
Lash, Ephrem 78, 99
Lassner, Jacob 359, 375
Latyshev, B. 90, 100
Lauxtermann, Marc 55–56, 69
Lawrence, Marion 173, 200
Leemhuis, Fred 355, 375
Leroy, Julien 40, 49
Leveto, Paula D. 313, 317
Lévi-Strauss, Claude 22, 31
Lévi, Israël 114–15, 119
Liddonici, Lynn 346, 375
Lidova, Maria v, 9, 121–22, 125–28, 130, 133–34, 136, 138–39, 161, 378

Lieber, Andrea 346, 375
Limberis, Vasiliki 95, 100, 112, 116, 119, 150, 161
Lindsay, Wallace M. 211–12, 229
Lloyd, J. Barclay 123, 136, 161
Lodahl, Michael E. 353, 360, 375
Loewe, Gustavus 212, 230
Lowden, John 138, 162, 179, 200
Luff, Robert 298, 317
Lutterbach, Hubertus 324, 342
Lybarger, Loren D. 371, 375
Maas, Paul 83, 87, 100, 111, 119
Mackie, Gillian Vallance 148, 162, 189, 200
Magdalino, Paul 13, 31
Maggioni, Bruno 205, 230
Maguire, Henry 129, 141, 145–46, 157, 162
Maltese, Enrico Valdo 35, 46, 49
Mandel, Paul 107, 119
Mango, Cyril 29, 31, 53, 69, 72, 81, 87, 89, 100, 132, 140, 145, 149, 153, 162
Mansi, Giovan Domenico 145, 162
Martindale, J. R. 55, 69
Mathews, Thomas F. 169, 201
Matons, Jean/José Grosdidier de 33, 49, 87, 100
Maunder, Chris 71, 100, 121, 122, 143, 156, 159, 162, 164
Mayeski, Marie Anne 289, 292, 294, 317
Mayr-Harting, Henry 191, 193, 201
Mazzoleni, Danilo 168, 201
McCash, June Hall 170, 201, 275–76
McClanan, Anne L. 170, 201
McGuckin, John A. 125, 162
McKitterick, Rosamond 195, 201, 317
McMillin, Linda A. 314, 317
McNamara, Jo Ann 277, 317
McVey, Kathleen E. 111, 119
Meens, Rob 327, 329, 332–33, 342
Meerson, Michael 103, 119–20
Menna, Maria Raffaella 124, 162
Menz-von der Mühll, Marguerite 191, 201
Meyvaert, Paul 148, 159
Michel, Thomas 355, 375
Mietke, Gabriele 136, 158
Mimouni, Simon Claude 84, 90, 100
Mitchell, John 121, 129, 156, 191, 201
Moffatt, Ann 52, 69
Moretti, Paola Francesca 279, 317
Morey, Charles Rufus 190, 201
Morganti, Giuseppe 174, 197
Morris, Rosemary 57, 69
Moussy, Claude 239–40, 257
Muehlberger, Ellen 148, 154, 162
Mullett, Margaret 13, 31
Munitiz, Joseph A. 136, 162
Munzi, Luigi 244, 257
Muzj, Maria Giovanna 168, 201
Nöldeke, Theodor 347, 375
Nardi, Eva 34, 37, 49
Navoni, Marco 133, 163
Neale, John Mason 154, 163
Nedungatt, George 39–40, 48
Neel, Carol 281, 317
Nelson, Janet L. 28–83, 317
Neri, Elisabetta 129, 163
Neuwirth, Angelika 345–46, 348, 370–71, 375
Neville, Leonora 13, 32
Newman, Hillel 104, 119
Nicolai, Vincenzo Fiocchi 168, 201
Nielsen, Christina M. 194, 201
Nilgen, Ursula 173, 201
Noble, Thomas F. X. 186, 201
Noga-Banai, Galit 171, 201
Noort, Edward 352, 375
Nordhagen, Per Jonas 134, 163, 182, 186, 201
Norelli, Enrico 305, 318
Oikonomidès, Nikolas 132, 163
Olkinuora, Jaakko 80, 100
Olovsdotter, Cecilia 163
Orchard, Andy 243, 257
Orléans, Jonas d' 218, 283, 285, 291, 318
Osborne, John 174–75, 185–86, 197, 202
Pace, Valentino 190, 202
Pagani, Ileana 209, 230

Palazzo, Éric   193–94, 198, 202–3, 299, 306, 309–10, 313, 315–16, 318–19
Pallas, Demetrios I.   145, 163
Parani, Maria   147, 163
Paranikas, Matthaios   89, 97
Parker, John Henry   280, 318
Parlato, Enrico   186, 202
Parrinello, Rosa Maria   v, 7, 33, 35, 37, 40, 49, 378
Peers, Glenn   130, 137, 145, 148, 151, 163
Peltomaa, Leena Mari   75, 87, 97, 100, 111, 119, 121–22, 129, 150, 158–59, 163
Pentcheva, Bissera V.   71–72, 95, 100, 121, 163, 175, 202
Perels, Ernst   262–63, 265–67, 275
Peroni, Adriano   193, 202
Pettit, Emma   243, 257
Pitra, Jean-Baptiste   89, 100
Podskalsky, Gerhard   145, 164
Pokorny, Rudolf   327, 330–31, 333, 336–37, 341
Prenner, Karl   355, 375
Price, Richard M.   122, 164
Prochno, Joachim   193, 202
Proverbio, Cecilia   145, 164
Rademacher, Franz   123, 164
Raheb, Mitri   348, 376
Rahlfs, A.   67, 100
Ravasi, Gianfranco   205, 230
Réau, Louis   312, 318
Reims, Hinkmar von   10, 312, 324, 341–42
Reynolds, Philip L.   324, 342–43
Rhijn, Carine van   333, 342
Riché, Pierre   281, 284, 286–88, 290, 293–94, 296, 298, 318
Rivington, J.   280, 318
Rivington, J. G. F.   280, 318
Rizzardi, Clementina   181, 202
Rochow, Ilse   51, 53–54, 58, 69
Romano, Serena   123, 155, 186, 189, 197, 202
Rosano, Luigi   167, 202
Rosenthal, Erwin   188, 202

Rosier, James L.   243, 256
Rosso, Stefano   42, 50
Rouche, Michel   284, 318
Rudolph, Wilhelm   347, 376
Russo, Daniel   193–94, 198, 202–3, 299, 306, 310, 313, 315–16, 318–19
Russo, Eugenio   176, 203
Rutschowscaya, Marie-Hélène   138, 164
Said, Edward W.   347, 376
Salis, Ludwig Rudolf von   328, 336–37, 343
Salmi, Mario   141, 157
Salvian of Marseilles   214, 223, 230
Santini, Giovanni   237, 257
Santorelli, Paola   277–78, 318
Savigni, Raffaele   283, 295, 318
Scaravelli, Irene   299, 319
Schäfer, Peter   103–5, 119–20
Scheck, Helene   307, 312–13, 319
Schibille, Nadine   129, 163
Schimmel, Annemarie   373, 376
Schmeller, Andreas   316
Schmitz, Hermann Joseph   328–30, 336, 343
Schreiner, Stefan   346–47, 376
Schüssler Fiorenza, Elisabeth   13–14, 25, 32
Schweizer, Harald   357, 376
Schwind, Ernst Maria Augustin   327, 329, 338, 343
Seeliger, Hans Reinhard   136, 158
Sena Chiesa, Gemma   133, 157, 159, 163–64, 171
Ševčenko, Nancy Patterson   145, 160
Shandrovskaya, Valentina   123, 164
Shepherd, Dorothy G.   138, 164, 179, 203
Sherry, Kurt   54, 57–58, 60, 69
Shoemaker, Stephen J.   72–74, 84, 91–93, 100–1, 122, 164, 192, 203
Sidéris, Georges   147, 164
Sidonius   242, 244, 257
Signori, Gabriela   299, 319
Silvas, Anna M.   v, 7, 9, 45–46, 51, 55, 69, 378

Simić, Kosta 58, 61–63, 69
Sinai, Nicolai 346, 376
Sivertsev, Alexei M. 116–17, 120
Slavazzi, Fabrizio 133, 164
Smythe, Dion 14, 32, 55, 69
Spain, Suzanne 125, 164, 171, 203
Spawforth, Antony 133, 160
Speyer, Heinrich 347, 376
Spier, Jeffrey 136, 164
Spieser, Jean-Michel 151, 164
Spirito, Giuseppe de 126, 165
Stafford, Pauline 290, 319
Steenberg, M. C. 77, 101
Steigerwald, Gerhard 125–26, 134, 165
Steiner, George 271, 276
Stella, Francesco vi, 5, 231, 233, 237, 249, 257, 280, 283, 318, 378
Stern, Henri 127, 165
Stevenson, Jane 259–60, 276, 313, 319
Stiegemann, Christoph 138, 165
Stone, Rachel 285, 319
Stout, Ann M. 172, 175, 203
Stratmann, Martina 327, 330–31, 333, 336–37, 341
Strecker, Karl 256, 306, 308–9, 311, 316, 319
Stroll, Mary 173, 203
Strycker, Émile de 74, 101
Studer, Basil 125, 165
Stuhlfauth, Georg 123, 165
Summit, Jennifer 274–76
Swanson, Robert Norman 71–72, 75, 78, 96–97, 101, 121, 151, 157, 165, 171, 192, 198, 201
Talbot, Alice-Mary 15, 25, 28–33, 50, 52, 68, 74, 101
Tavard, George Henry 180, 203
Tea, Eva 134, 165
Terry, Ann 141, 162
Thayer, Anne T. 253, 257–58
Theobald, Michael 330–31, 343
Thiébaux, Marcelle 281, 287, 319
Thomson, H. J. 242, 258
Thunø, Erik 176, 180, 189–90, 203

Toniolo, Ermanno M. 73, 101, 150, 165, 168, 201
Toubert, Hélène 312, 319
Touliatos, Diane 55, 69
Traube, Ludwig 245, 256, 309, 316
Treadgold, Warren T. 56, 69
Tripolitis, Antonia 58, 61–62, 64–65, 67, 69
Trypanis, C. A. 64, 69, 83, 87, 100, 111, 119
Tsironis, Niki 72, 75, 83–84, 87, 89, 101
Ubl, Karl 324, 329, 343
Uguccione, da Pisa 212–13, 230, 377
Underwood, Paul A. 131, 143, 161, 165
Urbano, Arthur 128, 165
Ussani Jr., Vincenzo 212, 229
Utro, Umberto 168, 203
Vassilaki, Maria 71–73, 75, 88, 99–102, 109, 118, 123, 131–32, 137, 143, 151, 155–58, 160, 165, 180, 192, 203
Veglery, Alexander 123, 166
Venetz, Hermann-Josef 339, 343
Vergani, Graziano Alfredo 137, 166
Veronese, Francesco 283, 319
Veyrard-Cosme, Christiane vi, 7–8, 259, 268, 270, 276, 279, 379
Viller, Marcel 83, 102
Vinay, Gustavo 303, 319
Vinson, Martha 109, 120
Volger, W. 191, 203
Wadud, Amina 349, 376
Wailes, Stephen L. 299, 313–15, 317, 319–20
Waldman, Marilyn R. 348, 376
Walker, G. S. M. 328–29, 336, 343
Walker, Jeffrey 23, 32
Waquet, Françoise 271, 276
Wasselynck, René 286, 320
Wasserschleben, F. W. H. 327–30, 333, 335–36, 343
Weber, Ines vi, 9–10, 321, 323–26, 328, 335, 338, 340, 343–44, 379
Weber, Robertus 205, 230
Weitzmann, Kurt 137–38, 166–67, 180–81, 183, 200, 203

Wellen, Gerard A.	136, 166
Wemhoff, Matthias	138, 165
Wenger, A.	84, 90, 92–93, 102
Wensinck, Arent J.	368, 376
Werminghoff, A.	332–35, 337, 344
Werner, Martin	184, 204
Whatley, E. Gordon	277, 317
Wheeler, Brannon M.	355, 376
Wilpert, Josef	134, 166
Wilson, Katharina M.	299–300, 310, 312–13, 320
Winterfeld, Paul	256, 309, 316
Wolf, Gerhard	146, 166, 177–78, 204
Woodruff, Helen	187, 204
Woollcombe, K. J.	78, 99
Wormald, Francis	180, 204
Wortley, John	18–19, 32
Wright, David H.	183, 204
Wright, William	149, 166
Young, Frances	78, 102
Zacos, Georgios	123, 166
Zakarian, Lilit	181, 204
Zanichelli, Giuseppa Z.	v, 7, 122, 167, 188, 204, 379
Zeller, Dieter	330, 344
Zeumer, Karl	322, 326–29, 332, 336–37, 344
Ziadé, Raphaëlle	109–10, 120
Zibawi, Mahmoud	176, 178, 198
Zotto, Carla Del	299, 320

www.ingramcontent.com/pod-product-compliance
Lightning Source LLC
Chambersburg PA
CBHW032144010526
44111CB00035B/1188